TOWARD A THEORY
OF NEUROPLASTICITY

TOWARD A THEORY OF NEUROPLASTICITY

Christopher A. Shaw
Jill C. McEachern
University of British Columbia

PSYCHOLOGY PRESS

Taylor & Francis Group

USA	Publishing Office:	PSYCHOLOGY PRESS
		A member of the Taylor & Francis Group
		325 Chestnut Street
		Philadelphia, PA 19106
		Tel: (215) 625-8900
		Fax: (215) 625-2940
	Distribution Center:	PSYCHOLOGY PRESS
		A member of the Taylor & Francis Group
		7625 Empire Drive
		Florence, KY 41042
		Tel: 1-800-624-7064
		Fax: 1-800-248-4724
UK		PSYCHOLOGY PRESS
		A member of the Taylor & Francis Group
		27 Church Road
		Hove
		E. Sussex, BN3 2FA
		Tel.: +44 (0) 1273 207411
		Fax: +44 (0) 1273 205612

TOWARD A THEORY OF NEUROPLASTICITY

1 2 3 4 5 6 7 8 9 0

Printed by Edwards Brothers, Lillington, NC, 2000.
Cover design by Curt Tow.

A CIP catalog record for this book is available from the British Library.
   The paper in this publication meets the requirements of the ANSI Standard Z39.48-1984 (Permanence of Paper).

Library of Congress Cataloging-in-Publication Data

Toward a theory of neuroplasticity / edited by Christopher A. Shaw, Jill C. McEachern.
   p. ; cm.
   Includes bibliographical references and index.
   ISBN 1-84169-021-X (alk. paper)
      1. Neuroplasticity.   I. Shaw, Christopher A. (Christopher Ariel)   II. McEachern, Jill C.
   [DNLM: 1. Neuronal Plasticity.   2. Adaptation, Physiological.   3. Learning—physiology.
   4. Memory—physiology.   5. Nervous System—growth & development. WL 102 T737 2001]
   QP363.3 .T69   2001
   612.8—dc21   00-055382

ISBN 1-84169-021-X (case)

JCM: For Sterling and Maureen McEachern and Hilda Bennett, constant sources of support and inspiration.

CAS and JCM: In honor of their spirit, courage, and ability to inspire, this book is also dedicated to Paul Pena and Kondar-ol Ondar.

ABOUT THE COVER

The cover design symbolizes the editors' conception of the interrelationships between different levels of the nervous system, particularly as these bear upon neuronal plasticity. The use of a web as background is intended to suggest the interactions within and across various levels of neural organization, beginning with the genetic code at the center of the web and moving outward to increasing levels of neural complexity. Each level is connected to, and dependent on, the ones above and below, and further interconnected laterally within the same level. In order, as they are depicted in this illustration from the center outward are the following: genetic code, molecule/synapse, single neuron, neural circuit, neural system, and behavioral outcome (represented by the spider spinning the web). Each level contains emergent properties derived from the ones at lower levels. The systems depicted are: retina (bottom outside web), olfactory system (top outside), and a generalized cortical laminar organization (left outside).

The general concept and design for this illustration was by C. A. Shaw, J. C. McEachern, and R. J. Simpson. Original sketches were made by R. J. Simpson. Art and computer graphics were provided by C. Calvert.

CONTENTS

CONTRIBUTORS

Hymie Anisman
Life Sciences Research Centre, Institute of Neuroscience, Carleton University, Ottawa, Ontario, Canada

Gytis Baranauskas
Department of Physiology, Northwestern University Medical School, Chicago, Illinois, USA

Donald P. Cain
Department of Psychology, University of Western Ontario, London, Ontario, Canada

Sic L. Chan
Laboratory of Neurosciences, National Institute on Aging, Baltimore, Maryland, USA

William M. DeBello
Department of Neurobiology, Stanford University Medical Center, Stanford, California, USA

Niraj S. Desai
Department of Biology and Center for Complex Systems, Brandeis University, Waltham, Massachusetts, USA

Gernot S. Doetsch
Section of Neurosurgery, Medical College of Georgia, Augusta, Georgia, USA

Wenzhen Duan
Laboratory of Neurosciences, National Institute on Aging, Baltimore, Maryland, USA

Liisa A. M. Galea
Department of Psychology, University of British Columbia, Vancouver, British Columbia, Canada

Robbin Gibb
Department of Psychology and Neuroscience, University of Lethbridge, Lethbridge, Alberta, Canada

Claudia L. R. Gonsalez
Department of Psychology and Neuroscience, University of Lethbridge, Lethridge, Alberta, Canada

Zhihong Guo
Laboratory of Neurosciences, National Institute on Aging, Baltimore, Maryland, USA

S. Hayley
Life Sciences Research Centre, Institute of Neuroscience, Carleton University, Ottawa, Ontario, Canada

Gregory S. Hickok
Department of Developmental and Cell Biology, University of California, Irvine, California, USA

Jon H. Kaas
Department of Psychology, Vanderbilt University, Nashville, Tennessee, USA

J. Lee Kavanau
Department of Organismic Biology, Ecology and Evolution, Los Angeles, California, USA

Eric I. Knudsen
Department of Neurobiology, Stanford University School of Medicine, Stanford, California, USA

Bryan Kolb
Department of Psychology and Neuroscience, University of Lethbridge, Lethbridge, Alberta, Canada

Howard M. Lenhoff
Department of Developmental and Cell Biology, University of California, Irvine, California, USA

Lidong Liu
Research Institute of Hospital for Sick Children, Department of Laboratory Medicine and Pathobiology, University of Toronto, Toronto, Canada

Mark P. Mattson
Laboratory of Neurosciences, National Institute on Aging, Baltimore, Maryland, USA

Jill C. McEachern
Department of Physiology, University of British Columbia, Vancouver, British Columbia, Canada

M. J. Meaney
Douglas Hospital Research Centre, Montreal, Quebec, Canada

Z. Merali
School of Psychology & Pharmacology, University of Ottawa, Ottawa, Ontario, Canada

Alison R. Mercer
Department of Zoology and the Neuroscience Research Centre, University of Otago, Dunedin, New Zealand

George D. Mower
Department of Anatomical Sciences and Neurobiology, Health Sciences Center, University of Louisville School of Medicine, Louisville, Kentucky, USA

David Neill
Department of Psychiatry, South Tyneside District Hospital, Tyne and Wear, United Kingdom

Sacha Nelson
Department of Biology and Center for Complex Systems, Brandeis University, Waltham, Massachusetts, USA

Helen J. Neville
Department of Psychology, University of Oregon, Eugene, Oregon, USA

Miguel Nicolelis
Department of Neurobiology, Duke University Medical Center, Durham, North Carolina, USA

Brandi K. Ormerod
Department of Psychology, University of British Columbia, Vancouver, British Columbia, Canada

Oligario Perales
Department of Developmental and Cell Biology, University of California, Irvine, California, USA

Catharine H. Rankin
Department of Psychology, University of British Columbia, Vancouver, British Columbia, Canada

Josef P. Rauschecker
Georgetown Institute for Cognitive and Computational Sciences, Georgetown University Medical Center, Washington, DC, USA

Jacqueline K. Rose
Department of Psychology, University of British Columbia, Vancouver, British Columbia, Canada

Minoru Saito
Department of Neurobiology, Tokyo Metropolitan Institute for Neuroscience, Tokyo, Japan

Christopher A. Shaw
Department of Ophthalmology, University of British Columbia, Vancouver, British Columbia, USA

William Staines
Department of Cellular and Molecular Medicine, University of Ottawa, Ottawa, Ontario, Canada

Yoichi Sugita
Laboratory for Neural Information Processing, National Institute of Bioscience and Human Technology, Tsukuba, Japan

G. Campbell Teskey
Department of Psychology, University of Calgary, Calgary, Alberta, Canada

Timothy J. Teyler
Department of Neurobiology and Pharmacology, Northeast Ohio College of Medicine, Rootstown, Ohio, USA

Gina G. Turrigiano
Department of Biology and Center for Complex Systems, Brandeis University, Waltham, Massachusetts, USA

Yu Tian Wang
Research Institute of Hospital for Sick Children, Department of Laboratory Medicine and Pathobiology, University of Toronto, Toronto, Canada

Norman M. Weinberger
Department of Neurobiology and Behavior, University of California, Irvine, California, USA

Marina Wolf
Department of Neuroscience, Finch University of Health Sciences, The Chicago Medical School, North Chicago, Illinois, USA

PREFACE

When you can measure what you are speaking about, and express it in numbers, you know something about it; but when you cannot measure it, when you cannot express it in numbers, your knowledge is of a meager and unsatisfactory kind: it may be the beginning of knowledge, but you have scarcely, in your thoughts, advanced to the stage of science.

—Lord Kelvin

It is always undesirable to make an effort to increase precision for its own sake— especially linguistic precision—since this usually leads to loss of clarity. . . . One should never try to be more precise than the problem situation demands.

—Karl Popper

The term *neuroplasticity* means change in the nervous system, an idea at the same time so fundamental to the very nature of a "nervous" system and yet often so vaguely defined as to be nearly meaningless. Seemingly, the field of neuroplasticity research is paralyzed between these two poles: in need of a working definition and framework for the field as a whole, but too diverse for any but the most general ones to work.

For many in the neurosciences, the terms *plasticity* and *neuroplasticity* are conceptual cliches approaching those of "motherhood and apple pie" as general statements of belief. Most neuroscientists would claim to be interested in neuroplasticity in one or many of its forms, and it is rare to find a grant application or public talk by members of the profession that does not refer to it. But what does neuroplasticity mean? What does it refer to? Many neuroscientists use the word habitually as a generic term as if there were consensus on its meaning and on what it implies for the function of individual neurons or the nervous system at large. But definitions, where given, tend to be vague, leading to the problem that different scientists mean very different things by it. At the same time, the myriad levels and complexities of nervous system plasticity may defy a composite definition, for precision in one aspect may exclude other equally important elements.

The goal of this book is to address the nature of neuroplasticity and to attempt a synthesis of the diverse areas that may fall within it. In other words, we seek to find the common ground between the extremes, which, if it exists, will allow a general theory of neuroplasticity to emerge. The questions this book seeks to answer are the following: Is neuroplasticity a single phenomenon or many? What are the implications of either conclusion for understanding the human nervous system in sickness and health, for treating neurological disorders or enhancing normal neural function? If unitary, does it use the same elements in different parts of the nervous system and across different species? Are components of one level of the nervous system more important than those at another level (e.g., genetic instructions versus activity in systems of neurons)? If neuroplasticity is a collection of unrelated phenomena, what are the dividing lines; that is, does it differ by level of neural organization, type of system, species or genus, etc.?

We have structured this book with a viewpoint based loosely on different levels of organization in the nervous system. In part this perspective was derived from a 1996 NIH miniconference entitled *Traversing Levels of Organization*, which seemed to us to provide a framework that would approach neuroplasticity from all levels, behavioral to genetic. Our hope was that we would achieve at least a partial analysis at each level, with each level linked sequentially to the ones above and below. Included within each section of the book, based on level of organization, are chapters dealing with quite different preparations and species. This organization, obviously, reflects our view that the "cut" to be made is across such levels of organization, rather than by other characteristics. This assumption may be incorrect and, if so, this fact will emerge as the reader contemplates the following chapters, particularly the last. For completeness, we have also included sections on developmental and "pathological" neuroplasticity, areas that are clearly part of the story and need to be addressed in any search for a theory of neuroplasticity.

It is important to stress at this point important caveats to the organization of the book: the goal of providing a wide coverage across the field of neuroplasticity came at the expense of depth in any particular area, the latter due, in part, to imposed constraints on final book size. The other consequence of this approach was that gaps between subfields occur for areas that did not allow for overlapping coverage, or due to attrition of some of the originally invited contributors.

The choice of authors for this volume was, of course, an arbitrary selection reflecting our own perspective on how to achieve some order from the vast subject matter that can be contained under the neuroplasticity rubric. No slight is intended to the very many extremely talented scientists working in the field who we did not approach and whose work could fill many such volumes. Those who did contribute were asked, first, to discuss research on neuroplasticity in their own subfield. Second, they were asked to attempt to place these subfields into a broader perspective in order to attempt a crossing of levels of organization. To us, this aspect seemed fundamental to the search for a theory of neuroplasticity. And, once again, the reader will be the judge of whether or not this effort has succeeded.

To the best of our knowledge, this book is the first to attempt a comprehensive synthesis of this broad area of the neurosciences. Whether this attempt has succeeded or failed, the crucial part has been the attempt *toward* synthesis, as indicated by the title. Our hope is that, even falling short of providing a unified theory of all the phenomena, this book will spark thought, debate, and continued efforts by the neuroscience community to create a theory, or theories, of neuroplasticity.

No book is ever completed without the contributions of many individuals. We thank all the contributors for their time and efforts; each has provided a fascinating glimpse into the various areas that make up neuroplasticity. Reading these chapters has been one of the most enjoyable aspects of editing the book, allowing us the opportunity to learn from the various content specialists. In particular, we wish to thank Drs. Cam Teskey and Norman Weinberger, who made many valuable suggestions for organizing the book. We are also indebted to Dr. Howard Lenhoff for his unfailing encouragement. Belated thanks to Drs. Peter Hillman and Uri Yinon and many other former colleagues of the Hebrew University of Jerusalem whose inspiration (to C.A.S.) lingers still. We are grateful to James Fiumara and Stephanie Weidel of Taylor & Francis for all of their assistance. Many thanks to Craig Calvert for the beautiful rendering of the concept for the cover page. We also note with deepest gratitude Margaret Wong and Rebecca Simpson's crucial assistance in many stages in this project. Finally, we thank members of the 6th Field Engineer Squadron for valuable lessons on bridging gaps, lessons that were invaluable for compiling this book!

Christopher A. Shaw
Jill C. McEachern

☐ References

Schlipp, P. A. (Ed.). (1974). *The philosophy of Karl Popper*. La Salle, IL: Open Court.

Kargon, R., & Achinstein, P. (Eds.). (1987). *Kelvin's Baltimore lectures and modern theoretical physics: Historical and philosophical perspectives*. Cambridge, MA: MIT Press.

I

INTRODUCTION TO NEUROPLASTICITY

1

CHAPTER

Christopher A. Shaw
Jill C. McEachern

Is There a General Theory of Neuroplasticity?

Research is essentially a dialogue with Nature. The important thing is not to wonder about Nature's answer—for she is always honest—but to closely examine your question to her.

—*A. Szent-Györgyi*

Neuroplasticity may be viewed as a fundamental property of neurons and the nervous system at all levels and across all species. As such, it could be said that it is the basis for all of the neurosciences insofar as almost any aspect of the study of the nervous system involves the changing properties of neural elements, either during development, due to natural or artificial alterations in input, or in cases of neural trauma. This fundamental aspect has long been recognized and has been commented on by many of the pioneers of neuroscience. In Chapter 2, G. C. Teskey provides a brief overview of the history of neuroplasticity research (see also Teskey & Valentine, 1998).

Given the central importance of neuroplasticity, an outsider would be forgiven for assuming that it was well defined and that a basic and universal framework served to direct current and future hypotheses and experimentation. Sadly, however, this is not the case. While many neuroscientists use the word neuroplasticity as an umbrella term, it means different things to researchers in different subfields. Relatively few workers have seemingly been willing or able to look beyond their own quite reductionist models of neuroplasticity to probe for similarities or differences in other models. In brief, a mutually agreed upon framework does not appear to exist. The innumerable studies of the various types of neuroplastic phenomena cannot be easily compared or synthesized, neither within nor across subfields, due to variations in preparation, system, level of analysis, and, not least, the overwhelming complexity that seems to typify neuroplasticity. It may not be hyperbole to claim that there are far more basic questions than answers. Some of these include the following: What is neuroplasticity exactly? Where does it occur; that is, are all types of neurons comparable? What are the mechanisms that govern it? What is it good for? Are there deleterious as well as beneficial forms? As an example for the latter question: Do memory and cell death share common mechanisms?

How do different types of plasticity measured *in vitro*, for example, long-term potenti- ation (LTP), compare with behavioral learning or developmental alterations in neural function? What are the factors that determine and distinguish the various subtypes? Are such types interconvertible, for example, do normal processes such as those involved in learning go awry to cause neurological disease? Do the subtypes of neuroplasticity depend on type of neuron or system, age or other peculiarities of the animal, method of experimentation or analysis? And the really big issue: Based on the answers to each of the above, is it possible to formulate a general theory of neuroplasticity, or are the phe- nomena too varied and multifaceted to be encompassed by a single theory? And, lastly, what are the implications for a single theory versus multiple theories of neuroplasticity?

The organization of the book was intended to provide for exploration of neuroplas- ticity through a series of levels of neural organization, moving systematically from the "highest" level (behavioral) to the "lowest" (genetic). The hope was that the reader when traversing these levels would see both the interconnection between levels and the similarities (or dissimilarities) in the underlying processes. Additional sections dealing with development and "pathological" plasticity were added as separate parts in order to provide for further elaboration of the phenomena without introducing too much complexity to the sections dealing with the separate levels of organization. Authors were asked to attempt the difficult task of summarizing work in their own subfield in relation to their own studies and to provide at least a partial crossing of levels of neural organization to those above and below their own. In many cases, the latter re- quest proved difficult. This is not the fault of the authors, but rather reflects two clear observations that have emerged in the writing of this book: (a) the field, for the most part, is highly reductionist, and (b) gaps in the framework between levels are difficult to bridge. We return to these problems in more detail in the summary chapter.

As an introduction to these problems, however, we present a summary of the outcome of the first task given to the authors of the various chapters, that is, to provide a defini- tion of neuroplasticity. In comparing definitions, we note similarities across subfields, for example, the notion that neuroplasticity refers to an induced change in some prop- erty of the nervous system that results in a corresponding change in function and/or behavior. However, with the changing focus of authors discussing different levels of neural organization (e.g., synaptic modifications vs. modifications of sensory maps), it becomes difficult to know if fundamental processes remain the same at each level in the absence of analysis at all levels in each preparation. With this uncertainty, it becomes difficult to know if the definitions provided can be cross-referenced to each other. The contributors seem divided on the following: whether there is *one fundamental process* for all forms of neuroplasticity or whether there are distinct families of neuroplasticity, the latter only united by the fact that each contains some change in final neural activity or behavioral response. The implications are the following: a general or "united" theory would suggest that fundamental principles, if not molecules and structures, underlie all forms of neuroplasticity. This view would suggest that each critical experiment, from any preparation or level of organization, would contribute to a comprehensive edifice that could then be probed to understand and/or influence both adaptive and maladaptive forms of the phenomenon, especially as it relates to human brain function. In contrast, a conclusion that neuroplasticity is a myriad of differing phenomena would suggest rather different conclusions: (a) each preparation and system must be under- stood independently of the others, and (b) most of these will have little relevance for understanding human brain function. In addition, any unified theory will be subject to a great variety of constraints, mostly in the form of the diverse experimental data. A theory postulating different plasticities has no such constraint.

The various contributors to this volume will suggest their own interpretations. We, as editors, have had the advantage of having seen all the chapters, and this advantage allows us the particular perspective that will form the summary chapter to this book.

☐ References

Limbird, L. E. (1996). *Cell surface receptors: A short course in theory and methods* (2nd ed.). Boston: Kluwer.

Teskey, G. C., & Valentine, P. A. (1998). Post-activation potentiation in the neocortex of awake freely moving rats. *Neuroscience and Biobehavioural Reviews, 22,* 195–207.

2

G. Campbell Teskey

A General Framework for Neuroplasticity Theories and Models

Plasticity of the nervous system has long been an important theme in psychology and the neurosciences. It has long been thought that the brain was responsible for behavior, and formal speculations concerning the relation between brain activity and behavior have existed for more than 100 years. Pioneering anatomical work by Golgi and Ramón y Cajal allowed microscopic visualization of the anatomy of the whole neuron, including the cell body, dendrites, and axons. This was an important step leading to the neuron doctrine: the principle that neurons are the basic signalling units of the nervous system and that each neuron is a cell that forms contacts with other neurons. Based on the neuron doctrine, Tanzi (1893) and Ramón y Cajal (1894) independently proposed that brain plasticity probably takes place at the junctions between neurons. Later, Sherrington (1906) named these junctions *synapses*. The idea that the brain is composed of interconnected neurons and that a change in behavior is mediated by a change in cellular and synaptic properties continues to serve as the basis for theories concerning neuroplasticity.

The search for the basic organization of brain structures as well as the rules and mechanisms of how the brain changes has occupied researchers for the last century. Sensory physiologists discovered excitatory and inhibitory neurons and the macro-organization of groups of these neurons into receptive fields. Lashley (1929, 1950) contributed to the modern view of plasticity by stating that the brain is unlikely to store a specific memory in a single neuron, but rather that the memory was distributed throughout the cortex. He further concluded that the neural tissue responsible for the storage of memories for sensory discrimination (i.e., vision) were established in the same sensory cortex (i.e., visual cortex). Wood-Jones and Porteus (1928) made a clear statement of the synaptic hypothesis for plasticity, as a lowering of the synaptic resistance (facilitation). In his highly influential book, *Organization of Behavior*, Hebb (1949) extended James's (1890) law of association by clearly articulating the "coincidence rule" (or Hebb rule) of use-dependent neural plasticity as the basis for information storage in the central nervous system. More recently we have learned that synaptic potentiation or depression can take place on millisecond time scales, that synapses can be added or pruned on hourly time scales, that dendritic arborizations can grow or regress over several hours, and that new neurons can be added or deleted over days. Thus, plastic changes occur on many time scales in organized networks of excitatory and inhibitory neurons, through changes in cellular and synaptic function according to multiple rule-based systems. Today, a working theory of neuroplasticity that is designed to account for changes in behavior still rests upon these historical foundations.

A simple definition of neuroplasticity as any change in neuronal form or function does little to help us with the construction of theories or the development of model systems. What is needed is a general framework in which theories and models of neuroplasticity can be developed and tested. Such a framework exists and I will articulate it below. But first, I will introduce a constraint or consideration, which I feel is a necessary starting point. It is my opinion that the primary function of the brain is to generate behavior. More specifically, the brain was designed to generate appropriate behavior in particular contexts. Thus, animals have brains that are not only sensitive to context, but also able to change an animal's behavior with both experience and life stage. Furthermore, the brain must hold behavior constant, through either regenerative or compensatory mechanisms, in the face of degeneration or damage. Therefore, any general theory of neuroplasticity or research with neuroplastic models should be related to behavior. While the study of the insertion of a specific protein into a lipid bilayer or the relative distribution of $GABA_B$ receptors in the telencephalon can be considered neuroscience, it is my position that, ultimately, these phenomena need to be related to the generation of behavior. Given this, the goal of neuroscience is to discover the details of the relationship between brain activity, including plasticity, and behavior.

The framework that I believe provides the most utility for asking and answering questions of behavior was developed by the ethologist Niko Tinbergen (1963, 1968). I have adapted his framework for questions of neuroplasticity, based on the monist philosophical position and the central tenet of neuroscience, which is that the brain, in concert with its effectors, is the sole generator of behavior. Thus, frameworks for understanding behavior should, and in my opinion do, map onto frameworks for understanding brain activity. Tinbergen suggested that there are four problems common to all areas of biology, including behavior, each of which requires its own explanation. These four explanations correspond to mechanism (proximate causation), ontogeny (development), phylogeny (genealogy), and evolution (function). All of these explanations are necessary for a complete understanding of behavior and, thus, neuroplasticity. Furthermore, these multiple explanations complement each other and, together with rigorous qualitative description and quantitative measurement, provide a rich fabric of knowledge. I will now expand on the four explanations with reference to an example, that of olfactory memory in sheep.

The proximate explanation is the one most utilized by neuroscientists. It refers to the direct mechanisms that cause a particular behavior as well as those that cause a change in a particular behavior. Proximate explanations usually describe phenomena on relatively short time scales. This explanation answers the question, "How?" For example, we could ask the question, "How is it that ewes learn the scent of their own lambs?" In order to satisfactorily answer this question, proximate mechanisms are described at a number of organizational levels: individual, brain, structure, network, intercellular communication, cellular, subcellular, biochemical, and genetic. Using our example, sheep have been shown to recognize the odors of their lambs within 2 hours of giving birth (Kendrick, 1994). That is to say that the behavior of the ewe has been altered by an experience with a specific odor soon after parturition. The individual's brain, spinal cord, peripheral nervous system, and muscles are doing new things. At the brain level there likely have been alterations in blood flow, and glial support. At the structural level there are, presumably, changes to the olfactory bulbs. At the network level, groups of interconnected neurons are likely behaving in a modified fashion. There probably has been a change in intercellular communication, mediated by pheromones, hormones, growth factors, or neurotransmitters. At the cellular level, new cells could be incorporated into the system and old cells replaced. Subcellularly, there may be alterations in the functioning of organelles such as mitochondria and ribosomes. At a biochemical level, there may have been a plethora of changes, including protein conformation, ion concentration, and enzyme mobilization, to name but a few. These biochemical alterations may cause changes in neuronal activity over relatively short periods of time without interacting with genome, but some of the biochemical changes will interact with genome and cause longer term changes. At the genetic level, alterations in transcription, translation, and posttranslational modification can also lead to neuronal modification. All these levels from individual to biochemical and genetic are proximate mechanisms that need to be adequately described and measured before we can fully account for a change in behavior. Furthermore, the interaction and relationship between the levels of the proximate mechanisms must also be described in order to achieve an integrated understanding of neuroplasticity. It is worth pointing out that because of ethical and technical limitations, we are probably prohibited from a complete investigation of all aspects of the proximate mechanisms. It is, however, critical that we understand the limitations of a particular technology or model when we interpret the significance of our discoveries. Hopefully, with more technological advances in measurement techniques as well as data acquisition and analysis, many of these limitations may diminish.

Tinbergen's ontological consideration is an approach to behavioral phenomena that incorporates a life-span or developmental perspective. When we ask the question, "What are the behaviors that a sheep expresses at different times in its life?" we are asking a question from this perspective. The developmental perspective is also concerned with the developmental history of an organism as well as those mechanisms that change organisms and their behaviors over the course of their lives. Developmental explanations of behavior usually refer to those changes that occur over longer periods of time than proximate explanations. The developmental mechanisms, like the hormonal changes that underlie the reorganization of a juvenile into an adult and that ultimately lead to new behaviors (i.e., sexual activity), *are* also neuroplastic. Historically, neuroscientists have made, perhaps somewhat arbitrary, distinctions between developmental mechanisms and proximate mechanisms, with the former concerned with the building of a general structure (i.e., olfactory bulb) and the latter concerned with particular modifications to the functioning of that structure (i.e., olfactory memory). Regardless, we can envisage a temporal continuum of developmental/proximate neuroplastic mechanisms that are responsible for behavioral change.

The phylogenetic explanation of behavior is an account of the evolutionary progression by which that behavior, and the underlying brain mechanisms, has been formed out of some preexisting organization. While I cannot offer a good phylogenetic account of olfactory learning and memory in sheep, I can make hypotheses. For example, an olfactory memory mechanism in sheep might have evolved from the normal developmental machinery that allowed olfactory detection in an ancestor. In practice, phylogenetic explanations of behavior are relatively neglected. However, knowledge of phylogenetic relationships is relevant for understanding the particular neuroplastic mechanisms available to a particular species. When considering sheep olfactory memory we must remember to consider both the abilities and limitations of that species. Phylogenetic considerations also recognize the genealogical relationship between all life forms. It is because we are related that animal models for human conditions have validity. Because evolution works by tinkering with what already exists and has been operating over billions of generations, many proximate mechanisms will be highly conserved. This fact allows some neuroscientists to study relatively simple invertebrates, which are more amenable to study, as models for more complex systems. Thus studying other animals can lead to important insights for our species. There is, however, an important limitation that must be addressed. Because different species diverged at earlier times and/or have different behavioral ecologies, we must be careful to recognize when behaviors, and their neurobiological generators, are analogous (solve similar problems with different solutions) or homologous (solve similar or different problems with similar solutions). Clearly, we need to use homologous animal models for human conditions.

The final explanation is that of adaptive significance. This is the evolutionary or functional answer that addresses the question, "Why?" For example, we can ask the question, "Why do ewes learn the specific scent of their lambs?" The general answer to this question states that, historically, animals in this lineage that were able to learn the specific scent of their lambs had a competitive (reproductive) advantage over other individuals without this phenotype. The evolutionist holds that the neuroplastic mechanisms that underlie this learned behavior were created, and then maintained, by natural selection operating against a backdrop of variation. Since natural selection is the only known force to give rise to complex biological phenomena, termed *adaptations*, the phenomena have been *designed*. That is to say that as a consequence of reproductive success, adaptations arose that solved a long-standing problem. This is of immense value for both theorists and empiricists because we can determine if a neuroplastic mechanism has the characteristics of good design (i.e., economy and efficiency) and whether there is a "fit" between the neuroplastic mechanism and the problem it solved (i.e., keeping track of your offspring). Thus, evolutionary considerations act as a heuristic in guiding us in our search for proximate and developmental mechanisms. For instance, in contrast to the view that developing organisms reach their pinnacle when they achieve reproductive capability, evolutionists would say that an organism is adapted to its historical environment at all stages of its life. Stated another way, animals face predictably different adaptive problems at various points in their lives and have designed sets of solutions (adaptations) for dealing with those problems. Juveniles face the problem of survival, but not the problem of mating. Problems of mating are faced before problems of parenting. So developmental and proximate neuroplastic mechanisms, which move an organism from one life stage and context to the next, must not critically interfere with the organism's ability to function. More specifically, the process of changing (developing or learning) must either not put the organism at a relatively higher risk or be very rapid if, for that intervening time, it does put the organism at a competitive disadvantage.

Explanations of adaptive significance also make a distinction between those neuroplastic mechanisms that are operating normally and those that do not appear to be operating correctly due to some pathology (i.e., tumor). Adaptations operating in an environment that no longer resembles the historical environment in which the adaptation arose may also appear to be operating incorrectly (modern context problem). Therefore, when considering whether a system is acting typically versus atypically, an evolutionary (functionalist) perspective is vital. Finally, when considering the ecological validity versus the artificiality of a neuroplastic model, the distinction is also informed by an evolutionary viewpoint.

In summary, neuroplasticity is a biological phenomenon, and its nature and origins can best be elucidated within a biological framework. To make proper use of Tinbergen's

(1963, 1968) framework, one must understand the multiple types of explanation in order to develop comprehensive theories of neuroplasticity. Neuroplasticity and its relationship to behavior needs to be understood in terms of physiological control over many time scales, developmental and evolutionary history, as well as adaptive significance.

☐ References

Hebb, D. O. (1949). *The organization of behavior*. New York: Wiley.

James, W. (1890). *Psychology: Briefer course*. Cambridge, MA: Harvard University Press.

Kendrick, K. M. (1994). Neurobiological correlates of visual and olfactory recognition in sheep. *Behavior Proceedings, 33*, 89–112.

Lashley, K. S. (1929). *Brain mechanisms and intelligence: A quantitative study of injuries to the brain*. Chicago: University of Chicago Press.

Lashley, K. S. (1950). In search of the engram. *Symposium of the Society for Experimental Biology, 4*, 454–82.

Ramón y Cajal, S. (1894). La fine structure des centres nerveux. *Proceedings of the Royal Society of London, 55*, 444–468.

Sherrington, C. S. (1906). *The integrative action of the nervous system*. New York: Scribner's.

Tanzi, E. (1893). I fatti e le induzioni nell'odierna isolgia del sistema nervoso. *Rev. Sper. Freniatr. Med. Leg., 19*, 419–72.

Tinbergen, N. (1963). On aims and methods of ethology. *Zeitschrift fur Tierpsycholgie, 20*, 410–433.

Tinbergen, N. (1968). On war and peace in animals and man. *Science, 160*, 1411–1418.

Wood-Jones, F., & Porteus, S. D. (1928). *The matrix of the mind*. Honolulu, HI: Mercantile.

BEHAVIORAL AND SYSTEMS APPROACHES TO EXPERIENCE, LEARNING, AND MEMORY

William M. DeBello
Eric I. Knudsen

Adaptive Plasticity of the Auditory Space Map

☐ Introduction

The auditory localization pathway in the midbrain of birds and mammals creates a map of space that is used to guide orienting movements. The optic tectum (OT), which is the highest stage of this pathway, contains mutually aligned auditory and visual maps of space that form a unified, topographic representation of the animal's surroundings. The auditory space map is highly plastic, particularly in young animals, displaying a topography and precision that is dependent on both auditory and visual experience. In this chapter we describe the auditory map, experimental manipulations that have been used to reveal its plastic nature, and some of the cellular and molecular mechanisms that underlie this plasticity. We propose that these mechanisms are general mechanisms of experience-dependent plasticity employed widely in the central nervous system to adjust its performance to the needs and environment of the individual.

The location of an auditory stimulus in space is not represented topographically in the cochlea, but instead must be derived by the central nervous system from the evaluation of a variety of cues that arise from the interaction of the head and ears with incoming sounds. These cues include interaural timing differences (ITDs), interaural level differences (ILDs), and the amplitude spectrum at each ear (Cohen & Knudsen, 1999; Middlebrooks & Green, 1991). Because auditory localization cues depend upon the size and shape of the head and ears, they vary in magnitude across species, across individuals, and even for an individual during development. Moreover, changes in the relative sensitivities of the ears that may occur during the lifetime of an individual will alter the perceived cue values that correspond with particular stimulus locations. In order to establish and maintain an accurate representation of auditory space, the central auditory system shapes its interpretation of cue values on the basis of experience.

Experience-guided plasticity occurs in parallel pathways in the midbrain and forebrain (King, 1993; Knudsen, 1983; Miller & Knudsen, 1999). Both the midbrain and forebrain pathways are capable of deriving spatial information from frequency-specific localization cues and of guiding attention and orienting behavior (Cohen & Knudsen,

1999; Knudsen, Knudsen, & Masino, 1993). Although experience can cause dramatic changes in the representation of spatial information in both of these pathways, our knowledge of the mechanisms that underlie this plasticity comes exclusively from studies of the midbrain pathway. This is because the midbrain pathway represents space as a topographic map, which allows the effects of experience to be assessed easily and reliably. Consequently, this chapter will focus on the characteristics and mechanisms of plasticity in the midbrain auditory localization pathway.

☐ The Auditory Space Map

The map of space that is synthesized in the midbrain pathway reflects the associations between cue values and locations in space that have been established by the central auditory system (Figure 3.1). At the site of map formation, in the external nucleus of the inferior colliculus (ICX), these associations are encoded in the tuning of auditory neurons for localization (Moiseff & Konishi, 1981). Cue-location associations can be ascertained more easily and precisely, however, at the next level in the midbrain pathway, the optic tectum (OT, also referred to as the superior colliculus). Here, the nervous system merges the auditory space map with the visual space map (and other sensory maps) to create a multimodal representation of space. Because the auditory and visual space maps are mutually aligned in the OT, the auditory and visual tuning of individual OT neurons indicates the associations between auditory cue values and locations in the visual field that have been formed by this pathway (Figure 3.1b).

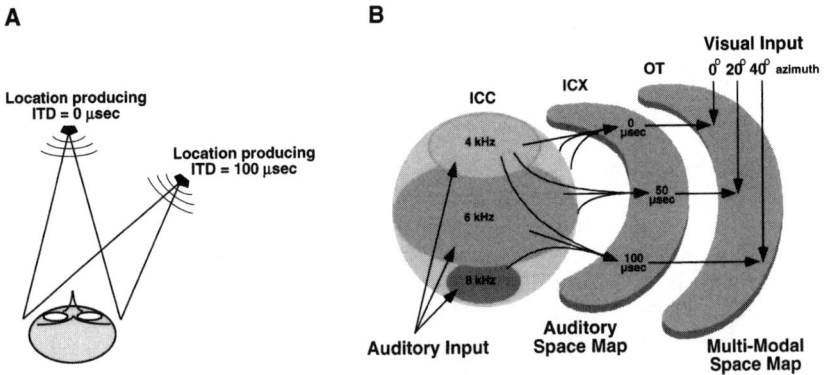

Figure 3.1. The auditory space map. (a) ITDs result from differences in the pathlengths that sound must follow to reach the two ears. An auditory stimulus located directly in front of the animal reaches both ears simultaneously, resulting in an ITD of 0 μsec. The same stimulus, when located to the right of the animal, produces a right-ear-leading ITD; for a barn owl, a sound located 40° to the right produces an ITD of 100 μsec. (b) Schematic representation of the midbrain localization pathway in the barn owl. The midbrain auditory map emerges from a series of feedforward projections linking inferior colliculus (ICC) to ICX to OT. This space map is constructed in the ICX and is then relayed to the OT, where it merges with visual input to create a multimodal map of space. In the OT, frontal space is represented rostrally and contralateral space is represented caudally.

The midbrain auditory space map has been described in several species, including the barn owl, bat, guinea-pig, mouse, ferret, cat, and monkey. Although the particular cues exploited by each species to create the map appear to vary (King, 1993; Olsen, Knudsen, & Esterly, 1989; Wise & Irvine, 1985), the gross topography of the map is similar in all: auditory spatial tuning changes systematically along the rostral-caudal dimension of the OT, with the representation of frontal space located rostrally and the representation of contralateral space located caudally. However, both receptive field size and the topographic precision of the map (i.e., the tightness of the correlation between a neuron's auditory spatial tuning and its anatomical location in the OT) is highly species dependent. For example, the map observed in guinea-pigs (King & Palmer, 1983) is less precise than that observed in cats and ferrets (King & Hutchings, 1987; Middlebrooks & Knudsen, 1984) and is much less precise than that observed in barn owls (Knudsen, 1982), indicating a relationship between the auditory localization ability of a species and the precision of its map.

In addition to its exceptional precision, the auditory space map in the barn owl is distinctive in two other ways. First, the auditory cues that underlie spatial tuning of individual neurons (or units) is well understood: the principal cues for azimuth are ITDs (Brainard, Knudsen, & Esterly, 1992; Olsen et al.), whereas in other species they appear to be ILDs (King, 1993; Wise & Irvine, 1985). In barn owls, however, ILDs at high frequencies are the principal cues for elevation, due to an asymmetry in the orientation of the outer ear structures (Olsen et al.). Second, in barn owls, neurons that respond to both auditory and visual stimuli are found throughout all layers of the OT, and in fact account for the vast majority of sensory cells in the OT (Knudsen, 1984). This is in contrast to mammals, where auditory responses occur only in the deep layers of the OT.

☐ Early Sensory Experience Affects Map Structure

The effects of early auditory experience on the development of the auditory map has been explored using a variety of auditory manipulations. These manipulations, performed on young animals, have included chronic exposure to noise, removal of the sound-collecting structures of the external ears, and monaural occlusion with various kinds of devices. The results of these experiments demonstrate that early auditory experience can play an important role in shaping the auditory map (Gold & Knudsen, 1999; King, Hutchings, Moore, & Blakemore, 1988; Knudsen, 1983; Knudsen, Esterly, & Olsen, 1994; Mogdans & Knudsen, 1992, 1993; Schnupp, King, & Carlile, 1998; Withington-Wray, Binns, & Keating, 1990a). In the interest of brevity, these results will be not be discussed further.

Early visual experience also exerts a powerful influence on the auditory space map. That visual signals calibrate the auditory space map in the OT is not surprising, because the primary function of the OT is to orient the eyes toward targets of interest (Stein & Meredith, 1993). This function requires that the auditory representation of space match with the visual representation, so that auditory signals lead to accurate foveation of the sound source. This chapter focuses on visually guided plasticity of the auditory space map.

Early Visual Deprivation Disrupts Map Development

The degree to which the properties of the auditory space map depend on visual experience varies with age and species. The most dramatic effects of visual deprivation occur in juvenile guinea-pigs: keeping guinea-pigs in total darkness during a 4-day critical period results in (a) auditory spatial receptive fields that are abnormally large, and (b) no systematic representation of auditory space along the rostral-caudal dimension of the OT (Withington-Wray, Binns, & Keating, 1990b). Thus, total visual deprivation prevents auditory map development.

An alternative, less severe method of visual deprivation is bilateral eyelid suture (blind rearing). Blind rearing attenuates and blurs incoming visual signals but does not completely eliminate them. In guinea-pigs that are blind-reared from birth, the auditory map is only mildly degraded relative to normal, with most sites exhibiting normal spatial tuning and topography (Withington, 1992). Thus blind rearing, unlike dark rearing, does not eliminate the basic features of the guinea-pig auditory map.

The effects of blind rearing on the auditory space map in barn owls is similar to that in guinea-pigs. The auditory map that develops in blind-reared owls is abnormal in several ways (Knudsen, Esterly, & du Lac, 1991): individual units tend to habituate and are often unimodal rather than bimodal, and the topography of the map is degraded, especially in the representation of elevation, which is either stretched or even flipped upside-down. On the other hand, several key features of the map are not affected by blind rearing: unit tuning for azimuth is sharp, both azimuth and elevation are represented topographically (although the representation of elevation may be flipped), and the portion of the map that represents frontal space is always correctly calibrated. These results demonstrate that patterned visual experience is required for some, but not all, aspects of map development in barn owls. The consistently normal tuning and topography in the representation of frontal space indicates that vision is not essential for the development of this portion of the map. This could reflect the fact that the ITD and ILD values that correspond with frontal regions are predictably small (i.e., near 0), change little throughout development, and are relatively frequency independent, all of which permit, in principle, a genetically controlled developmental mechanism.

In blind-reared ferrets, also, the auditory map in the OT develops but is degraded (King & Carlile, 1993). As in barn owls, the representation of elevation is often stretched, but in contrast to barn owls, the most dramatic effects are on the representation of azimuth. ILD cues appear to be the dominant cues for azimuth in ferrets, as they are for elevation in barn owls. This suggests that the representation of ILD cues in the OT map depends heavily on visual calibration. This may reflect the large variability of ILD values across individuals and across frequencies (Keller, Hartung, & Takahashi, 1998; Knudsen et al., 1991; Middlebrooks & Green, 1991).

Adaptive Adjustments to Visual Manipulations

The effects of blind rearing demonstrate that patterned vision, though not required for auditory map formation, is required for refining the topography of the map. Since visual experience is necessary for this refinement, systematic displacement of the visual field should also influence the auditory space map. This is, indeed, the case.

Eye Deviation

Displacement of the visual field in ferrets has been accomplished by surgical rotation of one eye (by cutting the medial rectus muscle) and removal of the opposite eye (King et al., 1988). This procedure, performed before the age of eyelid opening, results in a 15°–20° lateral deviation of the eye compared to age-matched adults. Lateral deviation of the eye causes the visual map in the OT to shift commensurately to represent a more contralateral field than normal. In animals that experience eye deviation from birth, there is a corresponding shift in the auditory map. Thus, the auditory map appears to adapt to the deviated visual field. One confound of this procedure, however, is that the auditory map has been shown to be sensitive to changes in eye position (Jay & Sparks, 1984), which could, in principle, account for the effect.

Prism Rearing

Displacement of the visual field has been accomplished using a different manipulation in barn owls: by mounting prismatic spectacles in front of the eyes. Because owls do not alter the positions of their eyes by more than a few degrees, this manipulation dissociates the effects of eye position from those of visual field displacement.

Prisms cause the auditory and visual worlds of the owl to be misaligned. Because owls cannot rotate their eyes in their heads, they experience a chronic, systematic shift in the correspondence between auditory cue values and the locations in the visual field that produce them. In order to bring their auditory and visual worlds back into alignment, they must learn the new relationship between auditory cue values and locations in the visual field. This is what they do.

Neurons in the OT of prism-reared owls become tuned for sounds produced at the location of their optically displaced visual receptive fields (Figure 3.2a). Adaptive shifts in auditory spatial tuning have been observed for visual displacements of up to 34° (Knudsen & Brainard, 1991). Large adaptive shifts occur only in the portion of the map that represents the displaced portion of the visual field. The rest of the map, which represents portions of the visual field that are either blocked or unaffected by the spectacles, are either shifted minimally or normal. These results illustrate that (a) vision provides a powerful instructive signal that can guide adaptive plasticity in the space map, (b) different parts of the map can shift differentially, and (c) the range of auditory locations represented in the map, as well as the amount of the map that is devoted to the representation of particular locations, can be specified by visual instruction.

The basis for the shift in the auditory spatial receptive fields in the OT is a shift in the tuning of OT units for binaural localization cues (Brainard & Knudsen, 1993). For example, in owls that are raised with a 23° horizontal displacement of the visual field, the tuning of OT neurons to ITDs is shifted in the appropriate direction by 30–60 μsec (Figure 3.2b,c), to values of ITDs that were previously ineffective or even inhibitory to the neuron. Thus, experience can alter the auditory tuning of OT neurons dramatically so that they come to respond to the values of auditory cues produced by a sound source located in their visual receptive fields.

☐ Dynamics of Adaptive Plasticity

The process of shifting the auditory map from a normal to a learned map involves several stages (Brainard & Knudsen, 1995). These stages are apparent in the barn owl in the tuning of OT neurons for ITDs. Initially, individual OT neurons respond only to a narrow range of ITDs, hereafter referred to as normal responses. As shown in Figure 3.3 (left panel) even after 2 weeks of prism rearing, normal responses still dominate. As the map begins to adjust, responses appear to ITDs that are produced at the location of the optically displaced visual receptive field. These responses will hereafter be referred to as *learned responses*. During this transition stage, normal responses are co-expressed with learned responses (Figure 3.3, middle panel). In the final stage of the adjustment process,

A

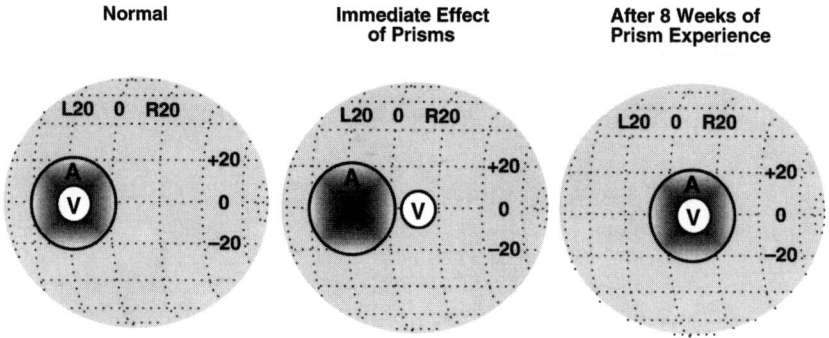

B   **C**

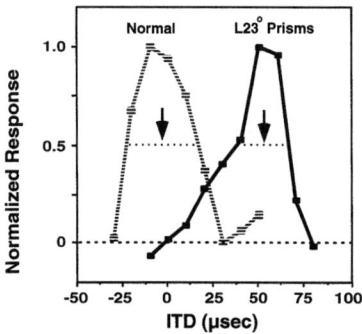   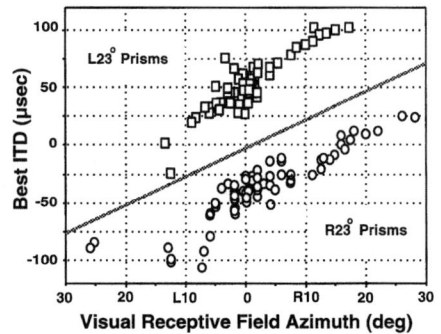

Figure 3.2. Effects of prism rearing on the auditory map. (a) Prism experience shifts the locations of auditory receptive fields in the OT. Left panel: The auditory (A) and visual (V) receptive fields of an OT neuron in a normal juvenile before prism experience. Center panel: Prisms displace the visual field, in this case to the right, causing an immediate misalignment between the auditory and visual receptive fields. Right panel: After 8 weeks of experience with the prisms, the auditory receptive field is aligned with the prismatically displaced visual receptive field. (b) ITD tuning curves recorded in the OT before (dashed line) and after (solid line) prism experience. In both cases, the visual receptive field was straight ahead (azimuth = 0°). Auditory responses were assessed using broad-band noise bursts presented through earphones inserted into the ear canals. The best ITD (arrows) for each site was calculated as the midpoint of the ITD range that elicited more than 50% of maximum response. Negative values of ITDs indicate left-ear leading. (c) The relationship between best ITDs and visual receptive field location for normal and prism-reared owls. The diagonal line represents the least-squares regression for data from normal owls. For prism-reared owls, best ITDs are displaced from normal, over a large portion of frontal space, in the direction that realigns the auditory receptive field with the displaced visual receptive fields: experience with L23° prisms causes best ITDs to become more right-ear leading (squares); conversely, experience with R23° prisms causes best ITDs to become more left-ear leading (circles).

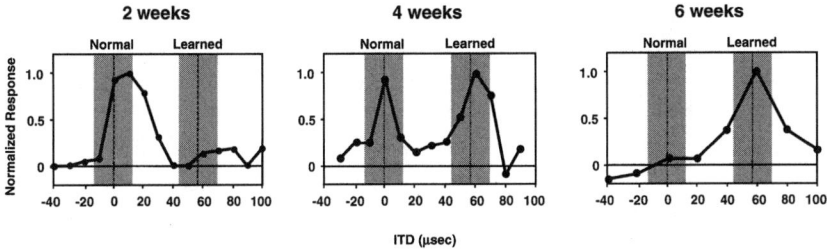

Figure 3.3. Stages of adaptive adjustment. Changes in ITD tuning measured at a single, chronically recorded site in the OT in response to experience with L23° prisms. The cumulative time of prism experience is indicated above each curve. Normal responses for this site are to 0 μsec ITD, and learned responses are to 57 μsec ITD. The data show three stages in the adjustment process (see text for discussion).

normal responses are eliminated, so that only the learned map is expressed (Figure 3.3, right panel). Later in the chapter, the mechanisms that underlie the acquisition of learned responses and the elimination of normal responses will be discussed.

Sensitive Periods for Adaptive Plasticity

The plasticity of the auditory space map is developmentally regulated: the same manipulations of auditory or visual experience that induce adaptive adjustments in young animals may result in little or no adaptive adjustment in adults. When owls are exposed to a standard 23° horizontal displacement of the visual field, the map of ITDs in owls younger than 200 days (d) old shifts adaptively by up to 60 μsec within 60 d, as shown in Figure 3.4b (the shift of the population tuning curve is shown in Figure 3.4a, left panel). In owls older than 200 d, the equivalent sensory manipulation leads to only a small shift in ITD tuning, even after a much longer period of prism experience (over 6 months; Figures 3.4b and 3.4a, center panel). Barn owls approach sexual maturity at about 200 d. Thus, as owls reach adulthood, the plasticity of the auditory space map decreases markedly (Brainard & Knudsen, 1998).

During this sensitive period, the capacity of the auditory space map to shift substantially depends on the richness of the animal's environment (Brainard & Knudsen, 1998). In owls that are younger than 60 d, prism experience can cause large changes in the map even when the animal is housed in a small cage. In older owls (60–200 d) that are kept in the same small cages, the same experience causes little or no change in the map. Thus, a small cage, that for nestlings (owls leave the nest at about 60 d) is an adequate environment, becomes a deprived environment, and one that no longer induces plasticity, once the animal reaches the age at which it would normally leave the nest. In order to induce plasticity in these older owls, they must be exposed to a richer environment, as provided, for example, by a large flight room containing many other individuals.

Traces of Juvenile Plasticity Revealed in Adults

When prisms are removed from owls that have acquired a shifted map, the map returns to normal, even in adult animals (Brainard & Knudsen, 1998). If, after 6 months of normal experience, these owls are reexposed to the same prismatic displacement to which they

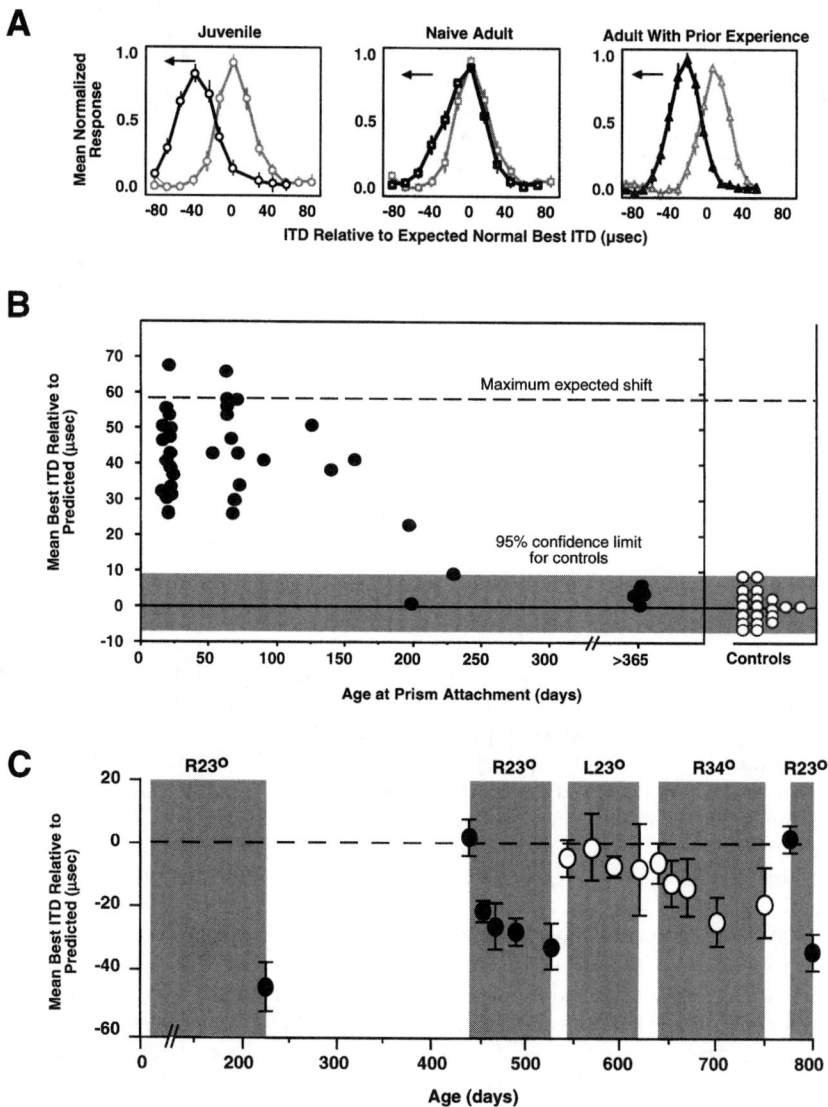

Figure 3.4. Effects of age on plasticity. (a) Large-scale plasticity occurs only in juvenile owls and adult owls that have adjusted to prisms previously as juveniles. These are population curves for a juvenile owl raised with prisms (left), a normal owl exposed to prisms as an adult (center), and a prism-reared adult owl that is reexposed to the same prisms (right). Each curve is based on ITD tuning curves from 10–18 different sites recorded before (grey), and after (black) prism experience. ITD tuning curves were aligned relative to their expected normal best ITD (derived from the visual receptive field; see Figure 3.2c), normalized, and averaged together to produce the population curves, which represent the average ITD tuning in the auditory map. (b) The sensitive period for prism-induced plasticity in barn owls exposed to 23° prisms. Best ITDs were measured for a population of sites in each owl after at least 2 months of prism experience. None of the owls that

had adjusted as juveniles, they rapidly re-acquire a learned map (Figures 3.4a, right panel, and 3.4c). In contrast, and as previously discussed, in owls that are subjected to a 23° prismatic displacement for the first time as adults, the map does not adjust (Figure 3.4a, compare center panel to right panel). These results demonstrate that the acquisition of a learned map during the sensitive period leaves an enduring trace in this pathway that enables re-acquisition of the novel map in adulthood under appropriate sensory conditions (Knudsen, 1998). This trace persists despite a protracted period (6 months), during which the learned map is not used and, indeed, is maladaptive.

Owls that acquire a left-shifted map as a juvenile can re-acquire a left- but not a right-shifted map as an adult (Figure 3.4c). In addition, in owls raised with a 23° displacement and then reexposed to a 34° displacement as adults, the map of ITDs shifts no further than it does in response to a 23° displacement. Therefore, the capacity to re-acquire a learned map of ITDs in adulthood is limited in direction and magnitude to the plasticity that occurred during the sensitive period (Knudsen, 1998).

The ICX: A Site of Plasticity in the Barn Owl

Plasticity in the auditory space map is usually assessed at the level of the OT. However, this plasticity reflects changes that occur largely at an earlier stage in the localization pathway, in the ICX, where the map of space is synthesized (Brainard & Knudsen, 1993). This conclusion is based, in part, on a comparison of the reconstructed maps of ITDs in the central nucleus of the inferior colliculus (ICC), external nucleus of the interior colliculus (ICX), and optic tectum (OT) in normal and prism-reared owls. These reconstructions show that, in prism-reared owls, the maps in both the ICX and OT are shifted adaptively by similar amounts. In contrast, the map of ITD in the ICC is normal. In addition, the learned responses in the ICX have latencies that are as short as those of the normal responses (5–8 ms). These short latencies indicate that plasticity takes place in the direct ascending pathway, either in the ICX itself or in the projection from the ICC to the ICX.

Prism Rearing Leads to Anatomical Remodeling

An anatomical correlate of the functional plasticity in the auditory space map has been found in the pattern of axonal projections from the ICC to the ICX in prism-reared owls (Feldman & Knudsen, 1997). In normal owls, this projection is topographic, as revealed by retrograde labeling of ICC neuronal cell bodies by small injections placed in the ICX (Figure 3.4a): injections in the rostral ICX label cell bodies in the rostral ICC while injections at progressively caudal sites in the ICX label neurons at progressively caudal locations in the ICC.

←

were older than 200 d at the time the prisms were mounted exhibited substantial ITD adjustment. Data from 20 normal owls are plotted for comparison. (c) Juvenile prism experience leaves a trace in the midbrain pathway that can be re-activated in adults. The history of one prism-reared owl is shown, with shaded areas indicating times of prism exposure. As a juvenile, this owl adjusted its map of ITDs in response to experience with R23° prisms. As an adult, the owl was able to express a normal map of ITDs or reexpress an adaptive map for R23° prisms, and a partially adaptive map for R34° prisms, but was not able to acquire a new map of ITD in response to L23° prisms.

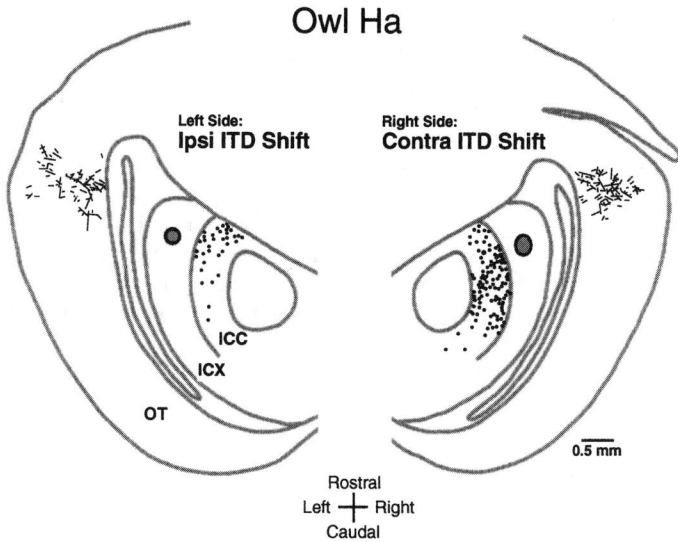

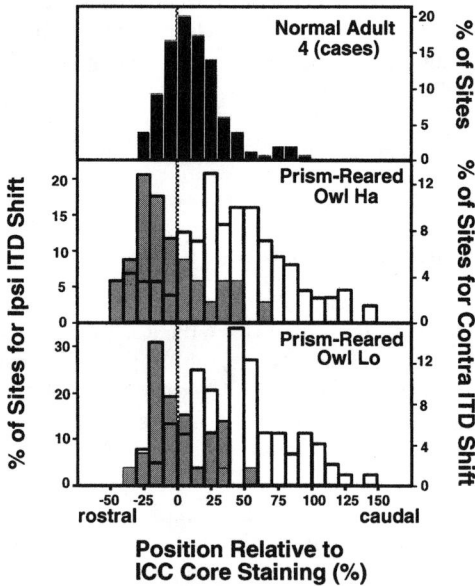

Figure 3.5. Prism-rearing alters the anatomy of the ICC-ICX projection. (A) Retrograde labeling of neuronal cell bodies in the ICC resulting from small iontophoretic injections of biotinylated dextran amine (BDA) made in the ICX of a prism-reared owl. These are camera lucida drawings of horizontal sections through the tectal lobes on both sides of the brain. Injections (shaded areas) were made at equivalent sites

In prism-reared adults that express a shifted map of ITD in the ICX, the pattern of labeled neurons in the ICC is altered systematically: Many retrogradely labelled neurons appear at abnormal locations, which are predicted by the direction of the physiologically measured shift of the ITD map (Figure 3.5a,b). These data are consistent with the hypothesis that a novel axonal projection from the ICC to the ICX conveys the learned responses. In addition, many labelled neurons also appear at normal locations, but, interestingly, these normal connections are not functionally expressed. The basis for this phenomenon will be discussed below.

NMDA Receptors Differentially Support Newly Learned Responses

During plasticity, ICX neurons pass through an intermediate stage in which they express both normal and learned responses (Figure 3.3). At this stage, the pharmacology of the normal and learned responses can be compared directly. AP-5 (an NMDA-receptor antagonist), when applied locally in the ICX at this stage, blocks learned responses far more effectively than it blocks normal responses, as shown in Figure 3.6a (Feldman, Brainard, & Knudsen, 1996, 1998b). This effect is specific for NMDA receptors, as the AMPA-receptor antagonist CNQX has the reverse effect and the broad spectrum glutamate-receptor antagonist kynurenic acid blocks both responses equally (Figure 3.6b,c). These results demonstrate that the newly learned responses are differentially dependent on NMDA-receptor activation for their expression. This heavy dependence of newly functional connections on NMDA receptors is similar to results from developmental studies on glutamatergic, suggesting that adaptive plasticity may exploit at least some of the cellular mechanisms that are utilized during early development (Feldman & Knudsen, 1998a).

Elimination of Inappropriate Responses

Adaptive adjustments of the auditory space map require not only that neurons gain responses to instructed cue values, but also that they lose responses to inappropriate values. The loss of inappropriate responses could be accomplished by decreasing the strength of underlying excitatory connections or by inhibiting responses to them. Both mechanisms are employed in the barn owl ICX during prism-induced plasticity (Zheng & Knudsen, 1999). The ICX contains a high density of GABAergic neurons and terminals (Carr, Fujita, & Konishi, 1989), and blocking inhibition mediated by $GABA_A$ receptors with the antagonist bicuculline leads to a dramatic increase in neuronal responses to all ITD channels that drive a site (Fujita & Konishi, 1991; Zheng & Knudsen). In the normal ICX, the magnitude of this increase is equal on both flanks of the ITD

---

in the ICX on both sides. The position of each labeled cell body in the ICC is indicated by a solid dot. Anterograde labeling is shown in the OT. Due to bilateral symmetry of the ITD map, the map on the two sides of the brain shifted in opposite directions: the map shifted caudally on the left side (ipsi ITD shift) and rostrally on the right side (contra ITD shift). (B) The distribution of labeled cell bodies in the ICX on both sides of the brain in normal and prism-reared owls. Top panel, composite distribution for normal owls; middle panel, the case shown in (A) (left side as gray bars, right side as open bars); bottom panel, another prism-reared owl.

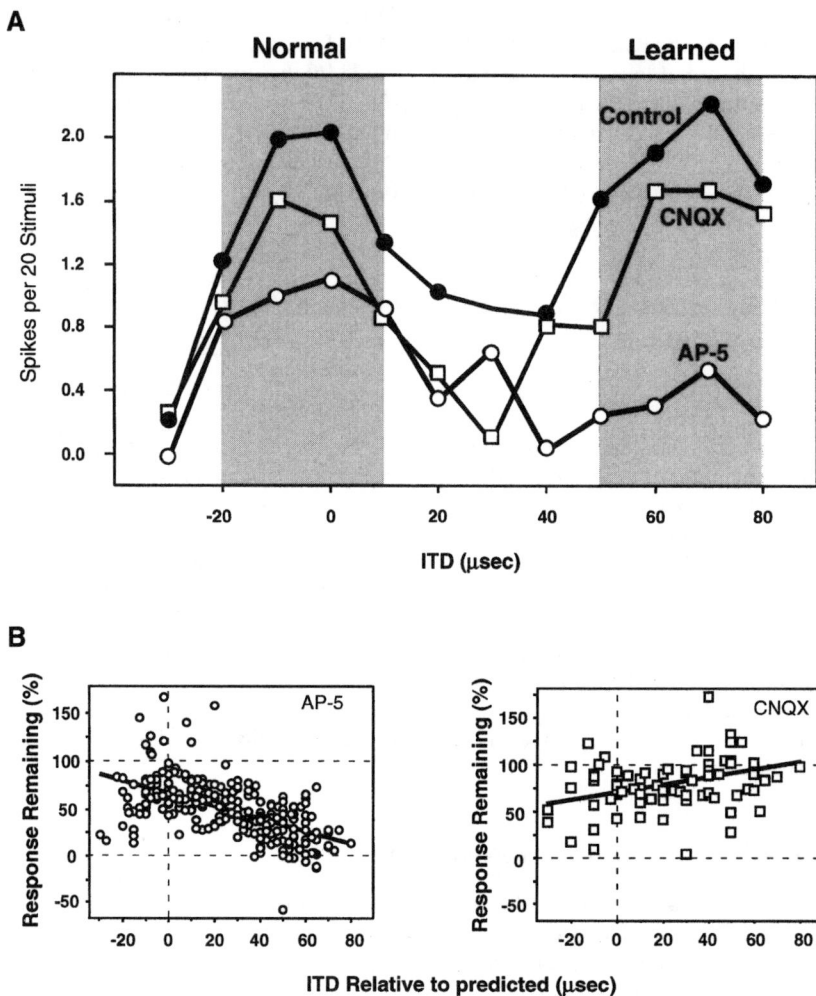

Figure 3.6. Differential contribution of NMDA receptors to learned responses. (a) ITD tuning curves recorded at a single site in the OT during iontophoreatic drug application at a spatially matched site in the ICX. This juvenile owl was at an intermediate stage in adjusting to L23° prisms. The control curve (filled circles) shows that this site responds equally well to both the normal and learned ranges of ITDs. Application of CNQX (open squares) blocks the same proportion of response in the normal and learned ranges. Application of AP-5 (open circles) has a much greater effect on the learned than on the normal responses. (b) The proportion of responses that are blocked by AP-5 (left panel, open circles) and CNQX (right panel, open squares) is ITD dependent. Percentage response remaining was derived from values such as those shown in (a). Only tuning curves that exhibited transition-state tuning (see text) were included in this analysis.

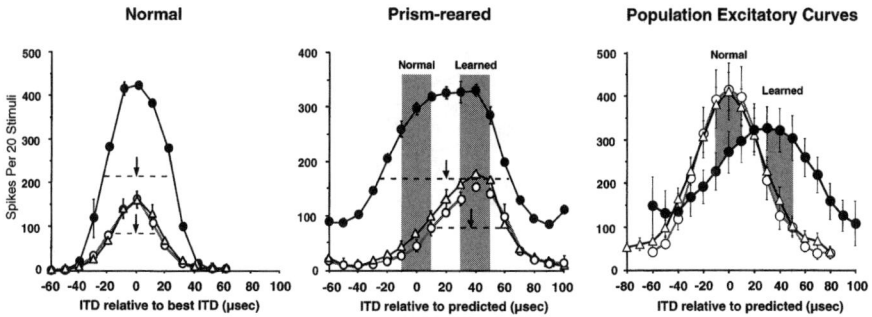

Figure 3.7. Effects of blocking GABA$_A$ inhibition in normal and prism-reared owls. These ITD tuning curves were measured before (open circles), during (closed circles), and after (open triangles) iontophoreatic application of bicuculline in the ICX. The curves are aligned relative to predicted normal best ITDs, based on the location of the recording site in the ICX. Dashes indicate the width at 50% of maximum response. Arrows indicate the center of this range, the best ITD. (a) Data from a normal owl. (b) Data from a prism-reared owl with shifted ITD tuning in the ICX. Responses to normal ITDs increase disproportionately following GABA$_A$-receptor blockade. (c) Population excitatory curves (see Figure 3.4 caption) recorded with inhibition blocked in normal (open circles), prism-reared (filled circles), and prism-removed (open triangles) owls. In the process of shifting the map of ITDs, excitatory drive decreases for normal ITDs and increases for learned ITDs.

tuning curve, as shown in Figure 3.7, left panel. In contrast, in an ICX that is expressing a fully shifted map of ITD, blocking GABA$_A$-mediated inhibition unmasks disproportionately strong excitatory responses to normal ITDs (Figure 3.7, center panel). This result indicates that strong excitatory connections, supporting responses to normal ITDs, persist but are suppressed by unusually strong inhibition. As a consequence, the ratio of inhibition to excitation for the normal ITD input channel is unusually high.

In addition to this increase in the inhibition of the normal ITD channel, the strength of the excitatory drive for the normal ITD channel decreases. Excitatory drive can be quantified from the strength of responses with inhibition suppressed with bicuculline (Zheng & Knudsen, 1999). When compared between normal and prism-reared owls, responses to normal ITD values are slightly but significantly weaker (Figure 3.7, right panel). Thus the elimination of responses to normal values of ITDs in an ICX that is expressing a shifted map of ITDs involves both a decrease in excitatory drive and an increase in inhibition of normal ITD channels.

In contrast, in prism-reared owls that have had the prisms removed and in which the ITD map has returned to normal, blocking inhibition does not unmask strong excitatory responses for the previously learned ITD values (Zheng & Knudsen, 1999). This indicates that the learned responses can be eliminated completely by decreasing the strength of their excitatory inputs alone. The inability to eliminate responses to the normal ITD channel solely by decreasing the strength of the excitatory drive suggests that the connections supporting normal responses are privileged relative to learned functional connections. This may explain the capacity of the ITD map to return to normal at any age when the animal is exposed to a normal sensory environment.

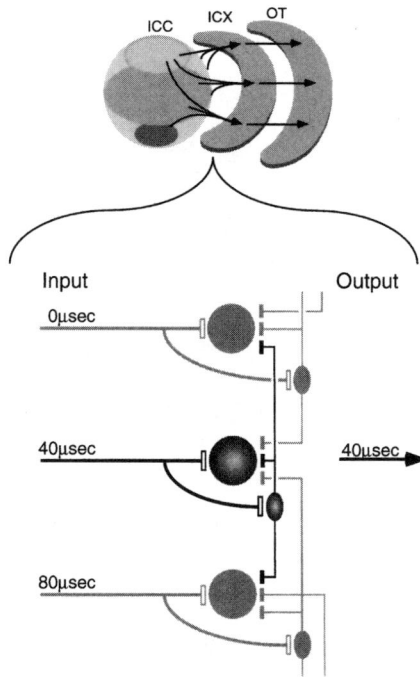

Figure 3.8. Model of the native ICX network. Excitatory (output) neurons are represented by large circles; inhibitory interneurons are represented by smaller ovals. Synaptic contacts are shown as rectangles: open for excitatory synapses and filled for inhibitory synapses. The relative sizes of rectangles reflect the relative strengths of the synapses. Neurons and synapses that are activated by a 40 μsec ITD stimulus are darkened. All other neurons and connections are grey. Only the middle excitatory and inhibitory neurons are activated by this stimulus.

☐ Model for the Cellular Basis of Adaptive Plasticity

Adaptive plasticity of the auditory space map can be studied at the behavioral, systems, and cellular levels. Thus, it provides an excellent paradigm for analyzing cellular mechanisms of learning. To focus this effort, we present a simple model for the cellular basis of plasticity in the barn owl ICX (Figure 3.8), which can account for all of the cellular results that have been discussed thus far.

The model is based on a linear feedforward network, analogous to other known biological networks in the superior colliculus, hippocampus, and cerebellum. In our model, input coming from the ICC is organized in ITD-specific channels; for each ITD channel, ICC input contacts both excitatory (output neurons) and inhibitory interneurons in the ICX. Activation of a channel (for example, by a 40 μsec ITD stimulus) leads to direct excitation and indirect inhibition of the output neuron. For the native ICX network shown in Figure 3.8, the strength of the excitatory drive to the output neuron exceeds the strength of the inhibitory drive, producing activity in the normal output channel.

In normal owls, inhibition sharpens the ITD tuning of ICX neurons (Fujita & Konishi, 1991; Zheng & Knudsen, 1999). Assuming linear summation of excitatory and inhibitory

Acquisition of Learned Responses   Elimination of Normal Responses

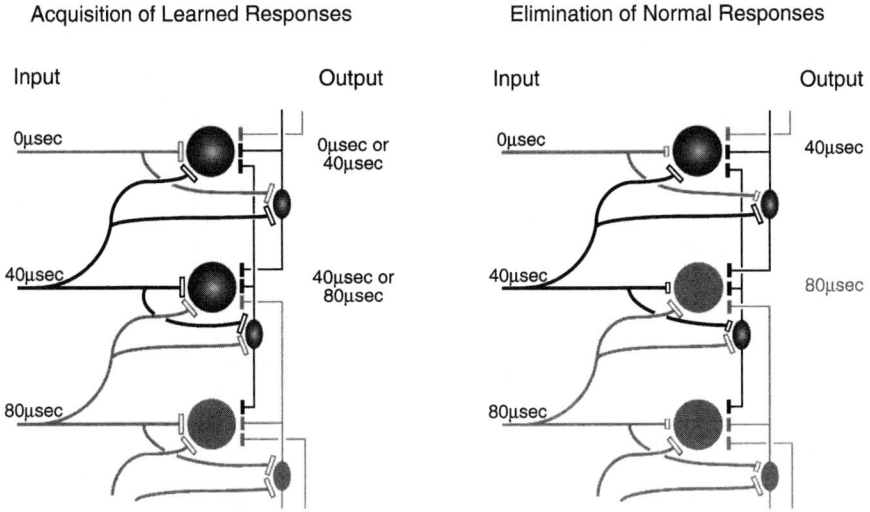

Figure 3.9. Model of the cellular basis of adaptive plasticity. Left panel: Acquisition of learned responses. All symbols are as defined in Figure 3.8. Functional connections that support learned responses are accounted for by new connections that cross ITD channels and form indiscriminately on both excitatory and inhibitory neurons (see text for discussion). The top output neuron responds to a stimulus at either 0 μsec or 40 μsec ITD, while the middle output neuron responds to either a 40 μsec or an 80 μsec ITD. Right panel: Elimination of normal responses. All symbols as defined in Figure 3.8. The strength of the normal excitatory synapses onto output neurons and inhibitory interneurons have been diminished. Consequently, the middle output neuron no longer responds to a 40 μsec ITD and responds only to an 80 μsec ITD.

inputs, this result implies that the pattern of inhibition across ITD channels differs from the pattern of excitation. This property is represented in the model by the lateral connections of the inhibitory interneurons, as shown in Figure 3.8.

The changes to this native ICX network that are induced by prism rearing are shown in Figure 3.9. During the acquisition of learned responses, newly functional connections are formed across ITD channels (left panel). These newly functional connections could result from axonal outgrowth and synaptogensis, or potentiation of preexisting weak or silent synapses, or both. In either case, the simplest assumption is that these newly functional connections are formed indiscriminately on both excitatory and inhibitory neurons, as in the native network. As a result of these newly functional connections, output neurons in the ICX will be activated by both the normal and learned channels. This accounts for the appearance of transition-state ITD tuning curves (Figure 3.3, center panel).

The final stage of plasticity involves the elimination of the normal responses (Figure 3.3, right panel). This could, in principle, be due to either loss of excitatory drive from the normal ITD channel or to abnormally strong inhibition resulting from the activation of the normal channel. Inspection of the model reveals that both of these mechanisms could be causally related. As indicated in the right panel of Figure 3.9, even a partial decrease in the strength of the excitatory drive from the normal ITD input channel results in an unusually high ratio of inhibition to excitation. This is due to the effect of the cross-ITD channel connections onto inhibitory interneurons that formed during the acquisition phase. This connection conveys the strong inhibition associated with the activation of the normal ITD channel through its lateral connections. The net result is a substantial decrease in, or loss of, normal responses.

This model can also account for results from prism-reared owls that have had their prisms removed (Zheng & Knudsen, 1999). In response to prism removal, the excitatory drive from the normal channel increases, while the cross-ITD channel excitatory drive from the learned channel decreases and eventually disappears. The network now functions exactly like a native network, and blocking inhibition does not reveal any excitatory drive in response to the previously learned ITD channel. Interestingly, a network trained in this fashion retains the capability to reform the learned, cross-ITD connections rapidly should they become adaptive later in adult life (Figure 3.4).

☐ Conclusions

The midbrain auditory localization pathway, like many pathways in the nervous system, is shaped powerfully by experience, and especially by experience that occurs during early life. The midbrain pathway synthesizes a map of auditory space based on the tuning of neurons for sound localization cues. This map merges with a visual space map in the OT. The effect of experience on the auditory localization pathway manifests as changes in the tuning of tectal neurons for sound localization cues. These changes are instructed by a visually based signal and are adaptive in that they tend to restore alignment of the auditory and visual maps of space in the tectum.

In the barn owl, the cellular and molecular mechanisms that underlie the plasticity of the auditory space map are beginning to be understood. Experience-dependent changes involve the acquisition of "learned" neuronal responses as well as the elimination of inappropriate "normal" responses. Acquisition of learned responses is accompanied by anatomical remodeling and is supported primarily by NMDA-receptor currents. Elimination of inappropriate normal responses is achieved by weakening of normal excitatory connections and differentially strong inhibition of normal responses. Once the midbrain pathway has acquired an alternative map of localization cues as a result of juvenile experience, this alternative map can be reexpressed later in adult life in response to appropriate sensory experience. A simple neuronal network model can account for these results and provides a conceptual framework for further inquiry into the cellular mechanisms of plasticity in both juvenile and adult animals.

☐ References

Brainard, M. S., & Knudsen, E. I. (1993). Experience-dependent plasticity in the inferior colliculus: A site for visual calibration of the neural representation of auditory space in the barn owl. *Journal of Neuroscience, 13* (11), 4589–4608.

Brainard, M. S., & Knudsen, E. I. (1995). Dynamics of visually guided auditory plasticity in the optic tectum of the barn owl. *Journal of Neurophysiology, 73* (2), 595–614.

Brainard, M. S., & Knudsen, E. I. (1998). Sensitive periods for visual calibration of the auditory space map in the barn owl optic tectum. *Journal of Neuroscience, 18* (10), 3929–3942.

Brainard, M. S., Knudsen, E. I., & Esterly, S. D. (1992). Neural derivation of sound source location: Resolution of spatial ambiguities in binaural cues. *Journal of the Acoustical Society of America, 91* (2), 1015–1027.

Carr, C. E., Fujita, I., & Konishi, M. (1989). Distribution of GABAergic neurons and terminals in the auditory system of the barn owl. *Journal of Comparative Neurology, 286* (2), 190–207.

Cohen, Y. E., & Knudsen, E. I. (1999). Maps versus clusters: Different representations of auditory space in the midbrain and forebrain. *Trends in Neuroscience, 22* (3), 128–135.

Feldman, D. E., Brainard, M. S., & Knudsen, E. I. (1996). Newly learned auditory responses mediated by NMDA receptors in the owl inferior colliculus. *Science, 271* (5248), 525–528.

Feldman, D. E., & Knudsen, E. I. (1997). An anatomical basis for visual calibration of the auditory space map in the barn owl's midbrain. *Journal of Neuroscience, 17* (17), 6820–6837.

Feldman, D. E., & Knudsen, E. I. (1998a). Experience-dependent plasticity and the maturation of glutamatergic synapses. *Neuron, 20* (6), 1067–1071.

Feldman, D. E., & Knudsen, E. I. (1998b). Pharmacological specialization of learned auditory responses in the inferior colliculus of the barn owl. *Journal of Neuroscience, 18* (8), 3073–3087.

Fujita, I., & Konishi, M. (1991). The role of GABAergic inhibition in processing of interaural time difference in the owl's auditory system. *Journal of Neuroscience, 11* (3), 722–739.

Gold, J. I., & Knudsen, E. I. (1999). Hearing impairment induces frequency-specific adjustments in auditory spatial tuning in the optic tectum of young owls. *Journal of Neurophysiology, 82*(5), 2197–2209.

Jay, M. F., & Sparks, D. L. (1984). Auditory receptive fields in primate superior colliculus shift with changes in eye position. *Nature, 309* (5966), 345–347.

Keller, C. H., Hartung, K., & Takahashi, T. T. (1998). Head-related transfer functions of the barn owl: Measurement and neural responses. *Hearing Research, 118* (1–2), 13–34.

King, A. J. (1993). The Wellcome Prize Lecture. A map of auditory space in the mammalian brain: Neural computation and development. *Experimental Physiology, 78* (5), 559–590.

King, A. J., & Carlile, S. (1993). Changes induced in the representation of auditory space in the superior colliculus by rearing ferrets with binocular eyelid suture. *Experimental Brain Research, 94* (3), 444–455.

King, A. J., & Hutchings, M. E. (1987). Spatial response properties of acoustically responsive neurons in the superior colliculus of the ferret: A map of auditory space. *Journal of Neurophysiology, 57* (2), 596–624.

King, A. J., Hutchings, M. E., Moore, D. R., & Blakemore, C. (1988). Developmental plasticity in the visual and auditory representations in the mammalian superior colliculus. *Nature, 332* (6159), 73–76.

King, A. J., & Palmer, A. R. (1983). Cells responsive to free-field auditory stimuli in guinea-pig superior colliculus: Distribution and response properties. *Journal of Physiology (London), 342,* 361–381.

Knudsen, E. I. (1982). Auditory and visual maps of space in the optic tectum of the owl. *Journal of Neuroscience, 2* (9), 1177–1194.

Knudsen, E. I. (1983). Early auditory experience aligns the auditory map of space in the optic tectum of the barn owl. *Science, 222* (4626), 939–942.

Knudsen, E. I. (1984). Auditory properties of space-tuned units in owl's optic tectum. *Journal of Neurophysiology, 52* (4), 709–723.

Knudsen, E. I. (1998). Capacity for plasticity in the adult owl auditory system expanded by juvenile experience. *Science, 279* (5356), 1531–1533.

Knudsen, E. I., & Brainard, M. S. (1991). Visual instruction of the neural map of auditory space in the developing optic tectum. *Science, 253* (5015), 85–87.

Knudsen, E. I., Esterly, S. D., & du Lac, S. (1991). Stretched and upside-down maps of auditory space in the optic tectum of blind-reared owls; acoustic basis and behavioral correlates. *Journal of Neuroscience, 11* (6), 1727–1747.

Knudsen, E. I., Esterly, S. D., & Olsen, J. F. (1994). Adaptive plasticity of the auditory space map in the optic tectum of adult and baby barn owls in response to external ear modification. *Journal of Neurophysiology, 71* (1), 79–94.

Knudsen, E. I., Knudsen, P. F., & Masino, T. (1993). Parallel pathways mediating both sound localization and gaze control in the forebrain and midbrain of the barn owl. *Journal of Neuroscience, 13* (7), 2837–2852.

Middlebrooks, J. C., & Green, D. M. (1991). Sound localization by human listeners. *Annual Review of Psychology, 42,* 135–159.

Middlebrooks, J. C., & Knudsen, E. I. (1984). A neural code for auditory space in the cat's superior colliculus. *Journal of Neuroscience, 4*(10), 2621–2634.

Miller, G. L., & Knudsen, E. I. (1999). Early visual experience shapes the representation of auditory space in the forebrain gaze fields of the barn owl. *Journal of Neuroscience, 19* (6), 2326–2336.

Mogdans, J., & Knudsen, E. I. (1992). Adaptive adjustment of unit tuning to sound localization cues in response to monaural occlusion in developing owl optic tectum. *Journal of Neuroscience, 12* (9), 3473–3484.

Mogdans, J., & Knudsen, E. I. (1993). Early monaural occlusion alters the neural map of interaural level differences in the inferior colliculus of the barn owl. *Brain Research, 619* (1–2), 29–38.

Moiseff, A., & Konishi, M. (1981). Neuronal and behavioral sensitivity to binaural time differences in the owl. *Journal of Neuroscience, 1* (1), 40–48.

Olsen, J. F., Knudsen, E. I., & Esterly, S. D. (1989). Neural maps of interaural time and intensity differences in the optic tectum of the barn owl. *Journal of Neuroscience, 9* (7), 2591–2605.

Schnupp, J. W. H., King, A. J., & Carlile, S. (1998). Altered spectral localization cues disrupt the development of the auditory space map in the superior colliculus of the ferret. *Journal of Neurophysiology, 79* (2), 1053–1069.

Stein, B. E., & Meredith, M. A. (1993). *The merging of the senses.* Cambridge, MA: MIT Press.

Wise, L. Z., & Irvine, D. R. (1985). Topographic organization of interaural intensity difference sensitivity in deep layers of cat superior colliculus: Implications for auditory spatial representation. *Journal of Neurophysiology, 54* (2), 185–211.

Withington, D. J. (1992). The effect of binocular lid suture on auditory responses in the guinea-pig superior colliculus. *Neuroscience Letters, 136,* 153–156.

Withington-Wray, D. J., Binns, K. E., & Keating, M. J. (1990a). The maturation of the superior collicular map of auditory space in the guinea pig is disrupted by developmental auditory deprivation. *European Journal of Neuroscience, 2,* 693–703.

Withington-Wray, D. J., Binns, K. E., & Keating, M. J. (1990b). The maturation of the superior collicular map of auditory space in the guinea pig is disrupted by developmental visual deprivation. *European Journal of Neuroscience, 2,* 682–692.

Zheng, W., & Knudsen, E. I. (1999). Functional selection of adaptive auditory space map by GABA$_A$-mediated inhibition. *Science, 284* (5416), 962–965.

4

CHAPTER

Norman M. Weinberger

Learning and Receptive Field Plasticity in the Auditory Cortex: Identification of a Memory Code?

☐ Introduction

Investigations of neuroplasticity cover an exceptionally broad span of neuroscience, including development, aging, brain insult, and learning. This chapter concerns the latter, specifically the receptive field plasticity that develops in the primary auditory cortex during normal behavioral learning. This line of inquiry has not only revealed that the primary sensory cortex is specifically retuned by learning but also that receptive field plasticity permits the potential discovery of memory codes.

By a *memory code* I mean a relationship that describes the transformation of an experience into an enduring neural form. As there seem to be no prior systematic writings about neurobiological memory codes, the concept may be highly novel and this definition may seem vague at this point. However, the concept of a memory code is explicated in the balance of this chapter. The experimental support for a particular candidate code will also be presented. This is the memory code for the learned behavioral importance of events. We suggest that the memory code for the acquired behavioral importance of a stimulus is the amount of receptive field retuning toward or to that stimulus. In short, more cells become tuned to important stimuli and fewer cells become tuned to less important stimuli.

☐ Developmental and Adult Sensory System Neuroplasticity

The inclusion of receptive field plasticity as a substrate of memory involves a marked departure from the traditional assumption that sensory systems are not involved in learning and memory or are at best substrates only of "perceptual learning," such as improved acuity over thousands of trials and scores of training days (Karni, 1996; Karni & Sagi, 1993). The literature now strongly supports the conclusion that the primary sensory cortex fully participates in the acquisition and storage of experience (reviewed in Weinberger, 1995). That learning in the adult involves substantial and systematic plasticity in the sensory cortex breaks with traditional conceptions of sensory system function but is no more revolutionary than the past discovery that early experience leaves its strong imprint on the developing sensory system, a now-accepted fact that was unknown and unpredicted before the findings of Hubel and Weisel in the 1960s.

Because early sensory exposure shapes the domain of possible perceptions, the resultant individual structural and functional sensory system architectures can be considered "long-term memories," but largely only in a metaphorical sense, because such memories have little if any content. Although they reflect past experience, such organizational substrates appear to delimit possibilities rather than comprise the repository of the "stuff" of experience, the detailed stream of explicitly or implicitly remembered events. Nonetheless, developmental plasticity in sensory systems may be considered the first stage of sensory system storage of experience, a process now known to continue throughout the life-span.

While there is every reason to believe that the storage of the experiential stuff or contents—the details of memory—also occurs in the primary sensory cortex during development, this is largely an unexplored area. But this line of inquiry has been conducted in adult animals, including humans, in which learning and developmental processes can be disentangled. The structural changes that are likely to occur in the adult sensory cortex are no doubt far more subtle than the large-scale changes observed during development. However, there are marked and highly specific functional plasticities within adult primary sensory cortices and these involve the storage of actual behavioral experiences themselves. This discovery has led to a broader conception of the functions of primary sensory cortices and also provided a novel approach to the problem of memory codes.

☐ What Is a Memory Code?

The term memory code may bring to mind the term *memory encoding*. Of course, encoding in memory is neither a new nor a neglected topic. However, it has been approached mainly with respect to discovering which aspects of experience in humans (and sometimes other animals) attain memory. This important issue provides insight into the principles that govern what may be called the contents of memory, or the "attributes of experience." However, issues of memory encoding largely concern psychological constructs and more recently the detection of regions of the brain whose changes in activity levels seem to correlate with encoding various types of information.

What about encoding has been neglected? We believe a fundamental issue has been ignored, perhaps because it is too daunting: the actual neural codes used by the brain to store cardinal features of experience. Such neural codes operate at a deeper, that is, more reductionistic, level than encoding because they would constitute the actual neural representation of the characteristics of memory. We hypothesize that memory codes operate at the level of the transformation of current dynamic neural activity into long-lasting *alterations of neural tissue*, which are more latent in character.

We propose two principles, explicitly:

1. The brain actually uses memory codes to represent stored experience. We believe that memory codes exist in the same general sense in which sensory codes exist.
2. Neural encoding is governed by principles that are related to the type of information stored. This chapter discusses a code for stimulus importance, but we hypothesize that other codes are used to represent other aspects of experience. There may be different memory codes for different classes of information.

☐ What Are Attributes of Stored Experience?

Given that the storage of experience must include detail, we can ask what attributes of an experience may be stored. Several attributes are listed here, without attempting to be exhaustive.

1. Background stimuli, that is, those stimuli relatively constant in the learning situation, including the location or place in which the experience occurs.
2. Changing of stimuli, which are usually brief (milliseconds to seconds).
3. Any and all sensory parameters of background and phasic stimuli: sensory modality (e.g., visual), sensory dimension (e.g., sound frequency), location, intensity, duration, pattern, etc.
4. Physiological effects of receiving appetitive or aversive stimulation: sensory feedback, hormonal release and feedback, autonomic feedback.
5. Motivational/affective: appetitive, aversive, novel.
6. General physiological state, as exemplified by state-dependent learning, state of general arousal, state of sexual arousal, state of hunger, etc.
7. Time of day, month, and season.

In short, attributes of experience include all afferentation to the brain plus various brain states themselves.

There is a paradoxical aspect of encoding: the fact that the encoding of experience into memory simultaneously encompasses both less and more than we directly sense. With regard to the "less" side, consider the construct of the *sensorium*, which is defined as the totality of sensory receptor epithelia. The state of the sensorium at any instant comprises a representation of all the sensory events that may attain processing within a nervous system and that therefore ultimately may be stored as components of memory. However, on both reasonable empirical and conceptual grounds, the complete state of the sensorium at any one instant does not attain the status of memory, defined as enduring for minutes or longer. Not all sensory events are stored. Thus, memory, regardless of which type or form, contains less than did the sensorium.

As to the "more" side, encoding includes factors that are not and never can be present in the sensorium. These are the more abstract features of experience. For example, a subject may encode whether or not a stimulus is novel or unexpected in a given context, by comparing it with stored information. Another encoded abstraction is that of the acquired behavioral significance of a stimulus. This certainly occurs in associative conditioning, as when a conditional stimulus (CS) acquires significance by its predictive value as a signal for an unconditional stimulus (US). However, virtually all learning situations involve "tagging" or "assigning" significance or importance to experience, from the simplest habituation situation in invertebrates to the most sophisticated cognitive processes in humans.

☐ Engrams and Memory Codes are Different

Continuing an explication of memory codes, we now come to the question of how such codes are related to engrams. Engrams and memory codes are related, but they are not at all the same sort of things. As originally coined by Semon (1921), and still in common use, *engrams* are generally considered to be the totality of neural changes that comprise a memory. One seeks engrams, or at least places where particular engrams exist (Lashley, 1950; Thompson, 1976). When found in whole, or more likely in part, engrams can be subjected to reductionistic analyses at circuit, cellular, and molecular levels.

Memory codes are not the substrates of neural memories themselves. Each separate memory for the unique experiences of individual organisms may involve an individual engram. In contrast, we consider that memory codes comprise a finite class of relationships that denote an aspect of memories. More specifically, a memory code denotes a particular type of "input-output" function. A memory code describes the transform function from, for example, patterns of sensory-derived neuronal discharges (input) into long-lasting changes in nervous tissue (output). The long lasting changes in neural organization constitute an engram.

Memory codes need be no more conceptually mysterious than are sensory codes, although they are much more difficult to find. A sensory code describes the input-output relationship between a pattern of energy on a receptor epithelium (input) and the discharges of sensory neurons (output). A well-known sensory code is the increase in rate of discharge (output) as stimulus intensity increases (input). The code is described by the input-output function, that is, stimulus intensity versus rate of discharge.

To help clarify the relationship between an engram and a memory code, consider the example of the auditory memory for your own name. This "sonic engram" presumably consists of various types of linked neuronal changes (at the levels of circuits, cells, and subcellular processes) perhaps localized mainly in the left hemisphere in one or more parts of the auditory cortex. What might be one of the involved memory codes? Because one's own name is very important, the memory needs to be encoded not only along acoustic dimensions but also in terms of relative behavioral importance. Therefore, a memory code for behavioral importance would be involved. It might be "increase the number of neurons that process and store highly important sensory stimuli."

Whether or not this is a memory code that would operate on one's own name is unknown. However, we believe that this may be the code for stimulus importance, based on evidence from the use of pure tone stimuli in guinea-pigs and rats. We now turn to the findings that have led us to this hypothesis.

☐ Learning Retunes the Primary Auditory Cortex

We originally developed the use of receptive field analysis in learning to bridge the gap between sensory physiology and the neurobiology of learning and memory. More specifically, we thought that the determination of how the brain changed in response only to training sensory stimuli, such as conditioned stimuli that were paired (CS+) or not paired (CS−) with a US, provided a less than comprehensive data set with which to probe the representation of stored experience. Therefore, we combined techniques from the two fields to ask how various types of learning might affect the receptive fields of neurons, in the auditory thalamus and primary auditory cortex.

Although this line of research was not originally conceived with reference to memory codes, it seems to have provided an entry point into the search for such codes. In effect, the receptive field studies have used the output of a sensory code to seek a memory code for acquired stimulus importance. The output in question is the receptive field for acoustic frequency. As commonly defined, a sensory receptive field of a neuron is comprised of all of the stimuli whose presence affects the neuron's activity. As used here, the frequency receptive field is the set of pure tone frequencies whose presentation alters the discharges of one or more neurons. (We focus on excitatory responses while recognizing that cells can be inhibited by stimuli.) The frequency receptive field is commonly displayed as a graph of the number of discharges versus acoustic frequency. This graph is often called a "tuning curve" and we will use this term synonymously with "frequency receptive field" (or simply RF within the context of auditory experiments). The question we addressed was whether or not frequency RFs in the auditory cortex are systematically transformed when an animal learns that a single pure tone frequency is a signal for another event.

The basic behavioral situation used to discover that learning specifically modifies neuronal receptive fields in the primary auditory cortex is rapid Pavlovian cardiac conditioning. An adult guinea-pig receives a 6 s tone (CS) followed at tone offset by a brief, mild pawshock (US). Thirty trials are presented at approximately 1.5-minute intervals in a single session lasting approximately 45 minutes. Receptive field plasticity is also induced during two-tone discriminative Pavlovian conditioning. Moreover, it develops during instrumental avoidance conditioning, both for one-tone training and in two-tone discrimination training. This commonality across tasks and types of learning supports the view that the shifts in the tuning of receptive fields denote the operation of a general code for acquired stimulus significance. The findings will be summarized only briefly (for review, see Weinberger, 1998).

The fundamental experiment consists of a hybrid design in which a sensory physiology paradigm is combined with a learning and memory paradigm. Following prior chronic implantation of microelectrodes in the primary auditory cortex (hereafter, "auditory cortex" or ACx), there are three basic stages.

1. Receptive fields are obtained in an acoustic chamber by presenting brief tone pips (50–100 ms) of many frequencies (and often much intensity) to the contralateral ear under conditions of acoustic control. The peak of the resultant frequency tuning curve (best frequency, BF) is noted, and a nonbest frequency is selected to serve as the CS; the rationale for choosing a non-BF is that this permits the detection of a shift in tuning toward, or all the way to, the frequency of the CS.
2. The subject is moved to a different experimental room where it undergoes classical (or instrumental avoidance) conditioning in a single session. For classical conditioning, heart rate is recorded. After several trials of habituation to the CS alone, the cardiac deceleration conditioned response develops within 5–10 trials (Edeline & Weinberger, 1993).
3. The animal is returned to the acoustic chamber and receptive fields are obtained using the tone stimulus set identical to that employed in stage 1. RFs may be obtained repeatedly over days; the longest time employed has been about 60 days.

The findings can be summarized as follows. Receptive fields are changed in a systematic way to favor processing of the frequency of the CS; responses to the CS frequency are relatively increased, whereas responses to the pretraining BF and many other frequencies are reduced or less changed. The simultaneous opposite changes may be sufficiently

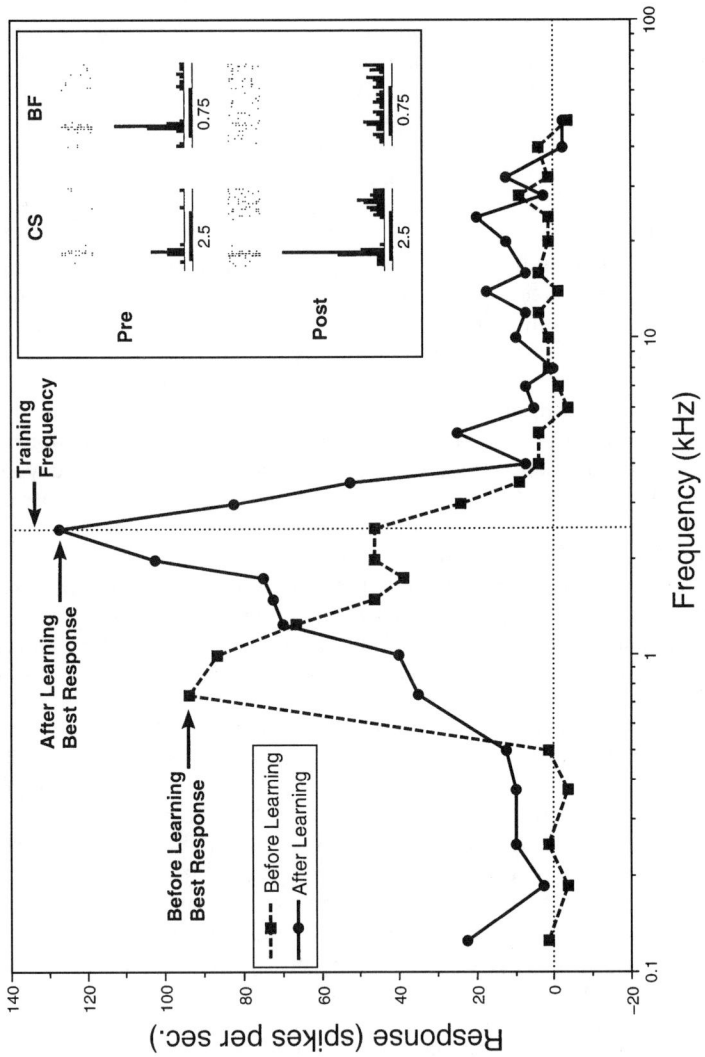

Learning that a Sound (Frequency) is Important Shifts Tuning ("Retunes") Auditory Cortex Cells to the Important Frequency

large to actually shift the RF toward or even to the frequency of the conditioned stimulus (Figure 4.1).

This RF plasticity is associative because random presentation of the CS and US does not induce tuning shifts but only a general increase in response across frequency (Bakin, Lepan, & Weinberger, 1992; Figure 4.2a, b). Note that because conditioning and sensitization both produce increased response to the frequency of the CS, one would conclude that conditioning and sensitization have the same effect if only responses to this frequency had been studied. Habituation produces specific decreased responses at the frequency of the repeated stimulus (Figure 4.2c).

RF plasticity is also discriminative: responses to a reinforced frequency (CS+) increase, whereas responses to a nonreinforced (CS−) frequency and other frequencies decrease (Edeline & Weinberger, 1993). The tuning shifts are not spontaneous because the shifts are toward, not equally away from, the frequency of the CS. Finally, CS-specific RF plasticity is not due to putative arousal to the CS frequency during the posttraining determination of receptive fields, for at least four reasons. First, subjects exhibit no behavioral arousal (e.g., cardiac response) to this frequency when it is presented in RF assays for 100 ms intermixed with all the other frequencies instead of as a CS of 6 s. Second, the latency of arousal is greater than the latency of tone-elicited neuronal discharges (~150 ms vs ~10 ms, respectively). Third, neural responses to the succeeding tone presented only a few hundred milliseconds after the occurrence of the CS frequency do not exhibit increased responses, which would be predicted by an arousal explanation. Fourth, RF plasticity that is induced when animals are awake can be expressed when they are under deep barbiturate anesthesia, during which state stimuli cannot and do not produce arousal (Weinberger, Javid, & Lepan, 1993).

RF plasticity has other important characteristics in addition to being associative and stimulus specific. It is induced very rapidly, in as few as five trials (Edeline, Pham, & Weinberger, 1993). Of particular importance, RF plasticity is retained for very long periods of time. It is present as long at 2 months after a single training session of 30 trials; this is the longest retention interval tested to date (Weinberger et al., 1993). Finally, RF plasticity exhibits consolidation, that is becomes stronger over hours

---

Figure 4.1. The effects of associative learning on the frequency receptive fields of a cell in the primary auditory cortex of a guinea-pig. The subject underwent 30 trials of classical conditioning, during which a 6 s tone (CS) was followed by a mild pawshock at stimulus offset. The subject developed a cardiac decelerative conditioned response, used to indicate that associative conditioning had been successful. Preconditioning, the cell's BF was 0.75 kHz. After conditioning with a CS of 2.5 kHz, the tuning had shifted so that the frequency of the CS became the peak of the tuning curve, that is, the new BF. Note the opposite sign changes, with increased responses to the frequency of the CS and adjacent frequencies but decreased responses to the preconditioning BF and its adjacent frequencies. The inset shows the poststimulus time histograms (PSTHs) for the frequency of the CS and the BF pre- and postconditioning. Rasters show all spike discharges during the 20 repetitions of all frequencies used to determine the tuning curves. (Not illustrated are PSTHs for other frequencies.) Note the increased response to the frequency of the CS and the decreased response to the preconditioning BF; the consistency of response to the CS frequency in the postconditioning rasters shows that the increase of response was characteristic of each presentation of the CS frequency in the postconditioning receptive field.

TABLE 4.1. Some characteristics of associative memory and learning-induced receptive field plasticity.

Characteristic	Associative memory	Receptive field plasticity
Associative?	Yes	Yes
Highly specific?	Yes	Yes
Discriminative?	Yes	Yes
Rapidly acquired?	Yes	Yes
Long-lasting?	Yes	Yes
Consolidates?	Yes	Yes

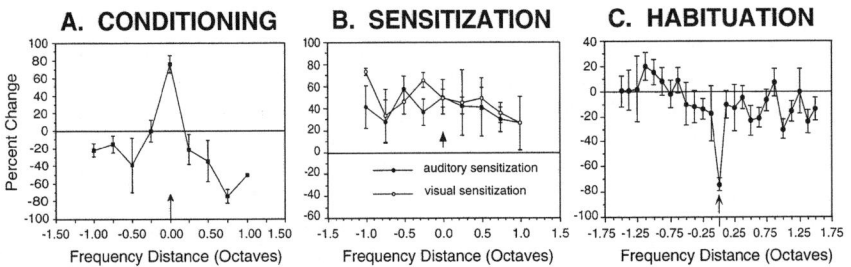

Figure 4.2. Classical conditioning produces specific, associative receptive field plasticity in the primary auditory cortex. Each panel shows group average receptive field difference functions (post-training minus pre-training or control). The abscissa is frequency distance (octaves) from a reference frequency, either the frequency of the CS during conditioning (A), sensitization training (B), or a repeated tone during habituation (C). A. Conditioning produces a highly specific increase in the receptive field such that response is increased only to the frequency of the CS, while the responses to all other frequencies show no change or actually are decreased ("side-band suppression"). B. Sensitization training (tone or light presented randomly with shock) produces a non-specific increase in responses to all frequencies. Note that training with a light produces the same general effect as training with a tone, showing that general sensitized effects are not specific to the auditory modality. C. Habituation (repetition of a single tone for several minutes) produces a specific decrease at the frequency of the repeated stimulus.

(Edeline & Weinberger, 1993) and even days (Galvan et al., 1998) without further training.

Table 4.1 summarizes the characteristics of RF plasticity with those of at least some forms of associative memory. RF plasticity possesses all of these characteristics. Therefore, it is a viable candidate to encode specific attributes of a learning experience. As previously noted, the stimulus attribute that we believe is so encoded is the acquired behavioral importance of the frequency of the CS.

These findings show that acoustic frequencies that acquire behavioral importance as signals for reinforcement or for the opportunity to avoid an aversive event achieve greater control of cortical processing than frequencies that do not serve as relevant behavioral signals. At the level of single neurons, this is observed as increased response to signal frequencies and decreased response to nonsignal frequencies. But this individual retuning of receptive fields has implications for the overall functional organization of the primary auditory cortex because the frequency map is comprised of the receptive fields or, more specifically, is denoted by the best frequencies of cells at various loci. Therefore, after having found RF plasticity in the primary auditory cortex, we specifically hypothesized that learning would produce an increased representation of signal important frequencies across the map (Weinberger et al., 1990). This prediction was subsequently verified in the owl monkey (Recanzone, Schreiner, & Merzenich, 1993). The code for stimulus importance, then, may be the number of cells (i.e., amount of cortex) that become tuned to a stimulus.

☐ Some Functional Implications

There are several functional implications for a memory code that represents the behavioral significance of a stimulus by increasing the number of neurons that are tuned toward or to that stimulus, that is, biasing a cortical field to that stimulus (Weinberger et al., 1990).

First, detection of that stimulus in a noisy situation could be increased because the probability of engaging cells that preferentially process that stimulus would be increased. This does not mean that the cells are "grandmother" cells, that is, that they are tuned so specifically that they would only respond to a highly specific and unique stimulus such as one's own grandmother. Rather, we suggest that whatever the degree of tuning across a population of cells, their aggregate neuronal synaptic and spike activity to that stimulus will be greater than otherwise simply because the tuning of more neurons has been biased toward responding to that stimulus.

A second implication is that the stimulus in question might be more effective in gaining attention in any situation, again on the hypothesis that the aggregate amount of response would be positively related to the behavioral salience of a stimulus.

Third, there are more likely to be errors of perceptual commission for that stimulus because highly similar stimuli will also command greater neural response than otherwise. A common example is that we often "hear" our name (particularly in a noisy environment) when it hasn't been called at all. Moreover, we are more likely to respond to words similar or identical to our name when they refer to something else. For example, with a nickname of "Norm," I find it difficult to listen to discussions about statistical "norms" without beginning to react as if to my name.

Fourth, there might be a neuroprotective function in the form of an increased "safety" margin for processing and responding to important stimuli in the presence of cerebral damage or other compromised functioning, such as fatigue, drugged states, and the like.

☐ Neuroepistemology

There are other sorts of implications, both of learning-induced retuning of the sensory cortex and of a memory code that employs numbers of synapses and neurons to encode the behavioral importance of stimuli. These cannot be adequately discussed in the current forum. However, one is worth mentioning, with apologies to professional philosophers.

Epistemelogy, the philosophical inquiry into the sources of human knowledge (e.g., "How do we come to know what we know?") is related to the neurobiological considerations summarized above. During a substantial historical period two opposing views were rationalism and empiricism. Overly simplified, knowledge was considered to be achievable by thought alone (e.g., Descartes) or to come to the tabula rasa of mind only from experience (e.g., Locke, Hume). To break the deadlock, Kant argued that experience, while the source of much knowledge, was processed by a structured mind that contained a priori "information" in the form of categories and rules through which all experience was organized. The latter included, for example, built-in knowledge of cause and effect.

Considerations of developmental plasticity indicate that experience itself shapes sensory systems. However, after they have been "shaped" in development, information ("knowledge") is processed within the constraints and opportunities provided by these systems. This would appear to roughly coincide with some of the a priori knowledge of Kant. That the behavioral importance of stimuli may be coded by the number of neurons tuned to respond preferentially to these stimuli suggests a further refinement of the sensory cortex. Thus, whether an experience is transformed from a sensory event into a long-term memory and whether it elicits a behavioral response may be functions of the prior tuning of the sensory cortex. Therefore, experience would seem to be a source not only of knowledge in the sense of daily experience but also in the sense of providing the functional substrate through which experience is "filtered."

In Kantian terms, another a priori factor would have been added. It would not actually be a priori but serve an a priori function of determining the organization of experience. I refer to continual shaping of the neural material through which experience is processed. There seem to be two types of experience-based sensory plasticity: (a) developmental plasticity that determines what types of sensory experience can later be processed; and (b) learning-induced plasticity that determines the tuning of sensory cortical neurons, providing a finer-grain shaping of the system, reallocating neuronal resources on the basis of behavioral importance of past experiences, and thus encoding a key aspect of memory. Whether or not cause and effect and other hypothesized a priori factors exist is a question for another occasion.

☐ Toward Testing the Hypothesis of a Memory Code for Stimulus Importance

We have hypothesized that memory codes exist and that the code for acquired stimulus importance is increasing the number of cells tuned toward or to that stimulus. How might these hypotheses be tested? Obviously, it is insufficient to identify a neural correlate; this is merely an initial step. One method is to determine if related findings have been observed in other sensory systems. There is such evidence (Weinberger, 1995). While such findings strengthen the generality of the relationship between learning and increased representation of behaviorally important stimuli, they are still correlative.

Behavioral validation would be a more direct test and it might be accomplished by several means. For example, the functional implications discussed above could be examined by training animals to a stimulus to various degrees and predicting that the more behaviorally important a stimulus, the greater will be its representation in the sensory cortex. A more compelling approach would be to induce increased tuning to a specific stimulus in primary sensory cortices in the absence of behavioral training and then to predict that the specific stimulus will be treated behaviorally as if the increased tuning had occurred during normal learning. Such findings would speak to the issue of sufficiency. Necessity could be tested by reversibly changing the amount of preferential tuning and determining whether or not the behavior in question was degraded as a function of the amount of reduced tuning in the cortex.

☐ Overview

The central issue addressed here concerns the transformation of sensory experiences into memories of those experiences. We have proposed that these transformations are unique at the level of the individual engrams, which encode the details of each experience, but that general principles govern the production of engrams. We believe that these principles are embodied in memory codes and have presented evidence that the memory code for the learned behavioral importance of a stimulus is to increase the number of cells that preferentially process, that is, become tuned to, that stimulus.

To the best of our knowledge, the concept of memory codes has not been presented previously. Therefore, we provide a summary of the place of memory codes within a larger context. Figure 4.3 provides a simplified but useful hypothetical picture of the transformation of experience into memory. Three levels of processing are shown:

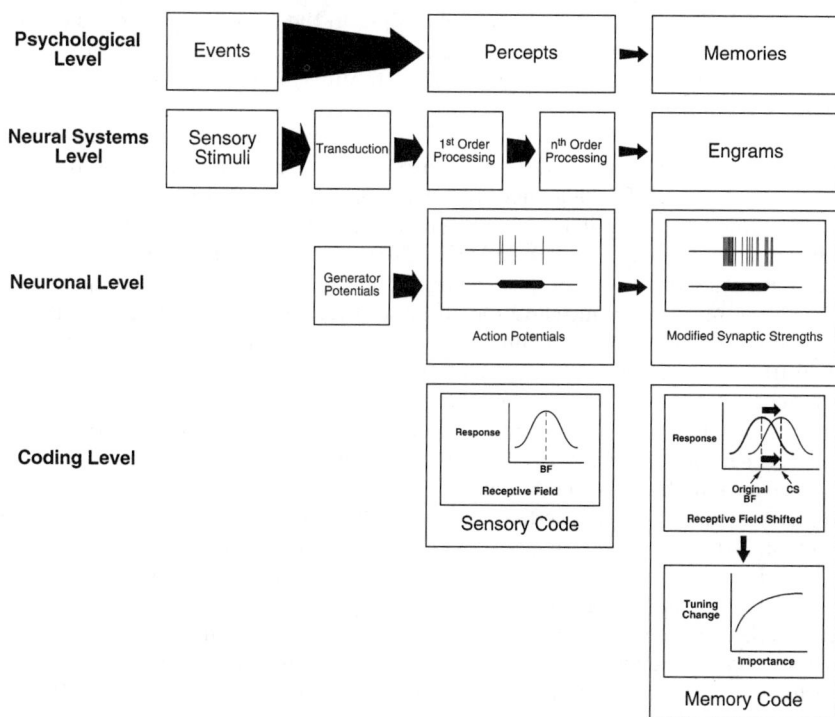

Figure 4.3. Schematic showing the hypothesized place of a memory code within a multi-level framework (psychological, neural systems, neuronal, and coding levels) that relates experience (percepts) to memory. See text for details.

psychological, neural systems, and neuronal. Also shown are the places within the processing stream at which two neural codes operate, sensory codes and memory codes (coding level).

At the psychological level, events occur in the environment and are experienced as percepts. Some fraction of percepts become memories, hence the arrow from percepts to memories is smaller than the arrow from events to percepts.

At the neural systems level, the events are treated as sensory stimuli. These are transduced in sensory receptors, but transduction is not viewed as part of perception. Rather, perception is seen as being coextensive with processing within central sensory systems; two parts are schematized, first- and nth-order processing, to indicate the hierarchical nature of sensory system operation. The highest order may be taken to be cortical processing. Some fraction of stimuli processed in sensory systems become engrams, the neural substrate of memories. Once again, as only a fraction of sensory stimuli become engrams, the arrow to the latter is smaller than those within sensory processing proper.

The next reductionist level, the neuronal level, occurs entirely within the nervous system. Transduction at the systems level is more or less coextensive with generator potentials, which give rise to action potentials at all orders of a sensory system. Perception and sensory processing are coextensive at the neuronal level with the discharges (and of course synaptic potentials) of single cells in response to sensory stimuli (indicated by the bar below the illustrated spike train). Illustrated here are pre-learning responses of a cell to a frequency that will later be used as the conditional stimulus. The effects of learning are illustrated in the box to the right, in the memories/engrams column. This cell's response to the frequency of the CS is increased after learning because of presumptive increased synaptic strength for this stimulus. (Not illustrated are decreased responses to non-CS frequencies.)

At the coding level are illustrated a sensory code and a memory code. The sensory code is the relationship between the frequency of pure tones and the rate of discharge. Thus, the sensory code for frequency is given by the tuning curve or frequency receptive field. Illustrated to the right are receptive fields before (thin line) and after (thick line) conditioning to the frequency labeled "CS." Note the shift in tuning from the original BF to the frequency of the CS. The memory code specifies the relationship between acquired stimulus importance and the amount of tuning change, which is illustrated as a monotonic increasing function. In short, the greater the acquired importance of a tonal frequency, the greater will be the magnitude of tuning shifts toward and to the frequency of the CS, and the number of cells that develop the tuning shifts. Thus, sensory codes are viewed as the initial specification of how an event is (transiently) encoded in sensory systems, whereas memory codes are considered to be engaged only when percepts are transformed into memories.

This schematic summary is perhaps oversimplified, but we hope not overly simplistic. This initial formulation of the concept of memory codes and the explication of findings that have led us to postulate such codes is only an appropriate starting point. It is our hope that the concept of memory codes will engage others in theoretical and empirical studies of the neurobiology of memory encoding. It is surely worthwhile to seek general principles that have evolved to solve problems of the transformation of experience into enduring neural representations of the behaviorally meaningful world. If it turns out that the first neurobiological memory code has been discovered, there may be substantial implications for understanding memory and the brain. If not, perhaps the search to date will nonetheless prove illuminating.

☐ Acknowledgments

This research was supported by the following research grants from the National Institutes of Health: MH-57235, DC 02346, and DC 02938. I wish to thank Jacquie Weinberger for preparation of the manuscript and Gabriel Hui and Dewey McLin III for assistance with figures and for insightful discussions.

☐ References

Bakin, J. S., Lepan, B., & Weinberger, N. M. (1992). Sensitization induced receptive field plasticity in the auditory cortex is independent of CS-modality. *Brain Research, 577*, 226–235.

Edeline, J. M., Pham, P., & Weinberger, N. M. (1993). Rapid development of learning-induced receptive field plasticity in the auditory cortex. *Behavioral Neuroscience, 107*, 539–551.

Edeline, J. M., & Weinberger, N. M. (1993). Receptive field plasticity in the auditory cortex during frequency discrimination training: Selective retuning independent of task difficulty. *Behavioral Neuroscience, 107*, 82–103.

Galvan, V. V., Chen, J., & Weinberger, N. M. (1998). Local field potentials reveal learning-induced receptive field plasticity in the primary auditory cortex of the guinea pig. *Society for Neuroscience Abstracts, 28*, 561.

Karni, A. (1996). The acquisition of perceptual and motor skills: A memory system in the adult human cortex. *Brain Research. Cognitive Brain Research, 5*, 39–48.

Karni, A., & Sagi, D. (1993). The time course of learning a visual skill. *Nature, 365*, 250–252.

Lashley, K. S. (1950). In search of the engram. In *Physiological mechanisms in animal behaviour* (pp. 454–482). Cambridge, England: Cambridge University Press.

Recanzone, G. H., Schreiner, C. E., & Merzenich, M. M. (1993). Plasticity in the frequency representation of primary auditory cortex following discrimination training in adult owl monkeys. *Journal of Neuroscience, 13*, 87–103.

Semon, R. W. (1921). *The mneme.* London: G. Allen & Unwin.

Thompson, R. F. (1976). The search for the engram. *American Psychologist, 31*, 209–227.

Weinberger, N. M. (1995). Dynamic regulation of receptive fields and maps in the adult sensory cortex. *Annual Review of Neuroscience, 18*, 129–158.

Weinberger, N. M. (1998). Physiological memory in primary auditory cortex: Characteristics and mechanisms. *Neurobiology of Learning and Memory, 70*, 226–251.

Weinberger, N. M., Ashe, J. H., Metherate, R., McKenna, T. M., Diamond, D. M., & Bakin, J. S. (1990). Retuning auditory cortex by learning: A preliminary model of receptive field plasticity. *Concepts in Neuroscience, 1*, 91–132.

Weinberger, N. M., Javid, R., & Lepan, B. (1993). Long-term retention of learning-induced receptive-field plasticity in the auditory cortex. *Proceedings of the National Academy of Sciences of the United States of America, 90*, 2394–2398.

5

Yoichi Sugita

Global Plasticity of Adult Visual System

☐ The Approach

We perceive objects in a fixed setting, although the retinal image continually changes as we move. Consequently, the location constancy appears to be familiar, natural, and ordinary. However, unusual conditions show that the constancy strongly depends on past experience. For example, experiments that use special glasses to distort the retinal image demonstrate the importance of learning in constancy.

In a classic study conducted around the end of 19th century, Stratton (1897) fitted himself with lenses that not only inverted the visual field, so that he saw the world upside down, but also reversed it, so that objects appearing on the left were actually located on the right and vice versa. Although, initially, the visual world seemed to lose its stability, the location constancy was gradually restored after a few days of wearing the spectacles. When he removed the glasses, he again needed time to adjust before he regained his old visual-motor habits. Since then, similar experiments have been carried out with comparable results, but with different arguments regarding the underlying mechanisms of the adaptation. To clarify the mechanisms physiologically it is, therefore, very important to understand the nature of this adaptation to visual distortion. It will also provide a new model for investigating the functional change in cortical neurons and circuits.

☐ Behavioral Change During the Course of Adaptation to Visual Transformation

Human subjects have shown a remarkable ability to regain location constancy in a visually rearranged world (Kohler, 1964). For instance, adapted subjects were able to perform such daily tasks as washing and eating and could even perform more complex tasks such as skiing or riding a motorcycle. These subjects adapted to the visual distortion by the following steps. First, appropriate visuomotor responses are learned within minutes (Held & Freedman, 1963). This can be demonstrated by simple experiments.

The odd number of light reflections creates upside-down inversion and left-right reversal of the visual scene. A hand mirror is sufficient to invert the scene. It may be a bit difficult to touch or grasp an object while looking at the object through the mirror. However, it becomes easy with only a few minutes of training. Second, there is a change in perceived hand location (Harris, 1964). In the disarranged world, subjects cannot see their hands where they expect to see them. When proprioception and vision provide conflicting information, proprioception gives way. The subjects come to feel that their hand is where they see it. Third, eye movement becomes coordinated with head movement (Gonshor & Melvill Jones, 1976). When one's head moves horizontally, the visual field moves in the opposite direction to the head movement. Visual field reversal reverses this relationship: the head movement becomes associated with the movement of the visual field in the same direction. Thus, it becomes very difficult to keep looking at an object while one's head is moving. However, after approximately 1 month of visual field reversal, the functional reversal in the relationship between the direction of head and eye movement was gradually achieved. Finally, visual perception itself undergoes a transformation. Some attributes of the visual scene appear normal, whereas others remain in the reversed or inverted form (Kohler, 1964). In addition to this so-called "piecemeal" adaptation, there are dramatic changes in stereoscopic depth perception. Left-right reversing spectacles also reverse the relationship between the direction of perceived depth and the direction of binocular depth cue. After prolonged exposure to the left-right reversed vision, however, the relation between perceived depth and disparity was adaptively reversed (Shimojo & Nakajima, 1981).

☐ Responsible Loci for the Adaptation

The adaptation to the transformation of the retinal image consists of several different behavioral changes. Correspondingly, there should be several different loci in the brain that are responsible for the adaptation.

For simple motor learning primary, premotor, and supplementary motor areas might be involved. Indeed, it was recently found that the ventral part of the premotor cortex plays an important role in recalibrating visual and motor coordinates (Kurata & Hoshi, 1999). Monkeys could easily learn a simple visually guided reaching task, even when the visual target was displaced with wedge prisms. However, it became very difficult when the ventral premotor cortex was inactivated by muscimol injection, indicating that the ventral premotor cortex is involved in this adaptation.

The cerebellum may also be involved in the motor learning because it has been shown that complex spikes of cerebellar purkinje cells contribute both to the initiation of arm movements and to the gradual improvement of motor skills (Kitazawa, Kimura, & Yin, 1998).

Using positron emission tomography (PET), Clower et al. (1996) localized changes in regional cerebral blood flow in subjects performing a prism adaptation task. Their subjects wore spectacles that displaced the visual field 17° to the left or to the right. During the PET scan, the subjects made visually guided attempts to reach targets that were viewed through laterally displacing prisms. It was found that the posterior parietal cortex, contralateral to the reaching hand, was strongly activated during the adaptation.

The frontal lobe may also be related to the adaptation. This suggestion is based on very rare, curious cases of frontal lobe disease (see Solms, Kaplan-Solms, Saling, & Miller, 1988), where the patients reported that their vision suddenly inverted and remained upside-down for a few minutes. Their complaint was seldom chronic and disappeared as general recovery progressed. However, it is enough to consider the frontal lobe as a possible candidate for the responsible loci.

☐ Advantage and Disadvantage of Visual Distortion

Monkeys and humans show a remarkable ability to adapt to visual distortion. There should be functional changes in several cortical loci as a result of the adaptation, although the nature of the change has not been clarified yet. The functional changes require no specific training but only the displacement, inversion, or reversal of the visual field. These distortions are easily achieved either by wearing appropriate spectacles or by the surgical rotation of eyes. Furthermore, simple visuomotor responses can be learned quite easily, especially when the visual field is shifted to the left or to the right.

However, it is not so easy to observe perceptual changes when the left-right reversal or the upside-down inversion of the visual field is employed. Adaptive change in the relationship between the perceived depth and binocular depth cue, for example, was observed after 14 days (on average, 46 days at the longest) in human subjects in our laboratory.

It takes a very long time for mammals to adapt to the visual distortion. Monkeys are capable of the behavioral adaptations to the left-right reversed vision just as human subjects are; however, they initially closed their eyes and would not move by themselves at first. Extensive manipulations were necessary for them to regain normal behavior: taking them out of their home cage to a large play field, making them search for their favorite food, etc. It has not been observed that adult birds and reptiles adapt to the visual field reversal.

☐ Functional Reorganization in Primary Visual Cortex

As mentioned above, monkeys would not move by themselves for the first few weeks after visual field reversal. Most cells in the primary visual cortex (V1) apparently lost responsiveness during this period. However, prolonged exposure to left-right reversed vision leads to dramatic changes in V1 (Sugita, 1996). Some V1 cells began to respond to stimuli presented not only in the contralateral visual field but also in the ipsilateral visual field. These changes were observed only after visuomotor adaptation had completed and disappeared soon after the removal of reversing prisms. The functional change in V1 cells would, therefore, be related to the adaptation to the visual reversal.

The cells with bilateral receptive fields had several characteristic response properties. They showed no selectivity to orientation or direction of motion, but responded well to a flash of light. Although they tended to respond to the contralateral stimulation more vigorously than to the ipsilateral stimulation, they responded to both in a similar way (Figure 5.1). For example, if a cell responded transiently to the onset of contralateral stimulation, it also responded transiently to ipsilateral stimulation. Newly formed ipsilateral receptive fields were located bisymmetrically to the original contralateral receptive fields; that is, the distance from the center of the ipsilateral receptive field to the vertical midline was almost equal to that for the contralateral receptive field. Also, the size of the ipsilateral receptive field was much larger than that of the original contralateral field.

The cells with bilateral receptive fields should receive inputs from higher cortical areas that have strong interhemispheric connections. Cortical visual areas are organized

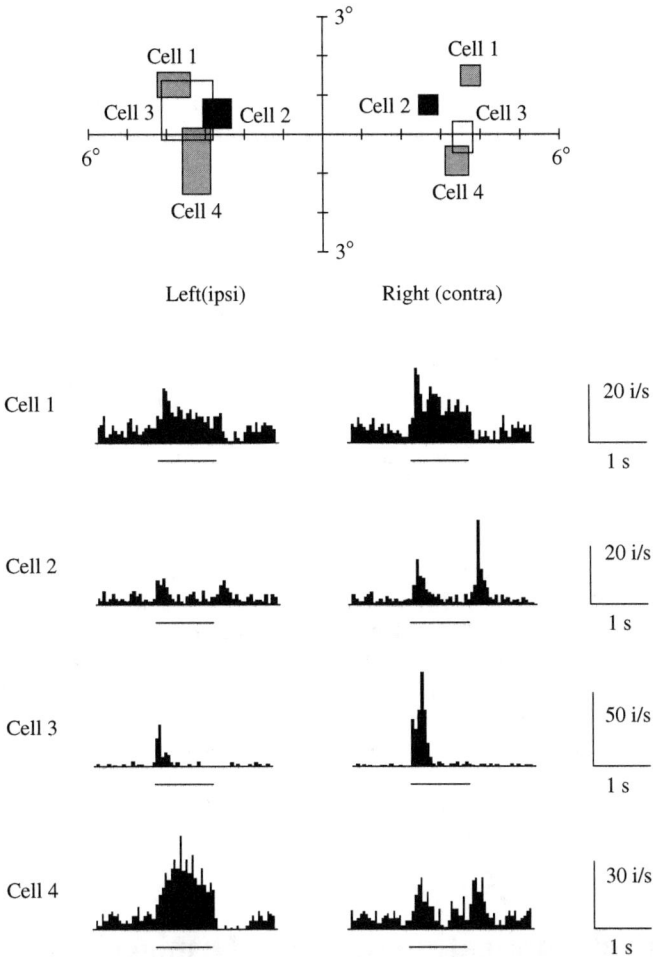

Figure 5-1. Receptive fields of four V1 cells in the left hemisphere of Japanese monkeys (and peristimulus time histograms [PSTHs] for a light spot of 1 s duration). The animals had been continuously exposed to visual field reversal for about 2 months. The stimulus was presented to the left eye for each cell. The underlined section below each histogram represents the period of stimulation. PSTHs of the responses for the preferred stimulus size were made on the basis of at least seven trials. i/s: impulses per second. From "Global Plasticity in Adult Visual Cortex Following Reversal of Visual Input," by Y. Sugita, 1996, *Nature, 380,* 523–526. Reprinted with permission.

in a reciprocal fashion (van Essen & Maunsell, 1983). An area not only sends signals to, but also receives them from, another area. The interhemispheric connections have already been demonstrated in the secondary visual cortex, as well as in a part of V1 (Cusick, Gould, & Kaas, 1984; Spatz & Kunz, 1984). Furthermore, the connections were observed at regions of high cytochrome oxidase activity, where the cells show no preference to either the orientation or the direction of motion. It is therefore very likely that the cells with bilateral receptive fields receive signals from the cells of regions rich in cytochrome oxidase.

Cells in higher visual areas, such as V4, middle temporal area (MT), and medial superior temporal area (MST) were also tested. Some V4 cells responded to ipsilateral stimulation, although the response was much weaker than that to contralateral stimulation. These cells also showed no preference to the orientation. In MT and MST areas, however, cells did not respond to ipsilateral stimulation at all.

The visual system has two separate pathways: one that is specialized for spatial vision and follows a dorsal route from occipital to parietal lobes, and the other that is for object vision and follows a ventral route from occipital to inferior temporal lobes (Ungerleider & Mishkin, 1982). It was expected that, if cells had shown functional change for the adaptation to displaced vision, these cells would have belonged to the occipitoparietal pathway. However, all cells with bilateral receptive fields apparently belonged to the occipitotemporal pathway. Obviously the number of objects we have to learn is far more than the number of spatial arrangements in the retinal image. It is, therefore, likely that cells in the occipitotemporal pathway are more plastic and the visual system employs this plasticity to adapt to the visual reversal.

Functional reorganization has also been reported in the somatosensory cortex after sensory deafferentation by the cutting of sensory nerve roots as they enter the spinal cord (Pons et al., 1991). Two different mechanisms have been proposed to explain this reorganization. First, the cortical deactivation produced by cutting sensory nerves would result in sprouting both within and beyond the framework of the existing connections (Florence, Taub, & Kaas, 1998). Second, the deafferentation would result in the degeneration, and subsequent rearrangement, of thalamic nuclei if the injury led to the death of dorsal root ganglion neurons (Jones & Pons, 1998). In this case, connectional sprouting within the thalamus would be the principal basis of the cortical reorganization. In the case of reorganization in the visual cortex, however, it seems very likely that the connections are normally present and the adaptation to left-right reversed vision induces the enhancement of synaptic efficiency.

☐ Clinical Application of Visual Displacement

Right-hemisphere stroke patients often show hemispatial neglect. They have difficulty paying attention to, and even perceiving stimuli presented in, their left side. Several sensory manipulations (for example, caloric stimulation, neck vibration, and optokinetic stimulation) have been tried to rehabilitate this neglect. However, despite more than 20 years of extensive research efforts, the effects of the sensory manipulations only last several minutes.

Rossetti et al. (1998) investigated the effect of prism adaptation on the neglect symptoms. Their patients were exposed to a 10° optical shift of the visual field to the right. The patients were asked to point straight ahead before and after the exposure. Their subjective midline was initially shifted to the right. However, after several minutes of exposure to the visual field shift, they showed a close-to-normal performance. It was also found that the prism adaptation could improve other clinical manifestations of neglect. For example, the patients showed clear improvement in the Gainotti test, in which they were asked to copy a simple drawing made of five items (Figure 5.2). Furthermore, these improvements were observed even with a delay of a few hours after the prism exposure.

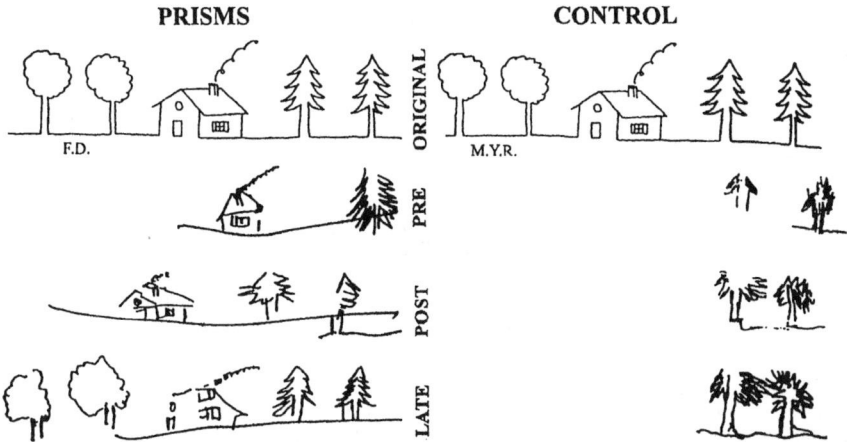

Figure 5-2. Gainotti test. An example from a patient (left) in which the drawing made before prism exposure demonstrates the complete neglect of three items. Soon after the prism removal, one item is added to the patient's drawing. Two hours after the removal, all items are drawn. By contrast, another patient (right), who was exposed to neutral glasses, did not show any improvement. From "Prism Adaptation to a Rightward Optical Deviation Rehabilitates Left Hemispherical Neglect," by Y. Rossetti et al., 1998, *Nature, 395,* pp. 166–169. Reprinted with permission.

☐ Signal for Visual Adaptation

The functional reorganization in V1 and the improvement of hemispatial neglect suggest that a signal is given to the brain that induces the enhancement of synaptic efficiency and the alteration of neural circuitry. This signal stimulates neural plasticity and the natural recovery processes. The main signal for the adaptation does not originate from the visual system alone. Without body movement, a subject would not be aware that the visual field is left-right reversed or shifted to the right or to the left. The signal is the discrepancy observed between the expected visual scene and the actual retinal image. When the subject tries to touch a visual target, he would notice that the shape and position of his hand is completely different from his expectation. The subject would also notice that the movement of his visual field is not as anticipated when his head moves. Hence, the activity of the motor system is invaluable for the adaptation, although it remains to be investigated how the activity affects the functional reorganization and the natural recovery processes in the visual system.

☐ Summary

Several different behavioral changes are involved in the adaptation to visual transformation which involves the sensorimotor system as well as the visual. Adaptation to the reversal induces functional reorganization of early visual processing. A clinical application of visual displacement involves exposing patients with left hemispatial neglect to a right optical shift of the visual field, which can result in rehabilitation. The signal for the adaptation stems from the discrepancy between the expected visual scene and the actual retinal image, although it remains unclear how this signal is generated and how it affects the visual system.

☐ References

Clower, D. M., Hoffman, J. M., Voraw, J. R., Faber, T. L., Woods, R. P., & Alexander, G. E. (1996). Role of posterior parietal cortex in the recalibration of visually guided reaching. *Nature, 383,* 618–621.

Cusick, C. G., Gould, H. J. III, & Kaas, J. H. (1984). Interhemispheric connections of visual cortex of owl monkeys (*Aotus trivirgatus*), marmosets (*Callithrix jacchus*), and galagos (*Galago crassicaudatus*). *Journal of Comparative Neurology, 230,* 311–336.

Florence, S. L., Taub, H. B., & Kaas, J. H., (1998). Large-scale sprouting of cortical connections after peripheral injury in adult macaque monkeys. *Science, 282,* 1117–1121.

Gonshor, A., & Melvill Jones, G. (1976). Extreme vestibulo-occular adaptation induced by prolonged optical reversal of vision. *Journal of Physiology (London), 256,* 381–414.

Harris, C. S. (1964). Adaptation to displaced vision: Visual, motor, or proprioceptive change? *Science, 140,* 812–813.

Held, R., & Freedman, S. J. (1963). Plasticity in human sensorimotor control. *Science, 142,* 455–462.

Jones, E. G., & Pons, T. P. (1998). Thalamic and brainstem contributions to large-scale plasticity of primate somatosensory cortex. *Science, 282,* 1121–1125.

Kitazawa, S., Kimura, T., & Yin, P. (1998). Cerebellar complex spikes encode both destinations and errors in arm movements. *Nature, 392,* 494–497.

Kohler, I. (1964). The formation and transformation of the perceptual world. *Psychological Issues, 3,* 1–173.

Kurata, K., & Hoshi, E. (1999). Reacquisition deficits in prism adaptation after muscimol microinjection into the ventral premotor cortex of monkeys. *Journal of Neuropysiology, 81,* 1927–1938.

Pons, T. P., Garraghty, P. E., Ommaya, A. K., Kaas, J. H., Taub, E., & Mishkin, M. (1991). Massive cortical reorganization after sensory deafferentation in adult macaques. *Science, 252,* 1857–1860.

Rossetti, Y., Rode, G., Pisella, L., Farne, A., Li, L., Boisson, D., & Perenin, M. (1998). Prism adaptation to a rightward optical deviation rehabilitates left hemispatial neglect. *Nature, 395,* 166–169.

Shimojo, S., & Nakajima, Y. (1981). Adaptation to the reversal of binocular depth cues: Effects of wearing left-right reversing spectacles on stereoscopic depth perception. *Perception, 10,* 391–402.

Solms, M., Kaplan-Solms, K., Saling, M., & Miller, P. (1988). Inverted vision after frontal lobe disease. *Cortex, 24,* 499–509.

Spatz, W. B., & Kunz, B. (1984). Area 17 of anthropoid primates does participate in visual callosal connections. *Neuroscience Letters, 48,* 49–53.

Stratton, G. M. (1897). Vision without inversion of the retinal image. *Psychological Review, 4,* 341–360, 463–481.

Sugita, Y. (1996). Global plasticity in adult visual cortex following reversal of visual input. *Nature, 380,* 523–526.

Ungerleider, L. G., & Mishkin, M. (1982). Two cortical visual systems. In D. J. Ingle, M. A. Goodale, & R. J. W. Mansfield, (Eds). *Analysis of Visual Behavior,* (pp. 549–586). Cambridge, MA: MIT Press.

Van Essen, D. C., & Maunsell, J. H. R. (1983). Hierarchical organization and functional streams in the visual cortex. *Trends in Neuroscience, 6,* 370–375.

J. Lee Kavanau

Reinforcement of Memory During Sleep

☐ Introduction

The concept that brain circuitry benefits from sleep traces back at least to De Manacéïne (1897), who stated with remarkable prescience that dreams "have a direct salutary influence insofar as they serve to exercise regions of the brain which in the waking state remain unemployed" (p. 312). After a lengthy hiatus, Moruzzi (1966) proposed that sleep facilitates recovery processes in circuitry for learned acts, while Roffwarg, Musio, and Dement (1966) conjectured that spontaneous, repetitive activations of circuitry in the central nervous system during rapid-eye-movement (REM) sleep in the human embryo facilitate circuit development and maintenance. They suggested that such activations during sleep could maintain circuitry throughout life. Since then, many studies have supported the view that the brain's repetitive, self-generated activations during sleep reinforce memory circuits.

Concepts of memory circuit maintenance were formalized in terms of a paradigm of functional and nonutilitarian reinforcement (also referred to as "dynamic stabilization," reviewed in Kavanau, 1994, 1996). According to this paradigm, "dedicated" or functional synaptic efficacies become established initially by a tailoring of their values in the course of repeated circuit use for specific functions. These dedicated efficacies are maintained in the brain's long-term memory stores by two principal means: first, by continued frequent use during activity ("functional" reinforcement), and second, by self-generated activations induced largely, but not exclusively, by low-frequency oscillatory potentials (slow waves) during quiet wakefuness and sleep ("nonutilitarian" reinforcement). Self-generated activations during these phases of inactivity preserve dedicated synaptic efficacies by maintaining sufficient concentrations of essential, but unstable, peptide and protein molecules (by virtue of use-dependent synaptic plasticity; Steward, 1993). Since they usually do not trigger circuit functions, because of lesser or lower frequency inducing potentials or temporarily increased activation thresholds, they are referred to as being "nonutilitarian." Examples of possibly reinforcing, self-generated slow waves are reviewed in Kavanau (1997, 1998a).

☐   Synaptic Efficacy Maintenance

Possessing only nonplastic synapses, an animal merely would respond passively to external stimuli. Responses might vary with physiological state, but behavioral responses would be limited essentially to successions of fixed reflexive actions. The first evolutionary advance beyond stereotypic reflexive behavior doubtless involved the development of synapses with activity-dependent plasticity, that is, synapses that respond adaptively, or "learn." Such synapses confer the potential to evolve virtually unlimited behavioral adaptations.

Synaptic Efficacy Maintenance Through Use (Functional Reinforcement)

Efficacies could be maintained indefinitely at dedicated levels if functional reinforcement was sufficiently frequent, sufficing, as it does, in many (particularly non-sleeping) animals. However, supplemental mechanisms (reviewed in Matthies, 1989; McEachern & Shaw, 1996; Shaw, Lanius, & van den Doel, 1994) of later evolutionary origin provide greater flexibility, whereby functional reinforcement prolongs synaptic efficacies more lengthily than merely minutes to days, thereby requiring less frequent use for long-term maintenance.

Maintaining dedicated efficacy values in synapses by repeated activation is only one aspect of lengthily encoding information in neural circuits. Other aspects include activity-dependent alterations of synaptic morphology, number, and patterns of connectivity (reviewed in Kavanau, 1994; see also Bailey & Kandel, 1995). But functional and/or nonutilitarian reinforcement of the altered circuitry very likely is required for these other alterations to persist. With reinforcement being nonovert, but synaptic alterations being visible, the impression is conveyed that the alterations play the greatest role in information storage and maintenance (Greenough & Chang, 1985).

Synaptic Efficacy Maintenance by Nonutilitarian Reinforcement

The Precise States of Synaptic Efficacies During Refreshment. Preservation of authentic memories in a circuit entails maintenance of the dedicated values of synaptic efficacies for the circuit's specific functions. By what mechanism does nonutilitarian reinforcement maintain these efficacies in infrequently used circuits at the different dedicated values that encode each memory? Two crucial questions, almost completely untreated until very recently (Kavanau, 1998a, 1999), pertain to the precise states of the synaptic efficacies in circuits being reinforced and to the precise conditions that constitute dedicated synaptic efficacies.

Specifically, is a dedicated synaptic efficacy value sharply defined, with a slightly different value having a deleterious effect on circuit function? Or, does the value cover a range, outside of which the circuit becomes "incompetent"? Or, is the value merely a minimum, with the synapse retaining its specific function at higher values? And does each synapse retain a "record" of its dedicated strengths, with refreshment ceasing when the values are reached? Also, what is the magnitude of the time normally required to achieve dedicated values, and does refreshment occur gradually (incrementally) or in a single step?

In seeking answers to these questions, several recent findings and other considerations treated here provide guidance. For long-term refreshment of the efficacies of hippocampal CA3–CA1 synapses, at least, efficacy enhancement appears to occur on an all-or-none basis, with individual synapses having different induction thresholds (Petersen, Malenka, Nicoll, & Hopfield, 1998). This suggests that individual synapses keep "records" of their dedicated efficacies. On the other hand, for efficacy refreshments that require protein synthesis, synaptic activations lead to a local dendritic accumulation of newly synthesized messenger RNA (mRNA) and proteins (Steward, Wallace, Lyford, & Worley, 1998) and to polyadenylation of certain mRNAs (Wu et al., 1998). These findings suggest that the efficacies of these synapses are refreshed by a gradual, rather than an abrupt, process.

Other answers to some of these questions may be implicit in the preceding treatment. With unstable protein and peptide molecules being essential in the establishment of dedicated synaptic efficacies, and with maintenance of the dedicated values being dependent largely on appropriate replenishment of essential molecules, it appears highly improbable that dedicated efficacy values are sharply defined. Maintenance of precise values of synaptic efficacies for weeks, days, or even only hours, and over the course of highly varied schedules of synaptic use, would seem to require the existence of impossibly fine-tuned, molecular replacement mechanisms.

It seems warranted, then, to conclude that one of the two remaining conditions applies to dedicated synaptic efficacies, that is, that they either are minimum values or cover a range. Minimum values, which also would include lower limits of ranges, perhaps correspond to the experimentally determined thresholds. These two candidate conditions, however, are more likely to be equivalent than alternatives. This follows because it is very likely that the process of refreshment is inherently self-limiting (probably involving diffusive molecular exchanges; see Kavanau, 1994, 1996) upon attainment of an exchange equilibrium occurring at the level of the individual synapse. This process would provide an upper limit to dedicated synaptic efficacies in both circumstances. Covering a range, then, becomes the most feasible condition for dedicated synaptic efficacies.

"Incompetent" Circuits and Incremental Refreshment.

The knowledge that synaptic efficacies are exposed continuously to deleterious influences, are refreshed by slow waves during lengthy periods of sleep, and probably cover a range, and that efficacy increases by individual activations commonly are additive (e.g., presynaptic facilitation), leads to two significant, partially interdependent, implications. First, efficacy refreshment of many synapses may, as suggested above, be an incremental process that often requires considerable time—even many hours—not necessarily completed in a single night. Second, synaptic efficacy refreshment by slow waves sometimes may act on synapses whose efficacies are partially degraded, hence, on circuits that have become incompetent, encoding faulty information (Kavanau, 1999, 2000). Because of the enormous inherent complexity of the memory system, it is a reasonable supposition that, though the vast majority of synaptic strengths are in dedicated ranges, with refreshments merely augmenting them from lower to upper reaches of these ranges, the efficacies of a small fraction of the synapses (among the many trillions that exist) are, by chance, below their dedicated values at any given time.

It is directly relevant, then, to ask what would occur if, in the distributed circuitry representing a scene in a dream or memory, the efficacies of a small fraction of the synapses—of the millions that may be involved—were altered from their dedicated values for the authentic scene. In answer to this question, one would not expect the image to be degraded beyond recognition as a scene; rather, novel, unpredictable, but probably relatively minor alterations might occur—distortions, background or location changes, altered temporal settings or identities, etc.—depending partly on the degree of parallel processing and redundancy involved in encoding and recalling the scene.

☐ Reinforcement Priorities and Permanent Error Accumulation

There evidently is a high priority for reinforcing significant memories of the same day (the "day residues"), other recently acquired memories, for events arousing emotions, and other actions and perceptions with survival value. In this connection, the well-known gradual weakening and loss of many memories over time has a significant implication. Taking a cue from accumulation of mutations in genotypes, that other, but much less complex, system for encoding and storing biological information, the following assumption seems warranted: old memory circuits, even though reinforced regularly during sleep, accumulate permanent synaptic efficacy errors in proportion to the circuits' ages, as a result of extraneous influences (e.g., infections, chemical insults, radiation). Since error accumulation would tend to eliminate useless old memories and provide a substrate for new memories, it probably would be adaptive and favored by natural selection. These considerations concerning the origin of temporarily and permanently weakened synaptic efficacies are of significance for the genesis of illusory dreams, illusory awake states, and mental disorders, the latter also involving brain-wave abnormalities (Kavanau, 1999, 2000).

☐ The Major Function of the Awake Brain

The essence of awake brain function in the absence of volitional activity is the processing of sensory input, predominantly visual (Llinás & Paré, 1991). Much visual input is processed at a low level, without visual attention (Rafal & Robertson, 1995). Wide regions of cortex, including many cortical fields, interact during even simple visual tasks (Kaas, 1989).

Of over 52 regions of macaque monkey neocortex, 25 are devoted solely to visual processing, including visuomotor performance. Another 7 regions process visual information but are multimodal, some also processing auditory and/or somatosensory inputs. The 32 regions together cover over half the surface of the brain (Rolls, 1991; Van Essen, Anderson, & Felleman, 1992). A very rich subcortical network interconnects the neocortical visual regions (Young, 1992). For example, each visual region in the owl monkey (Aotis trivirgatus) projects to about 5–15 subcortical structures, many closely related to motor performance (Jacobson, 1991).

☐ The Fundamental Dogma

An intrinsic basis—"the fundamental dogma" (Rauschecker, 1995)—for potential incompatibilities between the brain's endogenous processing of information simultaneously with reception of sensory input is that learning and memory processing and storage involve changes in synaptic strengths in many of the same cortical regions that process sensory information and control motor output (Squire, 1986; Ungerleider, 1995). For example, neuronal activity circulating in cortical and thalamic networks is modified by activity engendered by incoming sensory information (Verzeano, 1980).

A classical example of sensory interference is blocking of the alpha rhythm by alerting stimuli (Niedermeyer & Lopes da Silva, 1993). Interference tends to occur, not in primary areas (i.e., neurons of the first synaptic level, where the accurate registration of new inputs necessitates a rapid return to a narrowly tuned baseline), but at more downstream levels, such as associative and limbic areas (Mesulam, 1998).

The Selective Pressure for Primitive Sleep

As nonsleeping animals acquired increasingly complex brains, behavioral repertoires, and visual competencies, together with ever-enlarging stores of experiential and inherited memories, increased needs for reinforcement of memory circuits existed during periods of quiet wakefulness. Like sleep, quiet wakefulness in present-day vertebrates is not an exclusive function of external circadian rhythms, but is determined by additional internal regulatory mechanisms (Tobler, 1985).

Eventually, with continued evolutionary advances in brain complexity, a condition would have been attained in which greatly increased needs for reinforcement of memory circuits led to significant conflicts with other circuit activities of quiet wakefulness. These circuit activities would have involved chiefly the processing of sensory inputs, predominantly visual. The selective pressure for the evolutionary origin of primitive sleep may have been the need to achieve a lesser state of brain responsiveness to (lesser states of attention and potential arousability by) these sensory inputs during reinforcement of circuitry than usually occurs during quiet wakefulness.

If, under this selective pressure, the brain were relieved of extensive needs to deal with environmental input, reinforcement could have proceeded unimpededly. Such relief occurs during sleep; with the thalamus and cortex engaged in synchronous oscillations, only a minor part of thalamocortical connectivity in the sleeping brain is devoted to the transfer of sensory inputs. Accordingly, perception of most sensory inputs (and their arousal value) is depressed during much of sleep (Hobson & McCarley, 1977; Hobson & Schmajuk, 1988; Llinás & Paré, 1991). In consequence, the forebrain tends to become isolated from (or inattentive to) distracting environmental influences, with its activities confined largely to functions of internally generated activations (Hobson, 1995; Steriade, Jones, & Llinás, 1990).

Ancillary Benefits of Sleep

The proposed origin and primal function of primitive sleep would not rule out the subsequent or concomitant evolution of ancillary benefits that may have become essential in some forms. Indeed, for almost all mammals and birds, ancillary benefits, such as bodily rest and rejuvenation, physiological restoration, regulation of hormonal secretions, and reinforcing of the immune system, also appear to come into play, as well as deep-seated, circadian rhythmical changes that engage many physiological systems (Everson, 1995; Vertes, 1990). The physiological and thermoregulatory continuities between sleep and hibernation (shallow and deep torpor) in some mammals and birds suggest that energy conservation also is an ancillary benefit of sleep (see Kavanau, 1997, 1999). On the other hand, continuous swimming by many fishes shows conclusively that some ancillary benefits, such as bodily rest and rejuvenation, physiological restoration, and energy conservation, are not inherently indispensable (Kavanau, 1998a, 1998b).

☐ The Need for Sleep in Blind Mammals

Having advanced the thesis that a conflict between the enormous requirements for visual information processing and reinforcement of memory circuits was the selective pressure for the evolutionary origin of, and continuing need for, sleep, the need of blind mammals for sleep might seem paradoxical. The resolution of the seeming disparity hinges on two circumstances: the warm-bloodedness of mammals and the existence of the same amount of "visual" cortex in need of extensive nonutilitarian reinforcement in both sighted and blind mammals.

In elucidating the first of these circumstances, nonsleeping, cold-blooded, lamnoid sharks were compared to warm-blooded, genetically blind mole rats, taking into account the total absence of brain waves in small mammals during 1–3 weeks at subzero temperatures of deep torpor. It was concluded that the need for sleep in warm-blooded animals hinges partly on their relatively high rate of degradation and functional depletion of molecules essential for synaptic function. In consequence of this relatively high rate, there is a correspondingly more frequent need for the replenishment of these molecules by nonutilitarian reinforcement during sleep (Kavanau, 1997, 1998a, 1999).

A clue to the second circumstance is provided by findings in nongenetically blind mammals. Many neurological and neurophysiological studies in humans and/or cats have given uniform results. Although the optic nerve, optic chiasm, and lateral geniculate nucleus may degenerate, neocortical visual regions undergo no size reduction and show no evidence of organic change. They remain highly active metabolically and electrically, with highest activity in striate and prestriate regions (Breitenseher et al., 1998; Ishikawa, Nishijo, Satou, Takeda, & Itai, 1995; Phelps et al., 1981; Riddle, Lo, & Katz, 1995; Wanet-Defalque et al., 1988; Yaka, Yinon, & Wollberg, 1999). In monkeys and cats visually deprived since birth, the activity that develops spontaneously in neurons of visual regions resembles activity in nondeprived animals (Roder, Rosler, & Hennighausen, 1997).

These observations probably are accounted for partly by the development of cross-modal plasticity in many visual neocortical regions, which take on supplementary auditory and tactile functions. All cells, in fact, become responsive to audition in some regions of the feline visual cortex (Yaka et al., 1999). This plasticity is not unexpected, as the neocortex generally is highly adaptable (Rauschecker, 1995), and many visual regions normally also process auditory and somatosensory inputs (Rolls, 1991; Van Essen et al., 1992). Some nonsensory neocortical regions, however, are not as adaptable; they may atrophy after years of deprivation (see, e.g., Rymer, 1993).

Thus, in addition to the influence of high metabolic rate, the continued need for sleep and large amounts of nonutilitarian reinforcement by blind mammals, no less than by the sighted, would appear to hinge on the circumstances that the "visual" neocortex develops its typical size and complex initial patterning of functional architecture during ontogeny (dependent on patterning mechanisms intrinsic to neocortex; Miyashita-Lin, Hevner, Wassarman, Martinez, & Rubenstein, 1999), that it is retained throughout life, and that it takes on additional nonvisual functions.

Retention of neural circuits for unused functions is a well-known phenomenon in other animals. Such circuits may be retained for many millions of years, either capable of, but not implementing, the functions, with the functions occurring only during certain developmental stages or pathological states, or in the absence of effectors (e.g., muscles). Some examples are widespread behavioral atavisms (characteristics inherited adventitiously from remote ancestors), some are superficial reflexes (e.g., Babinski's sign), and many are relict avian behaviors (Kavanau, 1987, 1990).

Sleep States and Reinforcement of Memory Circuitry

Putative Circuit Reinforcement Largely During REM Sleep

The seminal contributions of Roffwarg et al. (1966) were mentioned earlier. Steriade (1978) and Hobson and Steriade (1986) extended the concept of reinforcement by repetitive activations to experiential memories. Fishbein and Gutwein (1981) conjectured that REM sleep facilitates memory consolidation, and thereafter promotes long-term maintenance of the consolidated memories. Winson (1985, 1997) suggested that the theta rhythm of REM sleep is involved in reprocessing previously acquired information into memory, while Siegel (1995) proposed that some neurons reinforced during REM sleep are being compensated for inactivity during non-REM (NREM) sleep, others for awake inactivity.

Findings based largely on sleep deprivation studies strongly support the view that REM sleep periods facilitate learning retention. The facilitating portions of REM sleep—the REM "windows"—are characterized by their uniquely more intense phasic characteristics, as gauged by distribution and density of rapid eye movements (REMs; Smith & Lapp, 1986; additional refs. in Kavanau, 1997). Information processing during postlearning REM sleep is thought to complement the processing initiated during active wakefulness (De Koninck, 1995; Hennevin, Hars, Maho, & Bloch, 1995).

Karni, Tanne, Rubenstein, Askenazi, and Sagi (1994) showed that human performance gains for a visual discrimination task can occur either after a normal night's sleep or during wakefulness. Gains while awake do not begin until up to 8 hours posttraining (Karni & Sagi, 1993). If REM sleep, but not NREM sleep, was disrupted, there was no gain. In other words, consolidation of procedural memory for a visual discrimination task occurs during both wakefulness and REM sleep.

Using a different approach, namely, looking directly at cortical activity, Hennevin et al. (1995) demonstrated that the memory processing that occurs during REM sleep is enhanced by stimulation of the mesencephalic reticular formation.

Putative Circuit Reinforcement Largely During NREM Sleep

Steriade's (1988) original suggestion of consolidation of labile memories during NREM sleep was amplified by Steriade and coworkers (Steriade, Contreras, Curró Dossi, & Nuñez, 1993; Steriade, McCormick, & Sejnowski, 1993). Reinforcement in cortical associative neurons is thought to be mediated by cyclic trains of single spikes or rhythmic spike bursts in thalamocortical axons resulting from spindle and delta oscillations, as well as by continuous synaptic bombardment from the intrinsic cortical networks that generate the slow sleep rhythm.

Reinforcement of neural pathways during NREM (and REM) sleep received direct support from a study by Pavlides and Winson (1989). Learning associated with the firing of given rat hippocampal complex-spike "place cells" in the CA1 subfield led to increases in firing rates (up to 10-fold), in sharp spike burst rates, and in the number of bursts with multiple spikes and short interspike intervals. Increased activity of the place cells during NREM sleep, and accompanying unrestricted transmission through the CA1 subfield, appears to represent processing of information acquired during prior active wakefulness.

The specific firing correlations determined by Wilson and McNaughton (1994) extended this study, showing that the CA1 place cells that tended to fire together during experimental periods also tended to fire together during subsequent sleep (see also Shen, Kudrimoti, McNaughton, & Barnes, 1998). They also focused more sharply on periods of synchronous sharp spike bursts of NREM sleep as periods of maximal information transfer. Thus, place-cell firing correlations were greatest during the synchronized burst phase of NREM sleep. Based on these data and other evidence, Wilson and McNaughton (1994) support the paradigm of consolidation of neocortical memory circuits by hippocampal "replay" (see below).

A pursuit rotor task study by Smith and MacNeill (1994) provided further evidence for circuit reinforcement during NREM sleep. EEG comparisons of controls and experimental groups (variously deprived of sleep) identified stage-2 NREM sleep as the probable period of memory consolidation for the task. REM sleep deprivation was without effect. The motor circuits employed for the pursuit rotor task are in very frequent use during active wakefulness. Hence, from the present perspectives, they would be expected to require little or no reinforcement during REM sleep. The memory circuits being reinforced during stage-2 NREM sleep may include not circuits involved in movement execution, but circuits that play other roles in motor output (see Kavanau, 1997).

☐ Putative Circuit Alterations Involving Both REM and NREM Sleep

Krueger, Obál, Kapas, and Fang (1995) propose that reinforcement of synapses occurs during both sleep states but at different neuraxial levels. Noting that multiple single-neuron recording in the hippocampus suggests that reinforcement occurs during NREM sleep (see Wilson & McNaughton, 1994), McClelland, McNaughton, and O'Reilly (1995) proposed that structured knowledge stored in the neocortex could be similarly reinforced. Events reactivated in the hippocampus during NREM sleep may prime related neocortical memory traces, so that these become available for reactivation during REM sleep.

Recordings from the hippocampus and entorhinal cortex of the rat by Buzsáki (1989) and Chrobak and Buzsáki (1994) indicate that communication between the neocortex and the hippocampus depends on the vigilance state of the animal. During exploration, sensory input flows into the neocortex, and from there into the hippocampus, whereas during quiet wakefulness and slow-wave sleep (SWS = NREM sleep stages 3 and 4), information flows in the reverse direction ("playback"). With the onset of REM sleep, the flow pattern reverses; sharp-wave potentials and transmission out of the hippocampus cease and transmission into the hippocampus reappears together with hippocampal theta waves. Using a visual discrimination task, the findings of Stickgold and collaborators (see Stickgold, 1998) also suggest a two-step process of memory consolidation requiring SWS followed by REM sleep.

From comparisons of learning abilities following periods of wakefulness and sleep, Plihal and Born (1997) suggested that REM sleep plays a larger role in consolidation of procedural memories (for paired associates) and SWS in consolidation of declarative memories (for mirror writing).

☐ Circuit Reinforcement Solely During NREM Sleep

While memory mechanisms doubtlessly are sufficiently complex to accommodate aspects of many of the processes reviewed above, some marine mammals with excellent memories (dolphins and sea porpoises) do not engage in REM sleep, but almost entirely in unihemispheric NREM sleep. The total absence of REM sleep is associated with the animals being perpetually active (thus requiring very little motor or visual circuit reinforcement; see also the following section, "Dream Genesis"), and correlates with the large role played by REM sleep in motor and visual circuit reinforcement (Kavanau, 1997, 1998b). Sleep in an intermediate form, the Northern fur seal (*Callorhinus ursinus*), the only marine mammal that engages in unihemispheric sleep and spends some time sleeping on land, accords with expectations for reinforcement needs. It requires some REM sleep (90 min) for reinforcement of motor and visual circuitry, but engages mostly in NREM sleep (7 h), approximately 50% of it being unilateral (see Kavanau, 1998a, 1998b).

In view of these circumstances, it would appear that, as marine mammals that previously engaged in both sleep states evolved the ability to remain active and alert continuously, by sleeping unihemispherically (with continuous motor and visual activity), absence of a need for nonutilitarian reinforcement of motor and visual circuitry was accompanied by loss of a need for REM sleep. Concomitantly, the other specializations that REM sleep had acquired for circuit reinforcement either no longer were needed or could be accomplished during NREM sleep.

☐ Dream Genesis

Viewed from the perspective of nonutilitarian reinforcement, certain implications emerge concerning various aspects of dreams. In the views of Hobson and McCarley (1977), Greenberg (1981), and Antrobus (1991, 1993), dreaming is a by-product of, and tightly linked to, the mental activities that normally occur during REM sleep. Implications of nonutilitarian reinforcement are consonant with the views cited above, identifying the "mental activities" as reinforcement that achieves the consolidation and maintenance of circuits encoding memories, but not restricting their time of occurrence to REM sleep.

Expressed from another point of view by Llinás and Paré (1991, p. 525), "REM sleep can be considered as a modified attentive state in which attention is turned away from the sensory input, toward memories" and as "favoring a free processing mode operating mostly on previously stored representations" (Paré & Llinás, 1995, p. 1165). The "attention" would appear to consist of reinforcement of memory circuits, with memories involving motor circuitry being reinforced primarily during REM sleep. The large role played by motor activity in dreams, most of which occur during REM sleep (Hobson & Stickgold, 1995; Pivik, 1994), is consistent with this proposal (68% of REM dream reports describe motion; Porte & Hobson, 1996).

Visual memories also must be reinforced largely during REM sleep, because dreams usually are highly visual. An association of reinforcement of motor and visual circuitry during dreaming accords with the existence of numerous visuomotor neocortical regions (Rolls, 1991; Van Essen et al., 1992). It can be suggested that, because of this abundance of visuomotor circuits, many visual and motor memories are activated by default during nonutilitarian reinforcement, even frequently used circuits that are not in need of such reinforcement.

☐ References

Antrobus, J. (1991). Dreaming: Cognitive processes during cortical activation and high afferent thresholds. *Psychological Review, 98*, 96–120.

Antrobus, J. (1993). Dreaming: Can we do without it? In A. Moffitt, M. Kramer, & R. Hoffman (Eds.), *The functions of dreaming* (pp. 548–558). Albany: State University of New York Press.

Bailey, C., & Kandel, E. (1995). Molecular and structural mechanisms underlying long-term memory. In M. S. Gazzaniga (Ed.), *The cognitive neurosciences* (pp. 19–33). Cambridge, MA: MIT Press.

Breitenseher, M., Uhl, F., Prayer Wimberger, D., Deecke, L., Trattnig, S., & Kramer, J. (1998). Morphological dissociation between visual pathways and cortex: MRI of visually-deprived patients with congenital peripheral blindness. *Neuroradiology, 40*, 424–427.

Buzsáki, G. (1989). Two stage model of memory trace formation: A role for "noisy" brain states. *Neuroscience, 31*, 551–570.

Chrobak, J. J., & Buzsáki, G. (1994). Selective activation of deep layer (V-VI) retrohippocampal cortical neurons during hippocampal sharp waves in the behaving rat. *Journal of Neuroscience, 14*, 6160–6170.

De Koninck, J. (1995). Intensive learning, REM sleep, and REM sleep mentation. *Sleep Research Society Bulletin, 1*, 39–40.

De Manacéïne, M. (1897). Sleep: Its physiology, pathology, hygiene and psychology (E. Jaubert, Trans.). London: W. Scott.

Everson, C. A. (1995). Functional consequences of sustained sleep deprivation in the rat. *Behavioural Brain Research, 69*, 43–54.

Fishbein, W., & Gutwein, B. M. (1981). Paradoxical sleep and a theory of long-term memory. In W. Fishbein (Ed.). *Sleep, dreams, and memory* (pp. 147–182). New York: SP Medical and Scientific Books.

Greenberg, R. (1981). Dreams and REM sleep - An integrative approach. In W. Fishbein (Ed.), *Sleep, dreams, and memory* (pp. 125–133). New York: SP Medical and Scientific Books.

Greenough, W. T., & Chang, F.-L. F. (1985). Synaptic structural correlates of information storage in mammalian nervous systems. In C. W. Cotman (Ed.), *Synaptic plasticity* (pp. 335–372). New York: Guilford.

Hennevin, E., Hars, B., Maho, C., & Bloch, V. (1995). Processing of learned information in paradoxical sleep. *Behavioural Brain Research, 69*, 125–135.

Hobson, J. A. (1995). *Sleep.* New York: Scientific American Library.

Hobson, J. A., & McCarley R. (1977). The brain as a dream state generator: An activation-synthesis hypothesis of the dream process. *American Journal of Psychiatry, 134*, 1335–1348.

Hobson, J. A., & Schmajuk, N. A. (1988). Brain state and plasticity: An integration of the reciprocal interaction model of sleep cycle oscillation with attentional models of hippocampal function. *Archives of Italian Biology, 126*, 209–224.

Hobson, J. A., & Steriade, M. (1986). Intrinsic regulatory systems of the brain. *Handbook of Physiology, IV*, 701–823.

Hobson, J. A., & Stickgold, R. (1995). The conscious state paradigm: A neurocognitive approach to waking, sleeping, and dreaming. In M. S. Gazzaniga (Ed.), *The cognitive neurosciences* (pp. 1373–1389). Cambridge, MA: The MIT Press.

Ishikawa, N., Nishijo, K., Satou, M., Takeda, T., & Itai, Y. (1995). Study on the primary visual cortex of visually impaired subjects by means of 123I-IMP Spect and MRI. *Annals of Nuclear Medicine, 9*, 105–108.

Jacobson, M. (1991). *Developmental neurobiology.* New York: Plenum Press.

Kaas, J. H. (1989). Why does the brain have so many visual areas? *Journal of Cognitive Neuroscience, 1*, 121–134.

Karni, A., & Sagi, D. (1993). The time course of learning a visual skill. *Nature, 365*, 250–252.

Karni, A., Tanne, D., Rubenstein, J. S., Askenasy, J. J., & Sagi, D. (1994). Dependence on REM sleep of overnight improvement of a perceptual skill. *Science, 265*, 676–679.

Kavanau, J. L. (1987). *Lovebirds, cockatiels, budgerigars: Behavior and evolution.* Los Angeles: Science Software Systems.

Kavanau, J. L. (1990). Conservative behavioural evolution, the neural substrate. *Animal Behaviour 39*, 758–767.

Kavanau, J. L. (1994). Sleep and dynamic stabilization of neural circuitry: A review and synthesis. *Behavioural Brain Research, 63*, 111–126.

Kavanau, J. L. (1996). Memory, sleep, and dynamic stabilization of neural circuitry: Evolutionary perspectives. *Neuroscience and Biobehavioral Reviews, 20*, 289–311.

Kavanau, J. L. (1997). Memory, sleep, and the evolution of mechanisms of synaptic efficacy maintenance. *Neuroscience, 79*, 7–44.

Kavanau, J. L. (1998a). *Memory, sleep, and the evolution of mechanisms of synaptic efficacy maintenance, Revision F* (pp. 1–146). Los Angeles: UCLA Document Services.

Kavanau, J. L. (1998b). Vertebrates that never sleep: Implications for sleep's basic function. *Brain Research Bulletin, 46*, 269–279.

Kavanau, J. L. (1999). Adaptations and pathologies linked to dynamic stabilization of neural circuitry. *Neuroscience and Biobehavioral Reviews, 23*, 635–648.

Kavanau, J. L. (2000). Sleep, memory maintenance and mental disorders. *The Journal of Neuropsychiatry and Clinical Neurosciences.*

Krueger, J. M., Obál, F., Jr., Kapas, L., & Fang, J. (1995). Brain organization and sleep function. *Behavioural Brain Research, 69*, 177–185.

Llinás, R. R., & Paré, D. (1991). Of dreaming and wakefulness. *Neuroscience, 44*, 521–535.

Matthies, H. (1989). In search of cellular mechanisms of memory. *Progress in Neurobiology, 32*, 277–349.

McClelland, J. L., McNaughton, B. L., & Reilly, R. C. (1995). Why there are complementary learning systems in the hippocampus and neocortex: Insights from the successes and failures of connectionist models of learning and memory. *Psychological Reviews, 102*, 419–457.

McEachern, J. C., & Shaw, C. A. (1996). An alternative to LTP orthodoxy: A plasticity-pathology continuum model. *Brain Research Reviews, 22*, 51–92.

Mesulam, M.-M. (1998). From sensation to cognition. *Brain, 121*, 1013–1052.

Miyashita-Lin, E. M., Hevner, R., Wassarman, K. M., Martinez, S., & Rubenstein, J. L. R. (1999). Early neocortical regionalization in the absence of thalamic innervation. *Science, 285*, 906–909.

Moruzzi, G. (1966). The functional significance of sleep with particular regard to the brain mechanisms underlying consciousness. In J. C. Eccles (Ed.), *Brain and conscious experience* (pp. 345–388). New York: Springer-Verlag.

Niedermeyer, E., & Lopes da Silva, F. (1993). *Electroencephalography: Basic principles, clinical applications and related fields* (3rd ed). Baltimore: Williams and Wilkins.

Paré, D., & Llinás, R. R. (1995). Conscious and pre-conscious processes as seen from the standpoint of sleep-waking cycle neurophysiology. *Neuropsychologia, 33*, 1155–1168.

Pavlides, C., & Winson, J. (1989). Influences of hippocampal place cell firing in the awake state on the activity of these cells during subsequent sleep episodes. *Journal of Neuroscience, 9*, 2907–2918.

Petersen, C. C. H., Malenka, R. C., Nicoll, R. A., & Hopfield, J. J. (1998). All-or-none potentiation at CA3-Ca1 synapses. *Proceedings of the National Academy of Sciences USA, 95*, 4732–4737.

Phelps, M. E., Mazziotta, J. C., Kuhl, D. E., Nuwer, M., Packwood, J., Metter, J., & Engel, J., Jr. (1981). Tomographic mapping of cerebral metabolism visual stimulation and deprivation. *Neurology, 31*, 517–529.

Pivik, R. T. (1994). The psychophysiology of dreams. In M. H. Kryger, T. Roth, & W. C. Dement (Eds.), *Principles and practice of sleep medicine* (pp. 384–393). Philadelphia: Saunders.

Plihal, W., & Born, J. (1997). Effects of early and late nocturnal sleep on declarative and procedural memory. *Journal of Cognitive Neuroscience, 9*, 534–547.

Porte, H. S., & Hobson, J. A. (1996). Physical motion in dreams: One measure of three theories. *Journal of Abnormal Psychology, 105,* 329–335.

Rafal, R., & Robertson, L. (1995). The neurology of visual attention. In M. Gazzaniga (Ed.), *The cognitive neurosciences* (pp. 625–648). Cambridge, MA: The MIT Press.

Rauschecker, J. P. (1995). Developmental plasticity and memory. *Behavioral Brain Research, 66,* 7–12.

Riddle, D. R., Lo, D. C., & Katz, L. C. (1995). NT-4-mediated rescue of lateral geniculate neurons from effects of monocular deprivation. *Nature, 378,* 189–191.

Roder, B., Rosler, F., & Hennighausen, E. (1997). Different cortical activation patterns in blind and sighted humans during encoding and transformation of haptic images. *Psychophysiology, 34,* 292–307.

Roffwarg, H. P., Muzio, J. N., & Dement, W. C. (1966). Ontogenetic development of the human sleep-dream cycle. *Science, 152,* 604–619.

Rolls, E. T. (1991). Information processing in the temporal lobe visual cortical areas of macaques. In M. A. Arbib & J.-P. Ewert (Eds.), *Visual structures and integrated functions* (pp. 339–352). Berlin: Springer-Verlag.

Rymer, R. (1993). *Genie: A scientific tragedy.* London: Penguin Books.

Shaw, C. A., Lanius, R. A., & van den Doel, K. (1994). The origin of synaptic neuroplasticity: Critical molecules or a dynamical cascade? *Brain Research Reviews, 19,* 241–263.

Shen, J., Kudrimoti, H. S., McNaughton, B. L., & Barnes, C. A. (1998). Reactivation of neuronal ensembles in hippocampal dentate gyrus during sleep after spatial experience. *Journal of Sleep Research, 7* (Suppl. 1), 6–16.

Siegel, J. M. (1995). Phylogeny and the function of REM sleep. *Behavioural Brain Research, 69,* 29–34.

Smith, C., & Lapp, L. (1986). Prolonged increases in both PS and number of REMs following a shuttle avoidance task. *Physiology and Behavior, 36,* 1053–1057.

Smith, C., & MacNeill, C. (1994). Impaired motor memory for a pursuit rotor task following stage 2 sleep loss in college students. *Journal of Sleep Research, 3,* 206–213.

Squire, L. R. (1986). Mechanisms of memory. *Science, 232,* 1612–1619.

Steriade, M. (1978). Cortical long-axoned cells and putative interneurons during the sleep-waking cycle. *Behavioral Brain Science, 2,* 465–514.

Steriade, M. (1988). New vistas on the morphology, chemical transmitters, and physiological actions of the ascending brainstem reticular system. *Archives of Italian Biology, 126,* 225–238.

Steriade, M., Contreras, D., Curró Dossi, R., & Nuñez, A. (1993). The slow (<1 Hz) oscillation in reticular thalamic and thalamocortical neurons: Scenario of sleep rhythm generation in interacting thalamic and neocortical networks. *Journal of Neuroscience, 13,* 3284–3299.

Steriade, M., Jones, E. G., & Llinás, R. R. (1990). *Thalamic oscillations and signaling.* New York: Wiley.

Steriade, M., McCormick, D. A., & Sejnowski, T. J. (1993). Thalamocortical oscillations in the sleeping and aroused brain. *Science, 262,* 679–685.

Steward, O. (1993). Molecular sorting in neurons: Cell biological processes that play a role in synapse growth and plasticity. In M. Baudry, R. F. Thompson, & J. L. Davis (Eds.), *Synaptic plasticity* (pp. 13–43). Cambridge, MA: The MIT Press.

Steward, O., Wallace, C. S., Lyford, G. L., & Worley, P. F. (1998). Synaptic activation causes the mRNA for the IEG Arc to localize selectively near activated postsynaptic sites on dendrites. *Neuron, 21,* 741–751.

Stickgold, R. (1998). Sleep: Off-line memory reprocessing. *Trends in Cognitive Science, 2,* 484–492.

Tobler, I. (1985). Deprivation of sleep and rest in vertebrates and invertebrates. In S. Inoue & A. A. Borbély (Eds.), *Endogenous sleep substances and sleep regulation* (pp. 57–66). Tokyo: Japan Scientific Societies Press.

Ungerleider, L. G. (1995). Functional brain imaging studies of cortical mechanisms for memory. *Science, 270,* 769–775.

Van Essen, D. C., Anderson, C. H., & Felleman, D. J. (1992). Information processing in the primate visual system: An integrated systems perspective. *Science, 255,* 419–423.

Vertes, R. P. (1990). Brainstem mechanisms of slow-wave sleep and REM sleep. In W. R. Klemm & R. P. Vertes (Eds.), *Brainstem mechanisms of behavior* (pp. 535–583). New York: Wiley.

Verzeano, M. (1980). Activity of neuronal networks in cognitive function. In R. F. Thompson, L. H. Hicks, & V. R. Shvyrkov (Eds.), *Neural mechanisms of goal-directed behavior in learning* (pp. 353–373). New York: Academic Press.

Wanet-Defalque, M.-C., Veraart, C., DeVolder, A., Metz, R., Michel, C., Dooms, S., & Gofinet, A. (1988). High metabolic activity in the visual cortex of early blind human subjects. *Brain Research, 446,* 369–373.

Wilson, M. A., & McNaughton, B. L. (1994). Reactivation of hippocampal ensemble memories during sleep. *Science, 265,* 676–679.

Winson, J. (1985). *Brain and psyche: The biology of the unconscious.* New York: Anchor Press, Doubleday.

Winson, J. (1997). The meaning of dreams. In *Mysteries of the mind* (pp. 58–67). New York: Scientific American.

Wu, L., Wells, D., Tay, J., Mendis, D., Abbott, M. A., Barnitt, A., Quinlan, E., Haynen, A., Fallon, J. R., & Richter, J. D. (1998). CREB-mediated cytoplasmic adenylation of the regulation of experience-dependent translation of alpha-CaMKII mRNA at synapses. *Neuron, 21,* 1129–1139.

Yaca, R., Yinon, U., & Wollberg, Z. (1999). Auditory activation of cortical visual areas in cats after early visual deprivation. *European Journal of Neuroscience, 11,* 1301–1312.

Young, M. P. (1992). Objective analysis of the topological organization of the primate cortical visual system. *Nature, 358,* 152–155.

Alison R. Mercer

The Predictable Plasticity of Honey Bees

☐ Introduction

Honey bees have quite a reputation to live up to: their behavioral ecology has been a focus of attention for centuries, but still they continue to surprise us. Insect behavior was once thought to be entirely stereotyped and the insect nervous system "hard-wired," but evidence contradicting these views is now overwhelming. Adaptive neural regulation enables honey bees to optimize brain function in the face of changing demands and to modify behavior as a result of experience. There is, nonetheless, an underlying predictability in much of what the honey bee does that provides unique opportunities for exploring the cellular basis of behavioral plasticity using this remarkable insect.

Adult worker honey bees have a rich and interesting behavioral repertoire. Not only do they change their behavior with age, but also the sequence of tasks they perform is highly predictable (Figure 7.1a). From a multitude of activities, four distinct but overlapping temporal castes have been identified. These are characterized by the following duties: (1) cell cleaning and capping, (2) tending the queen and developing larvae, (3) comb building, food handling, and cleaning debris from the hive, and (4) duties outside the hive, such as guarding, ventilation, and foraging (Winston, 1987). Very young bees (cell cleaners) and foragers tend to be task specific, but "middle-aged" bees may perform a range of activities during the course of a day. Average ages of between 7 and 13 days have been reported for nurses, the mean age for comb-builders is around 15 days, and foraging flights generally begin at around 20 days after adult emergence (Winston, 1987). However, worker bees can alter their normal pattern of behavioral development in response to the needs of the colony. A shortage of foragers, for example, induces young bees to forage precociously, whereas a shortage of nurses can delay the shift to foraging and induce forager bees to revert to duties within the hive (Lindauer, 1961). This behavioral plasticity is also highly predictable and can be used to disentangle effects on the brain of age versus activity.

Changes in behavior have a significant impact on the structure of the brain. To explore the origins and consequences of this structural plasticity we have chosen to focus

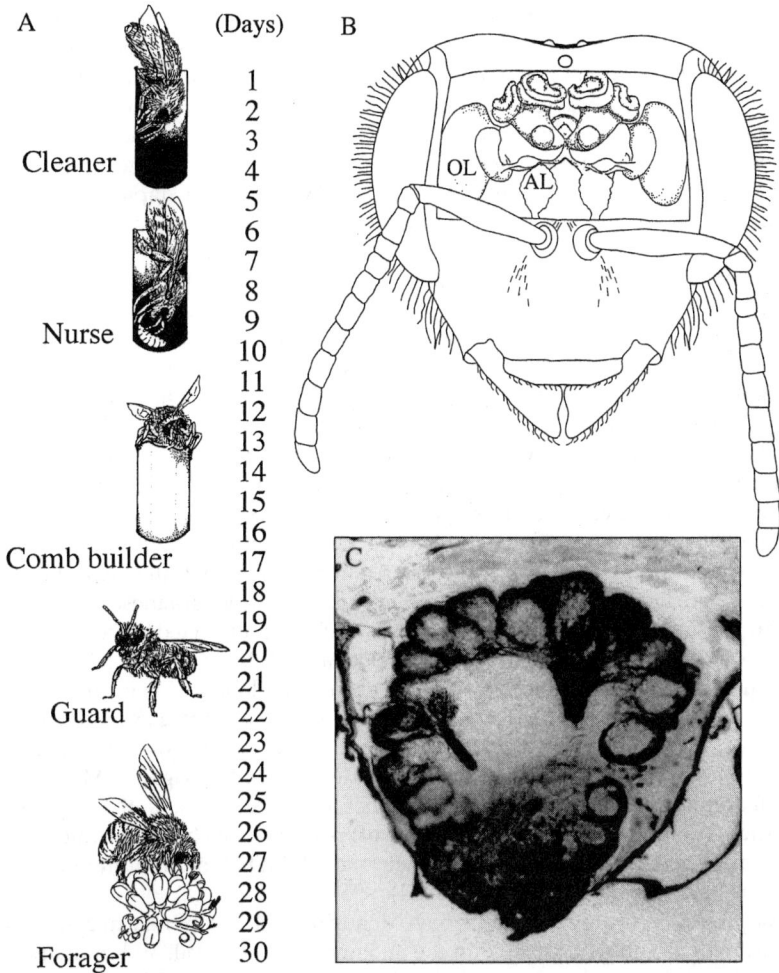

Figure 7.1. (A) Adult worker honey bees change their behavior with age. Illustrations in the left-hand column show some of the different behaviors performed. Approximate ages in days since adult emergence are indicated in the column to the right. Mean ages reported for "nurses," which feed the developing larvae, range from 7 to 13 days, the mean age for comb-builders is around 15 days, and foraging flights generally begin at around 20 days of age (Winston, 1987). While very young bees (cell cleaners) and foragers tend to be task specific, "middle-aged" bees generally perform a range of activities during the course of a day (Winston, 1987). (B) Multimodal sensory information gathered by the antennae is essential to many honey bee behaviors. Antennal sensory information is conveyed to the deutocerebrum via the antennal nerve. A large proportion of the primary sensory afferent neurons project to the antennal lobes (ALs), where they terminate within discrete subcompartments (glomeruli) at the periphery of the antennal-lobe neuropil (see [C]). (C) Filling antennal sensory afferent neurons with cobalt reveals their terminal arbors in the outer (cortical) layer of each glomerulus (G). The arrow points to primary sensory afferents entering the lobe in Tract 1, which innervates glomeruli in the anterior and dorsal regions of the antennal lobe (see Figure 2a).

on the antennal lobes, which are the primary antennal-sensory centers of the insect brain (Figure 7.1b). Most tasks performed by adult worker honey bees rely, at least in part, on sensory information gathered by the antennae. An interesting array of sensilla distributed across each antennal flagellum reflects the multifunctional role of these remarkable organs. Olfactory receptors, mechanoreceptors, and contact chemoreceptors have been identified on the antennae, along with receptors for detecting changes in temperature, carbon dioxide levels, and humidity (Masson & Mustaparta 1990; Esslen & Kaissling, 1976). Within the darkness of the hive, odors, mechanosensory stimuli, and chemosensory cues provide communication signals that are essential to the survival of all members of the colony. Not surprisingly, a significant proportion of the brain neuropil is dedicated to the processing of antennal sensory inputs.

Antennal sensory receptor neurons enter the brain at the level of the deutocerebrum. A large proportion of these primary sensory afferents, including most, if not all, chemosensory receptor neurons, project to the antennal lobes, where they terminate in discrete spheres of synaptic neuropil, called glomeruli (Figures 7.1c, 7.2a). A smaller population of antennal sensory afferents projects to an area immediately posterior to the antennal lobe, known as the dorsal lobe (Figure 7.2a), which is the antennal motor and mechanosensory center of the brain (Kloppenburg, 1995; Kloppenburg, Kirchhof, & Mercer, 1999). Fibers extending beyond the dorsal lobes and antennal lobes of the deutocerebrum, either dorsally into the protocerebrum or posteroventrally toward the suboesophageal ganglion, have also been identified, but the functions of these neurons remain unclear. The antennal lobe and ipsilateral dorsal lobe are connected by deutocerebral interneurons with arborizations in both lobes (Flanagan & Mercer, 1989b). Presumably as a consequence of these interconnections, local antennal-lobe interneurons respond not only to chemosensory signals (Flanagan & Mercer, 1989b; Fonta, Sun, & Masson, 1993; Sun, Fonta, & Masson, 1993) and to changes in humidity (Itoh, Yokohari, & Tominaga, 1991), but also to mechanical stimuli, such as puffs of air (Flanagan & Mercer, 1989b). The integrative properties of the antennal lobes are reflected also in the response characteristics of antennal-lobe projection (output) neurons, which convey information to higher order centers of the brain. These neurons exhibit bi- and multimodal responses to antennal sensory input (Homberg, 1984).

Most projection (output) neurons have dendritic arbors confined to a specific subcompartment, or glomerulus, within the antennal-lobe neuropil, and in many cases it is possible to identify the glomerulus in question (e.g., Figure 7.2b). The number of glomeruli in the antennal lobes of the adult worker honey bee is relatively small (about 160), their layout is highly conserved across individuals, and approximately one quarter are readily identifiable from one individual to the next (e.g., Figures 7.2a, 7.3a; Arnold, Masson, & Budharugsa, 1985; Flanagan & Mercer, 1989a; Galizia, McIlwrath, & Menzel, 1999). Recent studies have shown that antennal stimulation evokes spatially defined patterns of activity across the glomerular array (Galizia, Sachse, Rappert, & Menzel, 1999; Joerges, Küttner, Galizia, & Menzel, 1997; Lieke, 1993). Unique patterns of activity in the antennal lobes resulting from integration of multimodal inputs could play a role in communication, orientation behavior, and flower recognition, and provide an important substrate for context-specific learning.

In addition to the terminal arbors of primary sensory afferent neurons (e.g., Figure 7.1c) and the dendrites of projection (output) neurons (e.g., Figure 7.2b), each glomerulus contains processes of local interneurons (e.g., Figure 7.2c) and ramifications of centrifugal neurons that project to the antennal lobe from elsewhere in the brain. Evidence suggests that centrifugal inputs contribute significantly to antennal lobe plasticity (see the section on "Underlying Mechanisms," below).

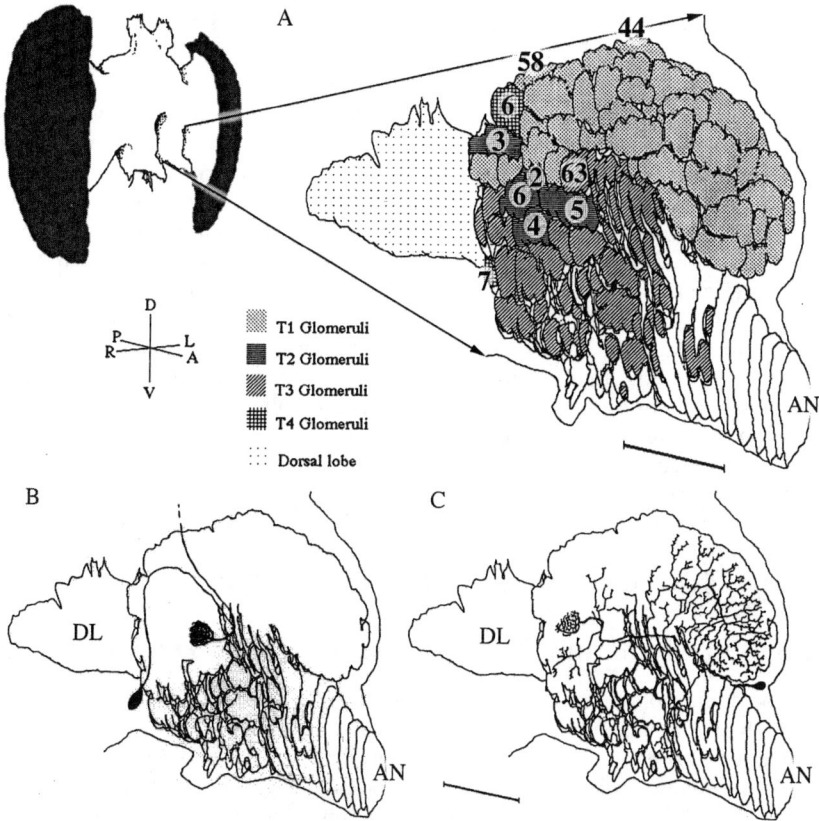

Figure 7.2. (A) Computer reconstruction of the left antennal lobe of the adult worker honey bee. The medial surface of the lobe is viewed anteriorly from 60° to the right of a direct frontal aspect. Major divisions of the deutocerebral neuropil are explained in the key provided. Readily identifiable glomeruli are numbered in the reconstructions. The whole-brain reconstruction on the left-hand side indicates the position of the antennal lobe in the brain of the honey bee. Many antennal-lobe neurons can be identified according to their glomerular projections (e.g., see [B], [C]). (B) Partial reconstruction of a projection (output) neuron that has dendritic arbors restricted to glomerulus T2-1(5). (C) Reconstruction of a local interneuron with a concentration of arbors in the identifiable glomerulus, T2-1(6). This neuron also sends sparse projections into a number of T1 glomeruli toward the anterior of the antennal lobe. Not all local interneurons exhibit a heterogeneous distribution of arbors within the glomerular neuropil; some have a more homogeneous appearance and are therefore more difficult to identify. Reconstructions redrawn from "An Atlas and 3-D Reconstruction of the Antennal Lobes in the Worker Honey Bee, *Apis mellifera* L. (Hymenoptera: apidal)" by D. Flanagan and A. R. Mercer, 1989, *International Journal of Insect Morphology & Embryology, 18,* pp. 145–159. Copyright © Pergamon Press. Used with permission. Anterior (A), antennal nerve (AN), dorsal (D), dorsal lobe (DL), left (L), posterior (P), right (R), T1–T4 region of the antennal lobe innervated by Tracts 1–4, respectively, ventral (V). Scale bars = 100 μm.

☐ Structural Plasticity of the Antennal Lobes

Antennal lobes undergo constant modification during the lifetime of the adult worker bee. The volume of the antennal-lobe neuropil increases significantly during the first 4–6 days of adult life, and a second burst of growth is apparent as bees reach foraging age (Winnington, Napper, & Mercer, 1996). Some, but not all, glomeruli share this pattern of growth (e.g., Figure 7.3b–f). For example, glomerulus T1-44, a large glomerulus in the dorsal (T1) region of the antennal lobe (Figure 7.3a) increases in volume significantly during the first 6 days of adult life, but shows very little growth thereafter, even in bees of foraging age (Figure 7.3b). In contrast, in the posterior (T4) region of the lobe, glomerulus T4-2(1) (Figure 7.3a), not only shows significant growth during the first 4 days postemergence, but increases in volume further in bees of foraging age (Figure 7.3e). Growth patterns remarkably similar to those described above are apparent in bees arranged according to predicted age but selected on the basis of their behavioral activities at the time of capture. For example, in a colony with a normal age structure, the volume of glomerulus T4-2(1) is significantly larger in nurses and comb-builders than in newly emerged adult workers, but significantly smaller in nurses and comb-builders than in foragers (Figure 7.4a). In contrast, the volume of T1-44 in nurses and comb-builders is similar to that seen in foragers, but is significantly larger in each of these groups than in newly emerged workers (Figure 7.4c).

Changes in Glomerular Volume: Age or Activity Dependent?

If increases in the volume of glomerulus T4-2(1) occur as a consequence of activities performed while foraging, one would predict that precocious foraging behavior should be accompanied by premature enlargement of this glomerulus. Removing bees of foraging age from the colony induces some young workers to begin foraging at a much earlier age than normal (Lindauer, 1961). Precocious foraging can be induced also by treating bees with juvenile hormone (Jaycox, 1976) or the juvenile hormone analog, methoprene (Robinson 1985, 1992). Behavioral manipulations of this kind provide strong evidence in support of the view that changes in glomerular volume are, at least in part, activity dependent. For example, glomerulus T4-2(1), which was found to be significantly larger in normal-aged foragers than in nurses (Figure 7.4a), is also significantly larger in precocious foragers than in bees of the same age performing duties within the hive (Figure 7.5d). As predicted from age-based studies, the volume of glomerulus T1-44, which under normal colony conditions is similar in nurses, comb-builders, and foragers, was not affected by a precocious shift to foraging activities (Sigg, Thompson, & Mercer 1997).

Evidence that the growth of T4-2(1) is enhanced by activities performed while foraging is supported by behavioral reversion experiments. Removing nurses and comb-builders from a colony induces some workers that are already foraging to revert to duties within the hive. Winnington et al. (1996) found that foragers that reverted to nursing duties exhibited significantly smaller T4-2(1) volumes than bees that continued foraging (see Figure 7.4b). Foragers that reverted to comb-building activities exhibited T4-2(1) volumes intermediate in size between those of nurses and foragers (Figure 7.4b) and behavioral reversion had no significant impact on the volume of glomerulus T1-44 (Figure 7.4d). Together, these studies provide strong support for the hypothesis that changes in behavior can have a significant impact on the structure of the brain. Similar studies reveal also that activity-dependent structural plasticity is not restricted to the antennal-lobe neuropil.

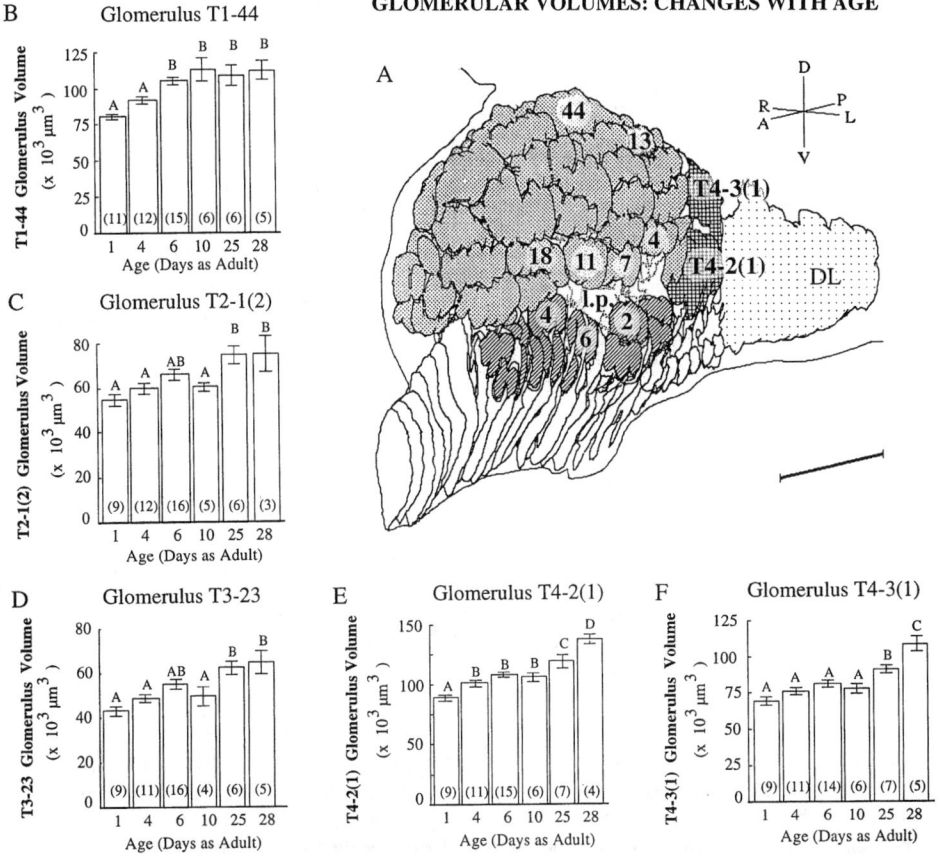

GLOMERULAR VOLUMES: CHANGES WITH AGE

Figure 7.3. (a) Computer reconstruction of the lateral surface of the left antennal lobe of the adult worker honey bee viewed anteriorly from 60° to the left of a direct frontal aspect. Major divisions of the deutocerebral neuropil are explained in the key provided in Figure 7.2. Readily identifiable glomeruli are numbered in the reconstruction. Reconstruction redrawn from "An Atlas and 3-D Reconstruction of the Antennal Lobes in the Worker Honey Bee, *Apis mellifera* L. (Hymenoptera: apidal)" by D. Flanagan and A. R. Mercer, 1989, *International Journal of Insect Morphology & Embryology, 18*, pp. 145–159. Copyright © Pergamon Press. Used with permission. Anterior (A), antennal nerve (AN), dorsal (D), dorsal lobe (DL), left (L), lateral passage (lp), posterior (P), right (R), T1–T4 region of the antennal lobe innervated by antennal-nerve Tracts 1–4, respectively, ventral (V). Scale bar = 100 μm. (b)–(f) Changes in mean glomerular volume (±S.E.M.) with age in five readily identifiable glomeruli: T1-44, T2-1(2), T3-23, T4-2(1), and T4-3(1), respectively. The graphs reveal that volumetric changes in the glomerular neuropil of the antennal lobes are site specific. Changes in glomerular volume are also highly predictable, but not invariant. The *n* value for each group is shown in parentheses. Within each graph, letters above the bars indicate which groups differ significantly from one another. Groups that do not share one or more letters differ significantly (Student-Newman-Keuls test, $p < 0.05$). Data redrawn from "Structural Plasticity of Identified Glomeruli in the Antennal Lobes of the Adult Worker Honey Bee," by A. P. Winnington, R. M. Napper, and A. R. Mercer, 1996, *Journal of Comparative Neurology, 365*, pp. 479–490. Copyright © Wiley-Liss. Used with permission.

A   T4-2(1) Volumes vs Behavior

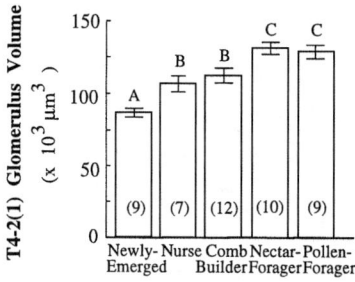

B   Reversion Experiment T4-2(1)

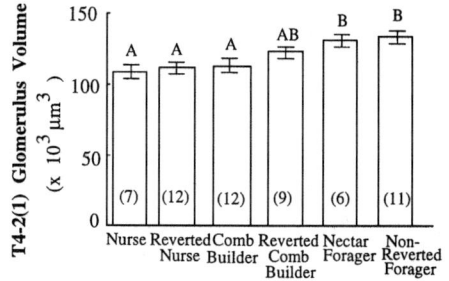

C   T1-44 Volumes vs Behavior

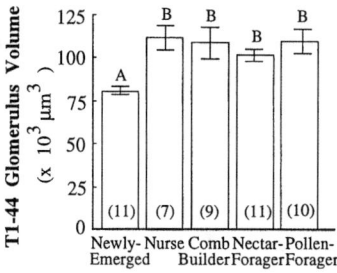

D   Reversion Experiment T1-44

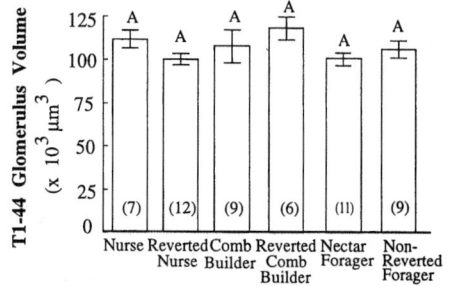

Figure 7.4. (a), (c) Mean volume (±S.E.M.) of glomerulus T4-2(1) (a) and glomerulus T1-44 (c) in adult worker bees performing different behavioral tasks. Arranging the groups according to predicted age reveals patterns of glomerular growth remarkably similar to those observed in age-based studies (see Figure 7.3e, b respectively). (b), (d) Comparison of mean glomerular volumes (±S.E.M.) of worker bees from a normal colony (nurse, comb-builder, nectar forager) and in workers from a colony in which young bees had been removed in order to induce bees that were already foraging to revert to duties within the hive (reverted nurse, reverted comb-builder). As predicted from the results of age-based studies, T4-2(1) volumes in reverted nurses were significantly smaller than in nectar foragers and nonreverted foragers (b). Effects of inducing foragers to revert to duties within the hive on T1-44 volumes were not statistically significant (d). These results reveal that in some cases, increases in glomerular volume can be reversed by manipulating the behavioral activities of the bee. In each graph, groups with different letters are significantly different from one another (Student-Newman-Keuls test, $p < 0.05$). The n value for each group is shown in parentheses. Data redrawn from "Structural Plasticity of Identified Glomeruli in the Antennal Lobes of the Adult Worker Honey Bee," by A. P. Winnington, R. M. Napper, and A. R. Mercer, 1996, *Journal of Comparative Neurology, 365*, pp. 479–490. Copyright © Wiley-Liss. Used with permission.

Parallel Changes in the Mushroom Bodies of the Brain

The pattern of volumetric changes in the antennal lobes is reflected in higher order centers, such as the mushroom bodies (see Figure 1b) of the brain (Durst, Eichmüller, & Menzel, 1994; Fahrbach, & Robinson, 1996; Withers, Fahrbach, & Robinson, 1993, 1995).

Projection (output) neurons transfer information from the antennal lobes to the "lip" of the mushroom body calyces and to the lateral lobes of the protocerebrum (Mobbs, 1985). Durst et al. (1994) found that the volume of the lip was significantly larger in bees performing nursing duties than in newly emerged workers. In contrast, the "collar" of the mushroom body calyces, which receives input from the optic lobes, was found to be remarkably similar in volume in these two groups, perhaps reflecting the limited amount of visual stimulation experienced by "in house" bees. Consistent with this explanation, Durst and colleagues (1994) found that irrespective of the age of the bee, the volume of both the lip and the collar of the mushroom bodies increased significantly with the onset of foraging. It is not surprising that a bee's entry into a visual world has a significant impact on the structure of the brain. Bees begin performing new behavioral activities at this time, and demands on their sensory information–processing capabilities increase significantly.

☐ Causes and Consequences of Structural Plasticity

In some insect species, such as the house cricket (*Acheta domesticus*), undifferentiated cells in the mushroom bodies of the brain divide and give rise to cortical interneurons during adult life (Cayre, Strambi, & Strambi, 1994). While changes in cell number could contribute to volumetric changes in the brain of some species, there is no evidence of cell proliferation in the brain of the adult worker honey bee (Fahrbach, Strande, & Robinson, 1995; Malun, 1998). We assume, therefore, that alterations to the size and complexity of existing cell profiles are most likely to be responsible for volumetric changes in the antennal lobes of the brain. In light of the age-related changes in behavior apparent in honey bee workers, it seems likely that the antennal lobes, like other regions of the brain, are constantly being optimized for tasks that are important to the bee at the time. Structural alterations to the dendritic arbors of antennal-lobe neurons have recently been described that could reflect the fine tuning of neuronal connectivities within the glomerular neuropil of the antennal lobes (Devaud & Masson, 1999). Changes in spine morphology that correlate temporally with the first orientation flights of bees have been identified also on the dendritic abors of mushroom body intrinsic neurons (Brandon & Coss, 1982; Coss, Brandon, & Globus, 1980), but whether the formation or retraction of synapses and changes in dendritic morphology contribute to volumetric changes in the brain has yet to be clearly established. The possibility that changes in volume may be accompanied by site-specific changes in synapse counts (Gascuel & Masson, 1987, 1991) is being examined currently at the ultrastructural level using stereological techniques (Brown, Napper, & Mercer, 2000).

Division of labor results in adult workers using their antennae in different ways. For example, brood pheromones induce nurses to feed the developing larvae, tactile receptors at the tips of the antennae are used by comb-builders to measure the thickness of cell walls, and foragers rely on antennal olfactory receptors to detect the complex blends of volatiles that form the floral signatures used by bees for flower recognition. Changes in antennal usage are reflected in the dynamic properties of the antennal lobes (Sigg et al., 1997; Winnington et al., 1996). This is strongly reminiscent of structural plasticity in the somatosensory cortex of the vertebrate brain (e.g., Buonomano & Merzenich, 1998). It has recently been shown in humans, for example, that increasing the relative activity of specific subpopulations of sensory neurons, such as the tactile receptors in the index (reading) finger of a Braille reader (Pascual-Leone & Torres, 1993), can result in representational expansions in the cortex. Studies of the somatosensory cortex reveal two important features of this use-dependent plasticity that seem likely to be directly relevant

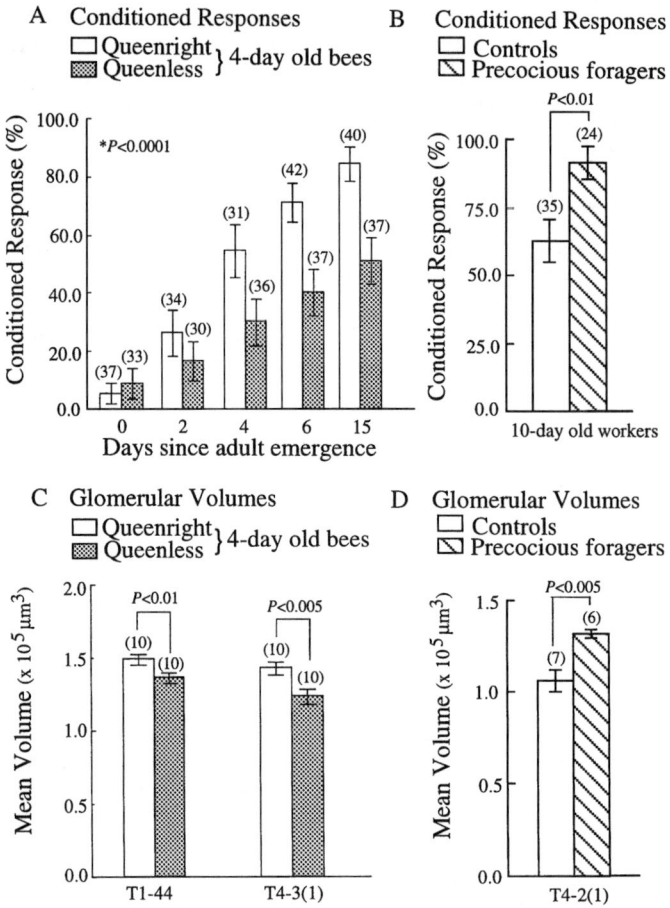

Figure 7.5. Correlations between changes in glomerular volume and olfactory learning behavior in the bee. (a) The effect of queenlessness on the percentage of bees 0 to 15 days of age exhibiting conditioned responses to lavender odor after a single conditioning trial. Logistic regression analysis revealed that learning levels of workers from a queenright colony (white bars) were significantly higher than those observed after the same colony had been rendered queenless (gray bars). Data shown are means ± standard errors of the proportions. Data redrawn from "The Effects of Queenlessness on the Maturation of the Honey Bee Olfactory System," by S. M. Morgan, V. Butz Huryn, S. R. Downes, and A. R. Mercer, 1998, *Behavioral Brain Research, 91*, pp. 115–126. Copyright © Elsevier Science B. V. Used with permission. (b) Precocious foragers (striped bar) exhibited significantly higher levels of conditioned responses than bees of the same age performing duties within the hive (controls, white bars). A Chi-squared test was used in this analysis and the data shown are means ± standard errors of the proportions. Data are redrawn from "Activity-Dependent Charges to the Brain and Behavior of the Honey Bee, *Apis mellifera* L.," by D. Sigg, C. M. Thompson, and A. R. Mercer, 1997, *Journal of Neuroscience, 17*, pp. 7148–7156. Copyright © Society for Neuroscience. Used with permission. (c) Removing the queen from the colony had a significant impact on the glomerular neuropil of the antennal lobes in young worker bees. Readily identifiable glomeruli, such as T1-44 and

to structural plasticity in the brain of the honey bee. First, structural reorganization of cortical maps requires that sensory stimulation occur within a behaviorally relevant context: passive stimulation seems to be ineffective (Recanzone, Merzenich, Jenkins, Grajski, & Dinse, 1992). Second, in Braille readers, where tactile discrimination has to be fast and accurate, improved tactual capabilities have been shown to coincide with structural changes to the cortex (e.g., Sterr et al., 1998). Changes in the use of peripheral sensory pathways associated with age-related polyethism will have strong behavioral relevance for the bee, but whether this is an essential component of activity-dependent plasticity in the antennal lobes has yet to be explored. While it is also unclear whether a bee's perception is altered as a result of structural changes in the brain, perceptual changes may underlie some of the interesting correlations described below that exist between changes in glomerular volume and olfactory learning performance in the bee.

Experience, Learning, and Memory

Most honey bees learn rapidly to associate a floral odor with a food reward, an ability that contributes significantly to their success as foragers (Mauelshagen & Greggers, 1993; Menzel & Müller, 1996). Associative learning has been studied extensively in bees using the proboscis conditioning paradigm. Touching the antenna of a bee with sugar water induces reflex extension of the proboscis. If a floral odor is presented to the bee immediately prior to eliciting this reflex response, and the bee is allowed to drink from the sugar-water droplet, the bee learns rapidly to associate the odor with a food reward. In subsequent tests, a bee that has made this association will exhibit a conditioned response (proboscis extension) when the odor alone is presented in the absence of the unconditioned stimulus (sugar-water stimulation of the antennae) or a food reward. Approximately 60% to 80% of foragers tested in this way exhibit the conditioned response after a single conditioning trial (e.g., Menzel, Erber, & Masuhr, 1974; Smith, 1991). However, newly emerged adults generally perform poorly in this task (Morgan, Butz Huryn, Downes, & Mercer, 1998; Ray & Ferneyhough, 1997). Significant improvements in olfactory learning performance that occur during the first week of adult life (Figure 7.5a) correlate temporally with site-specific increases in the glomerular-neuropil volume of the antennal lobes (e.g., Figure 7.3, Winnington et al., 1996; Morgan et al., 1998). Similar parallels between changes in glomerular volume and olfactory learning performance have been observed in behavioral manipulation studies. Sigg et al. (1997)

T4-3(1), were significantly larger in 4-day-old bees from a queenright colony (white bars) than in bees of the same age from the same colony rendered queenless (gray bars). Two-sample t-tests were used in this analysis. Data shown are means ±S.E.M. Data redrawn from "The Effects of Queenlessness on the Matulation of the Honey Bee Olfactory System," by S. M. Morgan, V. Butz Huryn, S. R. Downes, and A. R. Mercer, 1998, *Behavioral Brain Research, 91*, pp. 115–126. Copyright © Elsevier Science B. V. Used with permission. (d) In precocious foragers (striped bar), the volume of glomerulus T4-2(1) was found to be significantly larger than in bees of the same age performing duties within the colony. Two-sample t-tests were used also in this analysis. Data shown are means ±S.E.M. and are redrawn from "Activity-Dependent Charges to the Brain and Behavior of the Honey Bee, *Apis mellifera* L.," by D. Sigg, C. M. Thompson, and A. R. Mercer, 1997, *Journal of Neuroscience, 17*, pp. 7148–7156. Copyright © Society for Neuroscience. Used with permission.

compared levels of conditioned olfactory responses in precocious foragers and bees of the same age performing duties within the hive. Not only were learning levels after a single conditioning trial significantly higher in the precocious foragers (Figure 7.5b), but also glomeruli such as T4-2(1) were significantly larger in the antennal lobes of precocious foragers than in same-age controls (Figure 7.5d). Effects of sensory deprivation on the glomerular neuropil of the antennal lobes are reflected also in the olfactory learning behavior of the bee. Removing the queen from the colony illustrates such effects well. Queen pheromones are distributed widely as volatile odors and as nonvolatiles spread through antennation and food-sharing activities of the bees, and they affect both the behavior and physiological state of adult workers (Seeley, 1985; Winston, 1987). Morgan et al. (1998) found that removing the queen from a colony not only impaired the development of olfactory learning behavior in young (4-day-old) adult workers (Figure 7.5a, gray bars), but also had a significant impact on the structure of the antennal-lobe neuropil (Figure 7.5c). Glomeruli such as T1-44 and T4-3(1) were significantly smaller than normal in bees that emerged as adults after removal of the queen.

Removing the queen did not affect the learning performance of all members of the colony. The percentage of pollen foragers that exhibited conditioned olfactory responses after a single conditioning trial was almost identical before and after the queen had been removed. The absence of any impact on the learning levels of these bees suggests that learning performance may be affected only if the olfactory system of the bee is undergoing a critical period of maturation at the time the queen is removed from the colony. However, improvements with age in the learning performance of queen-deprived bees suggest that even bees deprived of a queen during early adult life may eventually display learning levels not significantly different from those of foragers from queenright hives.

☐ Underlying Mechanisms

Biogenic amines have been strongly implicated in the development and plasticity of the nervous system, and they seem likely to play a central role in mediating the structural and functional plasticity of the antennal lobes. In the vertebrate olfactory bulb, the density of fibers in the glomerular layer that contain the biogenic monoamine serotonin (5-hydroxytryptamine, 5HT) increases significantly during postnatal development (Philpot, Jazaeri, & Brunjes, 1994). The volume of the glomerular layer increases also (Pomeroy, La Mantia, & Purves, 1990), and it has been postulated that serotonergic fibers serve to sculpt the formation of synaptic contacts within the glomeruli during this period (McLean & Shipley, 1987). Pharmacological depletion of 5HT not only impairs olfactory performance in rats (McLean, Darby-King, Sullivan, & King, 1993) but also causes shrinkage of the glomerular layer of the olfactory bulb (Moriizumi, Tsukatani, Sakashita, & Miwa, 1994). In bees, a single 5HT-immunoreactive neuron projects to most, if not all, glomeruli in the antennal lobe (Rehder, Bicker, & Hammer, 1987). Exogenously applied 5HT has been shown to enhance the growth of antennal-lobe neurons in vitro (Mercer, Kirchhof, & Hildebrand, 1996) and, in the sphinx moth *Manduca sexta*, 5HT not only increases the excitability of antennal-lobe interneurons (Kloppenburg & Hildebrand, 1995; Mercer, Hayashi, & Hildebrand, 1995; Mercer, Kloppenburg, & Hildebrand, 1996) but also enhances the responsiveness of male-specific antennal-lobe neurons to female sex pheromone (Kloppenburg, Ferns, & Mercer, 1999). Both input and output synapses have been identified between 5HT-immunoreactive processes and the processes of other neurons in the glomerular neuropil of the antennal lobe (Salecker & Distler, 1990; Sun, Tolbert, & Hildebrand, 1993). One possible consequence of this arrangement could be the site-specific release of 5HT resulting from activity-dependent events within local (glomerular) circuits. In vitro studies suggest that in addition to its influence on cell excitability, 5HT would promote the growth and elaboration of cell processes within the glomerular neuropil (Mercer, Kirchhof, & Hildebrand, 1996). Interestingly, 5HT levels in the antennal lobes of the sphinx moth fluctuate significantly over a 24-hour period and are highest when the moths are most active (Kloppenburg, Ferns, & Mercer, 1999). Moreover, in honey bees, regardless of their age, levels of 5HT (and octopamine) have been found to be higher in the antennal lobes of foragers than in nurses (Schulz, & Robinson, 1999) Ferns, & mercer. Taken together, these results suggest that biogenic amines contribute not only to the structural and functional plasticity of the antennal-lobe neuropil but also to the performance of odor-dependent behaviors.

Dopamine and octopamine have been identified also in the antennal lobes of the honey bee (Mercer, Mobbs, Davenport, & Evans, 1983; Schulz & Robinson, 1999) and both are strong candidates for involvement in the structural and functional plasticity of the brain. Processes of dopamine-immunoreactive neurons project around the base of each glomerulus (Kirchhof, Homberg, & Mercer, 1999; Schäfer & Rehder, 1989; Schürmann, Elekes, & Geffard, 1989) and are well placed to influence the development, as well as the subsequent plasticity, of the glomerular neuropil. During the first days of adult life, there is a dramatic increase in the density of D_1-like dopamine receptors in the brain of the adult worker bee (Kokay & Mercer, 1997). While the functional significance of this dopamine receptor up-regulation has yet to be determined, it correlates temporally with changes in both brain structure and the behavior of the bee. In bees of foraging age, dopamine injected into the midbrain before or after one-trial olfactory conditioning, or applied directly to the antennal lobes, reduces the percentage of bees responding to the conditioned stimulus (Macmillan & Mercer, 1987; Menzel, Michelsen, Ruffer, & Sugawa, 1988; Mercer & Menzel, 1982; Michelsen, 1988) and has a significant effect on information relayed to the mushroom bodies of the brain (Mercer & Erber, 1983). Interestingly, *Drosophila* mutants that have reduced levels of the enzyme dopa decarboxylase, and therefore synthesize lower than normal levels of dopamine, also perform poorly in olfactory learning tasks (Temple, Livingstone, & Quinn, 1984), but how and where dopamine acts in the insect brain has yet to be clearly established. The identification and pharmacological characterization of several distinct dopamine receptor subtypes in the insect brain (Blenau, Erber, & Baumann, 1998; Blenau, May, & Erber, 1995; Ebert, Rowland, & Toma, 1998; Feng et al., 1996; Gotzes, Balfanz, & Baumann, 1994; Han, Millar, Grotewiel, & Davis, 1996; Kokay & Mercer, 1996; Reale, Hannan, Hall, & Evans, 1997; Sugamori, Demchyshyn, McConkey, Forte, & Niznik, 1995) and analyses of their expression in situ (Blenau et al., 1998; Kokay, McEwan, and Mercer 1998) and in antennal lobe neurons in vitro (Kirchhof & Mercer, 1997) are providing important first steps toward identifying the modulatory role(s) that dopamine plays in the antennal lobes.

In 1993, Martin Hammer described the morphology and response characteristics of a ventral unpaired median neuron in the suboesophageal ganglion (VUMmx1) that sends projections not only to the antennal lobes, but also to the mushroom bodies and lateral protocerebrum. Evidence suggests that VUMmx1 contains octopamine (Kreissl, Eichmüller, Bicker, Rapus, & Eckert, 1994), a phenolamine that enhances the responsiveness of bees to sensory cues (Bicker & Menzel, 1989; Erber, Kloppenburg, & Scheidler, 1993; Mercer & Menzel, 1982). Octopamine injected into the antennal lobes evokes a rapid and transient activation of cAMP-dependent PKA activity, an effect that can be mimicked by stimulation of the bee's antenna with sucrose solution (Hildebrandt & Müller, 1995a, 1995b). Sucrose stimulation of the antennae enhances a bee's responsiveness to odor stimuli (Greggers & Menzel, 1993) and evokes a long-lasting discharge in VUMmx1 (Hammer, 1993). Hammer found that in olfactory conditioning trials, such as those described above, appropriate stimulation of VUMmx1 could serve the reinforcing function of the unconditioned stimulus (sugar-water stimulation of the antennae), and moreover, that learned odors excited VUMmx1 (Hammer, 1997). This elegant work revealed that octopamine mediates nonassociative behavioral changes, such as sensitization and arousal, as well as serving an instructive (reinforcing) function during associative learning (reviewed by Hammer & Menzel, 1998). 5HT has the same dual function in the marine mollusc, *Aplysia californica* (reviewed by Byrne & Kandel, 1996). Moreover, in *Aplysia*, long- term changes in synaptic efficacy are accompanied by 5HT-induced changes in synaptic morphology (Bailey & Kandel, 1993). It is well established in honey bees that associative learning of odors that predict a food reward can induce long-lasting, odor-specific memories (see Hammer & Menzel, 1995). Recent evidence suggests also that multiple conditioning trials lead not only to an increase in protein kinase C activity in the antennal lobes of the honey bee (Grünbaum & Müller, 1998; see also Müller, 1999), but also to changes in the patterns of activity across the glomerular array elicited by the conditioned olfactory stimulus (Faber, Joerges, & Menzel, 1999). While it is tempting to speculate that changes in glomerular volume may contribute to the formation of long-term olfactory memories in the bee, this has yet to be clearly established. The ability to detect temporally correlated events at the level of the antennal lobes could be used also to drive neurons engaged by behaviorally important stimuli to respond in a more temporally coherent manner, a property fundamental to antennal lobe function (Laurent, 1997; Stopfer, Bhagavan, Smith, & Laurent, 1997).

In bees, brain amine levels are affected by age, time of day, season, and conditions within the colony (Fuchs, Dustmann, Stadler, & Schürmann, 1989; Harris & Woodring, 1992; Kokay & Mercer, 1997; Purnell, Mitchell, Taylor, Kokay, & Mercer, 2000; Schulz & Robinson, 1999; Taylor, Robinson, Logan, Laverty, & Mercer, 1992; Wagener-Hulme, Kuehn, Schulz, & Robinson, 1999) and amine receptor densities, and their pattern of expression in the brain, also change dramatically during the lifetime of the bee (Kokay & Mercer, 1997). A new generation of questions is beginning to emerge as attention turns to the modulation of modulatory systems in the brain of the bee. In the words of Karl von Frisch: "The life of the bee is like a magic well, the more you draw from it, the more there is to draw" (Lindauer, 1987). The same could surely be said of the nervous system and its most fundamentally important feature, neuroplasticity.

☐ Acknowledgment

I am indebted to Mr. Ken Miller for his assistance with the illustrations and, in particular, for his preparation of Figure 7.1a.

☐ References

Arnold, G., Masson, C., & Budharugsa, S. (1985). Comparative study of the antennal lobes and their afferent pathway in the worker bee and the drone (*Apis mellifera*). *Cell & Tissue Research, 242,* 593–605.

Bailey, C. H., & Kandel, E. R. (1993). Structural changes accompanying memory storage. *Annual Review of Physiology, 55,* 397–426.

Bicker, G., & Menzel, R. (1989). Chemical codes for the control of behaviour in arthropods. *Nature, 337,* 33–39.

Blenau, W., Erber, J., & Baumann, A. (1998). Characterization of a dopamine D1 receptor from *Apis mellifera*: Cloning, functional expression, pharmacology and mRNA localization in the brain. *Journal of Neurochemistry, 70,* 15–23.

Blenau, W., May, T., & Erber, J. (1995). Characterization of a dopamine-sensitive [^{3}H]LSD binding site in honeybee (*Apis mellifera*) brain. *Comparative Biochemistry & Physiology, 110C,* 197–205.

Brandon, J., & Coss, R. (1982). Rapid dendritic spine stem shortening during one-trial learning: The honeybee's first orientation flight. *Brain Research, 252,* 51–61.

Brown, S. M., Napper, R. M., & Mercer, A. R. (2000). Analysis of structural plasticity in the honey bee brain using the Cavalieri estimator of volume and the disector method. *Image Analysis and Stereotype, 19,* 139–144.

Buonomano, D. V., & Merzenich, M. M. (1998). Cortical plasticity: From synapses to maps. *Annual Review of Neuroscience, 21,* 149–186.

Byrne, J. H., & Kandel, E. R. (1996). Presynaptic facilitation revisited: State and time dependence. *Journal of Neuroscience, 16,* 425–435.

Cayre, M. C., Strambi, C., & Strambi, A. (1994). Neurogenesis in an adult insect brain and its hormonal control. *Nature, 368,* 57–59.

Coss, R. G., Brandon, J. G., & Globus, A. (1980). Changes in morphology of dendritic spines on honeybee calycal interneurons associated with cumulative nursing and foraging experiences. *Brain Research, 192,* 49–59.

Devaud, J. M., & Masson, C. (1999). Dendritic pattern development of the honeybee antennal lobe neurons: A laser scanning confocal microscopic study. *Journal of Neurobiology, 15,* 461–474.

Durst, C., Eichmüller, S., & Menzel, R. (1994). Development and experience lead to increased subcompartments of the honeybee mushroom body. *Behavior and Neural Biology, 62,* 259–263.

Ebert, P. R., Rowland, J., & Toma, D. P. (1998). Isolation of seven unique biogenic amine receptor clones from the honey bee by library scanning. *Insect Molecular Biology, 7,* 151–162.

Erber, J., Kloppenburg, P., & Scheidler, A. (1993). Neuromodulation by serotonin and octopamine in the honeybee: Behaviour, neuroanatomy and electrophysiology. *Experientia, 49,* 1073–1083.

Esslen, J., & Kaissling, K. E. (1976). Zahl und Verteilung antennaler Sensillen bei der Honigbiene. *Zoomorphologie, 83,* 227–251.

Faber, T., Joerges, J., & Menzel, R. (1999). Associative learning modifies neural representations of odors in the insect brain. *Nature Neuroscience, 2,* 74–78.

Fahrbach, S. E., & Robinson, G. E. (1996). Juvenile hormone, behavioral maturation, and brain structure in the honey bee. *Developmental Neuroscience, 18,* 102–114.

Fahrbach, S. E., Strande, J. L., & Robinson, G. E. (1995). Neurogenesis is absent in the brain of adult honey bees and does not explain behavioral neuroplasticity. *Neuroscience Letters, 197,* 145–148.

Feng, G., Hannan, F., Reale, V., Hon, Y. Y., Kousky, C. T., Evans, P. D., & Hall, L. M. (1996). Cloning and functional characterization of a novel dopamine receptor from *Drosophila melanogaster*. *Journal of Neuroscience, 16,* 3925–3933.

Flanagan, D., & Mercer, A. R. (1989a). An atlas and 3-D reconstruction of the antennal lobes in the worker honey bee, *Apis mellifera* L. (Hymenoptera: apidae). *International Journal of Insect Morphology & Embryology, 18,* 145–159.

Flanagan, D., & Mercer, A. R. (1989b). Morphology and response characteristics of neurons in the deutocerebrum of the brain in the honeybee *Apis mellifera*. *Journal of Comparative Physiology A, 164,* 483–494.

Fonta, C., Sun, X. J., & Masson, C. (1993). Morphology and response characteristics of neurons in the deutocerebrum of the brain in the honey bee *Apis mellifera*. *Chemical Senses, 18,* 101–119.

Fuchs, E., Dustmann, J. H., Stadler, H., & Schürmann, F. W. (1989). Neuroactive compounds in the brain of the honeybee during imaginal life. *Comparative Biochemistry & Physiology, 92C,* 337–342.

Galizia, C. G., McIlwrath, S. L., & Menzel, R. (1999). A digital three-dimensional atlas of the honeybee antennal lobes based on optical sections acquired by confocal microscopy. *Cell & Tissue Research, 295,* 383–394.

Galizia, C. G., Sachse, S., Rappert, A., & Menzel, R. (1999). The glomerular code for odor representation is species specific in the honey bee, *Apis mellifera*. *Nature Neuroscience, 2,* 473–478.

Gascuel, J., & Masson, C. (1987). Influence of olfactory deprivation on synapse frequency in developing antennal lobe of the honey bee *Apis mellifera*. *Neuroscience Research Communications, 1*, 173–180.

Gascuel, J., & Masson, C. (1991). Developmental study of afferented and deafferented bee antennal lobes. *Journal of Neurobiology, 22*, 795–810.

Gotzes, F., Balfanz, S., & Baumann, A. (1994). Primary structure and functional characterization of a *Drosophila* dopamine receptor with high homology to human $D_{1/5}$ receptors. *Receptors and Channels, 2*, 131–141.

Greggers, U., & Menzel, R. (1993). Memory dynamics and foraging strategies of honeybees. *Behavioral Ecology and Sociobiology, 32*, 17–29.

Grünbaum, L., & Müller, U. (1998). Induction of a specific olfactory memory leads to a long-lasting activation of protein kinase C in the antennal lobes of the honeybee. *The Journal of Neuroscience, 18*, 4384–4392.

Hammer, M. (1993). An identified neuron mediates the unconditioned stimulus in associative learning in honeybees. *Nature, 366*, 59–63.

Hammer, M. (1997). The neural basis of associative reinforcement learning in honeybees. *Trends in Neurosciences, 20*, 252–458.

Hammer, M., & Menzel, R. (1995). Learning and memory in the honeybee. *Journal of Neuroscience, 15*, 1617–1630.

Hammer, M., & Menzel, R. (1998). Multiple sites of associative odor learning as revealed by local brain microinjections of octopamine in honeybees. *Learning & Memory, 5*, 146–156.

Han, K. A., Millar, N. S., Grotewiel, M. S., & Davis, R. L. (1996). DAMB, a novel dopamine receptor expressed specifically in *Drosophila* mushroom bodies. *Neuron, 16*, 1127–1135.

Harris, J. W., & Woodring, J. (1992). Effects of stress, age, season, and source colony on levels of octopamine, dopamine and serotonin in the honeybee (*Apis mellifera* L.) brain. *Journal of Insect Physiology, 38*, 29–35.

Hildebrandt, H., & Müller, U. (1995a). Octopamine mediates rapid stimulation of protein kinase A in the antennal lobes of honeybees. *Journal of Neurobiology, 27*, 44–50.

Hildebrandt, H., & Müller, U. (1995b). PKA activity in the antennal lobe of honeybees is regulated by chemosensory stimulation in vivo. *Brain Research, 679*, 281–288.

Homberg, U. (1984). Processing of antennal information in extrinsic mushroom body neurons of the bee brain. *Journal of Comparative Physiology A, 154*, 825–836.

Itoh, T., Yokohari, F., & Tominaga, Y. (1991). Response to humidity change of deutocerebral interneurons of the honeybee, *Apis mellifera* L. *Naturwissenschaften, 78*, 320–322.

Jaycox, E. R. (1976). Behavioral changes in worker honey bees (*Apis mellifera* L.) after injection with synthetic juvenile hormone (Hymenoptera: Apidae). *Journal of the Kansas Entomological Society, 49*, 165–170.

Joerges, J., Küttner, A., Galizia, C. G., & Menzel, R. (1997). Representation of odours and odour mixtures visualized in the honeybee brain. *Nature, 387*, 285–288.

Kirchhof, B. S., Homberg, U., & Mercer, A. R. (1999). Development of the dopamine-immunoreactive neurons associated with the antennal lobes of the honey bee, *Apis mellifera*. *The Journal of Comparative Neurology, 411*, 643–653.

Kirchhof, B. S., & Mercer, A. R. (1997). Antennal-lobe neurons of the honey bee, *Apis mellifera*, express a D2-like dopamine receptor *in vitro*. *The Journal of Comparative Neurology, 383*, 189–198.

Kloppenburg, P. (1995). Anatomy of the antennal motor neurons in the brain of the honeybee (*Apis mellifera*). *The Journal of Comparative Neurology, 363*, 333–343.

Kloppenburg, P., Ferns, D., & Mercer A. R. (1999). Serotonin enhances central olfactory neuron responses to female sex pheromone in the male sphinx moth, *Manduca sexta*. *Journal of Neuroscience, 19*, 8172–8181.

Kloppenburg, P., & Hildebrand, J. G. (1995). Neuromodulation by 5-hydroxytryptamine in the antennal lobe of the sphinx moth *Manduca sexta*. *Journal of Experimental Biology, 198*, 603–611.

Kloppenburg, P., Kirchhof, B. S., & Mercer, A. R. (1999). Voltage-activated currents from honey bee (*Apis mellifera*) antennal motoneurons recorded *in vitro* and *in situ*. *Journal of Neurophysiology, 81*, 39–48.

Kokay, I. C., McEwan, J., & Mercer, A. R. (1998). Autoradiographic localisation of [³H]-SCH23390 and [³H]-spiperone binding sites in honey bee brain. *The Journal of Comparative Neurology, 394,* 29–37.

Kokay, I. C., & Mercer, A. R. (1996). Characterisation of dopamine receptors in insect (*Apis mellifera*) brain. *Brain Research, 706,* 47–56.

Kokay, I. C., & Mercer, A. R. (1997). Age-related changes in dopamine receptor densities in the brain of the honey bee, *Apis mellifera. Journal of Comparative Physiology A, 181,* 415–423.

Kreissl, S., Eichmüller, S., Bicker, G., Rapus, J., & Eckert, M. (1994). Octopamine-like immunore-activity in the brain and suboesophageal ganglion of the honeybee. *The Journal of Comparative Neurology, 348,* 583–595.

Laurent, G. (1997). Olfactory processing: Maps, time and codes. *Current Opinion in Neurobiology, 7,* 547–553.

Lieke, E. (1993). Optical recording of neuronal activity in the insect central nervous system: Odorant coding by the antennal lobes of honeybees. *European Journal of Neuroscience, 5,* 49–55.

Lindauer, M. (1961). *Communication among social bees.* Cambridge, MA: Harvard University Press.

Lindauer, M. (1987). Karl von Frisch, a pioneer in sensory physiology and experimental sociobi-ology. In R. Menzel & A. R. Mercer (Eds.), *Neurobiology and behavior of honey bees* (pp. 1–6). Berlin: Springer-Verleg.

Macmillan, C. S., & Mercer, A. R. (1987). An investigation of the role of dopamine in the antennal lobes of the honeybee, *Apis mellifera. Journal of Comparative Physiology A, 160,* 359–366.

Malun, D. (1998). Early development of mushroom bodies in the brain of the honeybee *Apis mellifera* as revealed by BrdU incorporation and ablation experiments. *Learning and Memory, 5,* 90–101.

Masson, C., & Mustaparta, H. (1990). Chemical information processing in the olfactory system of insects. *Physiological Reviews, 70,* 199–245.

Mauelshagen, J., & Greggers, U. (1993). Experimental access to associative learning in honeybees. *Apidologie 24,* 249–266.

McLean, J. H., Darby-King, A., Sullivan, R. M., & King, S. R. (1993). Serotonergic influence on olfactory learning in the neonate rat. *Behaviour & Neural Biology, 60,* 152–162.

McLean, J. H., & Shipley, M. T. (1987). Serotonergic afferents to the rat olfactory bulb: II. Changes in fiber distribution during development. *The Journal of Neuroscience, 7,* 3029–3039.

Menzel, R., Erber, J., & Masuhr, T. H. (1974). Learning and memory in the honey bee. In L. Barton-Brown (Ed.), *Experimental analysis of insect behaviour* (pp. 195–217). Berlin: Springer-Verlag.

Menzel, R., Michelsen, B., Ruffer, P., & Sugawa, M. (1988). Neuropharmacology of learning and memory in honey bees. In G. Hertting & H. C. Spatz (Eds.), *Modulation of synaptic transmission and plasticity in nervous systems* (pp. 333–350). Berlin, Heidelberg: Springer-Verlag.

Menzel, R., & Müller, U. (1996). Learning and memory in honeybees: From behaviour to neural substrates. *Annual Review of Neuroscience, 19,* 379–404.

Mercer, A. R., & Erber, J. (1983). The effects of amines on evoked potentials recorded in the mushroom bodies of the bee brain. *Journal of Comparative Physiology, 151,* 469–476.

Mercer, A. R., Hayashi, J. H., & Hildebrand, J. G. (1995). Modulatory effects of serotonin on voltage-activated currents in cultured antennal lobe neurons of the sphinx moth, *Manduca sexta. Journal of Experimental Biology, 198,* 613–627.

Mercer, A. R., Kirchhof, B. S., & Hildebrand, J. G. (1996). Enhancement by serotonin of the growth *in vitro* of antennal lobe neurons of the sphinx moth, *Manduca sexta. Journal of Neurobiology, 29,* 49–64.

Mercer, A. R., Kloppenburg, P., & Hildebrand, J. G. (1996). Serotonin-induced changes in the excitability of cultured antennal lobe neurons of the sphinx moth, *Manduca sexta. Journal of Comparative Physiology A, 178,* 21–31.

Mercer, A. R., & Menzel, R. (1982). The effects of biogenic amines on conditioned and uncondi-tioned responses to olfactory stimuli in the honeybee *Apis mellifera. Journal of Comparative Physiology A, 145,* 363–368.

Mercer, A. R., Mobbs, P. G., Davenport, A. P., & Evans, P. D. (1983). Biogenic amines in the brain of the honey bee, *Apis mellifera. Cell & Tissue Research, 234,* 655–677.

Michelsen, D. B. (1988). Catecholamines affect storage and retrieval of conditioned odour stimuli in honey bees. *Comparative Biochemistry & Physiology, 91C*, 479–482.

Mobbs, P. G. (1985). Brain Structure. In G. A. Kerkut & L. I. Gilbert (Eds.), *Comprehensive insect physiology, biochemistry and pharmacology*, Vol. 5. *Nervous system structure and motor function* (pp. 299–370). Oxford England: Pergamon Press.

Morgan, S. M., Butz Huryn, V., Downes, S. R., & Mercer, A. R. (1998). The effects of queenlessness on the maturation of the honey bee olfactory system. *Behavioural Brain Research, 91*, 115–126.

Moriizumi, T., Tsukatani, T., Sakashita, H., & Miwa, T. (1994). Olfactory disturbance induced by deafferentation of serotonergic fibers in the olfactory bulb. *Neuroscience, 61*, 733–738.

Müller, U. (1999). Second messenger pathways in the honeybee brain: Immunohistochemistry of protein kinase A and protein kinase C. *Microscopy Research and Technique, 45*, 165–173.

Pascual-Leone, A., & Torres, F. (1993). Plasticity of the sensorimotor cortex representation of the reading finger in Braille readers. *Brain, 1160*, 39–52.

Philpot, B. D., Jazaeri, A. A., & Brunjes, P. C. (1994). The development of serotonergic projections to the olfactory bulb of *Monodelphis domestica* (the grey, short-tailed opossum). *Developmental Brain Research, 77*, 265–270.

Pomeroy, S. L., La Mantia, A.-S., & Purves, D. (1990). Postnatal construction of neural circuitry in the mouse olfactory bulb. *Journal of Neuroscience, 10*, 1952–1966.

Purnell, M. T., Mitchell, C. J., Taylor, D. J., Kokay, I. C., & Mercer, A. R. (2000). The influence of endogenous dopamine levels on the density of [^{3}H]SCH23390-binding sites in the brain of the honey bee, *Apis mellifera* L. *Brain Research, 855*, 206–216.

Ray, S., & Ferneyhough, B. (1997). The effects of age on olfactory learning and memory in the honey bee *Apis mellifera*. *NeuroReport, 8*, 789–793.

Reale, V., Hannan, F., Hall, L. M., & Evans, P. D. (1997). Agonist-specific coupling of a cloned *Drosophila melanogaster* D$_1$-like dopamine receptor to multiple second messenger pathways by synthetic agonists. *Journal of Neuroscience, 17*, 6545–6553.

Recanzone, G. H., Merzenich, M. M., Jenkins, W. M., Grajski, K. A., & Dinse, H. R. (1992). Topographic reorganization of the hand representation in cortical area 3b of owl monkeys trained in a frequency-discrimination task. *Journal of Neurophysiology, 67*, 1031–1056.

Rehder, V., Bicker, G., & Hammer, M. (1987). Serotonin-immunoreactive neurons in the antennal lobes and suboesophageal ganglion of the honeybee. *Cell & Tissue Research, 247*, 59–66.

Robinson, G. E. (1985). Effects of a juvenile hormone analogue on honey bee foraging behavior and alarm pheromone production. *Journal of Insect Physiology, 31*, 277–282.

Robinson, G. E. (1992). Regulation of division of labour in insect societies. *Annual Reviews of Entomology, 37*, 637–665.

Salecker, I., & Distler, P. (1990). Serotonin-immunoreactive neurons in the antennal lobes of the American cockroach *Periplaneta americana*: Light- and electron-microscope observations. *Histochemistry, 94*, 463–473.

Schäfer, S., & Rehder, V. (1989). Dopamine-like immunoreactivity in the brain and suboesophageal ganglion of the honeybee. *Journal of Comparative Neurology, 280*, 43–58.

Schulz, D. J., & Robinson, G. E. (1999). Biogenic amines in the honey bee brain: Behaviorally-related changes in the antennal lobes and age-related changes in the mushroom bodies. *Journal of Comparative Physiology A, 184*, 481–488.

Schürmann, F. W., Elekes, K., & Geffard, M. (1989). Dopamine-like immunoreactivity in the bee brain. *Cell & Tissue Research, 256*, 399–410.

Seeley, T. D. (1985). *Honeybee ecology.* Princeton, NJ: Princeton University Press.

Sigg, D., Thompson, C. M., & Mercer, A. R. (1997). Activity-dependent changes to the brain and behavior of the honey bee, *Apis mellifera* L. *Journal of Neuroscience, 17*, 7148–7156.

Smith B. H. (1991). The olfactory memory of the honey bee *Apis mellifera*. I. Odorant modulation of short- and intermediate-term memory after single-trial conditioning. *Journal of Experimental Biology, 161*, 367–382.

Sterr, A., Müller, M. M., Elbert, T., Rockstroh, B., Pantev, C., & Taub, E. (1998). Changed perceptions in Braille readers. *Nature, 391*, 134–135.

Stopfer, M., Bhagavan, S., Smith, B. H., & Laurent, G. (1997). Impaired odour discrimination on desynchronization of odour-encoding neural assemblies. *Nature, 390,* 70–74.

Sugamori, K. S., Demchyshyn, L. L., McConkey, F., Forte, M. A., & Niznik, H. B. (1995). A primordial dopamine D1-like adenylyl cyclase-linked receptor from *Drosophila melanogaster* displaying poor affinity for benzazepines. *FEBS Letters, 362,* 131–138.

Sun, X. J., Fonta, C., & Masson, C. (1993). Odour quality processing by bee antennal lobe interneurones. *Chemical Senses, 18,* 355–377.

Sun, X. J., Tolbert, L. P., & Hildebrand, J. G. (1993). Ramification pattern and ultrastructural characteristics of the serotonin-immunoreactive neuron in the antennal lobe of the moth *Manduca sexta*: A laser scanning confocal and electron microscopic study. *Journal of Comparative Neurology, 338,* 5–16.

Taylor, D. J., Robinson, G. E., Logan, B. J., Laverty, R., & Mercer, A. R. (1992). Changes in brain amine levels associated with the morphological and behavioural development of the worker honeybee. *Journal of Comparative Physiology A, 170,* 715–721.

Temple, B. L., Livingstone, M. S., & Quinn, W. G. (1984). Mutations in the dopa decarboxylase gene affect learning in *Drosophila. Proceedings of the National Academy of Sciences of the United States of America, 81,* 3577–3581.

Wagener-Hulme, C., Kuehn, J., Schulz, D. J., & Robinson, G. E. (1999). Biogenic amines and division of labor in honey bee colonies. *Journal of Comparative Physiology A, 184,* 471–479.

Winnington, A. P., Napper, R. M., & Mercer, A. R. (1996). Structural plasticity of identified glomeruli in the antennal lobes of the adult worker honey bee. *Journal of Comparative Neurology, 365,* 479–490.

Winston, M. L. (1987). *The biology of the honey bee.* Cambridge, MA: Harvard University Press.

Withers, G. S., Fahrbach, S. E., & Robinson, G. E. (1993). Selective neuroanatomical plasticity and division of labour in the honeybee. *Nature, 364,* 238–240.

Withers, G. S., Fahrbach, S. E., & Robinson, G. E. (1995). Effects of experience and juvenile hormone on the mushroom bodies of honey bees. *Journal of Neurobiology, 20,* 130–144.

CIRCUIT, CELLULAR, AND SYNAPTIC ASPECTS OF NEUROPLASTICITY

8

Brandi K. Ormerod
Liisa A. M. Galea

Mechanism and Function of Adult Neurogenesis

☐ Definition of Neuroplasticity

Neuroplasticity is a morphological and/or physiological modification in a cell or group of cells that changes intercellular communication. Specifically, these changes could occur via modifications in electrophysiological properties, receptor number or sensitivity, synapse number, and cell number that either independently or interdependently alter cell signalling. Events that precipitate neuroplasticity can be environmental (learning, repeated stress, or enriched housing) or hormonal (adolescence, pregnancy, menopause, or disease) in nature. Neuroplasticity, in turn, permits us to incorporate experience into adaptive responses to our environment.

History of Neurogenesis Research

Perhaps an extreme form of neuroplasticity would be the complete remodeling of a brain region via a turnover or an increase/decrease in neurons. Recent evidence has shattered traditional dogma by demonstrating that at least two areas of the adult mammalian brain incorporate new neurons. Altman (1962) discovered neurogenesis in the dentate gyrus of adult rats and subsequently introduced the concept that "undifferentiated cells" within the subgranular zone of the dentate gyrus become "differentiated" after migrating into the granular cell layer (GCL; Altman & Das, 1965). Despite published evidence that ^{3}H-thymidine is incorporated into the DNA of replicating cells (Leblond & Walker, 1959) few studies of adult neurogenesis immediately followed Altman's work. Many reasons could account for this: (a) techniques for positively identifying new neurons versus new glial cells were not yet available; (b) reliable stereological methods had not yet been developed to dispel the idea that cell proliferation in rodents was too low level to affect existing circuitry; and (c) the concepts of neuronal stem cells and advanced differentiated neuroblast division were very preliminary (Rakic & Sidman, 1968; Kaplan & Hinds, 1980).

Interest in adult neurogenesis was sparked in the 1980s after Nottebohm and his colleagues published evidence of season-dependent neurogenesis in the song system of adult canaries (Goldman & Nottebohm, 1983), with higher rates being related to seasons accompanying song acquisition (Alvarez-Buylla, Kirn, & Nottebohm, 1990). However, hopes that the human hippocampus harbored regenerative potential were diminished when Rakic and his colleagues reported that although cell division occurred within the dentate gyrus of adult rhesus monkeys, the neuronal phenotype of the progeny could not be definitively verified (Rakic, 1985a, 1985b).

Fortunately, new stereological and immunohistochemical methods were created to count and identify the phenotype of new cells. Using immunohistochemistry, Cameron, Woolley, McEwen, & Gould (1993) confirmed Altman & Das's (1965) hypothesis that many labeled cells within the dentate gyrus of adult rats acquire a neuronal phenotype. Subsequent stereological analyses demonstrated that neurogenesis in the dentate gyrus of adult rodents is abundant. In fact, as many as 4,000 granule neurons could be produced in the dentate gyrus of young adult rats following 2 hours of proliferation (see Gould, Beylin, Tanapat, Reeves, & Shors, 1999a). Many of these neurons mature and likely form functional connections among the estimated other 1.2 million neurons within the GCL (West, Slomianka, & Gunderson, 1991).

In 1997, Gould, McEwen, Tanapat, Galea, and Fuchs discovered new granule neurons in the dentate gyrus of the adult tree shrew, an insectivore phylogenetically related to primates. Subsequently, Gould, Tanapat, McEwen, Flügge, and Fuchs (1998) reported neurogenesis in the dentate gyrus of adult marmoset monkeys and, concurrently with Kornack and Rakic (1999), adult macaque monkeys (Gould, Reeves, Fallah et al., 1999). At about the same time, a group headed by Eriksson and Gage (Eriksson et al., 1998) found new neurons in the brain tissue of human patients that had received the DNA marker bromodeoxyuridine to monitor tumor growth prior to succumbing to cancer. The discovery of neurogenesis within the dentate gyrus of adult humans confirmed that studying adult mammalian neurogenesis could profoundly impact therapeutic approaches geared toward reversing neurotraumatic injury or neurodegenerative disease, such as Alzheimer's disease (AD).

☐ Neurogenesis in the Adult Brain

Both the dentate gyrus and olfactory bulbs of adult mammals incorporate new neurons into their existing circuitry. In the dentate gyrus, precursor cells located between the GCL and hilus (in the subgranular zone) divide. One or both of the progeny migrate, probably along radial glia (Cameron, Woolley, McEwen, & Gould, 1993), into the GCL, where they may differentiate into neurons (see Kempermann & Gage, 1999 and Figure 8.1). In contrast, precursor cells located in the subventricular zone (SVZ) divide and their progeny migrate tangentially into the olfactory bulbs, where they may differentiate into neurons (Lois & Alvarez-Buylla, 1993). Recent evidence suggests that some SVZ progenitor–derived neuroblasts migrate to neocortical association areas in adult macaque monkeys (Gould, Reeves, Graziano, & Gross, 1999c) and possibly in rodents (Kolb, Gibb, Gorny, & Whishaw, 1998).

The hippocampus, SVZ, and olfactory bulbs may be the most plastic structures of the adult brain, and these areas degenerate in patients with AD and Parkinson's disease (Laasko et al., 1996). However, the dentate gyrus remains relatively intact in AD (West, Coleman, Flood, & Troncoso, 1994), possibly due to continued proliferation, while regions such as CA1 degenerate. By elucidating the mechanisms that control cell proliferation in the healthy adult brain it may become possible to induce them to reverse

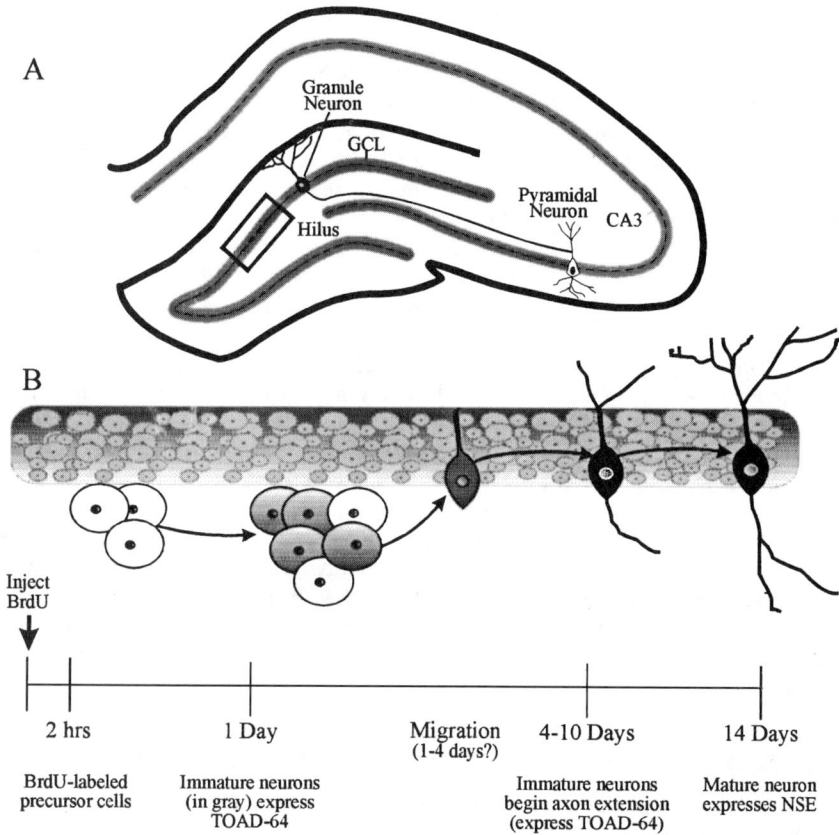

Figure 8.1. Representation of a coronal hippocampal section and inset depicting the time course of cell division and maturation. (a) Mature granule neuron with dendrites extended to the molecular layer and an axon extended to region CA3. (b) Precursor cells incorporate BrdU during mitosis. Neuroblasts can be identified 24 hours after division, when they begin to express immature neuron-specific proteins. Neuroblasts migrate deeper into the GCL and, 4–10 days after birth, extend dendrites and an axon. Once a functional synapse is established (2–3 weeks) the neuron expresses mature neuron-specific proteins.

the neuronal loss and symptoms associated with neurodegenerative disorders. We will focus the remainder of this chapter on neurogenesis in the dentate gyrus of the adult hippocampus.

Determining Neuronal Phenotype

A combination of procedures can be used to demonstrate that, in vivo, precursor cells have divided and that a proportion of the daughter cells have acquired a neuronal phenotype. Dividing cells are visualized autoradiographically or immunohistochemically in the brain tissue of animals that have been injected with either ^{3}H-thymidine (Altman & Das, 1965; Bayer, 1982) or the thymidine-analogue bromodeoxyuridine (BrdU), respectively (Dolbeare, 1994). Both compounds are incorporated into the DNA of cells during the synthesis phase of mitosis. Cells labeled 2 h postinjection are dividing precursors because this amount of time is sufficient for ^{3}H-thymidine- or BrdU-uptake but not sufficient for the completion of mitosis (Lewis, 1978). Mitosis lasts approximately 16 h in the developing rodent (Cai, Hayes, & Nowakowski, 1997). Therefore, in adult rodents, cells labeled 24 h postinjection (adjusted for postnatal cell-cycle length) are precursors and/or their progeny (Cameron, Woolley, McEwen, & Gould, 1993). During development, mitosis in the primate takes 2–5 times longer than in the rodent (Kornack & Rakic, 1998); thus in adult primates, labeled cells 2–5 days postinjection would likely be precursors and/or their progeny.

Many labeled cells acquire a neuronal phenotype that can be verified by antibodies raised against neuron-specific proteins. For example, anti-Turned-On-After-Division-64kD detects CRMP-4, the earliest known protein expressed by neurons throughout differentiation and axon extension (Minturn, Geschwind, Fryer, & Hockfield, 1995). Recently, Hastings and Gould (1999) demonstrated that new granule cells complete axon extension 4–10 days after mitosis. However, new neurons only begin to express neuron-specific enolase (NSE) approximately 2 weeks after birth (Cameron, Woolley, & Gould, 1993), which may coincide with the formation of mature synaptic contacts as observed during postnatal development of the GCL (Schmechel, Brightman, & Marangos, 1980).

Evidence that many ^{3}H-thymidine- or BrdU-labeled cells become neurons is fourfold. Labeled neurons (a) extend axons into the mossy fiber pathway, targeting CA3 pyramidal neurons (Hastings & Gould, 1999; Stanfield & Trice, 1988); (b) exhibit granule cell morphology (Cameron, Woolley, & Gould, 1993); (c) have postsynaptic densities (Kaplan and Hinds, 1977); and (d) express neuron-specific proteins often coincident with specific stages of neuronal maturation (see Table 8.1).

TABLE 8.1. Neuron-specific proteins used to verify the phenotype of cells, immunohistochemically.

Protein	Cell cycle	Association	References
Polysialated neural adhesion molecule (PSA-NCAM)	Early postmitotic neurons	Migration and process extension	Seki and Arai, 1993
Turned-on-after-division 64kD (TOAD-64kD)	Early postmitotic neurons	Migration and process extension	Minturn et al., 1995
Microtubule-associated protein 2 (MAP-2)	Postmitotic neurons	Process extension	Bernhardt and Matus, 1984
Class III ‡-tubulin	Early neuronal differentiation	Process extension	Easter, Ross, and Frankfurter, 1993; Lee, Rebhun, and Frankfurter, 1990
Calcium binding protein (Calbindin)	Mature neurons	Cell signalling	Sloviter, 1989
Neuronal nucleii (NeuN)	Mature neurons	Terminal differentiation	Mullen, Buck, and Smith, 1992
N-methyl-d-aspartate receptor subunit 1	Mature neurons	Cell signalling	Cameron, Woolley, McEwen, and Gould, 1993
Neuron specific enolase (NSE)	Mature neurons	Nuclear protein	Schmechel et al., 1978

TABLE 8.2. The effect of various factors on cell proliferation and granule neuron survival.

Factor	Proliferation	Survival
Adrenal steroids	↓	NC
Aging (rats)	↓	Possibly↓
Adrenalectomy	↑	↑
Dentate gyrus lesions	↑	↑
NMDA	↓	
NMDAr antagonist	↑	↑
Running (mice)	↑	
High levels of estradiol (rats, voles, and canaries)	↑	Possibly↑
Serotonin (rats)	↑	
Hippocampal-dependent learning (rats)	NC	↑
Short photoperiod (voles, hamsters, chickadees, canaries)	↑	↑
Rearing in enriched environments (mice)	NC	↑
Kindling (rats)	↑	NC
Exposure to stress (rats, tree shrews, marmoset monkeys)	↓	Possibly↓

To understand the mechanisms and function of adult neurogenesis, the factors that affect cell proliferation must be delineated from those that affect cell survival. Factors that affect cell proliferation either suppress or induce mitosis in precursor cells. Factors that affect cell survival either promote or prevent the differentiation, migration, and/or maturation of labeled cells into functional neurons. Therefore, a manipulation administered prior to or during uptake of a DNA marker will affect cell proliferation (the number of cells that will be labeled), whereas a manipulation administered after the uptake of a DNA marker will affect the survival of new labeled neurons that are in the process of migration, differentiation, or maturation. Conversely, studies could address an effect on survival by assessing the percentage of new cells that mature into neurons (approximately 3 weeks postlabel). Many factors affect either cell proliferation or cell survival; for example, a hippocampal-dependent learning task (Gould, Beylin et al., 1999) enhances the survival of new neurons but does not alter cell proliferation. Table 8.2 summarizes the effect of various factors on cell proliferation and survival.

☐ Regulation of Adult Neurogenesis

Corticosteroids

Type I and Type II glucocorticoid receptors are expressed predominantly within the hippocampus (McEwen, DeKloet, & Rostene, 1986) and mediate widespread adrenal steroid-induced effects on the dentate gyrus. For example, high levels of adrenal steroids decrease cell proliferation and low levels increase cell proliferation. Specifically, adrenalectomy (ADX) increases the number of new cells in the dentate gyrus of adult rats, and the majority of these cells express NSE by three weeks (Cameron & Gould, 1994). Alternatively, corticosterone (CORT) administration decreases the number of new cells in the dentate gyrus of adult rats (Cameron & Gould, 1994). Because new granule cells express Type I and Type II receptors at 24 h and 2 weeks after mitosis, respectively (Cameron, Woolley, & Gould, 1993), cell proliferation must be indirectly regulated by CORT. Recent work has demonstrated that the CORT mechanism involves downstream NMDA receptor activation (Cameron, Tanapat, & Gould, 1998).

Rodriguez and colleagues (1998) found that ADX increases PSA-NCAM (polysialylated neural cell adhesion molecule)-immunoreactivity in the dentate gyrus of young adult rats in association with increasing cell proliferation. In developing rats, PSA-NCAM is expressed by immature neurons during migration and differentiation and is expressed in regions that incorporate new neurons during adulthood (Seki & Arai, 1993). Rodriguez and colleagues (1998) found that CORT replacement immediately reversed ADX-induced increases in cell proliferation but that one circadian fluctuation of CORT was required to normalize the expression of PSA-NCAM.

Glutamate

The primary source of glutamatergic input to the mammalian GCL, via N-methyl-D-aspartate (NMDAr) receptor activation (Collingridge, 1989), is the perforant pathway that originates in the entorhinal cortex (Steward, 1976). High-level NMDAr activation decreases cell proliferation and low-level NMDAr activation increases cell proliferation in the dentate gyrus of adult rats. Specifically, NMDA injections rapidly suppress granule cell proliferation but injections of either a competitive (CGP 37849) or noncompetitive (MK-801) NMDAr antagonist or entorhinal cortex lesions increase granule neuron production (Cameron, McEwen, & Gould, 1995).

Cameron, Tanapat, and Gould (1998) demonstrated that cell proliferation is coregulated by both CORT and NMDAr activation. Specifically, NMDA injections rapidly block the ADX-induced increase in cell proliferation, whereas MK-801 injections block the CORT-induced suppression of cell proliferation. Thus, NMDAr activation regulates cell proliferation downstream of CORT. Because granule cell precursors do not express the NMDAr subunit, NR1 (a necessary component of functional NMDArs; Luo, Wang, Yasuda, Dunah, & Wolfe, 1997), another factor in addition to CORT and NMDAr activation, must regulate cell proliferation via this mechanism in the dentate gyrus of adult rodents.

Estradiol

Separate studies have demonstrated that estradiol (E_2) regulates neurogenesis in the adult rodent. Cell proliferation rates are inversely related to circulating E_2 levels in wild-(Galea & McEwen, 1999) and laboratory-reared meadow voles (Ormerod & Galea, 1999). During the breeding season (long photoperiod), when E_2 levels are high, the rate of cell birth is significantly lower than during the nonbreeding season (short photoperiod), when E_2 levels are low. In contrast, Tanapat, Hastings, Reeves, & Gould (1999) found that proestrus (high-level) E_2 transiently increases neurogenesis in the dentate gyrus of adult female rats. Our ongoing work with female meadow voles indicates that while E_2 increases the rate of cell proliferation within 4 hours but suppresses cell proliferation within 48 hours (Figure 8.2). E_2 also elevates circulating CORT (Buckingham, Döhler, & Wilson, 1978; Carey, Deterd, de Koning, Helmerhorst, & de Kloet, 1995), which may mediate the E_2-induced suppression in the rate of cell proliferation at 48 hours. The effect of E_2 on granule neuron production could be indirect, as estrogen α receptors are found on interneurons within the hilus (Weiland, Orikasa, Hayashi, & McEwen, 1997) but could also be mediated directly by estrogen β receptors.

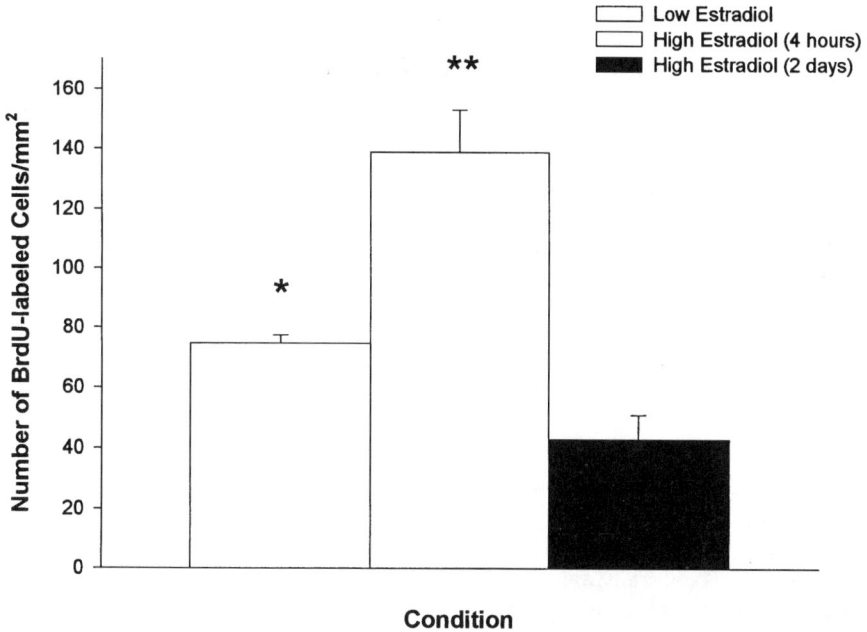

Figure 8.2. Density of BrdU-labeled cells in the dentate gyrus of adult female meadow voles as a function of estradiol (E_2) level and time after BrdU administration. Low E_2 (open bar) was achieved by housing females in a short photoperiod. High E_2 (4 h; gray bar) was achieved by injecting females with 10 μg of E_2 4 hours before BrdU. High E_2 (black bar) was induced by housing females in a long photoperiod and introducing a male cage partner 48 hours before BrdU. *p = 0.0116; **p = 0.004.

Serotonin

Recent work suggests that serotonin (5-HT) influences adult neurogenesis. Brezun and Daszuta (1999) found that either parachlorophenylalanine (PCPA, which blocks 5-HT synthesis) administration or lesioning dorsal raphe nucleii (the main serotonergic input to the GCL) suppresses cell proliferation in the dentate gyrus of adult rats. This finding complements preliminary evidence that 8-OH-DPAT (5-HT1$_A$ receptor agonist) or fenfluramine (promotes 5-HT release) administration increases granule cell proliferation (Jacobs, Tanapat, Reeves, & Gould, 1998). 5-HT may work upstream from NMDAr activation to increase cell birth as NMDAr antagonists increase 5-HT levels in the brain (Whitton, Richards, Briggs, & Fowler, 1994).

Dopamine

Dopamine (DA) alters glutamatergic transmission in the perforant pathway (Otmakhova & Lisman, 1990), suggesting that dopamine can influence the rate of cell proliferation downstream of NMDAr activation. Acute haloperidol (D$_2$-receptor antagonist) administration increases cell proliferation (Dawirs, Hildebrandt, & Teuchert-Noodt, 1998), while methamphetamine (a DA and NE agonist) administration attenuates cell proliferation (Teuchert-Noodt, Dawirs, & Hildebrandt, 2000) in the dentate gyrus of adult gerbils. In addition, a single dose of methamphetamine given to juvenile gerbils attenuates their adulthood rate of cell proliferation, which can then be restored by multiple haloperidol doses (Hildebrandt, Teuchert-Noodt, & Dawirs, 1999).

☐ Behavioral Function of Adult Neurogenesis

Although the function of adult neurogenesis is unknown, rates of cell proliferation are related to experience. Experiences that influence cell proliferation and/or survival include exposure to a stressor, aging, experimentally induced pathologies, season (photoperiod), hippocampal-dependent learning, and exposure to a complex environment (see Table 8.2).

Stress

Studies have separately shown that exposure to ecologically relevant stressors rapidly suppresses cell proliferation in the dentate gyrus of adult rats, tree shrews, and marmoset monkeys (Galea, Tanapat, & Gould, 1996; Gould et al., 1997; Gould et al., 1998). Predator odor is naturally aversive to rodents (Weldon, 1990) and rapidly suppresses cell proliferation within the dentate gyrus of rats relative to controls (Galea et al., 1996). Tree shrews acquire subordinate/dominant relationships, and exposure to a dominant male is stressful to the subordinate male (von Holst, 1972). Gould et al. (1997) found that subordinate tree shrews have suppressed rates of cell proliferation in the dentate gyrus following exposure for 1 h to a dominant male. Finally, "intruder" (non resident) marmoset monkeys exposed to the home cage of another marmoset monkey for 1 h have suppressed rates of cell proliferation in the dentate gyrus (Gould et al., 1998).

Exposure to a stressful event elevates circulating adrenal steroids and, depending upon the stressor, increases glutamate, acetylcholine, and/or serotonin release within the hippocampus (Gilad, 1984; Kirby, Chou-Green, Davis, & Lucki, 1997; Moghaddam, 1993). Because these factors independently influence cell proliferation, each could potentially mediate stressor-induced suppressions in cell proliferation. Preliminary evidence indicates that predator-odor-induced suppression of cell proliferation is regulated via a cholinergic mechanism. Injections of scopolamine (a muscarinic receptor antagonist) block the predator-odor-induced suppression of cell proliferation in rats (Galea et al., 1996).

Aging

Gage and colleagues found that the rate of granule neuron proliferation is diminished in the dentate gyrus of senescent rodents. They found fewer labeled cells 12 h after BrdU uptake and fewer labeled neurons 6 weeks after BrdU uptake in 21- versus 6-month-old rats. They also found that decreased cell proliferation was related to decreased PSA-NCAM expression (Kuhn, Dickinson-Anson, & Gage, 1996). Interestingly, Montaron and colleagues (1999) found that ADX increases the rate of cell proliferation but does not upregulate PSA-NCAM expression in the dentate gyrus of senescent rats, suggesting that cell survival during migration may also be diminished. In addition, Cameron and McKay (1999) found that ADX restores the level of cell proliferation in aged rats to the level observed in young adult rats.

Experimentally Induced Pathologies

Research utilizing a variety of experimentally induced brain pathologies in rodents has demonstrated that compensatory increases in neurogenesis may be induced by damage. Kindling to class-5 seizure intensity (Racine, 1972) increases the production of new neurons in the dentate gyrus of adult rats. For example, Parent, Janumpalli, McNamara, and Lowenstein (1998) found that amygdala-kindled rats have significantly more new granule neurons following nine seizures but not following five seizures compared to sham-kindled rats. In contrast, Scott, Wang, Burnham, De Boni, & Wotjowicz (1998) reported that rats amygdala-kindled to four seizures have more new neurons than sham-kindled rats. The differences between results are intriguing because they could indicate that the mechanism of kindling-induced neurogenesis in the dentate gyrus is desensitized by repeated stimulation. For example, Scott and colleagues (1998) injected BrdU just prior to the rats' second, third, fourth seizures (although rats were kindled for 10 more days), while Parent and colleagues (1998) injected on each of the 3 days following the last (fifth or ninth) seizure. Parent et al. (1998) found that cells continued to divide at an accelerated rate after nine seizures but not after five seizures when labeling is done poststimulation, while Scott et al. (1998) found that cells do indeed divide at an accelerated rate on the second, third, and fourth seizure day when labeling is done *prior* to stimulation. Alternatively, Scott et al. (1998) may have enhanced the survival of newborn cells by stimulating for 10 days after BrdU labeling, via an unidentified mechanism.

The rate of cell proliferation in the dentate gyrus of adult rats is increased six- to eightfold following chemical-induced seizures, and the majority of new cells differentiate into mature neurons (Parent et al., 1997). Continuous electrical stimulation of the perforant pathway for 6 h (no damage produced) or 24 h (hippocampal damage produced) induces seizure activity and increases the number of new neurons ($\cong$163%) in the dentate gyrus of adult rats (Parent et al., 1997). The increase in cell proliferation is even more pronounced in rats given single ($\cong$283%) or intermittent ($\cong$574%) CA1 region electrical stimulation (Bengzon et al., 1997).

In gerbils, global ischemia produces an increase in cell proliferation that is proportional to the duration of ischemia; longer episodes produce more new cells (Liu et al., 1998). Gould and Tanapat (1997) suggested that there may be a signal in dying granule cells that stimulates cell birth in the dentate gyrus of rats. They found that the extent of unilateral lesion-induced GCL damage was positively correlated with the number of proliferating cells on the side of the lesion, many of which acquired a neuronal phenotype. Taken together, these results suggest that increases in neurogenesis may be mediated by compensatory mechanisms that are activated by damaged cells.

Season

Birds.   Brain nuclei in many avian species undergo seasonal increases in neurogenesis. During the breeding season, when male canaries must learn songs from conspecific males to attract mates and defend territories, the song system incorporates new neurons (Nordeen & Nordeen, 1990). Specifically, more new neurons are born into the higher vocal center (HVC) of adult male canaries in the spring when they modify their songs than during the fall when the male canary song is stable (Nottebohm, O'Loughlin, Gould, Yohay, & Alvarez-Byulla, 1994). In female canaries, testosterone mediates seasonal changes within the HVC by enhancing the survival of new neurons (Rasika, Nottebohm, & Alvarez-Buylla, 1994). The avian hippocampus also undergoes seasonal changes in neurogenesis that are related to food-storing behavior. For example, in adult black-capped chickadees the hippocampus incorporates more new neurons during October when the chickadees increase food-storing behavior in preparation for winter (Barnea and Nottebohm, 1994).

Rodents.   Previously, we discussed our finding that the rate of cell proliferation in the dentate gyrus of wild- or laboratory-reared female meadow voles is season dependent. Spatial learning in the laboratory and territory size in the wild is also season dependent in these animals (Galea, Kavaliers, Ossenkopp, & Hampson, 1995; Madison, 1985; Sheridan & Tamarin, 1988). Female meadow voles learn a spatial task better when E_2 levels are low relative to when E_2 levels are high (Galea et al., 1995). Perhaps analogously, wild female meadow voles expand their territory range during the nonbreeding season compared to the breeding season (Madison, 1985; Sheridan & Tamarin, 1988). Therefore, better spatial performance in the laboratory and larger territory size accompany the season in which rates of cell proliferation are elevated in female meadow voles. Similarly, male golden hamsters display an increased number of new neurons when housed in short photoperiods compared to long photoperiods (Huang, DeVries, & Bittman, 1998).

Hippocampal-Dependent Learning

Gould, Beylin, and colleagues (1999) found that hippocampal-dependent learning enhances granule neuron survival. Specifically, they found more labeled neurons in rats trained on hippocampal-dependent versus nonhippocampal-dependent tasks, when they injected BrdU 1 week prior to learning. However, van Praag, Kempermann & Gage (1999) found that hippocampal-dependent learning neither increased cell proliferation nor the survival of new neurons when BrdU was injected over the first 12 learning trials. Greenough, Cohen, and Juraska (1999) suggested that hippocampal-dependent learning may "rescue" new cells from death if the learning occurs at an optimal time during their maturation. For example, hippocampal-dependent learning enhances the survival of 7-day-old neurons for at least 2 weeks but reversal learning does not enhance the survival of 12-day-old neurons over a 4-week period (Gould, Beylin et al., 1999; van Praag et al., 1999). Thus, hippocampal-dependent learning appears to affect the survival of new neurons during phases of migration and axon extension rather than maturation, by a presently unknown mechanism.

Experience

Kempermann, Kuhn, and Gage (1997) found that mice living in an enriched environment had more 4-week-old labeled neurons but not more 24-h-old labeled cells than mice living in standard housing and therefore concluded that enriched housing enhances the survival of new neurons rather than cell proliferation. Consistent with previous work, they also found that mice living in an enriched environment outperform mice living in standard housing on the Morris water maze task. Hence, factors that promote cell survival are correlated with better performance on hippocampal-dependent learning tasks. Interestingly, neurogenesis which is diminished in senescent rodents can be enhanced by placing the animals in enriched housing, which suggests that the survival of new neurons in an aged brain can be upregulated (Kempermann, Kuhn, & Gage, 1998).

Environment or experience also influences neurogenesis in avian species. Although neurogenesis is season dependent in black-capped chickadees the effect can be potentiated by environmental experience. For example, wild black-capped chickadees have more proliferating cells and labeled neurons in the hippocampus than laboratory-reared black-capped chickadees during the food-caching season (Barnea & Nottebohm, 1994). In addition, juvenile marsh tits given three to eight opportunities to retrieve and store sunflower seeds had higher rates of cell proliferation than naïve marsh tits (Patel, Clayton, & Krebs, 1997).

☐ How and When Are New Neurons Functional?

Perhaps counterintuitively, many factors that promote cell proliferation also impair learning in adult rodents. For example, hippocampal-dependent learning is impaired by ADX (Conrad, Lupien, Thanasoulis, & McEwen, 1997), NMDAr antagonists (Bannerman et al., 1995), high levels of estradiol (Galea et al., 1995), hippocampal lesions (Sutherland, Whishaw, & Kolb, 1983), and kindling (Robinson, McNeill, & Reed, 1993), which are all factors that increase cell proliferation within the dentate gyrus of adult rodents. The same factors that increase cell proliferation are not necessarily advantageous for hippocampal-dependent behavior, at least shortly after their administration. However, factors that promote cell survival, such as rearing in a complex environment (Kempermann et al., 1997), generally augment hippocampal-dependent learning.

Independent regulation of cell proliferation and survival of new neurons makes adaptive sense. When certain conditions change (such as environmental complexity) it may become advantageous to rapidly incorporate immature neurons into existing circuitry (thus, up-regulate survival) to enhance behavior such as spatial ability. Hippocampal-dependent learning promotes the survival of cells (cells that are in the early stages of neuronal maturation) that possibly have the greatest influence on immediate function. New neurons in the process of axon extension and/or maturation are excellent candidates for incorporating new information because they are very plastic electrophysiologically. For example, Wang, Scott, and Wojtowicz (2000) found that long-term potentiation (LTP) can always be induced in new granule neurons by low-threshold stimulation. Furthermore, LTP is completely unaffected by GABAergic inhibition in young granule neurons, whereas it is never produced in mature granule neurons when GABAergic inhibition is intact (Wang, Scott, & Wojtowicz, 2000).

Although neurons are only generated in the dentate gyrus and SVZ in the adult mammal, precursor (perhaps stem) cells isolated from these areas have multilineage potential (Kukekov et al., 1999). Indeed, Gage and his colleagues found that adult hippocampal-derived progenitor cells survived 8 weeks following transplant into the subventricular zone, dentate gyrus, and cerebellum of adult recipient rats (Suhonen, Peterson, Ray, & Gage, 1996). Furthermore, hippocampal-derived progenitor cells transplanted into the subventricular zone acquired the phenotype of neurons indigenous to the area (Suhonen et al., 1996). Thus, this line of research has far-reaching implications for treating neurodegenerative disorders and neurotraumatic injury. In conclusion, neuroplasticity permits us to incorporate experience into adaptive responses to our environment, and increasing/decreasing the number of neurons within the dentate gyrus gives us a strong mechanism by which we can incorporate these experiences.

☐ Acknowledgments

We wish to extend our thanks to Erin Falconer and Melissa Holmes for reviewing this chapter and to Stan Floresco for preparing our figure that outlines neurogenesis in the dentate gyrus.

☐ References

Altman, J. (1962). Are new neurons formed in the brains of adult mammals? *Science, 135,* 1127–1128.

Altman, J., & Das, G. D. (1965). Autoradiographic and histological evidence of postnatal hippocampal neurogenesis in rats. *Journal of Comparative Neurology, 124,* 319–336.

Alvarez-Buylla, A., Kirn, J. R., & Nottebohm, F. (1990). Birth of projection neurons in adult avian brain may be related to perceptual or motor learning. *Science, 249,* 1444–1446.

Barnea, A., & Nottebohm, F. (1994). Seasonal recruitment of hippocampal neurons in adult free ranging black capped chickadees. *Proceedings of the National Academy of Sciences USA, 91,* 11217–11221.

Bannerman, D. M., Good, M. A., Butcher, S. P., Ramsay M., & Morris, R. G. M. (1995). Distinct components of spatial learning revealed by prior training and NMDA receptor blockade. *Nature, 378,* 182–186.

Bayer, S. A. (1982). Changes in the total number of dentate gyrus cells in juvenile and adult rats: A correlated volumetric and ^{3}H-thymidine autoradiographic study. *Experimental Brain Research, 46,* 315–323.

Bengzon, J., Kokaia, Z., Elmér, E., Nanobashvili, A., Kokaia, M., & Lindvall, O. (1997). Apoptosis and proliferation of dentate gyrus neurons after single and intermittent limbic seizures. *Proceedings of the National Academy of Sciences USA, 94,* 10432–10437.

Bernhardt, R., & Matus, A. (1984). Light and electron microscopic studies of the distribution of microtubule associated protein 2 in adult rat brain: A difference between dendritic and axonal cytoskeletons. *Journal of Comparative Neurology, 226,* 203–221.

Brezun, J. M., & Daszuta, A. (1999). Depletion in serotonin decreases neurogenesis in the dentate gyrus and the subventricular zone of adult rats. *Neuroscience, 89,* 999–1002.

Buckingham, J. C., Döhler, K.-D., & Wilson, C. A. (1978). Activity of the pituitary-adrenocortical system and thyroid gland during the oestrus cycle of the rat. *Journal of Endocrinology, 78,* 359–366.

Cai, L., Hayes, N. L., & Nowakowski, R. S. (1997). Local homogeneity of cell cycle length in developing mouse cortex. *The Journal of Neuroscience, 17,* 2079–2087.

Cameron, H. A., & Gould, E. (1994). Adult neurogenesis is regulated by adrenal steroids in the dentate gyrus. *Neuroscience, 61,* 203–209.

Cameron, H. A., McEwen, B. S., & Gould, E. (1995). Regulation of adult neurogenesis by excitatory input and NMDA receptor activation in the dentate gyrus. *The Journal of Neuroscience, 15,* 4687–4692.

Cameron, H. A., & McKay, R. (1999). Restoring production of hippocampal neurons in old age. *Nature Neuroscience, 2,* 894–897.

Cameron, H. A., Tanapat, P., and Gould, E. (1998). Adrenal steroids and N-methyl-D-aspartate receptor activation regulate neurogenesis in the dentate gyrus of adult rats through a common pathway. *Neuroscience, 82,* 349–354.

Cameron, H. A., Woolley, C. S., & Gould, E. (1993). Adrenal steroid receptor immunoreactivity in cells born in the adult rat dentate gyrus. *Brain Research, 611,* 342–346.

Cameron, H. A., Woolley, C. S., McEwen, B. S., & Gould, E. (1993). Differentiation of newly born neurons and glia in the dentate gyrus of the adult rat. *Neuroscience, 56,* 337–344.

Carey, M. P., Deterd, C. H., de Koning, J., Helmerhorst, F., & de Kloet, E. R. (1995). The influence of ovarian steroids on hypothalamic-pituitary-adrenal regulation in the female rat. *Journal of Endocrinology, 144,* 311–321.

Collingridge, G. L. (1989). Synaptic function of N-methyl-D-aspartate receptors in the hippocampus. In V. Chan-Palay and C. Kohler (Eds.), *The hippocampus, new vistas* (Vol. 52, pp. 329–346). New York: Liss.

Conrad, C. D., Lupien, S. J., Thanasoulis, L. C., & McEwen, B. S. (1997). The effects of Type I and Type II corticosteroid receptor agonists on exploratory behavior and spatial memory in the Y-maze. *Brain Research, 759,* 76–83.

Dawirs, R. R., Hildebrandt, K., & Teuchert-Noodt, G. (1998). Adult treatment with haloperidol increases dentate granule cell proliferation in the gerbil hippocampus. *Journal of Neural Transmission, 105,* 317–327.

Dolbeare, F. (1994). Bromodeoxyuridine: A diagnostic tool in biology and medicine. Part 1: Historical perspectives, histochemical methods and cell kinetics. *Histochemistry Journal, 27,* 339–369.

Easter, S. S., Ross, L. S., & Frankfurter, A. (1993). Initial tract formation in the mouse brain. *Journal of Neuroscience, 13,* 285–299.

Eriksson, P. S., Perfilieva, E., Björk-Eriksson, T., Alborn, A., Nordberg, C., Peterson, D. A., & Gage, F. H. (1998). Neurogenesis in the adult human hippocampus. *Nature Medicine, 4,* 1313–1317.

Galea, L. A. M., Kavaliers, M., Ossenkopp, K.-P., & Hampson, E. (1995). Gonadal hormone levels and spatial learning performance in the Morris water maze in male and female meadow voles Microtus Pennsylvanicus. *Hormones and Behavior, 29,* 106–125.

Galea, L. A. M., & McEwen, B. S. (1999). Sex and seasonal differences in the rate of cell proliferation in the dentate gyrus of adult wild meadow voles. *Neuroscience, 89,* 955–964.

Galea, L. A. M., Tanapat, P., & Gould, E. (1996). Exposure to predator odor suppresses cell proliferation in the dentate gyrus of adult rats via a cholinergic mechanism. *Society for Neuroscience Abstracts, 22,* 1196.

Gilad, G. M. (1984). The stress-induced response of the septo-hippocampal cholinergic system. A vectorial outcome of psychoneuroendocrinological interactions. *Psychoneuroendocrinology, 12,* 167–184.

Goldman, S. A., & Nottebohm, F. (1983). Neuronal production, migration, and differentiation in a vocal control nucleus of the adult female canary brain. *Proceedings of the National Academy of Sciences USA, 80,* 2390–2394.

Gould, E., Beylin, A., Tanapat, P., Reeves, A., & Shors, T. J. (1999). Learning enhances adult neurogenesis in the hippocampal formation. *Nature Neuroscience, 2,* 260–264.

Gould, E., McEwen, B. S., Tanapat, P., Galea, L. A. M., & Fuchs, E. (1997). Neurogenesis in the dentate gyrus of the adult tree shrew is regulated by psychosocial stress and NMDA receptor activation. *The Journal of Neuroscience, 17,* 2492–2498.

Gould, E., Reeves, A. J., Fallah, M., Tanapat, P., Gross, C. G., & Fuchs, E. (1999). Hippocampal neurogenesis in adult old world primates. *Proceedings of the National Academy of Sciences USA, 96,* 5263–5267.

Gould, E., Reeves, A. J., Graziano, M. S. A., & Gross, C. G. (1999). Neurogenesis in the neocortex of adult primates. *Science, 286,* 548–552.

Gould, E., & Tanapat, P. (1997). Lesion-induced proliferation of neuronal progenitors in the dentate gyrus of the adult rat. *Neuroscience, 80,* 427–436.

Gould, E., Tanapat, P., McEwen, B. S., Flügge, G., & Fuchs, E. (1998). Proliferation of granule cell precursors in the dentate gyrus of adult monkeys is diminished by stress. *Proceedings of the National Academy of Sciences USA, 95,* 3168–3171.

Greenough, W. T., Cohen, N. J., & Juraska, J. M. (1999). New neurons in old brains: Learning to survive? *Nature Neuroscience, 2,* 203–205.

Hastings, N. B., & Gould, E. (1999). Adult-generated granule cells rapidly extend axons into the CA3 region: A combined BrdU-labeling and retrograde tracer study. *Journal of Comparative Neurology, 413,* 146–154.

Heale, V. R., Vanderwolf, C. H., & Kavaliers, M. (1994). Components of weasel and fox odors elicit fast wave bursts in the dentate gyrus of rats. *Behavioral Brain Research, 63,* 159–165.

Hildebrandt, K., Teuchert-Noodt, G., & Dawirs, R. R. (1999). A single neonatal dose of methamphetamine suppresses dentate granule cell proliferation in adult gerbils which is restored by acute doses of haloperidol. *Journal of Neural Transmission, 106,* 549–558.

Huang, L., DeVries, G. J., & Bittman, E. L. (1998). Photoperiod regulates neuronal bromodeoxyuridine labeling in the brain of a seasonally breeding mammal. *Journal of Neurobiology, 36,* 410–420.

Jacobs, B. L., Tanapat, P., Reeves, A. J., & Gould, E. (1998). Serotonin stimulates the production of new hippocampal granule neurons via the 5HT1A receptor in the adult rat. *Society for Neuroscience Abstracts, 24,* 1992.

Kaplan, M. S., & Hinds, J. W. (1977). Neurogenesis in the adult rat: Electron microscopic analysis of light autoradiographs. *Science, 197,* 1092–1094.

Kaplan, M. S., & Hinds, J. W. (1980). Gliogenesis of astrocytes and oligodendrocytes in the neocortical grey and white matter of the adult rat: Electron microscope analysis of light autoradiographs. *Journal of Comparative Neurology, 193,* 711–727.

Kempermann, G. & Gage, F. H. (1999). New nerve cells for the adult brain. *Scientific American, May*, 48–53.

Kempermann, G., Kuhn, H. G., & Gage, F. H. (1997). More hippocampal neurons in adult mice living in an enriched environment. *Nature, 386*, 493–495.

Kempermann, G., Kuhn, H. G., & Gage, F. H. (1998). Experience-induced neurogenesis in the senescent dentate gyrus. *The Journal of Neuroscience, 18*, 3206–3212.

Kirby, L. G., Chou-Green, J. M., Davis, K., & Lucki, I. (1997). The effects of different stressors on extracellular 5-hydroxytyptamine and 5-hydroxyindoleacetic acid. *Brain Research, 760*, 218–230.

Kolb, B., Gibb, R., Gorny, G., & Whishaw, I. Q. (1998). Possible regeneration of rat medial frontal cortex following neonatal frontal lesions. *Behavioral Brain Research, 91*, 127–141.

Kornack, D. R., & Rakic, P. (1998). Changes in cell cycle kinetics during the development and evolution of the primate cortex. *Proceedings of the National Academy of Sciences USA, 95*, 1242–1246.

Kornack, D. R., & Rakic, P. (1999). Continuation of neurogenesis in the hippocampus of the adult macaque monkey. *Proceedings of the National Academy of Sciences USA, 96*, 5768–5773.

Kuhn, H. G., Dickinson-Anson, H., & Gage, F. H. (1996). Neurogenesis in the dentate gyrus of the adult rat: Age-related decrease of neuronal progenitor proliferation. *The Journal of Neuroscience, 16*, 2027–2033.

Kukekov, V. G., Laywell, E. D., Suslov, O., Davies, K., Scheffler, B., Thomas, L. B., O'Brien, T.F., Kuskabe, M., & Steindler, D. A. (1999). Multopotent stem/progenitor cells with similar properties arise from two neurogenic regions of the adult human brain. *Experimental Neurology, 156*, 333–344.

Laasko, M. P., Partanen, K., Riekkinen, P., Lehtovirta, M., Helkal, E. L., Hallikainen, M., Hanninen, T., Vainio, P., Soininen, H. (1996). Hippocampal volumes in Alzheimer's disease, Parkinson's disease with and without dementia, and in vascular dementia: An MRI study. *Neurology, 46*, 678–681.

Leblond, C. P., & Walker, B. E. (1959). Renewal of cell populations. *Physiological Review, 36*, 255–276.

Lee, M. K., Rebhun, L. I., & Frankfurter, A. (1990). Posttranslational modification of class III β-tubulin. *Proceedings of the National Academy of Sciences USA, 87*, 7195–7199.

Lewis, P. D. (1978). Kinetics of cell proliferation in the postnatal rat dentate gyrus. *Neuropathology and Applied Neurobiology, 4*, 191–195.

Liu, J., Solway, K., Messing, R. O., & Sharp, F. R. (1998). Increased neurogenesis in the dentate gyrus after transient global ischemia in gerbils. *The Journal of Neuroscience, 18*, 7768–7778.

Lois, C., & Alvarez-Buylla, A. (1993). Proliferating subventricular zone cells in the adult mammalian forebrain can differentiate into neurons and glia. *Proceedings of the National Academy of Sciences USA, 90*, 2074–2077.

Luo, J., Wang, Y., Yasuda, R. P., Dunah, A. W., & Wolfe, B. B. (1997). The majority of N-methyl-D-aspartate receptor complexes in adult rat cortex contain at least three different subunits (NR1/NR2/NR2B). *Molecular Pharmacology, 51*, 79–86.

Madison, D. M. (1985). Activity rhythms and spacing. In R. H. Tamarin (Ed.), *Biology of new world microtus* (pp. 373–419). Boston, MA: American Society for Mammologists.

McEwen, B. S., DeKloet, E. R., & Rostene, W. (1986). Adrenal steroid receptors and actions in the nervous system. *Physiological Review, 66*, 1121–1187.

Minturn, J. E., Geschwind, D. H., Fryer, H. J. L., & Hockfield, S. (1995). Early post-mitotic neurons transiently express TOAD-64, a neural specific protein. *Journal of Comparative Neurology, 355*, 369–379.

Moghaddam, B. J. (1993). Stress preferentially increases extraneuronal levels of excitatory amino acids in the prefrontal cortex: Comparison to hippocampus and basal ganglia. *Journal of Neurochemistry, 60*, 1650–1657.

Montaron, M. F., Petry, K. G., Rodriguez, J. J., Marinelli, M., Aurousseau, C., Rougon, G., Le Moal, M., & Abrous, D. N. (1999). Adrenalectomy increases neurogenesis but not PSA-NCAM expression in aged dentate gyrus. *European Journal of Neuroscience, 11*, 1479–85.

Mullen, R. J., Buck, C. R., & Smith, A. M. (1992). NeuN, a neuronal specific nuclear protein in vertebrates. *Development, 116*, 201–211.

Nordeen, E. J., & Nordeen, K. W. (1990). Neurogenesis and sensitive periods in avian song learning. *Trends in Neuroscience, 13*, 31–36.

Nottebohm, F., O' Loughlin, B., Gould, K., Yohay, K., & Alvarez-Buyulla, A. (1994). The life span of new neurons in a song control nucleus of the adult canary brain depends on time of year when these cells are born. *Proceedings of the National Academy of Sciences, 91*, 7849–7853.

Ormerod, B. K., & Galea, L. A. M. (1999). Survival of newly born granule cells in the dentate gyrus of the adult female meadow vole, Microtus Pennsylvanicus, is influenced by reproductive status. *Society for Neuroscience Abstracts, 24*, 863–864.

Otmakhova, N. A., & Lisman, J. E. (1990). Dopamine selectively inhibits the direct cortical pathway to the CA1 hippocampal region. *Journal of Neuroscience, 19*, 1437–1445.

Parent, J. M., Janumpalli, S., McNamara, J. O., & Lowenstein, D. H. (1998). Increased dentate granule cell neurogenesis following amygdala kindling in the adult rat. *Neuroscience Letters, 247*, 9–12.

Parent, J. M., Yu, T. W., Leibowitz, R. T., Geschwind, D. H., Sloviter, R. S., & Lowenstein, D. H. (1997). Dentate granule cell neurogenesis is increased by seizures and contributes to aberrant network reorganization in the adult rat hippocampus. *The Journal of Neuroscience, 17*, 3727–3738.

Patel, S. N., Clayton, N. S., & Krebs, J. R. (1997). Spatial leaning induces neurogenesis in the avian brain. *Behavioral Brain Research, 89*, 115–128.

Racine, R. J. (1972). Modification of seizure activity by electrical stimulation II. Motor Seizure. *Electroencephalography and Clinical Neurophysiology, 32*, 281–294.

Rakic, P. (1985a). DNA synthesis and cell division in the adult primate brain. *Annals of the New York Academy of Sciences, 457*, 193–211.

Rakic, P. (1985b). Limits of neurogenesis in primates. *Science, 227*, 1054–1056.

Rakic, P., & Sidman, R. L. (1968). Subcommissural organ and adjacent ependyma: Autoradiographic study of their origin in the rat brain. *American Journal of Anatomy, 122*, 317–336.

Rasika, S., Nottebohm, F., & Alvarez-Buylla, A. (1994). Testosterone increases the recruitment and/or survival of new high vocal center neurons in adult female canaries. *Proceedings of the National Academy of Sciences, 91*, 7854–7858.

Robinson, G. B., McNeill, H. A., & Reed, G. D. (1993). Comparison of the short- and long-lasting effects of perforant path kindling on radial maze learning. *Behavioral Neuroscience, 107*, 988–995.

Rodriguez, J. J., Montaron, M. F., Petry, K. G., Aurousseau, C., Marinelli, M., Premier, S., Rougon, G., Le Moal, M., & Abrous, D. N. (1998). Complex regulation of the expression of the polysialated form of the neuronal cell adhesion molecule by glucocorticoids in the rat hippocampus. *European Journal of Neuroscience, 10*, 2994–3006.

Schmechel, D., Marango, P. J., Zis, A. P., Brightman, M., & Goodwin, F. K. (1978). Brain enolases as specific markers of neuronal and glial cells. *Science, 199*, 313–315.

Scott, B. W., Wang, S., Burnham, W. M., De Boni, U., & Wotjowicz, J. M. (1998). Kindling-induced neurogenesis in the dentate gyrus of the rat. *Neuroscience Letters, 248*, 73–76.

Seki, T., & Arai, Y. (1993). Highly polysialated neural cell adhesion molecule (NCAM-H) is expressed by newly generated granule cells in the dentate gyrus of the adult rat. *Journal of Neuroscience, 13*, 2351–2358.

Sheridan, M., & Tamarin, R. H. (1988). Space use, longevity and reproductive success in meadow voles. *Behavior, Ecology and Sociobiology, 22*, 85–90.

Sloviter, R. S. (1989). Calcium-binding protein (calbindin-D28k) and paralbumin immunocytochemistry: Localization in the rat hippocampus with specific reference to the selective vulnerability of hippocampal neurons to seizure activity. *Journal of Comparative Neurology, 280*, 183–196.

Stanfield, B. B., & Trice, J. E. (1988). Evidence that granule neurons generated in the dentate gyrus of adult rats extend axonal projections. *Experimental Brain Research, 72*, 399–406.

Steward, O. (1976). Topographic organization of the projections from the entorhinal area to the hippocampal formation of the rat. *Journal of Comparative Neurology, 167*, 285–314.

Suhonen, J. O., Peterson, D. A., Ray, J., & Gage, F. H. (1996). Differentiation of adult hippocampus-derived progenitors into olfactory neurons *in vivo*. *Nature, 383*, 624–627.

Sutherland, R. J., Whishaw, I. Q., & Kolb, B. (1983). A behavioural analysis of spatial localization following electrolytic, kainate- or colchicine-induced damage to the hippocampal formation in the rat. *Behavioural Brain Research, 7*, 133–153.

Tanapat, P., Hastings, N. B., Reeves, A. J., & Gould, E. (1999). Estrogen stimulates a transient increase in the number of new neurons in the dentate gyrus of the adult female rat. *The Journal of Neuroscience, 19*, 5792–5801.

Teuchert-Noodt, G., Dawirs, R. R., & Hildebrandt, K. (2000). Adult treatment with methamphetamine transiently decreases dentate granule cell proliferation in the gerbil hippocampus. *Journal of Neural Transmission, 107*, 133–143.

van Praag, H., Kempermann, G., & Gage, F. (1999). Running increases cell proliferation and neurogenesis in the adult mouse dentate gyrus. *Nature Neuroscience, 2*, 266–270.

von Holst, D. (1972). Social stress in the tree-shrew: Its causes and physiological and ethological consequences. In R. D. Martin, G. A. Doyle, and A. C. Walker (Eds.), *Prosimian Biology* (pp. 389–411), Philadelphia: University of Pittsburgh Press.

Wang, S., Scott, B. W., & Wojtowicz, J. M. (2000). Plasticity of the putative adult-generated neurons in the rat dentate gyrus. *Journal of Neurobiology, 42*, 248–257.

Weiland, N. G., Orikasa, C., Hayashi, S., & McEwen, B. S. (1997) Distribution and hormone regulation of estrogen receptor immunoreactive cells in the hippocampus of male and female rats. *The Journal of Comparative Neurology, 388*, 603–612.

Weldon, P. (1990). Responses by vertebrates to chemicals from predators. In D. W. Macdonald, D. Muller-Schwarze, and S. E. Natynczuk (Eds.), *Chemical signals in vertebrates* (Vol. 5, pp. 500–521). New York: Oxford University Press.

West, M. J., Coleman, P. D., Flood, D. G., & Troncoso, J. C. (1994). Differences in the pattern of hippocampal neuronal loss in normal ageing and Alzheimer's disease. *Lancet, 344*, 769–772.

West, M. J., Slomianka, L., & Gunderson, H. J. G. (1991). Unbiased stereological estimation of the total number of neurons in the subdivisions of the rat hippocampus using the optical fractionator. *The Anatomical Record, 231*, 482–497.

Whitton, P. S., Richards, D. A., Briggs, C. S., & Fowler, L. J. (1994). N-methyl-D- aspartate receptors modulate extracellular 5-hydroxytryptamine concentration in rat hippocampus and striatum in vivo. *Neuroscience Letters, 169*, 215–218.

9

CHAPTER

Timothy J. Teyler

LTP and the Superfamily of Synaptic Plasticities

☐ What Is Long-Term Potentiation?

Long-term potentiation (LTP) is defined as an enduring alteration in synaptic efficacy or gain following repeated afferent activation (Figure 9.1). LTP is usually considered an NMDA receptor-dependent mechanism underlying memory storage in the brain and is usually studied in brain areas closely associated with the storage of behavioral memory, for example, the hippocampal formation and, to a lesser extent, cerebral neocortex. While this is a reasonable operational definition of the features of LTP, it provides a limited view regarding the biological function of this form of synaptic alteration. The reason that LTP is favored as a neural system underlying memory storage is due to its unique phenomenology. Almost alone among those functional changes known to exist in the brain, LTP has the induction characteristics and longevity necessary to place it firmly as a candidate for the storage of experiential memory in the brain. That is, LTP is induced only by sufficient levels of afferent activity, it displays an induction threshold, and it can be induced in an associative fashion such that a strong and weak input when active together will result in LTP at the weak input (which normally would not induce LTP). Associativity is a feature close to the hearts of learning theorists, who view the association of a strong and weak stimulus as an important associative consideration in the establishment of cognitive memory (Teyler & DiScenna, 1987).

Among neurophysiological phenomena, LTP is clearly the most enduring functional phenomenon known (but see also Chapter 24 of this volume, by Teskey, on kindling). For decades, neurophysiologists have sought functional changes at synaptic junctions that might subserve memory. The commonly accepted model of the storage of experiential information (e.g., memory) involves the establishment of networks of neurons interconnected in such a way as to encode the salient aspects of the experience. These neural networks, which may be quite extensive and potentially involve thousands, if not millions, of neurons, come to represent the experience itself (Kudrimoti, Barnes, & McNaughton, 1999). This is opposed to a more hierarchical conceptualization, wherein

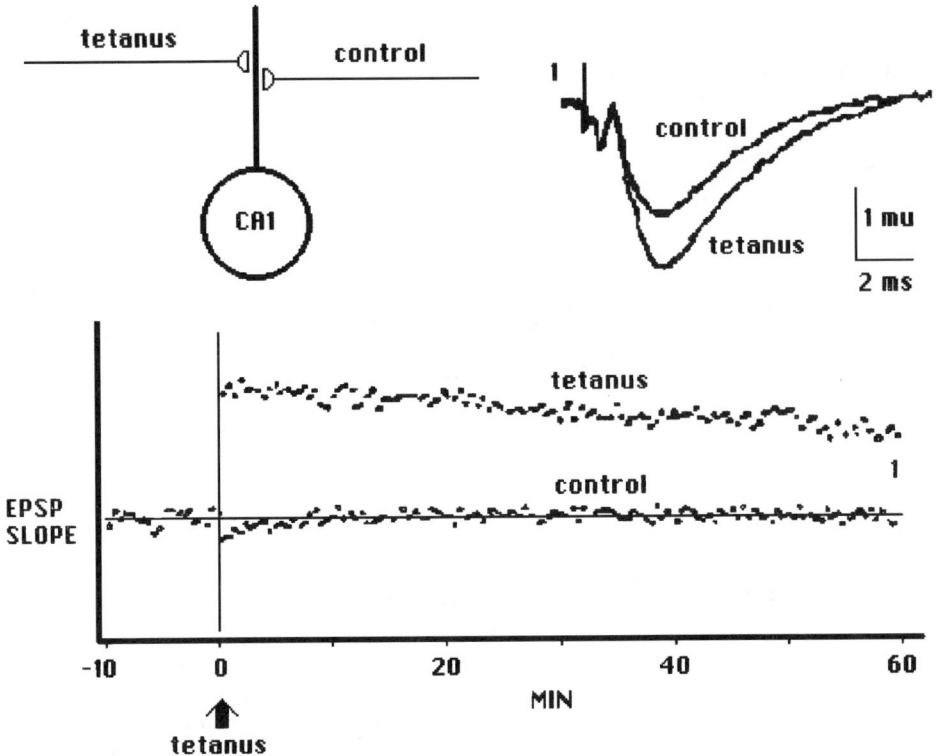

Figure 9.1. LTP is defined as an enduring alteration in synaptic efficacy or gain following repeated afferent activation. In this example, two independent inputs are selected onto a CA1 hippocampal neuron. The input to be potentiated receives a tetanus, whereas the control input only receives infrequent test stimulation. Following the tetanus (bottom) the tetanus pathway shows a large increase in the size of the field EPSP (fEPSP; upper right), whereas the control pathway remains unchanged (measured at 1 h posttetanus). This result indicates: (a) the induction of LTP requires suprathreshold afferent activation, (b) the potentiation is specific to the input tetanized, and (c) the potentiated response is long-lasting.

succeeding levels of feature extraction come to represent experience in a smaller and smaller set of "executive" neurons, such that ultimately one might conceive that particular experiences are stored in a small set of neurons at the top of the hierarchy. The current view suggests that this is incorrect and that a distributed network encoding the salient aspects of experience represents the cerebral encoding of that experience (Teyler & DiScenna, 1985).

LTP is often defined as a change in synaptic gain that underlies memory storage. Such a definition, however, tends to equate memory storage with single synapses. A more accurate definition would emphasize that the memory is represented in networks of interconnected neurons and that LTP may be a means by which the networks are formed and maintained. Such a view suggests that synaptic gain changes must occur over widespread areas of the brain (particularly the neocortex) in order to establish the complex networks believed to underlie the storage of experience.

Such a model requires that networks be capable of being formed rapidly and that the interconnectedness or geometry of the network be preserved over time, lest the experience be forgotten. Such a conceptualization also posits that reactivation of the neuronal network will result in the experiencing of the stored information, for example, recall. Similarly, the partial activation of a network (perhaps by a few salient cues) is sufficient to, in turn, activate the entire network, for example, recognition.

Thus, the rapidity of network formation and its stability across time are important characteristics for this view of neural network information storage. Given this view, LTP fulfills most of the desired characteristics, as it is an enduring change that occurs at single synapses following suprathreshold amounts of afferent activity. It is thus easy to conceive how the neural representation of experience can activate specific neuronal ensembles and how these ensembles may become interconnected by periods of coherent neuronal activity leading to LTP, which then serves as the glue to hold the network together.

While such a conceptualization has been helpful in thinking about properties of synaptic plasticity and as an impetus driving much of the research into LTP, it is in this author's view an overly limited view of the function of synaptic plasticity.

☐ A Widespread Role for LTP

There have been many reviews of the potential role of LTP in memory both from electrophysiological studies in reduced preparation (brain slices) as well as in behavioral studies wherein LTP was usually manipulated by pharmacological manipulations or genetic knock-out experiments. Less often considered are the roles LTP plays in other forms of neural function.

As an early player in the developing nervous system, glutamate and, in particular, the NMDA glutamate receptor subtype is present early in development and plays a critical role in carving features of brain development that may endure for the lifespan of the organism. As one example of these processes, consider the role of the NMDA receptor in the development of ocular dominance columns. Here, blockade of NMDA receptors and LTP by pharmacological antagonists or by genetic knockouts disrupts the formation of ocular dominance columns and thus the subsequent development of binocularity (Bear, Kleinschmidt, Gu, & Singer, 1990). LTP has been reported in the visual neocortex (Aroniadou, Grover, & Teyler, 1991) and, in conjunction with modulatory inputs, has been suggested to modulate receptive field properties of visual neurons (Kirkwood, Rozas, Kirkwood, Perez, & Bear, 1999). Synaptic plasticity also has been documented in the motor cortex (Aroniadou & Keller, 1995) and cerebellum (Crepel & Jaillard, 1991), and interference with the normal operation of NMDA systems is known to interfere with a variety of learned motor patterns, including those mediating through the vestibular-ocular reflex (VOR; Lisberger & Pavelko, 1986).

It is thus clear that LTP can be experimentally induced widely in a variety of brain functions, structures, and developmental times. If it is true that naturally occurring LTP is equally widespread, it is thus more appropriate to think of LTP as a cellular mechanism that brain circuits utilize whenever enduring alterations in synaptic gain need to be made, as opposed to the more limiting view that LTP encodes behavioral experience.

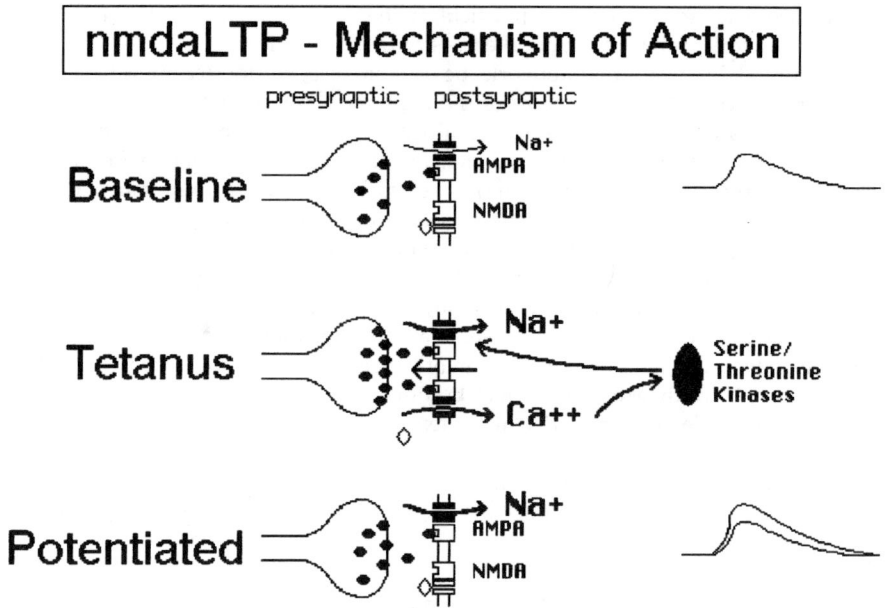

nmdaLTP - Mechanism of Action

Figure 9.2. The most widely studied form of LTP is induced by activation of the NMDA glutamate receptor. Under baseline conditions, the NMDAR-channel complex is blocked by Mg^{2+} and postsynaptic EPSPs are mediated by the AMPAR channel. During a tetanus (a brief period of heightened afferent activity), sufficient glutamate is released presynaptically to depolarize the postsynaptic cell sufficient to relieve the Mg^{2+} block of the NMDAR and allow the influx of Ca^{2+} into the postsynaptic cell. The Ca^{2+} activates a variety of serine/threonine kinases, one of whose effects is to phosphorylate the AMPAR. In the potentiated state, the AMPAR remains phosphorylated and, as such, gates more Na^+ into the cell resulting in a potentiated fEPSP. Other factors, most notably the involvement of various retrograde messengers (arrow), also play a role in LTP induction.

☐ Cellular Mechanisms of LTP

LTP was discovered in 1973 and since then has generated thousands of papers investigating its cellular mechanism of action, its phenomenology, and its significance. It wasn't until the 1980s that the role of the NMDA receptor subtype of glutamate synapses was identified as playing a key role in LTP (Figure 9.2). The current status of the role of the NMDA receptor (NMDAR) in LTP posits that the induction of LTP is triggered by the influx of calcium through an activated NMDAR. Normally, the NMDAR, which is a ligand-gated receptor, is blocked by physiological concentrations of magnesium. This voltage-dependent block is alleviated given sufficient depolarization of the postsynaptic cell. Upon relief from the magnesium block, the NMDAR channel is opened, allowing the flux of sodium, potassium, and, significantly, calcium. The stimulus for achieving sufficient postsynaptic depolarization and thus the triggering of the NMDAR is either an increased activity of glutaminergic afferents and the resulting depolarization from binding to AMPA receptors, or a reduction in hyperpolarizing GABAergic influences onto postsynaptic cells, thus contributing to the depolarization required to activate the NMDAR, or a combination of the two phenomena. Thus, LTP mediated by NMDAR (hereafter termed nmdaLTP) is induced by alterations in synaptic activity onto target cells, resulting in their increased depolarization (Cavus & Teyler, 1996).

The postsynaptic expression of LTP is dependent upon a transient increase in cytosolic calcium levels induced by NMDAR activation. The transiently induced increases in cytosolic calcium concentration bind to a variety of calcium-binding proteins in the postsynaptic cell, setting off signal transduction cascades that lead to the expression and maintenance of LTP (Lisman & Fallon, 1999). Among the calcium-binding proteins known to be activated by NMDAR activation are a variety of serine/threonine kinases (PKA, PKC, CaMKII). The activated kinases, some of which are autophosphorylated as a result of their activation (thus ensuring their continued activity in the absence of the calcium transient), serve to phosphorylate their substrates. Many of the receptors, channels, and enzymes present postsynaptically have phosphorylation sites which, when activated, result in increases in postsynaptic responsivity. While the precise identity of many of the substrates are unknown, two of the major substrates for serine/threonine kinase activation are the AMPA and NMDA receptors. The expression of LTP immediately following a tetanus is primarily due to phosphorylation of the AMPAR. As we shall see later, the phosphorylation sites on the AMPAR and other substrates can be dephosphorylated through the action of phosphatases (Coussens & Teyler, 1996b). Thus, the reader should not assume that the phosphorylation of a substrate, even by an autophosphorylated enzyme, represents a permanent state of affairs.

Other targets of the serine/threonine phosphorylation include signal transduction pathways such as the transcription factor CREB (Alberini, Ghirardi, Hguang, Nguyen, & Kandel, 1995; Chapter 15 of this volume, Saitoe & Tully), which ultimately lead to alterations in gene expression following LTP (Schulz, Siemer, Krug, & Hollt, 1999), and the Ras-MAPK signaling pathway (Orban, Chapman, & Brambilla, 1999). The details of the signal transduction cascade(s) activated during LTP are far from clear, and this is an active area of research made difficult by the existence of multiple complex signal transduction pathways that interact with each other (Lisman & Fallon, 1999). Nonetheless, it is assumed that for the long-term maintenance of synaptic change, there must be a signal sent to the nucleus to alter the patterns of gene expression and thus protein synthesis. This is so because the elements involved in the expression of LTP, the receptors, channels, and enzymes, are all proteins whose number and activity must be maintained for long periods of time—far longer than can be accommodated by the transient and reversible alterations in phosphorylation state.

☐ Revised Definition of LTP

Based on the above suggestions, a better definition of LTP is one that emphasizes that LTP is a generic mechanism for increasing synaptic gain throughout the brain whenever increases in synaptic strength are needed. Thus, while LTP may play a role in the storage of experiential memory, that is only one of the many roles that LTP plays in the brain. LTP should better be considered as a general purpose mechanism by which synapses can increase their influence on the postsynaptic cell regardless of the kind of circuit in which they are embedded. LTP is a mechanism responsible for establishing or strengthening neural circuits responsible for specific jobs. Some of those jobs may be to organize networks underlying binocular vision (ocular dominance columns), motor programs to accomplish specific movements, or the establishment of networks supporting the development of perceptual constancies, to name a few.

☐ Long-Term Depression

Long-term depression (LTD) is the decremental counterpart of LTP (Figure 9.3). LTD is found at the same forebrain synapses as is LTP and may be considered to be the opposite side of the synaptic plasticity coin from LTP. Its mechanism of action appears to also utilize calcium influx through NMDARs, leading to the obvious question of how calcium fluxing through the same receptor can, under one set of circumstances, result in LTP, an increase in synaptic gain, and, under another set of circumstances, result in LTD, a decrease in synaptic gain. While the question remains somewhat controversial, a leading hypothesis suggests that the amount of calcium entering the postsynaptic cell is critical in determining which form of synaptic plasticity will be expressed (Teyler et al., 1994). Evidence for this comes from observations of the conditions required

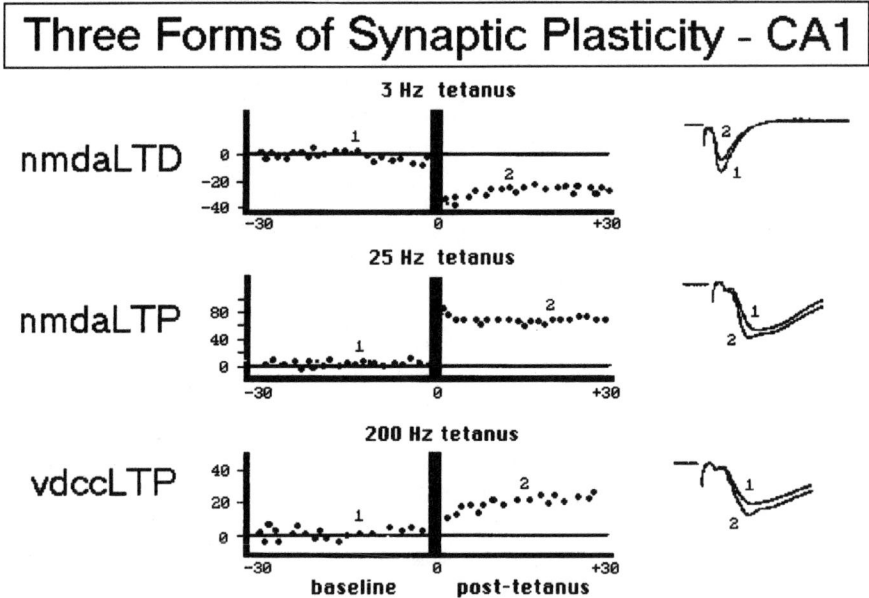

Figure 9.3. Synapses of CA1 hippocampus and elsewhere display at least three different forms of synaptic plasticity. At low levels of afferent activation (~3Hz), the posttetanic response shows a long-lasting *decrease* in fEPSP magnitude. Since this depression is initiated by low levels of Ca^{2+} via the NMDAR, it is called NMDAR-dependent long-term depression, or nmdaLTD. At moderate levels of afferent activity (>25Hz) the posttetanic response is an LTP mediated by Ca^{2+} entering the postsynaptic cell via NMDARs, or nmdaLTP. At higher levels of afferent activity, the postsynaptic cell is depolarized sufficiently to activate voltage-dependent calcium channels (VDCCs) and induce a form of LTP that has different properties and mechanisms of action from the NMDAR-mediated form. This form is called vdccLTP.

for the induction of LTP versus LTD. LTP induction is seen following high-frequency afferent activity, whereas LTD is seen following prolonged low-frequency activation. The former is likely to lead to quick increases in postsynaptic cytosolic calcium levels, whereas the latter should lead to much lower levels of free calcium in the postsynaptic cell. According to this view, low levels of calcium in the postsynaptic cell bind with high-affinity calcium binding sites on protein phosphotases, whose action is to dephosphorylate the same substrates that are targets of serine/threonine kinases. Thus, LTD acts to dephosphorylate sites that have been phosphorylated by the action of protein kinases. Thus, LTP and LTD (or phosphorylation and dephosphorylation, or kinases and phosphatases) exist in a "yin/yang" or opposing relationship (Coussens & Teyler, 1996b).

Some terminology: A previously potentiated synapse can be "depotentiated" by the subsequent induction of LTD. This is termed *depotentiation*. In addition, a naïve synapse can be depressed below baseline (the EPSP magnitude decreases) by the application of the same treatment. This is termed LTD. While not all workers would agree, the position taken in this chapter is that the two phenomena, depotentiation and LTD, reflect the operation of a common underlying cellular process.

There is ample evidence to demonstrate that LTD is dependent upon the activity of protein phosphatases for its expression (e.g., Mulkey, Herron, & Malenka, 1993). What is less clear is the physiological or network function of LTD. While it is clear that this is the decremental counterpart to LTP and has the ability of reversing increases in synaptic gain mediated by nmdaLTP, the significance of this observation is far from being clearly understood. Should LTD be considered as an "erasure" mechanism for LTP or as a tool for sculpting neuronal networks in its own right?

Modeling studies, wherein neuronal networks are created in software or hardware, suggest that a neuronal network that possesses only synapses that increment (e.g., only LTP) will quickly saturate because all synapses will become maximally potentiated, allowing for no further synaptic plasticity and thus no further ability to store information. Thus, neuronal models would suggest that there needs to be some means of normalization to reset the synapse. This could occur through passive decay, as nmdaLTP is known to decay to baseline over time or through an active process like LTD. It is known from studies of the decay kinetics of LTP that this increase in synaptic gain is not a permanent alteration in synaptic efficacy, but decays back to baseline with varying kinetics depending upon the nature of induction, but never longer than several months. The decay of nmdaLTP, however, creates theoretical difficulties for LTP as a memory substrate, because if it decays back to baseline over time, what is it that retains information for periods beyond months? As we shall see later, there is a different form of LTP that may resolve this difficulty.

A different view of LTD suggests that it plays a role in network formation and maintenance by sculpting the architecture of the neuronal network. A reduction in synaptic gain is just as efficacious as an increase in synaptic gain if one is attempting to define the architecture of a neuronal network. An automobile route is affected equally by closed roads as by open ones. Thus, it may be that the switching off of a subset of neurons is equally as important as the turning on of other sets of neurons in forming central networks representing experience. A related suggestion is that LTD is a means of increasing the cellular signal-to-noise ratio between potentiated synapses and neighboring non-potentiated synapses. Experiments have shown that potentiating the synapses onto a limited segment of dendrite is accompanied by the depression of proximal and distal synapses (Coussens & Teyler, 1996a). The hypothesis suggests that potentiated dendritic synapses are embedded in regions of synaptic depression to further accentuate the potentiated synapses. A similar phenomenon occurs in the familiar patterns of surround and lateral inhibition in sensory systems.

While it remains unclear what the role of LTD is in the formation and establishment of neuronal networks, it is relatively clear that nmdaLTP is readily reversed by LTD. Thus, this example of synaptic gain change can be relatively quickly undone by the invocation of LTD. Given this, it may be more appropriate to think of nmdaLTP as a temporary, reversible, or buffer information storage system, rather than as a permanent sculpting of the network's underlying structure. If this is the case, are there other forms of synaptic plasticity that might underlie long-term network stability?

☐ Another Form of LTP

In hippocampus and neocortex (and probably elsewhere) there exists a second form of LTP which does not depend upon calcium entry through the NMDA receptor for its induction (Figure 9.4). This form of LTP utilizes calcium entry through voltage-dependent calcium channels (VDCCs) to induce a form of LTP which differs from that seen by the induction of nmdaLTP (Grover & Teyler, 1990). We shall term this form of LTP vdccLTP to distinguish it from nmdaLTP. VdccLTP is initiated by depolarizing the postsynaptic cell sufficient to activate L-type VDCCs and allow an influx of calcium into the postsynaptic cell. By requiring sufficient depolarization of the postsynaptic cell it is similar to the induction of nmdaLTP. The difference, however, lies in the details. The

	Induction	Ca^{2+} Channel	Blockers	Signaling Pathway
nmdaLTD	1-3 Hz	NMDA	APV MK-801	Serine/ Threonine Phosphatase
nmdaLTP	25+ Hz	NMDA	APV MK-801	Serine/ Threonine Kinase
vdccLTP	50+ Hz	VDCC	Nifedipine Verapamil	Tyrosine Kinase

Figure 9.4. The three forms of synaptic plasticity seen at many central synapses are all Ca^{2+} dependent, yet result in different responses and kinetics (left panel). Two of the forms, nmdaLTD and nmdaLTP, gate Ca^{2+} into the postsynaptic cell via NMDARs and act on serine/threonine phosphatases and kinases, respectively. VdccLTP gates Ca^{2+} into the postsynaptic cell via VDCCs and activates tyrosine kinase pathways. Each form can be blocked by antagonists of their respective calcium channels or by inactivation of elements of the enzymatic pathways activated (not shown). Which form of synaptic plasticity induced depends upon the amount of Ca^{2+} entering the cell, which is in turn governed by the amount of postsynaptic depolarization induced by afferent activity. Thus, there exists a relationship between degree of afferent activity and form of synaptic plasticity induced.

depolarization requirements for the induction of vdccLTP are more stringent than for nmdaLTP: the postsynaptic cell must be more greatly depolarized to induce vdccLTP. This means that either the degree of afferent activity must lead to a higher level of postsynaptic depolarization or that other elements must assist in the establishment of appropriate levels of depolarization to induce this form of LTP. There are two known means by which cellular processes contribute to the induction of vdccLTP. The first is through the simultaneous induction of nmdaLTP, which contributes depolarization to the postsynaptic cell and thus helps to achieve the conditions for the activation of VDCCs. The second is by reducing the inhibitory drive onto the postsynaptic cell to facilitate the induction of vdccLTP.

The cellular targets of calcium fluxing through VDCCs appear to be different from the calcium fluxing through NMDA channels in that enzyme inhibitors of serine/threonine kinases that block nmdaLTP have no effect on the induction or expression of vdccLTP (Figure 9.5; see also Grover & Teyler, 1995). The localization of calcium to specific cytosolic targets is suggested to be a result of calcium compartmentalization resulting

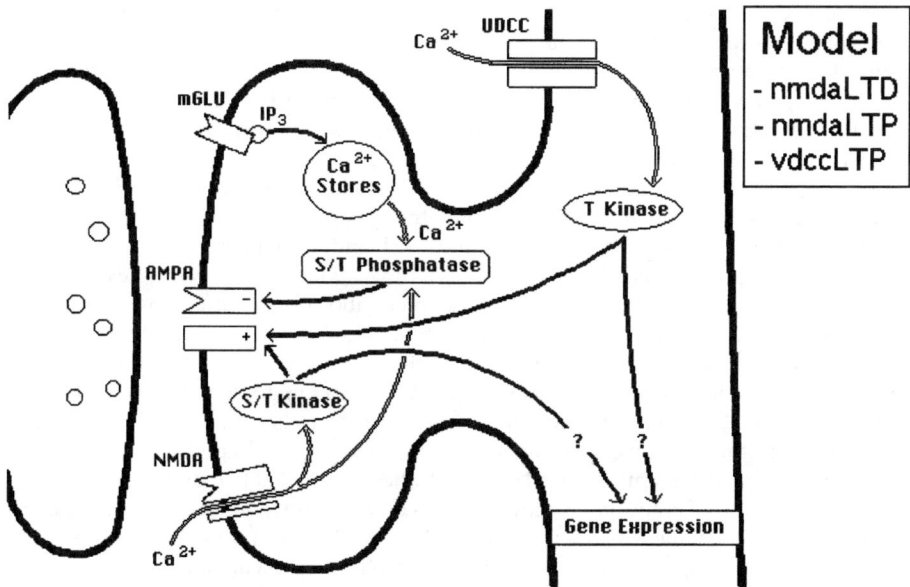

Figure 9.5. A model of the signal transduction pathways involved in the three forms of synaptic plasticity. nmdaLTP is associated with low-frequency synaptic activation, weak depolarization, and low levels of Ca^{2+} entry. The serine/threonine phosphatases have the highest affinity for Ca^{2+} and are thus activated in nmdaLTD. Given more afferent activity, postsynaptic depolarization, and Ca^{2+} entry, serine/threonine kinases are activated. Both kinases and phosphatases are simultaneously active and, under the right conditions, the actions of the kinases and phosphatases can cancel, resulting in no synaptic gain change. A sufficiently depolarized cell will activate VDCCs leading to Ca^{2+} entry via that route and activation of tyrosine kinase pathways. The metabotropic glutamate receptors (mGLU) also contribute to plastic change, but in ways that are incompletely understood. Both kinase pathways also appear to influence gene expression and interact with one another in a complex manner.

from anatomically different channel sites coupled with the limited diffusion of free calcium in the cytosol (Teyler et al., 1994). It is now known that vdccLTP depends upon the activation of a separate set of enzymes, tyrosine kinases, and involves the participation of tyrosine receptor kinases (*trk*'s), the receptors for neurotrophins (Cavus & Teyler, 1996). The induction of vdccLTP leads to an increase in CREB phosphorylation (Alberini et al., 1995), the release of the neurotrophins BDNF and NT3 (Patterson, Grover, Schwartzkroin, & Bothwell, 1992), as well as an up-regulation in the *trk* B receptor for BDNF, showing that vdccLTP (and not nmdaLTP) leads to involvement of this important class of cellular growth mediators. Similarly, the application of BDNF to naive hippocampal slices results in the appearance of a form of potentiation that appears to share many of the characteristics of vdccLTP (Kang & Schuman, 1995).

Since nmdaLTP has been shown to be reversible through the action of phosphatases, the question arises as to whether vdccLTP can be reversed through the action of tyrosine phosphatases. When a depotentiating stimulus is supplied to a hippocampal slice that has recently expressed vdccLTP, there is no apparent reduction in the magnitude of vdccLTP. In contrast, nmdaLTP will be reversed. It appears that once activated, the VDCC form of LTP is more resistant to reversal than its NMDA counterpart (Martinez, Coussens, Cruce, & Teyler, 1997). Given the growth-promoting and damage-reversing roles of the neurotrophins, it is quite possible that the unique activation of neurotrophins and their receptors via the mechanisms underlying vdccLTP leads to the activation of signal transduction cascades which result in alterations in gene expression, making the underlying synaptic machinery relatively permanent, that is, a form of synaptic plasticity that is enduring.

The above suggests that the two forms of LTP differ primarily in their permanence. NmdaLTP, which is primarily represented by the phosphorylation of AMPA receptors (Barria, Muller, Derkash, Griffith, & Soderling, 1997) and subsequent increases in AMPA channel conductance (Derkash, Barria, & Soderling, 1999), can be readily reversed by different patterns of synaptic activation (depotentiation). Thus, it can be considered a temporary or transient form of network alteration. VdccLTP, on the other hand, is more resistant to decay and thus may be involved in the longer term aspects of network integrity and thus information storage. It is appealing to view the two forms of LTP as working together to induce changes transiently and, if the alteration is of significant magnitude, relatively permanently. The proof of this hypothesis is not to be found in the literature. This is because most studies have failed to distinguish between the two forms of LTP and have actually induced both forms simultaneously (called compound LTP). While this may be what occurs in the intact animal (Figure 9.6), it makes disentangling the contribution of the two cellular mechanisms experimentally difficult.

In an attempt to test this hypothesis, we have recently undertaken a behavioral experiment in which the two forms of LTP were selectively blocked by using channel blockers to NMDA receptors (to block nmdaLTP) and/or to VDCCs (to block vdccLTP). These channel blockers were systemically administered to animals being trained in an eight-arm spatial maze task, a task known to be disrupted by blockers of NMDARs, as well as a task that requires an intact hippocampal network for its successful solution. The performance of the animals was measured when subjected to doses of channel blockers known to block LTP induction in vivo (Morgan & Teyler, 1999). The results of this experiment show that the NMDA receptor blockade (nmdaLTP) interferes with the ability of the animal to remember the correct arms from day to day (Figure 9.7). The animals receiving calcium channel blockade (vdccLTP), however, seem to learn this aspect of the task without difficulty, but fail to retain what they have learned over a week-long

Multiple Channels Contribute to LTP

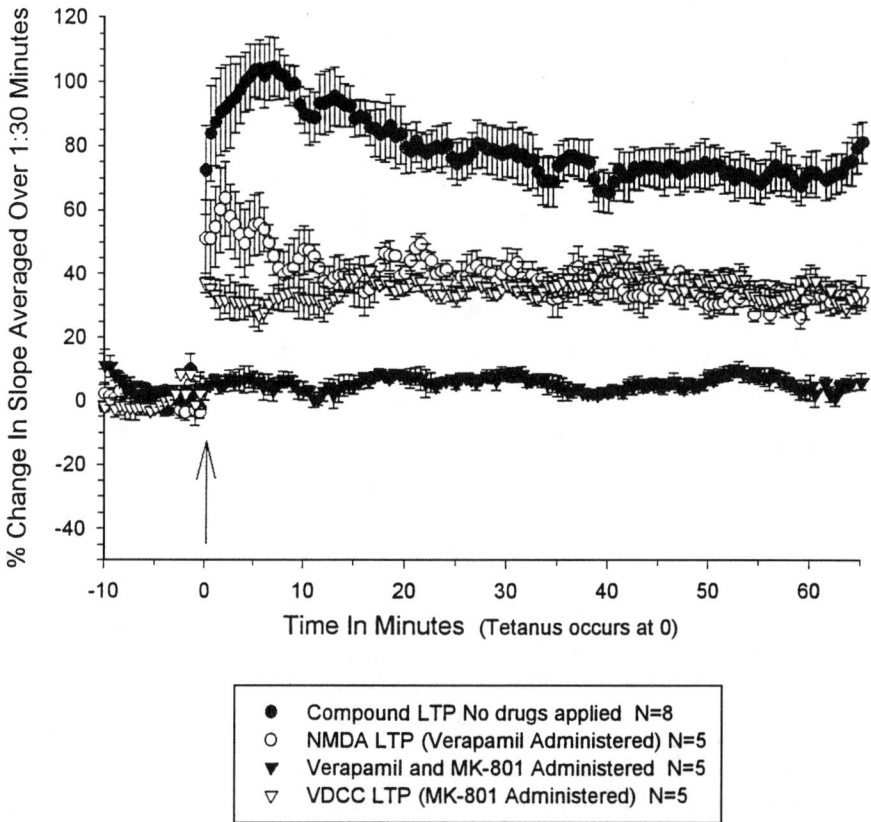

Figure 9.6. The two forms of LTP are usually simultaneously expressed. In this experiment, a tetanus was applied to Schaffer collateral fibers in an intact rat with no channel blockers present (compound LTP expressed; filled circles), with only nmdaLTP expressed (verapamil, 10mg/kg; open circles), with only vdccLTP expressed (MK-801, 0.1mg/kg; open triangles), or with both forms of LTP blocked (closed triangles). From this figure it can be seen that compound LTP is the sum of nmdaLTP and vdccLTP. From "VDCCs and NMDARs underlie two forms of LTP in CA1 hippocampus *in vivo*," by S. L. Morgan and T. J. Teyler, 1999, *Journal of Neurophysiology, 82,* 736–740.

retention interval (the NMDAR-blocked animals perform normally across the retention interval). This data suggests that the two forms of LTP encode information of different temporal domains, with nmdaLTP operating over a shorter time span than vdccLTP (Woodside, Hammonds, & Teyler, 1999). However, it also emphasizes that the normal process of information registration and storage in the intact brain involves the interplay between the two systems, because animals that had combined blockade of the channels inducing both forms of LTP both failed to learn and failed to remember over the retention interval.

LTP and Spatial Memory

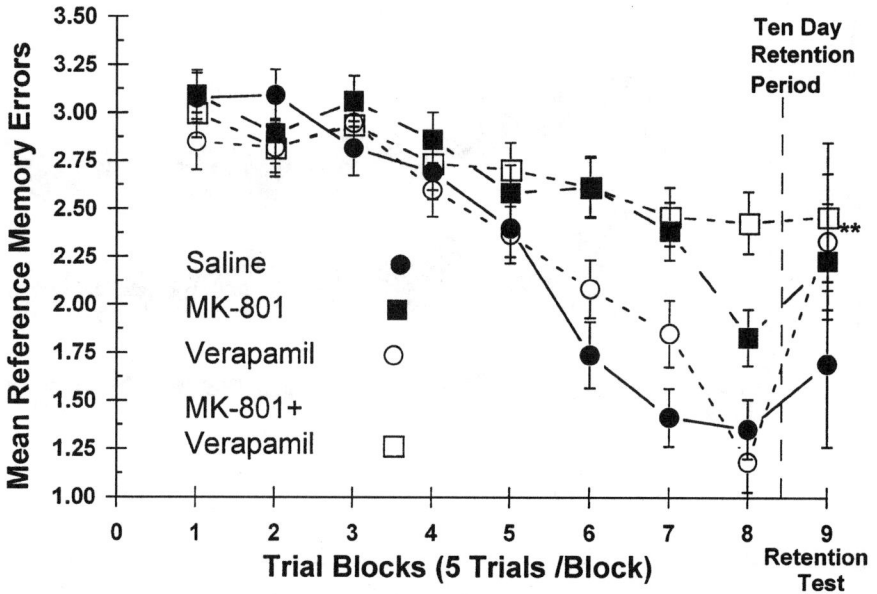

Figure 9.7. The selective blockade of nmdaLTP and vdccLTP has different behavioral consequences. Rats trained on a 4/8 radial arm maze task were trained and tested for memory retention in the presence of blockers of nmdaLTP (MK-801, 0.1mg/kg), vdccLTP (verapamil, 10mg/kg), or both drugs, administered IP prior to daily training/testing. Compared to saline-injected control animals, the nmdaLTP-blocked group shows slowed acquisition but normal levels of retention over a 10-day period. In contrast, the vdccLTP-blocked group shows normal acquisition but impaired retention. The combined drug group displayed poor acquisition and retention performance. These results indicate that vdccLTP operates over a longer time frame than does nmdaLTP. From "VdccLTP and nmdaLTP Mediate Different Aspects of Acquisition and Retention in the 4/8 Radial Arm Maze Task," by B. L. Woodside, M. D. Hammonds, and T. J. Teyler, 1999, *Society for Neuroscience Abstracts, 25*, A354.6.

☐ A Superfamily of Synaptic Plasticities

It appears that the different forms of LTP and LTD are members of a larger class of synaptic plasticities whose phenomonology (temporal duration, induction parameters) and mechanisms of action differ across different neuronal networks or at nodes within a neuronal network. Thus there appears to be a related family of synaptic plasticities. All members of the family display similar characteristics: they either increment or decrement synaptic gain. However, they do so utilizing different mechanisms with different cellular consequences; some are more permanent, some are more transient, some are reversible, and some are relatively irreversible. These varied forms of synaptic plasticity are expressed in various combinations, leading to further complexity and an increased ability

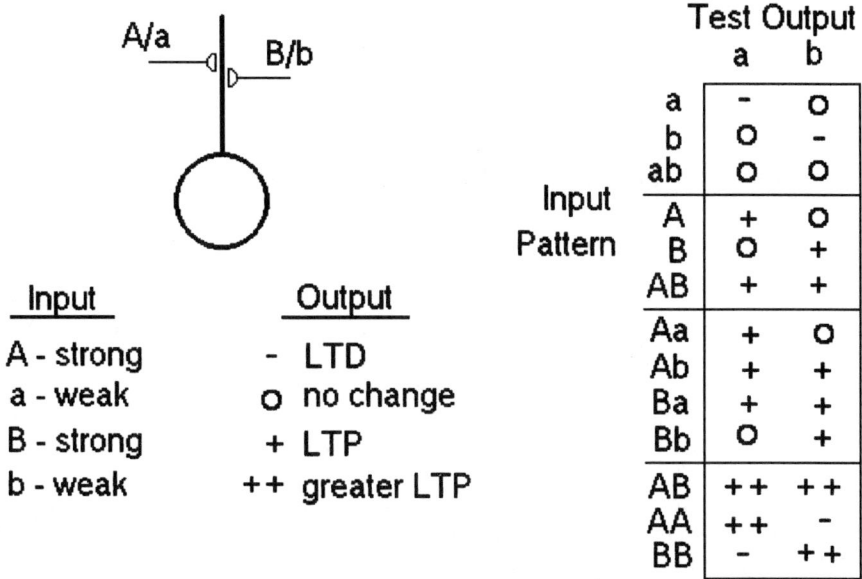

Figure with diagram labeled A/a, B/b, a circle (cell body).

Input	Output
A - strong	- LTD
a - weak	o no change
B - strong	+ LTP
b - weak	++ greater LTP

Input Pattern	Test Output a	Test Output b
a	-	o
b	o	-
ab	o	o
A	+	o
B	o	+
AB	+	+
Aa	+	o
Ab	+	+
Ba	+	+
Bb	o	+
AB	++	++
AA	++	-
BB	-	++

Figure 9.8. Hypothetical results from the activation of just two sets of synapses onto a forebrain pyramidal cell. Each of the sets of synapses experiences either a weak (a, b) or strong (A, B) activation, either alone or in combination with another input (or the same input activated again). As a result of this "experience" the output of the cell can show LTD, no change, LTP, or a greater magnitude LTP. The entries in the "Test Output" table represent hypothetical results from the weak test stimulation of either input a or b following the "experience." The results are based on the observation that the type of synaptic plasticity induced is a function of the degree of postsynaptic depolarization attained in a small segment of dendrite where influences interact.

of neural networks to process and store information. Figure 9.8 presents some hypothetical results from the interaction of just two sets of synapses. It is in the subtle details that the true dynamics of information storage in the nervous system will be fully appreciated.

What is the evidence that multiple forms of synaptic plasticity exist? In addition to the three forms already mentioned, it is known that a form of LTP exists in the CA3 synapse and in the neostriatum which features presynaptic mechanisms of action as opposed to the primarily postsynaptic inducing mechanisms of action reviewed above (Groves et al., 1995). Whereas forms of LTP and LTD are present throughout the brain, it can be expected that the mechanisms of action and consequences of those mechanisms may vary from brain region to brain region. An understanding of these variations will have a great deal to say regarding the function of the neuronal networks in which those synapses are embedded. While the variance represented by family members within the plasticity family will make understanding their roles and mechanisms of action experimentally difficult, the possibility that the forms of plasticity represented by specific tissues can be altered by the past history of the neuron will make such searches even more problematic. The expression of specific receptor and channel subunits can be changed by the activation of different promoters and repressors which can be regulated by the activity of synaptic neuromodulators interacting with second messenger systems. It is thus not difficult to imagine that the protein substrates underlying synaptic plasticity (the enzymes, channels, and receptors) and the subunits which confer the details of their functionality may be under the experiential control of the neuron and thus may change as a function of the prior history of the cell or synapse.

☐ Homeostasis Versus Homeodynamics

A building block of biology is the concept of homeostasis: the maintenance of stable conditions in the face of change. As applied to a number of physiological systems (water balance, temperature, receptor regulation) the concept is well proven. However, as applied to synaptic plasticity, the concept requires modification (Goodwin, 1997). Experience-induced synaptic plasticity that endures (e.g., memory) requires that neural networks and their constituent synapses change and retain that change over the long term. If synapses maintained stable conditions in the face of change, synaptic plasticity would not be possible. If networks could not form as a result of changing experience, memory would not be possible.

Once synaptic plasticity has occurred and the mechanisms that govern the expression of synaptic change have run to completion, this new state of affairs must be retained over the long term. If we assume, for the sake of argument, that the endpoint of synaptic plasticity is an alteration in gene expression and consequently an enhanced synthesis of the cellular machinery responsible for expressing synaptic change (AMPA receptors, enzymes, etc.), then this new state of affairs must be maintained. Brain proteins have an average half-life of less than a month. If the alterations in gene expression induced during the induction of synaptic plasticity are not maintained, then the protein basis for the altered synaptic gain will gradually disappear. If, however, the altered gene expression is maintained—if it is made constitutively permanent—then the molecular infrastructure of the memory can be retained indefinitely. (See also Kavanau, Chapter 6 of this volume, for details on a synaptic gain "refresh" mechanism.)

What is needed is a mechanism by which a new homeostasis can be established and the new setpoint defended against change. Such a mechanism does not eliminate the need for homeostatic machinery; rather, it requires that the concept be modified to allow for the establishment of a dynamic setting of homeostatic parameters: a homeodynamic process. The cellular mechanisms by which such a process might work are only dimly perceived at present. We can imagine how such a process might work with respect to the maintenance of LTP at a subset of synapses on the distal dendrites of a cortical pyramidal cell. To carry our earlier speculation further, we would need a process by which the additional AMPA receptors would be replaced when they are naturally degraded, thereby keeping the new AMPA receptor total the same. Such a process must be able to target the replacement receptors to the synapses that were potentiated, and no others. It is difficult to imagine a process other than local control to accomplish this (See Liu & Wang, Chapter 12 of this volume, for details of one such process). A local homeostatic process could replace degraded receptors by withdrawing them from a circulating pool. Withdrawals from the circulating pool could then stimulate the central synthesis of more receptor to replenish the pool.

If such a process is found to exist, then our concept of homeodynamic regulation might take the following form. The induction of stable forms of synaptic plasticity activates mechanisms that insert new AMPA receptors in specific synapses (or functionalize existing silent ones). The eventual degradation of these receptors will be replaced under local (dendritic spine) control from a centrally maintained circulating pool. Such a system retains the powerful regulatory control of classical homeostasis, yet allows for the establishment of a new setpoint locally.

Why Have Multiple Forms of Synaptic Plasticity?

There are two possibilities. One possibility is that the differences between the various forms of synaptic plasticity represent synapse-specific solutions to the requirements of synaptic gain change capability. In such a case, the differences may carry no particular functional consequences and represent different mechanistic solutions based on the particular genetic endowment of the cell or synapse. A second possibility is that the differences have evolved to confer different functional consequences to the synapses and the networks in which they are found.

An examination of the synapses wherein something specific is known about the phenomenology and mechanisms of synaptic plasticity suggests that no two synapse types share identical properties. While they may appear to be phenomenologically identical, differences appear upon closer analysis. Take the case of the well-studied synapses onto CA1 hippocampal pyramidal cells. Synapses in the apical dendrites and those in the basilar dendrites receive afferents from CA3 and other cells, and both display similar-appearing LTP. Yet, on closer analysis, the magnitude of the nmdaLTP induced in basal synapses is larger than that induced in apical dendrites (Leung & Shen, 1995), basal synapses possess a lower LTP induction threshold (Arai, Black, & Lynch, 1994) and respond differently to various tetanus frequencies (Leung, Shen, & Kaibara, 1992), the effect of vdccLTP signal transduction inhibitors is more pronounced in basal dendrites (Cavus & Teyler, 1998), the *trk*B receptor is absent in basal dendrites (Teyler, Morgan, Russell, & Woodside, 1999), endothelial NO synthase is present in apical but not basal dendrites (Kantor et al., 1996), and the two dendritic regions respond differently to inhibitory synaptic inputs (Kaibara & Leung, 1993). While these synapses behave similarly at a molar level (both show several forms of synaptic plasticity), they differ subtly under finer scrutiny. Similar differences are accumulating as phenomenological and mechanistic details emerge for other synapses.

It is possible that these fine differences carry no particular consequence and merely reflect variations on a theme that different synapses employ to accomplish similar tasks. On the other hand, differences in NO, *trk*B, and vdccLTP signal transduction pathways may indicate markedly different functions for the apical versus basal synapses of these cells. At present the functional significance of these differences is unknown. Ultimately, we will need to understand these synapses in the networks in which they are embedded to fully appreciate their contribution to network function and maintenance. Some networks will probably require an extremely stable and persistent presence (perceptual constancies, for example), whereas other networks will be typified by rapid evolution and change (encoding dynamic experience). In the other chapters of this book, the reader can appreciate the breadth and diversity of synaptic plasticity and appreciate the various solutions the brain employs to process a variety of kinds of information.

References

Alberini, C. M., Ghirardi, M., Hguang, Y. Y., Nguyen, P. V., & Kandel, E. R. (1995). A molecular switch for the consolidation of long-term memory: cAMP-inducible gene expression. *Annals of the New York Academy of Sciences, 758*, 261–286.

Arai, A., Black, J., & Lynch, G. (1994). Origins of the variations in long-term potentiation between synapses in the basal versus apical dendrites of hippocampal neurons. *Hippocampus, 4,* 1–10.

Aroniadou, V. A., Grover, L. M., & Teyler, T. J. (1991). Long-term potentiation (LTP) and depression (LTD) in rat visual cortex; role of NMDA receptor-mediated- and polysynaptic components. *Brain Research, 562,* 136–143.

Aroniadou, V. A., & Keller, A. (1995). Mechanisms of LTP induction in rat motor cortex in vitro. *Cerebral Cortex, 5,* 353–362.

Barria, A., Muller, D., Derkash, V. A., Griffith, L. C., & Soderling, T. R. (1997). Regulatory phosphorylation of AMPA-type glutamate receptors by CaMKII during long-term potentiation. *Science, 276,* 2042–2045.

Bear, M., Kleinschmidt, A., Gu, Q., & Singer, W. (1990). Disruption of experience-dependent synaptic modifications in striate cortex by infusion of an NMDA receptor antagonist. *Journal of Neuroscience, 10,* 909–925.

Cavus, I., & Teyler, T. J. (1996). Two forms of long-term potentiation in area CA1 activate different signal transduction pathways. *Journal of Neurophysiology, 76,* 3038–3047.

Cavus, I., & Teyler, T. (1998). NMDA receptor-independent LTP in basal versus apical dendrites of CA1 pyramidal cells in rat hippocampal slice. *Hippocampus, 8,* 373–379.

Coussens, C. M., & Teyler, T. J. (1996a). LTP induction induces synaptic plasticity at nontetanized adjacent synapses. *Learning & Memory, 3,* 106–114.

Coussens, C. M., & Teyler, T. J. (1996b). Protein kinase and phosphatase activity regulate the form of synaptic plasticity expressed. *Synapse, 24,* 97–103.

Crepel, F., & Jaillard, D. (1991). Pairing of pre- and postsynaptic activities in cerebellar Purkinje cells induces long-term changes in synaptic efficacy in vitro. *Journal of Physiology (London), 432,* 123–141.

Derkach, V. V., Barria, A., & Soderling, T. R. (1999). Ca^{2+}/calmodulin-kinase II enhances channel conductance of AMPA type glutamate receptors. *Proceedings of the National Academy of the Sciences of the United States of America, 96,* 3269–3274.

Goodwin, B. C. (1997). Temporal organization and disorganization in organisms. *Chronobiology International, 14,* 531–536.

Grover, L. M., & Teyler, T. J. (1990). Two components of long-term potentiation induced by different patterns of afferent activation. *Nature, 347,* 477–479.

Grover, L. M., & Teyler, T. J. (1995). Different mechanisms may be required for maintenance of NMDA receptor-dependent and independent forms of long-term potentiation. *Synapse, 19,* 121–133.

Groves, P. M., Garcia-Monoz, M., Linder, J. C., Manley, M. S., Martone, M. E., & Young, S. J. (1995). Elements of the intrinsic organization and information processing in the neostriatum. In J. C. Houk, J. L. Davis, & D. G. Beiser (Eds.), *Models of information processing in the basal ganglia* (pp. 51–96). Boston: MIT Press.

Kaibara, T., & Leung, L. S. (1993). Basal versus apical dendritic long-term potentiation of commissural afferents to hippocampal CA1: A current-source density study. *Journal of Neuroscience, 13,* 2391–2404.

Kang, H., & Schuman, E. (1995). Long-lasting neurotrophin-induced enhancement of synaptic transmission in the adult hippocampus. *Science, 267,* 1658–1662.

Kantor, D. B., Lanzrein, M., Stary, S. J., Sandoval, G. M., Smith, W. B., Sullivan, B. M., Davidson, N., & Schuman, E. M. (1996). A role for endothelial NO synthase in LTP revealed by adenovirus-mediated inhibition and rescue. *Science, 274,* 1744–1748.

Kirkwood, A., Rozas, C., Kirkwood, J., Perez, F., & Bear, M. F. (1999). Modulation of long-term synaptic depression in visual cortex by acetylcholine and norepinephrine. *Journal of Neuroscience, 19,* 1599–1609.

Kudrimoti, H. S., Barnes, C. A., & McNaughton, B. L. (1999). Reactivation of hippocampal cell assemblies: Effects of behavioral state, experience, and EEG dynamics. *Journal of Neuroscience, 19,* 4090–4101.

Leung, L. S., Shen, B., & Kaibara, T. (1992). Long-term potentiation induced by patterned stimulation of the commissural pathway to hippocampal CA1 region in freely moving rats. *Neuroscience, 48,* 63–74.

Leung, S. L., & Shen, B. (1995). Long-term potentiation at the apical and basal dendritic synapses of CA1 after local stimulation in behaving rats. *Journal of Neurophysiology, 73*, 1938–1946.

Lisberger, S. G., & Pavelko, T. A. (1986). Vestibular signals carried by pathways subserving plasticity of the vestibular-ocular-reflex in monkeys. *Journal of Neuroscience, 6*, 346–354.

Lisman, J. E., & Fallon, J. R. (1999). What maintains memories? *Science, 283*, 339–340.

Martinez, J. S., Coussens, C. M., Cruce, W. L. R., & Teyler, T. J. (1997). The time required to depotentiate vdccLTP varies with stimulation frequency. *Society for Neuroscience Abstracts, 23*, A316.11.

Morgan, S. L., & Teyler, T. J. (1999). VDCCs and NMDARs underlie two forms of LTP in CA1 hippocampus *in vivo*. *Journal of Neurophysiology, 82*, 736–740.

Mulkey, R. M., Herron, C. E., & Malenka, R. C. (1993). An essential role for protein phosphatases in hippocampal long-term depression. *Science, 261*, 1051–1055.

Orban, P. C., Chapman, P. F., & Brambilla, R. (1999). Is the Ras-MAPK signaling pathway necessary for long-term memory formation? *Trends in Neuroscience, 22*, 38–44.

Patterson, S. L., Grover, L. M., Schwartzkroin, P. A., & Bothwell, M. (1992). Neurotrophin expression in rat hippocampal slices: A stimulus paradigm inducing LTP in CA1 evokes increases in BDNF and NT-3 mRNAs. *Neuron, 9*, 1081–1088.

Schulz, S., Siemer, H., Krug, M., & Hollt, V. (1999). Direct evidence for biphasic cAMP responsive element-binding protein phosphorylation during long-term potentiation in the rat dentate gyrus in vivo. *Journal of Neuroscience, 19*, 5683–5692.

Teyler, T. J., & DiScenna, P. (1985). The role of hippocampus in memory: A hypothesis. *Neuroscience and Biobehavioral Reviews, 9*, 377–389.

Teyler, T. J., & DiScenna, P. (1987). Long-term potentiation. *Annual Review of Neuroscience, 10*, 131–161.

Teyler, T. J., Cavus, I., Coussens, C., DiScenna, P., Grover, L. M., Lee, Y. P., & Little, Z. (1994). The multideterminant role of calcium in hippocampal synaptic plasticity. *Hippocampus, 4*, 623–634.

Teyler, T. J., Morgan, S. L., Russell, R. N., & Woodside, B. L. (in press). Synaptic plasticity and secondary epileptogenesis. In J. E. Engel, D. H. Lowenstein, S. L. Moshe, & P. A. Schwartzkroin (Eds.), *Brain plasticity and epilepsy*, International Review of Neurobiology. San Diego, CA: Academic Press.

Woodside, B. L., Hammonds, M. D., & Teyler, T. J. (1999). VdccLTP and nmdaLTP mediate different aspects of acquisition and retention in the 4/8 radial arm maze task. *Society for Neuroscience Abstracts, 25*, A354.6.

10

CHAPTER   D. P. Cain

Synaptic Models of Neuroplasticity: What Is LTP?

☐ Introduction

The term *neuroplasticity* can refer to an enormous range of neural processes, from cellular development and axonal outgrowth early in life, to pathological events in old age. The subject of this chapter is the relation between adaptive behavioral change that results from experience and a particular class of neuroplastic phenomena. In broad terms, this is the relation between learning and memory, and the neural changes that might underlie them. For this chapter, neuroplasticity is defined as synaptic change that underlies learning.

An important early idea about this kind of neuroplasticity was contained in Donald Hebb's 1949 book *Organization of Behavior*. In it he described what has became known as the "Hebb synapse," a modifiable synapse that increases in efficiency when it is repeatedly activated. Hebb was describing the establishment of an engram in the brain, which could represent learned information. He acknowledged that his modifiable synapse was highly speculative and that he had no empirical evidence to support it. However, subsequent research has shown that something like the Hebb synapse might well exist; thus, Hebb's is one of the most-cited ideas in the history of neuroscience.

Some years later Terje Lomo discovered a neuroplastic event in the hippocampus of the rabbit using electrophysiological stimulation and recording. He called this *frequency potentiation* (Lomo, 1966). Tim Bliss and Lomo later published a more detailed report of the potentiation phenomenon (Bliss & Lomo, 1973). The potentiation appeared to embody Hebb's idea of increased synaptic efficiency resulting from repeated activation. The effect is now referred to generally as long-term potentiation (LTP). As defined by Bliss and Lomo, LTP was a lasting increase in the excitatory postsynaptic potential that resulted from brief, high frequency electrical stimulation of afferent pathways. They acknowledged that the function of LTP was not known, but it seemed to provide a model of neuroplasticity that might be related to learning and memory.

☐ The Relevance of LTP to Learning

The fact that LTP was first demonstrated in the hippocampus fit with the view that the hippocampus was important for learning, which arose from the fact that removal of the medial temporal lobes in epileptic patients led to disturbances in learning and memory. Later research with rats revealed "place cells" in the hippocampus that fired when the rat was in a specific place in a familiar environment. Place cells seemed to code spatial locations, giving support to the idea that the hippocampus served as a spatial map that was important for navigation. The fact that damage to the hippocampus and related structures impaired behaviors involving accurate navigation, such as the Morris water maze task, was consistent with this idea. One current view is that place cell selectivity is established by a neuroplastic process like hippocampal LTP. Of course, many other places in the brain also support robust LTP, and one wonders whether the course of research and theory on LTP would have been the same if LTP had first been found in a brain region other than the hippocampus that was unrelated to learning. A very different view of the role of LTP might have dominated the field.

The research literature on LTP is enormous. In what follows, only basic LTP phenomena will be discussed, with emphasis on the aspects that are most relevant to its possible relation to learning and memory. Some important issues are not discussed here. Excellent reviews are available (Bliss & Collingridge, 1993), including two that deal with issues of LTP's relevance to learning (McEachern & Shaw, 1996; Shors & Matzel, 1997). A goal here will be to evaluate research designed to explicitly test whether the N-methyl-D-aspartate (NMDA) receptor–dependent form of LTP is required for certain kinds of learning.

As many researchers acknowledge, the view that LTP might underlie learning is to some extent an act of faith. Although some of the early studies seemed to support a causal link to learning, subsequent work has raised serious questions about this link. On the other hand, some recent work has again given support for a role for LTP in certain forms of learning. The data aside, a major feature of LTP that makes it so appealing as a learning model is that it has many of the properties that a learning model should have. We turn to those properties now.

☐ Basic Phenomena of LTP

As a laboratory model of neuroplasticity, LTP is easily induced in the hippocampus using standard electrophysiological techniques, which have the advantage of providing information about synaptic events. This is because the hippocampus is an organized and laminar structure, and appropriate electrical stimulation can evoke a field potential that reflects the synchronous activity of a large population of synapses. With detailed information about the source-sink relations in the responses (Lomo, 1971) it is possible to interpret the significance of individual waveforms and changes in those waveforms in terms of synaptic activity or unit firing. This would otherwise be possible only with technically more difficult intracellular unit recording, which would not be usable with awake, behaving animals.

LTP is usually induced with repeated application of short trains of electrical pulses (each 0.1 ms long) delivered at high frequency (100 to 400 Hz). When trains of 8 to 50 pulses are applied to hippocampal inputs, there is an increase in the response. The increase is documented by comparing the responses to single test pulses given before the high-frequency trains are delivered to the responses to the same test pulses given after the high-frequency trains. The synaptic component is typically measured as the slope of the rising phase of the evoked potential and is regarded as a population EPSP (excitatory postsynaptic potential). The discharge of cells fired by the EPSP is measured as the amplitude of the population spike that occurs when a sufficiently strong test pulse is given. Increases of from 10% to 30% in the slope of the population EPSP, and from 40 to 200 percent in the amplitude of the population spike are common. The increases are thought to reflect an increase in the efficacy of synaptic transmission.

Detailed study of the physiology and chemistry of LTP is usually done using brain slices kept alive in a dish (Schwartzkroin & Wester, 1975), and most of the research on the neural mechanisms of LTP has used this approach. However, as a strategy for evaluating whether LTP underlies learning and memory, this technique has limitations. For example, it cannot be used to monitor the possible development of LTP as rats progressively learn a task.

The ability of areas outside the hippocampus to support LTP was established by Racine, who found that most pathways and regions tested supported LTP, including the neocortex and cerebellum (Racine, Milgram, & Hafner, 1983; Racine, Wilson, Gingell, & Sunderland, 1986; Wilson & Racine, 1983). Racine and colleagues performed their research in intact, awake rats with chronic electrodes, which allowed them to follow the time course of LTP decay. They found that two distinct time courses of induction and decay occurred, which they referred to as short-term potentiation (STP) and LTP. They found that STP decayed after minutes, but that LTP could persist for a number of weeks in the hippocampus. More recent work has shown that LTP can persist for as long as 8 weeks in the neocortex, which was the longest retention time tested (Trepel & Racine, 1998). This finding is consistent with theories positing that LTP should last longer in the neocortex than in subcortical areas because the neocortex is the site where engrams for long-term memory are established. However, no one has shown that LTP can persist as long as behavioral learning can.

One property that makes LTP attractive as a learning model is cooperativity, also called associativity. Simultaneous activation of weak and strong synaptic inputs produces LTP of the weak input, whereas activation of the weak input alone fails to produce LTP (Levy & Steward, 1979). In general, LTP that is produced by simultaneous activation of different inputs is greater than the sum of LTP that is produced by separate activation of those inputs (McNaughton, Barnes, & Andersen, 1981). This is reminiscent of the associativity of learning (Levy & Steward, 1979) and may have its neural basis in the way that NMDA receptors function in the presence of strong postsynaptic depolarization from multiple inputs (Bliss & Collingridge, 1993). This kind of NMDA receptor–dependent LTP is the best known form, but other forms exist (Harris & Cotman, 1986). The multiplicity of forms emphasizes that LTP is not a unitary phenomenon.

This description of LTP is only an outline. There are more ways of inducing potentiation effects than have been discussed here, some of which do not involve electrical stimulation at all (see McEachern & Shaw, 1996). Indeed, the very definition of LTP frequently differs among researchers. Also, the opposite of LTP, long-term depression (LTD) has been described. LTD involves a reduction in the strength of an evoked response following electrical stimulation. Although LTD is of great potential interest in learning research, little has been done to investigate its role in learning. An extensive discussion of these topics is beyond the scope of this chapter, but they are considered further by McEachern & Shaw (1996). For our purposes the discussion will center around NMDA receptor–dependent LTP induced in dentate gyrus, hippocampal area CA1, or the neocortex by high-frequency electrical stimulation.

☐ Evaluating the Role of LTP in Learning and Memory

However attractive LTP is as a learning mechanism, until it is causally linked with behavioral learning in experiments with awake, behaving organisms it remains only a laboratory model of neuroplasticity. The pursuit of functional links between LTP and learning has been difficult, and the outcome remains uncertain. In this context, a number of points are worth making.

First, the majority of work on LTP has been done with brain slices. This technique is useful for studying the neural mechanisms of LTP, but it has limitations for studying whether LTP underlies behavioral learning. The focus of the discussion here will be on work with intact, awake animals. Second, LTP involves laboratory techniques that are crude relative to the subtle and detailed anatomy and workings of the mammalian brain. The simultaneous activation of thousands of neurons by electrical pulses from a laboratory stimulator is unlikely to simulate what occurs naturally. If learning selectively alters synapses in a distributed manner throughout a number of brain regions, as many researchers believe, it may be difficult or impossible to detect the altered synapses using current LTP methods. Third, nearly all of the work has concerned hippocampal LTP. Work involving other subcortical regions is sparse, and work with neocortical LTP has only recently begun to appear. Fourth, a necessary requirement for the validation of LTP as a learning mechanism is that LTP be found to occur during actual behavioral learning. As two well-known researchers put it,

> [N]o amount of research studying whether LTP is necessary for learning will ever be persuasive in the absence of studies definitively establishing that LTP occurs naturally during learning. Uncomfortable as it is, we have to face up to the complications of demonstrating that this synaptic mechanism is actually engaged during learning." (Morris & Davis, 1994, p. 368)

There have been three main research strategies used in LTP-learning research. The first involves correlating field potential data with behavioral learning data (the correlation strategy). The second involves saturating LTP to asymptote before behavioral training and examining the animal's ability to learn (the saturation strategy). The third involves blocking LTP during training and examining the animal's ability to learn and retain the learning (the blockade strategy). The second and third strategies overlap in their conceptual basis, since it is assumed that both manipulations impair or block the formation of new LTP during training. Due to the many issues and difficulties involved, it is not likely that a definitive answer will come from the use of a single strategy. The best approach is to make use of multiple strategies to try to obtain converging evidence on the question.

The Correlation Strategy

An early study required rats to learn which of many holes on a large board led to a dark enclosure hidden beneath the board (Barnes, 1979). This is an example of "spatial," or "place" learning that requires a rat to learn the location of a place with respect to distal cues in the environment or to keep track of its movements by path integration. A correlation was found between the amount of LTP that could be induced electrophysiologically and the behavioral performance that was exhibited in the task (Barnes).

To fulfill Morris and Davis's (1994) requirement discussed above, other studies searched for LTP that was induced by behavioral training. These studies reported LTP-like changes in the hippocampus as a result of training in various nonspatial tasks (e.g., Skelton, Scarth, Wilkie, Miller, & Phillips, 1987). LTP-like changes were also found in rats that explored a novel, complex environment (Sharp, McNaughton, & Barnes, 1985). The rationale for the studies was that the hippocampus might be involved in the learning. However, hippocampal damage does not interfere with learning these tasks, so the likelihood of finding hippocampal LTP as a result of the learning seems uncertain. In any case, the studies gave early support to the LTP learning hypothesis.

Subsequent work raised questions about this conclusion. One problem is what has been called "Vanderwolf's dilemma" (Morris & Baker, 1984), which results from two facts. First, evoked potentials are known to vary in amplitude depending on the moment-to-moment behavior of the animal; the amplitude is low when the animal is walking or moving its head and is higher when the animal is immobile, whether the animal is learning something or not (Vanderwolf, Harvey, & Leung, 1987). Second, animals display systematic changes in their behavior as a result of learning. Vanderwolf's dilemma says that with spontaneously behaving animals, it is impossible to tell whether a change in a potential has occurred because the underlying neural circuitry has changed (e.g., LTP has occurred during the learning process), or because the animal is now exhibiting different behavior as a result of the training, which is associated with changes in evoked potential amplitude. In the latter case, some mechanism completely unconnected with LTP might be underlying learning at the neural level. Unfortunately, in the studies cited in the previous paragraph this problem was not controlled for.

Vanderwolf's dilemma can be dealt with by holding behavior constant while the potentials are being recorded. This is easily done by delivering test pulses only when the animal is immobile. When this was done in studies involving radial arm maze, avoidance, and water maze tasks, hippocampal and neocortical potentials did not change as a result of the training (Beiko & Cain, 1998; Hargreaves, Cain, & Vanderwolf, 1990).

A further issue is the fact that motor activity increases body and brain temperature. The brain temperature increase can alter potentials in a way that strongly resembles LTP (Cain, Hargreaves, & Boon, 1994; Moser, Mathiesen, & Andersen, 1993). In one study on learning and LTP, the changes in brain temperature accounted for all of the changes in the evoked potentials (Moser et al., 1993). However, when the effects of brain temperature were accounted for in a second study, exploration of novel objects in an open field led to increases in the potentials (Moser, Moser, & Andersen, 1994).

Other recent studies made use of auditory fear conditioning and recorded responses in the amygdala to auditory conditioned stimuli or electrical activation of the auditory thalamus (McKernan & Shinnick-Gallagher, 1997; Rogan, Staubli, & LeDoux, 1997). Increases in the responses that were electrophysiologically similar to the changes that occurred in electrophysiological LTP of the same pathway were found. Another study found that motor skill learning in a reaching task increased the strength of field potentials in the motor cortex in the hemisphere opposite the trained limb but not in the contralateral hemisphere, and that less electrophysiological LTP was inducible in the motor cortex after the experiment as a result (Rioult-Pedotti, Friedman, Hess, & Donoghue, 1998). Control procedures ruled out confounds due to ongoing behavior in these experiments. None of the studies proved that LTP was critical for the learning, but the results were consistent with LTP playing a causal role.

In sum, the results emphasize the importance of controlling for confounding variables that can affect the potentials used to document LTP. When confounds are eliminated, a few of the studies appear to document LTP-like changes that may result from learning. However, it remains to be seen whether the changes are identical to, and make use of the same neural mechanisms as, laboratory LTP. As with all correlations, concluding that there is a causal relation between the potentiation and behavioral learning is not possible. The other two strategies, to which we now turn, are intended to deal with this limitation.

The Saturation Strategy

This strategy involves "using up" all of the available LTP in a circuit by applying enough high-frequency trains to saturate LTP to asymptote. The rationale is that if all of the available LTP is used up in the circuit, and if the circuit is required for the learning, saturation of LTP should interfere with or prevent the learning. Much of the research in the rest of this chapter made use of the Morris water maze, which is well suited to the research because the learning occurs rapidly and can be analyzed in detail. This task also depends on an important natural ability, spatial navigation. It requires an animal to swim in a pool of water about 1.5 meters in diameter and learn the location of a small platform hidden just below the surface. The platform cannot be seen, and its location must be learned either in relation to distal cues in the room or by the self-monitoring of navigation movements. Rats or mice with chronic electrode implants can be trained in this task, which allows comparisons between LTP and behavioral learning in the same animal. The fact that the hippocampus is involved in spatial navigation in rodents made it useful to study hippocampal LTP in this task.

In initial studies, LTP in the dentate gyrus was saturated and impairments in learning were found (Castro, Silbert, McNaughton, & Barnes, 1989; McNaughton, Barnes, Rao, Baldwin, & Rasmussen, 1986). In the second of these studies, which used the water maze, an impairment was present while LTP saturation was complete, but the same rats learned the task after LTP had decayed back to baseline. This was a very important result and provided some of the strongest evidence that LTP was causally involved in learning. Other labs attempted to replicate and extend the research, but the attempts failed to substantiate the original finding (Cain et al., 1993; Jeffery & Morris, 1993). Similarly, saturation of LTP did not affect radial arm maze learning, another form of spatial learning (Robinson, 1992).

The saturation approach was pursued by Moser's group (Moser, Krobert, Moser, & Morris, 1998), who used a more effective means of saturating LTP. They found an impairment in spatial learning that was related to the degree of LTP saturation. However, more recent work by the same research group calls this result into question. In this work (Otnaess, Brun, Moser, & Moser, 1999) the rats were first pretrained to find a hidden platform in one pool. A week later they received LTP saturation and were again trained to find a hidden platform, but this time it was done using a different pool in a different room, involving the use of different visual cues. The pretrained rats learned the location of the hidden platform in room 2 after LTP saturation as quickly as control rats, indicating that the LTP saturation had not impaired spatial learning ability (Otnaess et al., 1999). In the original experiment, Moser had used naïve rats, and the LTP saturation impaired their performance in the water maze. There are two possible explanations for the behavioral impairment in the naïve rats. First, if LTP is not required for spatial navigation, it may be crucial for learning the strategies needed for the water maze task, and LTP saturation might prevent this learning. This possibility is discussed further in the next section. Second, the electrical stimulation itself, and not the LTP that it induced, might have disrupted the functioning of neural circuits required for either use of the water maze strategies in the task or for the spatial learning. In addition to inducing LTP, the stimulation no doubt triggered the expression of various genes and other physiological and molecular consequences in activated circuits. It is not known whether it was the LTP or other consequences of the high-frequency stimulation that caused the behavioral impairment.

A variation on the saturation strategy involves the induction of less than asymptotic amounts of LTP and predicts that this should facilitate transmission through the affected circuits, thus facilitating learning. This result was obtained in an early study (Berger, 1984), but was not obtained in a later, more complete study in which both initial and reversal learning of a nictitating membrane–conditioned response were unaffected by LTP (Rioux & Robinson, 1995).

In sum, the saturation strategy provided early support for a link between LTP and learning, but more recent work suggests that LTP is not required for spatial navigation.

The Blockade Strategy

Much of the work with the blockade strategy has made use of drugs to block LTP. A limitation of drug treatment is that it is often difficult to know whether the treatment impaired performance in the task by specifically blocking a learning mechanism or by impairing some nonlearning process that is crucial for behavioral performance of the task. Among the latter are sensorimotor mechanisms to initiate and guide behavior or mechanisms for acquiring the basic behavioral strategies that are necessary to cope with and acquire appropriate information for solving the task.

Nonspatial pretraining was developed by Morris (1989) to deal with this problem. Morris nonspatially pretrained the rats by letting them swim in the pool with black curtains around it to prevent them seeing the visual cues in the room and by moving the hidden platform to a new location after every trial. He argued that to acquire the water maze task, two kinds of learning were required. First, the rats had to learn the particular strategies needed in the task: how to swim; that the only refuge in the pool was an unseen platform; to swim away from the wall to find the platform; and that if the platform was contacted, to get onto it. Second, the rats had to learn the exact location of the platform with respect to visual cues in the room. For rats to be able to learn a platform location, they had to learn the strategies first, because only appropriate use of the strategies would enable them to obtain the information needed to learn the platform location. Use of nonspatial pretraining made it possible to separate the two kinds of learning. Training in the water maze is also stressful for rats, as indicated by behaviors such as squealing, which is especially strong in drugged rats, and by strong elevation in blood corticosterone levels in naïve rats (J. Beiko, unpublished observations, June, 1999). Blood corticosterone levels are much lower after pretraining. Thus, pretraining also reduces the stress of the handling and swimming, allowing them to make better use of the strategies learned during the pretraining.

Early research with the water maze showed that hippocampal damage or cholinergic antagonists severely impaired performance (Morris, Garrud, Rawlins, & O'Keefe, 1982; Sutherland, Kolb, & Whishaw, 1982). Based on the fact that most hippocampal LTP depends on NMDA receptors, Morris extended this work by blocking hippocampal LTP with an NMDA antagonist (Morris, Anderson, Lynch, & Baudry, 1986). The rats performed poorly in the pool, and a later study reported the same finding with nonspatially pretrained rats (Morris, 1989).

Our work with this approach has led to a different conclusion. When we administered an NMDA receptor antagonist to naïve rats they could not learn the platform's location, but they also had marked sensorimotor disturbances in the pool, including repeated swimming around the edge of the pool and failure to climb onto the hidden platform when it was contacted (Cain, Saucier, Hall, Hargreaves, & Boon, 1996). Some rats even swam right over the platform and off the other side without stopping (Cain, 1998), which probably resulted from the hyperactivity that NMDA antagonists produce (Hargreaves & Cain, 1992). The rats also had a small but reliable visual impairment (Cain, Saucier, & Boon, 1997). All of these effects would be expected to contribute to poor learning measures even if LTP is not involved in the learning.

To our surprise, nonspatially pretrained rats given the same NMDA antagonist performed the required strategies and learned the platform location as effectively as controls (Cain et al., 1996). We then tried other NMDA receptor antagonists, given systemically to block NMDA receptors throughout the brain and spinal cord, and again obtained the same result (Cain et al., 1997; Saucier & Cain, 1995). We were able to confirm that the NMDA antagonist blocked hippocampal LTP in these rats (Cain et al., 1997; Saucier & Cain, 1995). Excellent learning in rats with LTP blocked was also obtained by Morris's group using a two-pool pretraining technique (Bannerman, Good, Butcher, Ramsay, & Morris, 1995). Our technique involved systemic administration in most cases, which produced more sensorimotor disturbances in naïve rats than the technique that Morris used. The fact that nonspatially pretrained rats performed as well as controls under these challenging conditions, with LTP completely blocked, underlines the fact that robust spatial learning can occur in the absence of the most common form of hippocampal LTP.

In these experiments the nonspatially pretrained rats learned the task strategies without drug present. Could they learn the strategies when LTP was blocked, and could they then use the strategies to learn the location of a hidden platform? We examined this by giving rats nonspatial pretraining, followed by conventional spatial training. We also asked whether the rats could learn a reversal: a new platform location that was different from the first location they learned. The rats were given the NMDA antagonist before each of these three phases of training. What was different about this experiment and earlier ones was the separation of the strategy-learning phase, the spatial-learning phase, and the reversal-learning phase into three distinct stages of training. We found that the rats were able to learn the required strategies, then use them to learn the platform location, and then learn another platform location as quickly as controls did, despite the blockade of hippocampal LTP (Hoh, Beiko, Boon, & Cain, 1999).

Taken together, these results indicate that, while hippocampal LTP normally may be engaged during strategy or spatial learning, it is not essential. If LTP plays an important role in learning we would expect some decline in performance when it is blocked. The fact that there was none suggests that either there was complete redundancy between LTP and some other learning mechanism or that LTP plays no role in the learning.

Task difficulty may be an important factor in these studies (Hoh et al., 1999). For example, particularly difficult versions of the water maze task involving a large pool, small hidden platform, the need to learn new platform locations in a single trial, and long delays between training and retention testing yield a performance deficit in nonspatially pretrained rats given an NMDA receptor antagonist (Steele & Morris, 1999), where one did not occur with a less difficult version of the task (Bannerman et al., 1995). In interpreting the results of blockade strategy studies it is crucial to include nonspatially pretrained controls and to take task difficulty into account.

An important variation on the blockade strategy involves gene manipulation to block LTP. Although a complete discussion of this approach is beyond the scope of this chapter, as with the other approaches, there have been mixed results. An early study found that mice with a null mutation of the *fyn* gene had deficient LTP and were impaired in the water maze (Grant et al., 1992). However, later work showed that the swimming of the mutant mice was not normal, and that they floated a large part of the time. The long platform search times that were found in the original study had been interpreted to indicate that the animals were impaired in learning the platform location. However, if the mice were induced to swim by manually stimulating their feet with a thin wooden stick, they swam and learned the platform location as quickly as controls (Huerta, Scearce, Farris, Empson, & Prusky, 1996). Subsequent work has found both impaired (Tsien, Huerta, & Tonegawa, 1996) and normal water maze learning (Meiri, Sun, Segal, & Alkon, 1998; Zamanillo et al., 1999) in mutant mice with hippocampal LTP blocked. Difficulties of interpreting the data from mutant animals and issues of the ethological relevance of the behavioral tasks used are important for this strategy (Gerlai, 1996; Gerlai & Clayton, 1999).

In sum, some studies show that blockade of LTP using drugs or gene manipulation can produce impairments in learning tasks, but it is not clear that the effects are due to specific impairment in an LTP-dependent learning mechanism. Other studies clearly show that animals can learn the tasks when LTP is blocked.

☐ General Conclusions

No definitive conclusion whether LTP subserves any form of learning and memory is available as yet. Results with the correlation strategy show that changes in evoked potentials can occur in some tasks, but there is no evidence that the potentiation involves the same neural mechanisms as laboratory LTP. Strictly speaking, Daniel Alkon is correct in saying that "LTP has never been observed to occur during learning and memory, period" (Russo, 1999). The blockade strategy has produced mixed results, with some studies implicating a causal role for LTP in learning particularly difficult spatial tasks, but others clearly showing that robust learning can occur in the water maze task when LTP is completely blocked. And the saturation strategy has recently provided evidence that LTP is not required for spatial learning.

Additional work needs to be done to determine whether LTP plays a causal role in learning. Crucial controls, such as nonspatially pretrained groups in water maze research, together with sophisticated behavioral analysis, are all-important. Inferring unseen events such as "learning" and "memory" from the behavior of rodents and functionally linking LTP to learning and memory are fraught with difficulty (Cain, 1998; Cain & Saucier, 1996; Gerlai & Clayton, 1999; McEachern & Shaw, 1996; Shors & Matzel, 1997).

For many researchers the idea that LTP has no functional importance is difficult to accept. I am among this group. Since LTP is found in most circuits in the brain and is theoretically interesting, it is worth considering the possibility that it may be involved in functions other than learning. In considering possibilities, it might be useful to compare the time course of potentiation with the time course of behavioral events that LTP might underlie. STP is induced within seconds and decays within minutes; LTP is induced within minutes and decays within hours, days, or weeks. The time course of behavioral or cognitive events that overlap these include attention mechanisms (Shors & Matzel, 1997), changes in emotional state or tone (Cain, 1997), and many others. To date little has been done to evaluate whether LTP is involved in anything other than learning and memory (*but see references for a possible LTP-pathology connection in Shaw & McEachern, Chapter 29 of this volume*). The time seems ripe for this to be done.

☐ References

Barnes, C. A. (1979). Behavioral deficits associated with senescence: A neurophysiological and behavioral study in the rat. *Journal of Comparative and Physiological Psychology, 93*, 74–104.

Bannerman, D. M., Good, M. A., Butcher, S. P., Ramsay, M., & Morris, R. G. M. (1995). Distinct components of spatial learning revealed by prior training and NMDA receptor blockade. *Nature, 378*, 182–186.

Beiko, J., & Cain, D. P. (1998). The effect of water maze spatial training on posterior parietal cortex transcallosal evoked potentials in the rat. *Cerebral Cortex, 8*, 407–414.

Berger, T. W. (1984). Long-term potentiation of hippocampal synaptic transmission affects rate of behavioral learning. *Science, 224*, 627–630.

Bliss, T. V. P., & Collingridge, G. H. (1993). A synaptic model of memory: Long-term potentiation in the hippocampus. *Nature, 361*, 31–39.

Bliss, T. V. P., & Lomo, T. (1973). Long-lasting potentiation of synaptic transmission in the dentate area of the anaesthetized rabbit following stimulation of the perforant path. *Journal of Physiology, 232*, 331–356.

Cain, D. P. (1997). Importance of behavior in LTP research. *Behavioral and Brain Sciences, 20*, 615–616.

Cain, D. P. (1998). Testing the NMDA, long-term potentiation, and cholinergic hypotheses of spatial learning. *Neuroscience & Biobehavioral Reviews, 22*, 181–193.

Cain, D. P., Hargreaves, E. L., Boon, F., & Dennison, Z. (1993). An examination of the relations between hippocampal long-term potentiation, kindling, after discharge, place learning in the water maze. *Hippocampus, 3*, 153–164.

Cain, D. P., Hargreaves, E. L., & Boon, F. (1994). Brain temperature- and behavior-related changes in the dentate gyrus field potential during sleep, cold water immersion, radiant heating, and urethane anesthesia. *Brain Research, 658*, 1235–1244.

Cain, D. P., Saucier, D., Hall, J., Hargreaves, E. L., & Boon, F. (1996). Detailed behavioral analysis of water maze acquisition under APV or CNQX: Contribution of sensorimotor disturbances to drug-induced acquisition deficits. *Behavioral Neuroscience, 110*, 86–102.

Cain, D. P., & Saucier, D. (1996). The neuroscience of spatial navigation: Focus on behavior yields advances. *Reviews in the Neurosciences, 7*, 215–231.

Cain, D. P., Saucier, D., & Boon, F. (1997). Testing hypotheses of spatial learning: The role of NMDA receptors and NMDA-mediated long term potentiation. *Behavioral Brain Research, 84*, 179–193.

Castro, C. A., Silbert, L. H., McNaughton, B. L., & Barnes, C. A. (1989). Recovery of spatial learning deficits after decay of electrically induced synaptic enhancement in the hippocampus. *Nature, 342*, 545–548.

Gerlai, R. (1996). Gene-targeting studies of mammalian behavior: Is it the mutation or the background genotype? *Trends in Neurosciences, 19*, 177–181.

Gerlai, R., & Clayton, N. S. (1999). Analysing hippocampal function in transgenic mice: An ethological perspective. *Trends in Neurosciences, 22*, 47–51.

Grant, S. G. N., O'Dell, T. J., Karl, K. A., Stein, P. L., Soriano, P., & Kandel, E. R. (1992). Impaired long-term potentiation, spatial learning, and hippocampal development in fyn mice. *Science, 258*, 1903–1910.

Hargreaves, E. L., & Cain, D. P. (1992). Hyperactivity, hyper-reactivity, and sensorimotor deficits induced by low doses of the N-methyl-D-aspartate non competitive channel blocker MK-801. *Behavioral Brain Research, 47*, 23–33.

Hargreaves, E. L., Cain, D. P., & Vanderwolf, C. H. (1990). Learning and behavioral-long-term potentiation: Importance of controlling for motor activity. *Journal of Neuroscience, 10*, 1472–1478.

Harris, E. W., & Cotman, C. W. (1986). Long-term potentiation of guinea pig mossy fiber responses is not blocked by N-methyl-D-aspartate antagonists. *Neuroscience Letters, 70*, 132–137.

Hebb, D. O. (1949). *The organization of behavior. A neuropsychological theory.* New York: Wiley.

Hoh, T., Beiko, J., Boon, F., & Cain, D. P. (1999). Complex behavioral strategy and reversal learning in the water maze without NMDA receptor-dependent long-term potentiation. *Journal of Neuroscience, 19*, RC2 1–5.

Huerta, P. T., Scearce, K. A., Farris, S. M., Empson, R. M., & Prusky, G. T. (1996). Preservation of spatial learning in fyn tyrosine kinase knockout mice. *Neuroreport, 7*, 1685–1689.

Jeffery, K. J., & Morris, R. G. M. (1993). Cumulative long-term potentiation in the rat dentate gyrus correlates with, but does not modify, performance in the watermaze. *Hippocampus, 3*, 133–140.

Levy, W. B., & Steward, O. (1979). Synapses as associative memory elements in the hippocampal formation. *Brain Research, 175*, 233–245.

Lomo, T. (1966). Frequency potentiation of excitatory synaptic activity in the dentate area of the hippocampal formation. *Acta Physiologica Scandinavica, 68*, supplement 277, 128.

Lomo, T. (1971). Patterns of activation in a monosynaptic cortical pathway: The perforant path input to the dentate area of the hippocampal formation. *Experimental Brain Research, 12*, 18–45.

McEachern, J. C., & Shaw, C. A. (1996). An alternative to the LTP orthodoxy: A plasticity-pathology continuum model. *Brain Research Reviews, 22*, 51–92.

McKernan, M. G., & Shinnick-Gallagher, P. (1997). Fear conditioning induces a lasting potentiation of synaptic currents in vitro. *Nature, 390*, 607–661.

McNaughton, B. L., Barnes, C. A., & Andersen, P. (1981). Synaptic efficacy and EPSP summation in granule cells of rat fascia dentata studied in vitro. *Journal of Neurophysiology, 46*, 952–966.

McNaughton, B. L., Barnes, C. A., Rao, G., Baldwin, J., & Rasmussen, M. (1986). Long-term enhancement of hippocampal synaptic transmission and the acquisition of spatial information. *Journal of Neuroscience, 6*, 563–571.

Meiri, N., Sun, M. K., Segal, Z., & Alkon, D. L. (1998). Memory and long-term potantiation (LTP) dissociated: Normal spatial memory despite CA1 LTP elimination with Kv1.4 antisense. *Proceedings of the National Academy of Science, 95*, 15037–15042.

Morris, R. G. M. (1989). Synapitic plasticity and learning: Selective impairment of learning in rats and blockade of long-term potentiation in vivo by the N-methyl-D-aspartate receptor blocker AP5. *Journal of Neuroscience, 9*, 3040–3057.

Morris, R. G. M., Anderson, E., Lynch, G. S., & Baudry, M. (1986). Selective impairment of learning and blockade of long-term potentiation by an N-methyl-D-aspartate receptor antagonist, AP5. *Nature, 319*, 774–776.

Morris, R. G. M., & Baker, M. (1984). Does long-term potentiation/synaptic enhancement have anything to do with learning or memory? In L. Squire & N. Butter (Eds.), *Neuropsychology of memory* (pp. 521–535). New York: Guilford.

Morris, R. G. M., & Davis, M. (1994). The role of NMDA receptors in learning and memory. In L. Collingridge & J. C. Watkins (Eds.), *The NMDA receptor* (2nd ed., pp. 340–375). New York: Oxford University Press.

Morris, R. G. M., Garrud, P., Rawlins, J. N. P., & O'Keefe, J. (1982). Place navigation impaired in rats with hippocampal lesions. *Nature, 297*, 681–683.

Moser, E., Krobert, K., Moser, M.-B., & Morris, R. G. M. (1998). Impaired spatial learning after saturation of long-term potentiation. *Science, 281*, 2038–2041.

Moser, E., Mathiesen, J., & Andersen, P. (1993). Association between brain temperature and dentate field potentials in exploring and swimming rats. *Science, 259*, 1324–1326.

Moser, E. I., Moser, M.-B., & Andersen, P. (1994). Potentiation of dentate synapses initiated by exploratory learning in rats: Dissociation from brain temperature, motor activity, and arousal. *Learning & Memory, 1*, 55–73.

Otnaess, M. K., Brun, V. H., Moser, M.-B., & Moser, E. I. (1999) Pretraining prevents spatial learning impairment following saturation of hippocampal long-term potentiation. *Journal of Neuroscience, 19*, RC49.

Racine, R. J., Milgram, N. W., & Hafner, S. (1983). Long-term potentiation phenomena in the rat limbic forebrain. *Brain Research, 260*, 217–231.

Racine, R. J., Wilson, D. A., Gingell, R., & Sunderland, D. (1986). Long-term potentiation in the interpositus and vestibular nuclei in the rat. *Experimental Brain Research, 63*, 158–162.

Rioult-Pedotti, M. -S., Friedman, D., Hess, G., & Donoghue, J. P. (1998) Strengthening of horizontal cortical connections following skill learning. *Nature Neuroscience, 1*, 230–234.

Rioux, G. F., & Robinson, G. B. (1995). Hipppocampal long-term potentiation does not affect either discrimination learning or reversal learning of the rabbit nictitating membrane response. *Hippocampus, 5*, 165–170.

Robinson, G. B. (1992). Maintained saturation of hippocampal long-term potentiation does not disrupt acquisition of the eight-arm radial arm maze. *Hippocampus, 2,* 389–396.

Rogan, M. T., Staubli, U., & LeDoux, J. (1997). Fear conditioning induces associative long-term potentation in the amygdala. *Nature, 390,* 604–607.

Russo, E. (1999). Controversy surrounds memory mechanism. *The Scientist, 13,* 1–6.

Saucier, D., & Cain, D. P. (1995). Spatial learning without NMDA receptor-dependent long-term potentiation. *Nature, 378,* 186–189.

Schwartzkroin, P. A., & Wester, K. (1975). Long-lasting facilitation of a synaptic potential following tetanization in the in vitro hippocampal slice. *Brain Research, 89,* 107–119.

Sharp, P. E., McNaughton, B. L., & Barnes, C. A. (1985). Enhancement of hippocampal field potentials in rats exposed to a novel, complex environment. *Brain Research, 339,* 361–365.

Shors, T. J., & Matzel, L. D. (1997). Long-term potentiation: What's learning got to do with it? *Behavioral and Brain Sciences, 20,* 597–655.

Skelton, R., Scarth, A., Wilkie, D., Miller, J., & Phillips, A. (1987). Long-term increases in dentate granule cell responsivity accompany operant conditioning. *Journal of Neuroscience, 7,* 3081–3087.

Steele, R. J., & Morris, R. G. M. (1999). Delay-dependent impairment of a matching-to-place task with chronic and intrahippocampal infusion of the NMDA antagonist D-AP5. *Hippocampus, 9,* 118–136.

Sutherland, R. J., Kolb, B., & Whishaw, I. Q. (1982). Spatial mapping: Definitive disruption by hippocampal or medial frontal cortical damage in the rat. *Neuroscience Letters, 31,* 271–276.

Trepel, C., & Racine, R. (1998). Long-term potentiation in the neocortex of the adult, freely moving rat. *Cerebral Cortex, 8,* 719–729.

Tsien, J. Z., Huerta, J., & Tonegawa, S. (1996). The esssential role of hippocampal CA1 NMDA receptor-dependent synaptic plasticity in spatial memory. *Cell, 87,* 1327–1338.

Vanderwolf, C. H., Harvey, G. C., & Leung, L.-W. S. (1987). Transcallosal evoked potentials in relation to behavior in the rat: Effects of atropine, p-chlorophenylalanine, reserpine, scopamine and trifluoperazine. *Behavioral Brain Research, 25,* 31–48.

Wilson, D. A., & Racine, R. J. (1983). The postnatal development of post-activation potentiation in the rat neocortex. *Developmental Brain Research, 7,* 271–276.

Xu, L., Anwyl, R., & Rowan, M. J. (1998). Spatial exploration induces a persistent reversal of long-term potentiation in rat hippocampus. *Nature, 394,* 891–894.

Zamanillo, D., Sprengel, R., Hvalby, Ø., Jensen, V., Burnashev, N., Rozov, A., Kaiser, K., Koster, H., Borchardt, T., Worley, P., Lubke, J., Frotscher, M., Kelly, P., Sommer, B., Andersen, P., Seeburg, P., & Sakmann, B. (1999). Importance of AMPA receptors for hippocampal synaptic plasticity but not for spatial learning. *Science, 284,* 1805–1811.

Niraj S. Desai
Sacha B. Nelson
Gina G. Turrigiano

11

CHAPTER

Homeostatic Regulation of Cortical Networks

The sound of neuroplasticity:
One buzzed synapse learns;
Thousands gently homeostase;
Chaos averted.

☐ Introduction

Neural plasticity processes can be classified according to several different schemes. One could, for example, divide them by behavioral context (e.g., development, associative learning, habituation) or by neural mechanism (e.g., plasticity of synaptic weights, connectivity, or intrinsic electrical properties). Which classification scheme is most appropriate depends upon the kinds of questions one is asking. In this chapter the dividing line we choose is between Hebbian (or correlation-based) plasticity and homeostatic plasticity. The former should be familiar to nearly all readers because it is widely believed that Hebbian plasticity mechanisms underlie such functions of the nervous system as the development of neural circuitry and several distinct kinds of learning (Bear & Malenka, 1994; Hebb, 1949; Katz & Shatz, 1996; Stent, 1973). The latter, on the other hand, has only recently emerged as the topic of intensive study; but its potential importance for the nervous system seems evident given the dramatic changes in the number and strength of synaptic connections that can be produced by the Hebbian processes responsible for development and learning. Such changes, if left unchecked, can threaten the stability of neural circuits, suggesting the need for homeostatic regulatory mechanisms aimed at preventing Hebbian processes from disrupting the overall functioning of neural circuits (Bear, 1995; Bienenstock, Cooper, & Munro, 1982; Craig, 1998; Miller, 1996; Turrigiano, 1999).

Much recent work on homeostatic plasticity has been motivated by the need to address two concrete problems of this sort faced by cortical neurons during development and learning. The first problem is the question of how neurons keep their firing rates from saturating or falling silent if the average level of synaptic input rises too high or falls too low. This is an important consideration for cortical neurons because synapses are continually being formed and eliminated during development; sensory input to developing neurons can shift abruptly in response to events such as eye opening; and many putative learning mechanisms, such as long-term potentiation and depression (LTP and LTD), rely upon experience-dependent rules of synaptic modification (Bear & Malenka, 1994; Katz & Shatz, 1996). As a result the synaptic input received by a cortical neuron might vary by orders of magnitude on several different time scales. The second problem is created by the nature of Hebbian rules for synaptic modification. Under these rules correlated firing increases the synaptic strength linking two neurons, while uncorrelated firing has the opposite effect. Such rules have been the most influential model of how information is stored in neural circuits, but they are peculiarly liable to alter synaptic connections in possibly unstable ways because of positive feedback; the strengthening of the synapse between two cells causes the presynaptic cell to drive the postsynaptic one more strongly, this in turn strengthens the synapse even more, which leads to more driving and so on (Miller & MacKay, 1994). Both of these problems may be going on concurrently, and what they have in common is that they suggest the need for homeostatic regulatory mechanisms that can keep neuronal firing rates and synaptic strengths within functional boundaries.

In this chapter we will review evidence that suggests the existence of homeostatic mechanisms that promote stability through activity-dependent modifications of both synaptic strengths and intrinsic neuronal excitability. In the former case, which has been called "synaptic scaling," excitatory and inhibitory currents onto cortical neurons are scaled up or down multiplicatively depending upon the neuron's recent history of activity (Lissin et al., 1998; Ramakers, Kloosterman, Van Hulten, Van Pelt, & Corner, 1998; Turrigiano, Leslie, Desai, Rutherford, & Nelson, 1998); in the latter case, what is modified by activity is the neuron's distribution of intrinsic ionic conductances, which in turn determines spike threshold and firing frequency (Desai, Rutherford, & Turrigiano, 1999a, 1999b). These two mechanisms appear to work in distinct but complementary ways to preserve stability in neuronal circuits subject to the potentially destabilizing side-effects of other plasticity processes, principally those that rely upon correlation-based synaptic modifications. While our emphasis here is on evidence from cultured cortical neurons, it is important to keep in mind that similar processes have been described in quite different preparations (e.g., the neuromuscular junction and the crustacean stomatogastric ganglion), raising the intriguing possibility that a general homeostatic principle is at work in many systems in which learning, memory, and developmental mechanisms tend to threaten stability (Craig, 1998; Davis & Goodman, 1998; O'Brien et al., 1998; Turrigiano, 1999; Turrigiano, Abbott, & Marder, 1994).

☐ Synaptic Scaling

Evidence that homeostatic regulatory mechanisms act, on slow time scales, to keep synaptic strengths within functional boundaries comes from a number of recent studies on cultured mammalian central neurons. In particular, one clear-cut set of experiments involves pyramidal neurons in cultures of rat neocortex (Rutherford, Nelson, & Turrigiano 1998; Turrigiano et al., 1998). Neurons in these cultures form extensive synaptic connections over time, and these in turn produce significant spontaneous activity. Pharmacological manipulations of this activity are found to produce striking changes in both excitatory and inhibitory synaptic transmission. Preventing pyramidal neurons from firing action potentials for two days doubles the quantal amplitude of both

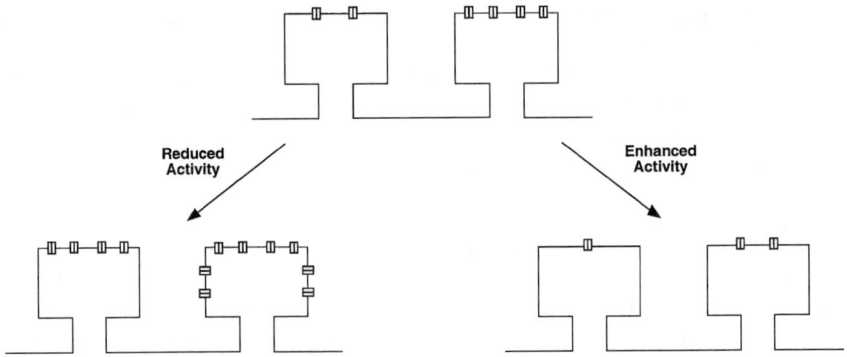

Figure 11.1. Global, multiplicative scaling of synaptic strengths between neocortical pyramidal neurons. Experiments on neurons in neocortical cultures indicate that the quantal amplitudes of excitatory synaptic currents onto pyramidal neurons depend upon their recent history of activity. When average activity is low, excitatory synaptic currents are increased in strength, possibly to move firing rates up to a target or functional range. Conversely, when average activity is high, excitatory synaptic currents are decreased in strength. These changes in synaptic strength appear to be global and multiplicative, as illustrated in the cartoon above. Depicted are two excitatory synapses, one with twice the number of receptors as the other. A prolonged reduction in activity causes the receptor density at each to be increased by a multiplicative factor, but it does not change the ratio of receptors at the two synapses. Similarly, a prolonged increase in activity decreases densities, but again preserves the ratio. Consequently, not only does "synaptic scaling" allow synaptic strengths to be regulated homeostatically in response to changes in activity, but it does so in such a way as to preserve relative differences in strength, such as those produced by learning mechanisms.

AMPA- and NMDA-mediated excitatory postsynaptic currents (EPSCs), whereas increasing neuronal firing above control levels for the same period nearly halves them (Figure 11.1; Turrigiano et al., 1998; Watt, Van Rossum, MacLeod, Nelson, & Turrigiano, 2000). These changes in quantal amplitude translate into corresponding changes in spike-mediated transmission and are likely mediated by postsynaptic changes in receptor number (Watt et al., 1999). By contrast, inhibitory currents are regulated in the other direction: blocking action potentials significantly decreases the size and frequency of inhibitory currents onto pyramidal neurons as well as the GABA content of neuronal cultures (Rutherford, DeWan, Lauer, & Turrigiano, 1997), whereas prolonged depolarization, which is presumably analogous to enhanced activity, increases GABA expression (Ramakers, Van Galen, Feenstra, Corner, & Boer, 1994). Together these data suggest that activity manipulations alter the balance between the excitatory and inhibitory inputs received by pyramidal neurons—in favor of the former when average activity is low, in favor of the latter when it is high.

One particularly striking difference between this homeostatic synaptic regulation and correlation-based synaptic plasticity is that the former appears to be global in its effects, whereas the latter is generally synapse specific or otherwise localized. The global character of homeostatic synaptic plasticity takes on an especially intriguing form: all excitatory synaptic strengths appear to be scaled up or down by the same multiplicative factor (Turrigiano et al., 1998). Multiplicative scaling of synaptic strengths is valuable because it preserves relative differences between inputs, such as those produced by correlation-based modifications, while allowing a neuron to adjust the total amount of excitation it receives (Figure 11.1). This suggests that synaptic scaling, working on a slow time scale (hours), can help preserve stability without interfering with correlation-based learning or development.

Results from other preparations also offer evidence for synaptic scaling's role in the central nervous system, though some of these studies do not agree in detail. The closest agreement with the neocortical findings comes from a study on cultures of spinal neurons, which found that increasing excitatory synaptic activity led to a decrease in the quantal amplitude of AMPA-mediated EPSCs, while decreasing such activity led to an increase (O'Brien et al., 1998). Using quantitative immunohistochemistry to measure internal and surface expression of synaptic AMPA receptors, O'Brien et al. provided a compelling argument that this regulation of synaptic currents was accomplished by regulating the turnover of AMPA receptors. This explanation might serve equally well for the neocortical experiments, as a fluctuation analysis of synaptic currents also identified changes in channel density as the mechanism of synaptic scaling (Watt et al., 1999). The hypothesis is further buttressed by related radioligand binding studies of ionotropic receptors, which suggest that activity manipulations that lead to receptor phosphorylation or dephosphorylation affect receptor sequestration and recycling (Pasqualotto & Shaw, 1996; Shaw, Lanius, & van den Doel, 1994).

Somewhat more ambiguous results have been obtained in hippocampal cultures, though these too have indicated that some kind of synaptic scaling mechanism is at work (Liao, Zhang, O'Brien, Ehlers, & Huganir, 1999; Lissin et al., 1998; Rao & Craig, 1997). Chronic enhancement of network activity by blockade of GABAergic transmission was found in one study to regulate differentially the synaptic surface expression of subtypes of glutamate receptors (Lissin et al., 1998). The number of virally expressed epitope-tagged clusters of the AMPA receptor subunit GluR1 was decreased by the manipulation, while that of tagged clusters of NMDA receptor subunit NR1 was unaltered. This result appears to be at odds with an earlier immunocytochemical study of hippocampal cultures in which activity blockade was found to have no effect on the distribution of GluR1 subunits, but to increase greatly the number of clusters of NMDA receptors (Rao & Craig, 1997). Moreover, both studies do not quite agree with a different immunocytochemical study that found that both AMPA and NMDA receptors could be manipulated by activity: AMPA receptor blockade increased the number of AMPA receptor clusters, while NMDA receptor blockade both increased the number of NMDA receptor clusters and decreased that of AMPA receptor clusters (Liao et al., 1999). The origin of the differences between the three studies is not clear; they may have been caused by differences in the developmental age of the neurons, in the kinds of drugs used, or in a culture parameter like cell density (Craig, 1998; Liao et al., 1999).

Also, it must be noted that some of the immunohistochemical hippocampal results cannot be easily reconciled with the electrophysiological neocortical results cited above (Turrigiano et al., 1998; Watt et al., 2000). Here one must consider the question of what fraction of the receptors visualized by immunostaining methods are in fact functional, as well as differences between the neocortex and the hippocampus. This second point is especially important. While both regions likely require some form of homeostatic synaptic regulation, it is not at all clear that the form should be the same for both, as their patterns of connectivity and the kinds of input they receive are very different. Making sense of these differences is certain to be the subject of much future study, but what can be said is that some mechanism(s) of homeostatic regulation of synaptic strengths is apparently at work in a number of parts of the central nervous system.

☐ Regulation of Intrinsic Excitability

Circuit dynamics are determined by a complex interplay between the synaptic connections between neurons and the intrinsic electrical properties of individual neurons. While plasticity mechanisms that regulate synaptic transmission have received extensive attention, mechanisms that regulate intrinsic properties (such as the action potential threshold or the amount of spike frequency adaptation) have been much less well studied. Despite this imbalance there are very good reasons for examining how experience, in the form of activity, shapes a neuron's intrinsic distribution of ionic conductances: throughout life there is a continual turnover of the channels underlying these conductances, and during development neurons can change size and shape. Moreover, experimental work on both vertebrate and invertebrate preparations has indicated that activity is important in modulating intrinsic neuronal excitability (Franklin, Fickbohm, & Willard, 1992; Li, Jia, Fields, & Nelson, 1996; Linsdell, & Moody, 1995; Moody, 1998a, 1998b; Turrigiano et al., 1994; Turrigiano, LeMasson, & Marder, 1995). This suggests that to achieve and maintain appropriate electrical activity, neurons must continually and selectively adjust not only the strengths of their synaptic connections, but also their intrinsic electrical properties.

Evidence that this is true of neocortical neurons comes from the same cell culture preparation that indicated the existence of synaptic scaling (Desai et al., 1999a, 1999b). Chronic activity blockade for one or two days increased the excitability of neocortical pyramidal neurons substantially. In response to injected current, neurons that had been activity deprived fired more rapidly than did their control counterparts once the activity blockade was lifted, both initially and later on in the spike train; and the slope of the initial part of the f-I curve (constructed by plotting the initial firing frequency versus the current amplitude) for activity-deprived neurons was nearly double that for control neurons (Figure 11.2). Also, the spike threshold was significantly lower: after activity deprivation the average threshold (rheobase) current was nearly halved, while the average threshold potential was decreased by several millivolts. As was true of synaptic scaling, the increase in intrinsic excitability proceeded on a slow time scale: the increase produced by 24 h activity blockade was noticeably smaller than that produced by 48 h blockade.

These effects were not simply the result of changes in passive cell properties, as they were not accompanied by changes in whole cell capacitance, resting input resistance, or resting potential. Instead the increased excitability was accomplished by an activity-dependent regulation of voltage-gated channels (Desai et al., 1999b). Voltage-clamp experiments revealed that 48 h activity blockade increased the density of sodium currents by almost a third, decreased that of persistent potassium currents by more than a third, and left those of calcium and transient potassium currents unchanged. No changes were detected in the voltage dependence of any of these currents, or in their kinetics, suggesting that what was being regulated was the density of each channel type.

This activity-induced regulation of current densities goes on at the same time as developmental changes in current densities, which might lead one to hypothesize that

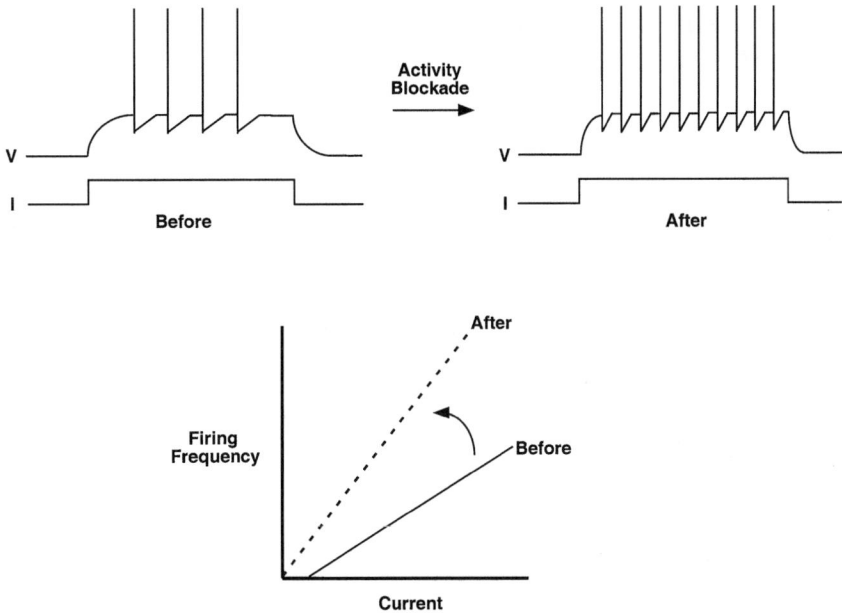

Figure 11.2. Activity-dependent regulation of the intrinsic excitability of neocortical neurons. Neurons in cortical cultures that are deprived of activity for a prolonged period adjust their balance of intrinsic inward and outward currents so as to become more excitable. In response to injected current, activity-deprived neurons fire more quickly (top) and in response to smaller amounts of current. This point may be illustrated most clearly by measuring f-I curves, constructed by plotting firing frequency versus current amplitude (bottom). After activity blockade, such curves are shifted upwards and to the left, indicating both that firing frequencies are higher and that the spike threshold is lower. This change in intrinsic excitability, which is mediated by a differential regulation of sodium and persistent potassium currents, serves as another way of homeostatically regulating network activity, distinct from but complementary to synaptic scaling.

activity's role is to modify the dynamics of a developmental process. But this does not appear to be the case, as activity deprivation has qualitatively different effects on individual currents than development does. In normal cortical development, sodium, sustained potassium, and high-voltage-activated calcium current densities all increase in the early postnatal period, whereas transient potassium current densities decrease (Huguenard, Hamill, & Prince, 1988; Klee, Ficker, & Heinemann, 1995; Moody, 1998a, 1998b; Spigelman, Zhang, & Carlen, 1992; Spitzer, 1991; Tarasenko, Isaev, Eremin, & Kostyuk, 1998; Yaari, Hamon, & Lux, 1987). The rather different changes induced by activity blockade suggest that this process is distinct from developmental processes. On the other hand, the effects of activity blockade on neocortical current densities are broadly consistent with earlier studies on amphibian and nonneocortical mammalian preparations, which showed that blocking activity can increase sodium channel number and mRNA and decrease persistent potassium currents (Brodie, Brody, & Sampson, 1989; Desarmenien & Spitzer, 1991; Linsdell & Moody, 1995; Offord & Catterall, 1989; Tayag, Ge, & Niesen, 1997).

☐ How Are the Synaptic and Intrinsic Processes Linked?

The cortical synaptic and intrinsic plasticity processes described above appear to be complementary: both tend to regulate firing rates homeostatically, making pyramidal neuron firing more likely when average activity is low, and making it less likely when average activity is high. And indeed, direct measurements of firing rates in cortical cultures bear out this idea (Ramakers et al., 1998; Ramakers, Corner, & Habets, 1990; Rutherford et al., 1997; Turrigiano et al., 1998). After chronic activity blockade is lifted, pyramidal neuron firing rates rise dramatically, to as much as ten times control levels; conversely, after pharmacologically induced enhancement of activity is ended, firing rates drop by as much as a factor of 4.

Yet there are important differences between synaptic scaling and the regulation of intrinsic excitability. For example, the increase in intrinsic excitability produced by activity blockade appears to be independent of the identity of the target neuron; inhibitory interneurons are made more excitable by activity blockade, just as pyramidal neurons are, though to a lesser extent (Desai et al., 1999a). By contrast, while activity blockade strengthens excitatory synapses onto pyramidal neurons, it has no effect on excitatory synapses onto interneurons, presumably because one would not wish, in conditions of low activity, to increase the amount of inhibitory drive received by pyramidal neurons (Rutherford et al., 1998). The differences between the two processes may be important because changes in synaptic strengths and changes in intrinsic excitability are unlikely to be functionally equivalent. While synaptic scaling can modify excitation and inhibition independently, a change in the slope of the f-I curve will alter the effectiveness of both excitatory and inhibitory inputs, thus modifying the neuron's sensitivity to all synaptic drive. Consequently it seems likely that the two processes must work conjointly to regulate firing behavior. To do this, there should be some biophysical mechanism that ties them together.

While such a mechanism has yet to be identified and explored, there is substantial reason to believe that, at least for neocortical neurons, it involves the regulation of the neurotrophin brain-derived neurotrophic factor (BDNF; Ramakers et al., 1998; Rutherford et al., 1998). BDNF is released by pyramidal neurons, possibly in an activity-dependent way, and can act on both pyramidal neurons and interneurons by binding to the TrkB receptors that both neuron classes possess (Cabelli et al., 1996; Cellarino, Maffei, & Domenici, 1996; Kokaia et al., 1993; McAllister, Katz, & Lo, 1999; Miranda, Sohrabji, & Toran-Allerand, 1993). In pyramidal neurons, BDNF prevents both the increase in excitatory quantal amplitude and the increase in intrinsic excitability produced by activity blockade (Desai et al., 1999a; Rutherford et al., 1998). Blocking the action of endogenous BDNF, on the other hand, reproduces both of these effects. In interneurons, BDNF increases the strength of excitatory synapses onto these inhibitory cells and prevents the effects of activity blockade both on expression of GABA and on intrinsic excitability (Desai et al., 1999a; Rutherford et al., 1997; Rutherford et al., 1998). Taken together, these results suggest that activity affects synaptic strengths and intrinsic excitability by manipulating the availability of BDNF. A possible scenario for this process is as follows (Figure 11.3): When average activity is low, relatively little BDNF is released; this in turn increases the prevalence of excitation, reduces that of inhibition, and reduces the spike threshold. On the other hand, when average activity is high, relatively more BDNF is released; this then reduces excitation, increases inhibition, and raises the spike threshold.

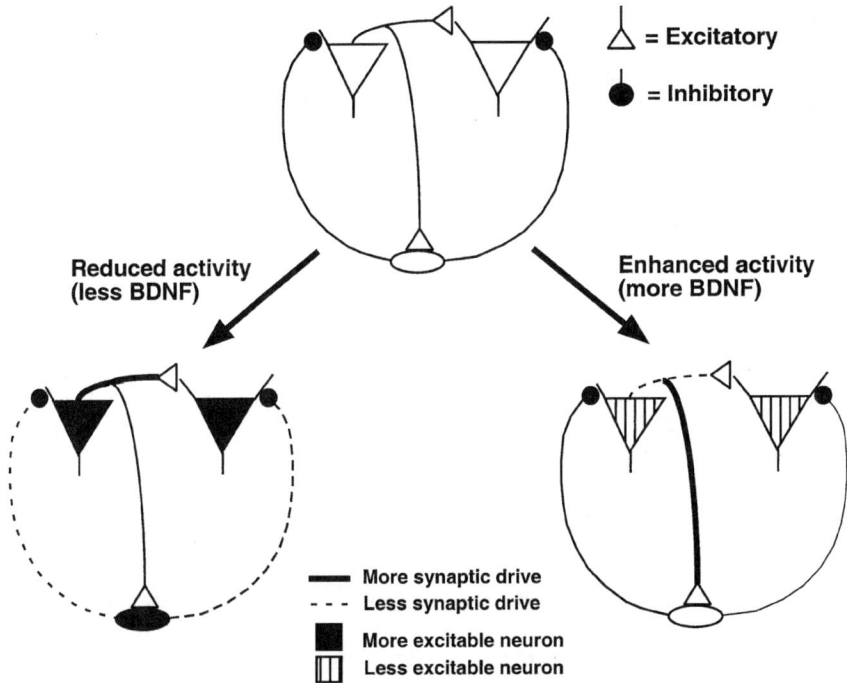

Figure 11.3. Activity- and BDNF-dependent regulation of synaptic and intrinsic properties. It has been hypothesized that BDNF release depends upon pyramidal neuron firing rates. This idea, together with recent cortical experiments on BDNF's effects on synaptic and intrinsic properties, suggests a model of how activity and BDNF interact to regulate cortical activity. Consider a simple network of two excitatory neurons and one inhibitory neuron. (Left) When pyramidal neuron firing rates fall (reduced activity), comparatively less BDNF is released. This causes excitatory connections between pyramidal neurons to increase in strength and reduces inhibition from inhibitory neurons. It also increases the intrinsic excitability of pyramidal neurons to a large extent and that of inhibitory bipolar interneurons to a lesser extent. The net result is an increase in the excitatory drive received by pyramidal neurons, which serves to raise pyramidal firing rates. (Right) When firing rates rise above basal levels (enhanced activity), comparatively more BDNF is released. This strengthens excitatory connections onto inhibitory neurons, thus increasing the feedback inhibition onto pyramidal neurons. It also reduces the intrinsic excitability of pyramidal neurons. Together, these effects tend to lower pyramidal firing rates back to basal levels.

That BDNF might play such a role is not surprising given what in vivo and in vitro experiments have previously revealed about its expression and action in the visual cortex and hippocampus (Bonhoeffer, 1996; Lesser, Sherwood, & Lo, 1997; McAllister et al., 1999; Sherwood, Lesser, & Lo, 1997; Thoenen, 1995). While neurotrophins have traditionally been studied with respect to their constitutive release and long-term trophic functions, recent work has demonstrated that certain neurotrophins can also be expressed in response to physiological activity and can act on time scales fast enough and length scales local enough to affect synaptic efficacy (Berninger & Poo, 1996; Gonzalez &

Collins, 1997; McAllister et al., 1999; Thoenen, 1995; Wetmore, Olson, & Bean, 1994). This is especially true of BDNF. To cite just a few examples, experiments to date have indicated that BDNF affects the activity-dependent development of the visual cortex, the induction of LTP and LTD in both hippocampus and neocortex, and the size and frequency of synaptic currents in cultured neurons (Cabelli, Hohn, & Shatz ,1995; Cabelli, Shelton, Segal, & Shatz, 1997; Castrén, Zafra, Thoenen, & Lindholm, 1992; Kang & Schuman, 1995; Maisonpierre et al., 1990; McAllister et al., 1999). The roles postulated for BDNF are numerous and disparate, and in no case completely understood. But one idea does emerge rather clearly from the experimental evidence: how BDNF acts depends upon the context in which it acts. Specifically, BDNF can have very different effects on different classes of neurons, when acting on short or long time scales, on neurons from young versus old animals, and on synapses that have been recently active or potentiated versus those that have not. This context-dependence makes BDNF an attractive candidate molecule to mediate between different forms of plasticity, though it also suggests that disentangling the different functions of BDNF will be a difficult experimental and theoretical task.

☐ Homeostatic Regulation and Metaplasticity

Synaptic scaling and the homeostatic regulation of intrinsic excitability are not the only possible mechanisms for neural circuits to address the problems posed by large fluctuations in synapse number or strength during development and learning. Indeed a number of alternative proposals have been made (Bienenstock et al., 1982; Miller, 1996; Turrigiano, 1999). One deserves special consideration because it is backed by a significant body of experimental evidence and has elicited substantial attention. This is the idea that the ability of a synapse to undergo Hebbian, or other correlation-based, modifications depends upon its history of use. This idea that the plasticity processes associated with learning and development are themselves plastic has been termed "metaplasticity" and was put in its best-known form by Bienenstock, Cooper, and Munro (BCM; see Bienenstock et al., 1982; see also Abraham & Bear, 1996 and Bear, 1995). In the BCM formulation, one assumes that individual synapses can undergo both potentiation and depression, and whether a synapse is strengthened or weakened by presynaptic activity depends upon whether postsynaptic activity is above or below some threshold. The threshold itself is a function of the average postsynaptic activity, with the average taken over a slow time scale. When postsynaptic activity is high, the threshold slides so as to make depression more likely; when postsynaptic activity is low, the threshold slides in the other direction, making potentiation more likely (Figure 11.4). Clearly activity can be kept homeostatically within bounds in such a scheme, assuming the threshold is an appropriate function of average activity.

The most compelling evidence for the existence of sliding threshold processes comes from experiments on the visual cortex of dark-reared rats (Kirkwood, Rioult, & Bear, 1996). Both LTP and LTD can be induced in this preparation. High-frequency stimulation induces the former, low-frequency stimulation the latter. There is then a frequency threshold between potentiation and depression. The threshold here is explicitly a presynaptic one, not a postsynaptic one, but one can make a connection with the BCM model by assuming that postsynaptic firing tracks presynaptic stimulation closely. Depriving postnatal rat pups of visual stimuli by dark rearing, and presumably thereby reducing activity in the visual cortex, causes this threshold to slide down; that is, LTP becomes

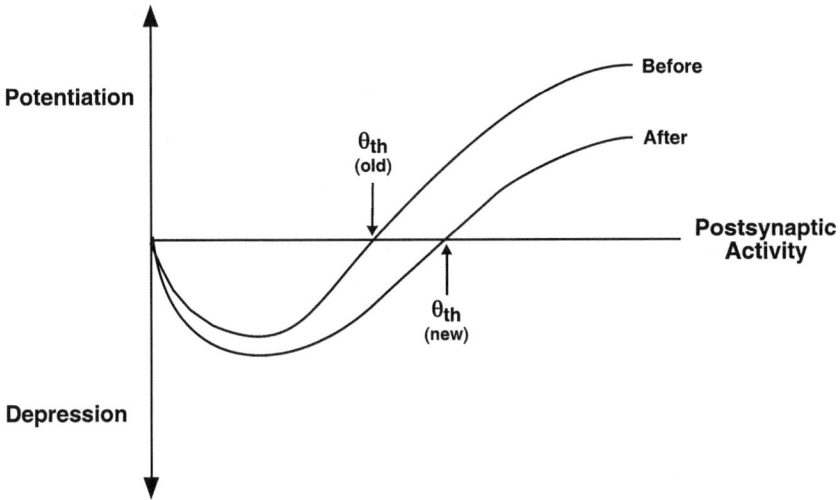

Figure 11.4. The BCM theory of potentiation and depression. An influential model of how network activity is regulated homeostatically is the BCM theory. Here one assumes that individual synapses can undergo both potentiation and depression. The former results when presynaptic input is strong enough to produce postsynaptic activity c above some threshold θ_{th} (that is, $c > \theta_{th}$); the latter results when presynaptic input can only produce postsynaptic activity below the threshold ($c < \theta_{th}$). The threshold itself is a function of average activity, with the average taken over a time scale slow compared to that of potentiation or depression: $\theta_{th} = \theta_{th}(\langle c \rangle)$. This rule can keep cortical activity within bounds. For example, as illustrated above, if activity were to increase above basal levels as a result of much potentiation, the threshold would slide to the right. This would shift the balance in future in favor of depression and against potentiation. Conversely, a depression of synapses that resulted in reduced activity would cause the threshold to shift the other way, making potentiation more likely in future.

easier to induce, LTD harder. How is this change in threshold accomplished? The answer is as yet unknown, but one interesting, if speculative, idea is that it is mediated by the homeostatic synaptic and intrinsic processes discussed above. Scaling all synaptic strengths up should make potentiation easier to induce; scaling them down should do the same for depression. Moving the spike threshold up or down would have similar effects. This compatibility is not itself evidence, but it strongly suggests the need to investigate how synaptic scaling, regulation of intrinsic excitability, and the sliding threshold hypothesis are related, especially given that all three have been shown to occur in the rat visual cortex on the same slow time scale of one or more days.

More broadly, it is important to investigate how homeostatic plasticity processes affect all kinds of correlation-based, synapse-specific plasticity. This is particularly true of synaptic scaling because experiments on neocortical cultures have shown that AMPA and NMDA receptors are coregulated by activity (Watt et al., 2000). Not only do activity blockade and enhancement have the same effects on the densities of the two receptor types, but the regulation appears to be done in such a way that the ratio of AMPA to NMDA receptors is held constant. This fact may have profound implications for correlation-based mechanisms like LTP and LTD, for which calcium influx through NMDA receptors is thought to be crucial (Zucker, 1999). In particular, scaling of NMDA receptors up or down might be the determining factor in whether synapses are strengthened or weakened by a given stimulus. This in turn might mediate the sort of activity-dependent competition between synapses thought important in the fine-tuning of synaptic connections during development (Miller, 1996). Imagine that some inputs are strengthened in response to a stimulus in such a way as to boost overall activity, while others are not. Synaptic scaling would then weaken all synapses, whether active or not, multiplicatively, making depression of the weakest synapses even more likely in the future. If, as has been hypothesized, synaptic weakening is a prelude to synapse elimination, then the weakest synapses might be eliminated altogether at some point (Colman, Nabekura, & Lichtman, 1997; Lo & Poo, 1991). Synaptic scaling then could be said to have promoted competition between synapses, even as it preserved total synaptic strength.

☐ Conclusion

Work from a variety of systems has indicated the existence of homeostatic plasticity mechanisms that serve to counter the potentially destabilizing effects of other kinds of plasticity, particularly those that depend upon correlation-based modifications of synapses. These results have not always agreed in detail, but several broadly defined features can, even now, be seen. The main one is that, on a time scale of hours or days, both synapses and intrinsic excitability are modulated to keep neuronal firing rates within functional boundaries. Prolonged reductions or increases in activity are met with a complex, differentiated response that tends to counter the changes. Because the time scale of these homeostatic effects appears to be much longer than that associated with correlation-based plasticity (e.g., the induction of LTP), the different plasticity processes can coexist in principle, with some involved directly in learning and development and others in maintaining network stability despite learning and development.

At the same time, it is clear that several questions have to be answered before the nature and biological importance of synaptic scaling and the regulation of intrinsic excitability will be known. What is activity? Experiments to date, particularly in the cortex, have not distinguished clearly such features of activity as postsynaptic firing rate or level of synaptic activation, and so it is not clear what is being regulated. How do changes in synaptic and ionic conductances jointly regulate neuronal networks? The varied nature of the homeostatic response, involving synapses among different classes of neurons as well as changes in intrinsic conductances, suggests the need for a biophysical signal that can coordinate the homeostatic response. Considerable evidence suggests that the signal is the neurotrophin BDNF. But the precise mechanism by which BDNF mediates homeostatic plasticity is as yet unknown. Nor is it known whether there are functional differences between synaptic scaling and the regulation of intrinsic excitability. How are these homeostatic responses related to the idea of metaplasticity? Synaptic scaling and excitability regulation should affect not only average activity levels, but also the ability of synapses to be altered by other plasticity mechanisms. Investigating their relation to these other mechanisms, particularly to the "sliding threshold" hypothesis, is important if they are to be understood in context. Finally, what differences exist between in vitro preparations and the intact nervous system? Almost all the relevant results in the cortex have been obtained from culture or slice preparations. Demonstrating homeostatic plasticity in vivo is perhaps the single most important experimental task.

☐ References

Abraham, W. C., & Bear, M. F. (1996). Metaplasticity: The plasticity of synaptic plasticity. *Trends in Neuroscience, 19*, 126–130.

Bear, M. F. (1995). Mechanism for a sliding synaptic modification threshold. *Neuron, 15*, 1–4.

Bear, M. F., & Malenka, R. C. (1994). Synaptic plasticity: LTP and LTD. *Current Opinion in Neurobiology, 4*, 389–399.

Berninger, B., & Poo, M.-M. (1996). Fast actions of neurotrophic factors. *Current Opinion in Neurobiology, 6*, 324–330.

Bienenstock, E. L., Cooper, L. N., & Munro, P. W. (1982). Theory for the development of neuron selectivity: Orientation specificity and binocular interaction in the visual cortex. *Journal of Neuroscience, 2*, 32–48.

Bonhoeffer, T. (1996). Neurotrophins and activity-dependent development of the neocortex. *Current Opinion in Neurobiology, 6*, 119–126.

Brodie, C., Brody, M., & Sampson, S. R. (1989). Characterization of the relation between sodium channels and electrical activity in cultured rat skeletal myotubes: Regulatory aspects. *Brain Research, 488*, 186–194.

Cabelli, R. J., Allendoerfer, K. L., Radeke, M. J., Welcher, A. A., Feinstein, S. C., & Shatz, C. J. (1996). Changing patterns of expression of subcellular localization of TrkB in the developing visual system. *Journal of Neuroscience, 14*, 7965–7980.

Cabelli, R. J., Hohn, A., & Shatz, C. J. (1995). Inhibition of ocular dominance column formation by infusion of NT-4/5 or BDNF. *Science, 267*, 1662–1666.

Cabelli, R. J., Shelton, D. L., Segal, R. A., & Shatz, C. J. (1997). Blockade of endogenous ligands of TrkB inhibits formation of ocular dominance columns. *Neuron, 19*, 63–76.

Castrén, E., Zafra, F., Thoenen, H., & Lindholm, D. (1992). Light regulates expression of brain-derived neurotrophic factor mRNA in rat visual cortex. *Proceedings of the National Academy of Science of the United States of America, 89*, 9444–9448.

Cellarino, A., Maffei, L., & Domenici, L. (1996). The distribution of brain-derived neurotrophic factor and its receptor TrkB in parvalbumin-containing neurons of the rat visual cortex. *European Journal of Neuroscience, 8*, 1190–1197.

Colman, H., Nabekura, J., & Lichtman, J. W. (1997). Alterations in synaptic strength preceding axon withdrawal. *Science, 275*, 356–361.

Craig, A. M. (1998). Activity and synaptic receptor targeting: The long view. *Neuron, 21*, 459–462.

Davis, G. W., & Goodman, C. S. (1998). Synapse-specific control of synaptic efficacy at the terminals of a single neurons. *Nature, 392*, 82–86.

Desai, N. S., Rutherford, L. C., & Turrigiano, G. G. (1999a). BDNF regulates the intrinsic excitability of cortical neurons. *Learning & Memory, 6*, 284–291.

Desai, N. S., Rutherford, L. C., & Turrigiano, G. G. (1999b). Plasticity in the intrinsic excitability of cortical pyramidal neurons. *Nature Neuroscience, 2*, 515–520.

Desarmenien, M. G., & Spitzer, N. C. (1991). Role of calcium and protein kinase C in development of the delayed rectifier potassium current in *Xenopus* spinal neurons. *Neuron, 7*, 797–805.

Franklin, J. L., Fickbohm, D. J., & Willard, A. L. (1992). Long-term regulation of neuronal calcium currents by prolonged changes of membrane potential. *Journal of Neuroscience, 12*, 1726–1735.

Gonzalez, M., & Collins, W. F., III. (1997). Modulation of motoneuron excitability by brain-derived neurotrophic factor. *Journal of Neurophysiology, 77*, 502–506.

Hebb, D. O. (1949). *The organization of behavior: A neurophysiological theory*. New York: Wiley.

Huguenard, J. R., Hamill, O. P., & Prince, D. A. (1988). Developmental changes in Na^+ conductances in rat neocortical neurons: Appearance of a slowly inactivating component. *Journal of Neurophysiology, 59*, 778–795.

Kang, H., & Schuman, E. M. (1995). Long-lasting neurotrophin-induced enhancement of synaptic transmission in the adult hippocampus. *Science, 267*, 1658–1662.

Katz, L. C., & Shatz, C. J. (1996). Synaptic activity and the construction of cortical circuits. *Science, 274*, 1133–1138.

Kirkwood, A., Rioult, M. C., & Bear, M. F. (1996). Experience-dependent modification of synaptic plasticity in visual cortex. *Nature, 381*, 526–528.

Klee, R., Ficker, E., & Heinemann, U. (1995). Comparison of voltage-dependent potassium currents in rat pyramidal neurons acutely isolated from hippocampal regions CA1 and CA3. *Journal of Neurophysiology, 74*, 1982–1995.

Kokaia, Z., Bengzon, J., Metsis, M., Kokaia, M., Persson, H., & Lindvall, O. (1993). Coexpression of neurotrophins and their receptors in neurons of the central nervous system. *Proceedings of the National Academy of Sciences of the United States of America, 90*, 6711–6715.

Lesser, S. S., Sherwood, N. T., & Lo, D. C. (1997). Neurotrophins differentially regulate voltage-gated ion channels. *Molecular and Cellular Neurosciences, 10*, 173–183.

Li, M., Jia, M., Fields, R. D., & Nelson, P. G. (1996). Modulation of calcium currents by electrical activity. *Journal of Neurophysiology, 76*, 2595–2607.

Liao, D., Zhang, X., O'Brien, R. O., Ehlers, M. D., & Huganir, R. L. (1999). Regulation of morphological postsynaptic silent synapses in developing hippocampal neurons. *Nature Neuroscience, 2*, 37–43.

Linsdell, P., & Moody, W. J. (1995). Electrical activity and calcium influx regulate ion channel development in embryonic *Xenopus* skeletal muscle. *Journal of Neuroscience, 15*, 4507–4514.

Lissin, D. V., Gomperts, S. N., Carroll, R. C., Christine, C. W., Kalman, D., Kitamura, M., Hardy, S., Nicoll, R. A., Malenka, R. C., & von Zastrow, M. (1998). Activity differentially regulates the surface expression of AMPA and NMDA glutamate receptors. *Proceedings of the National Academy of Sciences of the United States of America, 95*, 7097–7102.

Lo, Y.-J., & Poo, M.-M. (1991). Activity-dependent synaptic competition in vitro: Heterosynaptic suppression of developing synapses. *Science, 254*, 1019–1020.

Maisonpierre, P. C., Belluscio, L., Friedman, B., Alderson, R. F., Wiegand, S. J., Furth, M. E., Lindsay, R. M., & Yancopoulos, G. D. (1990). NT-3, BDNF, and NGF in the developing rat nervous system. *Neuron, 5*, 501–509.

McAllister, A. K., Katz, L. C., & Lo, D. C. (1999). Neurotrophins and synaptic plasticity. *Annual Review of Neuroscience, 22*, 295–318.

Miller, K. D. (1996). Synaptic economics: Competition and cooperation in synaptic plasticity. *Neuron, 17*, 371–374.

Miller, K. D., & MacKay, J. D. C. (1994). The role of constraints in Hebbian learning. *Neural Computation, 6*, 100–126.

Miranda, R. C., Sohrabji, F., & Toran-Allerand, C. D. (1993). Neuronal colocalization of mRNAs for neurotrophins and their receptors in the developing central nervous system suggests a potential for autocrine interactions. *Proceedings of the National Academy of Sciences of the United States of America, 90*, 6439–6443.

Moody, W. J. (1998a). Control of spontaneous activity during development. *Journal of Neurobiology, 37*, 97–109.

Moody, W. J. (1998b). The development of voltage-gated ion channels and its relation to activity-dependent developmental events. *Current Topics in Developmental Biology, 39*, 159–185.

O'Brien, R. J., Kamboj, S., Ehlers, M. D., Rosen, K. R., Fischbach, G. D., & Huganir, R. L. (1998). Activity-dependent modulation of synaptic AMPA receptor accumulation. *Neuron, 21*, 1067–1078.

Offord, J., & Catterall, W. A. (1989). Electrical activity, cAMP, and cytosolic calcium regulate mRNA encoding sodium channel α subunits in rat muscle cells. *Neuron, 2*, 1447–1452.

Pasqualotto, B. A., & Shaw, C. A. (1996). Regulation of ionotropic receptors by protein phosphorylation. *Biochemical Pharmacology, 51*, 1417–1425.

Ramakers, G. J. A., Corner, M. A., & Habets, A. M. (1990). Development in the absence of spontaneous bioelectric activity results in increased stereotypic burst firing in cultures of dissociated cerebral cortex. *Experimental Brain Research, 79*, 157–166.

Ramakers, G. J. A., Kloosterman, F., Van Hulten, P., van Pelt, J., & Corner, M. A. (1998). Activity-dependent regulation of neuronal network excitability. In V. Torre & J. Nicholls (Eds.), *Neural circuits and networks* (pp. 41–47). New York: Springer-Verlag.

Ramakers, G. J. A., Van Galen, H., Feenstra, M. G., Corner, M. A., & Boer, G. J. (1994). Activity-dependent plasticity of inhibitory and excitatory amino acid transmitter systems in cultured rat cerebral cortex. *International Journal of Developmental Neuroscience, 12,* 611–621.

Rao, A., & Craig, A. M. (1997). Activity regulates the synaptic localization of the NMDA receptor in hippocampal neurons. *Neuron, 19,* 801–812.

Rutherford, L. C., DeWan, A., Lauer, H. M., & Turrigiano, G. G. (1997). BDNF mediates the activity-dependent regulation of inhibition in neocortical cultures. *Journal of Neuroscience, 17,* 4527–4535.

Rutherford, L. C., Nelson, S. B., & Turrigiano, G. G. (1998). BDNF has opposite effects on the quantal amplitude of pyramidal neuron and interneuron excitatory synapses. *Neuron, 21,* 521–530.

Shaw, C. A., Lanius R. A., & van den Doel, K. (1994). The origin of synaptic neuroplasticity: Crucial molecules or a dynamical cascade? *Brain Research Review, 19,* 241–263.

Sherwood, N. T., Lesser, S. S., & Lo, D. C. (1997). Neurotrophin regulation of ionic currents and cell size depends on cell context. *Proceedings of the National Academy of Sciences of the United States of America, 94,* 5917–5922.

Spigelman, I., Zhang, L., & Carlen, P. L. (1992). Patch-clamp study of postnatal development of CA1 neurons in rat hippocampal slices: Membrane excitability and K^+ currents. *Journal of Neurophysiology, 68,* 55–69.

Spitzer, N. C. (1991). A developmental handshake: Neuronal control of ionic currents and their control of differentiation. *Journal of Neurobiology, 22,* 659–673.

Stent, G. S. (1973). A physiological mechanism for Hebb's postulate of learning. *Proceedings of the National Academy of Sciences of the United States of America, 70,* 997–1001.

Tarasenko, A. N., Isaev, D. S., Eremin, A. V., & Kostyuk, P. G. (1998). Developmental changes in the expression of low-voltage-activated Ca^{2+} channels in rat visual cortical neurones. *Journal of Physiology, 509,* 385–394 (1998).

Tayag, E. C., Ge, S., & Niesen, C. E. (1997). *Society for Neuroscience Abstracts, 23,* 1740.

Thoenen, H. (1995). Neurotrophins and neuronal plasticity. *Science, 270,* 593–598.

Turrigiano, G. G. (1999). Homeostatic plasticity in neuronal networks: The more things change, the more they remain the same. *Trends in Neuroscience, 22,* 221–227.

Turrigiano, G. G., Abbott, L. F., & Marder, E. (1994). Activity-dependent changes in the intrinsic properties of cultured neurons. *Science, 264,* 974–977.

Turrigiano, G. G., Leslie, K. R., Desai, N. S., Rutherford, L. C., & Nelson, S. B. (1998). Activity-dependent scaling of quantal amplitude in neocortical neurons. *Nature, 391,* 892–896.

Turrigiano, G. G., LeMasson, G., & Marder, E. (1995). Selective regulation of current densities underlies spontaneous changes in the activity of cultured neurons. *Journal of Neuroscience, 15,* 3640–3652.

Watt, A. J., Van Rossum, M. C. W., MacLeod, K. M., Nelson, S. B., & Turrigiano, G. G. (2000). Activity co-regulates quantal AMPA and NMDA currents at neocortical synapses. *Neuron, 26,* 659–670.

Wetmore, C., Olson, L., & Bean, A. J. (1994). Regulation of brain-derived neurotrophic factor (BDNF) expression and release from hippocampal neurons is mediated by non-NMDA type glutamate receptors. *Journal of Neuroscience, 14,* 1688–1700.

Yaari, Y., Hamon, B., & Lux, H. D. (1987). Development of two types of calcium channels in cultured mammalian hippocampal neurons. *Science, 235,* 680–682.

Zucker, R. S. (1999). Calcium- and activity-dependent synaptic plasticity. *Current Opinion in Neurobiology, 9,* 305–313.

MOLECULAR AND GENETIC DETERMINANTS OF NEUROPLASTICITY

12
CHAPTER

Lidong Liu
Yu Tian Wang

Regulation of Postsynaptic Receptor Trafficking: A Novel Means of Generating Synaptic Plasticity

Neuroplasticity is often referred to as the ability of the nervous system to undergo adaptive functional and morphological modifications in response to internal and/or external environmental changes. Neuroplasticity can occur in all species and may be expressed in a variety of forms depending upon the systems studied. Synaptic plasticity (i.e., changes in the strength or efficacy of synaptic transmission), one of many forms of neuroplasticity, has attracted a great deal of attention because of its potential role in the development of neural circuitry, learning, and memory, as well as a number of neuropathologies (Chen & Tonegawa, 1997; Klintsova & Greenough, 1999; Nicoll & Malenka, 1995). While several different forms of synaptic plasticity have been found throughout the mammalian central nervous system (CNS) during the past several decades (Chen & Tonegawa, 1997; Frey & Morris, 1998; Klintsova & Greenough, 1999; McBain & Maccaferri, 1997), the most extensively studied examples are the long-term changes in synaptic efficacy observed at the glutamatergic synapses of the CA1 region of the hippocampus (Malinow & Mainen 1996; Zhuo & Hawkins 1995). Within these synapses high-frequency stimulation has been shown to induce a long-term potentiation (LTP) of synaptic transmission, while a prolonged low-frequency-stimulation (LFS) often causes a long-term depression (LTD). As both LTP and LTD are considered prime candidates for cellular mechanisms for learning and memory (Bliss & Collingridge 1993; Fujii et al. 1996; Lisman, 1997), understanding mechanisms mediating these forms of synaptic plasticity has been one of the most intensively studied topics in the field of neuroscience (Bliss & Collingridge, 1993; Malenka & Nicoll, 1999; McBain & Maccaferri, 1997).

Fast glutamatergic synaptic transmission in the mammalian CNS is primarily mediated by ligand-gated glutamate receptors. Based on their sequence homologies and electrophysiological and pharmacological properties, these receptors can be divided into three major families: AMPA (α-amino-3-hydroxyl-5-methyl-4-isoxazolepropionic acid) receptors, which comprise various combinations of glutamate receptor subunits GluR1-4; kainate receptors, which consist of the GluR5-7 and KA1 and 2 subunits; and the NMDA (*N*-methyl-D-aspartate) receptors, which contain NR1 and NR2A-D (Bettler & Mulle, 1995; Hollmann & Heinemann, 1994). In most CNS excitatory synapses studied thus far, including the hippocampal CA1 synapse, normal excitatory postsynaptic currents (EPSCs) have been shown to contain two pharmacologically distinct components: an AMPA receptor–mediated fast component and an NMDA receptor–mediated slow component (Hestrin, Sah, & Nicoll, 1990; Hollmann & Heinemann, 1994). However, much slower EPSCs evoked by high-frequency stimulation in hippocampal CA3 cells have recently been shown to be mediated by kainate receptors (Castillo, Malenka, & Nicoll, 1997; Bortolotto et al., 1999).

While it is generally accepted that the induction of both LTP and LTD at the CA1 synapse is dependent upon postsynaptic Ca^{2+} influx through activated NMDA receptors, the mechanisms underlying their expression remain heavily debated. In all likelihood, both a presynaptic component (operating via the alteration of transmitter release) and a postsynaptic component (operating through the modification of AMPA receptors by changing the receptor channel gatings or numbers), are involved (Bolshakov, Golan, Kandel, & Siegelbaum, 1997; Malenka & Nicoll, 1999; Malinow, 1998; Stevens & Wang, 1993). The "silent synapse" is an attractive hypothesis that has recently been proposed to explain the postsynaptic locus of expression and that has gained considerable experimental support (Durand, Kovalchuk, & Konnerth, 1996; Kullman & Asztely, 1998; Shi et al., 1999; Malenka & Nicoll, 1997, 1999). According to this hypothesis, synapses have two states: active and silent (Malenka & Nicoll, 1999; Voronin, Volgushev, Chistiakova, Kuhnt, & Singer, 1996). A silent synapse contains functional NMDA receptors, but lacks functional AMPA receptors, and because NMDA receptors are inactive at normal resting potentials due to voltage-dependent Mg^{2+} blockade, these synapses are functionally nontransmitting. These synapses are activated during the induction of LTP by the recruitment of functional postsynaptic AMPA receptors (Durand et al., 1996; Liao, Hessler, & Malinow, 1995). By extrapolation, an active synapse may be silenced during LTD by a selective loss of functional AMPA receptors (Carroll, Lissin, von Zastrow, Nicoll, & Malenka, 1999; Voronin et al., 1996). Thus, a simple and unified mechanism involving either rapid addition or removal of functional AMPA receptors from the postsynaptic domain could underlie both LTP and LTD. One key question that remains to be resolved is how the number of postsynaptic AMPA receptors can be rapidly regulated, or in other words, how the synapses are switched between the two states during LTP/LTD.

Most integral plasma membrane proteins are constitutively trafficked between the plasma membrane and the intracellular compartments via vesicle-mediated membrane fusion (insertion) and endocytosis (internalization). Regulation of these processes has been shown to be an important means of controlling the cell-surface expression and function of these proteins (Chu, Murray, Lissin, & von Zastrow, 1997; Karoor, Wang, Wang, & Malbon, 1998; Pessin, Thurmond, Elmendorf, Coker, & Okada, 1999). By analogy, it is not unreasonable to speculate that plasma membrane expression of AMPA receptors is also subject to similar modes of regulation, and the regulation of plasma membrane insertion and removal of AMPA receptors could therefore be an attractive mechanism for switching synapses between states, thereby influencing expression of LTP and LTD. Indeed, evidence is emerging to support a critical role for facilitated postsynaptic membrane insertion and internalization of AMPA receptors in these forms of synaptic plasticity. Evidence for rapid translocation of postsynaptic AMPA receptors in influencing LTP/LTD expression has appeared in several recent reviews (Morales & Goda, 1999; Malenka & Nicoll, 1999) and will therefore not be the main subject of the present review. Rather, this chapter will focus on our current understanding of the mechanisms mediating vesicle-mediated rapid recruitment and/or removal of AMPA receptors, and their potential roles in LTP/LTD expression.

☐ Intracellular Trafficking of Integral Plasma Membrane Proteins

As illustrated in Figure 12.1, most integral plasma membrane proteins are trafficked between the plasma membrane and the intracellular compartments via vesicle-mediated membrane fusion (insertion) and endocytosis (internalization). The insertion of plasma membrane proteins into the plasma membrane surface is thought to be mediated primarily through vesicle-mediated protein transport which consists of several common steps (Schekman & Orci, 1996; Sudhof, 1995). Vesicles loaded with specific cargoes are formed at the level of the endoplasmic reticulum (ER) and Golgi body through complex coat protein-mediated membrane budding and fusion steps (Schekman & Orci, 1996). After release from the Golgi, the secretory vesicles are trafficked to the plasma

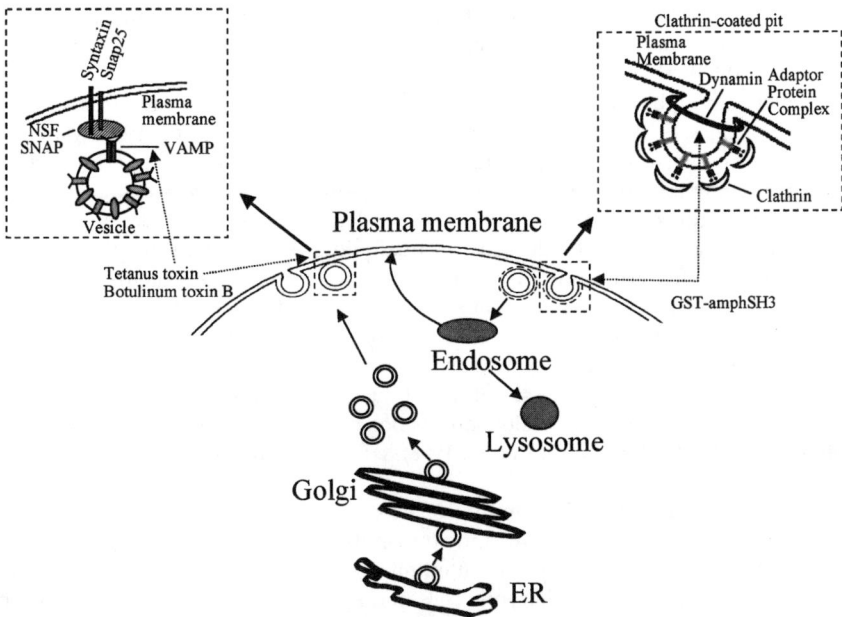

Figure 12.1. Hypothetical steps in vesicle-mediated trafficking of plasma membrane proteins. Tetanus toxin and botulinum toxins can specifically block the vesicle-mediated protein insertion by destroying proteins required in the membrane fusion step, and the GST-amphSH3 domain can selectively inhibit clathrin-mediated protein endocytosis by disrupting the recruitment of dynamin to the clathrin-coated pits.

membrane target, presumably through interactions with microtubules and microtubule-based motor proteins (Vallee & Sheetz, 1996). Following this, the secretory vesicles fuse with the plasma membrane, a process mediated by specific binding between proteins on the vesicle membrane with proteins on the targeted membrane, and cytosolic proteins such as N-ethylmaleimide-sensitive factor (NSF) and soluble NSF-attachment proteins (SNAPs) (Rothman, 1994; Sollner & Rothman, 1994). The proteins are inserted into the plasma membrane, where they remain and exert their biological influence until they are removed by the opposing process, endocytosis.

Most, but not all, plasma membrane proteins are removed by clathrin-mediated endocytosis, which involves clathrin and several associated clathrin adaptor protein complexes. The major function of clathrin in plasma membrane protein endocytosis is to provide the driving force for membrane deformation, thereby forming coated vesicles. The adaptor complexes recruit and concentrate the cargo proteins on the coated vesicles by binding with both the cargo proteins and clathrin (Goodman et al., 1998; Schmid, 1997). Although the detailed mechanisms involved may vary depending upon the specific cargo proteins being internalized, clathrin-mediated endocytosis involves a number of common steps. First, clathrin is recruited to the plasma membrane and linked to the receptors by adaptor proteins. While most G protein-coupled receptors employ a family of monomeric adaptor proteins known as β-arrestins (Ferguson, Zhang, Barak, & Caron, 1998; Goodman et al., 1998), most other plasma membrane receptors, including growth factor receptors, seem to be recruited to clathrin-coated pits by the adaptor protein AP2 (Schmid, 1997). The binding of adaptor proteins to receptors and to clathrin initiates clathrin-coat assembly, and membrane invagination is a process that can be inhibited by hypertonic sucrose (Hansen, Sandvig, & van Deurs, 1993). Vesicles then "pinch off" via a dynamin GTPase-dependent process, which can be blocked either by dominant negative dynamin mutants (Damke, Baba, Warnock, & Schmid, 1994; Herskovits, Burgess, Obar, & Vallee, 1993; Man et al, in press) or by interfering with amphiphysin recruitment of dynamin to the clathrin-coated pits using an amphiphysin SH3 domain peptide (Herskovits et al., 1993; Man et al., 2000; Shupliakov et al., 1997; Wang & Linden, 2000). The product of these processes is a clathrin-coated vesicle which is finally internalized from the plasma membrane surface to the intracellular compartment. The internalized proteins are then either recycled back to the plasma membrane or delivered to lysosomes for degradation (Bonifacino, Marks, Ohno, & Kirchhausen, 1996; Mellman, 1996; Schmid, 1997). With time it is becoming clear that both plasma membrane insertion and internalization of proteins are regulated processes and that such regulation is an important means of controlling cell-surface expression, and hence function, of these plasma membrane proteins (Chu et al., 1997; Karoor et al., 1998; Krupnick & Benovic, 1998; Pessin et al., 1999).

Although our current understanding of exocytosis and endocytosis has been derived largely from studies of presynaptic transmitter release, hormonal secretion, and various other receptor or transporter internalization, evidence is emerging that these processes are ubiquitous in eukaryotic cells and applicable to most, if not all, plasma membrane proteins (Schekman & Orci, 1996; Sudhof, 1995). As briefly reviewed below, evidence is accumulating to suggest that ligand-gated neurotransmitter receptors in the CNS, the AMPA receptors in particular, seem to be subjected to similar intracellular trafficking processes, and that regulating trafficking and plasma membrane expression of these receptors at the postsynaptic domain is an efficient means of both controlling synaptic efficacy and influencing the postsynaptic expression of LTP and LTD.

☐ Clathrin-Mediated AMPA Receptor Endocytosis and Its Role in LTD

Native AMPA receptors are largely assembled from heteromeric combinations of GluR1-4 (Hollmann & Heinemann, 1994). However, when expressed in mammalian cells, individual GluR subunits can form functional homomeric AMPA channels (Burnashev, Villarroel, & Sakmann, 1996). To study AMPA receptor surface expression, we inserted the hemagglutinin (HA) epitope in the N-terminal extracellular domains of GluR1 and GluR2 cDNAs. After transient transfection of these constructs into human embryonic kidney (HEK) 293 cells, we were able to use antibodies against the HA epitope to selectively visualize the trafficking of AMPA receptors expressed on the plasma membrane surface in live cells, and we found that both GluR1 and GluR2 receptors undergo constitutive endocytosis (Man et al., 2000). Several lines of evidence indicate that AMPA receptor endocytosis, like that of other plasma membrane receptors, is mediated by a clathrin-dependent mechanism. First, the endocytosed AMPA receptors are largely co-localized with EPS-15, an integral component protein of clathrin-coated pits (van Delft, Schumacher, Hage, Verkleij, & Bergen en Henegouwen, 1997), which suggests the presence of endocytosed AMPA receptors in clathrin-coated pits. Second, AMPA receptor endocytosis can be completely blocked by hypertonic sucrose treatment, consistent with the effect observed in clathrin-coat assembly in receptor endocytosis. One hallmark of clathrin-mediated receptor endocytosis is the requirement of dynamin GTPase activity (Schmid, 1997). We have found AMPA receptor endocytosis to be prevented by the transient co-expression of the dominant negative dynamin mutant, but not its wild-type counterpart, which strongly suggests endocytosis through a clathrin-dependent mechanism. Finally, AMPA receptors were specifically co-immunoprecipitated from brain homogenate with AP-2 clathrin adaptor proteins (Man et al., 2000). This result is of particular interest because, as the vesicle coating/uncoating process is rapid and under dynamic regulation, receptor-adaptor interactions have not always been observed, only demonstrated using co-immunoprecipitation in the few cases where high-affinity binding between the two partners may be involved (Vincent, Goffin, Rozakis-Adcock, Mornon, & Kelly, 1997; Kamiguchi et al., 1998). Thus, the co-immunoprecipitation of the AP-2 complex with the AMPA receptors may reflect a high-affinity interaction between the receptor and the AP-2 complex, thereby suggesting the involvement of this adaptor complex in clathrin-mediated AMPA receptor endocytosis. However, it should be noted that this internalization via the AP-2 adaptor does not exclude the possible involvement of other adaptor proteins such as β-arrestin and/or EPS-15 in the clathrin-mediated endocytosis.

In addition to constitutive endocytosis, there also appears to be a distinct regulated pathway for AMPA receptor endocytosis. We revealed this pathway by treating HEK cells expressing recombinant AMPA receptors with insulin, a hormone which is highly expressed in the CNS and known to be capable of regulating the cell-surface expression, and hence the function, of various plasma membrane proteins including ion channels and neurotransmitter receptors (Pessin et al., 1999; Kanzaki et al., 1999; Karoor et al., 1998). A 10-min insulin stimulation produced a dramatic enhancement of the rate and extent of GluR2, but not GluR1, receptor endocytosis (Man et al., 2000). Similar to the constitutive pathway, this insulin-stimulated one is also mediated by a clathrin-dependent mechanism as suggested by its blockade by hypertonic sucrose treatment and overexpression of dominant negative dynamin. However, there are several features associated with the regulated endocytosis that distinguish it from constitutive endocytosis. First, the facilitated endocytosis by insulin is capable of decreasing the number of AMPA receptors expressed on the plasma membrane surface. This indicates that insulin may be able to selectively facilitate the receptor endocytosis pathway without affecting receptor insertion, thereby resetting a new balance between receptor endocytosis and insertion that would maintain a lower number of cell-surface AMPA receptors. Consistent with this notion, we found that the reduction of cell-surface AMPA receptor expression by insulin could be completely prevented by overexpression of dominant negative dynamin, a manipulation that has previously been shown to affect the clathrin-mediated pathway without affecting vesicle-mediated membrane insertion (Damke et al., 1994). The regulated endocytosis is additionally long-lasting, and once initiated, the receptor removal can be maintained at the facilitated rate for more than 1 h following the wash-out of insulin. These results suggest that insulin functions as a trigger and is required for the initiation, but not the maintenance, of the regulated endocytosis. This feature, in conjunction with its ability to rapidly reduce cell-surface AMPA receptors, makes regulated endocytosis a very attractive mechanism for influencing synaptic plasticity in models such as LTD. Indeed, a similar mechanism appears to be critical in different forms of LTD (Man et al., 2000; Wang & Lindon, 2000; see below).

Finally, insulin-regulated endocytosis, unlike the constitutive pathway, is not shared across GluR receptor subunits, but is a GluR2-specific phenomenon. The GluR2 specificity is apparently mediated by unique sequences present in its carboxyl intracellular tail, which was demonstrated by exchanging its tail with that of GluR1 subunits (Man et al., 2000). In this regard, it is noteworthy that a number of intracellular proteins have recently been identified as AMPA receptor–interacting proteins, and that the majority of these proteins bind specifically to the GluR2 cytoplasmic tail (Nishimune et al., 1998; Osten et al., 1998; Song et al., 1998; Srivastava et al., 1998; Wyszynski, Kim, Yang, & Sheng, 1998; Xia, Zhang, Staudinger, & Huganir, 1999). Although the possible functions of these AMPA receptor–interacting proteins remain elusive, they may regulate endocytosis or other aspects of AMPA receptor vesicle trafficking via their binding to the GluR2 carboxy tail and thereby play an important role in controlling the AMPA receptor density in the postsynaptic membrane and thus the efficacy of synaptic transmission (Li et al., 1999; Lüthi et al., 1999; Noel et al., 1999).

Based upon the above-reviewed results there appear to exist two distinct clathrin-mediated endocytotic pathways involved in the removal of AMPA receptors from the cell surface. The constitutive endocytosis pathway may be a common mechanism shared by all GluRs, and its major function would be to counteract the constitutive receptor insertion pathway, thereby ensuring that a constant number of AMPA receptors are expressed on the cell surface. In contrast, the regulated pathway is GluR2 specific and rapidly regulates the cell-surface expression of AMPA receptors. Therefore, this pathway may play an important role in certain forms of GluR2-containing AMPA receptor–mediated synaptic plasticity.

Do these two forms of clathrin-mediated AMPA receptors occur in real neurons and are they therefore physiologically relevant? Using an "antibody feeding method" we (Man et al., 2000) and others (Carroll, Beattie et al., 1999) found that native AMPA receptors in cultured hippocampal neurons also undergo similar clathrin-mediated constitutive endocytosis. As we observed in GluR2 expressing HEK cells, a short period of insulin stimulation was also found to produce a dramatic enhancement of the AMPA receptor endocytosis in these neurons (Man et al., 2000). Both insulin and insulin receptors are expressed in discrete regions throughout the brain and localized in synapses (Baron-Van, Olichon-Berthe, Kowalski, Visciano, & Van, 1991; Abbott, Wells, & Fallon,

1999; Dore, Kar, Rowe, & Quirion, 1997). By stimulating the clathrin-dependent endocytosis of postsynaptic AMPA receptors, insulin has the potential to modulate the efficacy of synaptic transmission, thereby contributing to AMPA receptor–related synaptic plasticity, such as LTD. We have therefore examined the functional consequence of insulin-induced AMPA receptor endocytosis in CA1 synapses using an in vitro hippocampal slice preparation. Consistent with an endocytic removal of postsynaptic AMPA receptors, insulin treatment produced a clathrin-mediated selective LTD of AMPA, but not NMDA, EPSCs evoked by stimulation of the Schaffer collaterals, and in some cases insulin treatment produced silencing of AMPA receptor–mediated synaptic transmission (Man et al., 2000). These results suggest that enhancing clathrin-dependent endocytic removal of postsynaptic AMPA receptors can have profound effects on the efficacy of synaptic transmission and could therefore be a prime mechanistic candidate for CA1 homosynaptic LTD. This was indeed supported by our recent data involving mutual occlusion experiments. The induction of LTD using the LFS protocol prior to insulin application occluded the insulin-induced depression, and conversely, insulin application prevented the ability of LFS to induce LTD (Man et al., 2000). Thus, the mutual occlusion experiments demonstrated that LTD expression shares common mechanisms with insulin-induced AMPA depression, suggesting that this particular form of LTD is mediated by enhanced clathrin-dependent removal of postsynaptic AMPA receptors. This was further substantiated by the prevention of LTD expression by the application of the amphiphysin-SH3 domain peptide, which inhibits clathrin-mediated endocytosis by disrupting the binding of endogenous amphiphysin to dynamin (Man et al., 2000). These results are in line with recent reported data that suggest an indispensable role of postsynaptic clathrin-dependent endocytosis in the expression of CA1 LTD (Luscher et al., 1999).

The mediation of LTD expression by clathrin-dependent AMPA receptor endocytosis does not seem to be limited to hippocampal CA1 neurons. Cerebellar LTD is another well-characterized example of use-dependent synaptic plasticity. Application of insulin or insulin growth factor I produces a long-lasting depression of AMPA receptor–mediated currents by facilitating clathrin-dependent endocytosis of the AMPA receptors in cultured Purkinje neurons. Moreover, this insulin-induced depression occluded the cerebellar LTD production, and conversely, prior cerebellar LTD induction also prevented a further reduction of the AMPA receptor–mediated responses by insulin (Wang & Linden, 2000). Therefore, fairly strong evidence has now accumulated that rapid removal of postsynaptic AMPA receptors by a regulating clathrin-dependent endocytosis may be a common pathway in the expression of certain forms of LTD.

How a LTD induction protocol activates the clathrin-dependent endocytosis of AMPA receptors, thereby resulting in LTD, remains unclear. Considering that insulin is present in neurons and can be released from neurons in an activity-dependent manner, and that insulin receptors are highly expressed in the CNS and particularly concentrated on the postsynaptic density (Abbott et al., 1999; Dore et al., 1997; Wozniak, Rydzewski, Baker, & Raizada, 1993), one potential mechanism may involve the release of insulin from the presynaptic terminals in response to LFS during the LTD induction and activation of its receptors on the postsynaptic neurons facilitating the clathrin-dependent endocytosis of postsynaptic AMPA receptors. However, postsynaptic injection of the insulin receptor–neutralizing antibody, while blocking the insulin-induced depression of AMPA EPSCs, had little effect on either hippocampal homosynaptic LTD (Liu, Man, & Wang, 2000) or cerebellar LTD (Wang & Linden, 2000). These results do not support the notion that insulin is involved in mediating the expression of at least these forms of LTD but suggest that insulin and LTD induction stimuli may act at or through a convergent signal cascade that activates the clathrin-mediated endocytosis of AMPA receptors. Thus, understanding the mechanisms by which insulin regulates clathrin-mediated AMPA receptor trafficking, and how these mechanisms relate to the expression of CA1 and cerebellar LTD, may ultimately provide insight into the processes underlying brain insulin's effects on learning and memory in particular and the expression of LTD in general. Another potential signal that may be downstream of insulin receptor activation (and hence potentially shared with LTD induction) is protein kinase (PKC) activation, since insulin receptor activation is known to stimulate various isoforms of PKC (Sajan et al., 1999; Braiman, Sheffi-Friedman, Bak, Tennenbaum, & Sampson, 1999), and activation of PKC may stimulate clathrin-dependent endocytosis (Ferrari, Behar, Chorev, Rosenblatt, & Bisello, 1999). Along this line, it is relevant to note that stimulation of PKC by metabolic glutamate receptor activation is required for the induction of hippocampal LTD (see Zhuo & Hawkins, 1995, for review). Thus, it seems likely that multiple signal transduction pathways exist for the regulation of AMPA receptor trafficking.

☐ Evidence for AMPA Receptor Exocytosis and Its Potential Role in LTP

The constitutive/regulated endocytosis of AMPA receptors suggests that there must be a constitutive/regulated exocytotic pathway to deliver the receptors at a rate similar to their endocytic removal in order to continuously maintain a constant number of receptors on the cell surface under basal conditions, and the regulation of this pathway may contribute to synaptic plasticity. Unfortunately, unlike the endocytotic pathways, and despite vigorous research efforts, the vesicle-mediated exocytic pathways responsible for delivering AMPA receptors to the plasma membrane remain unidentified, and consequently the machineries involved and mechanisms regulating the process are unclear. Although little is known about the nature of AMPA receptor delivery to the plasma membrane, several studies from different laboratories have provided strong, albeit indirect, evidence suggesting that plasma membrane insertion of AMPA receptors may be mediated by membrane fusion similar to that involved in transmitter release at presynaptic terminals. Furthermore, the regulation of this process may play important roles in the generation of certain forms of synaptic plasticity, such as hippocampal LTP and LTD. Using the fluorescent dye FM1-43, Maletic-Savatic et al. (1998) first reported a calcium-dependent dentritic exocytosis in cultured neurons (Maletic-Savatic & Malinow, 1998) and more importantly that this dentritic exocytosis was mediated by calcium/calmodulin-dependent protein kinase II, a kinase that has been implicated in LTP (Malenka & Nicoll, 1999; Maletic-Savatic & Malinow, 1998). These studies provided the first evidence suggesting that vesicle-mediated membrane fusion events can occur in postsynaptic sites, presumably during LTP expression. More direct evidence for an involvement of membrane fusion events in LTP was reported by Lledo et al. (1998). In their studies, putative inhibitors that are believed to block membrane fusion at a number of different steps, when injected postsynaptically, impaired LTP, and introduction of recombinant SNAP into cells, which is required for membrane fusion, enhanced synaptic transmission and occluded LTP (Lledo et al., 1998). The clear implication of this data is that a membrane fusion step at the postsynaptic neuron is required for the production of LTP. However, it cannot rule out the possibility of exocytosis of a factor, other than the AMPA receptor itself, that is required for LTP induction and/or expression. Thus, this study falls short of providing direct evidence for the involvement of membrane fusion–dependent exocytosis of AMPA receptors during LTP. Such evidence was provided by a recent study by Shi et al. (Shi et al., 1999). To demonstrate the dynamic trafficking of intracellular pools of AMPA receptors during LTP, these authors transiently expressed green fluorescent protein (GFP)–tagged GluR1 subunits in cultured hippocampal slices and demonstrated that an LTP-inducing protocol could cause intracellularly localized GFP-GluR1 to rapidly translocate to synaptic sites including the cell-surface, thereby providing the first evidence for addition of postsynaptic AMPA receptors during LTP. There are, however, some limitations in this study (Malenka & Nicoll, 1999; Morales & Goda, 1999). The most critical is that while demonstrating the coincidence of the addition of new postsynaptic AMPA receptors during LTP induction, this work fails to show a direct contribution of these newly added receptors to the LTP-induced enhancement of synaptic efficacy. Consequently, whether the redistribution of AMPA receptors produced by the LTP-inducing protocol is a result of vesicle-mediated protein transport events and, if so, whether this increase in surface expression is due to an enhancement of the membrane fusion–dependent receptor insertion or due to depressing the clathrin-dependent receptor internalization, remain unknown.

Possibly the strongest line of evidence for the vesicle-mediated exocytosis of AMPA receptors in synaptic plasticity comes from recent work showing that NSF specifically binds and regulates cell-surface expression of AMPA receptors (Noel et al., 1999; Lin & Sheng, 1998). NSF was reported to bind directly and specifically to a defined region on the C-terminal domain of the GluR2 subunit (Nishimune et al., 1998; Osten et al., 1998; Song et al., 1998). Inhibition of this interaction by infusing either peptides corresponding to the binding domain of GluR2 (pep2m) or an anti-NSF antibody into the postsynaptic neuron resulted in a rapid decrease in AMPA receptor–mediated synaptic transmission and a reduction in the response of cultured neurons to local AMPA application. Viral expression of pep2m removes most surface-expressed GluR2-containing AMPA receptors (Noel et al., 1999). Taken together these studies have provided strong evidence for the rapid regulation of cell-surface expression of AMPA receptors, and hence synaptic plasticity, by the NSF-GluR2 specific interaction. However, how the interaction of NSF and GluR2 might play a role in the control of cell-surface expression of AMPA receptors, and hence in LTP or LTD remains unclear. Since NSF is a protein that is known to be critically important for the fusion of cargo-carrying vesicles and plasma membrane, one obvious possibility is that through binding to the GluR2 subunit, NSF might exert a chaperone-like role in vesicle-mediated plasma membrane insertion of AMPA receptors. If that is the case, one could then further speculate that activation or facilitation of NSF-dependent exocytotic insertion of AMPA receptors at postsynaptic sites may be a favorable mechanism for the conversion of silent synapses to active ones during LTP. Interestingly, two recent studies have reported that postsynaptic intracellular application of pep2m, the putative peptide inhibitor of NSF-GluR2 interaction, while producing a LTD of AMPA receptor–mediated synaptic transmission on its own, prevented the induction of LTD by the standard LFS inducing protocol, and conversely, prior LFS induction of LTD also reduced the ability of pep2m to induce depression in hippocampal CA1 neurons (Luscher et al., 1999; Lüthi et al. 1999). One obvious interpretation of this data is, as suggested by Lüthi et al. (1999), that interruption of the NSF-GluR2 interaction by pep2m impairs NSF-dependent AMPA receptor insertion to the postsynaptic membrane, and consequently causes the functional removal of AMPA receptors via normal internalization. However, a limitation of this explanation is that it relies heavily on an assumption that by binding to the GluR2 subunit, NSF functions as a chaperone protein, thereby playing a critical role in the vesicle-mediated exocytotic delivery of AMPA receptors. However, GluR2 is not a conventional SNAP protein, so unless strong evidence is obtained to support such a chaperone role of NSF in AMPA receptor insertion, how pep2m acts to reduces cell-surface AMPA receptors and hence contributes to LTD remains unclear. As mentioned previously, regulated clathrin-dependent endocytosis of AMPA receptors is also GluR2-subunit specific, and such enhanced endocytotic removal of AMPA receptors clearly contributes to the LTD. Moreover, a specific interaction of NSF with a component protein of clathrin-coated pit has recently been reported (McDonald et al., 1999). Thus, it might be equally plausible that the main function of the NSF-GluR2 interaction is to prevent regulated endocytosis of AMPA receptors by interfering with the interaction of GluR2 tails with machineries associated with clathrin-coated pits, such as AP2 or EPS-15 (Man et al., 2000). If that were the case, pep2m, by interrupting such a stabilization mechanism, could trigger the regulated AMPA receptor endocytosis (rather than inhibit membrane insertion of the receptors) to produce a rapid reduction in the number of receptors expressed on the postsynaptic membrane surface, producing the depression of AMPA receptor–mediated transmission and hence occluding the LFS LTD. Determining the effect of pep2m on LTP induction may provide useful insights into the role of NSF-GluR2 in either the exocytotic or endocytotic arms of AMPA receptor recycling since in the former case, pep2m should prevent the induction of LTP by impairing the NSF-dependent exocytotic insertion of AMPA receptors produced by the LTP-inducing stimulation, whereas in the latter case, the peptide may not be able to block LTP as enhanced exocytotic receptor insertion may still occur even in the presence of the pep2m-facilitated receptor endocytosis. Thus, while data from a number of studies using divergent sets of approaches strongly support the idea that regulation of vesicle-mediated exocytosis of AMPA receptors may be a very attractive means by which silent synapses are converted into active ones during LTP, direct evidence for the contribution of regulated exocytotic insertion of postsynaptic AMPA receptors to LTP is still lacking.

References

Abbott, M. A., Wells, D. G., & Fallon, J. R. (1999). The insulin receptor tyrosine kinase substrate p58/53 and the insulin receptor are components of CNS synapses. *Journal of Neuroscience, 19*, 7300–7308.

Baron-Van, E. A., Olichon-Berthe, C., Kowalski, A., Visciano, G., & Van, O. E. (1991). Expression of IGF-1 and insulin receptor genes in the rat central nervous system: A developmental, regional, and cellular analysis. *Journal of Neuroscience Research, 28*, 244–253.

Bettler, B., & Mulle, C. (1995). Review: neurotransmitter receptors. II. AMPA and kainate receptors. *Neuropharmacology, 34*, 123–139.

Bliss, T. V., & Collingridge, G. L. (1993). A synaptic model of memory: Long-term potentiation in the hippocampus. *Nature, 361*, 31–39.

Bolshakov, V. Y., Golan, H., Kandel, E. R., & Siegelbaum, S. A. (1997). Recruitment of new sites of synaptic transmission during the cAMP-dependent late phase of LTP at CA3-CA1 synapses in the hippocampus. *Neuron, 19*, 635–651.

Bonifacino, J. S., Marks, M. S., Ohno, H., & Kirchhausen, T. (1996). Mechanisms of signal-mediated protein sorting in the endocytic and secretory pathways. *Proceedings of the Association of American Physicians, 108*, 285–295.

Bortolotto, Z. A., Clarke, V. R., Delany, C. M., Parry, M. C., Smolders, I., Vignes, M., Ho, K. H., Miu, P., Brinton, B. T., Fantaske, R., Ogden, A., Gates, M., Ornstein, P. L., Lodge, D., Bleakman, D., & Collingridge, G. L. (1999). Kainate receptors are involved in synaptic plasticity. *Nature, 402*, 297–301.

Braiman, L., Sheffi-Friedman, L., Bak, A., Tennenbaum, T., & Sampson, S. R. (1999). Tyrosine phosphorylation of specific protein kinase C isoenzymes participates in insulin stimulation of glucose transport in primary cultures of rat skeletal muscle. *Diabetes, 48*, 1922–1929.

Burnashev, N., Villarroel, A., & Sakmann, B. (1996). Dimensions and ion selectivity of recombinant AMPA and kainate receptor channels and their dependence on Q/R site residues. *Journal of Physiology (London), 496,* 165–173.

Carroll, R. C., Beattie, E. C., Xia, H., Scher, C., Altschuler, Y., Nicoll, R. A., Malenka, R. C., & von Zastrow, M. (1999). Dynamin-dependent endocytosis of ionotropic glutamate receptors. *Proceedings of the National Academy of Sciences of the United States of America, 96,* 14112–14117.

Carroll, R. C., Lissin, D. V., von Zastrow, M., Nicoll, R. A., & Malenka, R. C. (1999). Rapid redistribution of glutamate receptors contributes to long-term depression in hippocampal cultures. *Nature Neurosci., 2,* 454–460.

Castillo, P. E., Malenka, R. C., & Nicoll, R. A. (1997). Kainate receptors mediate a slow postsynaptic current in hippocampal CA3 neurons. *Nature, 388,* 182–186.

Chen, C., & Tonegawa, S. (1997). Molecular genetic analysis of synaptic plasticity, activity-dependent neural development, learning, and memory in the mammalian brain. *Annual Review of Neuroscience, 20,* 157–184.

Chu, P., Murray, S., Lissin, D., & von Zastrow, M. (1997). Delta and kappa opioid receptors are differentially regulated by dynamin-dependent endocytosis when activated by the same alkaloid agonist. *Journal of Biological Chemistry, 272,* 27124–27130.

Damke, H., Baba, T., Warnock, D. E., & Schmid, S. L. (1994). Induction of mutant dynamin specifically blocks endocytic coated vesicle formation. *Journal of Cell Biology, 127,* 915–934.

Dore, S., Kar, S., Rowe, W., & Quirion, R. (1997). Distribution and levels of [125I]IGF-I, [125I]IGF-II and [125I]insulin receptor binding sites in the hippocampus of aged memory-unimpaired and -impaired rats. *Neuroscience, 80,* 1033–1040.

Durand, G. M., Kovalchuk, Y., & Konnerth, A. (1996). Long-term potentiation and functional synapse induction in developing hippocampus. *Nature, 381,* 71–75.

Ferguson, S. S., Zhang, J., Barak, L. S., & Caron, M. G. (1998). Role of beta-arrestins in the intracellular trafficking of G-protein-coupled receptors. *Advances in Pharmacology, 42,* 420–424.

Ferrari, S. L., Behar, V., Chorev, M., Rosenblatt, M., & Bisello, A. (1999). Endocytosis of ligand-human parathyroid hormone receptor 1 complexes is protein kinase C-dependent and involves beta-arrestin2. Real-time monitoring by fluorescence microscopy. *Journal of Biology Chemistry, 274,* 29968–29975.

Frey, U., & Morris, R. G. (1998). Synaptic tagging: Implications for late maintenance of hippocampal long-term potentiation. *Trends in Neuroscience, 21,* 181–188.

Fujii, S., Kuroda, Y., Miura, M., Furuse, H., Sasaki, H., Kaneko, K., Ito, K., Chen, Z., & Kato, H. (1996). The long-term suppressive effect of prior activation of synaptic inputs by low-frequency stimulation on induction of long-term potentiation in CA1 neurons of guinea pig hippocampal slices. *Experimental Brain Research, 111,* 305–312.

Goodman, O. B., Jr., Krupnick, J. G., Santini, F., Gurevich, V. V., Penn, R. B., Gagnon, A. W., Keen, J. H., & Benovic, J. L. (1998). Role of arrestins in G-protein-coupled receptor endocytosis. *Advances in Pharmacology, 42,* 429–433.

Hansen, S. H., Sandvig, K., & van Deurs, B. (1993). Clathrin and HA2 adaptors: Effects of potassium depletion, hypertonic medium, and cytosol acidification. *Journal of Cell Biology, 121,* 61–72.

Herskovits, J. S., Burgess, C. C., Obar, R. A., & Vallee, R. B. (1993). Effects of mutant rat dynamin on endocytosis. *Journal of Cell Biology, 122,* 565–578.

Hestrin, S., Sah, P., & Nicoll, R. A. (1990). Mechanisms generating the time course of dual component excitatory synaptic currents recorded in hippocampal slices. *Neuron, 5,* 247–253.

Hollmann, M., & Heinemann, S. (1994). Cloned glutamate receptors. *Annual Review of Neuroscience, 17,* 31–108.

Isaac, J. T., Nicoll, R. A., & Malenka, R. C. (1995). Evidence for silent synapses: Implications for the expression of LTP. *Neuron, 15,* 427–434.

Kamiguchi, H., Long, K. E., Pendergast, M., Schaefer, A. W., Rapoport, I., Kirchhausen, T., & Lemmon, V. (1998). The neural cell adhesion molecule L1 interacts with the AP-2 adaptor and is endocytosed via the clathrin-mediated pathway. *Journal of Neuroscience, 18,* 5311–5321.

Kanzaki, M., Zhang, Y. Q., Masjedi, H., Li, L., Shibata, H., & Kojima, I. (1999). Translocation of a calcium-permeable cation channel induced by insulin-like growth factor-I. *Nature Cell Biology, 1,* 165–170.

Karoor, V., Wang, L., Wang, H. Y., & Malbon, C. C. (1998). Insulin stimulates sequestration of beta-adrenergic receptors and enhanced association of beta-adrenergic receptors with Grb2 via tyrosine 350. *Journal of Biological Chemistry, 273,* 33035–33041.

Klintsova, A. Y., & Greenough, W. T. (1999). Synaptic plasticity in cortical systems. *Curr. Opin. Neurobiol., 9,* 203–208.

Krupnick, J. G., & Benovic, J. L. (1998). The role of receptor kinases and arrestins in G protein-coupled receptor regulation. *Annual Review of Pharmacological Toxicology, 38,* 289–319.

Kullmann, D. M. (1994). Amplitude fluctuations of dual-component EPSCs in hippocampal pyramidal cells: Implications for long-term potentiation. *Neuron, 12,* 1111–1120.

Kullmann, D. M., & Asztely, F. (1998). Extrasynaptic glutamate spillover in the hippocampus: Evidence and implications. *Trends in Neuroscience, 21,* 8–14.

Li, P., Wilding, T. J., Kim, S. J., Calejesan, A. A., Huettner, J. E., & Zhuo, M. (1999). Kainate-receptor-mediated sensory synaptic transmission in mammalian spinal cord. *Nature, 397,* 161–164.

Liao, D., Hessler, N. A., & Malinow, R. (1995). Activation of postsynaptically silent synapses during pairing-induced LTP in CA1 region of the hippocampal slice. *Nature, 375,* 400–405.

Lin, J. W., & Sheng, M. (1998). NSF and AMPA receptors get physical. *Neuron, 21,* 267–270.

Lisman, J., Malenka, R. C., Nicoll, R. A., & Malinow, R. (1997). Learning mechanisms: The case for CaM-KII. *Science, 276,* 2001–2022.

Liu, L., Man, H. Y., & Wang, Y. T. (2000). Activation of calcineurin phosphatase mediates both insulin and LTD-induced clathrin-dependent endocytosis of postsynaptic AMPA receptors. *The Society for Neuroscience* (abstract).

Lledo, P. M., Zhang, X., Sudhof, T. C., Malenka, R. C., & Nicoll, R. A. (1998). Postsynaptic membrane fusion and long-term potentiation. *Science, 279,* 399–403.

Luscher, C., Xia, H., Beattie, E. C., Carroll, R. C., von Zastrow, M., Malenka, R. C., & Nicoll, R. C. (1999). Role of AMPA receptor cycling in synaptic transmission and plasticity. *Neuron, 24,* 649–658.

Lüthi, A., Chittajallu, R., Duprat, F., Palmer, M. J., Benke, T. A., Kidd, F. L., Henley, J. M., Isaac, J. T. R., & Collingridge, G. J. (1999). Hippocampal LTD expression involves a pool of AMPARs regulated by the NSF-GluR2 interaction. *Neuron, 24,* 389–399.

Malenka, R. C., & Nicoll, R. A. (1997). Silent synapses speak up. *Neuron, 19,* 473–476.

Malenka, R. C., & Nicoll, R. A. (1999). Long-term potentiation—a decade of progress? *Science, 285,* 1870–1874.

Maletic-Savatic, M., & Malinow, R. (1998). Calcium-evoked dendritic exocytosis in cultured hippocampal neurons. Part I: Trans-Golgi network-derived organelles undergo regulated exocytosis. *Journal of Neuroscience, 18,* 6803–6813.

Maletic-Savatic, M., Koothan, T., & Malinow, R. (1998). Calcium-evoked dendritic exocytosis in cultured hippocampal neurons. Part II: Mediation by calcium/calmodulin-dependent protein kinase II. *Journal of Neuroscience, 18,* 6814–6821.

Malinow, R. (1998). Silencing the controversy in LTP? *Neuron, 21,* 1226–1227.

Mellman, I. (1996). Endocytosis and molecular sorting. *Annual Review of Cell Development Biology, 12,* 575–625.

Malinow, R., & Mainen, Z. F. (1996). Long-term potentiation in the CA1 hippocampus. *Science, 271,* 1604–1605.

Man, H. Y., Lin, L., Ju, W. Ahmadian, G., Liu, L. D., Becker, L. E., Sheng, M., & Wang, Y. T. (2000). Regulation of AMPA receptor-mediated synaptic transmission by clathrin-dependent receptor internalization. *Neuron, 25,* 649–662.

McBain, C. J., & Maccaferri, G. (1997). Synaptic plasticity in hippocampal interneurons? A commentary. *Canadian Journal of Physiology Pharmacology, 75,* 488–494.

McDonald, P. H., Cote, N. L., Lin, F. T., Premont, R. T., Pitcher, J. A., & Lefkowitz, R. J. (1999). Identification of NSF as a beta-arrestin1-binding protein. Implications for beta2-adrenergic receptor regulation. *Journal of Biological Chemistry, 274,* 10677–10680.

Morales, M., & Goda, Y. (1999). Nomadic AMPA receptors and LTP. *Neuron, 23,* 431–434.

Nicoll, R. A., & Malenka, R. C. (1995). Contrasting properties of two forms of long-term potentiation in the hippocampus. *Nature, 377,* 115–118.

Nishimune, A., Isaac, J. T., Molnar, E., Noel, J., Nash, S. R., Tagaya, M., Collingridge, G. L., Nakanishi, S., & Henley, J. M. (1998). NSF binding to GluR2 regulates synaptic transmission. *Neuron, 21*, 87–97.

Noel, J., Ralph, G. S., Pickard, L., Williams, J., Molnar, E., Uney, J. B., Collingridge, G. L., & Henley, J. M. (1999). Surface expression of AMPA receptors in hippocampal neurons is regulated by an NSF-dependent mechanism. *Neuron, 23*, 365–376.

Osten, P., Srivastava, S., Inman, G. J., Vilim, F. S., Khatri, L., Lee, L. M., States, B. A., Einheber, S., Milner, T. A., Hanson, P. I., & Ziff, E. B. (1998). The AMPA receptor GluR2 C terminus can mediate a reversible, ATP-dependent interaction with NSF and alpha- and beta-SNAPS. *Neuron, 21*, 99–110.

Pessin, J. E., Thurmond, D. C., Elmendorf, J. S., Coker, K. J., & Okada, S. (1999). Molecular basis of insulin-stimulated GLUT4 vesicle trafficking. Location! Location! Location! *Journal Biological Chemistry, 274*, 2593–2596.

Rothman, J. E. (1994). Mechanisms of intracellular protein transport. *Nature, 372*, 55–63.

Sajan, M. P., Standaert, M. L., Bandyopadhyay, G., Quon, M. J., Burke, T. R., Jr., & Farese, R. V. (1999). Protein kinase C-zeta and phosphoinositide-dependent protein kinase-1 are required for insulin-induced activation of ERK in rat adipocytes. *Journal of Biological Chemistry, 274*, 30495–30500.

Schekman, R., & Orci, L. (1996). Coat proteins and vesicle budding. *Science, 271*, 1526–1533.

Schmid, S. L., (1997). Clathrin-coated vesicle formation and protein sorting: An integrated process. *Annual Review of Biochemistry, 66*, 511–548.

Shi, S. H., Hayashi, Y., Petralia, R. S., Zaman, S. H., Wenthold, R. J., Svoboda, K., & Malinow, R. (1999). Rapid spine delivery and redistribution of AMPA receptors after synaptic NMDA receptor activation. *Science, 284*, 1811–1816.

Shupliakov, O., Low, P., Grabs, D., Gad, H., Chen, H., David, C., Takei, K., De Camilli, P., & Brodin, L. (1997). Synaptic vesicle endocytosis impaired by disruption of dynamin-SH3 domain interactions. *Science, 276*, 259–263.

Sollner, T., & Rothman, J. E. (1994). Neurotransmission: Harnessing fusion machinery at the synapse. *Trends in Neuroscience, 17*, 344–348.

Song, I., Kamboj, S., Xia, J., Dong, H., Liao, D., & Huganir, R. L. (1998). Interaction of the N-ethylmaleimide-sensitive factor with AMPA receptors. *Neuron, 21*, 393–400.

Srivastava, S., Osten, P., Vilim, F. S., Khatri, L., Inman, G., States, B., Daly, C., DeSouza, S., Abagyan, R., Valtschanoff, J. G., Weinberg, R. J., & Ziff, E. B. (1998). Novel anchorage of GluR2/3 to the postsynaptic density by the AMPA receptor-binding protein ABP. *Neuron, 21*, 581–591.

Stevens, C. F., & Wang, Y. (1993). Reversal of long-term potentiation by inhibitors of haem oxygenase. *Nature, 364*, 147–149.

Sudhof, T. C. (1995). The synaptic vesicle cycle: A cascade of protein-protein interactions. *Nature, 375*, 645–653.

Vallee, R. B., & Sheetz, M. P. (1996). Targeting of motor proteins. *Science, 271*, 1539–1544.

van Delft, S., Schumacher, C., Hage, W., Verkleij, A. J., & Bergen en Henegouwen, P. M. (1997). Association and colocalization of Eps15 with adaptor protein-2 and clathrin. *Journal of Cell Biology, 136*, 811–821.

Vincent, V., Goffin, V., Rozakis-Adcock, M., Mornon, J. P., & Kelly, P. A. (1997). Identification of cytoplasmic motifs required for short prolactin receptor internalization. *Journal of Biological Chemistry, 272*, 7062–7068.

Voronin, L. L., Volgushev, M., Chistiakova, M., Kuhnt, U., & Singer, W. (1996). Involvement of silent synapses in the induction of long-term potentiation and long-term depression in neocortical and hippocampal neurons. *Neuroscience, 74*, 323–330.

Wan, Q., Xiong, Z. G., Man, H. Y., Ackerley, C. A., Braunton, J., Lu, W. Y., Becker, L. E., MacDonald, J. F., & Wang, Y. T. (1997). Recruitment of functional GABA(A) receptors to postsynaptic domains by insulin. *Nature, 388*, 686–690.

Wang, Y. T., & Linden, D. J. (2000). Expression of cerebellar long-term depression requires clathrin-mediated internalization of postsynaptic AMPA receptors. *Neuron, 25*, 635–647.

Wozniak, M., Rydzewski, B., Baker, S. P., & Raizada, M. K. (1993). The cellular and physiological actions of insulin in the central nervous system. *Neurochemistry International, 22*, 1–10.

Wyszynski, M., Kim, E., Yang, F. C., & Sheng, M. (1998). Biochemical and immunocytochemical characterization of GRIP, a putative AMPA receptor anchoring protein, in rat brain. *Neuropharmacology, 37*, 1335–1344.

Xia, J., Zhang, X., Staudinger, J., & Huganir, R. L. (1999). Clustering of AMPA receptors by the synaptic PDZ domain-containing protein PICK1. *Neuron, 22*, 179–187.

Zhuo, M., & Hawkins, R. D. (1995). Long-term depression: A learning-related type of synaptic plasticity in the mammalian central nervous system. *Review in Neuroscience, 6*, 259–277.

George D. Mower

Immediate Early Gene Expression and Critical Period Neuroplasticity in the Visual Cortex

☐ Introduction

An outstanding feature of the neonatal mammalian brain is its plasticity, the process whereby its functional capacities, which are loosely specified by genetic makeup, are sharpened and crystallized through interaction with the external environment. Characteristic of this developmental plasticity are "critical periods" during which specific interactions between the growing brain and its environment are required for normal development. Examples of critical periods are found in systems as diverse as imprinting, birdsong, sexual differentiation, social behavior, sound localization, binocular vision, and somatosensory maps. While this developmental plasticity provides the organism with adaptability to the external world, it also produces the risk of developmental abnormality when the brain/environment interaction is less than optimal.

Developmental critical periods are only one form of neuroplasticity. Other forms include phenomena such as learning and memory, injury and regeneration, neurogenesis and migration, axonal sprouting, and path finding. While the exact underlying molecular mechanisms of the plastic response undoubtedly differ among the various forms of plasticity, there are some common features, at least from the point of view of a single postsynaptic cell. A stimulus external to the cell (or one external to the organism) must result in a change in the immediate extrinsic cellular environment, such as the release of neurotransmitters or growth factors. That change must be "sensed" by the cell, presumably through membrane-bound receptors. Transmembrane events must then initiate intracellular changes that include voltage and conductance changes, activation of G proteins, and initiation of second messenger cascades. Intracellular signals then can operate by several pathways. One is regulation and modulation of local proteins that already exist in the neuron, such as protein kinases, phosphatases, and ion channels. A second is the regulation of gene transcription in the nucleus and the production of new proteins. The former pathway has been linked to phenomena such as short-term memory and the early phase of long-term potentiation (LTP). The latter pathway has been linked to the more enduring aspects of neuronal plasticity, such as long-term memory and the late phase of LTP, both of which depend upon gene transcription and new protein synthesis (Alberini, Ghirardi, Huang, Nguyen, & Kandel, 1995; Matthies, 1989). Communication between these pathways is also required in order to provide specificity in the targeting of new gene products to the appropriate synapses or other molecular domains (Frey & Morris, 1997). Recent evidence has indicated that within minutes of an activating stimulus, sophisticated changes such as insertion of receptors into synapses, formation of dendritic spine-like structures, and changes in receptor subunit composition can occur (Carroll, Lissin, von Zastrow, Nicoll, & Malenka, 1999; Quinlan, Philpot, Huganir, & Bear, 1999). Such changes could not only mediate rapid alterations in synaptic efficacy, but also serve as markers for directing new gene products to appropriate targets.

In the context of critical period plasticity, most progress has been made on the front end of this cellular cascade. To date, studies aimed at molecular mechanisms of critical period plasticity have concentrated on the signaling pathways from the cell surface to the nucleus. The most compelling evidence has been demonstrations that the anatomical and physiological effects of environmental input can be prevented by manipulation of neurotransmitters and growth factors (e.g., Bear, 1996; Cellerino & Maffei, 1996). Second messenger systems have also been implicated (e.g., Dudek & Bear, 1989; Reid, Daw, Gregory, & Flavin, 1996). Critical period plasticity is unique in that it can produce massive anatomical and physiological reorganization that often persists throughout life. It is likely that such dramatic effects depend more on the output of genetic processes than on rapid changes produced by intracellular signaling pathways. If changes in gene expression are the penultimate mechanism for long-term plasticity, then the interruption of neuroplastic phenomena seen with manipulation of neurotransmitters, growth factor, and intracellular messengers could be less provocative: breaking, at any point, the chain of events that leads to the changes in gene expression that ultimately control neural plasticity would prevent the plastic response. Whatever the relative contributions of signaling events versus changes in gene expression, it is certain that understanding the genetic mechanisms of neuroplasticity is a critical piece of the puzzle.

The purpose of this chapter is to review evidence relating a primary step in the control of gene expression, the regulation of transcription by immediate early genes (IEGs), to the best-understood model of neuroplasticity, the critical period in the visual cortex. A complete review of the literature is not intended, and excellent comprehensive reviews have been done (Herdegen & Leah, 1998; Hughes & Dragunow, 1995; Kaczmarek & Chaudhuri, 1997). The focus here will be the evidence supporting a role for IEGs in the critical period plasticity of the visual cortex, in addition and/or distinction to their role as activity markers. Emphasis will be placed on the results from cats because IEGs have been studied most systematically in relation to visual cortical plasticity in this species.

☐ IEGs: Candidates for a Role in Neuroplasticity

IEGs are rapidly and transiently induced by extracellular stimulation and they do not require new protein synthesis for their expression. Their protein products regulate the expression of target genes that contain the response elements for IEG proteins (P. K. Johnson & McKnight, 1989; Mitchell & Tjian, 1989). IEGs can be seen as third messengers; that is, they are genes that are switched on or off as a result of the activation of second messenger systems, and they act as messengers for changes in transcription. These properties suggest a role in coupling extracellular stimulation with transcriptional events leading to long-lasting changes in neural function (Morgan & Curran,

1991; Sheng & Greenberg, 1990). Classically, all IEGs were thought to be transcription regulators. It is now clear, however, that some genes induced as IEGs are not transcription regulators and serve different cellular functions. Such IEGs include well-known genes such as BDNF (Hughes, Beilharz, Gluckman, & Dragunow, 1993) as well as other molecules whose function is unclear (Lanahan & Worley, 1998). Here we will consider only IEGs that act as transcription factors.

Since IEGs are a large gene family, how can their activation translate specific extracellular events to specific changes in target gene expression? Mechanisms are beginning to be understood. One mechanism in the nervous system, as in other systems, is that different types of stimulation lead to distinct combinations of induced IEGs (Herdegen & Leah, 1998; Morgan & Curran, 1991). For example, while both *fos* and *egr-1* (early growth response gene, also known as *zif-268*, *ngfi-a*, and *krox-24*) are elevated in the hippocampus by electrical stimulation conditions that cause seizures, electrical stimulation conditions that result in LTP reliably induce *egr-1* but not *c-fos*. *c-jun* is inducible by trophic factors but not by depolarization, while *c-fos* is inducible by both. It appears that the selective activation of subsets of IEGs provides a mechanism by which the expression of specific target genes is regulated. A second mechanism of target specificity is added through interaction between induced IEGs (P. F. Johnson & McKnight, 1989; Mitchell & Tjian, 1989). For example, the proteins produced by members of the Fos and Jun families form heterodimeric complexes collectively termed AP-1, which are capable of binding to target genes and altering their transcriptional state. Genes involved in a wide array of cellular functions contain AP-1 binding sites in their regulatory elements. Specificity of effects upon transcription can be generated by the selective combinatorial interaction of different members of the Fos and Jun families. Heterodimers of Fos and c-Jun proteins appear to be capable of activating many genes. However, Fos and Jun-B protein heterodimers appear to be capable of both activating certain target genes and repressing other genes.

A third mechanism for IEG specificity on target genes is added by temporal differences in the time course of induction of different IEGs. For example, after an inducing event, different members of the *fos* and *jun* families can be activiated with different time courses (Sonnenberg, Macgregor-Leon, Curran, & Morgan, 1989). A single IEG-inducing event, therefore, can produce a unique combinatorial/dimeric/temporal signature of induced IEGs which, in turn, activate and repress a number of target genes. Expression of the target genes can then contribute to long-term structural and functional changes.

☐ IEGs and Visual Cortical Plasticity

The Critical Period in Cat Visual Cortex: A Brief Synopsis

The cat visual cortex is a particularly illustrative model for understanding critical period development and plasticity at the molecular level. In the cat, the geniculocortical pathway is immature at birth in terms of both its anatomy and its physiology. By 3 weeks of postnatal age, cellular migration has completed formation of the mature lamination pattern in the visual cortex, embryonic cells have largely disappeared, and geniculocortical afferents have reached their final position and begun the process of segregating into ocular dominance columns (Shatz & Luskin, 1986). Correlated with these anatomical events is the appearance of adult-like physiological response properties in visual cortical neurons by about 4 weeks of age, and little change in response properties occurs thereafter (Fregnac & Imbert, 1984). Over the next several months, these loosely established anatomical and physiological characteristics are stabilized under the guidance of visual experience. One major event during this period is synaptogenesis, which increases sharply from birth to a peak at about 40 days and then declines to adult levels at 3–4 months of age (Cragg, 1975; Winfield, 1983). Maturation of both glial and neurotransmitter systems also occurs gradually over the first several postnatal months (Muller, 1991; Skangiel-Kramska, 1988). The outstanding characteristic of this developmental phase is plasticity, that is, the capacity for anatomical and physiological development to be altered by visual experience. The clearest demonstration of such environmental effects is to rear cats with one eye sutured closed, a condition that leads to dramatic anatomical and physiological alterations (Shatz & Stryker, 1978; Wiesel & Hubel, 1963). Unlike in normal cats, where most visual cortical neurons are responsive to stimulation of either eye, in such monocularly deprived cats virtually every cortical neuron is responsive only to the eye that received visual input. This physiological takeover by the experienced eye involves a massive anatomical expansion of the territory occupied by afferent terminals representing that eye and a corresponding shrinkage of the territory occupied by afferents representing the deprived eye. The visual cortex is susceptible to monocular deprivation only during a critical period of postnatal life; monocular deprivation in older animals produces no anatomical or physiological effect.

Studies of animals dark-reared from birth have provided important information concerning this critical period. One major insight is that visual experience plays a role not only in determining the final outcome of development during the critical period but also in activating the critical period itself. After prolonged dark-rearing from birth, most visual cortical neurons are visually responsive and binocularly driven, but they lack selectivity for parameters of the visual stimulus and habituate rapidly (Fregnac & Imbert, 1984). When subsequently exposed to the visual environment, visual cortical cells of dark-reared cats develop many normal response properties. More importantly, if there is monocular exposure after dark-rearing, dramatic takeover by the open eye occurs at ages far beyond the limits of the normal critical period (Cynader & Mitchell, 1980; Mower, Berry, Burchfiel, & Duffy, 1981). This result indicates that the critical period is not a simple age-dependent maturational process; rather, visual input controls the timing of the underlying mechanisms that control visual cortical plasticity. Dark-rearing, therefore, provides a means to dissociate changes associated with the state of visual cortical plasticity from changes associated with the general maturation of the brain, and it is a frequently used paradigm in studies aimed at molecular mechanisms of visual cortical plasticity.

Evidence For a Role of IEGs in Visual Cortical Plasticity

If the presence of a particular molecular event, in this case IEG expression, is critically involved in plasticity during the visual cortical critical period, then several criteria should be met. Daw (1994) has provided a useful set of four such criteria based on plasticity-related phenomena that have been demonstrated to occur during the critical period. Here, evidence for IEGs meeting these criteria will be evaluated. Additionally, in the context of IEGs, an additional criterion is needed: their inducibility by visual input.

Induction of IEGs by Visual Input.   In light of what is known regarding regulation of gene expression by IEGs, the first criterion is that IEGs should be induced differentially in response to visual input. In cats, brief visual experience has been shown to produce dramatic transient inductions of *egr-1*, *c-fos*, and *jun-B* in the visual cortex but not the frontal cortex. Levels of *c-jun* and *c-myc* are not affected (Rosen, McCormack,

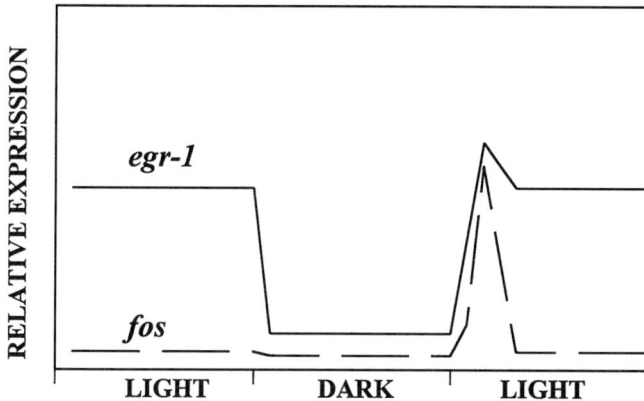

Figure 13.1. Schematic description of the differential responses of EGR-1 and Fos proteins to ambient light, darkness, and exposure to light after darkness. See text for details. Reprinted from "Immediate Early Gene Expression in Cat Visual Cortex During and After the Critical Period: Differences Between EGR-1 and Fos Proteins," by I. V. Kaplan, Y. Guo, and G. D. Mower, 1996, *Molecular Brain Research, 36*, p. 20. Copyright 1996 Elsevier Science. Reprinted with permission.

Villa-Komaroff, & Mower, 1992). Similar IEG-specific effects of visual input have been reported in rats (Kaminska, Kaczmarek, & Chaudhuri, 1996; Worley et al., 1991). Select combinatorial interactions of IEGs, therefore, could be an important step in the series of events by which visual input affects visual cortical structure and function. IEGs that are responsive to visual input also have been shown to have differential responses to the various phases of visual input (Kaplan, Guo, & Mower, 1996; Rosen et al., 1992). Such differences have been most clearly demonstrated for EGR-1 and Fos, as schematized in Figure 13.1. EGR-1 responds to visual input with sustained changes in its level of expression. It shows high basal levels, reduced expression in darkness, and rapid return to high constitutive levels with the introduction of light after prolonged darkness. Fos shows a markedly different profile. It has very low basal expression, which is not demonstrably affected by darkness, and its principal response is a marked transient induction upon exposure to light after darkness. In combination, therefore, these two IEGs (EGR-1:Fos) give different signatures to sustained light (high:low), sustained dark (low:low), and the transition from darkness to light (high:high). These unique changes in expression highlight the complexity of the response across IEGs to environmental input and suggest a genetic "on/off" signaling mechanism. The response of IEGs to visual input is not a simple or stereotyped response to visually driven neural activity. The multifaceted response within and across IEGs is consistent with a transcription factor program aimed at a critical sequence of activation and repression of distinct target genes.

IEG Expression Parallels the Critical Period.   Criterion 2 is that levels of IEG expression across development should parallel the time course of the critical period. In cats, susceptibility to monocular deprivation is very low until about 3 weeks, peaks at 4–5 weeks, then declines to low levels at 5 months and disappears by about 1 year of age (Daw, Fox, Sato, & Czepita, 1992). If IEG expression is related to the critical period, levels should increase to a peak during the rising phase of plasticity and

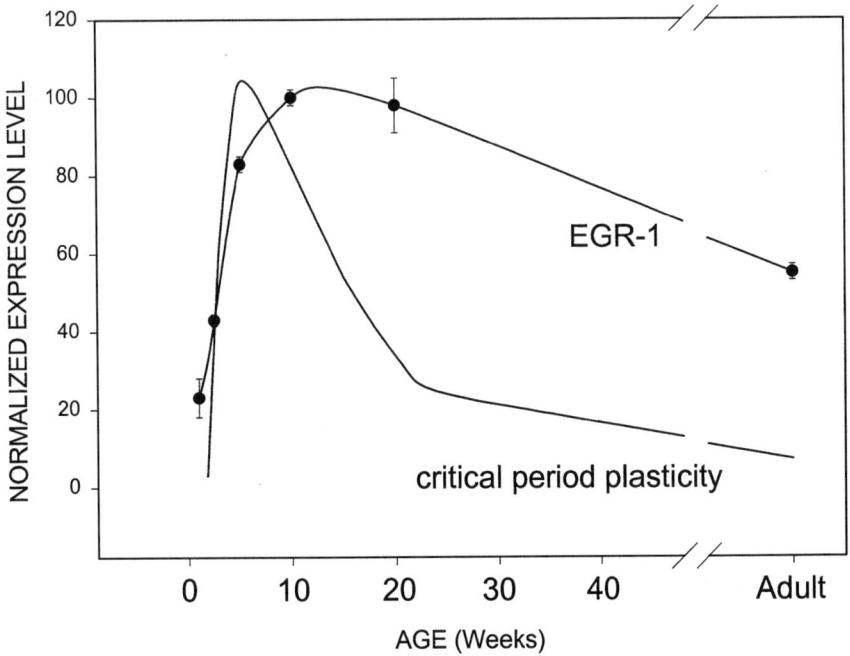

Figure 13.2. Developmental changes in the level of expression of EGR-1 protein (Mower & Kaplan, unpublished) and the level of plasticity, as measured by the physiological effect of monocular deprivation (data replotted from Daw, 1994) in the cat visual cortex. There is a close association of changes in EGR-1 expression and susceptibility to monocular deprivation during the rise of the visual cortical plasticity. Subsequently, both measures decline. See text for details.

decline thereafter. Northern blot and immunohistochemical analyses of basal mRNA (McCormack, Rosen, Villa-Komaroff, & Mower, 1992) and protein (Kaplan, Guo, & Mower, 1995) levels demonstrated that the expression of several IEGs shows a rise and decline in expression that parallels critical period plasticity. Figure 13.2 shows the developmental change in EGR-1 protein in relation to the critical period for monocular deprivation in the cat visual cortex. There is a close association of expression levels and plasticity during the rising phase of the critical period. At later ages, the decline in IEG expression is less marked than that of susceptibility to monocular deprivation, which could indicate involvement of these genes in other aspects of cortical plasticity (discussed below). Interestingly, IEGs that are inducible by visual input (*egr-1, c-fos, jun-B*) show this dynamic pattern of developmental regulation; IEGs that are not affected by visual input (*c-jun, c-myc*) are not developmentally regulated during the critical period.

Induced levels of IEG expression also show differences between cats at the peak of the critical period (5 weeks) and older cats that point to a relationship with the state of visual cortical plasticity. Analyses of *c-fos* and *egr-1* mRNA levels have indicated that both basal levels and the magnitude of induction of the two genes, as a result of exposure to light after darkness, are approximately double in the 5-week compared to the adult cat visual cortex (McCormack et al., 1992; Rosen et al., 1992). Western blot and immunohistochemical studies of Fos protein have also indicated a greater induction in young animals (Beaver, Mitchell, & Robertson, 1993; Mower, 1994; Mower & Kaplan, 1999). This age difference in the magnitude of IEG induction is difficult to explain in terms of activity levels. Physiological responsiveness of visual cortical neurons is more robust in adult than 5-week-old cats (Fregnac & Imbert, 1984). Moreover, a period of darkness (as used in these studies of induced IEG levels) leads to decreased responsiveness and degraded receptive field properties in visual cortical neurons of young kittens, but has little effect in older cats. The activity levels in the visual cortex in ambient light as well as those elicited by brief visual exposure after darkness, therefore, should be greater in adult than 5-week-old cats. IEG mRNAs and proteins, on the other hand, are more highly expressed in 5-week-old than adult cats.

In addition to the level of expression, changes in the pattern of IEG expression across visual cortical layers during postnatal development can be related to events that occur during the critical period. Because it shows high basal levels of expression, developmental changes in EGR-1 expression were studied systematically (Kaplan et al., 1995). In newborn kittens, EGR-1 protein expression is low and restricted to deep cortical layers (layer VI/Subplate). With increasing age, EGR-1 expression gradually progresses to more superficial layers in an inside-outside pattern and reaches its highest levels across all cortical layers by 5 weeks of age. Studies in the rat brain have indicated laminar and areal changes in the pattern of *egr-1* expression at the onset of temporally distinct critical periods in the somatosensory and visual cortex (Herms, Zurmohle, Schlingensiepen, Brysch, & Schlingensiepen, 1994; Schlingensiepen, Luno, & Brysch, 1991; Worley et al., 1991). In the cat visual cortex, EGR-1 expression stays at its maximum up to approximately 10 weeks of age and then begins to decline in layer IV with little change in supra- and infragranular layers. Therefore, in adult animals, EGR-1 immunoreactivity is much higher in supra- and infragranular layers than in layer IV.

The progressive laminar changes in EGR-1 protein expression parallel several events during maturation of the cat visual cortex. During the early process (0.5 to 2.5 weeks) of laminar maturation of EGR-1 immunoreactivity, there is initially dense staining in layer VI/subplate and then the appearance (at 1 week) of a prominently stained band of cells in the lowest part of layer IV. Recent evidence indicates that cells in this region of layer IV interact with subplate cells in early life and that this interaction is essential for the formation of ocular dominance columns (Ghosh & Shatz, 1994). EGR-1 immunoreactivity also reflects physiological changes during postnatal maturation of the cat visual cortex. The finding that EGR-1 expression originates in deep cortical layers and then spreads across the depth of the cortex in an inside-outside manner during the first 5 postnatal weeks parallels the progressive appearance of visual responsiveness and orientation selectivity in the developing visual cortex (Fregnac & Imbert, 1984). Orientation-selective properties begin to develop in deep cortical laminae (layers IV to VI) and progressively expand over the full cortical thickness by around 5 weeks of age. Finally, the developmental pattern in both the magnitude and laminar distribution of EGR-1 expression directly parallels physiologically assessed neuronal plasticity in the visual cortex, as discussed in the next section.

Laminar Changes in IEG Expression and Plasticity due to Age. Criterion 3 is that there should be differences in the laminar pattern of IEG expression in the visual cortex due to age. In young kittens near the peak of the critical period (5 weeks), cells in all visual cortical layers are highly plastic in term of modifiability of their receptive field properties in response to manipulation of visual input (Shatz & Stryker, 1978). With increasing age, plasticity declines, and the decline in plasticity occurs faster among cells in layer IV than in cells located outside of layer IV. Residual physiological plasticity in adult animals is limited to cells located above and below layer IV (Daw et al., 1992; Mower, Caplan, Christen, & Duffy, 1985). Immunohistochemical (Beaver et al., 1993; Kaplan et al., 1996; Mower, 1994) and in situ hybridization (Zhang et al., 1994) results indicate that IEG expression across cat visual cortical layers matches these laminar patterns. For both EGR-1 and Fos, the major difference between ages is in layer IV. In young animals, cells in all visual cortical layers show high levels of EGR-1 and Fos. In adults, expression is markedly greater in cells located above and below layer IV, and only faint labeling is seen within layer IV. Figure 13.3 shows immunohistochemical results for Fos which demonstrate the laminar differences due to age. Thus, the age differences in the laminar distribution of IEG expression directly parallel the state of physiological plasticity across layers in the cat visual cortex. Results in new world monkeys are similar to those in the cat (Silveira et al., 1996). In old world monkeys, some reports on laminar expression are similar to the cat (Van der Gucht, Arckens, Orban, & Vandesande, 1999); others are variable (Chaudhuri, Matsubara, & Cynader, 1995; Kaczmarek, Zangenehpour, & Chaudhuri, 1999).

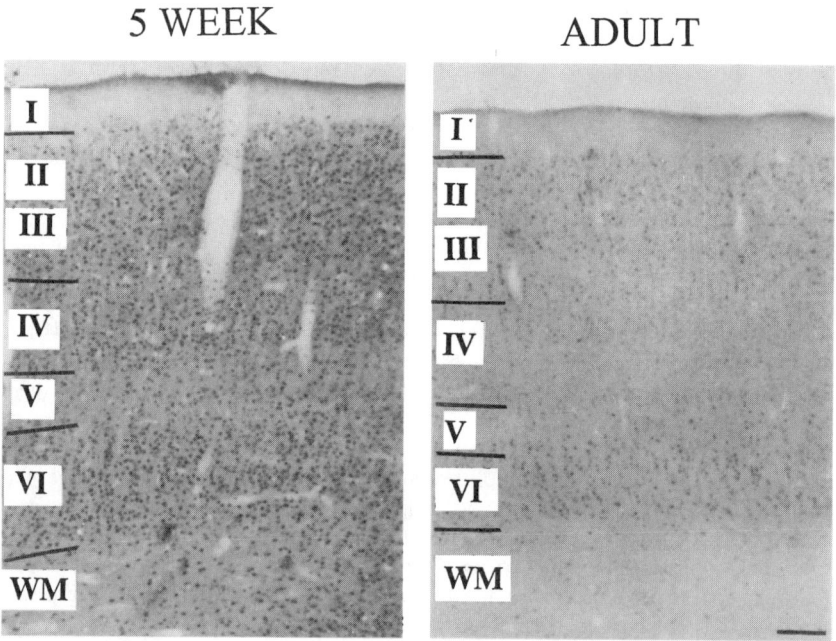

Figure 13.3. Normal age-related differences in the degree and laminar distribution of Fos protein induction (produced by exposure to the visual environment for 1 hour following a period of darkness) in 5-week-old and adult cat visual cortex. Visual cortical laminae are indicated. The magnitude of Fos induction is greater in 5-week-old cats. The laminar distribution of induced protein also differs with age: in 5-week-old cats, cells in all layers of the visual cortex show dramatic inductions, but in adults, Fos is mainly expressed in cells located above and below layer IV. Reprinted from "Immediate Early Gene Expression in Cat Visual Cortex During and After the Critical Period: Differences Between EGR-1 and Fos Proteins," by I. V. Kaplan, Y. Guo, and G. D. Mower, 1996. *Molecular Brain Research 36*, p. 19. Copyright 1996 Elsevier Science. Reprinted with permission.

The laminar differences between young and adult cats are also difficult to interpret simply in terms of activity levels. Metabolic markers, whose labeling intensity is highly correlated with neural activity levels, show that under binocular viewing conditions activity is much higher in layer IV and than in supra- and infragranular layers in adult animals (Wong-Riley, 1979). EGR-1 and Fos, on the other hand, are lowest in layer IV of adults and highest in supra- and infragranular layers. If EGR-1 and Fos immunoreactivity were reflecting only activity levels, they would be expected to mirror the metabolic markers and not be opposite to them.

The question arises as to why there is IEG expression in adults if these genes are involved in plasticity. Northern blots, western blots, and immunohistochemistry all indicate that IEG expression persists in older animals, but susceptibility to monocular deprivation disappears. This residual expression of IEGs could be related to other forms of residual plasticity in adults. By 1 year of age, plasticity of the visual cortex in response to monocular deprivation for a 3-month period is not evident; however, the visual cortex of animals older than 1 year is not immutable. More extreme manipulations of visual input can produce physiological reorganization in adult cats, and this reorganization, like IEG expression, appears mediated by neurons outside of layer IV (Darian-Smith & Gilbert, 1995; Singer, Tretter, & Yinon, 1982).

Dark Rearing Has Parallel Effects on Plasticity and IEG Expression.

Criterion 4 is that levels of IEG expression should be systematically altered by manipulations which change the time course of visual cortical plasticity. Rearing cats in total darkness from birth has been shown to extend the visual cortical critical period beyond its normal age limits and is thus an effective means for manipulating the level of plasticity during the critical period. Physiologically, the effect of dark-rearing is to slow the entire time course, both the rise and the decline, of visual cortical plasticity such that at young ages (5 weeks) normal cats are more plastic than dark-reared cats, while at later ages (20 weeks) dark-reared cats are more plastic than normal cats (Mower, 1991; N. W. Daw and C. J. Beaver, personal communication). Dark-rearing maintains plasticity primarily in cells located outside of layer IV. Anatomically, cats reared in total darkness show incomplete segregation of ocular dominance columns in layer IV (Mower et al., 1985; Swindale, 1988). By around 4 months of age, this state becomes permanent and neither binocular nor monocular visual experience can promote segregation of geniculocortical afferents. The physiological effects of visual experience after prolonged dark-rearing occur primarily in cells located outside of layer IV (Mower et al., 1985). The prolonged plasticity in dark-reared cats, therefore, appears to reflect mainly a mechanism of intracortical processing. Comparison of IEG expression in dark-reared and normal cats provides a means to test more stringently the notion that the expression of these genes is involved in visual cortical plasticity. If IEG expression is involved in visual cortical plasticity, then changing the time course of the critical period should also change IEG expression. Two stringent predictions regarding differences between normal and dark-reared cats can be made: (a) the level of IEG expression should be higher in normal than dark-reared cat visual cortex at 5 weeks of age, but higher in dark-reared than normal cat visual cortex at 20 weeks; (b) IEG expression in 20-week dark-reared cats should be selectively enhanced in super- and infragranular layers of the visual cortex. Western blotting and immunohistochemical results have confirmed prediction 1 for Fos (Mower & Kaplan, 1999; see Figure 13.4). The available data on effects of dark-rearing on IEG mRNA levels (Rosen et al., 1992; Worley et al., 1991) are also consistent with this prediction. Immunohistochemistry with a dilution series of primary antibody provided evidence in favor of prediction 2. In dark-reared 20-week-old cats,

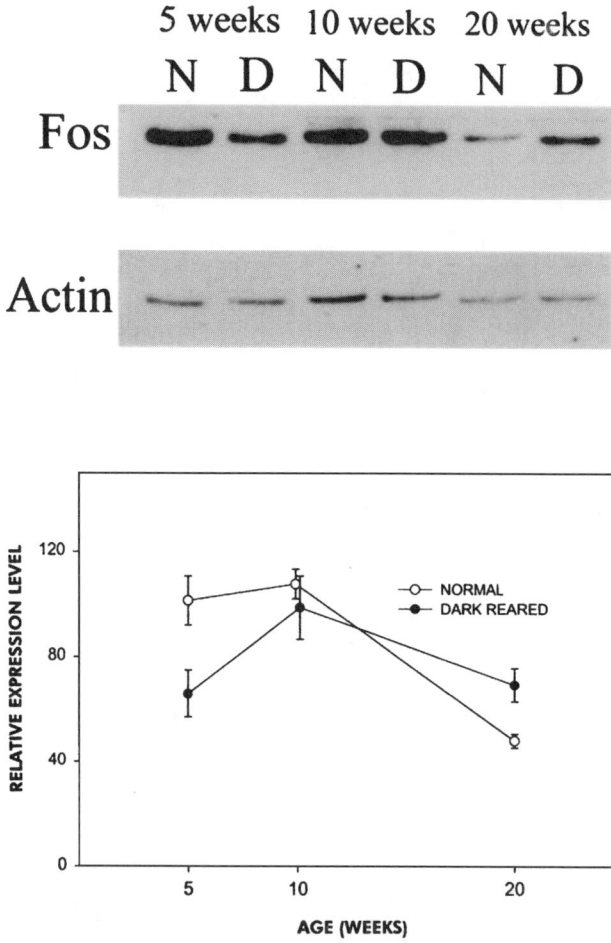

Figure 13.4. (Top) Portion of a western blot showing differences in the level of induced Fos between normal (N) and dark-reared (D) cat visual cortex at 5, 10, and 20 weeks of age. The blot was stripped and reprobed with an antibody against actin to correct for loading errors. (Bottom) Quantitative summary of differences in the levels of induced Fos between normal and DR cats at 5, 10, and 20 weeks of age. Dark-rearing has similar age-dependent effects on Fos induction, as it has on susceptibility to monocular deprivation in the visual cortex: at 5 weeks, levels of each were higher in normal than dark-reared cats, whereas, at 20 weeks, levels were higher in dark-reared than normal cats. See text for details. Reprinted from "Fos Expression During the Critical Period in Visual Cortex: Differences Between Normal and Dark Reared Cats," by G. D. Mower and I. V. Kaplan, 1999, *Molecular Brain Research, 64,* 265. Copyright 1999 Elsevier Science. Reprinted with permission.

Fos immunoreactivity persisted at greater antibody dilutions than in normal cats, and this elevated immunoreactivity was largely restricted to the supra- and infragranular layers. The elevation of Fos expression in 20-week-old dark-reared animals is difficult to explain in terms of neuronal activity levels since it takes several weeks for visual responsiveness to recover to normal levels (Cynader, 1983). Overall, dark-rearing appears to have very similar effects on Fos expression as it has on neuronal plasticity during the visual cortical critical period.

☐ Whither IEGs?

Are IEGs Necessary for Critical Period Plasticity in the Visual Cortex?

The final criterion for IEGs to be shown essential for visual cortical neuronal plasticity is that interfering with their expression should prevent neuronal plasticity during the critical period. Studies employing physiological analyses of the effects of antisense oligonucleotide interruption of IEG expression or IEG knockout mice may provide such evidence. Interference with gene expression tantalizingly suggests a role for IEGs in neuroplasticity. Infusion of antisense oligonucleotide to modify the expression of *c-fos* in the brain has been shown to block phenomena such as drug-induced rotation behavior, seizures in response to electrical stimulation, and light-induced changes in the circadian clock (see Chiasson, Hong, & Robertson, 1997, for review). Null mutation of *c-fos*, but not *egr-1*, impairs structural and functional plasticity in the kindling model of epilepsy (Watanabe et al., 1996; Zheng, Butler, & McNamara, 1998).

To date, only one preliminary report has analyzed IEG knockout mice in terms of visual cortical plasticity, and that study found no interference with the effect of monocular deprivation by disruption of *egr-1* (Mataga, Condie, & Hensch, 1998). While this result could be interpreted to indicate that *egr-1* is not necessary for critical period plasticity, it does not rule out a role for this IEG in the normal process. Application of gene knockout mice to visual cortical plasticity may present unique problems of interpretation. About half of *fos* knockout mice die before the visual cortical critical period (R. S. Johnson, Spiegelman, & Papaioannou, 1992), so even a positive result of the knockout on plasticity (elimination of the effect of monocular deprivation) could be due to indirect or nonspecific effects. Also, given the combinatorial nature of IEG actions, multiple simultaneous gene interruptions may be needed. Moreover, the critical period in mice may not be strictly analogous to that in binocular animals such as cats and monkeys. Physiological and anatomical analyses of the mouse visual cortical critical period indicate similarities but also major differences compared to cats and primates (Antonini, Fagiolini, & Stryker, 1999; Gordon & Stryker, 1996). Thus, it may not be appropriate to consider critical period plasticity in mouse visual cortex identical to that in highly binocular animals. Perhaps a better approach will be temporally and spatially controlled gene disruptions or improved antisense oligonucleotide treatments. Antisense technology provides direct control of the time and location of gene interruption and can be used in any species. Development of definitive experimental manipulations of IEG expression is a major need for assessing the role of these genes in visual cortical plasticity.

What Are the Targets of IEGs?

Changes at the level of IEGs are only a first step in the chain of events that ultimately leads to chronic modification of neuronal function. IEGs can be seen as a third messenger system that regulates other genes that effect the long-term changes. Identification of the target genes of the specific IEG combinations induced by the physiological stimulus would be a major advance. It was originally hoped that identification of the DNA binding sites for AP-1 and other IEG products would aid the search for potential target genes. It is now clear, however, that these binding sites are present in a vast number of genes. While there is suggestive evidence that many known genes are targets of IEGs, definitive evidence is generally lacking (see Herdegen & Leah, 1998). Moreover, the mechanisms of transcriptional regulation are extremely complex and controlled by factors such as the combinatorial nature of transcription factor induction, inter- and intrafamily protein-protein interactions between transcription factors, interaction between DNA binding sites, and postranslational modification of protein activity. This complex regulation is undoubtedly necessary to provide the flexibility and precision of gene expression required by a system as complex as the brain. However, it severely hampers the identification of relevant effector genes for a particular IEG-inducing event on the basis of the induced IEGs. Therefore, to bridge the gap between transcription factor inductions and long-term effector genes, investigators have taken an opposite direction approach, namely, to directly identify potential effector genes by differential screening of cDNA libraries or by differential display polymerase chain reaction (PCR) and related techniques. These techniques provide a means to identify genes whose expression is specifically elevated in one population compared to another. This approach has proven fruitful in identifying candidate effector genes involved in the neuroplastic response of hippocampal neurons to electrical and kainate acid stimulation (Nedivi, Hevron, Naot, Israel, & Citrl, 1993; Qian, Gilbert, Colicos, Kandel, & Kuhl, 1993). Such approaches are beginning to be applied to critical period plasticity in the visual cortex by identifying genes that are differentially expressed at the peak of the critical period (Prasad & Cynader, 1994) and genes that show age-dependent differences between normal and dark-reared cats (Yang, Silver, & Mower, 1999). Identification of candidate effector genes for neuroplasticity, and determination of whether they are regulated by IEGs or other means, is an exciting horizon for molecular neurobiology.

☐ Acknowledgments

Preparation of this chapter was supported by NSF EPSCoR grant OSR-9874767 and the Jewish Hospital Foundation, Louisville, KY, grant 970615-18.

☐ References

Alberini, C. M., Ghirardi, M., Huang, Y. Y., Nguyen, P. V., & Kandel, E. R. (1995). A molecular switch for the consolidation of long-term memory; cAMP-inducible gene expression. *Annals of the New York Academy of Sciences, 758*, 261–286.

Antonini, A., Fagiolini, M., & Stryker, M. P. (1999). Anatomical correlates of functional plasticity in mouse visual cortex. *Journal of Neuroscience, 19*, 4388–4406.

Bear, M. F. (1996). NMDA-receptor-dependent synaptic plasticity in the visual cortex. *Progress in Brain Research, 108*, 205–218.

Beaver, C. J., Mitchell, D. E., & Robertson, H. A. (1993). Immunohistochemical study of the pattern of rapid expression of c-fos protein in the visual cortex of dark reared cats following initial exposure to light. *Journal of Comparative Neurology, 333*, 469–484.

Carroll, R. C., Lissin, D. V., von Zastrow, M., Nicoll, R. A., & Malenka, R. C. (1999). Rapid redistribution of glutamate receptors contributes to long-term depression in hippocampal cultures. *Nature Neuroscience, 2,* 454–460.

Cellerino, A., & Maffei, L. (1996). The action of neurotrophins in the development and plasticity of the visual cortex. *Progress in Neurobiology, 49,* 53–71.

Chaudhuri, A., Matsubara, J. A., & Cyander, M.S. (1995). Neuronal activity in primate visual cortex assessed by immunostaining for the transcription factor Zif268. *Visual Neuroscience, 12,* 35–50.

Chiasson, B. J., Hong, M. G., & Robertson, H. A. (1997). Putative roles for the inducible transcription factor c-fos in the central nervous system: Studies with antisense oligonucleotides. *Neurochemistry International, 31,* 459–475.

Cragg, B. G. (1975). The development of synapses in the visual system of the cat. *Journal of Comparative Neurology, 160,* 147–166.

Cynader, M. (1983). Prolonged sensitivity to monocular deprivation in dark reared cats: Effects of age and visual exposure. *Brain Research: Developmental Brain Research, 8,* 155–164.

Cynader, M., & Mitchell, D. E. (1980). Prolonged sensitivity to monocular deprivation in dark reared cats. *Neurophysiology, 43,* 1026–1040.

Darian-Smith C., & Gilbert, C. D. (1995). Topographic reorganization in the striate cortex of the adult cat and monkey is cortically mediated. *Journal of Neuroscience, 15,* 1631–1647.

Daw, N. W. (1994). Mechanisms of plasticity in the visual cortex. The Friedenwald Lecture. *Investigative Ophthamology and Visual Science, 35,* 4168–4179.

Daw, N. W., Fox, K., Sato, H., & Czepita, D. (1992). Critical period for monocular deprivation in the cat visual cortex. *Journal of Neurophysiology, 67,* 197–202.

Dudek, S. M., & Bear M. F. (1989). A biochemical correlate of the critical period for synaptic modification in the visual cortex. *Science, 246,* 673–675.

Fregnac, Y., & Imbert, M. (1984). Development of neuronal selectivity in the primary visual cortex of the cat. *Physiological Reviews, 64,* 325–434.

Frey, U., & Morris, R. G. (1997). Synaptic tagging and long-term potentiation. *Nature, 385,* 533–536.

Ghosh, A., & Shatz, C. J. (1994). Segregation of geniculocortical afferents during the critical period: A role for subplate neurons. *Journal of Neuroscience, 14,* 3862–3880.

Gordon, J. A., & Stryker, M. P. (1996). Experience-dependent plasticity of binocular responses in the primary visual cortex of the mouse. *Journal of Neuroscience, 16,* 3274–3286.

Herdegen, T., & Leah, J. D. (1998). Inducible and constitutive transcription factors in the mammalian nervous system: Control of gene expression by Jun, Fos and Krox, and CREB/ATF proteins. *Brain Research Review, 28,* 370–490.

Herms, J., Zurmohle, U., Schlingensiepen, R., Brysch, W., & Schlingensiepen, K. H. (1994). Developmental expression of the transcription factor zif268 in rat brain. *Neuroscience Letters, 165,* 171–174.

Hughes, P., Beilharz, E., Gluckman, P., & Dragunow, M. (1993). Brain-derived neurotrophic factor is induced as an immediate early gene following N-methyl-D-aspartate receptor activation. *Neuroscience, 57,* 319–328.

Hughes, P., & Dragunow, M. (1995). Induction of immediate-early genes and the control of neurotransmitter-regulated gene expression within the nervous system. *Pharmacological Reviews, 47,* 133–178.

Johnson, P. F., & McKnight, S. L. (1989). Eukaryotic transcriptional regulatory proteins. *Annual Review of Biochemistry, 58,* 799–839.

Johnson, R. S., Spiegelman, B. M., & Papaioannou, V. (1992). Pleiotropic effects of a null mutation in the c-for proto-oncogene. *Cell, 71,* 577–586.

Kaczmarek, L., & Chaudhuri, A. (1997). Sensory regulation of immediate-early gene expression in mammalian visual cortex: Implications for functional mapping and neural plasticity. *Brain Research Review, 23,* 237–256.

Kaczmarek, L., Zangenehpour, S., & Chaudhuri, A. (1999). Sensory regulation of immediate-early genesc-fos and zif268 in monkey visual cortex at birth and throughout the critical period. *Cerebral Cortex, 9,* 179–187.

Kaminska, B., Kaczmarek, L., & Chaudhuri, A. (1996). Visual stimulation regulates the expression of transcription factors and modulates the composition of AP-1 in visual cortex. *Journal of Neuroscience, 16*, 3968–3978.

Kaplan, I. V., Guo, Y., & Mower, G. D. (1995). Developmental expression of the immediate early gene EGR-1 mirrors the critical period in cat visual cortex. *Brain Research: Developmental Brain Research, 90*, 174–179.

Kaplan, I. V., Guo, Y., & Mower, G. D. (1996). Immediate early gene expression in cat visual cortex during and after the critical period: Differences between EGR-1 and Fos proteins. *Molecular Brain Research, 36*, 12–22.

Lanahan, A., & Worley, P. (1998). Immediate-early genes and synaptic function. *Neurobiology of Learning and Memory, 70*, 37–43.

Mataga, N., Condie, B. G., & Hensch, T. K. (1998). Plasticity of visual cortex in the absense of the neuronal activity dependent marker Zif268/EGR-1. *Society for Neuroscience, 24*, 31.2.

Matthies, H. (1989). In search of cellular mechanisms of memory. *Progress in Neurobiology, 32*, 277–349.

McCormack, M. A., Rosen, K. M., Villa-Komaroff, L., & Mower, G. D. (1992). Changes in immediate early gene expression during postnatal development of cat cortex and cerebellum. *Molecular Brain Research, 12*, 215–223.

Mitchell, P. J., & Tjian, R. (1989). Transcriptional regulation in mammalian cells by sequence-specific DNA binding proteins. *Science, 245*, 371–378.

Morgan, J. I., & Curran, T. (1991). Stimulus-transcription coupling in the nervous system; involvement of the inducible proto-oncogenes fos and jun. *Annual Review Neuroscience, 14*, 421–451.

Mower, G. D. (1991). The effect of dark rearing on the time course of the critical period in cat visual cortex. *Developmental Brain Research, 58*, 151–158.

Mower, G. D. (1994). Differences in the induction of Fos protein in cat visual cortex during and after the critical period. *Molecular Brain Research, 21*, 47–54.

Mower, G. D., Berry, D., Burchfiel, J. L., & Duffy, F. H. (1981). Comparison of the effects of dark rearing and binocular suture on development and plasticity of cat visual cortex. *Brain Research, 220*, 255–267.

Mower, G. D., Caplan, C., Christen, W. G., & Duffy, F. H. (1985). Dark rearing prolongs physiological but not anatomical plasticity of the cat visual cortex. *Journal of Comparative Neurology, 235*, 448–466.

Mower, G. D., & Kaplan, I. V. (1999). Fos expression during the critical period in visual cortex: differences between normal and dark reared cats. *Molecular Brain Research, 64*, 264–269.

Muller, C. M. (1991). Astrocytes in cat visual cortex studied by GFAP and S-100 immunocytochemistry during postnatal development. *Journal of Comparative Neurology, 317*, 309–323.

Nedivi, E., Hevron, D., Naot, D., Israeli, D., & Citrl, Y. (1993). Numerous candidate plasticity related genes revealed by differential cDNA cloning. *Nature, 363*, 718–722.

Prasad, S. S., & Cynader, M. S. (1994). Identification of cDNA clones expressed selectively during the critical period for visual cortex development by subtractive hybridization. *Brain Research, 639*, 73–84.

Qian, A., Gilbert, M. E., Colicos, M. A., Kandel, E. R., & Kuhl, D. (1993). Tissue-plasminogen is induced as an immediate early gene during seizure, kindling, and long term potentiation. *Nature, 361*, 453–457.

Quinlan, E. M., Philpot, B. D., Huganir, R. L., & Bear, M. F. (1999). Rapid, experience-dependent expression of synaptic NMDA receptors in visual cortex in vivo. *Nature Neuroscience, 2*, 352–357.

Reid, S. N., Daw, N. W., Gregory, D. S., & Flavin, H. (1996). cAMP levels increased by activation of metabotropic glutamate receptors correlate with visual plasticity. *Journal of Neuroscience, 16*, 7619–7626.

Rosen, K. M., McCormack, M. A., Villa-Komaroff, L., & Mower, G.D. (1992). Brief visual experience induces immediate early gene expression in the cat visual cortex. *Proceedings of the National Academy of Sciences, 89*, 5437–5411.

Schlingensiepen, K. H., Luno, K., & Brysch, W. (1991). High basal expression of the zif/268 immediate early gene in cortical layers IV and VI, in CA1 and in the corpus striatum-an in-situ hybridization study. *Neuroscience Letters, 122.*

Shatz, C. J., & Luskin, M. B. (1986). The relationship between the geniculocortical afferents and their cortical target cells during development of the cat's primary visual cortex. *Journal of Neuroscience, 6*, 3655–3668.

Shatz, C. J., & Stryker, M. P. (1978). Ocular dominance in layer IV of the cat's visual cortex and the effects of monocular deprivation. *Journal of Physiology, 281*, 267–283.

Sheng, M., & Greenberg, M. E. (1990). The regulation of c-fos and other immediate early genes in the nervous system. *Neuron, 4*, 477–485.

Silveira, L. C., de Matos, F. M., Pontes-Arruda, A., Picanco-Diniz, C. W., & Muniz, J. A. (1996). Late development of Zif268 ocular dominance columns in primary visual cortex of primates. *Brain Research, 732*, 237–241.

Singer, W., Tretter, F., & Yinon, U. (1982). Evidence for long term functional plasticity in the visual cortex of adult cats. *Journal of Physiology, 324*, 239–248.

Skangiel-Kramska, J. (1988). Neurotransmitter systems in the visual cortex of the cat: Possible involvement in plastic phenomena. *Acta Neurobiologiae Experimentalis, 48*, 335–370.

Sonnenberg, J. L., Macgregor-Leon, P. F., Curran, T., & Morgan, J. I. (1989). Dynamic alteration occurs in the levels and composition of transcription factor AP-1 complexes after seizure. *Neuron, 3*, 359–369.

Swindale, N. V. (1988). Role of visual experience in promoting segregation of eye dominance patches in the visual cortex of the cat. *Journal of Comparative Neurology, 267*, 472–488.

Van der Gucht, E., Arckens, L., Orban, G. A., & Vandesande, F. (1999). A new cat specific c-fos antibody to assess different neuronal populations in cat and monkey visual system. *Society for Neuroscience, 25*, 874.9.

Watanabe, Y., Johnson, R. S., Butler, L. S., Binder, D. K., Spiegelman, B. M., Papaioannou, V. E., & McNamara, J. O. (1996). Null mutation of c-for impairs structural and functional plasticities in the kindling model of epilepsy. *Journal of Neuroscience, 16*, 3827–3836.

Wiesel, T. N., & Hubel, D. H. (1963). Single cell responses in striate cortex of kittens deprived of vision in one eye. *Journal of Neurophysiology, 26*, 1003–1017.

Winfield, D. A. (1983). The postnatal development of synapses in the different laminae of the visual cortex in the normal kitten and in kittens with eyelid suture. *Developmental Brain Research, 9*, 155–169.

Wong-Riley, M. (1979). Changes in the visual system of monocularly sutured or enucleated cats demonstrable with cytochrome oxidase histochemistry. *Brain Research, 171*, 11–28.

Worley, P. F., Christy, B. A., Nakabeppu, Y., Bhat, R. V., Cole, A. J., & Baraban, J. M. (1991). Constitutive expression of zif268 in neocortex is regulated by synaptic activity. *Proceedings of the National Academy of Sciences of the United States of America, 88*, 5106–5110.

Yang, C., Silver, B., & Mower, G. D. (1999). Identification of candidate genes for visual cortical plasticity by differential display PCR. *Society for Neuroscience, 25*, 702.3.

Zhang, F., Halleux, P., Arckens, L., Vanduffel, W., Van Bree, L., Mailleux, P., Vandesande, F., Orban, G.A., & Vanderhaeghen, J. J. (1994). Distribution of immediate early gene zif-268, c-fos, c-jun and jun-D mRNAs in the adult cat with special references to brain region related to vision. *Neuroscience Letters, 176*, 137–141.

Zheng, D., Butler, L. S., & McNamara, J. O. (1998). Kindling and associated mossy fibre sprouting are not affected in mice deficient of NGFI-A/NGFI-B genes. *Neuroscience, 83*, 251–258.

Jacqueline K. Rose
Catharine H. Rankin

Behavioral, Neural Circuit, and Genetic Analyses of Habituation in *C. elegans*

☐ Definition of Neuroplasticity

Neuroplasticity is a change (either a strengthening or weakening) in synaptic efficacy brought about through experience. Synapses can be strengthened or weakened through a number of mechanisms, including changes in activation properties of ionic channels in either the presynaptic or postsynaptic neurons, changes in second messenger systems within either cell, or altered gene activation and actual changes in cell morphology, either pre- or postsynaptically. Changes in synaptic strength can be reflected behaviorally as a change in either magnitude or probability of a given response. The maintenance of these altered synaptic connections is reflected in what is observed as "memory" for the earlier experience.

☐ Behavioral, Neural Circuit, and Genetic Analyses of Habituation in *C. elegans*

Use of Simple Systems

The use of physiologically and behaviorally simple animals (compared to higher order vertebrates) allows researchers to isolate mechanisms of behaviors such as learning and memory. When an animal expresses only simple forms of learning, it becomes an easier task to isolate the underlying mechanism, since fewer concurrent learning processes are capable of interfering and thus confounding the experimental conditions. Because these animals have a small, easily identifiable neuroanatomy, researchers can more accurately conclude that any cellular or biochemical changes observed following learning are due to the learning produced during the experiment.

Simple systems have been particularly useful in examining simple forms of learning such as habituation, dishabituation, sensitization, and classical conditioning. Studies of

Aplysia californica (for review, see Sahley & Crow, 1998) have shed light on the physiological basis of sensitization and classical conditioning. *Aplysia* has a nervous system that has large, easily identified, and easily accessed neurons. Electrophysiological studies of sensitization and classical conditioning have led to some major breakthroughs in understanding the roles of ion channels and second messenger systems. In addition, studies on long-term memory in *Aplysia* have demonstrated that changes in number and size of synapses occur as a result of experience (Bailey & Chen, 1988).

One simple system that has contributed to our understanding of the genes that play a role in mechanisms of learning and memory is *Drosophila melanogaster* (for review, see Saitoe and Tully, Chapter 15 of this volume). Many of the same proteins and enzymes involved in learning and memory in *Aplysia* are also involved in similar kinds of learning and memory in *Drosophila*. Genes that mediate long-term memory in *Drosophila* mediate long-term memory in *Aplysia* and in mammals as well. To date, many of the mechanisms that underlie plasticity in mammals were first identified in invertebrate simple systems (for review, see Sahley & Crow, 1998).

Background

C. elegans: Who, What and Why?   The large amount of information available about the *C. elegans* nervous system and genes makes it an ideal candidate for studies of the cellular mechanisms of learning and memory. Recent research has demonstrated that *C. elegans* shows several simple forms of learning such as habituation, sensitization, and context conditioning and is capable of long-term memory lasting at least 24 hours (Rankin, 2000; Rankin, Beck, & Chiba, 1990). *C. elegans* is a bacterivorous, self-fertilizing hermaphroditic nematode. The anatomy and connectivity of *C. elegans* 302 neurons has been mapped at the electron-microscope level, including a wiring diagram showing 5,000 putative electrical synapses and 10,000 putative chemical synapses (White, Southgate, & Durbin, 1988; White, Southgate, Thomson, & Brenner, 1986). In addition, the complete cell lineages of 1,000 somatic cells and their anatomical location across development have also been determined. The function of many of the neurons has been investigated through the use of mutant strains and laser ablation of individual identified neurons.

The genome of the worm has been physically mapped and sequenced, and from the genome sequence, the products of thousands of genes have been identified (for reviews of *C. elegans* research, see Riddle, Blumenthal, Meyer, and Preiss, 1997; Wood, 1988). Researchers are now able to manipulate the worm's genome and examine the phenotypic consequences. In addition, worms can survive freezing, and frozen mutant strains can be indefinitely maintained.

Importance of Habituation in Learning Studies

Habituation is a decrease in the rate and/or amplitude of a response due to repeated stimulation (Groves & Thompson, 1970). The behavioral characteristics outlined for habituation by Groves and Thompson (1970) have been consistent in all organisms studied to date, including a variety of invertebrates and vertebrates. Habituation forms the basis of selective attention and is thus the foundation of all other forms of learning. If habituation did not occur, an organism would give equal attention to all stimuli in the environment and would not be able to selectively attend to stimuli signaling food or danger. Despite its apparent simplicity and its importance for survival, remarkably little is known about the cellular mechanisms of habituation. However, since the behavioral rules characterizing habituation across many different organisms (ranging from single celled organisms to humans) are remarkably consistent (Groves & Thompson), and since habituation is so important to survival, it is likely that the mechanisms of habituation will be highly conserved across evolution. This makes it an ideal candidate for study in a simple system.

Behavioral Analyses

Short-Term Habituation.   Our research has focused on behavioral, neural and genetic studies of short- and long-term habituation of the response to a mechanical vibrational stimulus (a tap) in *C. elegans*. Worms exhibit a withdrawal response following a tap to the side of their Petri dish (for description of apparatus, see Gannon & Rankin, 1995). In adult worms (4-day-olds), this withdrawal response is seen as a reversal (swimming backwards for a brief distance) ~95% of the time. Rankin, Beck, and Chiba (1990) demonstrated that *C. elegans* was capable of nonassociative learning (habituation, dishabituation, and sensitization). Habituation was seen as a decrease in response amplitude following repeated tap stimulation. Dishabituation was the facilitation of the habituated response following the presentation of a brief electrical stimulus. Sensitization was seen as a facilitation of a nonhabituated, baseline response to a single tap by a strong train of taps. Rankin and Broster (1992) showed that in *C. elegans*, as in other organisms, habituation and spontaneous recovery from habituation are sensitive to the interstimulus intervals (ISIs) used during habituation training. Habituation was more rapid and showed greater decrement for the short ISI groups (2 and 10 sec) than for the longer ISI groups (30 and 60 s). ISI also played a major role in spontaneous recovery from habituation, with shorter ISIs resulting in faster and greater recovery than did longer ISIs (Figure 14.1). This effect of ISI on spontaneous recovery from habituation has been seen in other organisms and can be used as a way to distinguish habituation from either fatigue or sensory adaptation. With fatigue or adaptation, recovery should be more rapid the less fatigue or adaptation there is and therefore would not show the ISI-linked rates that we see with habituation. With habituation the less habituated group (the long ISI group) recovers more slowly than the group showing greater habituation (the short ISI group). Thus, one way to determine whether response decrement is habituation or fatigue is to look at the effect of ISI on recovery. In considering mechanisms of habituation, ISI must play a central role. Rankin and Broster showed that it is ISI that sets the recovery rate, not the number of stimuli or the amount of habituation. In this experiment, both the ISI of training stimuli and reaching asymptotic response levels for that ISI were critical features in determining the rate of spontaneous recovery from habituation. Thus, the neural machinery underlying habituation somehow encodes the ISI of training and "remembers" it for some time after the end of stimulation (worms recovered from training at a 10 s ISI within a few minutes, but did not recover from training at a 60 s ISI for over an hour). This led Rankin and Broster to the hypothesis that there were a number of different cellular processes underlying habituation, and that some would be common to all stimulus protocols while others would be preferentially recruited by either long or short ISIs.

Long-Term Habituation.   *C. elegans* has also been found to be capable of long-term (24-hour) retention of habituation. Beck and Rankin (1997) established a training procedure that consistently produced long-term habituation when worms were tested 24 hours after training (Figure 14.2). When stimuli were presented in a distributed training procedure with blocks of stimuli (ISI within blocks was 60 s) separated by an

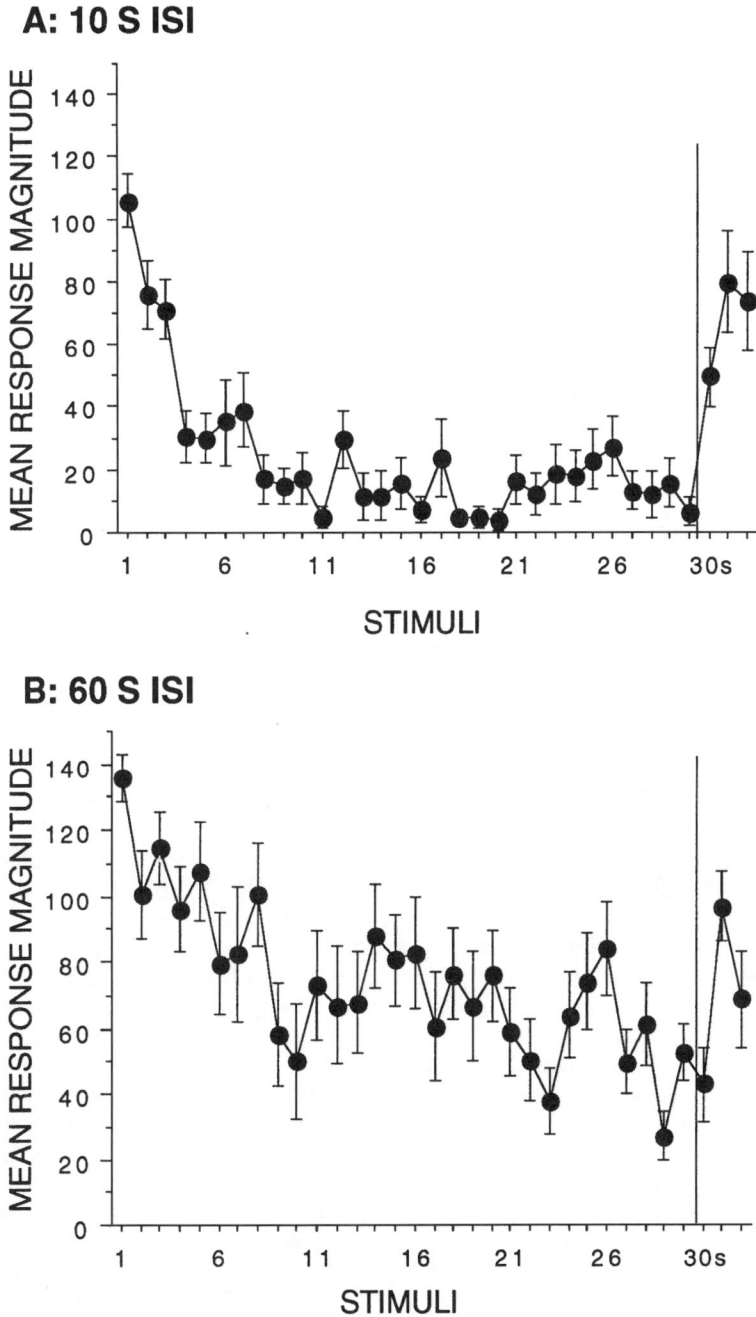

Figure 14.1. Habituation and spontaneous recovery from ($N = 20$ worms/group) (a) stimuli delivered at a 10 s ISI, (b) stimuli delivered at a 60 s ISI. Habituation at the 10 s ISI is more rapid, more complete, and recovers more rapidly at the 10 s ISI than at the 60 s ISI. Redrawn from "Factors Affecting Habituation and Rate of Recovery from Habituation in *C. elegans*," by C. H. Rankin and B. Broster, 1992, *Behavioral Neuroscience, 106*, 241–242.

A

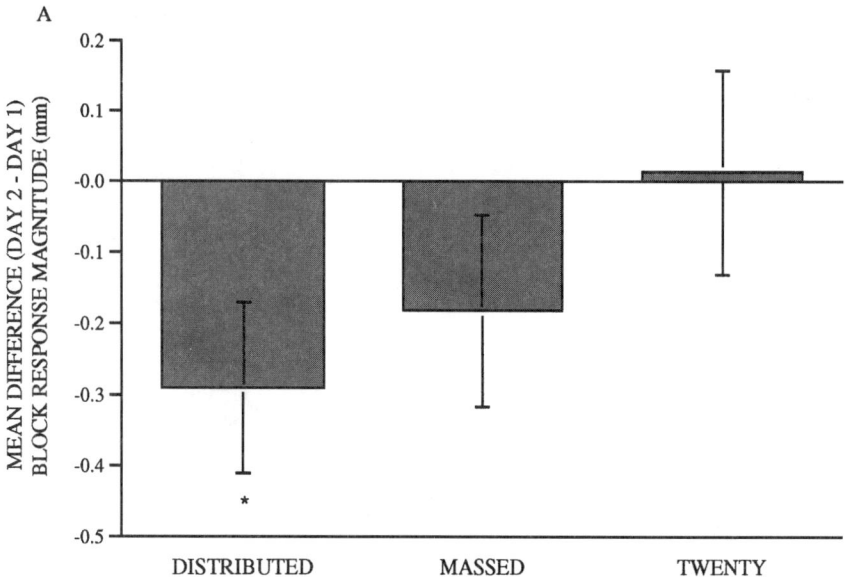

Figure 14.2. Long-term memory for habituation training. On day 1 the distributed training group received 60 tap stimuli in three blocks of 20 stimuli each (ISI within a block was 60 s) with 1 hour in between blocks. On day 1 the massed group received 60 stimuli at a 60 s ISI. On day 1 the 20-stimuli control group received 20 stimuli at a 60 s ISI. On day 2 all worms received 20 stimuli at a 60 s ISI. Data is shown as difference scores (mean day 2 response size − mean day 1 block 1 response size). There was significant retention of training in the distributed training condition but not in the massed or the 20-stimuli control conditions. Redrawn from "Long-Term Habituation Is Produced by Distributed Training at Long ISIs, and Not by Massed Training at Short ISIs in *Caenorhabditis elegans*," by C. D. Beck and C. H. Rankin, 1997, *Animal Learning and Behavior, 25,* 453.

hour there was significant retention 24 hours later. Distributed training with a within-block ISI of 10 s did not produce significant retention 24 hours later, nor did massed training at either a 60 s or a 10 s ISI. The inability of shorter ISIs to produce long-term habituation suggests that the effects of these different ISIs may have been due to different cellular mechanisms differentially recruited by short and long ISIs, as suggested by the studies of short-term habituation in *C. elegans* (Rankin & Broster, 1992).

The superiority of distributed training for the production of memory is consistent with the findings in other organisms. Both *Aplysia* and *Drosophila* show greater memory formation with distributed training. Genetic analyses with *Drosophila* have shown that distributed training induces protein synthesis that leads to lasting physiological change in the neural structures underlying the learning, while massed training does not induce protein synthesis (see Saitoe and Tully, Chapter 15 of this volume).

Beck and Rankin (1995) hypothesized that exposure to heat shock would attenuate protein synthesis and thus might disrupt the consolidation of long-term memory produced by distributed training. Worms were given distributed training. Heat shock administered prior to training or posttraining (directly prior to testing on day 2) had no effect on long-term memory. However, 3- to 45-minute blocks of heat shock administered during habituation training (during the rest periods) did attenuate long-term retention of habituation, although they had no effects on the short-term accumulation of habituation across training blocks. When heat shock was shortened to 15 minutes given in either the early, middle, or late portion of the 1-hour rest period, the results indicated that long-term memory was most disrupted when heat shock was administered in either the early or middle portion of the rest period. This suggested that the first half-hour following training is especially vulnerable to heat shock effects and may be a critical phase of long-term memory formation. These experiments demonstrate that *C. elegans* is capable of retaining information for long periods of time and thus provides a simple model system in which to study long-term memory.

Context Conditioning.   Historically, habituation has been viewed as strictly non-associative learning; however, researchers are now investigating whether, in fact, associations are made during habituation training between the stimulus and salient environmental cues. In context conditioning, it has been hypothesized that context cues may play a role in memory retrieval of earlier training (Wagner, 1976). Rankin (2000) examined context conditioning using *C. elegans*. To test this, worms were trained in one set of environmental conditions and then tested 1 hour later in either the same or different conditions. The context cue used was the presence or absence of .4M sodium acetate on the surface of the agar in the plate. Thus worms were trained with 30 tap stimuli on either plain agar plates or sodium acetate–treated plates, moved to plain plates for 1 hour, and then tested on either plain or sodium acetate plates. Those worms that were both trained and tested on sodium acetate at either a 10 s or 60 s ISI showed greater retention of the earlier training than worms that were trained and tested on different types of plates (Figure 14.3). The context effect could also be seen on plain agar if the agar was made distinctive by placing the worms on sodium acetate plates before training and during the 1-hour break between training and testing. If worms that were trained on sodium acetate were placed on sodium acetate for the hour in between training and testing, then the relationship between sodium acetate and taps was disrupted and extinction occurred. In addition, if worms were placed on sodium acetate plates for 1 hour prior to training on sodium acetate plates, this interfered with the relationship of the cue and the taps in a way termed by learning theorists *latent inhibition*. The results of these experiments showed that worms are capable of context conditioning to either sodium acetate or to plain agar, as long as the environment was not experienced in the absence of taps. It is amazing that such a simple animal is capable of what are considered to be relatively complex behaviors.

Neural Circuit Analyses

Circuit Identification.   To identify cellular mechanisms underlying learning it is first important to identify the neural circuitry of the response. The neural circuit underlying the backward swimming response to head touch and the forward swimming response to tail touch was characterized in the worm using laser ablation of identified neurons (Chalfie et al., 1985). The neural circuit for the tap withdrawal response (Wicks & Rankin, 1995; see Figure 14.4) was characterized by studying the effects of laser ablating cells from the touch circuits and cells that synapse onto them.

The mechanosensory (or touch) cells include bilaterally paired PLM neurons located in the tail and ALM neurons in the anterior body as well as one AVM neuron located at the midline. Ablation of the five touch cells (two PLMs, two ALMs, and the single AVM) eliminated the response to tap. Laser ablation of the three head touch cells (ALMs and AVM) produced worms that always swam forwards (accelerated) in response to

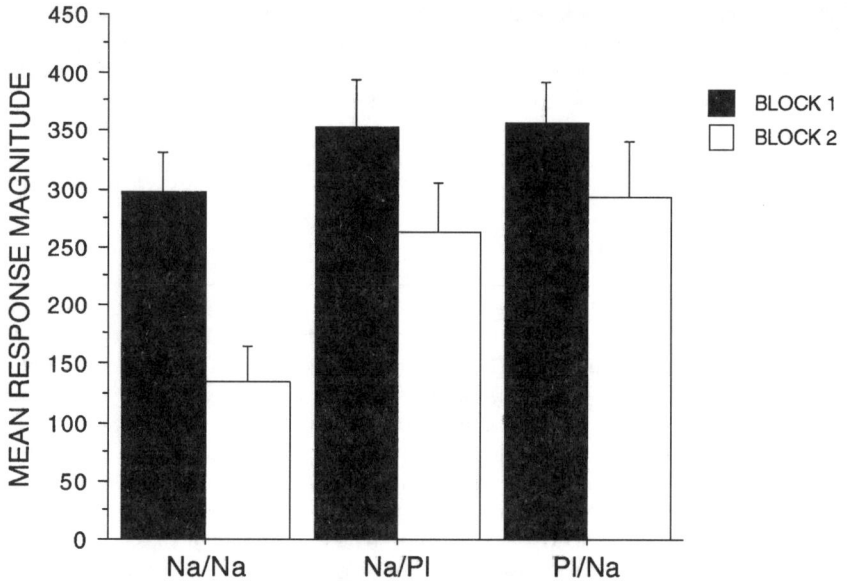

Figure 14.3. Context conditioning. Worms were given habituation training that consisted of 20 stimuli at a 10 s ISI on either plain agar plates (Pl) or agar plates treated with sodium acetate (Na). They were moved to a plain plate for 1 hour and then tested on either a plain plate or a sodium acetate–treated plate with 20 stimuli at a 10 s ISI. A comparison of mean response size during training and testing indicated that worms showed significantly greater retention of habituation training when trained and tested in the same context (Na/Na group) than when the training and testing contexts were different (Na/Pl or Pl/Na). Redrawn from "Context Conditioning in Habituation in the Nematode *C. Elegans*" by C. H. Rankin, 2000, *Behavioral Neuroscience, 114*, 501.

tap (Wicks & Rankin, 1995). Ablation of only the two ALM cells also resulted in worms that accelerated forward in response to tap; however, the accelerations were smaller than with ablation of ALM and AVM together. Ablation of just AVM resulted in a significant decrease in both the frequency and the magnitude of reversals to tap as well as an increased probability of acceleration to tap. AVM is not present at hatching, but is postembryonic and is not fully functional until the end of larval development. At younger (larval) stages of development worms have been shown to accelerate forward in response to tap 50% of the time and reverse the other 50% (Chiba & Rankin, 1990). The shift to predominantly reversals in adult worms has been hypothesized to be the result of the late development of AVM. Ablation of the two tail touch cells (PLMs) produced worms that always swam backwards in response to tap. These reversals were larger than the reversals of intact animals, suggesting that in the intact worms the effects of stimulation of the tail cells by the tap competes with the effects of stimulation of the head touch cells. Thus, the tap response of the intact worm is the result of the integration of competing responses produced by the head and tail touch circuits (Wicks & Rankin, 1995).

Chalfie et al. (1985) called the AVD and PVC interneurons, located in the head touch circuit and the tail touch circuit, respectively, "modulators." Chalfie et al. found that

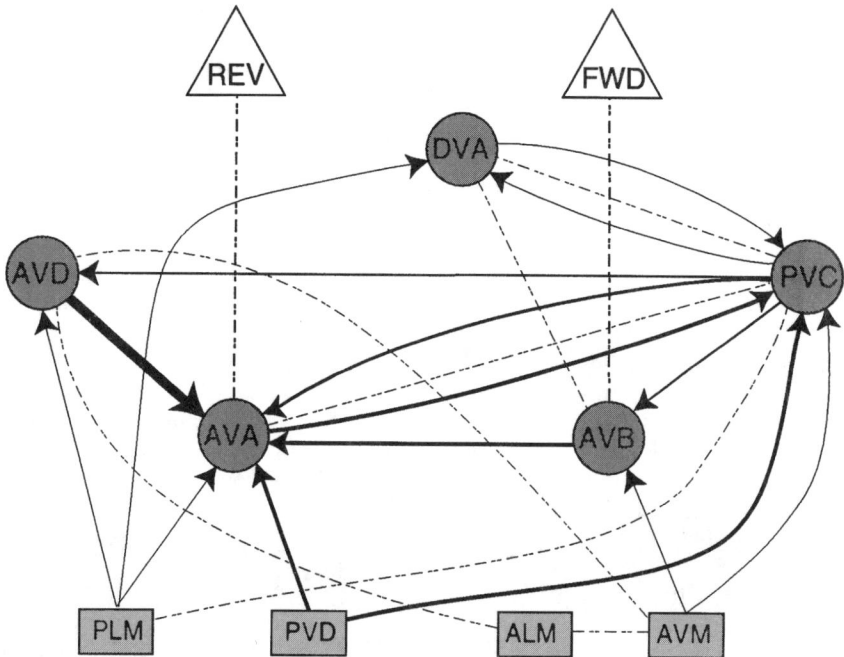

Figure 14.4. The neural circuit underlying response to tap. The squares represent sensory neurons, the circles represent interneurons, and the triangles represent large pools of motor neurons. Solid lines represent chemical connections, with the width of the line corresponding to the number of synapses between the two cells connected. Dashed lines represent electrical connections. The light shading on the sensory neurons represents the expression pattern for the *eat-4* gene; the darker shading on the interneurons represents the expression of a variety of types of glutamate receptors.

animals with PVC interneurons ablated were tail touch insensitive, while those with AVD interneurons ablated were head touch insensitive. A second group of interneurons, AVA in the head touch subcircuit and AVB in the tail touch subcircuit, were considered "drivers." These driver cells make electrical connections with motor neurons responsible for backward and forward motion, respectively, and are required for spontaneous locomotion. When AVA was ablated, animals were backward-uncoordinated (Unc); when AVB was ablated, animals were forward-Unc (Chalfie et al).

Ablation of one of the modulatory pair of interneurons (PVC) resulted in worms that reversed 100% of the time to tap; however, unlike the PLM-worms, the reversals seen in PVC worms were not significantly different in magnitude from control worms. The results support the hypothesis of Chalfie et al. (1985) that the PLM cells make inhibitory chemical connections to the head touch circuit interneurons (AVD and AVA): these connections remain intact following PVC ablation and continue to compete with the head cell stimulation. Chalfie et al. suggested that AVD acts as a connector between the head touch cells (AVM and ALM) and the backward locomotion driver cell (AVA). Thus the ablation of AVD would attenuate a putative excitatory input to the motor neurons responsible for backward locomotion, and therefore AVD animals should respond to tap with accelerations. Ablation of AVD resulted in animals that were capable of normal spontaneous locomotion but accelerated in response to tap.

Although the PVD cells have many of the genetic and anatomical characteristics of the touch cells, Chalfie et al. (1985) determined that they responded only to harsh touch and hypothesized that they were stretch receptors. The PVD neuron synapses onto both the head and the tail components of the circuit. When PVD was ablated there was a significant decrease in the number of tap reversals and the magnitude of reversals compared to controls (Wicks & Rankin, 1995). When PVD was ablated in conjunction with PLM (PVD, PLM-), animals consistently reversed to tap; however, the magnitude of these reversals was significantly smaller than those of the PLM-animals. PVD, ALM-ablated animals showed accelerations of decreased magnitude compared to the ALM-group. Thus, PVD played a role in both the reversals to tap mediated by the ALM, AVM circuit and the accelerations to tap mediated by the PLM circuit.

Like PVD, the DVA neurons synapse with both the AVA and PVC interneurons. Ablation of DVA alone resulted in a decrease in both the frequency and magnitude of reversals to tap (Wicks & Rankin, 1995). When DVA was co-ablated with PLM (DVA, PLM-) a decrease in the exaggerated PLM reversal magnitude was found. DVA, ALM-ablated animals demonstrated accelerations to tap that were also smaller than the acceleration following ALM-ablation. Thus, like PVD, DVA plays a role in both response types.

Roles of Identified Cells in Plasticity

By using laser ablation of the sensory neurons responsible for activating each of the two competing responses, Wicks and Rankin (1996) were able to investigate each of the subcircuits' contribution to habituation to tap.

Laser-ablating the posterior touch cells, the PLM neurons (Wicks & Rankin, 1995), prevented activation of the forward motion circuit. Laser-ablating the PVC interneuron, which eliminated electrical synaptic input from the PLM touch cells onto the interneurons, also altered the posterior circuit (which induces forward motion). The PLM- and the PVC-groups responded to tap consistently with reversals. All three groups (intact, PLM- and PVC-) habituated at both 10 s and 60 s ISIs. The habituation curve for the PLM-group showed a smaller initial slope than the intact animals, while the initial slope for the PVC-animals was virtually indistinguishable from the intact control group. All three groups habituated faster at the 10 s ISI than at the 60 s ISI; however, at each ISI the PLM-group had a higher asymptote than the control group. The difference in initial rate of habituation between the PLM- and the PVC-worms may be due to the fact that the PVC-ablation leaves the chemical synapse (putative inhibition) from the PLM neurons onto the interneurons intact, whereas the PLM ablation eliminates all input from the posterior mechanosensory field (Chalfie et al., 1985; Wicks & Rankin, 1995). The differential initial rate of habituation between the PLM- and PVC-groups led Wicks and Rankin (1996) to hypothesize that the activity of the chemical synapses from PLM to interneurons AVD, AVA, and DVA may contribute to this component of habituation.

Wicks and Rankin (1996) examined dishabituation in these groups (intact, PLM- and PVC-). Dishabituation is the facilitation of a decremented response following presentation of a novel stimulus (Groves & Thompson, 1970). After habituation training, dishabituation was assessed by analyzing responses to tap following a mild electric shock. The intact group showed significant dishabituation at both 10 s and 60 s ISIs, as did the PVC group. Interestingly, the PLM group only showed dishabituation when trained at 60 s ISI and not at 10 s ISI.

The effects of repeated stimulation on acceleration responses were analyzed by ablating the anterior touch cells (bilateral ALM neurons and a midline AVM cell; Wicks, &

Rankin , 1996). Both ALM- and ALM, AVM-ablations produced worms that accelerated in response to tap. Both of these groups habituated to repeated taps at both 10 s and 60 s ISIs. The AVM, ALM-group showed an initial facilitation of the response prior to response decrement, especially when stimulated at a 10 s ISI (Figure 14.5). Interestingly, both groups habituated slower at a 10 s ISI than a 60 s ISI, the opposite of the PLM- and PVC-groups. The AVM, ALM group had a higher response asymptote level at a 60 s ISI than at a 10 s ISI.

Dishabituation was also assessed for the acceleration response (Wicks & Rankin, 1996). The ALM- animals showed significant dishabituation following habituation training at both 10 s and 60 s ISIs. Like the PLM-animals, the AVM, ALM-animals only showed dishabituation at a 60 s ISI with no dishabituation at the 10 s ISI. This suggests that chemical synapses of touch cells onto interneurons of the tap circuit are important for normal dishabituation. The ablated groups that lost these chemical connections (PLM- and AVM, ALM-) show disrupted dishabituation at a 10 s ISI. This suggests that there may not be a single dishabituation process, but that different processes may occur in long versus short ISIs.

The habituation characteristics shown by the intact worm are an integration of different response kinetics in the two subcircuits. Reversals and accelerations habituate at different rates, thus their relative contribution to the intact response varies over the course of habituation (Figure 14.5). At a 10 s ISI the initial facilitation of the acceleration response has a greater influence on the total response, and the reversals seen in intact worms decrease in amplitude very quickly. Since accelerations habituate more slowly than do reversals they also have greater input towards the end of habituation training. This can be seen in intact worms that show an increase in accelerations near the end of habituation training. In order to understand habituation in the intact worm, it is necessary to understand not only the neural components that make up the response, but also the different cellular processes that may be activated in each of the cells.

Localization of Learning

The tap withdrawal circuit is comprised of two competing subcircuits: a head touch circuit inducing backward locomotion and a tail touch circuit inducing forward locomotion (Wicks & Rankin, 1995). The resultant response to tap is a composite response mediated by these two competing pathways. Laser ablation studies have shown that each of these subcircuits habituates, but that they do so with different kinetics (Wicks & Rankin, 1996). This suggests that the cellular mechanisms of habituation cannot be localized to a single cell, but must be in one or more cells in each subcircuit (and that different mechanisms may play a role in the decrement in each of the cells involved).

In order to rule out some of the possible sites for habituation, Wicks and Rankin (1997) characterized the effects of habituation of the tap withdrawal response on other, nonmechanosensory, withdrawal behaviors. There is a similarity in the magnitude of change in direction of movement in response to tap and in spontaneously occurring reversals. The neural trigger for spontaneous reversals is not known, however the interneurons and motor neurons of the tap withdrawal circuit play important roles in all forward and backward movement. Spontaneous reversals of animals with the touch cells ablated were compared to animals with ablations of the PVC interneuron (PVC-) and control group animals (Wicks & Rankin, 1997). There were no differences in the frequency and magnitude of spontaneous reversals between the control group and the touch cell ablation group; however, the PVC-group showed a greater frequency of reversals compared to controls. In addition, the reversals performed by the PVC-worms were smaller

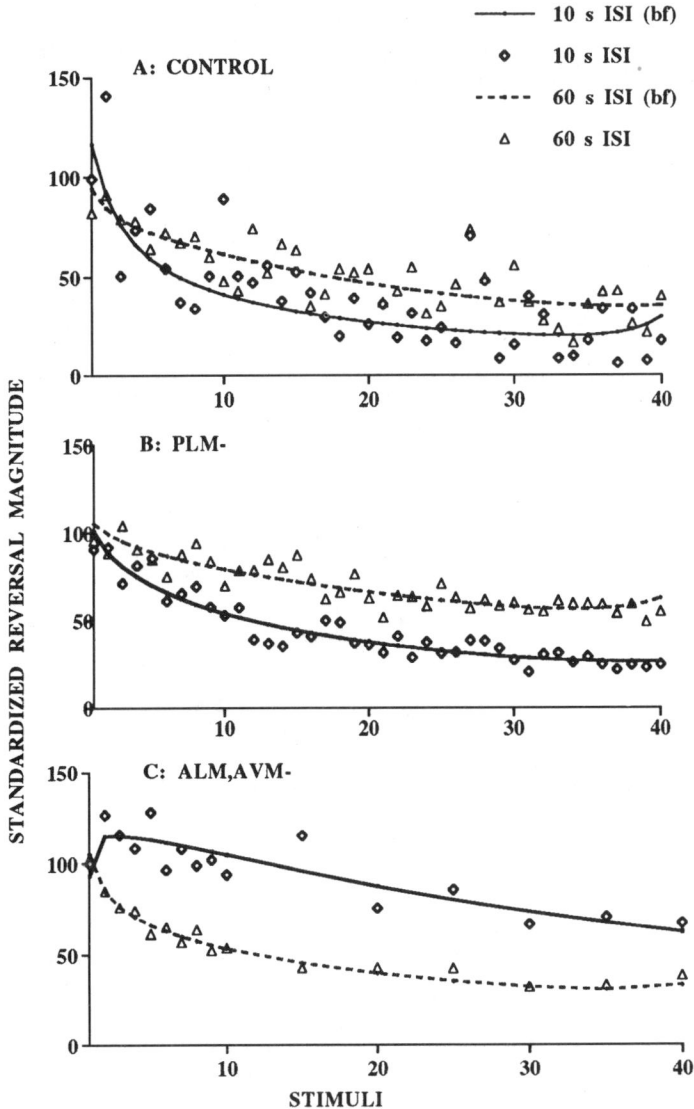

Figure 14.5. Habituation of worms missing sensory receptors from either the head or tail. The lines represent lines of best fit (bf), the diamonds represent responses to stimuli delivered at a 10 s ISI, and the triangles represent responses to stimuli delivered at a 60 s ISI. (a) Reversal responses of intact worms at 10 s and 60 s ISI. (b) Reversal responses of worms missing the PLM tail touch neurons. (c) Forward acceleration responses of worms missing the ALM and AVM head touch neurons. Modified from "The Integration of Antagonistic Reflexes Revealed by Laser Ablation of Identified Neurons Determines Habituation Kinetics of the *Caenorhabditis elegans* Tap Withdrawal Response, 1996, *Journal of Comparative Psychology A, 179,* 679. Habituation of reversals is slower than habituation of accelerations. The behavior of the intact worm is an integration of the behavior of the two subcircuits.

in magnitude. From this it was suggested that the PVC interneurons were likely involved in the initiation and maintenance of spontaneous locomotion under normal conditions. It also appears that the touch cells play no role in generating spontaneous locomotion.

If the locus of habituation is presynaptic to the level of interneurons, then neither the frequency nor the magnitude of spontaneous reversals should change as a result of habituation training to tap. However, if the locus of habituation is postsynaptic to the sensory neurons (interneurons or motor neurons), then habituation training may result in concurrent habituation of spontaneous reversals. Tap habituation training had no effect on the frequency or the magnitude of spontaneous reversals following habituation training (Wicks & Rankin, 1997), suggesting that the locus of habituation is unlikely to be in either the interneurons or the motor neurons.

Another study investigated whether habituation to tap would influence a reversal response triggered by another type of stimulus. For this experiment thermal stimulation was chosen, as the neurons that transduce thermal stimuli have been characterized and do not include the mechanosensory touch cells of the tap circuit (Mori & Ohshima, 1995). There was no difference between the magnitude of reversals away from a hot probe in a group that was habituated to tap and the magnitude of reversals away from a hot probe in a group that was not habituated to tap (Wicks & Rankin, 1997). Thus the magnitude of thermal-induced reversals was not affected by habituation training using taps. Therefore, it appears that habituation to tap is pathway-specific and that the locus of habituation is likely to be either in the sensory neurons themselves or in the synapses from the sensory neurons onto the interneurons.

Genetic Analyses

There is a growing body of evidence that suggests that the chemical synapses from the touch sensory neurons onto the interneurons are glutamatergic. Recently, genes homologous to two different classes of glutamate receptors have been isolated in *C. elegans* (AMPA-type: Hart, Sims, & Kaplan, 1995; Maricq, Peckol, Driscoll, & Bargmann, 1995; and NMDA-type: Brockie, Madsen, & Maricq, 1997) as well as genes for a third class of glutamate receptor: inhibitory glutamate-gated chloride channels (Dent, Davis, & Avery, 1997). All three of these receptor types have been found to be expressed on one or more of the four interneurons of the tap withdrawal circuit (AVA, AVB, AVD, and PVC).

Other evidence for glutamatergic transmission comes from studies on *eat-4* mutant worms. The EAT-4 gene has been hypothesized to positively regulate glutaminase activity, which is required for glutamate synthesis. Lee, Sawin, Chalfie, Horvitz, and Avery (1999) have postulated that EAT-4 may alter the rate of glutamate synthesis by modulating the activity of phosphate-activated glutaminase by inducing a high intracellular concentration of inorganic phosphate. In addition, Lee et al. (1999) have found that *eat-4* is expressed in the sensory neurons of the tap circuit (ALM, AVM, and PLM). Thus, there is now pre- and postsynaptic evidence to support the hypothesis that the chemical synapses between the sensory cells of the tap circuit and the interneurons are glutamatergic. If this is so, then worms deficient in one of the genes for either glutamate production or glutamate reception may alter tap-withdrawal responses and/or show a different pattern of habituation to tap than wild-type worms.

Rankin and Wicks (2000) examined *eat-4* mutant worms and their ability to habituate to tap. The *eat-4* worms' reversals to tap were of similar magnitude to wild-type worms. Therefore, it appears that EAT-4 has no specific role in responding to a single tap. There were, however, effects on responding to repeated stimulation. Like wild-type worms, *eat-4* worms showed faster and more complete habituation at a shorter 10 s ISI than at a 60 s ISI. However, at all ISIs *eat-4* worms showed very rapid response decrement and

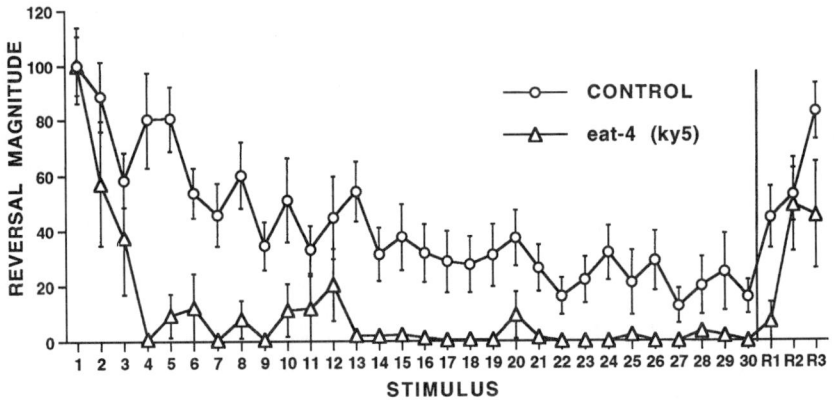

Figure 14.6. Habituation curves for wild-type control worms and mutant *eat-4 (ky5)* worms to taps delivered at a 10 s ISI. The *eat-4* worms show more rapid and complete habituation and slower recovery than the wild-type controls. Modified from "Mutations of the *C. elegans* Brain-Specific Inorganic Phosphate Transporter, *eat-4*, Affect Habituation of the Tap-Withdrawal Response Without Affecting the Response Itself," by C. H. Rankin and S. R. Wicks, 2000, *Journal of Neuroscience, 20,* 4340.

depressed asymptotic levels compared to controls (Figure 14.6). Recovery from habituation in *eat-4* worms was also ISI dependent, however it was slower than for wild-type worms. From these results it appears that the EAT-4 gene may not be required for glutamate transmission; however, it may serve to produce sustained (tonic) glutamate transmission.

A possible explanation for the behavior of *eat-4* worms during habituation training comes from an understanding of the electrical and chemical connections in the circuits. In intact *eat-4* worms both the anterior and posterior subcircuits of the tap withdrawal response are activated by electrical connections between the sensory and interneurons. The amount of neurotransmitter available may decrease rapidly with repeated stimulation in *eat-4* worms. With the two subcircuits simultaneously activated, and with little activation of the chemical synapses in the two subcircuits due to the depletion of glutamate, the two subcircuits may cancel each other out resulting in no response to the tap. This may explain why *eat-4* groups show no response by the end of habituation training.

One group of *eat-4* worms underwent laser ablation of the posterior touch cells (PLM), allowing analysis of the effects of EAT-4 on the pure reversal produced by the anterior touch cells (ALM and AVM). In *eat-4* worms with the PLM ablated (*eat-4*::PLM-) a similar pattern of habituation was seen, with rapid and more complete habituation and slower recovery than in wild-type worms with PLM ablated. Although there was more rapid decrement in the *eat-4*::PLM-worms the responses did not go to zero as they did in intact *eat-4* worms; that is, even at the end of the habituation training, worms were still responding to tap with reversals. In the *eat-4*::PLM-worms the repeated taps activate only the electrical connections from the sensory neurons onto the interneurons responsible for the reversal response. This suggests that the preserved electrical connections between the AVM and ALM neurons are sufficient to form a reversal response, especially without the competing inputs from the PLM. There is still a depression of response in the *eat-4*::PLM-worms as a result of repeated stimulation. Again the *eat-4* mutation may be depleting the amount of available glutamate rather than eliminating glutamate completely, thus a decrement would be noted in conditions where sustained glutamate activity is required (e.g., responding to repeated taps).

Habituation of the tap withdrawal response in *C. elegans* has been shown to dishabituate following presentation of a brief electric shock delivered to the agar on which the worm moves (Rankin, Beck, & Chiba, 1990). It was found that *eat-4* worms did not show a significant increase in response following shock (Rankin & Wicks, 2000). Although dishabituation has sometimes been considered a defining feature of habituation, sensitivity of spontaneous recovery to ISI may be a better feature; differential recovery to ISI is clearly a property of the same or related mechanisms involved in habituation, whereas little is known with regard to the relationship between the mechanisms of dishabituation and habituation. It has yet to be determined whether dishabituation is a reversal of the effects of habituation or a distinct facilitatory process superimposed on habituation. The *eat-4* worms are capable of habituation and demonstrate a sensitivity to ISI in recovery from habituation; however, dishabituation appears to be absent.

The *eat-4* mutant worms show a deficit in pharyngeal muscle relaxation. Lee et al. (1999) identified the *eat-4* gene and generated a genetic construct that rescued this pharyngeal deficit; Rankin and Wicks (2000) tested the effects of habituation on this transgenic worm strain. The transgenic strain (DA1242) that showed full rescue of the pharyngeal deficit also showed full rescue of the habituation and dishabituation deficits seen in the *eat-4* worms. This provides support for the hypothesis that the touch cells are glutaminergic and that the chemical transmission from the sensory to the interneurons plays a role in habituation of the tap withdrawal response.

The recent discovery of a number of types of glutamate receptors in *C. elegans* has led to the characterization of a number of mutant strains deficient in these receptors. Through the use of genetic markers such as green fluorescent protein (GFP) the expression pattern of these receptor subtypes has been determined. The GLR-1 gene encodes a glutamate receptor most homologous to the AMPA-type receptor (Hart et al., 1995; Maricq et al., 1995). It is expressed on a number of neurons in *C. elegans*, including the four interneurons of the tap withdrawal circuit (AVA, AVB, AVD, and PVC). Preliminary investigations indicate that the *glr-1* worms show smaller responses to tap and more rapid and complete habituation to tap than do wild-type worms. The NMR-1 gene encodes a glutamate receptor most homologous to the NMDA-type receptor (Brockie et al., 1997). It is expressed in approximately six of *C. elegans* neurons, including four of the interneurons in the tap withdrawal circuit (AVA, AVD, PVC, and DVA). Preliminary studies show that *nmr-1* worms show normal responses to tap and normal habituation to tap.

☐ Summary

What We Have Learned About *C. elegans* From These Studies of Habituation

This research offers the first detailed, controlled evidence that *C. elegans* is capable of changing its behavior as a result of experience. The experiments discussed in this chapter show that *C. elegans* is capable of short-term habituation, dishabituation, and sensitization, as well as associative context conditioning. The rules for these simple forms of learning are the same in *C. elegans* as they are in other organisms. In addition, both short- and long-term memory can be seen in *C. elegans*. The neural circuit analyses have shown that the response to tap is produced by two competing subcircuits whose responses are integrated to produce the response to tap. In addition, the responses of the two subcircuits were shown to habituate with different kinetics, indicating that all cells that habituate in *C. elegans* do not use the same mechanisms. The localization experiments suggested the hypothesis that the sites of plasticity underlying habituation were at the level of the sensory neurons. The investigation of the mutant strains of worms has led to a confirmation of the importance of the neurotransmitter glutamate in the touch cells and an investigation of the role of various glutamate receptors in habituation in *C. elegans*.

What We Have Learned About Habituation From These Studies of *C. elegans*

The studies of habituation in *C. elegans* have shown the importance of the ISI dependence in habituation, and spontaneous recovery from habituation, in the formation of long-term habituation, and possibly in dishabituation. These results suggest that habituation at long and short ISIs may recruit different (but overlapping) cellular mechanisms. ISI dependence is a defining characteristic of habituation that can be used along with or instead of dishabituation to distinguish habituation from fatigue or sensory adaptation. In the neural circuit analysis of habituation we have demonstrated that the locus of habituation is distributed across several neuronal classes and that the kinetics of habituation differ in these different neuronal classes. The integration of the kinetics of the different cell types is necessary for the production of the habituation curve of the intact worm. The studies of context conditioning have shown that it is possible to have an associative component to habituation and that the associative component shows extinction and latent inhibition. The examination of habituation in *eat-4* mutant worms shows that chemical synapses play a role in the observed response decrement and that the mechanisms of habituation, but not of dishabituation, operate independent of the amount of neurotransmitter available.

☐ Where to Next?

The analysis of neuroplasticity in *C. elegans* is just beginning. With the localization of the learning to specific cells, it will now be possible to use modern genetic techniques to manipulate gene expression in just those cells in order to investigate the roles of many compounds in plasticity. It will be possible to investigate the role of many compounds already identified in other organisms in learning and or in memory in *C. elegans*. The isolation of mutants that show deficits in either learning or memory in *C. elegans* will lead to identification of novel compounds not previously implicated as playing a role in plasticity. With its genome fully sequenced, and only 302 neurons, this small worm will likely make a significant contribution to our understanding of the cellular mechanisms underlying behavioral plasticity.

☐ References

Bailey, C. H., & Chen, M. (1988). Long-term sensitization in *Aplysia* increases the number of presynaptic contacts onto the identified gill motor neuron L7. *Proceedings of the National Academy of Sciences of the United States of America, 85*, 9356–9359.

Beck, C. D. O., & Rankin, C. H. (1995). Heat-shock disrupts long-term memory consolidation in *Caenorhabditis elegans*. *Learning and Memory, 2*, 161–177.

Beck, C. D. O., & Rankin, C. H. (1997). Long-term habituation is produced by distributed training at long ISIs and not by massed training at short ISIs in *Caenorhabditis elegans*. *Animal Learning and Behavior, 25*, 446–457.

Brockie, P. J., Madsen, D. M., & Maricq, A. V. (1997). Genetic analysis of two *C. elegans* putative NMDA receptor subunits *nmr-1* and *nmr-2*. *Society for Neuroscience Abstract, 23*, 936.

Chalfie M., Sulston J. E., White J. G., Southgate E., Thomson J. N., & Brenner, S. (1985). The neural circuit for touch sensitivity in *Caenorhabditis elegans*. *Journal of Neuroscience, 5*, 956–964.

Chiba, C. M., & Rankin, C. H. (1990). A developmental analysis of spontaneous and reflexive reversals in the nematode *Caenorhabditis elegans*. *Journal of Neurobiology, 21*, 543–554.

Dent, J. A., Davis, M. W., & Avery, L. (1997). *avr-15* encodes a chloride channel subunit that mediates inhibitory glutamatergic neurotransmission and ivermectin sensitivity in *Caenorhabditis elegans*. *EMBO, 16*, 5867–5879.

Gannon, T. N., & Rankin, C. H. (1995). Approaches to the analysis of *C. elegans* behavior. In D. Shakes (Ed.), *Methods in cell biology Vol. 48: Caenorhabditis elegans*. (pp. 205–223). San Diego, CA: Academic Press.

Groves, P. M., & Thompson, R. F. (1970). Habituation: A dual-process theory. *Psychological Review, 77*, 419–450.

Hart, A. C, Sims, S., & Kaplan, J. M. (1995). Synaptic code for sensory modalities revealed by *C. elegans* GLR-1 glutamte receptor. *Nature, 378*, 82–85.

Lee, R. Y. N., Sawin, E. R., Chalfie, M., Horvitz, H. R., & Avery, L. (1999). EAT-4, a homolog of a mammalian sodium-dependent inorganic phosphate co-transporter, is necessary for glutamatergic neurotransmission in *Caenorhabditis elegans*. *Journal of Neuroscience, 19*, 159–167.

Maricq, A. V., Peckol, E., Driscoll, M., & Bargmann, C. I. (1995). Mechansensory signalling in *C. elegans* mediated by the GLR-1 glutamate receptor. *Nature, 378*, 78–81.

Mori, I., & Ohshima, Y. (1995). Neural regulation of thermotaxis in *Caenorhabditis elegans*. *Nature, 376*, 344–348.

Rankin, C. H. (2000). Context conditioning in habituation in the nematode *Caenorhabditis elegans*. *Behavioral Neuroscience, 114*, 496–505.

Rankin, C. H., Beck, C., & Chiba, C. (1990). *Caenorhabditis elegans*: A new model system for the study of learning and memory. *Behavioral Brain Research, 37*, 89–92.

Rankin, C. H., & Broster, B. (1992). Factors affecting habituation and rate of recovery from habituation in *C. elegans*. *Behavioral Neuroscience, 106*, 239–249.

Rankin, C. H., & Wicks, S. R. (2000). Mutations of the *C. elegans* brain-specific inorganic phosphate transporter, *eat-4*, affect habituation of the tap-withdrawal response without affecting the response itself. *Journal of Neuroscience, 20*, 4337–4344.

Riddle, D. L., Blumenthal, T., Meyer, B. J., & Priess, J. (1997). *C. elegans II*. Cold Spring Harbor, NY: Cold Spring Harbor Laboratory Press.

Sahley, C., & Crow, T. (1998). Invertebrate learning: Current perspectives. In J. Martinez & R. Kesner (Eds.), *Neurobiology of learning and memory* (pp. 177–209). San Diego, CA: Academic Press.

Wagner, A. R. (1976). Priming in STM: An information-processing mechanism for self-generated or retrieval-generated depression in performance. In T. J. Tighe & R. N. Leaton (Eds.), *Habituation: Perspectives from child development, animal behavior, and neurophysiology* (pp. 95–128). Hillsdale, NJ: Erlbaum.

White, J. E., Southgate, E., & Durbin, R. (1988). Appendix 2. Neuroanatomy. In W. B. Wood (Ed.), *The nematode Caenorhabditis elegans* (pp. 433–455). Cold Spring Harbor, NY: Cold Spring Harbor Laboratory Press.

White J. E., Southgate E., Thomson J. N., & Brenner S. (1986). The structure of the nervous system of the nematode *Caenorhabditis elegans*. *Philosophical Transactions of the Royal Society of London. Series B: Biological Sciences, 314*, 1–340.

Wicks, S. R., & Rankin, C. H. (1995). Integration of mechanosensory stimuli in *Caenorhabditis elegans*. *Journal of Neuroscience, 15*, 2434–2444.

Wicks, S. R., & Rankin, C. H. (1996). The integration of antagonistic reflexes revealed by laser ablation of identified neurons determines habituation kinetics of the *Caenorhabditis elegans* tap withdrawal response. *Journal of Comparative Physiology A, 179*, 675–685.

Wicks, S. R., & Rankin, C. H. (1997). The effects of tap withdrawal response habituation on other withdrawal behaviors: the localization of habituation in *C. elegans. Behavioral Neuroscience. 111.* 1–12.

Wood, W. B. (Ed.). (1988). *The nematode Caenorhabditis elegans.* Cold Spring Harbor, NY: Cold Spring Harbor Laboratory Press.

15

CHAPTER

Minoru Saitoe
Tim Tully

Making Connections Between Developmental and Behavioral Plasticity in *Drosophila*

The brain is a unique organ, evolutionarily designed to sense its internal and external environment, to perceive causal relations among stimuli, and to change its responses adaptively. To accomplish this incredible task, a self-regulating network of 70 thousand genes directs the development of a cellular network of 1 trillion neurons with 70 trillion connections among them. To add to such staggering complexity, the computational activity generated by this neural network continually feeds back on the underlying gene network by regulating the expression of "plasticity" genes, which then alter neural connectivity.

This process originates early in vertebrate development (Goodman & Shatz, 1993). Activity-independent mechanisms control the differentiation of different cell types in the central nervous system (CNS) and the initial outgrowth of neuronal processes. These steps result in a largely stereotyped—although often crude—pattern of synaptic connections. Activity-dependent mechanisms then promote the sharpening and refinement of these circuits as synapses mature.

In the peripheral nervous system (PNS), a similar strategy underlies formation of the neuromuscular junction (Sanes & Lichtmann, 1999). Activity-independent guidance and recognition cues allow motor neurons many initial contacts with muscle fibers. Activity-dependent mechanisms then sharpen this innervation pattern through selective axonal withdrawal and synapse elimination so that each fiber within the muscle receives input from only one motor neuron. These two mechanisms ensure that a functioning circuit is tailored to its particular behavioral output.

Synaptic reorganization occurs within the adult brain itself (Kolb, 1995). Molecular and physiological insights have emerged both from behavioral investigations of learning and from cellular models of neuroplasticity. Adults and developing animals can modify their synapses with a host of common molecular components (Bailey & Kandel, 1993; Bear, Kleinschmidt, Gu, & Singer, 1990; Cline, 1998; Cline & Constantine-Paton, 1989; Mayford, Barzilai, Keller, Schacher, & Kandel, 1992; McKay, Purcell, & Carew, 1999; Pham, Impey, Storm, & Stryker, 1999; Tang et al., 1999; Weiler, Hawrylak, &

Greenough, 1995). These findings support the notion that mechanisms of adult learning and of developmental plasticity may be conserved.

Here, we summarize results from neurogenetic experiments on fruit flies supporting the notion that developmental plasticity and long-term memory (LTM) formation result from similar molecular mechanisms. Of particular interest are recent studies of activity-dependent synaptic plasticity at the larval neuromuscular junction (NMJ) in mutants originally isolated from assays of adult olfactory memory (Dubnau & Tully, 1998). These single-gene mutations have yielded a "genetic dissection" of olfactory memory formation, and all mutants evaluated to date also produce distinct lesions in synaptic structure and/or function at the larval NMJ. Thus, our approach yields novel links between molecular mechanisms of developmental and adult plasticity.

☐ Learning and Memory Mutants

Memory Phases

The memory of a new experience does not form all at once. Associative learning first produces a short-lived, disruptable form of memory. This early memory then is "consolidated" within a few hours into a longer lasting, stable form. In fact, pharmacological experiments in vertebrates have suggested at least three distinct memory phases: short-term memory (STM), middle-term memory (MTM), and LTM (Allweis, 1991; H. P. Davis & Squire, 1984; DeZazzo & Tully, 1995; McGaugh & Herz, 1972). Experiments in *Drosophila* largely support this view. Five genetically distinct temporal phases have been inferred: learning (LRN), STM, MTM, anesthesia-resistant memory (ARM), and LTM (DeZazzo & Tully, 1995; Dubnau & Tully, 1998; Tully, Preat, Boynton, & Del Vecchio, 1994; Tully et al., 1996).

Taken together, these studies suggest three important aspects of memory formation. First, memory of a new experience becomes disruption-resistant with time (McGaugh & Herz, 1972; Quinn & Dudai, 1976; Yamada, Sekiguchi, Susuki, & Mizukami, 1992). Second, memory formation from LRN to LTM involves both sequential and parallel processing. Third, memory formation for most tasks is stronger and longer lasting after spaced (distributed) rather than massed training (Quinn & Dudai, 1976; Yin, Del Vecchio, Zhou, & Tully, 1995; Yin et al., 1994).

Since detailed discussions of the properties of each memory phase already have been provided (Dubnau & Tully, 1998; DeZazzo & Tully, 1995; Tully et al., 1996), we briefly describe genetic variants that appear to affect these memory phases differentially (Figure 15.1a and Table 15.1). LRN mutants show reduced olfactory associative learning after a single training session, but the memory decay rate thereafter is normal. Such is the case for mutations in *latheo* (*lat*; Boynton & Tully, 1992; Pinto et al., 1999), *linotte* (*lio*; Bolwig, Del Vecchio, Hannon, & Tully, 1995; Dura, Preat, & Tully, 1993; Saitoe & Tully, 2000), *leonardo* (*leo*; Skoulakis & Davis, 1996), *DCO* (Skoulakis, Kalderon, & Davis, 1993), and *PKA-RI* (Goodwin et al., 1997). In reverse-genetic experiments, a mutant, constitutively active G_s alpha subunit also was shown to abolish associative learning (Connolly et al., 1996).

STM mutants show a reduction in initial learning and a rapid decay of memory within the first 30 minutes after training. STM defects are observed in *dunce* (*dnc*), *rutabaga* (*rut*), and *Volado* (*vol*) mutants (Chen, Denome, & Davis, 1986; Grotewiel, Beck, Wu, Zhu, & Davis, 1998; Levin et al., 1992; Tully & Quinn, 1985).

A.

B.

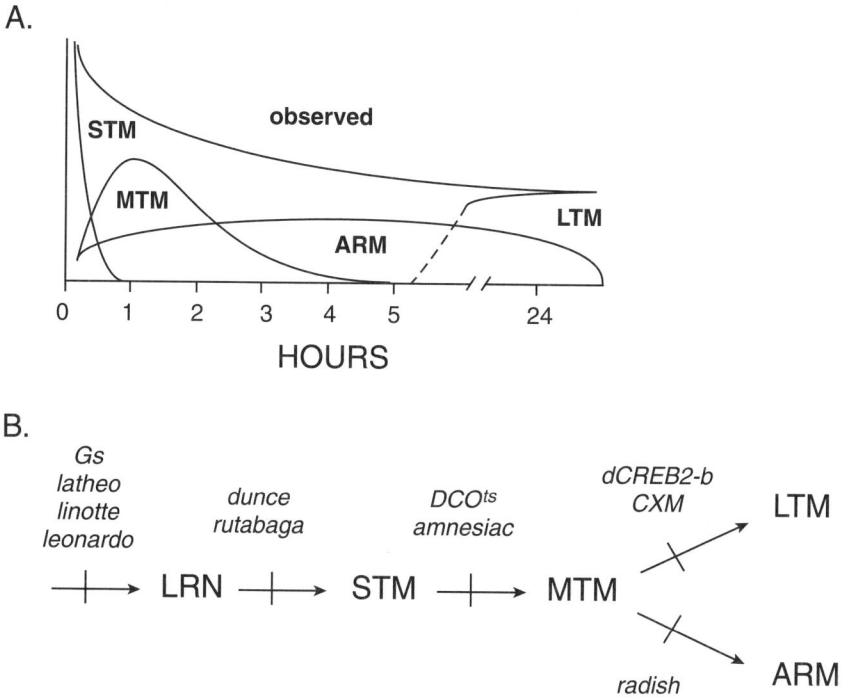

Figure 15.1. (a) Putative memory phases in *Drosophila*. Four functionally distinct memory phases underlie observed memory retention after acquisition of a new experience (LRN). STM, MTM, ARM, and LTM appear sequentially, and each has a progressively slower rate of decay. The kinetics of early memory components (STM and MTM) were derived by subtracting mutant memory retention curves from memory retention curves of wild type. The kinetics of ARM and LTM (except the initial induction of LTM, which remains unknown) were derived directly from pharmacological and/or genetic experiments. (b) Genetic pathway underlying memory formation after olfactory associative learning. Different memory phases appear to be blocked preferentially in different memory mutants. The pathway is sequential from LRN to MTM, but then it branches into two independent paths, ARM and LTM.

MTM mutants show near-normal learning and 7-h memory retention; between these time points, however, memory retention is deficient. *amnesiac* (*amn*) mutants and temperature-sensitive mutants of *DC0* (*DC0ts*) disrupt MTM preferentially (Feany & Quinn, 1995; Li, Tully, & Kalderon 1996; Moore et al., 1998; Tully et al., 1990).

Operationally defined, ARM is a consolidated memory, since it is not disrupted in retrograde amnesia experiments. Cold-shock anesthesia, when delivered immediately after training, almost completely abolishes 3-h memory. When delivered at progressively later times after training, however, 3-h retention becomes progressively resistant to cold-shock anesthesia. Within 2 h after a single training session, ARM appears asymptotic in normal flies and comprises about half of observed memory retention. This observation suggests that 3-h memory retention is composed of both ARM and

TABLE 15.1. Drosophila mutants and their affected olfactory memory phase, molecule, and synaptic plasticity.

Memory Phase	Mutants	Molecule	Synaptic Plasticity
LRN	*latheo*	ORC subunit	EJCs↑, facilitation↓, augmentation↓, no PTP
	linotte	novel	normal EJCs, facilitation↓, augmentation↓, no
	leonardo	14-3-3 protein	EJCs↓, facilitation↓, augmentation↓, no PTP
	DC0	PKA catalytic subunit	?
	PKA-RI	PKA regulatory subunit	?
	G-s	Stimulatory G	?
STM	*dunce*	PDE	EJCs↑, facilitation↓, no augmentation, no PTP
	rutabaga	AC	normal EJCs, facilitation↓, augmentation↓, no
	volado	integrin	?
MTM	*amnesiac*	(PACAPand/or GHRH)	?
	DC0ts	PKA catalytic subunit	?
ARM	*radish*	unknown	?
LTM	*hs-dCREBb*	CREB repressor	normal EJCs in *dnc* *hs-CREBb*
	hs-dCREBa	CREB activator	EJCs↑ in *50% Fas II* *hs-dCREBa*
?	*50% Fas II*	Fas II	increase synaptic site, normal EJCs
	hs-ala	Peptide inhibitor for CaMKII	increase synaptic site, EJCs↑, facilitation↓, augmentation↓, PTP↓

? = data not known.

an earlier, anesthesia-sensitive memory (ASM). ARM is absent in *radish* (*rsh*) mutants, as is 8-h retention after a single training session (Folkers, Drain, & Quinn, 1993; Tully et al., 1994). The latter observation implies that 8-h retention is composed entirely of ARM (unlike 3-h retention). Massed training (10 training sessions administered consecutively with no rest interval in between) produces more ARM (DelVecchio & Tully, 1995; Tully et al., 1994); consequently, memory after massed training lasts more than one day. Like 8-h memory after one training session, one-day memory after massed training is absent in *rsh* mutants. Importantly, LTM is normal in *rsh* mutants, indicating that ARM and LTM are functionally distinct (independent) memory phases (Tully et al., 1994; see below). Pharmacological data corroborate these genetic studies. ARM appears normal in cycloheximide (CXM)-fed flies, while LTM is abolished (Tully et al., 1994).

LTM, a second type of consolidated memory, is produced only after spaced training (10 training sessions with a 15-min rest interval between each) and lasts at least 7 days in normal flies. Seven-day memory is abolished in CXM-fed flies, thereby indicating that the induction of LTM depends on protein synthesis. Initial learning and one-day memory after spaced training in CXM-fed flies is similar to that normally produced by massed training. This observation suggests that, in addition to LTM, spaced training induces LRN, STM, MTM, and ARM to levels equivalent to those produced by massed training. Moreover, 1-day memory after spaced training appears to be composed of similar amounts of ARM and LTM, the former of which eventually decays away, while the latter of which persists. LTM specifically is disrupted by overexpression of CREB repressor transgene (dCREB2-b; Yin et al., 1994). Hence, memory retention after spaced or massed training appears similar in these transgenic animals. In striking contrast to these results, the induction of LTM is enhanced in transgenic flies overexpressing a CREB activator transgene (dCREB2-a). The requirements for extended training sessions and for a rest interval between them are abrogated; CREB2-a transgenic flies form maximal levels of LTM after only one training session (Yin et al., 1995).

Genetic Path of Memory Formation

These data suggest a genetic model of memory consolidation (Figure 15.1b). A new experience first is acquired during training (LRN). Memory processing then occurs in a sequential fashion from STM through MTM to ARM and LTM. Processing of ARM and LTM, however, then occurs in parallel. ARM is normal but LTM is blocked in CXM-fed flies or in CREB2-b transgenic flies. LTM is normal but ARM is blocked in *rsh* mutants. Thus, ARM and LTM represent two genetically and functionally distinct components of consolidated memory. Interestingly, this genetic dissection also reveals that one-day memory after spaced training is composed (additively) of both ARM and LTM. This observation suggests more generally that memory retention in other species/tasks may not consist solely of protein synthesis–dependent LTM, even after relatively long retention intervals.

Experiments combining the use of mutants and cold-shock anesthesia also suggest that 3-h retention after a single training session can be decomposed (additively) into ASM and ARM. Although memory becomes progressively more resistant to the cold shock with time, the asymptotic level of ARM (reached within 2 h) remains lower than the normal (observed) memory retention level. More complex manipulations of training protocols and mutants suggest that ASM can be subdivided further into MTM and STM (Tully et al., 1996). Consistent with this notion, MTM, but not STM or ARM, appears preferentially disrupted in $DC0^{ts}$ or *amn* mutants (Li et al., 1996; Tully et al., 1996). In fact, the memory curves of *amn* and $DC0^{ts}$ (at restrictive temperatures) are indistinguishable.

Why does the branch in information processing occur after MTM? This inference is derived from assessments of consolidated memories in *amn* mutants (Tully et al., 1996). Unlike the (opposing) cases for *rsh* and dCREB2-b, both ARM and LTM are defective in *amn* mutants. Hence, the independent functions of *rsh* and *dCREB2* both must be downstream of *amn* (in the simplest model).

This genetic model of memory formation serves now to direct new experiments and likely will be embellished in the future. The current model predicts, for instance, that LTM (and ARM) will be reduced in *lio* or *lat* (LRN) mutants. If, instead, LTM is found to be normal, such data would suggest that the branch in information processing actually occurs just after LRN, rather than after MTM. The model also predicts, and experiments confirmed, that 1-day memory after spaced training would be abolished completely in *rsh* mutants carrying the *CREB2-b* transgene (Yin et al., 1994).

☐ Biochemistry of Memory

One of the striking features obtained from these experiments is that several of the mutations that disrupt olfactory associative learning reside in genes that encode components of the cAMP signaling pathway. This strongly suggests that cAMP signaling plays a crucial role in behavioral plasticity. Interestingly, there is a striking correspondence between the position that a particular gene occupies in the cAMP pathway and when it affects memory formation (Table 15.1). Disruption of G protein function disrupts LRN; disruption of cAMP synthesis (*rut*) or hydrolysis (*dnc*) disrupts STM; (temperature-sensitive) disruptions of PKA (*DCO*) disrupt MTM; modulations of CREB affect LTM. One intriguing explanation for this correspondence is that these distinct effects on memory processing may reflect differences in the half-lives of various biochemical processes: cAMP levels, persistence of PKA activity, phosphorylation/dephosphorylation of PKA substrates, subcellular localization of newly synthesized proteins, etc. Alternatively, these observations may reflect differential recruitment of cAMP signaling in different anatomical regions of the "memory circuit." Future experiments with enhancer-trap technology may resolve these possibilities (cf. Connolly et al., 1996; Joiner & Griffith, 1999).

Obviously, some genes in our genetic pathway appear to participate in cAMP signaling but do not fit logically into the sequential memory process. The *amn* gene, for instance, encodes a neuropeptide homologous to vertebrate pituitary adenylyl cyclase activating peptide (PACAP). Given this presumed role as an activator of G protein–coupled receptors, one would expect *amn* mutations to affect LRN (as does disruption of G_s) rather than MTM. This apparent discrepancy may reflect another molecular role for *amn*, perhaps during development rather than during memory formation. To this end, *amn* is known also to encode a putative peptide with homology to growth hormone–releasing hormone (Moore et al., 1998) and to require expression during development for proper adult memory formation (DeZazzo, Xia, Christensen, Velinzon, & Tully, 1999b).

Similarly, cAMP levels appear reduced in *lio* mutants, even though the gene encodes a novel protein (Saitoe & Tully, 1999). This would imply a molecular role comparable to that for *rut*. The latter affects STM, however, while *lio* appears to affect LRN. In this case, the discrepancy may reside, in part, from differences in subcellular distribution. In adult mushroom bodies, RUT appears to be preferentially expressed in axonal neuropil, while LIO is expressed abundantly in both axonal and dendritic neuropil (Saitoe & Tully). Thus, LIO may participate upstream of RUT in an underlying memory circuit.

Finally, other genes in our genetic pathway are involved in cellular processes with no obvious molecular connection to cAMP signaling, or they remain unidentified. For example, 14-3-3 protein (*leonardo*) (a) interacts with rate-limiting enzymes in the synthesis of monoamine neurotransmitters, which are known to modulate AC; (b) binds to Raf kinase in Raf/MAPK signaling (B. Wang et al., 1999), and (c) regulates Ca^{2+}-dependent voltage-sensitive K^+ channels in a CaMKII-dependent manner (Zhou et al., 1999; see below). The *scabrous* (*Volado*) gene encodes an integrin, homologs of which are known to mediate cell-cell adhesion and cell contact–dependent signal transduction (Kauselmann et al., 1999). Finally, we recently have characterized *nalyot* mutants, which carry a hypomorphic lesion of the *Adf1* transcription factor (DeZazzo, Xia et al., 1999). After extended (spaced or massed) training of these mutants, ARM appears normal, while LTM is completely abolished. Perhaps the most perplexing discovery to date is *latheo*, which clearly has been shown to function as a subunit of the origin recognition complex (ORC). ORC is a constellation of nuclear proteins involved in DNA replication and, perhaps, in transcriptional regulation (Chesnokov, Gossen, Remus, & Botchan, 1999; Pinto et al., 1999). Nevertheless, LAT is expressed in presynaptic terminals of terminally differentiated neurons, where it appears to play a role in synaptic plasticity (Rohrbough, Pinto, Mihalek, Tully, & Broadie, 1999; see below)!

Experience-Dependent Structural Plasticity in the Adult Brain

Immunohistochemical analyses of some of these gene products have suggested some of the brain structures that subserve olfactory associative learning. Of primary importance is the role of the mushroom body (MB; Figure 15.2). DNC, RUT, PKA, PKA-RI, 14-3-3, SCAB, and LIO all are expressed preferentially in these adult brain structures (Goodwin et al., 1997; Grotewiel et al., 1998; Han, Levin, Reed, & Davis, 1992; Nighorn, Healy, & Davis, 1991; Saitoe & Tully, 2000; Skoulakis & Davis, 1996; Skoulakis, Kalderon, & Davis, 1993). MBs are large bilaterally symmetric structures, the cell bodies for which are located in the dorsoposterior region of the central brain. Each MB hemisphere consists of 2,500 Kenyon cells, which send dendrites dorsocaudally into the calyx (main input region) and project axons ventrorostrally into the alpha, beta, and gamma lobes. Chemical ablation of MB cells during development completely abolishes adult olfactory learning, without affecting sensorimotor responses to odors or footshock or associative learning to visual cues (de Belle & Heisenberg, 1994). Biochemical "jamming" of cAMP signaling in MBs via enhancer-driven expression of mutant (constitutively active) G_s protein also abolishes olfactory associative learning (Connolly et al., 1996). Thus, olfactory associative learning requires cAMP signaling in MBs.

Other central brain structures, most notably the central complex (CC), antennal lobe (AL), and lateral protocerebrum (LP), have been shown to make connections with MBs (Ito et al., 1998). The possibility that they participate in memory processing concerns an active area of research. Since the CC forms intricate connections to a variety of brain centers (including MBs), it likely functions as a control center for various behavioral responses (Hanesch, Fischbach, & Heisenberg, 1989; J. R. Martin, Raabe, & Heisenberg, 1999). The CC is positioned in the supraesophageal ganglia and is composed of four substructures: the ellipsoid body, the fan-shaped body, the nodulii, and the protocerebral bridge. Direct evidence that the CC is involved specifically in olfactory associative learning (rather than nonspecifically affecting sensorimotor responses) has not yet been reported. Expression of mutant G_s protein in some CC substructures, however, has no effect on olfactory associative learning (Connolly et al., 1996). Hence, MB currently is the only anatomical region of the adult brain known to be involved in olfactory associative learning in fruit flies. Since afferent inputs and efferent outputs (at least) also must be involved, future structure/function work likely will identify additional anatomies. Quite possibly, these anatomies will distinguish one or more memory phases.

As is the case in vertebrates, experience-dependent structural plasticity has been documented in adult *Drosophila* brains (Balling et al., 1987; Heisenberg, Borst, Wagner, & Byers, 1985; Technau, 1984; Technau & Heisenberg, 1982). Axonal projections from MB Kenyon cells normally undergo rearrangement during metamorphosis, first retracting and then reprojecting out from Kenyon cell bodies to (developing) adult alpha, beta, and gamma lobes. Flies reared in isolation end up with fewer axonal projections than those reared in "enriched environments" (Technau, 1984). Similarly, the dendritic neuropillar volume of MB calyces is reduced in visually deprived flies (Barth & Heisenberg, 1997). Importantly, these experience-dependent changes in MB structure do not occur normally in *dnc*, *rut*, and *amn* mutants (Balling et al., 1987; Hitier, Heisenberg, & Preat,

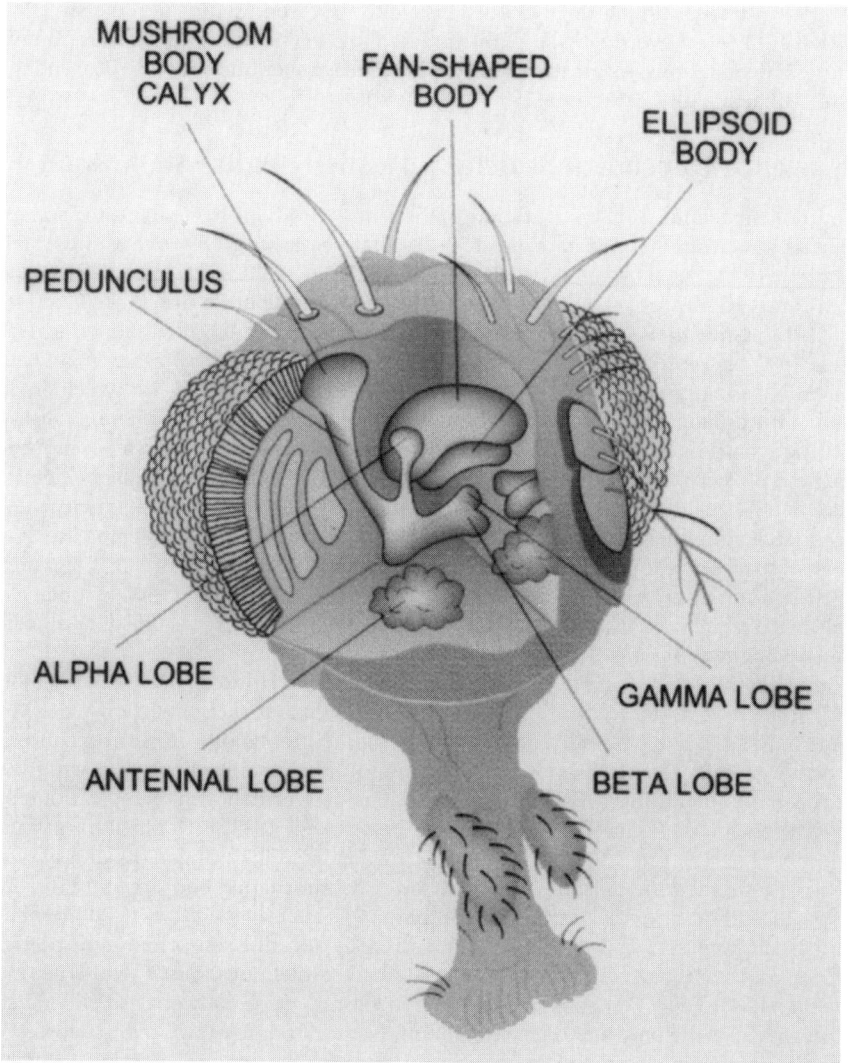

Figure 15.2. Anatomy of the *Drosophila* brain. MB neurons receive input from antennal lobes (AL), as well as from other brain regions, in the calyx region. Axonal projections from MB cells extend ventrally and anteriorly and divide into alpha/beta/gamma lobes. The central complex (CC), a motor output control center, receives input from a variety of brain centers. The CC is comprised of four substructures: the ellipsoid body and fan-shaped body (shown here) and the protocerebral bridge and nodulii (not shown). The MB and CC regions have been implicated as neural substrates for olfactory associative learning.

1998). This observation suggests a molecular link between some forms of developmental and behavioral plasticity. This neurogenetic link has been developed further at the larval NMJ.

Synaptic Plasticity at the Larval NMJ

Activity-Dependent Structural and Functional Changes. The larval NMJ is an excellent context in which to study synaptic plasticity during development (see Budnik & Gramates, 1999). As for vertebrate synapses in the CNS, glutamate is the primary excitatory neurotransmitter at the larval NMJ, with both pre- and postsynaptic biochemistries (and retrograde signaling) contributing to dynamic modulations of synaptic strength. Several forms of synaptic plasticity have been described, including paired-pulse facilitation (PPF), short-term facilitation (STF), augmentation (AUG), and posttetanic potentiation (PTP). As with memory formation in adults, genetic and pharmacological manipulations at the NMJ have dissected these forms of synaptic plasticity.

Long-lasting changes in neuronal activity at the NMJ lead to morphological changes in synaptic structure. Axonal outgrowth and path finding from motor neurons to embryonic muscle initially occur in an activity-independent manner. Soon after the postsynaptic target is contacted, however, further maturation of the NMJ depends on neural activity. Early on, this activity regulates the localization of glutamate receptors (Broadie & Bate, 1993b; Saitoe, Tanaka, Takata, & Kidokoro, 1997). At the time of initial synapse formation, these receptors form extrajunctional clusters associated in the vicinity of some muscle nuclei. In response to neural activity, these extrajunctional receptors recluster at the NMJ. In embryos of the paralytic temperature-sensitive mutant, $para^{ts\,1}$ (which encodes a Na^+ channel subunit; Loughney, Kreber, & Ganetzley, 1989), neural activity decreases drastically at restrictive temperatures (Suzuki, Grigliatti, & Williamson, 1971). When neural activity is blocked in this manner throughout synaptogenesis, glutamate receptors remain in the extrajunctional region and do not form junctional clusters (Saitoe et al., 1997).

Neural Activity Continues to Refine Synaptic Connections at the Postembryonic NMJ. Temperature-sensitive mutants of nap^{ts} (which encodes a protein that regulates expression of the *para* Na^+ channel; Kernan, Kuroda, Kreber, Baker, & Ganetzky, 1991) show reduced neuronal excitability and a slight reduction in synaptic arborization at restrictive temperatures. Temperature-sensitive mutations of sei^1 and *tip* also regulate expression of Na^+ current and show reduced neuronal excitability at restrictive temperatures (Feng, Deak, Kasbekar, Gil, & Hall, 1995; Kasbekar, Nelson, & Hall, 1987). When sei^1 and *tip* are raised at restrictive temperatures during a critical period from late embryogenesis to early first instar larvae, the number of ectopic connections on inappropriate muscle targets is increased (Jarecki & Keshishian, 1995). This critical period for refinement of synaptic connections is remniscent of that for the formation of ocular dominance columns in vertebrate visual cortex (cf. Z. J. Huang et al., 1999).

In contrast to these hypoexcitable mutants, double mutants of *eag Sh*, or *eag Hk* [*Shaker* (*Sh*), *ether-a-go-go* (*eag*), and *Hyperkinetic* (*Hk*) encode K^+ channel subunits and mutations lead to reduced K^+ channel conductance (Chouinard, Wilson, Schlimgen, & Ganetzky 1995; Ganetzky & Wu, 1983; Tempel, Papazian, Schwarz, Jan, & Jan, 1987; Warmke et al., 1991; Wilson, Wang, Chouinard, Griffith, & Ganetzky, 1998), are hyperexcitable, and show increases in the number of synaptic boutons and in transmitter release (Budnik, Zhong, & Wu, 1990). Similar changes in function and structure at the larval NMJ are seen when the *para* Na$^+$ channel is expressed at supranormal levels, alone or in combination with *Sh* mutations.

Exactly how neural activity translates into structural (and underlying functional) changes at the NMJ remains an active area of research. In addition to an ongoing exploration of basic components of synaptic vesicle release and recycling (Stimson & Ramaswami, 1999), recent work has revealed ensembles of proteins that work together to assemble and regulate synaptic transmission (Gramates & Budnik, 1999). FasII (NCAM homolog), GluR, Shaker, Eag, Slo (Slowpoke, calcium-dependent K$^+$ channel), Slob (Slo binding protein), DLG, CAMKII, 14-3-3, and PKA are all operating in this context to yield a synapse with bidirectional communication pre and post. More generally, perhaps, defects in synaptic function and/or structure have been identified for every "memory mutant" tested to date (see Hannan & Zhong, 1999).

cAMP at the NMJ

At the NMJ, cAMP signaling appears to play a central role in activity-dependent modulation of structure and function. Mutant *dnc* larvae show an abnormally large evoked excitatory junction current (EJC) accompanied by an increased probability of transmitter release, both of which appear to result from a decreased requirement for extracellular calcium. This primary synaptic defect also yields reductions in synaptic plasticity manifested as PPF, STF, and PTP (Zhong & Wu, 1991). Along with these effects on synaptic function, synaptic branching and bouton numbers at the NMJ are increased in mutant *dnc* larvae (Zhong, Budnik, & Wu, 1992). Notably, more severe structural defects are observed in *dnc eag* or *dnc Sh* double mutants and *dnc eag Sh* triple mutants, thereby suggesting an interaction between activity-dependent mechanisms and cAMP signaling.

Further support for this notion derives from studies of the NMJ in *rut* mutants. Just as the *rut^1* suppresses the supranormal basal levels of cAMP (Livingstone, Sziber, & Quinn, 1984) and the female sterility (Byers, Davis, & Kiger, 1981) of *dnc* mutants, so too are structural defects at the NMJ suppressed in *dnc rut* double mutants and in *dnc Sh rut* triple mutants (Zhong, Budnik, & Wu, 1991). Unlike *dnc* mutants, however, *rut* mutants alone do not show any structural defects at the NMJ, although functional defects in STF and PTP are observed (Zhong & Wu, 1991).

Postsynaptic overexpression of a constitutively active PKA catalytic subunit leads to a rapid decrease in quantal size, which is mediated via GluRIIA. Conversely, overexpression of a dominant-negative (cAMP-insensitive) PKA regulatory subunit leads to an increase in quantal size (G. W. Davis, DiAntonio, Petersen, & Goodman, 1998). In either case, changes in synaptic structure are not detected. Although the postsynaptic GluRIIA response diminishes in response to iontophoresed glutamate, no further investigations of PKA's role in synaptic plasticity have yet been done.

Manipulations of CREB alone yield no observable effects on synaptic structure or function at the NMJ (G. W. Davis, Schuster, & Goodman, 1996). Overexpression of CREB repressor in *dnc* mutants, however, reduces synaptic strength without affecting the supranormal structural defects. Conversely, overexpression of CREB activator in *fasII* mutants, which express only 50% normal levels of FasII, yields increases in both synaptic structure and function, whereas only changes in structure are observed in *fasII* mutants alone. These observations genetically dissect two distinct aspects of activity-dependent synaptic plasticity: a functional effect, mediated by CREB, and a structural effect, mediated by FasII. Although these two "branch pathways" of synaptic plasticity appear independent of each other, both nevertheless appear dependent on neural activity and "upstream" cAMP signaling.

The NMJ of Other Memory Mutants

The number of synaptic boutons is reduced in hypomorphic (*nalyot*) mutants of ADF1 and is increased when ADF1 is overexpressed. In both cases, however, no changes in basal synaptic transmission or synaptic plasticity are apparent. These observations suggest that ADF1 mediates activity-dependent changes in synaptic structure but not function (DeZazzo, Sandstrom et al., 2000).

Null *14-3-3* (*leonardo*) mutants show reduced EJC amplitudes, and the calcium dependency of synaptic transmission is shifted toward higher concentrations (Broadie, Rushton, Skoulakis, & Davis, 1997). *leonardo* mutants also show defects in AUG and PTP. Given 14-3-3's enriched expression in presynaptic terminals at the NMJ (Broadie et al., 1997), these observations suggest that 14-3-3 regulates transmitter release.

Null *lat* mutants show greatly increased EJCs with the calcium dependency of synaptic transmission shifted toward lower concentrations (Rohrbough et al., 1999). As in *dnc* mutants, these primary defects in *lat* mutants then give rise to severe disruptions of PPF, STF AUG, and PTP. Unlike *dnc* mutants, the number of synaptic boutons is slightly (but significantly) reduced. LAT also is predominantly expressed presynaptically (Rohrbough et al., 1999), again suggesting that LAT may regulate transmitter release.

In contrast to 14-3-3 and LAT, LIO appears predominantly expressed in postsynaptic muscle. Basal synaptic transmission appears normal in *lio* mutants, but PPF and PTP are reduced. cAMP levels are reduced in *lio* mutants, suggesting that LIO is a novel modulator of cAMP signaling (Saitoe & Tully, 2000). Hence, LIO may function upstream of PKA to regulate the postsynaptic response.

Other Genetic Interactions With Memory Mutants at the NMJ

To date, CAMKII has not yet been implicated in olfactory associative learning, although it clearly is involved in courtship suppression (Griffith et al., 1993). Nevertheless, CAMKII is expressed at the NMJ and functions acutely to modulate synaptic structure and function (Griffith, Wang, Zhong, Wu, & Greenspan, 1994; Wang et al., 1994). Overexpression of an inhibitory peptide in transgenic (*ala1*) larvae reduces CAMKII activity, increases EJC amplitude, produces defects in PPF, AUG, and PTP, and leads to an increase in the number of synaptic boutons. CAMKII also regulates Eag (and potassium channel function) and DLG (and FASII/Shaker clustering) via covalent modification (Griffith et al., 1994; Koh, Popova, Thomas, Griffith, & Budnik, 1999). O'Brien, Cutler, de la Fuente, & Tijan (2000) recently have shown that CAMKII also may phosphorylate ADF1, significantly decreasing ADF1-dependent gene transcription. Hence, the increases in synaptic structure observed by overexpression of *ala1* or *Adf1* may be mechanistically related.

Recently, 14-3-3 protein has been shown to interact with Slob, a novel protein that binds to Slowpoke (Adelman et al., 1992; Atkinson, Richtand, Schworer, Kuczenski, & Soderling, 1987; Schopperle et al., 1998) and regulates K_{Ca} channel gating by increasing voltage sensitivity (Zhou et al., 1999). Slob/14-3-3 binding is promoted by CAMKII-dependent phosphorylation of Slob. When 14-3-3 protein binds to the Slo/Slob complex, voltage sensitivity decreases.

Certain neuropeptides modulate synaptic plasticity. Pituitary adenylyl cyclase–activating polypeptide 38 (PACAP38) is a neuropeptide that activates adenylyl cyclase via a G protein–coupled receptor in vertebrates (Arimura, 1998; Spengler et al., 1993). PACAP38 immunoreactivity is observed at the larval NMJ, and application of PACAP38 produces a slow inward current followed by an enhancement of outward K^+ current (Zhong & Pena, 1995). The effect of PACAP38 can be mimicked by tetanic stimulation, which may release endogenous *Drosophila* PACAP-like peptide. In *rut* mutants, the PACAP response is suppressed, suggesting that the PACAP-like receptor is coupled to *rut* adenylyl cyclase postsynaptically (Zhong, 1995). Application of a cAMP analogue fails to mimic PACAP response, however. The PACAP response also is suppressed in *Ras* and *Raf* mutants, suggesting involvement of the *Ras/Raf* pathway in the PACAP response. Again, activation of the *Ras/Raf* pathway alone fails to mimic the PACAP response. Concomitant activation of cAMP and the Ras/Raf pathway, however, produces the PACAP response, suggesting that coactivation of these signaling pathways is required for the PACAP response (Zhong, 1995).

Further genetic dissection of the PACAP response has been carried out with mutants of the *Drosophila* neurofibromatosis type 1 (NF1) homolog (The, Hannigan, Cowley, Reginald, & Zhong, 1997). Human NF1 disease causes benign and malignant tumors of the peripheral nervous system and is accompanied by learning deficits (Gutman & Collins, 1993; North, Joy, Yuille, Cocks, & Hutchins, 1995). *NF1* mutant flies also show deficits in olfactory associative learning (Guo et al., 2000). Similar to *rut* and *Ras/Raf* mutants, *NF1* mutants do not show a PACAP response (Guo, The, Hannan, Bernards, & Zhong, 1997). The NF1 gene encodes a fragment similar to GTPase activating protein (GAP) and therefore inhibits Ras activity (Ras has GTPase activity and becomes active upon GTP binding; Ballester et al., 1990; Viskochil, White, & Cawthon, 1993; Xu et al., 1990). Hence, it has been assumed that the NF1 mutant defect(s) result from enhanced *Ras* activity. Surprisingly, the PACAP response is restored in *NF1* mutants by cAMP analogues and forskolin (an activator of adenylyl cyclase) and is not mimicked by mutations that increase levels of active Ras (Ras-GTP). At the larval NMJ, then, *NF1* appears to regulate *Rut* adenylyl cyclase rather than the *Ras/Raf* pathway.

☐ Synaptic Plasticity as a Molecular Mechanism for Experience-Dependent Changes in Behavior

Synaptic Plasticity and the *Drosophila* NMJ

Genetic dissection of activity-dependent plasticity at the NMJ suggests a basic model (Figure 15.3). Neural activity increases cAMP signaling (pre- and postsynaptically), which then regulates various forms of synaptic plasticity in the short term and eventually yields long-term changes in synaptic structure and function. This latter form of developmental plasticity involves two apparently independent transcription factor cascades: a CREB-dependent path, which modulates synaptic function (in a homeostatic fashion), and an ADF1-dependent path, which modulates synaptic structure perhaps via regulation of FASII expression. Below, we attempt to link more recent observations to this general model.

At NMJ presynaptic terminals, there exist two distinct pools of synaptic vesicles: an exo/endo cycling pool located in the periphery of synaptic boutons and a reserve pool located in the center (Kuromi & Kidokoro, 1998). During low-frequency stimulation, the size of the exo/endo cycling pool and quantal content are closely related (Kuromi & Kidokoro, 1999). Severing motor axons decreases the size of the exo/endo cycling pool and quantal content, while stimulation with forskolin increases both. Hence, the size of the exo/endo cycling pool represents the readily releasable pool (Gillis, Mossner, &

(A) Transcription-Independent Form

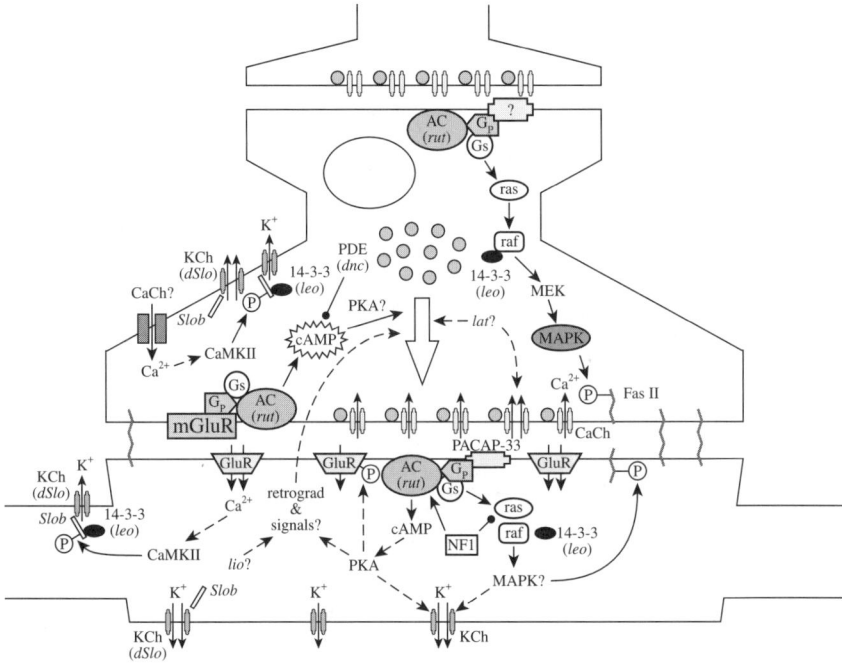

Figure 15.3. Putative molecular mechanisms of synaptic plasticity. (a) Biochemistries associated with transcription-independent early memories. Upon activation of cAMP, a change in the size of the exo/endo cycling pools leads to a change in transmitter release. MAPK also may induce internalization of Fas II via phosphorylation. In flies, the postsynaptic may be mediated by PACAP. (b) Signaling pathways implicated for transcription-dependent LTM. Generally, three kinases have been implicated in CREB-dependent gene expression: CaMKIV, PKA, and MAPK. Activation of CaMKIV likely results from Ca^{2+} influx. PKA and MAPK are activated by the cAMP and Ras/Raf pathways, respectively. For each kinase, translocation to (or localization in) the nucleus is critical for the regulation of gene expression. It is not yet clear which of these signaling cascades functions in flies to activate CREB.

Neher, 1996; Rosenmund & Stevens, 1996; Schneggenburger, Meyer, & Neher, 1999; Schweizer, Betz, & Augustine, 1995).

Pharmacological activation of adenylyl cyclase increases transmitter release at many vertebrate synapses (Chavez-Noriega & Stevens, 1994; Chavis, Mollard, Bockaert & Manzoni, 1998; Chen & Regehr, 1997; Dixon & Atwood, 1989; Trudeau, Emery, & Haydon, 1996). Most presynaptic group II mGluRs inhibit adenylyl cyclase (Prezeau et al., 1992; Tanabe, Masu, Ishii, Shigemoto, & Nakanishi, 1992). In a few cases, however, cAMP is elevated in response to mGluRII activation (Herrero, Miras-Portugal, & Sanchez-Prieto, 1992; Sciancalepore, Stratta, Fisher, & Cherubini, 1995; Winder & Conn, 1992). For enhancement of transmitter release, many mechanisms have been proposed (Capogna, Gahwiler, & Thompson, 1995; Gillis et al., 1996; Greengard, Valtorta, Czernik, & Benfenati, 1993; Meffert, Calakos, Scheller, & Schulman, 1996; Trudeau

(B) Transcription-Dependent Form

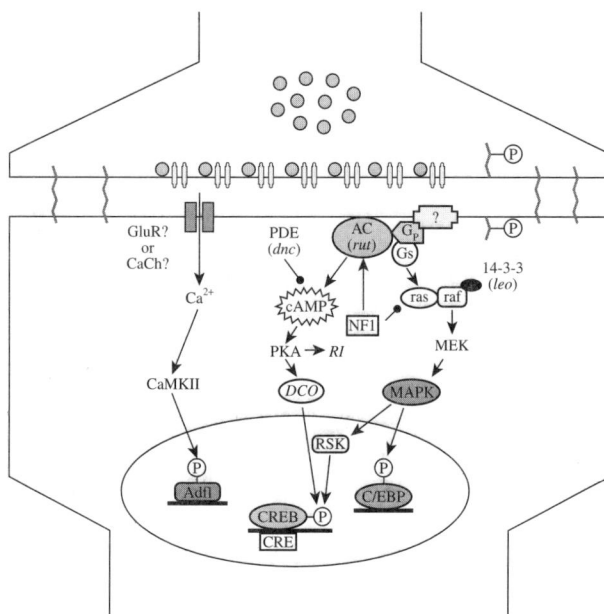

Figure 15.3. (*Continued*)

et al., 1996). At the NMJ, transmitter release is enhanced by activation of adenylyl cyclase (Zhang, Kuromi, & Kidokoro, 1999). Application of a Group II mGluR agonist increases the frequency of miniature synaptic currents, and this increase is suppressed by an adenylyl cyclase inhibitor. Moreover, the effect of a Group II mGluR agonist is reduced in *rut* mutants. These data suggest that presynaptic metabotropic glutamate receptors (mGluRs) may play a role in synaptic plasticity. Tetanic stimulation may activate presynaptic mGluRs and lead to a short-term increase in transmitter release.

14-3-3 and LAT are expressed in presynaptic terminals and colocalize with synaptic vesicles (Broadie et al., 1997; Rohrbough et al., 1999). The size of EJCs is reduced without changing the size of miniature EJCs in *leo* mutants, whereas the size of EJCs is enhanced without changing the size of miniature EJCs in *lat* mutants. These observations suggest that presynaptic release machinery is affected in these mutants and that synaptic plasticity is severely disrupted in both mutants, in accordance with the notion above (Broadie et al., 1997; Roth & Burgoyne, 1995). In *lat* mutants, Ca^{2+} dependency is shifted to lower Ca^{2+} concentrations (Rohrbough et al., 1999). Hence, *lat* may participate in the regulation of presynaptic Ca^{2+} dynamics at the release site. In *leo* mutants, the increased K^+ current (via its interaction with Slowpoke) may result in a decreased EJC. This also would affect the size of the exo/endo cycling (readily releasable) pool (Broadie et al., 1997; Roth & Burgoyne, 1995).

Postsynaptic mechanisms also contribute to synaptic plasticity at the NMJ. Manipulations of postsynaptic PKA affect quantal size, presumably via (direct or indirect) phosphorylation of a particular glutamate receptor subunit (DGluRIIA). Notably, quantal size is not affected in *dnc* mutants (Zhong & Wu, 1991), suggesting that Dnc may not function postsynaptically.

CaMKII also may function postsynaptically. CaMKII is expressed in the postsynaptic muscle fiber as well as in the presynaptic nerve terminal (J. Wang, Renger, Griffith, Greenspan, & Wu, 1994). Activation of postsynaptic glutamate receptors produces an increase in endogenous Ca^{2+}, which is restricted to the receptor site. In cultured myotubes, this calcium influx lasts for minutes (Saitoe, Koshimoto, Hirano, Suga, & Kidskoro, 1998).

Of particular interest is the observation (see above) that manipulations of postsynaptic PKA affect presynaptic quantal content (G. W. Davis et al., 1998). This implies the presence of a retrograde signal regulating presynaptic transmitter release—a signal not yet identified in *Drosophila*. The existence of a retrograde signal at vertebrate synapses also has been suggested. At developing *Xenopus* NMJ in culture, localized elevation of Ca^{2+} in the postsynaptic muscle suppresses neurotransmitter release (Cash, Dan, Poo, & Zucker, 1996). Postsynaptic injection of calcineurin inhibitors enhances synaptic transmission and decreased PPF. Postsynaptic density-95 (PSD95) mutant mice also show altered PPF (Migaud et al., 1998). In the lateral amygdala of rats, long-term potentiation (LTP) is induced postsynaptically (Y. Y. Huang & Kandel, 1998). Such LTP, however, is associated with PKA-dependent depression of PPF. Since PPF is thought to reflect a presynaptic mechanism (J. H. Wang & Kelly, 1997), these data suggest modulation of presynaptic release machinery via a retrograde signal. In this context, recent experiments on *lio* mutants are informative. LIO is expressed preferentially in NMJ muscle; nevertheless, PPF is defective in mutant larvae (Saitoe & Tully, 2000). Hence, LIO may be involved in retrograde signaling upstream of PKA (see above).

This pathway remains only a crude genetic framework with which to link developmental plasticity and behavioral plasticity via synaptic mechanisms. As more "memory" genes are identified and as synaptic plasticity at the NMJ is genetically dissected further, this genetic model assuredly will provide a more comprehensive explanation.

cAMP Signaling and Activity-Dependent Synaptic Plasticity

In the *Aplysia* sensorimotor cell culture system, one brief application of 5-HT produces STF lasting minutes, whereas five (spaced) applications of 5-HT induce a transcription-dependent long-term facilitation (LTF) lasting days (Montarolo et al., 1986; Rayport & Schacher, 1986). Both STF and LTF involve an enhancement of transmitter release induced by cAMP and mediated by the PKA (Brunelli, Castellucci, & Kandel, 1976; Ghirardi et al., 1992; Schacher, Castelluci, & Kandel, 1988; Scholz & Byrne, 1988). Repeated applications of 5-HT, however, activate PKA in the sensory neuron long enough to yield its translocation to the nucleus (Backsai et al., 1993; Bernier, Castellucci, Kandel, & Schwartz, 1982). Once sequestered (and persistently active) in the nucleus, PKA may act to phosphorylate CREB and to induce "downstream" gene expression (Kaang, Kandel, & Grant, 1993).

LTP in mammalian hippocampus is induced in three distinct regions: dentate gyrus (DG, synapses between the prefrontal pathway of the enthorrhinal cortex and granule cells in DG), CA3 (synapses between the mossy fiber pathway of granule cells and pyramidal cells in CA3), and CA1 (synapses between the Schaffer collateral pathway of pyramidal cells in CA1 and pyramidal cells in CA3). Among these regions, LTP is induced by two different mechanisms, which involve different glutamate receptors and pre- versus postsynaptic sites of induction (Bliss & Collingridge, 1993). In the DG and CA1 region, LTP induction is triggered postsynaptically via activation of NMDA receptors. The latter occurs only when glutamate is released presynaptically and NMDA receptors are activated simultaneously by membrane depolarization (a Hebbian contingency of events remniscent of associative learning). Calcium influx through activated NMDA receptors then initiates a short-term signaling cascade in the postsynaptic cell, which includes CaMKII, PKC, tyrosine kinases, and PKA. In the CA3 region, LTP is induced presynaptically (and thus is conceptually similar to nonassociative learning) and is independent of NMDA receptor activation. The short-term signaling cascade predominantly involves PKA. Both forms of short-term LTP (E-LTP) last 1–3 h and do not require gene transcription. In common to both mechanisms, however, is a long-lasting LTP (L-LTP) that requires cAMP signaling and new protein and RNA synthesis (Frey, Huang, & Kandel, 1993; Y.-Y. Huang, Li, & Kandel, 1994; Y.-Y. Huang & Kandel, 1994; Matthies & Reymann, 1993; Nguyen, Abel, & Kandel, 1994). Consistent with these observations, L-LTP (and LTM) are defective in mice double-mutant for Adenylyl cyclase 1 (AC1) and AC8 (Wong et al., 1999). Hence, cAMP-dependent gene expression seems to be a conserved mechanism for long-term synaptic plasticity.

CREB as a Switch for Long-Term Behavioral and Synaptic Changes

In normal flies, protein synthesis–dependent LTM is produced exclusively by spaced training (not by massed training or a single training session). Overexpression of CREB repressor blocks the formation of LTM, and overexpression of CREB activator induces LTM after a single training session (Yin et al., 1995). Thus, loss-of-function and gain-of-function manipulations of CREB have opposing effects on LTM formation. This satisfies the general definition of a molecular switch, which usually occupies a critical regulatory step in an underlying signaling pathway. The CREB activator–dependent enhancement of LTM also depends on phosphorylation of CREB at Ser231, which is equivalent to Ser133 of vertebrate CREB. This phosphorylation site is a target for PKA (and other kinases). Since a single training session is sufficient to induce maximum levels of LTM in transgenic flies overexpressing CREB activator, upstream signaling to CREB must be maximally induced after the first training session. Under these (transgenic) conditions, CREB activator, not PKA is clearly rate limiting for the induction of LTM.

These observations suggest two generalizations for long-term behavioral plasticity (Tully, 1997). First, the molecular ratio of CREB activators to repressors may constitute an initial "setpoint" for the CREB switch. Second, dynamic activating and inhibiting processes (involving both CREB activators and repressors or just activators) must function during the rest interval of spaced training to induce LTM (Dubnau & Tully, 1998; Yin et al., 1995; Yin & Tully, 1996). These two properties of the CREB switch are sufficient to explain the behavioral properties of LTM induction—even for traumatic events, which require only one training session for LTM to form (see below).

Similarly, CREB appears to act as a molecular switch at the NMJ. CREB repressor blocks the supranormal increase in synaptic strength usually observed in *dnc* mutants. Conversely, CREB activator enhances synaptic strength usually not observed in (50%) FasII mutants. (50%) FasII mutants show a supranormal increase in synaptic structure but not function in the absence of any CREB manipulations (Schuster, Davis, Fetter, & Goodman, 1996a). Nevertheless, FasII expression is suppressed by neural activity (in the hyperexcitable mutants) and by increases in cAMP levels (in *dnc* mutants; Schuster, Davis, Fetter, & Goodman, 1996b). These observations suggest that regulation of FasII expression is downstream of cAMP signaling in a "structural pathway" that is genetically distinct from a CREB-dependent "functional pathway." How ADF1-dependent transcription fits into this genetic path of synaptic plasticity promises to be informative. Nevertheless, these parallel effects of CREB manipulations on developmental plasticity at the NMJ and behavioral plasticity in adults constitute a strong causal link between the two phenomena—a link strengthened by a growing list of "memory" genes involved in a common site of synaptic plasticity.

Is CREB part of an evolutionarily conserved molecular switch for long-term synaptic plasticity? Evidence to date supports this notion (Dubnau & Tully, 1998; Frank & Greenberg, 1994; Tully, 1997, 1998). Mice lacking the alpha/delta isoforms of CREB show normal STM but defective LTM in both cued and contextual fear conditioning (Bourtchuladze et al., 1994; also see Gass et al., 1998). Consistent with these behavioral observations, L-LTP in the CA1 region of the hippocampus is severely disrupted, whereas E-LTP, PTP, and PPF are much less affected.

This (cued or contextual) fear conditioning task represents an example of "one-trial" LTM formation, a common result for traumatic experiences in many animals. From the CREB-centric perspective, this observation suggested the possibility that the CREB switch is set to "on" in neural circuits subserving fear by differentially up-regulating more activators than repressors. In CREB-mutant mice, activators, not repressors, were knocked out, thereby reducing the activator-to-repressor ratio. This led to speculation that the CREB switch in mutant mice might be set to an initial level similar to that for olfactory learning in normal flies. If so, then spaced training, but not massed training, would be expected to yield normal LTM in CREB-mutant mice. This is precisely what Kogan et al. (1996) found, providing strong support for the existence of a CREB switch in mice.

Impey et al. (1996) generated a transgenic mouse carrying a CRE-mediated beta-galactosidase reporter gene. These transgenic mice show CREB-dependent gene transcription in hippocampal slices after a tetanic stimulation protocol that produces L-LTP but not one that produces only E- LTP. Impey, Smith et al. (1998) also detected a report of CREB-dependent gene transcription in CA1 hippocampal neurons in vivo induced by a behavioral training protocol that produced LTM after fear conditioning but not after a training protocol that failed to produce LTM. More recent experiments in hippocampal neurons have suggested a concomitant role for ERK kinase signaling onto CREB during L-LTP induction (Impey, Obrietan et al., 1998). More generally, CREB has been shown to play a role in developmental plasticity of the visual cortex (Pham et al., 1999), of the barrel cortex (Glazewski et al., 1999), and in late-phase cerebellar long-term depression in cultured Purkinje cells (Ahn, Ginty, & Linden, 1999).

Experiments in rats also have revealed a role for CREB in LTM formation. Injection of antisense oligonucleotides into the hippocampus blocks LTM but not STM in water maze learning (Guzowski & McGaugh, 1997). Similar injections into the amygdala block LTM but not STM of conditioned taste aversion (Lamprecht, Hazvi, & Dudai, 1997). More recently, viral vector–mediated overexpression of CREB activator has been accomplished in amygdala. Memory of a fear-potentiated startle response in these viral-infected rats was supranormal after massed training and similar to memory retention levels normally produced by spaced training (Josselyn et al., 1998), a result quite analogous to that in flies.

In *Aplysia*, a siphon withdrawal reflex undergoes habituation or sensitization to tailshock. With only a few training trails, both forms of nonassociative learning decay away in minutes to hours. After several spaced training trials, however, protein synthesis–dependent long-term memories are induced, lasting days (Carew, Pinsker, & Kandel, 1972; Pinsker, Hening, Carew, & Kandel, 1973). A monosynapse between specific sensory and motor neurons was shown to contribute to behavioral sensitization and, more recently, has been used to elucidate cellular properties of the electrophysiological LTF that accompanies behavioral long-term sensitization (Bailey, Bartsch, & Kandel, 1996). In this cell culture system, five spaced applications of serotonin induce a protein synthesis–dependent LTF, while fewer applications induce a short-term form of facilitation that decays away (Castellucci, Blumenfeld, Goelet, & Kandel, 1989; Montarolo et al., 1986). The appearance of LTF is accompanied by a synaptic growth process that presumably contributes to the emergent increase in synaptic strength (Bailey & Kandel, 1993). Two CREB family members have been identified that play a role in LTF: CREB1 and CREB2 function as an activator and a repressor, respectively, of CRE-mediated transcription (Bartsch et al., 1995; Dash, Hochner, & Kandel, 1990). When an antibody against CREB2 is injected into the sensory neuron, CREB2 function is blocked, presumably "releasing" CREB1 function and thereby producing LTF after one serotonin pulse instead of the usual five spaced pulses—again a result quite analogous to that in flies and rats. Notably, this CREB-enhanced LTF also is accompanied by structural changes at the sensorimotor monosynapse (Bartsch et al., 1995; Bartsch, Casadio, Karl, Serodio, & Kandel, 1998). More recent experiments have revealed that five spaced pulses of serotonin induce translocations of both PKA and MAPK to the nucleus, where both may phosphorylate CREB (Bailey et al., 1997; K. Martin et al., 1997).

To effect gene trascription, CREB partners with CBP (CREB binding protein). CBP is a nuclear protein that binds specifically to CREB, when phosphorylated at Ser 133, and functions as a transcriptional coactivator that links CREB to the basal transcription complex (Chrivia et al., 1993). Two independent groups (Hardingham, Chawla, Cruzalegui, & Bading, 1999; Hu, Chrivia, & Ghosh, 1999) have shown that CBP is regulated via Ca^{2+} permeable glutamate receptors (NMDA receptors) and/or voltage-sensitive Ca^{2+} channels (L-type). Mutant CBP mice recently have been generated. Homozygous mutants are lethal, but heterozygous mice are viable and display deficits in LTM but not STM of passive avoidance and fear conditioning (Oike et al., 1999). Interestingly, these mutant CBP mice reproduce, in part, many of the other physical symptoms of patients suffering from Rubinstein-Taybi syndrome (RTS), including retarded growth, retarded osseous maturation, hypoplastic maxilla, and cardiac and skeletal abnormalities. Petrij et al. (1995) have shown that RTS patients are all carriers of mutations in CBP. RTS patients also suffer mental retardation, leading to the speculation that they do so because they are unable to form LTM normally.

Finally, CREB is expected to be an initial step in a more general transcription factor cascade involved in the appearance of an experience-dependent change in synaptic structure and function (see above). A few of these "downstream" genes now are being identified (Hegde, Goldberg, & Schwartz, 1993; Kennedy, Gawinowicz, Barzilai, Kandel, & Sweatt, 1988; Kuhl, Kennedy, Barzilai, & Kandel, 1992;). In *Aplysia*, one such downstream gene is C/EBP, an immediate early gene with CREB binding (CRE) sites in its promoter (Alberini, Ghirardi, Metz, & Kandel, 1994). When C/EBP function is blocked (by injecting antisense oligonucleotide or C/EBP antibody into the sensory neuron of the sensorimotor cocultures), LTF does not form. Sterneck et al. (1998) recently have extended this observation to the mouse C/EBP homolog. When the C/EBP delta isoform specifically is deleted, contextual fear conditioning selectively is enhanced.

Summary

cAMP signaling clearly is involved in various forms of synaptic plasticity in various species. An experience (learning) induces neural activity in the subserving circuitry. Neural activity (transmitter release, receptor binding) activates various signaling pathways, including calcium (CAMK), cAMP (PKA), and PKC. The activities of these upstream components participate in one or more functionally distinct memory phases that appear not to require gene transcription. The proper cadence of experience, however, can lead to sufficient activations of PKA and MAPK to produce their translocation to the nucleus and the phosphorylation of CREB. CREB then induces a transcription factor cascade involved in a "growth process" that yields changes in synaptic structure and function. This protein synthesis–dependent process is associated with the appearance of LTM.

Are other genes and molecules likely to be involved? Most certainly. The molecular players already named (and those that were covered in this review) will be joined by others as the discovery process continues. Gene discovery in *Drosophila* continues to contribute new components to the molecular puzzle. Novel genes have been implicated, as have novel functions for genes involved with other aspects of cell biology (such as *latheo* and cell proliferation). These unlikely connections begin to reveal a complex gene network underlying neuronal function.

Some of the extant molecular genetic components of synaptic plasticity have been implicated in both developmental and behavioral plasticity. CREB, for instance, is one such case (see above). Neurogenetic studies in *Drosophila* have contributed to this "synthesis" by comparing olfactory memory in adults and NMJ physiology in larvae. More insight is yet to come.

Acknowledgments

We thank Yoshi Kidokoro and Hiroshi Kuromi for their comments on the manuscript. This work has been supported by NIH grants HD32245 and NS36480, by the John A. Hartford Foundation, and by the Human Frontiers in Science Program (in support of T.T.).

☐ References

Adelman, J. P., Shen, K. Z., Kavanaugh, M. P., Warren, R. A., Wu, Y. N., Lagrutta, A., Bond, C. T., & North, R. A. (1992). Calcium-activated potassium channels expressed from cloned complementary DNAs. *Neuron, 9*(2), 209–216.

Ahn, S., Ginty, D., & Linden, D. (1999). A late phase of cerebellar long-term depression requires activation of CaMKIV and CREB. *Neuron, 23,* 559–568.

Alberini, C. M., Ghirardi, M., Metz, R., & Kandel, E. R. (1994). C/EBP is an immediate-early gene required for the consolidation of long-term facilitation in *Aplysia. Cell, 76,* 1099–1114.

Allweis, C. (1991). The congruity of rat and chick multiphasic memory-consolidation models. In R. J. Andrew (Eds.), *Neural and behavioural plasticity* (pp. 370–393). New York: Oxford University Press.

Arimura, A. (1998). Perspectives on pituitary adenylate cyclase activating polypeptide (PACAP) in the neuroendocrine, endocrine, and nervous systems. *Japan Journal of Physiology, 48*(5), 301–31.

Atkinson, J., Richtand, N., Schworer, C., Kuczenski, R., & Soderling, T. (1987). Phosphorylation of purified rat striatal tyrosine hydroxylase by Ca2+/calmodulin-dependent protein kinase II: Effect of an activator protein. *Journal of Neurochemistry, 49*(4), 1241–1249.

Backsai, B. J., Hochner, B., Mahaut-Smith, M., Adams, S. R., Kaang, B.-K., Kandel, E. R., & Tsien, R. Y. (1993). Spatially resolved dynamics of cAMP and protein kinase A subunits in *Aplysia* sensory neurons. *Science, 260,* 222–226.

Bailey, C., Bartsch, D., & Kandel, E. (1996). Toward a molecular definition of long-term memory storage. *Proceedings of the National Academy of Sciences USA, 93,* 13445–13452.

Bailey, C., Kaang, B.-K., Chen, M., Martin, K., Lim, C.-S., Casadio, A., & Kandel, E. (1997). Mutation in the phosphorylation sites of MAP kinase blocks learning-related internalization of apCAM in Aplysia sensory neurons. *Neuron, 18,* 913–924.

Bailey, C. H., & Kandel, E. R. (1993). Structural changes accompanying memory storage. *Annual Review of Physiology, 55,* 397–426.

Ballester, R., Marchuk, D., Bouguski, M., Saulino, A., Letcher, R., Wigler, M., & Collins, F. (1990). The NF1 locus encodes a protein functionally related to mammalian GAP and yeast IRA proteins. *Cell, 63,* 851–859.

Balling, A., Technau, G. M., & Heisenberg, M. (1987). Are the structural changes in adult *Drosophila* mushroom bodies memory traces? Studies on biochemical learning mutants. *Journal of Neurogenetics, 4,* 65–73.

Barth, M., & Heisenberg, M. (1997). Vision affects mushroom bodies and central complex in *Drosophila melanogaster. Learning and Memory, 4,* 219–229.

Bartsch, D., Casadio, A., Karl, K., Serodio, P., & Kandel, E. (1998). CREB1 encodes a nuclear activator, a repressor, and a cytoplasmic modulator that form a regulatory unit critical for long-term facilitation. *Cell, 95,* 211–223.

Bartsch, D., Ghirardi, M., Skehel, P. A., Karl, K. A., Herder, S. P., Chen, M., Bailey, C. H., & Kandel, E. R. (1995). Aplysia CREB2 represses long-term facilitation: Relief of repression converts transient facilitation into long-term functional and structural change. *Cell, 83*(6), 979–92.

Bear, M. F., Kleinschmidt, A., Gu, Q., & Singer, W. (1990). Disruption of experience-dependent synaptic modifications in striate cortex by infusion of an NMDA receptor antagonist. *Journal of Neuroscience, 10,* 909–925.

Bernier, L., Castellucci, V. F., Kandel, E. R., & Schwartz, J. H. (1982). Facilitatory transmitter causes a selective and prolonged increase in adenosine 3′:5′-monophosphate in sensory neurons mediating the gill and siphon withdrawal reflex in Aplysia. *Journal of Neuroscience, 2*(12), 1682–91.

Bliss, T. V. P., & Collingridge, G. L. (1993). A synaptic model of memory: Long-term-potentiation. *Nature, 361,* 31–39.

Bolwig, G. M., Del Vecchio, M., Hannon, G., & Tully, T. (1995). Molecular clonning of *linotte* in Drosophila: A novel gene that functions in adults during associative learning. *Neuron, 15,* 829–842.

Bourtchuladze, R., Frenguelli, B., Blendy, J., Cioffi, D., Schutz, G., & Silva, A. (1994). Deficient long-term memory in mice with a targeted mutation of the cAMP-responsive element-binding protein. *Cell, 79,* 59–68.

Boynton, S., & Tully, T. (1992). *Latheo,* a new gene involved in associative learning and memory in *Drosophila melanogaster* identified from P element mutagenesis. *Genetics, 131,* 655–672.

Broadie, K., & Bate, M. (1993). Innervation directs receptor synthesis and localization in Drosophilia embryo synaptogenesis. *Nature, 361,* 350–353.

Broadie, K., Rushton, E., Skoulakis, E. M. C., & Davis, R. L. (1997). Leonardo, a Drosophila 14-3-3 protein involved in learning, regulates presynaptic function. *Neuron, 19,* 391–402.

Brunelli, M., Castellucci, V., & Kandel, E. R. (1976). Synaptic facilitation and behavioral sensitization in Aplysia: Possible role of serotonin and cyclic AMP. *Science, 194*(4270), 1178–1181.

Budnik, V., & Gramates, L. S. (1999). *Neuromuscular junctions in Drosophila.* New York: Academic Press.

Budnik, V., Zhong, Y., & Wu, C.-F. (1990). Morphological plasticity of motor axons in Drosophila mutants with altered excitability. *Journal of Neuroscience, 10*(11), 3754–3768.

Byers, D., Davis, R. L., & Kiger, J. A., Jr. (1981). Defect in cyclic AMP phosphodiesterase due to the *dunce* mutation of learning in *Drosophila melanogaster*. *Nature, 289*, 79–81.

Capogna, M., Gahwiler, B. H., & Thompson, S. M. (1995). Presynaptic enhancement of inhibitory synaptic transmission by protein kinases A and C in the rat hippocampus in vitro. *Journal of Neuroscience, 15*(2), 1249–60.

Carew, T. J., Pinsker, H. M., & Kandel, E. R. (1972). Long-term habituation of a defensive withdrawal reflex in Aplysia. *Science, 175*, 451–454.

Cash, S., Dan, Y., Poo, M. M., & Zucker, R. (1996). Postsynaptic elevation of calcium induces persistent depression of developing neuromuscular synapses. *Neuron, 16*(4), 745–54.

Castellucci, V. F., Blumenfeld, H., Goelet, P., & Kandel, E. R. (1989). Inhibitor of protein synthesis blocks long-term behavioral sensitization in the isolated gill-withdrawal reflex of Aplysia. *Journal of Neurobiology, 20*, 1–9.

Chavez-Noriega, L. E., & Stevens, C. F. (1994). Increased transmitter release at excitatory synapses produced by direct activation of adenylate cyclase in rat hippocampal slices. *Journal of Neuroscience, 14*(1), 310–317.

Chavis, P., Mollard, P., Bockaert, J., & Manzoni, O. (1998). Visualization of cyclic AMP-regulated presynaptic activity at cerebellar granule cells. *Neuron, 20*(4), 773–81.

Chen, C., & Regehr, W. G. (1997). The mechanism of cAMP-mediated enhancement at a cerebellar synapse. *Journal of Neuroscience, 17*(22), 8687–8694.

Chen, C.-N., Denome, S., & Davis, R. L. (1986). Molecular analysis of cDNA clones and the corresponding genomic coding sequences of the *Drosophila* dunce+ gene, the structural gene for cAMP phosphodiesterase. *Proceedings of the National Academy of Sciences USA, 83*, 9313–9317.

Chesnokov, I., Gossen, M., Remus, D., & Botchan, M. (1999). Assembly of functionally active Drosophila origin recognition complex from recombinant proteins. *Genes & Development, 13*, 1289–96.

Chouinard, S. W., Wilson, G. F., Schlimgen, A. K., & Genetzky, B. (1995). A potassium channel beta subunit related to aldo-keto reductase superfamily is encoded by the Drosophila hyperkinetic locus. *Proceedings of the National Academy of Sciences USA, 92*(15), 6763–6767.

Chrivia, J. C., Kowk, R. P. S., Lamb, N., Hagiwara, M., Montminy, M. R., & Goodman, R. H. (1993). Phosphorylated CREB binds specifically to the nuclear protein CBP. *Nature, 365*, 855–859.

Cline, H. T. (1998). Topographic maps: Developing roles of synaptic plasticity. *Current Biology, 8*, R836–R839.

Cline, H. T., & Constantine-Paton, M. (1989). NMDA receptor antagonists disrupt the retinotectal topographical map. *Neuron, 3*, 413–426.

Connolly, J. B., Roberts, I. J., Armstrong, J. D., Kaiser, K., M., F., Tully, T., & O'Kane, C. J. (1996). Associative learning disrupted by impaired G_s signaling in Drosophila mushroom bodies. *Science, 274*, 2104–2107.

Dash, P., Hochner, B., & Kandel, E. (1990). Injection if the cAMP-responsive element into the nucleus of Aplysia sensory neurons blocks long-term facilitation. *Nature, 345*, 718–721.

Davis, G. W., DiAntonio, A., Petersen, S. A., & Goodman, C. S. (1998). Postsynaptic PKA controls quantal size and reveals a retrograde signal that regulates presynaptic transmitter release in *Drosophila*. *Neuron, 20*, 305–315.

Davis, G. W., Schuster, C. M., & Goodman, C. S. (1996). Genetic dissection of structural and functional components of synaptic plasticity. III. CREB is necessary for presynaptic functional plasticity. *Neuron, 17*, 669–679.

Davis, H. P., & Squire, L. R. (1984). Protein synthesis and memory: A review. *Psychology Bulletin, 96*(3), 518–559.

deBelle, J. S., & Heisenberg, M. (1994). Associative odor learning in Drosophila abolished by chemical ablation of mushroom bodies. *Science, 263*(5147), 692–5.

Del Vecchio, M., & Tully, T. (1995). Unpublished data.

DeZazzo, J., Sandstrom, D., deBelle, S., Velinzon, K., Smith, P., Grady, L., Del Vecchio, M., Ramaswami, M., & Tully, T. (2000). *Nalyot*, a mutation of the Drosophila myb-related Adf1 transcription factor, disrupts synapse formation and olfactory memory. *Neuron, 27*, 145–158.

DeZazzo, J., & Tully, T. (1995). Dissection of memory formation: From behavioral pharmacology to molecular genetics. *Trends in Neuroscience, 18*, 212–217.

DeZazzo, J., Xia, S., Christensen, J., Velinzon, K., & Tully, T. (1999). Rescue of the mutant memory defect reveals *amnesiac* to encode a peptide involved in neurodevelopment. *Journal of Neuroscience, 19*, 8740–8746.

Dixon, D., & Atwood, H. L. (1989). Adenylate cyclase system is essential for long-term facilitation at the crayfish neuromuscular junction. *Journal of Neuroscience, 9*(12), 4246–52.

Dubnau, J., & Tully, T. (1998). Gene discovery in *Drosophila:* New insights for learning and memory. *Annual Review of Neuroscience, 21*, 407–444.

Dura, J. M., Preat, T., & Tully, T. (1993). Identification of *linotte*, a new gene affecting learning and memory in *Drosophila melanogaster. Journal of Neurogenetics, 9*, 1–14.

Feany, M. B., & Quinn, W. G. (1995). A neuroeptide gene defined by the *Drosophila* memory mutant *amnesiac. Science, 268*, 869–873.

Feng, G., Deak, P., Kasbekar, D. P., Gil, D. W., & Hall, L. M. (1995). Cytogenetic and molecular localization of tipE: A gene affecting sodium channels in Drosophila melanogaster. *Genetics, 139*(4), 1679–1688.

Folkers, E., Drain, P. F., & Quinn, W. G. (1993). *radish*, a *Drosophila* mutant deficient in consolidated memory. *Proceedings of the National Academy of Sciences USA, 90*, 8123–8127.

Frank, D., & Greenberg, M. (1994). CREB: A mediator of long-term memory from mollusks to mammals. *Cell, 79*, 5–8.

Frey, U., Huang, Y., & Kandel, E. R. (1993). Effects of cAMP stimulate a late stage of LTP in hippocampal CA1 neurons. *Science, 260*, 1661–1664.

Ganetzky, B., & Wu, C. F. (1983). Neurogenetic analysis of potassium currents in Drosophila: synergistic effects on neuromuscular transmission in double mutants. *Journal of Neurogenetics, 1*(1), 17–28.

Gass, P., Wolfer, D. P., Balschum, D., Rudolph, D., Frey, U., Lipp, H.-P., & Schutz, G. (1998). Deficits in memory tasks of mice with CREB mutations depend on gene dosage. *Learning and Memory, 5*, 274–288.

Ghirardi, M., Braha, O., Hochner, B., Montarolo, P. G., Kandel, E. R., & Dale, N. (1992). Roles of PKA and PKC in facilitation of evoked and spontaneous transmitter release at depressed and nondepressed synapses in Aplysia sensory neurons. *Neuron, 9*(3), 479–89.

Gillis, K. D., Mossner, R., & Neher, E. (1996). Protein kinase C enhances exocytosis from chromaffin cells by increasing the size of the readily releasable pool of secretory granules. *Neuron, 16*(6), 1209–1220.

Glazewski, S., Barth, A., Wallace, H., McKenna, M., Silva, A., & Fox, K. (1999). Impaired experience-dependent plasticity in barrel cortex of mice lacking the alpha and delta isoforms of CREB. *Cerebral Cortex, 9*, 249–256.

Goodman, C. S., & Shatz, C. J. (1993). Developmental mechanisms that generate precise patterns of neuronal connectivity. *Cell/Neuron, 72/10 (Suppl.)*, 77–98.

Goodwin, S. F., Del Vecchio, M., Velinzon, K., Hogel, C., Russell, S. R. H., Tully, T., & Kaiser, K. (1997). Defective learning in mutants of the *Drosophila* gene for a regulatory subunit of cAMP-dependent protein kinase. *Journal of Neuroscience, 17*, 8817–8827.

Gramates, S. L., & Budnik, V. (1999). Assembly and maturation of the Drosophila larval neuromuscular junction. *International Review of Neurobiology, 43*, 93–117.

Greengard, P., Valtorta, F., Czernik, A. J., & Benfenati, F. (1993). Synaptic vesicle phosphoproteins and regulation of synaptic function. *Science, 259*, 780–785.

Griffith, L. C., Verselis, L. M., Aitken, K. M., Kyriacou, C. P., Danho, W., & Greenspan, R. J. (1993). Inhibition of calcium/calmodulin dependent protein kinase in Drosophila disrupts plasticity. *Neuron, 10*, 501–509.

Griffith, L. C., Wang, J., Zhong, Y., Wu, C.-F., & Greenspan, R. J. (1994). Calcium/calmodulin-dependent protein kinase II and potassium channel subunit Eag similary affect plasticity in Drosophila. *Proceedings of the National Academy of Sciences USA, 91*, 10044–10048.

Grotewiel, M. S., Beck, C. D., Wu, K. H., Zhu, X. R., & Davis, R. L. (1998). Integrin-mediated short-term memory in Drosophila. *Nature, 391*(6666), 455–460.

Guo, H. F., The, I., Hannan, F., Bernards, A., & Zhong, Y. (1997). Requirement of Drosophila NF1 for activation of adenylyl cyclase by PACAP38-like neuropeptides. *Science, 276*(5313), 795–798.

Guo, H. F., Tong, J., Hannon, F., Luo, L., & Zhong, Y. (2000). A neurofibro matosis-1-regulated pathway is required for learning in Drosophilia. *Nature, 403*, 895–898.

Gutman, D. H., & Collins, F. S. (1993). The neurofibromatosis type 1 gene and its protein product, neurofibromin. *Neuron, 10*, 334–343.

Guzowski, J., & McGaugh, J. (1997). Antisense oligodeoxynucleotide-mediated disruption of hippocampal cAMP response element binding protein levels impairs consolidation of memory for water maze training. *Proceedings of the National Academy of Sciences USA, 94*, 2693–2698.

Han, P.-L., Levin, L. R., Reed, R. R., & Davis, R. L. (1992). Preferential expression of the *Drosophila rutabaga* gene in mushroom bodies, neural centres for learning in insects. *Neuron, 9*, 619–627.

Hanesch, U., Fischbach, K. F., & Heisenberg, M. (1989). Neuronal architecture of the central complex in *Drosophila melanogaster*. *Cell and Tissue Research, 257*, 343–366.

Hannan, F., & Zhong, Y. (1999). Second messenger systems underlying plasticity at the neuromuscular junction. In V. Budnik & L. S. Gramates (Eds.), *International review of neurobiology* (pp. 119–138). New York: Academic Press.

Hardingham, G. E., Chawla, S., Cruzalegui, F. H., & Bading, H. (1999). Control of recruitment and transcription-activating function of CBP determines gene regulation by NMDA receptors and L-type calcium channels. *Neuron, 22*(4), 789–798.

Hegde, A. N., Goldberg, A. L., & Schwartz, J. H. (1993). Regulatory subunits of cAMP-dependent protein kinases are degraded after conjugation to ubiquitin: A molecular mechanism underlying long-term synaptic plasticity. *Proceedings of the National Academy of Sciences USA, 90*(16), 7436–40.

Heisenberg, M., Borst, A., Wagner, S., & Byers, D. (1985). Drosophila mushroom body mutants are deficient in olfactory learning. *Journal of Neurogenetics, 2*(1), 1–30.

Herrero, I., Miras-Portugal, M. T., & Sanchez-Prieto, J. (1992). Postitive feedback of glutamate exocytosis by metabotropic presynaptic receptor stimulation. *Nature, 360*, 163–166.

Hitier, R., Heisenberg, M., & Preat, T. (1998). Abnormal mushroom body plasticity in the *Drosophila* memory mutant *amnesiac*. *NeuroReport, 9*, 2717–2719.

Hu, S. C., Chrivia, J., & Ghosh, A. (1999). Regulation of CBP-mediated transcription by neuronal calcium signaling. *Neuron, 22*(4), 799–808.

Huang, Y. Y., & Kandel, E. R. (1994). Recruitment of long-lasting and protein kinase A-dependent long-term potentiation in the CA1 region of hippocampus requires repeated tetanization. *Learning and Memory, 1*, 74–82.

Huang, Y. Y., & Kandel, E. R. (1998). Postsynaptic induction and PKA-dependent expression of LTP in the lateral amygdala. *Neuron, 21*(1), 169–178.

Huang, Y.-Y., Li, X.-C., & Kandel, E. R. (1994). cAMP contributes to mossy fiber LTP by initiating both a covalently mediated early phase and macromolecular synthesis-dependent late phase. *Cell, 79*, 69–79.

Huang, Z. J., Kirkwood, A., Pizzorusso, T., Porciatti, V., Morales, B., Bear, M. F., Maffei, L., & Tonegawa, S. (1999). BDNF regulates the maturation of inhibition and the critical period of plasticity in mouse visual cortex. *Cell, 98*(6), 739–55.

Impey, S., Mark, M., Villacres, E., Poser, S., Chavkin, C., & Storm, D. (1996). Induction of CRE-mediated gene expression by stimuli that generate long-lasting LTP in area CA1 of the hippocampus. *Neuron, 16*, 973–982.

Impey, S., Obrietan, K., Wong, S., Poser, S., Yano, S., Wayman, G., Deloulme, J., Chan, G., & Storm, D. (1998). Cross talk between ERK and PKA is required for Ca2+ stimulation of CREB-dependent transcription and ERK nuclear translocation. *Neuron, 21*(1), 869–883.

Impey, S., Smith, D., Obrietan, K., Donahue, R., Wade, C., & Storm, D. (1998). Stimulation of cAMP respnse element (CRE)-mediated transcription during contextual learning. *Nature Neuroscience, 1*(7), 595–601.

Ito, K., Suzuki, K., Estes, P., Ramaswami, M., Yamamoto, D., & Strausfeld, N. J. (1998). The organization of extrinsic neurons and their implications in the functional roles of the mushroom bodies in Drosophila melanogaster Meigen. *Learning and Memory, 5*(1/2), 52–77.

Jarecki, J., & Keshishian, H. (1995). Role of neural activity during synaptogenesis in Drosophila. *Journal of Neuroscience, 15*(12), 8177–8190.

Joiner, M. A., & Griffith, L. C. (1999). Mapping of the anatomical circuit of CaM kinase-dependent courtship conditioning in Drosophila. *Learning and Memory, 6*(2), 177–192.

Josselyn, S., Carlezon, J. W. A., Shi, C.-J., Neve, R., Nestler, E., & Davis, M. (1998). Overexpression of CREB in the amygdala facilitates the formation of long-term memory measured with fear potentiated startle in rats. *Society for Neuroscience Abstracts, 28th Annual Meetng, 24*(1), 365.10.

Kaang, B. K., Kandel, E. R., & Grant, S. G. (1993). Activation of cAMP-responsive genes by stimuli that produce long-term facilitation in Aplysia sensory neurons. *Neuron, 10*(3), 427–35.

Kasbekar, D. P., Nelson, J. C., & Hall, L. M. (1987). Enhancer of seizure: A new genetic locus in Drosophila melanogaster defined by interactions with temperature-sensitive paralytic mutations. *Genetics, 116*(3), 423–431.

Kauselmann, G., Weiler, M., Wulff, P., Jessberger, S., Konietzko, U., Scafidi, J., Staubli, U., Bereiter-Hahn, J., Strebhardt, K., & Kuhl, D. (1999). The polo-like protein kinases fnk and snk associate with a Ca(2+)- and integrin-binding protein and are regulated dynamically with synaptic plasticity [In Process Citation]. *EMBO Journal, 18*(20), 5528–5539.

Kennedy, T. E., Gawinowicz, M. A., Barzilai, A., Kandel, E. R., & Sweatt, J. D. (1988). Sequencing of proteins from two-dimensional gels by using in situ digestion and transfer of peptides to polyvinylidene difluoride membranes: Application to proteins associated with sensitization in Aplysia. *Proceedings of the National Academy of Sciences USA, 85*(18), 7008–7012.

Kernan, M. J., Kuroda, M. I., Kreber, R., Baker, B. S., & Ganetzky, B. (1991). *Napts*, a mutation affecting sodium channel activity in Drosophila, is an allele of mle, a regulator of X chromosome transcription. *Cell, 66*(5), 949–59.

Kogan, J., Frankland, P., Blendy, J., Coblentz, J., Marowitz, Z., Schutz, G., & Silva, A. (1996). Spaced training induces normal long-term memory in CREB mutant mice. *Current Biology, 7*, 1–11.

Koh, Y. A., Popova, E., Thomas, U., Griffith, L. C., & Budnik, V. (1999). Regulation of DLG localization at synapses by CAMKII-dependent phosphorylation. *Cell, 98*, 353–363.

Kuhl, D., Kennedy, T. E., Barzilai, A., & Kandel, R. R. (1992). Long-term sensitization training in Aplsia leads to an increase in the expression of BiP, the major protein chaperon of the ER. *Journal of Cell Biology, 119*(December), 1069–1076.

Kuromi, H., & Kidokoro, Y. (1998). Two distinct pools of synaptic vesicles in single presynaptic boutons in a temperature-sensitive Drosophila mutant, shibire. *Neuron, 20*(5), 917–925.

Kuromi, H., & Kidokoro, Y. (1999). The optically determined size of exo/endo cycling vesicle pool correlates with the quantal content at the neuromuscular junction of Drosophila larvae. *Journal of Neuroscience, 19*(5), 1557–1565.

Lamprecht, R., Hazvi, S., & Dudai, Y. (1997). cAMP response element-binding protein in the amygdala is required for long- but not short-term conditioned taste aversion memory. *Journal of Neuroscience, 17*(21), 8443–8450.

Levin, L. R., Han, P.-L., Hwang, P. M., Feinstein, P. G., Davis, R. L., & Reed, R. R. (1992). The *Drosophila* learning and memory gene *rutabaga* encodes a Ca^{2+}/calmodulin—responsive adenylyl cylase. *Cell, 68*, 479–489.

Li, W., Tully, T., & Kalderon, D. (1996). Effects of a conditional *Drosophila* PKA mutant on learning and memory. *Learning and Memory, 2*, 320–333.

Livingstone, M. S., Sziber, P. P., & Quinn, W. G. (1984). Loss of calcium/calmodulin responsiveness in adenylate cyclase of rutabaga, a *Drosophila* learning mutant. *Cell, 137*, 205–215.

Loughney, K., Kreber, R., & Ganetzky, B. (1989). Molecular analysis of the para locus, a sodium channel gene in Drosophila. *Cell, 58*(6), 1143–54.

Martin, J. R., Raabe, T., & Heisenberg, M. (1999). Central complex substructures are required for the maintenance of locomotor activity in Drosophila melanogaster. *Journal of Comparative Physiology [A], 185*(3), 277–88.

Martin, K., Michael, D., Rose, J., Barad, M., Casadio, A., Zhu, H., & Kandel, E. (1997). MAP kinase translocates into the nucleus of the presynaptic cell and is required for long-term facilitation in aplysia. *Neuron, 18*, 899–912.

Matthies, H., & Reymann, K. G. (1993). Protein kinase A inhibitors prevent the maintenance of hippocampal long-term potentiation. *NeuroReport, 4*, 712–714.

Mayford, M., Barzilai, A., Keller, F., Schacher, S., & Kandel, E. R. (1992). Modulation of an NCAM-related adhesion molecule with long-term synaptic plasticity in Aplysia *Science, 256*, 638–644.

McGaugh, J. L., & Herz, M. L. (1972). *Memory consolidation*. San Francisco: Albion.

McKay, S. E., Purcell, A. L., & Carew, T. J. (1999). Regulation of synaptic function by neurotrophic factors in vertebrates and invertebrates: Implications for development and learning. *Learning & Memory, 6*, 193–215.

Meffert, M. K., Calakos, N. C., Scheller, R. H., & Schulman, H. (1996). Nitric oxide modulates synaptic vesicle docking fusion reactions. *Neuron, 16*(6), 1229–1236.

Migaud, M., Charlesworth, P., Dempster, M., Webster, L. C., Watabe, A. M., Makhinson, M., He, Y., Ramsay, M. F., Morris, R. G., Morrison, J. H., O'Dell, T. J., & Grant, S. G. (1998). Enhanced long-term potentiation and impaired learning in mice with mutant postsynaptic density-95 protein [see comments]. *Nature, 396*(6710), 433–439.

Montarolo, P. G., Goelet, P., Castellucci, V. F., Morgan, J., Kandel, E. R., & Schacher, S. (1986). A critical period for macromolecular synthesis in long-term heterosynaptic facilitation in Aplysia *Science, 234*, 1249–1254.

Moore, M., DeZazzo, J., Luk, A., Tully, T., Singh, C., & Heberlein, U. (1998). Ethanol intoxication in *Drosophila*: Genetic and pharmacological evidence for regulation by the cAMP signaling pathway. *Cell, 93*, 997–1007.

Nguyen, P. V., Abel, T., & Kandel, E. R. (1994). Requirement of a critical period of transcription for induction of a late phase of LTP. *Science, 265*(5175), 1104–1107.

Nighorn, A., Healy, M. J., & Davis, R. L. (1991). The cyclic AMP phosphodiesterase encoded by the *Drosophila dunce* gene is concentrated in the mushroom body neuropil. *Neuron, 6*, 455–467.

North, K., Joy, P., Yuille, D., Cocks, N., & Hutchins, P. (1995). Cognitive function and academic performance in children with neurofibromatosis type 1. *Developmental and Medical Child Neurology, 37*(5), 427–436.

O'Brien, T., Cutler, G., de la Fuente, L., & Tjian, R. (2000). Adf-1, a transcription factor implicated in neuroplasticity, is modulated by CaMKII. Manuscript submitted for publication.

Oike, Y., Hata, A., Mamiya, T., Kaname, T., Noda, Y., Suzuki, M., Yasue, H., Nabeshima, T., Araki, K., & Yamamura, K. (1999). Truncated CBP protein leads to classical Rubinstein-Taybi syndrome phenotypes in mice: implications for a dominant-negative mechanism. *Human Molecular Genetics, 8*(3), 387–396.

Petrij, F., Giles, R., Dauwerse, H., Saris, J., Hennekam, R., Masuno, M., Tommerup, N., van Ommen, G.-J. B., Goodman, R., Peters, D., & Breuning, M. (1995). Rubinstein-Taybi syndrome caused by mutations in the transcriptional co-activator CBP. *Nature, 376*, 348–351.

Pham, T., Impey, S., Storm, D., & Stryker, M. (1999). CRE-mediated gene transcription in neocortical neuronal plasticity during the developmental critical period. *Neuron, 22*, 63–72.

Pinsker, H. M., Hening, W. A., Carew, T. J., & Kandel, E. R. (1973). Long-term sensitization of a defensive withdrawal reflex in Aplysia. *Science., 198*, 1039–1042.

Pinto, S., Quintana, D. Q., Smith, P., Mihalek, R. M., Hou, Z.-H., Boynton, S., Jones, C. J., Hendricks, M., Velinzon, K., Wohlschlagel, J. A., Austin, R. J., Lane, W. S., Tully, T., & Dutta, A. (1999). *latheo* encodes a subunit of the origin replication complex and disrupts neuronal proliferation and adult olfactory memory formation when mutant. *Neuron, 23*, 45–54.

Prezeau, L., Manzoni, O., Homburger, V., Sladeczek, F., Curry, K., & Bockaert, J. (1992). Characterization of a metabotropic glutamate receptor: direct negative coupling to adenylyl cyclase and involvement of a pertussis toxin-sensitive G protein. *Proceedings of the National Academy of Sciences USA, 89*(17), 8040–4.

Quinn, W. G., & Dudai, Y. (1976). Memory phases in *Dosophila*. *Nature, 262*, 576–577.

Rayport, S. G., & Schacher, S. (1986). Synaptic plasticity in vitro: Cell culture of identified Aplysia neurons mediating short-term habituation and sensitization. *Journal of Neuroscience, 6*(3), 759–763.

Rohrbough, J., Pinto, S., Mihalek, R., Tully, T., & Broadie, K. (1999). *Latheo*, a Drosophila gene involved in learning, regulates functional synaptic plasticity. *Neuron, 23*, 55–70.

Rosenmund, C., & Stevens, C. F. (1996). Definition of the readily releasable pool of vesicles at hippocampal synapses. *Neuron, 16*(6), 1197–207.

Roth, D., & Burgoyne, R. D. (1995). Stimulation of catecholamine secretion from adrenal chromaffin cells by 14-3-3 proteins is due to reorganization of the cortical actin network. *FEBS Letters, 3745*, 77–81.

Saitoe, M., Koshimoto, H., Hirano, M., Suga, T., & Kidokoro, Y. (1998). Distribution of functional glutamate receptors in cultured embryonic Drosophila myotubes revealed using focal release of L-glutamate from caged compound by laser. *Journal of Neuroscience Methods, 80*(2), 163–170.

Saitoe, M., Tanaka, S., Takata, K., & Kidokoro, Y. (1997). Neural activity affects distribution of glutamate receptors during neuromuscular junction formation in Drosophila embryos. *Developmental Biology 184*(1), 48–60.

Saitoe, M., & Tully, T. (2000). The novel gene, *linotte*, contributes to synaptic plasticity and olfactory learning via cAMP signaling. *Manuscript* in preparation.

Sanes, J., & Lichtmann, J. W. (1999). Development of the vertebrate neuromuscular junction. *Annual Review of Neuroscience, 22*, 389–442.

Schacher, S., Castelluci, V. F., & Kandel, E. R. (1988). cAMP evokes long-term facilitation in *Aplysia* sensory neurons that requires new protein synthesis. *Science, 240*, 1667–1669.

Schneggenburger, R., Meyer, A. C., & Neher, E. (1999). Released fraction and total size of a pool of immediately available transmitter quanta at a calyx synapse. *Neuron, 23*(2), 399–409.

Scholz, K. P., & Byrne, J. H. (1988). Intracellular injection of cAMP induces a long-term reduction of neuronal K^+ currents. *Science, 240*, 1664–1666.

Schopperle, W. M., Holmqvist, M. H., Zhou, Y., Wang, J., Wang, Z., Griffith, L. C., Keselman, I., Kusinitz, F., Dagan, D., & Levitan, I. B. (1998). Slob, a novel protein that interacts with the Slowpoke calcium-dependent potassium channel. *Neuron, 20*(3), 565–73.

Schuster, C. M., Davis, G. W., Fetter, R. D., & Goodman, C. S. (1996a). Genetic dissection of structural and functional components of synaptic plasticity. I. Fasciclin II controls synaptic stabilization and growth. *Neuron, 17*, 641–654.

Schuster, C. M., Davis, G. W., Fetter, R. D., & Goodman, C. S. (1996b). Genetic dissection of structural and functional components of synaptic plasticity. II. Fasciclin II controls presynaptic structural plasticity. *Neuron, 17*, 655–667.

Schweizer, F. E., Betz, H., & Augustine, G. J. (1995). From vesicle docking to endocytosis: Intermediate reactions of exocytosis. *Neuron, 14*(4), 689–696.

Sciancalepore, M., Stratta, F., Fisher, N. D., & Cherubini, E. (1995). Activation of metabotropic glutamate receptors increase the frequency of spontaneous GABAergic currents through protein kinase A in neonatal rat hippocampal neurons. *J Neurophysiol, 74*(3), 1118–1122.

Skoulakis, E. M. C., & Davis, R. L. (1996). Olfactory learning deficits in mutants for *leonardo*, a *Drosophila* gene encoding a 14-3-3 protein. *Neuron, 17*, 931–944.

Skoulakis, E. M. C., Kalderon, D., & Davis, R. L. (1993). Preferential expression in mushroom bodies of the catalytic subunit of protein kinase A and its role in learning and memory. *Neuron, 11*, 197–208.

Spengler, D., Waeber, C., Pantaloni, C., Holsboer, F., Bockaert, J., Seeburg, P. H., & Journot, L. (1993). Differential signal transduction by five splice variants of the PACAP receptor. *Nature, 365*(6442), 170–175.

Sterneck, E., Paylor, R., Jackson-Lewis, V., Libbey, M., Przedborski, S., Tessarollo, L., Crawley, J. N., & Johnson, P. F. (1998). Selectively enhanced contextual fear conditioning in mice lacking the transcriptional regulator CCAAT/enhancer binding protein delta. *Proceedings of the National Academy of Sciences USA, 95*(18), 10908–10913.

Stimson, D. T., & Ramaswami, M. (1999). Vesicle recycling at the Drosophila neuromuscular junction. *International Review of Neurobiology, 43*, 163–89.

Suzuki, D. T., Grigliatti, T., & Williamson, R. (1971). Temperature-sensitive mutants in Drosophila melanogaster: A mutation (parats 1) causing reversible adult paralysis. *Proceedings of the National Academy of Sciences USA, 68*, 890–893.

Tanabe, Y., Masu, M., Ishii, T., Shigemoto, R., & Nakanishi, S. (1992). A family of metabotropic glutamate receptors. *Neuron, 8*(1), 169–79.

Tang, Y. P., Shimizu, E., Dube, G. R., Rampon, C., Kerchner, G. A., Zhu, M., Liu, G., & Tsien, J. Z. (1999). Genetic enhancement of learning and memory in mice. *Nature, 401,* 63–69.

Technau, G. (1984). Fiber number in the mushroom bodies of adult *Drosophila melanogaster* dependson age, sex and experience. *Journal of Neurogenetics, 1,* 113–126.

Technau, G., & Heisenberg, M. (1982). Neural reorganization during metamorphosis of the corpora pedunculata in *Drosophila melanogaster. Nature, 295,* 405–407.

Tempel, B. L., Papazian, D. M., Schwarz, T. L., Jan, Y. N., & Jan, L. Y. (1987). Sequence of a probable potassium channel component encoded at Shaker locus of Drosophila. *Science, 237,* 770–775.

The, I., Hannigan, G. E., Cowley, G. S., Reginald, S., & Zhong, Y. (1997). *Drosophila* NF1 acts in growth regulation and PKA-mediated signaling. *Science, 276,* 791–794.

Trudeau, L. E., Emery, D. G., & Haydon, P. G. (1996). Direct modulation of the secretory machinery underlies PKA-dependent synaptic facilitation in hippocampal neurons. *Neuron, 17*(4), 789–97.

Tully, T. (1997). Regulation of gene expression and its role in long-term memory and synaptic plasticity. *Proceedings of the National Academy of Sciences USA, 94,* 4239–4241.

Tully, T. (1998). Toward molecular biology of memory: The light's coming on! *Nature Neuroscience, 1*(7), 543–545.

Tully, T., Bolwig, G., Christensen, J., Connolly, J., Del Vecchio, M., DeZazzo, J., Dubnau, J., Pinto, S., Regulski, M., Svedberg, B., & Velinzon, K. (1996). *A return to genetic dissection of memory in Drosophila. Cold Spring Harbor Symposium on Quantitative Biology, 61,* 207–218.

Tully, T., Boynton, S., Brandes, C., Dura, J.-M., Mihalek, R., Preat, T., & Villella, A. (1990). Genetic dissection of memory formaton in *Drosophila melanogaster. Cold Spring Harbor Symp. Quant. Biol., 55,* 203–211.

Tully, T., Preat T., Boynton, S., & Del Vecchio, M. (1994). Genetic dissection of consolidated memory in Drosophila. *Cell, 79,* 35–47.

Tully, T., & Quinn, W. G. (1985). Classical conditioning and retention in normal and mutant Drosophila melanogaster. *Journal of Comparative Physiology, 157,* 263–277.

Viskochil, D., White, R., & Cawthon, R. (1993). The neurofibromatosis type 1 gene. *Annual Review of Neuroscience, 16,* 183–205.

Wang, B., Yang, H., Liu, Y. C., Jelinek, T., Zhang, L., Ruoslahti, E., & Fu, H. (1999). Isolation of highaffinity peptide antagonists of 14-3-3 proteins by phage display. *Biochemistry, 38*(38), 12499–12504.

Wang, J., Renger, J. J., Griffith, L. C., Greenspan, R. J., & Wu, C.-F. (1994). Concomitant alterations of physiological and developmental plasticity in Drosophila CaM kinase II-inhibited synapses. *Neuron, 13,* 1373–1384.

Wang, J. H., & Kelly, P. T. (1997). Attenuation of paired-pulse facilitation associated with synaptic potentiation mediated by postsynaptic mechanisms. *Journal of Neurophysiology, 78*(5), 2707–2716.

Warmke, J., Drysdale, R., & Ganetsky, B. (1991). A distinct potassium channel polypeptide encoded by the *Drosophila eag* locus. *Science, 252,* 1560–1562.

Weiler, I. J., Hawrylak, N., & Greenough, W. T. (1995). Morphogenesis in memory formation: Synaptic and cellular mechanisms. *Behavior and Brain Research, 66*(1/2), 1–6.

Wilson, G. F., Wang, Z., Chouinard, S. W., Griffith, L. C., & Ganetzky, B. (1998). Interaction of the K channel beta subunit, Hyperkinetic, with eag family members. *Journal of Biology and Chemistry, 273*(11), 6389–6394.

Winder, D. G., & Conn, P. J. (1992). Activation of metabotropic glutamate receptors in the hippocampus increases cyclic AMP accumulation. *Journal of Neurochemistry, 59*(1), 375–378.

Wong, S. T., Athos, J., Figueroa, X. A., Pineda, V. V., Schaefer, M. L., Chavkin, C. C., Muglia, L. J., & Storm, D. R. (1999). Calcium-stimulated adenylyl cyclase activity is critical for hippocampus-dependent long-term memory and late phase LTP. *Neuron, 23*(4), 787–798.

Xu, G., O'Connell, P., Viskochil, D., Cawthon, R., Robertson, M., Culver, M., Dunn, D., Stevens, J., Gesteland, R., White, R., & Weiss, R. (1990). The neurofibromatosis type 1 gene encodes a protein related to GAP. *Cell, 62,* 599–608.

Yamada, A., Sekiguchi, T., Susuki, H., & Mizukami, A. (1992). Behavioral analysis of internal memory states using cooling-induced retrograde amnesia in *Limax flavus*. *Journal of Neuroscience*, *12*, 729–735.

Yin, J., Del Vecchio, M., Zhou, H., & Tully, T. (1995). CREB as a memory modulator: Induced expression of dCREB2 activator isoform enhances long-term memory in Drosophila. *Cell*, *81*, 107–115.

Yin, J., Wallach, J., Del Vecchio, M., Wilder, E., Zhou, H., Quinn, W., & Tully, T. (1994). Induction of a dominant negative CREB transgene specifically blocks long-term memory in Drosophila. *Cell*, *79*, 49–58.

Yin, J. C., & Tully, T. (1996). CREB and the formation of long-term memory. *Current Opinions in Neurobiology*, *6*(2), 264–268.

Zhang, D., Kuromi, H., & Kidokoro, Y. (1999). Activation of metabotropic glutamate receptors enhances synaptic transmission at the Drosophila neuromuscular junction. *Neuropharmacology*, *38*(5), 645–657.

Zhong, Y. (1995). Mediation of PACAP-like neuropeptide transmission by coactivation of Ras/Raf and cAMP signal transduction oathways in Drosophila. *Nature*, *375*, 588–592.

Zhong, Y., & Pena, L. A. (1995). A novel synaptic transmission mediated by a PACAP-like neuropeptide in *Drosophila*. *Neuron*, *14*, 527–536.

Zhong, Y., Budnik, V., & Wu, C. F. (1992). Synaptic plasticity in Drosophila memory and hyperexcitable mutants: Role of cAMP cascade. *Journal of Neuroscience*, *12*, 644–651.

Zhong, Y., & Wu, C.-F. (1991). Altered synaptic plasticity in Drosophila memory mutants with a defective cyclic AMP cascade. *Science*, *251*, 198–201.

Zhou, Y., Schopperle, W. M., Murrey, H., Jaramillo, A., Dagan, D., Griffith, L. C., & Levitan, I. B. (1999). A dynamically regulated 14-3-3, Slob, and Slowpoke potassium channel complex in Drosophila presynaptic nerve terminals. *Neuron*, *22*(4), 809–818.

PART

V

DEVELOPMENTAL ASPECTS OF NEUROPLASTICITY

16

Bryan Kolb
Robbin Gibb
Claudia L. R. Gonzalez

CHAPTER

Cortical Injury and Neuroplasticity During Brain Development

☐ Introduction

It has been known for over 100 years that injury to the infant brain can have less severe consequences than similar injury in adulthood (for a review, see Finger & Almli, 1988). For example, Broca noticed in the late 1800s that damage to the speech zones of the left hemisphere during infancy did not interfere with the later development of language. It was discovered much later that this was due to the shifting of the speech zones either to the opposite hemisphere or, in some circumstances, within the left hemisphere (e.g., Rasmussen & Milner, 1977). Systematic study of the effect of early brain damage on functional development began with the studies of Margaret Kennard in the late 1930s, in which she showed that unilateral motor cortex impairments are less severe after motor cortex injury if the lesion occurs during infancy rather than adulthood (e.g., Kennard, 1942). Kennard proposed that there must be some change in the synaptic organization in the young animal that was supporting the functional recovery, although she was vague about what such changes might be. Thus, the general conclusion arising from Kennard's work was that brain injury early in life is associated with a better functional outcome than injury later because the developing brain can more easily reorganize than the adult brain. Teuber later labeled this idea the Kennard principle (Teuber, 1975), which is a term that is still often used.

One difficulty with the Kennard principle is that it does not account for those conditions under which early brain damage results in rather severe functional loss, such as in cerebral palsy or hemiplegia resulting from unilateral cerebral injury at birth. In fact, Donald Hebb noted that children with frontal lobe injuries in infancy showed little functional recovery in adulthood, and for some behaviors, such as social behaviors, these children might actually have more severe deficits than adults with similar injuries (e.g., Ackerly, 1964). Hebb concluded that at least some types of early injuries might prevent the development of certain intellectual capacities that are critical to normal cognitive development (e.g., Hebb, 1947, 1949). Thus, in Hebb's view, some forms of early injury might compromise the brain's capacity for later plastic changes.

The contradictory findings (and conclusions) of Kennard and Hebb are clearly important for a general theory of brain plasticity. In particular, we can pose three basic questions: (a) How plastic is the developing brain? (b) How do the plastic changes in the brain relate to function? And, (c) what factors influence this plasticity? In order to address these questions, we shall first consider the basic mechanisms of plasticity in the developing brain. Next, we shall examine the nature of synaptic change and functional improvement after cortical injury at different stages during development. Finally, we shall examine the factors that influence this plasticity.

Before we begin, however, we must first admit to several assumptions that guide our thinking on these issues. First, we are cortical chauvinists and our review will focus on the effects of cortical lesions. There are very few, parallel studies on noncortical structures but we have no a priori reason to anticipate that cortical results will not generalize, at least to forebrain or cerebellar structures. Second, we assume that functions are at least partially localized in the cortex. Functional localization occurs, in part, because particular cortical regions have specific inputs and outputs. For example, visual area V1 has its unique functions because it receives a unique set of inputs and it sends out a unique set of outputs. If V1 were completely lost to injury at any age, recovery would be impossible because the information normally generated in V1 could not be duplicated elsewhere. The implication of this fact is that recovery from cortical injury requires that at least part of a functional system remain intact. There are likely to be plastic changes within this remaining region that are important for understanding recovery. Third, the mechanisms of cortical plasticity that underlie functional recovery after early injury are likely to be at the synapse. This idea can be traced back at least to the Spanish anatomist, Ramón y Cajal (1928), who proposed that the process of learning might produce prolonged morphological changes in the efficiency of the synapse. It was not until the late 1940s, however, that Konorski (1948) and Hebb (1949) independently proposed similar mechanisms that could lead to synaptic change. For Hebb, the most important condition was that two neurons had to be coincidentally active, and if so, then the connection between them was strengthened. The general idea in the current context is that when neurons are active, such as when animals are engaged with sensory inputs, there is synaptic change. Fourth, the mechanisms of synaptic plasticity used by the brain are likely to be similar to those used for other forms of plasticity such as in learning, drug addiction, aging, etc. Furthermore, factors that influence plasticity in the normal brain will also influence plasticity (and thus functional recovery) in the injured brain. Finally, our focus will be on the rat, in large part because there is more known about plasticity, the effects of injury, and the role of different factors in recovery for rats than for any other species.

☐ Plasticity in the Normal Developing Brain

There are two key issues with respect to plasticity in the normal developing brain. First, there is the genetically programmed process of cell birth and differentiation. Second, there is the effect of various factors, and experience in particular, on all of the processes of brain development. We consider each in turn.

Stages of Brain Development

Like the brain of other vertebrates, the rat brain begins as a neural tube, which is the nursery for the cells that will form the brain (for reviews, see Bayer & Altman, 1991;

Uylings, van Eden, Parnavelas, & Kalsbeek, 1990). Neurons (and glia) arise from neural stem cells that reside in a layer of cells that surround the neural tube in a zone that is referred to as the ventricular zone. Later in development, these cells form a part of the ventricular zone and are referred to as the subependymal zone (SZ). Neural stem cells can divide symmetrically, to produce two stem cells, or asymmetrically, to produce a stem cell and a progenitor cell. As the brain grows into adulthood, stem cells remain active, although they may have a finite number of divisions before they die. It appears that progenitor cells that divide to produce neurons and/or glia can migrate away from the SZ and may lie quiescently in the white or gray matter. While in these locations they can be activated to produce neurons and/or glia, even in adulthood. (For a useful review, see Weiss et al., 1996.) In fact, it is now well documented that neurogenesis can continue throughout life, especially for neurons in the olfactory bulb and hippocampus (e.g., Gould, Tanapat, Hastings, & Shors, 1999; Kempermann & Gage, 1999). More surprising, however, is the increasing evidence that there are new cortical neurons produced well after birth, even in the human brain (e.g., Shankle et al., 1998).

The generation of the cells that will eventually form the cortex begins on embryonic day 12 and continues until about day 21. Rats are born on day 22, so neurogenesis is complete about the time of birth. As cells are generated in the brain they migrate to their appropriate locations, whether that be prefrontal or occipital cortex. This migration continues well into the first week of life, and is largely complete by 7–10 days of age. It is at this point that cell differentiation, which is the process whereby neuroblasts become a specific neuronal phenotype, begins. Cell differentiation is essentially complete by eye opening, which is on day 15, although neuron maturation, which includes the growth of dendrites, axons, and synapses is intense for 2–3 weeks and declines thereafter. One important feature of cortical development is that neurons appear to overproduce the number of synapses during the rapid growth phase and then later prune off excess synapses (e.g., Miller, 1988). This phenomenon is important because the pruning is presumably influenced by various events, including gonadal hormones, experience, and injury.

One feature of cortical development that emerges from the stages of growth is that the developing brain is very different in structure and organization at different ages. We should not be surprised, therefore, that the plastic responses of the brain both to experience and to injury will differ qualitatively at different times in development. Furthermore, we shall see that the brain's capacity for plastic change appears to vary with precise developmental age as well (Figure 16.1).

Experience-Dependent Changes During Brain Development

Development of the synaptic organization of the brain can be influenced, at least in principle, by any factors that influence any stage of brain development from mitosis to synaptogenesis and pruning (see also Greenough, Black, & Wallace, 1987; Greenough, & Chang, 1989). For example, any perturbation that prolongs neurogenesis or reinitiates neurogenesis will affect the number of neurons and/or glia in the brain. Similarly, events that stimulate activity in developing neurons are likely to affect the pattern of synaptic organization (e.g., Changeux, 1997). We can now identify a growing list of factors that can influence brain development including experience, gonadal hormones, stress, neuromodulators, neurotrophic factors, injury, and psychomotor stimulants. Few of these factors has been studied as thoroughly at different stages of development as experience, so we will focus here on experience-dependent changes in the developing brain. We then consider the effects of injury separately.

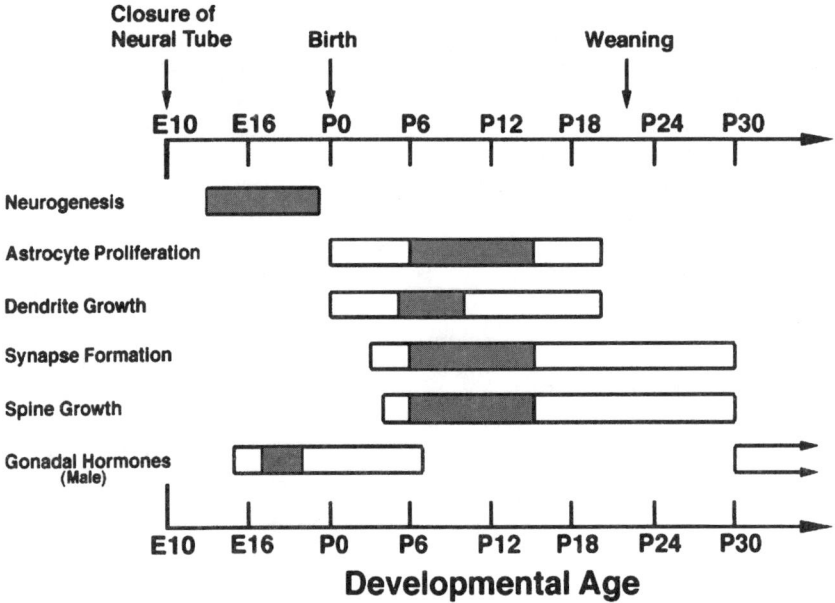

Figure 16.1. The main cellular events of cortical development in the rat. Bars indicate the approximate beginning and ending of different processes. The shaded areas reflect the intensity of the phenomenon.

One way to examine the effect of experience on plastic changes in the developing brain is to stimulate the brain at different times during development. One problem, of course, is that it is not possible to use the same stimulation at different ages, especially early in development, because the sensory systems are not fully developed. (Recall that the rat's eyes do not open until 15 days of age, so patterned visual stimulation cannot be given until at least 15 days of age.) We have approached this problem by using tactile stimulation during the first days of cortical development, both in utero and after birth (see Table 16.1). For the in utero stimulation the ventrum of pregnant dams is stimulated tactilely several times a day. For the postpartem stimulation, the infants are stimulated with a small camel-hair brush. In both cases the stimulation, which may last only about 10 days, produces a chronic change in behavior in adulthood. For example, tactile stimulation of infant rats produces an improvement in skilled forelimb reaching behavior in adulthood, relative to unstimulated animals, even though the stimulation was from postnatal days 4–18, which is before rats even show skilled reaching. Similarly, when animals are placed into complex environments for 3 months, beginning at weaning, there is an improvement in the later acquisition of various behaviors, including skilled reaching, relative to animals living in standard group-housed laboratory cages (e.g., Greenough & Chang, 1989; Juraska, 1990). Thus, in general it appears that the early stimulation, whether it be tactile in the youngest animals or more general experience in the older animals, produces chronic changes in adult behavior. It was our expectation, therefore, that these different experiences would likely have similar effects on the brain. We were mistaken. In fact, when the cortical neurons from brains of animals treated at these various times during development are compared, there are clear qualitative differences in the effects of the experiences. These data are summarized in Table 16.1.

TABLE 16.1. Summary of infant stimulation studies in normal animals.

Age at Stimulation	Type of Stimulation	Effect of Stimulation
Prenatal (E12–E21)[a]	Tactile stimulation	Heavier brain;?
Infant (P4–P18)[b]	Tactile stimulation spines	Heavier brain; same dendrites; fewer
Juvenile (P21–P120)[c]	Complex housing	Heavier brain; more dendrites; fewer spines
Adult (P120–P200)[d]	Complex housing	Heavier brain; more dendrites; more spines

[a] Gibb, Gonzalez, & Kolb, 2000.
[b] Kolb & Gibb, 2000.
[c] Kolb, Gibb, & Gorny, 2000.
[d] Greenough & Chang, 1989; Juraska, 1990

Our finding of a decrease in spine density in young animals is not without precedent. Wallhausser and Scheich (1987) presented newly hatched chicks with a hen or an acoustic stimulus with the goal of imprinting the chicks to the visual or auditory stimulus. The neurons in different regions of the hyperstriatum of the imprinted chicks were compared to those of isolated chicks: There was a decrease in spine density in the trained chicks when the brains were examined 7 days after training. There is an important caveat to this result, however. Patel and Stewart (1988) used a Golgi technique to impregnate chick brains 25 hours after training chicks to avoid a colored bead. They found a twofold increase in spine density in the neurons in a region of the hyperstriatum (intermediate medial hyperstriatum ventrale) in the "trained" chicks. They concluded that this represented an increase in synapses that reflected the learning. This interpretation was supported by a second study in which Patel, Rose, and Stewart (1988) trained chicks on the passive avoidance task described above but, in their experiment, half of the trained chicks were given a subconvulsive transcranial electroshock 5 minutes after training. This procedure rendered about half of the trained animals amnesic for the experience. The spine density was found to be higher in the chicks that remembered the aversive nature of the training stimulus compared to chicks rendered amnesic. This finding argues strongly in favor of a specific role for dendritic spines in experience-dependent memory formation in the chick. The critical difference between the Wallhausser and Scheich study and the Patel studies is the survival time. Thus, taken together the experiments show that there was an increase 25 hours after training but there was a decrease 7 days after training. The simplest conclusion from the chick studies is that the novel stimulation may cause an initial rapid increase in spine density, followed by a pruning. If we extrapolate to the current study we might predict that the juvenile animals showed an increase in spine density over the first hours or days in the condominiums, followed by a synaptic pruning. The critical experiment would be to examine brains of juvenile animals housed in the condominiums for varying periods of time.

Finally, we would be remiss if we did not point out that the paradox of a decrease in spine density per neuron at the same time as enhanced function might reflect the fact that the early stimulation actually increased the numbers of neurons in the brain. If the number of neurons was higher, then even with a decrease in spine density there would be a net increase in the number of cortical synapses. An increase in neuron number might happen either because the stimulation increased survival of the existing cells in the brain or because the stimulation induced the generation of new neurons. It is known that experience can increase the number of neurons in the hippocampus (e.g., Kempermann & Gage, 1999), but this remains to be shown for the cortex (see also Kolb, 1999).

☐ Plasticity in the Injured Developing Brain

In principle, there are three ways that the brain could show plastic changes that might support recovery. First, there could be changes in the organization of the remaining, intact circuits in the brain. The general idea is that the brain could reorganize in some way to do "more with less." It is unlikely that a complexly integrated structure like the cerebral cortex could undergo a wholesale reorganization of cortical connectivity, but rather, recovery from cortical injury would be most likely to result from a change in the intrinsic organization of local cortical circuits in regions directly or indirectly disrupted by the injury. Although it might be possible to produce significant reorganization of cortical connectivity in the young brain, the overwhelming evidence in experimental animals is that this is rare, and we shall see that it is just as likely to be associated with abnormal functioning as with recovery.

Second, there could be a generation of new circuitry. Cerebral reorganization can be stimulated by either some sort of behavioral therapy or the application of some sort of pharmacological treatment. In either event the stimulus could influence reparative processes in the remaining brain or could enhance the production of new circuitry. Once again, it seems most likely that the induced neuronal changes would be in the intrinsic organization of the cortex. One might predict that induced neuronal changes might be more extensive than in the case of endogenous change, in part because the treatment can act upon the whole brain rather than just on affected regions.

Third, there could be a generation of neurons and glia to replace at least some lost neurons. We saw earlier that the stem cells that give rise to the neurons and glia of the brain remain active in the SZ throughout life. It is thus possible that neurogenesis could be stimulated after injury, especially during development, and that these new neurons could replace those lost to injury or disease (e.g., Weiss et al., 1996).

We shall see that all three of these possibilities for cerebral plasticity after early injury appear to occur. We shall consider first the functional outcomes of early cortical injury in rats and then the nature of the plastic changes that underlie the observed behavioral changes.

Functional Outcome After Early Cortical Injury

We began this chapter by contrasting the results of studies by Kennard and Hebb, one showing a better outcome and one showing a worse outcome after early cortical injuries. It turns out that both are correct, the critical differences being the precise age at injury and the particular region injured (see also Villablanca, Hovda, Jackson, & Infante, 1993). Furthermore, the two different types of functional outcome are correlated with very different plastic responses in the cortex.

Over the past 20 years we have removed virtually every region of the cortical mantle of rats at varying ages ranging from embryonic day 18 to adolescence. Our general finding is that recovery varies with precise embryological age (Figure 16.2; Table 16.2). If the cortex is injured bilaterally during neurogenesis, there is virtually complete functional recovery. The ability of the brain to compensate for injury during the time of

TABLE 16.2. Summary of the effects of frontal cortical injury at different ages.

Age at Injury	Result	Basic Reference
E18	Functional recovery	Kolb, Cioe, & Muirhead, 1998
	Cortex regrows with odd structure	
P1–P6	Dismal functional outcome	Kolb & Whishaw, 1989
	Small brain, dendritic atrophy	Kolb et al., 1994
	Abnormal connectivity	Kolb et al., 1994
P7–P12	Functional recovery	Kolb & Whishaw, 1989
	Dendrite and spine growth	Kolb & Gibb, 1992
P120	Partial return of function	Kolb, 1995
	Dendritic atrophy, then regrowth	Kolb, 1995

Note. E18, embryonic day 18; Px, postnatal day x.

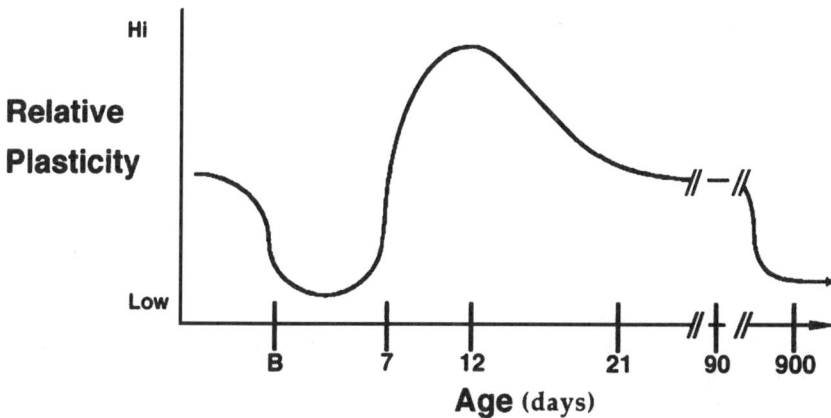

Figure 16.2. Cartoon illustrating the time-dependent differences in cortical plasticity. The cortex is relatively unplastic in the first few days after birth and then becomes very plastic in the second week.

neurogenesis is actually quite remarkable—Hicks demonstrated 40 years ago that if the developing brain was treated with X-radiation during the early stages of cortical neurogenesis, which effectively killed all of the cerebrum, the brain compensated by regenerating a substantial portion of the lost cells (Hicks & D'Amato, 1961). Thus, the cerebrum was killed by the treatment and the stem cells responded by overproducing new cortical neurons that rebuilt about 50% of the lost cerebrum. In contrast, however, if the cortex is injured in the first few days after birth in the rat, which is a time of neural migration and cell differentiation, the effect is functionally devastating, as animals show far more severe effects of injury than would be expected even in aging animals. This poor outcome is not a function of lesion size (Kolb & Cioe, 2000), nor is it localized to particular cortical areas (for a review, see Kolb, 1995). Rather, there is something about the cortex during this time that makes it especially vulnerable. For example, damage during this time may disturb the process of synaptogenesis or may even alter stem cell activity in some way. Once this phase of development is over, however, the brain is especially able to compensate for injury. Rats with cortical injuries at 7–12 days of age show behavioral capacities in adulthood that exceed those of animals with similar lesions at any other time. In fact, on some behavioral tests these animals show recovery that is virtually complete. Importantly, this recovery is far more extensive on cognitive tasks, such as the learning of various spatial navigation problems, than it is on tests of species-typical behaviors (e.g., Kolb & Whishaw, 1981a). This difference is important and likely reflects the relative ease of reorganizing cortical circuitry in supporting different types of behaviors. We must emphasize too that the extent of functional recovery is not equivalent with lesions in different cortical regions. The most extensive recovery is associated with lesions of the frontal areas, and the least extensive recovery is associated with damage to the primary sensory areas. For example, rats with occipital lesions show no recovery of visually guided behaviors. In contrast, they do show an enhanced somatosensory capacity that is not observed after similar lesions on day 4, which is consistent with the general idea that there is something special about the sequelae of injuries around 10 days of age (Kolb, Ladowski, Gibb, & Gorny, 1996).

One complication in our observations is seen when we increase our lesion size to remove all of the cortex (deneocortication) or all of the cortex of one hemisphere (hemidecortication). Totally deneocorticated rats show no functional recovery, regardless of the age at injury (Kolb & Whishaw, 1981b; Whishaw & Kolb, 1984). This result implies that the plastic changes underlying recovery from focal cortical lesions is likely occurring in the remaining cortex and not in subcortical structures. Hemidecortication produces a quite different outcome. Following hemidecortication there is maximal functional recovery the earlier the removal. (We have not made prenatal hemidecortications.) Thus, rats with hemidecortication on the day of birth have a far better functional outcome than do animals with later hemidecortications (e.g., Kolb & Tomie, 1988). One explanation for this result is that the lesion does not interfere with migration and differentiation in the intact hemisphere, which is presumably where the recovery is being mediated. We have tested this hypothesis by making very small lesions in the intact hemisphere of hemidecorticated neonates: recovery is substantially compromised (B. Kolb & R. Gibb, 1999).

Changes in Cortical Connectivity After Early Cortical Injury

It is reasonable to suppose that the best functional outcome would be correlated with the most extensive rewiring of the cerebrum, but this appears not to be the case. In one series of studies we compared the corticocortical, corticostriatal, and certain subcortical-cortical connections after frontal or parietal lesions on postnatal days 1 or 10 (e.g., Kolb, Gibb, & van der Kooy, 1994). The general finding was that adult rats with day 1 lesions had abnormalities in all types of connections examined. For example, there were aberrant thalamocortical connections such as projections from the medial geniculate to the visual cortex in the frontal animals. These abnormal connections likely were not formed after the lesions, however, as we also showed that newborn animals had such connections. These connections appear to be pruned off by day 7 or so. In contrast, rats with day 10 lesions had no obvious abnormalities in these connections. Hence, the day 1 animals had the worst functional outcomes, which were associated with the most extensive abnormalities in connectivity, whereas the day 10 animals had the best functional outcomes, which were associated with no obvious abnormalities. It is reasonable to hypothesize that the abnormal connections were interfering with the normal functioning of the remaining brain. This presumably reflects the fact that these connections are pathological and normally are eliminated during development. After early cortical injury this pruning appears to be attenuated or perhaps even stopped.

Similar results can be seen in animals with focal motor cortex injuries at different ages. In one series of studies we focused on the corticospinal projections following bilateral motor cortex injury on day 1, 10, or in adulthood (Kolb, Cioe, & Whishaw, 2000; Whishaw & Kolb, 1988). As with lesions elsewhere in the cortex, there was an age-related recovery in which day 10 animals performed better on various motor and cognitive tasks than did adult animals, whereas day 1 animals were as impaired as the adult animals on motor tasks and actually had deficits on spatial navigation tasks that were not observed in either of the other lesion groups. As in our studies with frontal animals, the day 1 motor cortex animals had significant abnormalities in cortical connectivity. In particular, in animals with bilateral lesions there was an enhancement of the corticospinal projections from the remaining hemisphere so that there were connections originating in regions of the visual and temporal cortex. It is likely that the novel spatial navigation deficits observed in these animals were related to the abnormal corticospinal projections. Again, these projections are likely aberrant ones that are normally pruned off during development (e.g., O'Leary, Ruff, & Dyck, 1994).

The results of unilateral motor cortex lesions were slightly different. When we examined the corticospinal projections of animals with unilateral lesions we found that there was an expansion of corticospinal projections from the normal hemisphere to the ipsilateral side in both the day 1 and day 10 animals, although it was more extensive in the day 1 animals. Both day 1 and day 10 animals showed a better functional outcome at skilled reaching tests than did the adult animals (Whishaw & Kolb, 1988). Thus, it appears that abnormal connections are not always detrimental and may be beneficial (see Castro, 1990, for a more extensive discussion of this point). This can be seen as well in the cortical connections of rats receiving hemidecortications in infancy (e.g., Kolb, Gibb, & van der Kooy, 1992). There are aberrant connections from the prefrontal regions in the normal hemisphere to the striatum of the contralateral, deneocorticated hemisphere. These abnormalities are greater the earlier the injury, which is correlated with the better functional outcome in the younger animals. These abnormal connections are truly anomalous, as they are not present in normal infants and must therefore reflect the growth of de novo connections.

Changes in Neuronal Morphology After Early Cortical Injury

The absence of obvious changes in cortical connectivity following bilateral cortical lesions on days 7–12 suggested to us that there may be changes in the intrinsic circuitry of the cortex, rather than in the longer corticocortical and corticosubcortical circuitry. The intrinsic circuitry is estimated to account for up to 70% of all cortical synapses, so changes in this circuitry could certainly have significant effects on cortical functioning. Because 95% of synapses on cortical pyramidal cells occur on the dendrites, we therefore examined the morphology of dendrites of cortical pyramidal neurons. Our hypothesis was that functional recovery would be related to an expansion of dendritic fields and perhaps in spine density. There were four major findings of our studies. First, rats with day 1 lesions showed an atrophy of dendritic fields and a decrease in spine density. Second, rats with day 10 lesions showed an expansion of dendritic fields and an increase in spine density. These first two findings imply that day 1 lesions are associated with synaptic loss, whereas day 10 lesions are associated with synaptic growth (Figure 16.3). Third, the increased dendritic growth seen in rats with day 10 lesions is relatively reduced in animals with extensive behavioral training. This is not because

Day 1   Day 10

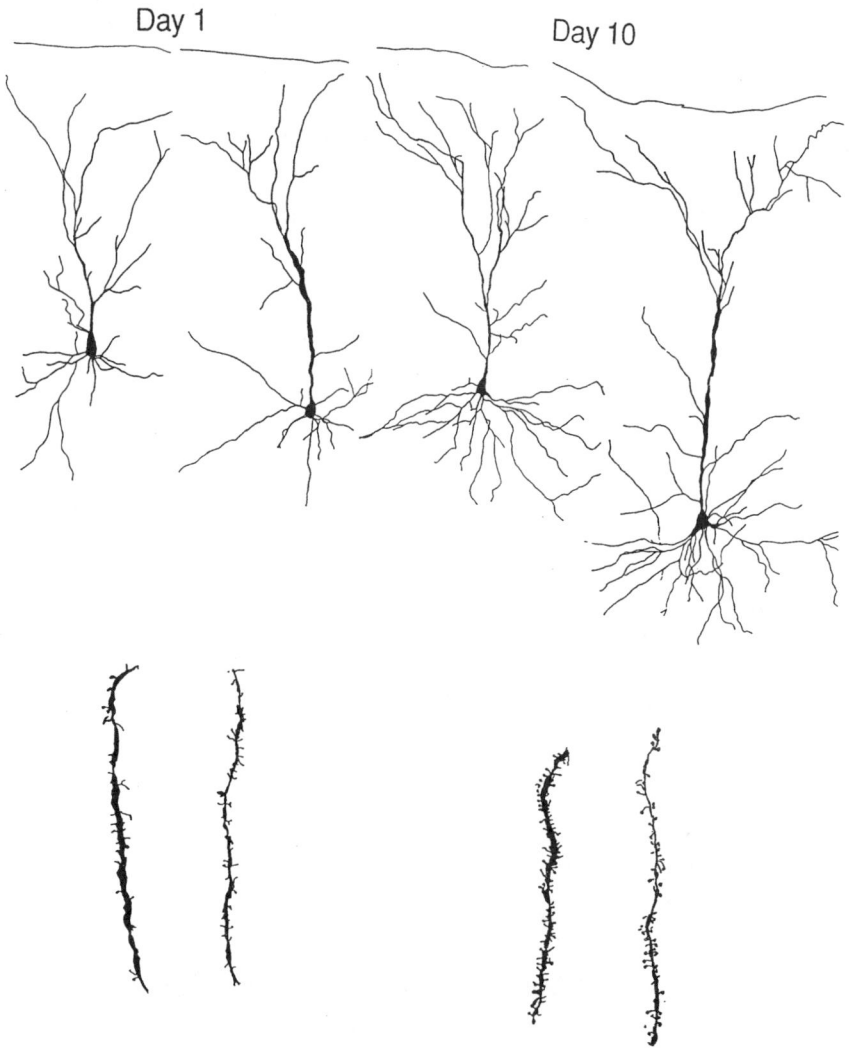

Figure 16.3. Representative examples of layer III pyramidal neurons from somatosensory cortex (top) and representative terminal dendritic segments (bottom) from the brain of a rat that had a P1 frontal lesion in one hemisphere and a P10 frontal lesion in the opposite hemisphere. There is an obvious difference both in dendritic arborization and in spine density.

the animals show a pruning of connections with the training but rather that the control and earlier lesion animals show relatively more synaptic growth in response to the training (Kolb, Gibb, & Gorny, 2000). This observation implies that there are limits to the plastic changes that occur after cortical injury during development and that if the brain changes "spontaneously" to support functional recovery, then there is less change possible in response to other experiences. (We return to this point below.) Finally, rats with hemidecortications on day 1 also show increased dendritic arborization and increased spine density, which correlates with their functional recovery. Furthermore, like rats with bilateral focal lesions on day 10, these animals show a relative reduction in dendritic growth if they have extensive behavioral training.

Neurogenesis After Early Cortical Injury

In the course of studying rats with restricted lesions of midline frontal cortex on day 10, we noticed that there was no lesion cavity when we examined the brains in adulthood (Figure 16.4). Although this cavity loss was most easily explained by a mechanical shifting of the remaining neural tissue, examination of the lesion area suggested that this was not too likely. Rather, it appeared that the midline tissue had regenerated. In fact, volume measurements showed that the midline cortex occupied about 65% of the normal volume in the adult brain (Kolb, Petrie, & Cioe, 1996). Furthermore, when animals were injected with the mitotic marker Bromo-deoxyuridine (BrdU) after the day 10 lesion we were able to show that there were newly generated neurons filling in the lesion cavity (Kolb, Gibb, Gorny, & Whishaw, 1998). When we examined the dendritic development of these neurons 2 weeks after the lesion we found them to be immature, as they had very simple dendritic fields (de Brabander & Kolb, 1997). By adulthood these dendritic fields had grown considerably, however, and did not differ in complexity from cells in normal brains. This is the result that one might anticipate if the cells in the filled-in cavity area had been born later. Injections of a retrograde tracer into the striatum or posterior parietal cortex showed that the new neurons had connections similar to those in the undamaged brains, although it appears that the long corticospinal projections from this region are absent. The failure of the long connections to grow may not be surprising given the complexity of fibers finding their route from the cortex to the spinal cord in a rapidly maturing brain. Furthermore, it is noteworthy that these animals show virtually complete recovery of cognitive functions but rather poor recovery of skilled forelimb reaching, which presumably reflects the absence of the corticospinal connections.

The regeneration of the midline cortical area appears to reflect a unique property of the midline telencephalon at about 7–12 days of age (Figure 16.4; Table 16.3). Thus, removal of the olfactory bulb or midline frontal cortex leads to regeneration, but removal of any other forebrain region does not. One unexpected finding occurred when we examined the effects of posterior midline removals at day 10. When the posterior cingulate cortex is removed, there is no regeneration of the lost tissue. In contrast, when the anterior cingulate cortex is removed along with the posterior cingulate cortex, there is partial regrowth of the posterior tissue (Gonzalez & Kolb, 1999). In other words, if the neural generation is stimulated by the removal of the anterior cortex, the cells appear to migrate beyond the damaged area and partially restore the posterior cortex. This regeneration again is correlated with substantial functional recovery.

Our demonstration that functional recovery is correlated with regeneration of the midline tissue does not prove that the new tissue is actually supporting recovery. The test of this would have to be either to prevent the growth of the tissue or to remove the regrown tissue, and in each case to demonstrate an absence of recovery. We have completed both experiments, and both support the hypothesis that the regrown tissue is supporting recovery. The regeneration was blocked by administering BrdU on embryonic day 13. This treatment appears to interfere with the stem cell activity when the brain is later given a frontal or olfactory bulb lesion on day 10. One difficulty with this experiment is that the BrdU treatment alone also produces behavioral impairments, although far less severe than seen in animals with the combined treatments (Kolb, Pedersen,

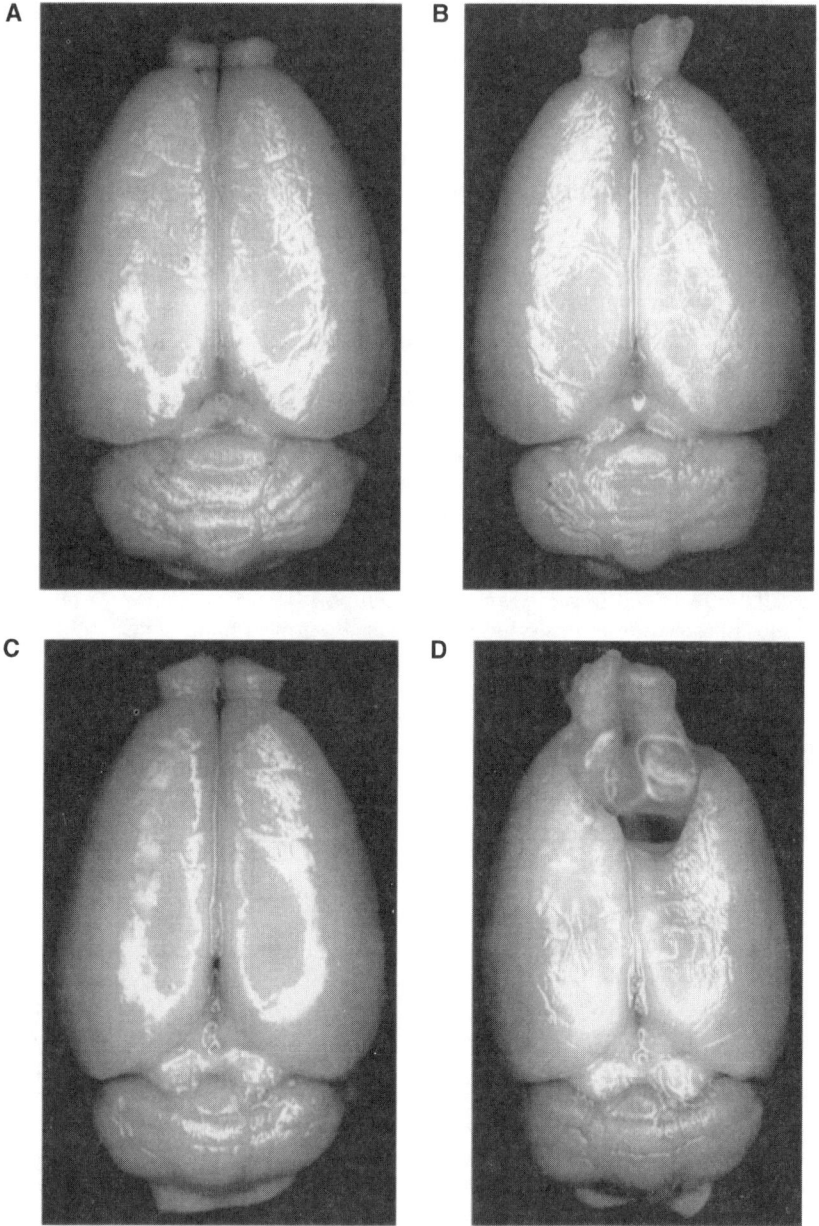

Figure 16.4. Photographs of brains of representative control: (A) P10 frontal lesion, (B) prenatal (E13) BrdU-treated, (C) and E13 BrdU plus P10 frontal lesion, (D) animals. Notice that the lesion cavity is filled after a P10 frontal lesion (B) but not if the animal is previously treated with BrdU (D). The BrdU interferes with stem cell activity and blocks cortical regeneration. (Abbreviation: BrdU, bromodeoxyuridine.)

TABLE 16.3. Summary of the evidence for neurogenesis after restricted midline telencephalic injury at day 10.

Age at Injury	Result	Basic Reference
P1–P6 Frontal	No cavity filling	Kolb et al., 1996
P1–P6 Olfactory bulb	No regeneration	Kolb et al., 1998
P1 Posterior cingulate	No regeneration	Gonzalez et al., 1999
P7–P12 Frontal	Cavity filling	Kolb et al., 1996
	New neurons formed	Kolb et al., 1998
	Some normal connections formed	Kolb et al., 1998
	New cells mature slower	de Brabander & Kolb, 1997
	Removal of tissue = lost recovery	Temesvary et al., 1998
	E13 BrdU blocks regeneration	Kolb et al., 1999
	Adult stem cell activity is reduced	Kolb et al., submitted
P10 Olfactory bulb	Regeneration	Kolb et al., 1998
P10 Posterior cingulate	Regeneration only when anterior cingulate also removed	Gonzalez & Kolb, 1999
P15–P600 Frontal	No cavity filling	Kolb et al., 1996
P1–P200 Other areas	No cavity filling	Kolb et al., 1998

Note. E13, embryonic day 13; Px, postnatal day x.

Ballerman, Gibb, & Whishaw, 1999). In a parallel experiment the regenerated tissue was removed in adulthood and the recovery was again blocked (Temesvary, Gibb, & Kolb, 1998). Taken together, these two experiments provide compelling evidence that the regrown medial frontal area is supporting functional recovery. As a final test, we recently placed stimulating electrodes in the regrown region and tested the animals for the capacity of the tissue to support the rewarding effects of intracranial self-stimulation (Kolb, Dallison, & Ruben, 1999). Medial frontal cortex stimulation normally supports a low but consistent rate of bar pressing for brain stimulation (Corbett, Silva, & Stellar, 1985), and this was true of the rats with regrown tissue as well. Thus, it appears that the regrown region is connected with the brain reward systems of the intact regions of the brain.

One question that arises in the regeneration studies is whether the generation of new neurons in the day 10 animals has any effect on the later activity of SZ stem cells. To test this we removed the midline frontal cortex of mice on postnatal day 7, and then in adulthood we removed the SZ stem cells and placed them in vitro with different growth factors. (Mice develop faster than rats, so day 7 for mice is about day 10 for rats.) Reynolds & Weiss (1992) had shown that SZ cells could be stimulated to generate spheres of new stem cells in vitro when they were exposed to the neurotrophic factors EGF (epidermal growth factor) or bFGF (basic fibroblast growth factor). We reasoned that if the stem cells were responsible for generating the new tissue infancy, then their later ability to produce new cells might be compromised. This was the case, as there was more than a 50% reduction in the production of neurospheres in vitro (Kolb, Martens, Gibb, Coles, & van der Kooy, 1999). Similar results were found in animals with E13 BrdU treatments, a result that may account for why the BrdU treatment blocks the regeneration of medial frontal tissue after day 10 lesions. In any event, our in vitro studies imply once again that the brain's capacity for plasticity may be limited. The

TABLE 16.4. Summary of the effects of factors on plasticity after early
cortical lesions.

Treatment	Result	Basic Reference
Tactile stimulation	Recovery after P4 frontal lesions; dendritic growth	Kolb & Gibb, 2000
	Recovery after P4 posterior parietal lesions; dendritic growth	Kolb & Gibb, 2000
Complex rearing	Enhanced recovery after P1–P5 frontal lesions; dendritic growth	Kolb & Elliott, 1987 Kolb, Gibb, & Gorny, 2000
Gonadal hormones	Sex differences in both recovery and dendritic changes after P7 frontal lesions	Kolb & Stewart, 1995
GDX	Block recovery after P7 frontal lesions Dendritic hypertrophy reduced	Kolb & Stewart, 1995
NA depletion	Blocks recovery after P7 frontal lesions; Blocks dendritic hypertrophy	Kolb & Sutherland, 1992
Choline supplement	Enhanced recovery after P4 frontal lesions; dendritic growth	Tees & Kolb, 1998

Notes. E18, embryonic day 18; Px, postnatal day x; GDX, gonadectomy.

generation of new cells in infancy may interfere with the brain's capacity to produce cells later in life. For instance, there may be a limited number of normal divisions of the stem cells, and after the vigorous activity after the infant lesion, the stem cells have a reduced proliferative potential. It would be particularly interesting to know if there is a reduction in the number of neurons generated for the hippocampus or olfactory bulb in adulthood in animals with midline frontal lesions that lead to regeneration in infancy.

Factors Influencing Plasticity After Early Cortical Injury

The normal brain is affected by a wide variety of factors, ranging from general sensory experience to gonadal hormones and psychoactive drugs (e.g., Kolb & Whishaw, 1998). It is reasonable to suppose that these factors will also influence the damaged brain, although it is possible that the factors might interact in some way with the injury. In Table 16.4 we summarize the effects of experience, neuromodulators, and gonadal hormones and, in addition, briefly consider the likely effects of neurotrophic factors and psychoactive drugs on the brain with a lesion in infancy (see Table 16.4).

Experience

There is now considerable evidence that experience can influence the course of recovery from cortical injury (e.g., Will & Kelche, 1992). One complication, however, is the observation that experience affects the brain differently at different stages of neural development (see above). We have therefore systematically varied the timing of experience after early cortical injury. Our guiding hypothesis has been that injuries sustained during the first week of age, when the brain is especially vulnerable to injury, will be the most responsive to experience, and particularly in the second and third weeks of life, after the lesions (see Figure 16.2). In contrast, injury later, such as around 7 days of age, when recovery is more complete, would not be much influenced by experience because the brain has used up much of its plastic capacity already. This is in fact the result.

When animals are given frontal or posterior parietal lesions on about postnatal day 3, and then are given tactile stimulation for the following 2 weeks, there is a dramatic effect upon functional recovery measured in adulthood. For example, when rats with P3 frontal lesions are given tactile stimulation in infancy they show marked recovery of both spatial navigation and skilled reaching behavior (Figure 16.5). This dramatic recovery is correlated with increased dendritic fields in the remaining cortex, as well as an increase in acetylcholinesterase throughout the cortex (Kolb, Gorny, & Gibb, 1994). In contrast, tactile stimulation of rats with P10 frontal lesions had no effect on either behavioral recovery or dendritic arborization.

In subsequent experiments we placed animals with P1–P3 frontal lesions in complex environments beginning at weaning or in adulthood. Although both treatments stimulated recovery and dendritic growth, the early enrichment had a greater effect than the similar experience in adulthood (Kolb, Gibb, & Gorny, 2000). Furthermore,when rats with frontal lesions on P7 received the same complex experience, there was only a small enhancement of their recovery. Dendritic analysis showed what might be expected: there were large increases in dendritic arborization for the complex-reared animals with P3 lesions but only a small increase for the animals with P7 lesions. We have also looked at the effect of similar complex experience on recovery of rats with frontal lesions in adulthood (Kolb & Gibb, 1991). The general result was that experience had no effect upon recovery in adulthood. In addition, in contrast to the young animals, who showed wide-scale changes in dendritic arborization, adult rats showed a change in response to the lesion but no additional change in response to experience after the injury. Once again, it appears that there are limits to plastic changes and thus subsequently to functional recovery.

Other Factors

There are two remaining factors that are likely to have a major impact upon the effect of recovery from early brain injury: neurotrophic factors and psychoactive drugs. There is now considerable evidence showing that both have significant effects upon the adult brain and on recovery from brain injury in adults, but to date there is little information with respect to early brain injury. Because of the potential importance of these factors after early brain injury, we will consider each briefly.

Basic neurobiological research over the past decade has shown that there are several proteins, which are referred to as neurotrophic factors, that have the property of stimulating neuromitosis as well as synaptogenesis during development and adulthood. These compounds have generated considerable interest both because of their potential for treatment of dementing diseases such as Alzheimer's disease (e.g., Hefti, Brachet, Will, & Christen, 1991) as well as for recovery from injuries (e.g., Hagg, Louis, & Varnon, 1993). For example, in one series of studies we administered nerve growth factor (NGF) into the ventricles of rats with large unilateral motor cortex lesions in adulthood (Kolb, Cote, Ribeiro-da-Silva, & Cuello, 1997) or we administered neutralizing antibodies

A. Morris Water Task

B. Par 1, Layer III, Basilar Dendrites

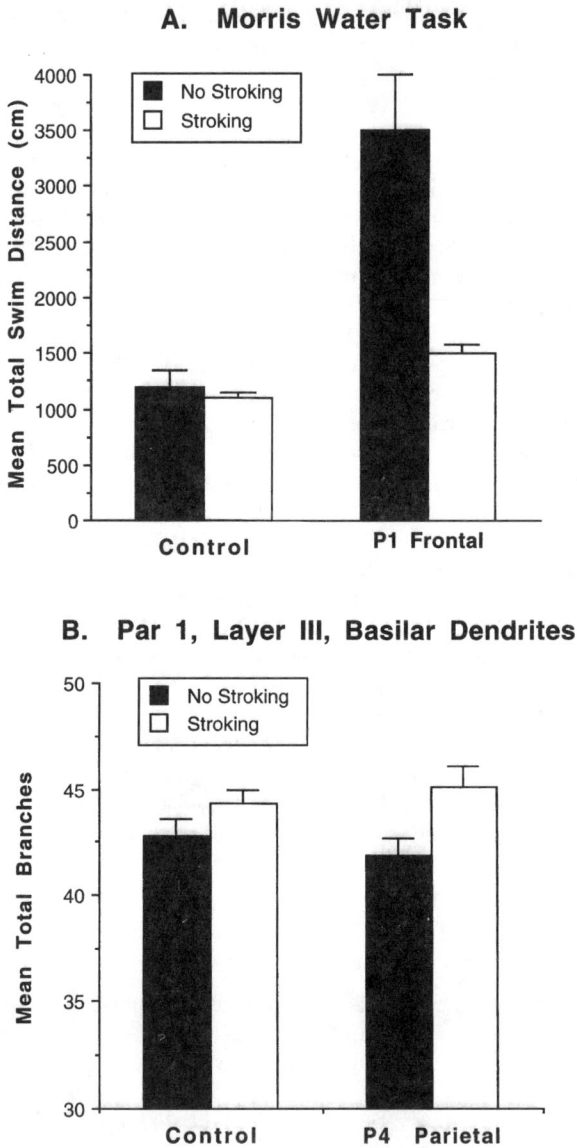

Figure 16.5. (a) The effects of tactile stimulation in infancy on recovery of Morris water task performance in adulthood after a P4 medial frontal lesion. (b) Dendritic arborization of layer III pyramidal cells in somatosensory cortex of rats with P4 posterior parietal lesions. Tactile stimulation reversed the cortical atrophy.

to another growth factor, basic fibroblast growth factor (Rowntree & Kolb, 1997). Stimulating NGF enhanced recovery and dendritic arborization, whereas blocking bFGF retarded recovery and produced dendritic atrophy. Although similar studies have not yet been completed using animals with early brain injury, it is known that subcutaneous injection of bFGF stimulates the generation of cells in the subventricular zone in infant rats (Wagner, Black, & DiCicco-Bloom, 1999). One prediction is that it might be possible to stimulate the regeneration of cortical tissue with bFGF treatment after neonatal cortical lesions in rats. These studies are in progress.

The repeated administration of psychostimulant drugs, such as amphetamine or cocaine, results in a variety of behavioral and anatomical adaptations that are thought to contribute to long-term sequelae associated with drug abuse, including tolerance, sensitization, dependence, and addiction. Sensitization refers to the phenomenon whereby repeated exposure to psychomotor stimulants renders individuals hypersensitive to the psychomotor activating effects of the drugs (e.g., Robinson & Becker, 1986). Most research on the neuroadaptations induced by psychostimulant drugs has focused on biochemical adaptations in brain monoamine systems (e.g., Kalivas & Stewart, 1991) and excitatory amino acid transmission (e.g., Wolf, 1998), but it has now become clear that both amphetamine and cocaine alters the structure of dendritic arborization in both the nucleus accumbens and prefrontal cortex (e.g., Robinson & Kolb, 1999). One prediction that could be made is that animals with damage to the motor cortex in infancy (or adulthood) might show enhanced recovery if synaptic change could be potentiated with psychomotor stimulants. In fact, Feeney and his colleagues have shown that amphetamine can enhance recovery after sensorimotor cortex lesions in adult rats (e.g., Feeney & Sutton, 1987). Although the anatomical basis of this recovery is not yet known, it is possible that this recovery is mediated by changes in dendritic organization of neurons in the prefrontal cortex, neurons that have been found to be chronically changed with amphetamine. It is a reasonable hypothesis that amphetamine would have similar actions in the injured developing brain, although we are unaware of any studies to date. Nonetheless, as described earlier, depletion of noradrenaline blocks recovery after early cortical injury and noradrenaline (NA) levels are known to be increased with amphetamine.

☐ Epilogue

As the preceding review has suggested, the developing cortex can be changed dramatically both by early injury and by various modulators. There is, however, an important proviso to make: there are limits to brain plasticity, and the plastic changes following injury during development may not easily be reversed later in life. We still do not know what determines the limits, nor in most cases what the limits might be. Nonetheless, it does appear that when the brain changes "spontaneously" after injury, during development there is a reduction in the plasticity of the affected regions later in life. In contrast, when the brain fails to change in response to injury there is considerable capacity for modification of cortical circuitry to be altered by various factors. In particular, it appears that behavioral therapies are very effective in stimulating restorative processes of plasticity after early injuries in infants that would otherwise show very little functional recovery. It seems likely that behavioral therapies will thus be most effective if they are initiated early in the postinjury period during development in order to ensure that the spontaneous changes can be influenced in such a way as to maximize functional recovery.

☐ References

Ackerly, S. S. (1964). A case of paranatal bilateral frontal lobe defect observed for thirty years. In J. M. Warren & K. Akert (Eds.), *The frontal granular cortex and behavior* (pp. 192–218). New York: McGraw-Hill.

Bailey, C. H., & Kandel, E. R. (1993). Structural changes accompanying memory storage. *Annual Review of Physiology, 55*, 397–426.

Bayer, S. A., & Altman, J. (1991). *Neocortical development*. New York: Raven Press.

Castro, A. (1990). Plasticity in the motor system. In B. Kolb & R. Tees (Eds.), *Cerebral cortex of the rat* (pp. 563–588). Cambridge, MA: MIT Press.

Changeux, J. P. (1997). Variation and selection in neural function. *Trends in Neuroscience, 7*, 291–293.

Corbett, D., Silva, L. R., & Stellar, J. R. (1985). An investigation of the factors affecting development of frontal cortex self-stimulation. *Physiology and Behavior, 34*, 89–95.

de Brabander, J., & Kolb, B. (1997). Development of pyramidal cells in medial frontal cortex following neonatal lesions of anterior midline cortex. *Restorative Neurology and Neuroscience, 11*, 91–97.

Feeney, D. M., & Sutton, R. L. (1987). Pharmacotherapy for recovery of function after brain injury. *CRC Critical Reviews in Neurobiology, 3*, 135–197.

Finger, S., & Almli, C. R. (1988). Margaret Kennard and her "principle" in historical perspective. In S. Finger, T. E. Le Vere, C. R. Almli, & D. G. Stein (Eds.), *Brain injury and recovery: Theoretical and controversial issues* (pp. 117–132). New York: Plenum.

Forgie, M., & Kolb, B. (1998). Sex differences in the effects of frontal cortex injury: Role of differential hormonal experience in early development. *Behavioral Neuroscience, 112*, 141–153.

Gibb, R., & Kolb, B. (2000). Comparison of the effects of pre- and postnatal tactile stimulation on functional recovery following early frontal cortex lesions in rats. *Society for Neuroscience Abstracts, 26*.

Gould, E., Tanapat, P., Hastings, N. B., & Shors, T. J. (1999). Neurogenesis in adulthood: A possible role in learning. *Trends in Cognitive Sciences, 3*, 186–191.

Gonzalez, C. L. R., & Kolb, B. (1999). Regeneration of functional tissue in infant rats after midline cortical lesions varies with age and locus. *Society for Neuroscience Abstracts, 25*.

Greenough, W. T., Black, J. E., & Wallace, C. S. (1987). Experience and brain development. *Child Development, 58*, 539–559.

Greenough, W. T., & Chang, F. F. (1988). Plasticity of synapse structure and pattern in the cerebral cortex. In: A. Peters & E. G. Jones (Eds). *Cerebral cortex* (vol. 7, pp. 391–440). New York: Plenum.

Hagg, T., Louis, J.-C, & Varnon, S. (1993). Neurotrophic factors and CNS regeneration. In A. Gorio (Ed.), *Neuroregeneration* (pp. 265–288). New York: Raven.

Hebb, D. O. (1947). The effects of early experience on problem solving at maturity. *American Psychologist, 2*, 737–745.

Hebb, D. O. (1949). *The organization of behaviour*. New York: McGraw-Hill.

Hefti, F., Brachet, P., Will, B., & Christen, Y. (1991). *Growth factors and Alzheimer's disease*. Berlin: Springer-Verlag.

Hicks, S., & D'Amato, C. J. (1961). How to design and build abnormal brains using radiation during development. In W. S. Fields & M. M. Desmond (Eds.), *Disorders of the developing nervous system* (pp. 60–79). Springfield, IL: Thomas.

Juraska, J. M. (1990). The structure of the rat cerebral cortex: Effects of gender and environment. In B. Kolb & R. Tees (Eds.) *The cerebral cortex of the rat* (pp. 483–506). Cambridge, MA: MIT Press.

Kalivas, P. W., & Stewart, J. (1991). Dopamine transmission in the initiation and expression of drug- and stress-induced sensitization of motor activity. *Brain Research Reviews, 16*, 224–244.

Kempermann, G., & Gage, F. H. (1999). New nerve cells for the adult brain. *Scientific American, 280*, 48–53.

Kennard, M. (1942). Cortical reorganization of motor function. *Archives of Neurology, 48*, 227–240.

Kolb, B. (1995). *Brain plasticity and behavior*. Mahwah, NJ: Erlbaum.

Kolb, B. (1999). Towards an ecology of cortical organization: Experience and the changing brain.

J. Grafman & Y. Christen (Eds.), *Neuronal plasticity: Building a bridge from the laboratory to the clinic* (pp. 17–34). New York: Springer-Verlag.

Kolb, B., & Cioe, J. (2000). Recovery from early cortical damage in rats, VIII. Earlier may be worse: Behavioural dysfunction and abnormal cerebral morphogenesis following perinatal frontal cortical lesions in the rat. *Neuropharmacology.*

Kolb, B., Cioe, J., & Muirhead, D. (1998). Cerebral morphology and functional sparing after prenatal frontal cortex lesions in rats. *Behavioural Brain Research, 91,* 143–155.

Kolb, B., Cioe, J., & Whishaw, I. Q. (2000). Is there an optimal age for recovery from unilateral motor cortex lesions? Behavioural and anatomical sequelae of unilateral motor cortex lesions in rats on postnatal days 1, 10, and in adulthood. *Restorative Neurology and Neuroscience.*

Kolb, B., Cote, S., Ribeiro-da-Silva, A., & Cuello, A. C. (1997). NGF stimulates recovery of function and dendritic growth after unilateral motor cortex lesions in rats. *Neuroscience, 76,* 1139–1151.

Kolb, B., Dallison, A., & Ruben, A. (1999). (Regenerated medial frontal tissue supports electrical self-stimulation). Unpublished observations.

Kolb, B., & Elliott, W. (1987). Recovery from early cortical damage in rats. II. Effects of experience on anatomy and behavior following frontal lesions at 1 or 5 days of age. *Behavioural Brain Research, 26,* 47–56.

Kolb, B., & Gibb, R. (1990). Anatomical correlates of behavioural change after neonatal prefrontal lesions in rats. *Progress in Brain Research, 85,* 241–256.

Kolb, B., & Gibb, R. (1991). Environmental enrichment and cortical injury: Behavioral and anatomical consequences of frontal cortex lesions. *Cerebral Cortex, 1,* 189–198.

Kolb, B., & Gibb, R. (1993). Possible anatomical basis of recovery of spatial learning after neonatal prefrontal lesions in rats. *Behavioral Neuroscience, 107,* 799–811.

Kolb, B., & Gibb, R. (1999). (Dendritic hypertrophy after hemidecortication is blocked by small lesions in the contralateral hemisphere). Unpublished observations.

Kolb, B., & Gibb, R. (1999). Manuscript submitted for publication.

Kolb, B., & Gibb, R. (2000). Tactile stimulation after cortical injury in infant rats facilitates functional recovery and neuronal changes. Manuscript in submission.

Kolb, B., Gibb, R., Biernaskie, J., Dyck, R. H., & Whishaw, I. Q. (1998). Regeneration of olfactory bulb or frontal cortex in infant and adult rats. *Society for Neuroscience Abstracts, 24:* 518.4.

Kolb, B., Gibb, R., & Gorny, G. (2000). Experience-dependent changes in dendritic arbor and spine density in neocortex vary with age and sex. Manuscript submitted for publication.

Kolb, B., Gibb, R., & Gorny, G. (2000). Experience-dependent changes in dendritic arbor and spine density in neocortex vary with age and sex. Manuscript in submission.

Kolb, B., Gibb, R., Gorny, G., & Whishaw, I. Q. (1998). Possible brain regrowth after cortical lesions in rats. *Behavioural Brain Research, 91,* 127–141.

Kolb, B., Gibb, R., & van der Kooy, D. (1992). Neonatal hemidecortication alters cortical and striatal structure and connectivity. *Journal of Comparative Neurology, 322,* 311–324.

Kolb, B., Gibb, R., & van der Kooy, D. (1994). Neonatal frontal cortical lesions in rats alter cortical structure and connectivity. *Brain Research, 645,* 85–97.

Kolb, B., Gorny, G., & Gibb, R. (1994). Tactile stimulation enhances recovery and dendritic growth in rats with neonatal frontal lesions. *Society for Neuroscience Abstracts, 20,* 1430.

Kolb, B., Ladowski, R., Gibb, R., & Gorny, G. (1996). Does dendritic growth underlie recovery from neonatal occipital lesions in rats? *Behavioural Brain Research, 77,* 125–133.

Kolb, B., Martens, D. J., Gibb, R., Coles, B., & van der Kooy, D. (1999). Proliferation of neural stem cells in vitro and in vivo is reduced by infant frontal cortex lesions or prenatal BrdU. *Society for Neuroscience Abstracts, 25.*

Kolb, B., Pedersen, B., Ballerman, M., Gibb, R., & Whishaw, I. Q. (1999). Embryonic exposure to BrdU produces chronic changes in brain and behavior in rats. *Journal of Neuroscience, 19,* 2337–2346.

Kolb, B., Petrie, B., & Cioe, J. (1996). Recovery from early cortical damage in rats. VII. Comparison of the behavioural and anatomical effects of medial prefrontal lesions at different ages of neural maturation. *Behavioural Brain Research, 79,* 1–13.

Kolb, B., & Stewart, J. (1995). Changes in neonatal gonadal hormonal environment prevent behavioral sparing and alter cortical morphogenesis after early frontal cortex lesions in male and female rats. *Behavioral Neuroscience, 109*, 285–294.

Kolb, B., Stewart, J., & Sutherland, R. J. (1997). Recovery of function is associated with increased spine density in cortical pyramidal cells after frontal lesions and/or noradrenaline depletion in neonatal rats. *Behavioural Brain Research, 89*, 61–70.

Kolb, B., & Sutherland, R. J. (1992). Noradrenaline depletion blocks behavioral sparing and alters cortical morphogenesis after neonatal frontal cortex damage in rats. *Journal of Neuroscience, 12*, 2221–2330.

Kolb, B., & Tomie, J. (1988). Recovery from early cortical damage in rats. IV. Effects of hemidecortication at 1, 5, or 10 days of age. *Behavioural Brain Research, 28*, 259–274.

Kolb, B., & Whishaw, I. Q. (1981a). Decortication of rats in infancy or adulthood produced comparable functional losses on learned and species typical behaviors. *Journal of Comparative and Physiological Psychology, 95*, 468–483.

Kolb, B., & Whishaw, I. Q. (1989). Plasticity in the neocortex: Mechanisms underlying recovery from early brain damage. *Progress in Neurobiology, 32*, 235–276.

Kolb, B., & Whishaw, I. Q. (1998). Brain plasticity and behavior. *Annual Review of Psychology, 49*, 43–64.

Konorski, J. (1948). *Conditioned reflexes and neuron organization*. Cambridge, England: Cambridge University Press.

Miller, M. W. (1988). Development of projection and local circuit neurons in neocortex. In A. Peters & E. G. Jones (Eds.), *Cerebral cortex, Vol. 7* (pp. 133–176). New York: Plenum.

O'Leary, D. D., Ruff, N. L., & Dyck, R. H. (1994). Development, critical period plasticity, and adult reorganizations of mammalian somatosensory systems. *Current Opinion Neurobiology, 4*, 535–544.

Patel, S. N., Rose, S. R. R., & Stewart, M. G. (1988). Training induced dendritic spine density changes are specifically related to memory formation processes in the chick, *Gallus domesticus. Brain Research, 463*, 168–173.

Patel, S. N., & Stewart, M. G. (1988). Changes in the number and structure of dendritic spines 25 hours after passive avoidance training in the domestic chick, *Gallus domesticus. Brain Research, 449*, 34–46.

Ramón y Cajal, S. (1928). *Degeneration and regeneration of the nervous system*. London: Oxford University Press.

Rasmussen, T., & Milner, B. (1977). The role of early left-brain injury in determining lateralization of cerebral speech functions. *Annals of the New York Academy of Sciences, 299*, 355–369.

Reynolds, B., & Weiss, S. (1992). Generation of neurons and astrocytes from isolated cells of the adult mammalian central nervous system. *Science, 255*, 1710–1727.

Robinson, T. E., & Becker, J. B. (1986). Enduring changes in brain and behavior produced by chronic amphetamine administration: A review and evaluation of animal models of amphetamine psychosis. *Brain Research Reviews, 11*, 157–198.

Robinson, T. E., & Kolb, B. (1999). Alterations in the morphology of dendrites and dendritic spines in the nucleus accumbens and prefrontal cortex following repeated treatment with amphetamine or cocaine. *European Journal of Neuroscience, 11*, 1598–1604.

Rowntree, S., & Kolb, B. (1997) Antibodies to bFGF block functional recovery and dendritic compensation after motor cortex lesions. *European Journal of Neuroscience, 9*, 2432–2442.

Shankle, W. R., Landing, B. H., Rafii, M. S., Schiano, A., Chen, J. M., & Hara, J. (1998). Evidence for a postnatal doubling of neuron number in the developing human cerebral cortex between 15 months and 6 years. *Journal of Theoretical Biology, 191*, 115–140.

Sutherland, R. J., Kolb, B., Becker, J. B., & Whishaw, I. Q. (1982). Cortical noradrenaline depletion eliminates sparing of spatial learning after neonatal frontal cortex damage in the rat. *Neuroscience Letters, 32*, 125–130.

Tees, R., & Kolb, B. (1998). (Prenatal choline stimulates recovery from neonatal medial frontal lesions in rats). Unpublished observations.

Temesvary, A. E., Gibb, R., & Kolb, B. (1998). Recovery of function after neonatal frontal lesions in rats: Function or fiction. *Society for Neuroscience Abstracts, 24*, 473.8.

Teuber, H.-L. (1975). Recovery of function after brain injury in man. In *Outcome of severe damage to the nervous system*, Ciba Foundation Symposium 34. Amsterdam: Elsevier North-Holland.

Uylings, H. B. M., van Eden, C. G., Parnavelas, J. G., & Kalsbeek, A. (1990). The prenatal and postnatal development of rat cerebral cortex. In B. Kolb & R. Tees (Eds.), *The cerebral cortex of the rat* (pp. 35–76). Cambridge, MA: MIT Press.

Villablanca, J. R., Hovda, D. A., Jackson, G. F., & Infante, C. (1993). Neurological and behavioral effects of a unilateral frontal cortical lesion in fetal kittens: II. Visual system tests, and proposing a 'critical period' for lesion effects. *Behavioural Brain Research, 57*, 79–92.

Wagner, J. P., Black, I. B., & DiCicco-Bloom, E. (1999). Stimulation of neonatal and adult brain neurogenesis by subcutaneous injection of basic fibroblast growth factor. *Journal of Neuroscience, 19*, 6006–6016.

Wallhausser, E., & Scheich, H. (1987). Auditory imprinting leads to differential 2-deoxyglucose uptake and dendritic spine loss in the chick rostral forebrain. *Developmental Brain Research, 31*, 29–44.

Weiss, S., Reynolds, B. A., Vescovi, A. L., Morshead, C., Craig, C. G., & van der Kooy, D. (1996). Is there a neural stem cell in the mammalian forebrain? *Trends in Neuroscience, 19*, 387–393.

Whishaw, I. Q., & Kolb, B. (1988). Sparing of skilled forelimb reaching and corticospinal projections after neonatal motor cortex removal or hemidecortication in the rat: Support for the Kennard Doctrine. *Brain Research, 451*, 97–114.

Will, B., & Kelche, C. (1992). Environmental approaches to recovery of function from brain damage: A review of animal studies (1981 to 1991). In F. D. Rose & D. A. Johnson (Eds.), *Recovery from brain damage: Reflections and directions* (pp. 79–104). New York: Plenum.

Wolf, M. E. (1998). The role of excitatory amino acids in behavioral sensitization to psychomotor stimulants. *Progress in Neurobiology, 54*, 679–720.

Josef P. Rauschecker

Developmental Neuroplasticity Within and Across Sensory Modalities

☐ Introduction

Representational plasticity, that is, expansion and reorganization of cortical maps, has been demonstrated most convincingly in the somatosensory cortex (Kaas, 1991; Kaas, Merzenich, & Killackey, 1983; Merzenich, Recanzone, Jenkins, Allard, & Nudo, 1988) and, more recently, also within the auditory cortex (Recanzone, Schreiner, & Merzenich, 1993). Mostly, such changes have been obtained as the result of enhanced experience within the *same* modality. By contrast, the majority of the studies summarized in this chapter describe an expansion of maps in one modality as a result of deprivation in another. In discussing the common theme of this book, a generalized theory of neuroplasticity, the question naturally arises what intermodal (or cross-modal) plasticity has in common with intramodal plasticity. At the single-neuron level, changes in tuning properties are observed in both intra- and intermodal plasticity (Rauschecker, 1991, 1995). Sharper tuning is thought to correspond to better resolution and thus better performance of the neural system. Better performance of the *neural* system is assumed to lead to better *behavioral* performance as well. Representational plasticity or expansion of maps seems to have the same effect: an increase in the number of elements participating in the encoding of the sensory world is thought to lead to better perceptual performance within the sensory modality corresponding to the expanded map regardless of the modality that causes the expansion.

The question of whether cross-modal plasticity existed at all had been a matter of debate for a long time (see Rauschecker, 1995, for review) and has recently received renewed attention from both animal and human studies. The evidence in favor of intermodal plasticity is now so strong that there can hardly be a doubt about its existence. While initial studies had suggested that experimental interventions had to be pretty drastic to enable cross-modal plasticity (Métin & Frost, 1989; Sur, Pallas, & Roe, 1990), it is now clear that simply withholding the normal pattern of sensory experience in one modality is sufficient to reorganize the neural representation of the remaining senses. Research now concentrates on the mechanisms governing map changes and reorganization across sensory modalities. It appears that the same synaptic mechanisms are invoked that also rule synaptic changes within the same modality. What is often less clear is how the signal initiating the compensatory changes reaches its destination. The interaction that is necessary for cross-modal plasticity to occur requires a convergence of signals from different modalities somewhere in the brain. Young animals, which generally show less specificity in their wiring, may therefore have a better chance for cross-modal reorganization than adults, in which multisensory convergence has been pared down to connections reaffirmed by associative learning and experience.

☐ Cross-Modal Effects of Early Blindness: Studies in Visually Deprived Animals

Auditory Compensation: Lid Suture and Development of Auditory Maps; Behavioral Evidence

Binocular lid suture has been established since the days of Wiesel and Hubel (1963) as an animal model of early blindness. It involves the use of a standardized procedure for the induction of visual deprivation, which leaves no doubt about the etiology of blindness and reduces the variability inherent in the study of human patients. Compared to enucleation it has the advantage that, after re-opening the eyelids, the eyes are perfectly intact and available for the testing of visual responses.

With regard to compensatory plasticity, it is extremely valuable to compare the behavioral performance of visually deprived animals with that of sighted controls. If the behavioral performance of blinded animals did not correspond to that of blind humans, they could not be considered a good animal model for the study of cross-modal compensation. Without behavioral data it would be unclear whether any neural changes were related to performance. Thankfully, behavioral data from auditory spatial testing after visual deprivation do exist in two mammalian species, cats (Rauschecker & Kniepert, 1994) and ferrets (King & Parsons, 1999). Both sets of data demonstrate that, indeed, auditory spatial acuity increases (and sound localization error decreases) in early blind animals. The most pronounced effects were found in lateral and rear positions of azimuth, where the differences to sighted controls were highly significant.

The above tests were all conducted using very brief sounds (40 ms), so that the animals had no chance to orient towards the sound source. However, if given the opportunity, visually deprived animals (just like blind humans) will use other strategies for the localization of sounds. Very frequently, binocularly lid-sutured cats can be observed to orient towards the azimuth position of a novel sound and then perform vertical scanning movements (in elevation) within that same azimuthal plane (Rauschecker & Henning, 2000). The frequency of these near-sinusoidal scanning movements in the vertical plane is about 1 Hz. Peak-to-peak amplitude covers a wide range from about 5° to 15° for pinna movements alone to over 40° when coordinated movements of head and pinnae are performed. These vertical scanning movements seem to utilize the directional characteristics of the pinnae. The behavior may help blind animals gain not only more refined information about the elevational location of objects in space, but also about their shape and surface texture.

Neural Changes in Visually Deprived Cats

Neurophysiologically, with regard to both intra- and intermodality effects of visual deprivation, the most extensive studies have been performed in cats. Cross-modal changes have been observed in the superior colliculus (SC; Rauschecker & Harris, 1983), where an increased number of auditory neurons was found in visually deprived cats compared to normal controls. These auditory neurons were situated at high density in intermediate and deep layers of the SC, but also occasionally in superficial layers, where normally only visual cells exist.

In the cortex of visually deprived cats, cross-modal changes were found primarily in association areas around the anterior ectosylvian sulcus (AES), the so-called AES region (Rauschecker & Korte, 1993). This cortical region normally contains a visual, an auditory, and a somatosensory area in close vicinity, with some overlap between the different modalities (Benedek, Mucke, Norita, Albowitz, & Creutzfeldt, 1988; Clarey & Irvine, 1990; Jiang, Leporé, Ptito, & Guillemot, 1994). In cats that were visually deprived from birth by means of binocular lid suture (and lids reopened for testing), the visual area (AEV) in the fundus of the AES had all but disappeared. However, neurons in this region did not become unresponsive to sensory stimulation at all. Instead, they were found to be briskly responsive to auditory and (to some extent) tactile stimulation. In other words, the neighboring auditory and somatosensory fields had expanded into the formerly visual territory, at the expense of the visual field (Rauschecker & Korte, 1993).

The response properties of the newly expanded auditory area (AEA) in the AES region were homogeneous with neighboring auditory fields. In particular, the auditory spatial tuning (the tuning for the location of a sound source in free field) was significantly sharper in the whole AES region (including the anterior auditory field, AAF, on the anterior ectosylvian gyrus) compared to sighted control animals (Korte & Rauschecker, 1993). Whereas the control group had roughly 50% spatially tuned cells (with a spatial tuning ratio of better than 2:1), the blind animals had close to 90% spatially specific auditory neurons in the AES region. In addition, neurons with spatial tuning ratios of 10:1 or better were much more abundant in blind cats.

The increased number of auditory neurons, together with their sharpened spatial filtering characteristics, is likely to improve the sampling density of auditory space and is thought to underlie the improved spatial abilities of early blind animals (Rauschecker, 1995). Sharper tuning increases the efficiency of a population code in the sense that fewer neurons are required to achieve a given acuity (Fitzpatrick, Batra, Stanford, & Kuwada, 1997). If the number of neurons stays the same (or even increases, as in our case), the resulting acuity increases as well. Related theoretical considerations lead to the conclusion that a tuning optimum for best performance can be found (Baldi & Heiligenberg, 1988), and it appears that the tuning values found in blind cats come closer to this optimum than the values prevailing in sighted cats.

Subsequent studies found improvements of similar magnitude in the spatial tuning of neurons in the primary auditory cortex (A1) and an overall more orderly organization of best azimuth in blind cats compared to normal controls (Henning & Rauschecker, 1995). However, the overall pattern of organization of auditory spatial information in the auditory cortex does not seem to take the form of a global space map as in the superior colliculus. Rather, the clustering suggests a pattern of piecewise continuous representations (Henning, Tian, & Rauschecker, 1995).

☐ Tactile Compensation: Binocular Enucleation and Somatosensory Barrel Cortex

Tactile Behavior in Visually Deprived Animals

Visually deprived cats use their vibrissae even more than sighted cats for spatial orientation. They explore the spatial layout of an unknown room first by walking along its walls. As in blind people using their white stick, this behavior helps to establish an internal representation of the explored space. Quantitative behavioral testing of binocularly lid-sutured cats in comparison to sighted controls was achieved in total darkness with the aid of an infrared camera. Run times through an obstacle course were measured and compared between the two groups. No significant difference was found (Rauschecker & Henning, 2000), which suggests that blind cats can indeed form a concept of spatial relationships without vision, in this case using primarily tactile means.

Tactile Compensation in Blind Animals

One of the earliest indications for a biological process of tactile compensation in early blindness equivalent to that of the auditory domain was the observation of increased whisker growth in binocularly lid-sutured cats (Rauschecker, Tian, Korte, & Egert, 1992). The same observation, which pertains to both length and diameter of the facial vibrissae, is true for binocularly enucleated (BE) mice (Rauschecker et al., 1992) and has also been replicated in BE rats (R. C. Tees, personal communication; Toldi, Farkas, & Volgyi, 1994). In addition to and corresponding with the extended growth of the vibrissae, BE mice also show an expansion of the whisker barrels, the neural representations of the vibrissae in the primary somatosensory cortex (Rauschecker et al., 1992). This has been demonstrated with cytochrome oxidase staining as well as conventional Nissl stains. The degree of correspondence between whisker growth and barrel expansion is quite astonishing: whiskers in lateral positions show the greatest hypertrophy (thus increasing the lateral range of the vibrissae as a tactile "organ"), and it is the barrels representing precisely those same positions in the brain that show the most significant expansion.

The mechanisms responsible for the peripheral increase in whisker growth are still only poorly understood. It seems unlikely that central factors would govern this process. Rather, it may be local growth factors, stimulated by increased usage of the whiskers, that lead to the observed hypertrophy. By contrast, the expansion of cortical barrels could very well be governed by central factors equivalent to the expansion of auditory territory. Thus, increased usage and stimulation of the whiskers is indeed the common cause of both processes, but different signals may be responsible on the two levels. Unlike compensatory map expansions in the auditory domain, which were first discovered in areas of association cortex such as the AES region, these compensatory changes of the somatosensory barrel system occur in the primary somatosensory cortex. It remains to be seen whether higher areas of the trigeminal system also reorganize as a result of visual deprivation. As argued below, the changes in the primary somatosensory cortex of the mouse could potentially come about as a result of retrograde changes originating in higher areas.

The graphic in Figure 17.1 sketches a possible scheme in which inputs from different sensory modalities are in competition with each other in a higher convergence area of the multimodal association cortex. As a result of visual deprivation, afferents from the nonvisual modalities are able to establish themselves more firmly in the multimodal

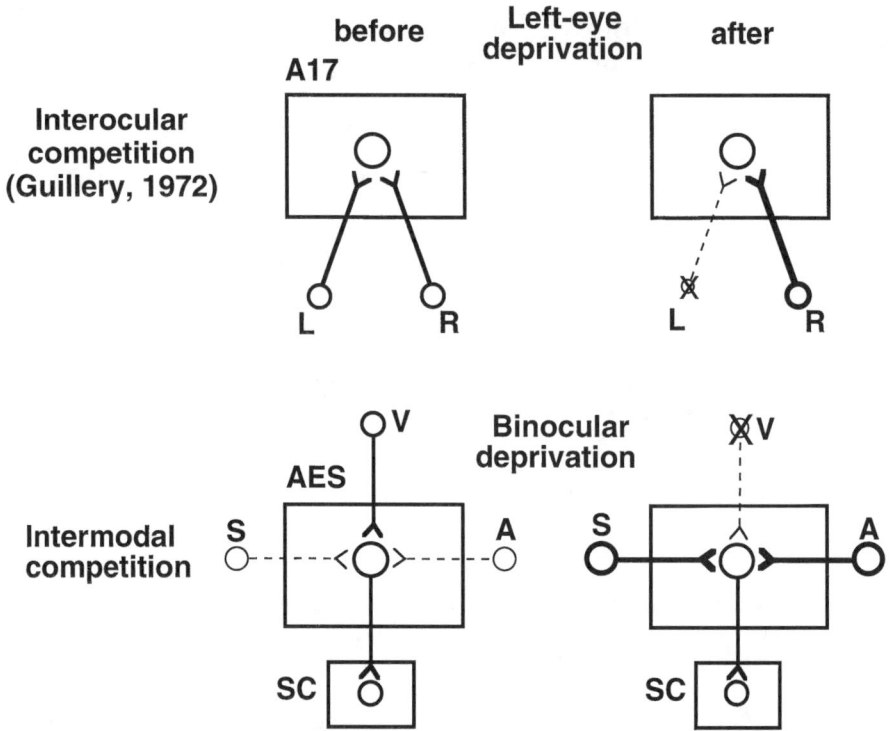

Figure 17.1. Comparison of interocular (top) and intermodal (bottom) competition for synaptic changes in the cerebral cortex. During monocular deprivation (occlusion or suture of, e.g., the left eye), geniculate afferents compete for synaptic space on the target neurons of area 17, which leads to a (retrograde) shrinkage of cell somata in the deprived layers of the lateral geniculate nucleus and an expansion of cell somata in the nondeprived layers. By analogy, inputs from different sensory modalities are in competition with each other in convergence areas of the multimodal association cortex, such as the cat's AES region. As a result of binocular visual deprivation, afferents from the nonvisual modalities are able to establish themselves more firmly in the multimodal target region, and cell somata in the somatosensory (and auditory) cortex sending their axons to the target regions get enlarged, whereas cells in visual areas shrink. The same hypothetical scheme could explain the increase of multimodal responses in the SC.

target region and expand their territory, as demonstrated in the AES region of the cat's cortex. By analogy with binocular competition of afferents from the lateral geniculate nucleus (LGN) in target regions of the primary visual cortex (Guillery & Stelzner, 1970), axon collaterals of the successful input fibers would be expected to proliferate and expand, whereas those belonging to the deprived pathway shrink. The size of cell bodies is known to covary with the extent of the terminal arbors they have to sustain. Therefore, like cell bodies in the LGN that have different sizes in deprived and nondeprived laminae (Guillery & Stelzner, 1970), cell somata in the mouse barrel cortex that send their axons to multimodal target regions would also get enlarged. This could conceivably be the major reason for the expansion of the barrel field in BE mice as a whole.

Measurements of cell soma size in the barrel fields of BE mice indeed showed a greater average soma size than in normal controls (Gelhard, Tian, & Rauschecker, 1993; Rauschecker, 1997). For that study, flat mounts of cerebral cortex in mice binocularly enucleated during their first week of life were cut at 50 μm and stained with cresyl violet. Number of cells, cell size, and cell density per unit area were analyzed quantitatively and compared to normal controls from the same litter. The increase in soma size was significant for every barrel position. No increased numbers of neurons were found in the enlarged barrels, which indicates that the expanded barrel size was not due to reduced cell death. However, a decreased cell density indicated that the network of fibers in the neuropil connecting the neurons with each other had also increased in size.

Extending the reasoning laid out above further, one may argue that "intermodal competition" (again, by analogy with binocular competition) should have a dual effect: while the representation of nonvisual modalities in the cortex expands, that of the visual modality should be diminished. Indeed, it is well established from studies of binocular enucleation in newborn rhesus monkeys that the visual cortex in these animals is reduced in size and contains smaller cell bodies (Rakic, 1988). This finding lends further credence to the hypothesis that cross-modal compensatory plasticity is in fact guided by the same principles as other forms of neural plasticity, including competition for synaptic space in the target region.

☐ Studies of Compensatory Plasticity in Blind Humans

Expansion of Auditory Representations; Behavioral Evidence

Early studies of sensory substitution in blind humans yielded controversial results (see Rauschecker, 1995, for review). The reasons for that were manifold, but clearly the following factors contributed to the confusion in the field: inhomogeneous patient populations with diverse etiology and unknown neurological status (partly due to unavailability of objective tests such as MRI), different ages of onset and duration of blindness, and small numbers of patients. Philosophical differences may have also influenced the interpretation of such data. Some researchers have always argued in favor of a compensatory adjustment after early blindness resulting in a behavioral improvement of other senses. By contrast, some have argued for a role of vision in the calibration of other senses resulting in the opposite effect, namely, a concomitant degradation of these senses after early blindness. Studies that resulted in no difference between blind and sighted subjects could then be interpreted as either a "glass half-full" or "glass half-empty" depending on one's philosophical bias. In reality, even the lack of a difference between blind and sighted subjects in their auditory or tactile performance speaks heavily in favor of compensatory mechanisms, because it demonstrates the independence of that performance from visual calibration. Obviously, nonvisual signals or motor feedback can accomplish the same thing.

Only recently have studies with large blind patient populations been undertaken that tested subjects with similar histories under stringent conditions (Lessard, Pare, Lepore, & Lassonde, 1998; Muchnik, Efrati, Nemeth, Malin, & Hildesheimer, 1991; Röder, et al., 1999). Invariably, these studies did *not* find a disadvantage of the blind in their sound localization abilities; they even showed them to be superior. Most interestingly, the study by Lessard et al. (1998) found patients with partial vision to be the worst of all three groups (fully sighted, completely blind, and partially sighted). The same study provided valuable hints as to the neural basis of the improvement of spatial tuning in the blind: the biggest improvement was found when monaural spectral cues had to be used for sound localization.

The recent study by Röder, Rösler, and Neville (1999) found the biggest improvements of sound localization in blind humans for lateral and rear positions of azimuth, precisely as had been demonstrated in visually deprived cats by Rauschecker and Kniepert (1994). Earlier studies by Rice, Feinstein, & Schusterman (1965), (1970) are also compatible with these findings in that they found significant improvements in the ability of the blind to judge the spatial direction of echoes, especially in lateral and rear positions.

Auditory Neuroimaging Studies in Blind Humans

With the advent of modern imaging techniques it became possible to map the distribution of neural activity during auditory stimulation in blind and sighted subjects directly in the human brain. Early studies of that kind had shown that the occipital cortex has metabolic rates in blind subjects that are as high as in sighted controls during visual stimulation (Wanet-Defalque et al., 1988). However, it did not become clear whether this increased rate was actually due to specific sensory activity until it could be shown that increased regional cerebral blood flow (rCBF) and metabolic rates were correlated with auditory stimulation (De Volder et al., 1999; Uhl, Franzen, Podreka, Steiner, & Deecke, 1993).

Studies using event-related potentials (ERP) then demonstrated that the extent of cortical activation by changes in the frequency, intensity, and location of a sound was expanded in blind people and shifted posteriorly into occipital areas (Kujala et al., 1995; Liotti, Ryder, & Woldorf, 1998; Röder, Rösler, Henninghausen, & Nacker, 1996). Comparing patients blind from birth with those who became blind later in life, one study found a posteriorly directed expansion also in late blind, which was intermediate in extent to the early blind (Kujala et al., 1997). The latter finding confirms the existence of at least partial cross-modal plasticity in the adult, which is consistent with behavioral findings in two visually deprived cats (Rauschecker & Kniepert, 1994).

A recent study using positron emission tomography (PET) in congenitally blind and sighted subjects showed massive activation of the occipital cortex during a sound localization task in virtual auditory space (Figure 17.2; Weeks et al., 2000). The sounds were presented via headphones and the spatial cues were programmed on the basis of

→

Figure 17.2. Statistical parametric maps of increased regional cerebral blood flow in a PET study of congenitally blind subjects in an auditory localization task compared to rest (Weeks et al., 2000). Copyright © 2000 by the Society for Neuroscience. Reprinted with permission. All areas shown are significant at $Z > 4.2$ after Bonferroni correction for multiple comparisons. (A) illustrates the within-group comparison of auditory localization and delayed matching compared to rest; (B) shows the comparison of auditory-localization-with-movement versus rest. The former task required subjects to compare a randomly presented sound location with one that was previously presented; the latter task required a joystick movement in the direction of the sound source. Both tasks led to increased activation in the occipital areas of blind subjects; the delayed matching task additionally activated regions in the prefrontal cortex, presumably involved in working memory.

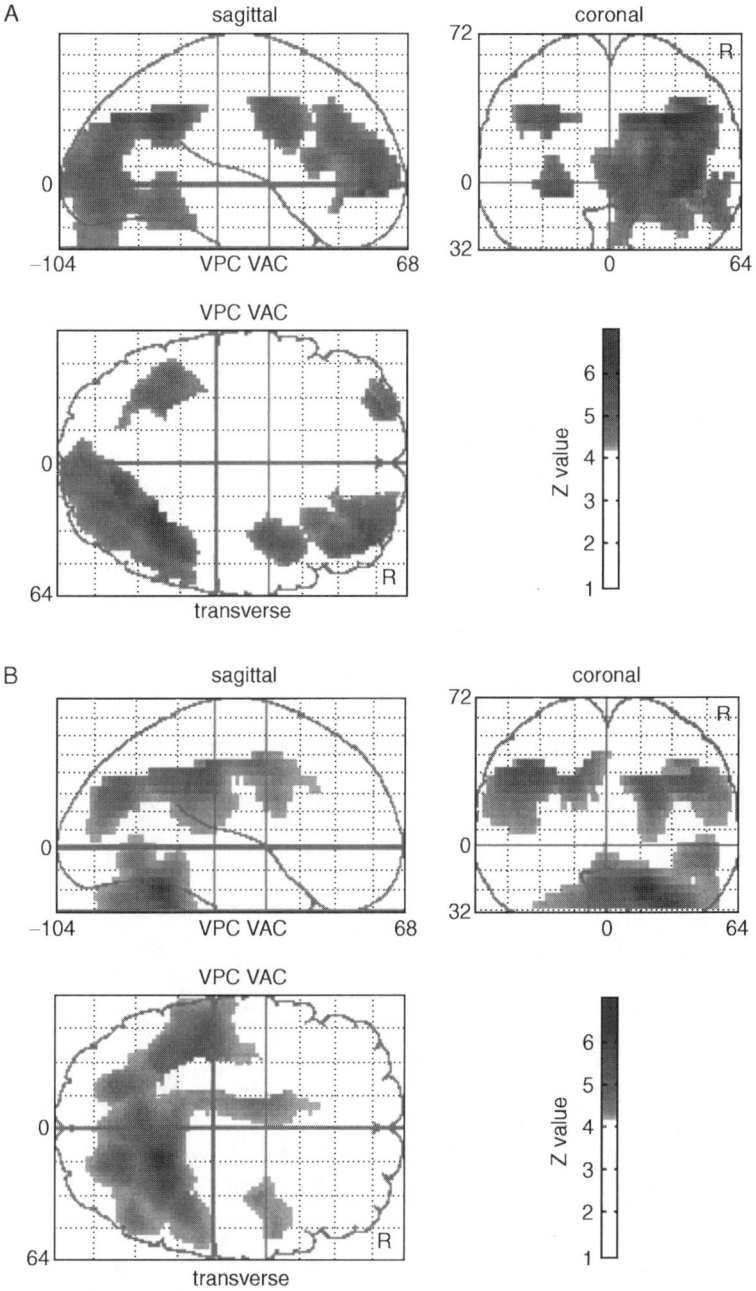

standardized head-related transfer functions (HRTF; Wightman & Kistler, 1989), taking into account monaural spectral cues in addition to binaural cues. The behavioral performance of the blind in localizing these sounds was just as good as that of the normal controls.

Localization of sounds in virtual auditory space by sighted subjects leads to activation of specific foci in the posterior parietal (IPL) and frontal cortices (Weeks et al., 1999; Bushara et al., 1999), with a slight bias towards the right hemisphere. The same foci light up in blind subjects but are vastly expanded towards parieto-occipital (area 7) and occipital locations (areas 18 and 19), and the right-hemisphere bias is more pronounced (Table 17.1). The areas of expansion may be homologous, in part, to higher visual areas shown to be activated by auditory or somatosensory stimuli in visually deprived cats (Rauschecker & Korte, 1993) and monkeys (Hyvärinen, Carlson, & Hyvärinen, 1981; Hyvärinen, Hyvärinen, & Linnankoski, 1981), but seem to include more primary areas in the occipital cortex, such as area 18, as well.

In neuroimaging studies, regional activation alone, in terms of increased activity relative to a control state, does not necessarily indicate functional involvement. Interregional correlation analysis (Horwitz, 1994) provides additional information regarding the function of the right occipital cortex during auditory localization in the blind. Using the right IPL as a reference region, correlation analysis reveals a functional network of connections involving inferior and posterior parietal and occipital areas of the right hemisphere (Weeks et al., 2000). Comparison of blind and sighted subjects revealed that there were significantly greater interregional correlations in the blind between the right IPL and the right parieto-occipital (areas 7/19), the right peristriate (BA 18), and right superior temporal cortices (area 22) (Table 17.1). This suggests that auditory signals from the temporal areas reach the occipital (formerly visual) cortex via parietal and parieto-occipital areas. Whether this involves the formation of new or the strengthening of existing connections remains to be elucidated. Potential anatomical pathways have recently been investigated in macaque monkeys (Romanski et al., 1999).

☐ Human Studies of Tactile Compensation

Interest in the question of whether blind humans develop enhanced capacities in their fingertips has been great since at least the days of Louis Braille. Early behavioral studies have been equally as controversial as in the auditory domain (Juurmaa & Suoni, 1975; Worchel, 1951; see Rauschecker, 1995, for review). Even those studies that demonstrated an improvement of spatial acuity in blind Braille readers often attributed the improvement to training effects, that is, greater opportunity to practice Braille reading.

Recent PET studies have begun to shine some light on this problem in neurobiological terms (Sadato et al., 1996). Activation of occipital areas by tactile Braille reading was demonstrated, and transcranial magnetic stimulation (TMS) of the occipital cortex disrupts the ability to recognize Braille characters (Cohen et al., 1997). The latter finding demonstrates unequivocally that the expanded region of cortex actually participates in the processing of tactile information. It has to be assumed that somatosensory regions normally participating in this task have expanded into formerly visual territory. How this somatosensory input and the auditory input observed in the other PET study mentioned above (Weeks et al., 2000) co-exist in the occipital cortex and share this territory remains to be elucidated by subsequent work testing auditory and somatosensory stimuli in the same blind subjects.

TABLE 17.1. Local maxima in occipital and temporal lobes for regional correlations of standardized rCBF during auditory localization for a reference voxel in the *right* inferior parietal lobule (Tailarach coordinates 42, −48, 32).

Sighted Subjects			Blind Subjects			Statistical Comparison		
Cerebral Regions and Brodmann Areas	Tailarach Coordinates	r Value	Cerebral Regions and Brodmann Areas	Tailarach Coordinates	r Value	Cerebral Regions and Brodmann Areas	Tailarach Coordinates	Z Score
R primary auditory cortex, BA 41/42	62, −28, 8	0.86	R Superior temporal gyrus, BA 42	40, −10, 0	0.76	R Superior temporal gyrus, BA 22	38, −38, 16	4.97
L inferior parietal lobule, BA 40	−44, −42, 36	0.86	L inferior parietal lobule, BA 40	−40, −54, 32	0.75	R fusiform gyrus, BA 37	26, −50, −12	4.92
R inferior temporal, BA 20/37	36, −38, −16	−0.81	R middle temporal gyrus, BA 21	48, −48, −4	0.83	R inferior temporal, BA 20	40, −28, −16	4.85
R inferior temporal, BA 37	34, −52, −8	−0.85	R inferior temporal gyrus, BA 20/21	40, −26, −16	0.78	R dorsal occipital cortex, BA 19	46, −70, 12	4.09
L peristriate cortex, BA 18	−12, −68, 4	−0.87	R dorsal occipital, BA 19	48, −70, 16	0.83	R peristriate cortex, BA 18	26, −84, 0	4.05
L parieto-occipital, BA 7/19	−12, −66, 28	−0.86	R ventral occipital, BA 19	50, −74, −12	0.75	R ventral occipital cortex, BA 19	50, −70, −16	5.51
R parieto-occipital, BA 7/19	6, −66, 24	−0.73	R parieto-occipital, BA 7/19	12, −60, 24	0.73	R parieto-occipital, BA 7/19	16, −60, 28	4.21
R ventral occipital, BA 18	30, −84, 0	−0.75	R peristriate cortex, BA 18	18, −80, 0	0.68			
			R ventral occ., BA 19	10, −66, −4	0.64			

Note. From "A Position Emission Tomographic Study of Auditory Localization in the Congenitally Blind," by R. Weeks et al., 2000, Journal of Neuroscience.

A more philosophical problem concerns the question of how blind individuals "see" their world. Does the activation of the occipital cortex by auditory and somatosensory stimuli evoke an "image" in the blind that can somehow be compared to "vision" because it is mediated by a brain region that was originally (by genetic design) dedicated to this sense? Or does the altered input change the function of these areas so fundamentally that they, in essence, turn into an extension of the auditory or somatosensory cortex, attaining some of their identities? In other words, is the perceptual and cognitive function determined by the recipient structure or by its inputs? Again, to answer this question requires further experimentation.

☐ Synthesis of Animal and Human Studies of Early Blindness

While many similarities between animal and human data can be found, even in great detail as described above, one major difference stands out: An expansion of the auditory-responsive cortex in visually deprived cats and monkeys was reported only for higher association areas; by contrast, ERP and neuroimaging studies of blind humans demonstrate a vast expansion of auditory activation into the occipital cortex, corresponding to primary and secondary visual areas. The explanation for this seeming discrepancy may be quite simple, however. Auditory responses were never tested in primary occipital areas of blind cats and monkeys because it seemed unlikely that auditory input could expand so far into normally visual territory. Cross-modal expansion was thought to be limited to neighboring areas with multimodal overlap, where competition could occur between overlapping input from different modalities. In light of the recent PET data, a reexamination of this view appears warranted. On the other hand, multimodal overlap and competition between different modalities may indeed occur even in the occipital cortex during early postnatal stages, when occipital areas are still wired to receive (transitory) input from the auditory cortex (Innocenti & Clarke, 1984).

Another area where comparison of animal and human data may help is the long-standing question of whether improved capacities of the blind can be attributed merely to increased attention. Even imaging studies demonstrating heightened activity levels cannot firmly prove that this increase is not just due to greater attention paid by blind subjects in comparison to sighted controls. Correlation techniques are better able to demonstrate functional connectivity, but are not the final proof either. This is the point where anatomical tracer techniques and electrophysiology in anesthetized animals come in as the ultimate test: changes demonstrated with these robust methods cannot be explained with changed levels of attention.

☐ Cross-Modal Effects of Congenital Deafness

Processes analogous to the auditory and tactile compensation in the blind have been demonstrated in congenitally deaf subjects. It can be shown with ERP as well as neuroimaging techniques that the brain of deaf subjects is reorganized profoundly. Visual motion areas in the right parietal cortex thought to be involved in the initial decoding of visual signals in American Sign Language (ASL) are expanded (Neville & Lawson, 1987). At the same time, "auditory" areas in the superior temporal cortex are also activated by sign language (Nishimura et al., 1999), but are not activated by the presentation of

English words, as they normally are in hearing subjects (Neville et al., 1998). However, areas responsible for the processing of language-specific contents develop normally, being fed through a different input system (Bavelier et al., 1997). Neurobiologically speaking, the mechanisms responsible for cross-modal reorganization during visual or auditory deprivation must be very similar. As has been argued above, the neural mechanisms are probably even the same for reorganization within and across modalities.

☐ Mechanisms of Neural Plasticity Within and Across Sensory Modalities

Representational Plasticity

It is clear that *representational plasticity* is only a short-hand term for changes that occur at the single-neuron or, even more succinctly, the synaptic level. Neural maps, whether they are sensory or computational in nature, consist of a dense web of neuronal elements that are tightly connected with each other. For maps to expand, shrink, or otherwise change, these neuronal elements have to change their connections with each other, or the input to at least some of these elements has to be modified. In the case of cross-modal plasticity, as described in this chapter, where cortical maps change their dominant sensory modality, single neurons actually have to receive new input connections (indirectly) from another sensory end-organ. This can only be achieved in one of two ways: (a) New connections grow from another nucleus or map that is already connected to that sense organ, or (b) the neurons in the map under consideration already receive input from that sense organ, but the input is too weak to drive the neurons or is suppressed by other, more dominant inputs. The latter hypothesis thus assumes the presence of "silent"' inputs that can be strengthened under certain circumstances (Merzenich et al., 1988).

Experimental evidence has been reported for both of these mechanisms. Although sprouting had long been assumed to require extended amounts of time because it was assumed to be a very slow process, it has been shown recently to be available on a much shorter time scale (Gilbert, 1998). For long-term deprivation studies of the type reported here (e.g., Rauschecker & Korte, 1993), the speed of change would not be of great concern. Nevertheless, activation of silent connections has to be considered as another possibility for map changes in the cerebral cortex.

Hebbian Synapses and NMDA Receptors

Experience-dependent synaptic changes must be brought about by neural activity. One form of activity-dependent synaptic modification is called Hebbian in reference to the Canadian psychologist Donald Hebb (1949), who proposed that synapses change their efficacy of transmission as a function of both pre- and postsynaptic activity. How this concept can be applied to developmental plasticity of sensory systems has been discussed previously (Rauschecker, 1991). A major boost for Hebb's theory came through the discovery of a specific type of glutamate receptors (the NMDA subtype) that regulate associated ion channels as a function not only of the transmitter but also of the postsynaptic potential (for summary, see Chapter 9 by Teyler and Chapter 10 by Cain, in this volume). However, a final proof of the specific involvement of NMDA receptors in cortical plasticity is still outstanding (Figure 17.3; Rauschecker, Egert, & Kossel, 1990).

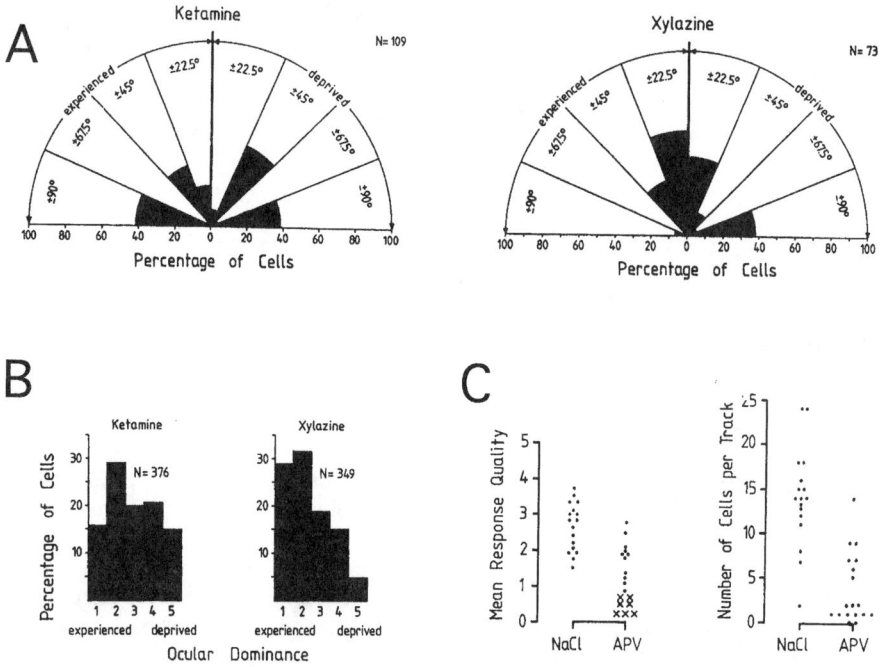

Figure 17.3. Effects of NMDA receptor blockade on response properties in the visual cortex (from Rauschecker et al., 1990). Two different protocols were used: In (a) and (b) kittens during the peak of the sensitive period of visual development were reared in the dark and exposed to visual patterns for brief periods each day, while one eye was occluded with an opaque contact lens. After each exposure, a systemic injection of the non-competitive NMDA channel blocker ketamine was given. In (c), the competitive NMDA antagonist APV was infused directly into the visual cortex of monocularly deprived kittens (cf. Bear et al., 1990). Systemic injections of ketamine not only prevented the expected ocular dominance shift (as visible in xylazine-injected controls) (b), but also entailed a larger number of neurons with unusually broad orientation tuning (a). Direct infusion of APV into the visual cortex significantly reduces response quality and recording density compared to saline-infused sham controls (c).

Work on the molecular basis of synaptic modification in the neocortex is ongoing (Fox, Henley, & Isaac, 1999; Quinlan, Philpat, Huganir, & Bear, 1999), although the hippocampus may still provide the safer substrate for this kind of research (Malenka & Nicoll, 1999). In the end, it appears unlikely that neuroplasticity can be reduced to a single molecule; rather it must be the result of a cascade of events involving a multitude of substances and processes acting at different time scales (Rauschecker, 1991; Shaw, Lanius, & van den Doel, 1994).

Gating Signals

Many influences play a role in plastic changes in the cerebral cortex. Specific sensory experience provides the most important shaping role, but "unspecific" influences such as attention, motivation, arousal, or emotional factors act in a gating capacity. These gating signals can ultimately decide whether the neural activity created by sensory signals are indeed converted into synaptic changes or not. In the case of cross-modal plasticity, the deprivation within one modality is a critical factor opening the door for competitive advantages of the remaining senses, as outlined in this chapter. At the same time, the intense training within these other modalities, tied with increased attention, is probably another main factor leading to the expansion of their representation. In real life, it is difficult to separate the two factors from each other, because it is hard to achieve the same amount of training in a single modality, say tactile Braille reading, without being forced to use it. It is clear that cross-modal plasticity, perhaps more than other forms of plasticity, demonstrates the adaptive value of synaptic changes, which are otherwise only discernable as deprivation effects and loss of function.

☐ Acknowledgments

I would like to thank Robert Gelhard, Jenny Van Lare, and Candace Pérez for assistance. This work was supported by grants R01DC03489, DAMD17-93-V-3018, and the NIMH-IRP.

☐ References

Baldi, P., & Heiligenberg, W. (1988). How sensory maps could enhance resolution through ordered arrangements of broadly tuned receivers. *Biological Cybernetics, 59*(4/5), 313–318.

Bavelier, D., Corina, D., Jezzard, P., Padmanabhan, S., Clark, V. P., Karni, A., Prinster, A., Braun, A., Lalwani, A., Rauschecker, J. P., Turner, R., & Neville, H. (1997). Sentence reading: A functional MRI study at 4 Tesla. *Journal of Cognitive Neuroscience, 9*(5), 664–686.

Bear, M. F., Kleinschmidt, A., Gu, Q., & Singer, W. (1990). Disruption of experience-dependent synaptic modifications in striate cortex by infusion of an NMDA receptor antagonist. *Journal of Neuroscience, 10*, 909–925.

Benedek, G., Mucke, L., Norita, M., Albowitz, B., & Creutzfeldt, O. D. (1988). Anterior ectosylvian visual area (AEV) of the cat: Physiological properties. *Progress in Brain Research, 75*, 245–255.

Bushara, K. O., Weeks, R. A., Ishii, K., Catalan, M.-J., Tian, B., Rauschecker, J. P., & Hallett, M. (1999). Modality-specific frontal and parietal areas for auditory and visual spatial localization in humans. *Nature Neuroscience, 2*(8), 759–766.

Clarey, J. C., & Irvine, D. R. F. (1990). The anterior ectosylvian sulcal auditory field in the cat: I. An electrophysiological study of its relationship to surrounding auditory cortical fields. *Journal of Comparative Neurology, 301*, 289–303.

Cohen, L. G., Celnik, P., Pascual-Leone, A., Corwell, B., Falz, L., Dambrosia, J., Honda, M., Sadato, N., Gerloff, C., Catala, M. D., & Hallett, M. (1997). Functional relevance of cross-modal plasticity in blind humans. *Nature, 389*(6647), 180–183.

De Volder, A. G., Catalan-Ahumada, M., Robert, A., Bol, A., Labar, D., Coppens, A., Michel, C., & Veraart, C. (1999). Changes in occipital cortex activity in early blind humans using a sensory substitution device. *Brain Research, 826*(1), 128–134.

Fitzpatrick, D. C., Batra, R., Stanford, T. R., & Kuwada, S. (1997). A neuronal population code for sound localization. *Nature, 388*(6645), 871–874.

Fox, K., Henley, J., & Isaac, J. (1999). Experience-dependent development of NMDA receptor transmission. *Nature Neuroscience 2*(4), 297–299.

Gelhard, R., Tian, B., & Rauschecker, J. P. (1993). Increased soma size underlies compensatory expansion of whisker barrels in somatosensory cortex of neonatally enucleated mice. *Society for Neuroscience Abstracts, 19*, 47.

Gilbert, C. D. (1998). Adult cortical dynamics. *Physiological Reviews, 78*(2), 467–485.

Guillery, R. W. (1972). Binocular competition in the control of geniculate cell growth. *Journal of Comparative Neurology, 144*, 117–130.

Guillery, R. W., & Stelzner, D. J. (1970). The differential effects of unilateral lid closure upon the monocular and binocular segments of the dorsal lateral geniculate nucleus in the cat. *Journal of Comparative Neurology, 139*(4), 413–421.

Hebb, D. O. (1949). *The Organization of Behavior*. New York: Wiley.

Henning, P., & Rauschecker, J. P. (1995). Organization of spatial tuning columns in the auditory cortex of normal and visually deprived cats. *Society for Neuroscience Abstracts, 21*, 668.

Henning, P., Tian, B., & Rauschecker, J. P. (1995). Piecewise continuous representation of azimuth and elevation in cat auditory cortex. *Association for Research in Otolarynogology Abstracts, 18*, 141.

Horwitz, B. (1994). Data analysis paradigms for metabolic flow data: Combining neural modeling and functional imaging. *Human Brain Mapping, 2*, 112–122.

Hyvärinen, J., Carlson, S., & Hyvärinen, L. (1981). Early visual deprivation alters modality of neuronal responses in area 19 of monkey cortex. *Neuroscience Letters, 4*, 239–243.

Hyvärinen, J., Hyvärinen, L., & Linnankoski, I. (1981). Modification of parietal association cortex and functional blindness after binocular deprivation in young monkeys. *Experimental Brain Research, 42*, 1–8.

Innocenti, G. M., & Clarke, S. (1984). Bilateral transitory projection from auditory cortex in kittens. *Developmental Brain Research, 14* (143–148).

Jiang, H., Leporé, F., Ptito, M., & Guillemot, J. P. (1994). Sensory modality distribution in the anterior ectosylvian cortex (AEC) of cats. *Experimental Brain Research, 97*(3), 404–414.

Juurmaa, J., & Suonio, K. (1975). The role of audition and motion in the spatial orientation of the blind and the sighted. *Scandinavian Journal of Psychology, 16*, 209–216.

Kaas, J. H. (1991). Plasticity of sensory and motor maps in adult mammals. *Annual Review of Neuroscience, 14*, 137–167.

Kaas, J. H., Merzenich, M. M., & Killackey, H. P. (1983). The reorganization of somatosensory cortex following peripheral nerve damage in adult and developing mammals. *Annual Review of Neuroscience, 6*, 325–356.

King, A. J., & Parsons, C. (1999). Improved auditory spatial acuity in visually-deprived ferrets. *European Journal of Neuroscience, 11*, 3945–3956.

Korte, M., & Rauschecker, J. P. (1993). Auditory spatial tuning of cortical neurons is sharpened in cats with early blindness. *Journal of Neurophysiology, 70*(4), 1717–1721.

Kujala, T., Alho, K., Huotilainen, M., Ilmoniemi, R., Lehtokoski, A., Leinonen, A., Rinne, T., Salonen, O., Sinkkonen, J., Standertskjold-Nordenstam, C., & Näätänen, R. (1997). Electrophysiological evidence for cross-modal plasticity in humans with early- and late-onset blindness. *Psychophysiology, 32*(2), 213–216.

Kujala, T., Alho, K., Kekoni, J., Hamalainen, H., Reinikainen, K., Salonen, O., Standertskjold-Nordenstam, C. G., & Näätänen, R. (1995). Auditory and somatosensory event-related brain potentials in early blind humans. *Experimental Brain Research, 104*(3), 519–526.

Lessard, N., Pare, M., Lepore, F. & Lassonde, M. (1998). Early-blind human subjects localize sound sources better than sighted subjects. *Nature, 395*(6699), 278–280.

Liotti, M., Ryder, K., & Woldorf, M. G. (1998). Auditory attention in the congenitally blind: where, when and what gets. *Neuroreport, 9*(6), 1007–1012.

Malenka, R. C., & Nicoll, R. A. (1999). Long-term potentiation—a decade of progress? *Science, 285*(5435), 1870–1874.

Merzenich, M. M., Recanzone, G., Jenkins, W. M., Allard, T. T., & Nudo, R. J. (1988). Cortical representational plasticity. In P. Rakic & W. Singer (Eds.), *Neurobiology of neocortex* (pp. 41–67). New York: Wiley.

Métin, C., & Frost, D. O. (1989). Visual responses of neurons in somatosensory cortex of hamsters with experimentally induced retinal projections to somatosensory thalamus. *Proceedings of the National Academy of Sciences of the United States of America, 86,* 357–361

Muchnik, C., Efrati, M., Nemeth, E., Malin, M., & Hildesheimer, M. (1991). Central auditory skills in blind and sighted subjects. *Scandinavian Audiology, 20,* 19–23.

Neville, H. J., Bavelier, D., Corina, D., Rauschecker, J. P., Karni, A., Lalwani, A., Braun, A., Clark, V., Jezzard, P., & Turner, R. (1998). Cerebral organization for language in deaf and hearing subjects: Biological constraints and effects of experience. *Proceedings of the National Academy of Sciences of the United States of America, 95,* 922–929.

Neville, H. J., & Lawson, D. (1987). Attention to central and peripheral visual space in a movement detection task: An event-related potential and behavioral study. II. Congenitally deaf adults. *Brain Research, 405*(2), 268–283.

Nishimura, H., Haskikawa, K., Doi, K., Iwaki, T., Watanabe, Y., Kusuoka, H., Nishimura, T., & Kubo, T. (1999). Sign language 'heard' in the auditory cortex. *Nature, 397*(6715), 116.

Quinlan, E. M., Philpot, B. D., Huganir, R., & Bear, M. F. (1999). Rapid, experience-dependent expression of synaptic NMDA receptors in visual cortex in vivo. *Nature Neuroscience, 2*(4), 352–357.

Rakic, P. (1988). Specification of cerebral cortical areas. *Science, 241,* 170–176.

Rauschecker, J. P. (1991). Mechanisms of visual plasticity: Hebb synapses, NMDA receptors and beyond. *Physiological Reviews, 71,* 587–615.

Rauschecker, J. P. (1995). Compensatory plasticity and sensory substitution in the cerebral cortex. *Trends in Neuroscience, 18,* 36–43.

Rauschecker, J. P. (1997). Mechanisms of compensatory plasticity in the cerebral cortex. In H. J. Freund, B. A. Sabel, & O. W. Witte (Eds.), *Brain plasticity/ advanced neurology, Vol. 73* (pp. 137–146). Philadelphia: Lippincott-Raven.

Rauschecker, J. P., Egert, U., & Kossel, A. (1990). Effects of NMDA antagonists on developmental plasticity in kitten visual cortex. *International Journal of Developmental Neuroscience, 8*(4), 425–435.

Rauschecker, J. P., & Hahn, S. (1987). Ketamine-xylazine anaesthesia blocks consolidation of ocular dominance changes in kitten visual cortex. *Nature 326,* 183–185.

Rauschecker, J. P., & Harris, L. R. (1983). Auditory compensation of the effects of visual deprivation in the cat's superior colliculus. *Experimental Brain Research, 50,* 69–83.

Rauschecker, J. P., & Henning, P. (2000). Crossmodal expansion of cortical maps in early blindness. In J. Kaas (Ed.), *The mutable brain* (pp. 243–260).

Rauschecker, J. P., & Kniepert, U. (1994). Enhanced precision of auditory localization behavior in visually deprived cats. *European Journal of Neuroscience, 6,* 149–160.

Rauschecker, J. P., & Korte, M. (1993). Auditory compensation for early blindness in cat cerebral cortex. *Journal of Neuroscience, 13,* 4538–4548.

Rauschecker, J. P., Tian, B., Korte, M., & Egert, U. (1992). Crossmodal changes in the somatosensory vibrissa/barrel system of visually deprived animals. *Proceedings of the National Academy of Sciences of the United States of America, 89,* 5063–5067.

Recanzone, G. H., Schreiner, C. E., & Merzenich, M. M. (1993). Plasticity in the frequency representation of primary auditory cortex following discrimination training in adult owl monkeys. *Journal of Neuroscience, 13,* 87–103.

Rice, C. E. (1970). Early blindness, early experience, and perceptual enhancement. *Research Bulletin (American Foundation for the Blind), 22,* 1–22.

Rice, C. E., Feinstein, S. H., & Schusterman, R. J. (1965). Echo-detection ability of the blind: Size and distance factor. *Journal of Experimental Psychology, 70,* 246–251.

Röder, B., Rösler, F., Henninghausen, E., & Nacker, F. (1996). Event-related potentials during auditory and somatosensory discrimination in sighted and blind human subjects. *Brain Research: Cognitive Brain Research, 4*(2), 77–93.

Röder, B., Teder-Salejärin, W., Sterr, A., Rösler, F., Hillyard, S. A., & Neville, H. J. (1999). Improved auditory spatial tuning in blind humans. *Nature, 400,* 162–166.

Romanski, L. M., Tian, B., Fritz, J., Mishkin, M., Goldman-Rakic, P. S., & Rauschecker, J. P. (1999). Dual streams of auditory afferents target multiple domains in the primate prefrontal cortex. *Nature Neuroscience, 2,* 1131–1136.

Sadato, N., Pascual-Leone, A., Grafman, J., Ibanez, V., Deiber, M.-P., Dold, G., & Hallett, M. (1996). Activation of the primary visual cortex by Braille reading in blind subjects. *Nature, 380,* 526–528.

Shaw, C. A., Lanius, R. A., & van den Doel, K. (1994) The origin of synaptic neuroplasticity: Crucial molecules or a dynamical cascade? *Brain Research: Brain Research Review, 19*(3), 241–263.

Sur, M., Pallas, S. L., & Roe, A. W. (1990). Cross-modal plasticity in cortical development: Differentiation and specification of sensory neocortex. *Trends in Neuroscience, 13,* 227–233.

Toldi, J., Farkas, T., & Volgyi, B. (1994). Neonatal enucleation induces cross-modal changes in the barrel cortex of rat. A behavioural and electrophysiological study. *Neuroscience Letters, 167,* 1–4.

Uhl, F., Franzen, P., Podreka, I., Steiner, M., & Deecke, L. (1993). Increased regional cerebral blood flow in inferior occipital cortex and cerebellum of early blind humans. *Neuroscience Letters, 150,* 162–164.

Wanet-Defalque, M. C., Veraart, C., De Volder, A., Metz, R., Michel, C., Dooms, G., & Goffinet, A. (1988). High metabolic activity in the visual cortex of early blind human subjects. *Brain Research, 446*(2), 369–373.

Weeks, R., Horwitz, B., Aziz-Sultan, A., Tian, B., Wessinger, C. M., Cohen, L., Hallett, M., & Rauschecker, J. P. (2000). A positron emission tomographic study of auditory localization in the congenitally blind. *Journal of Neuroscience, 20,* 2664–2672.

Weeks, R. A., Aziz-Sultan, A., Bushara, K. O., Tian, B., Wessinger, C. M., Dang, N., Rauschecker, J. P., & Hallett, M. (1999). A PET study of human auditory spatial processing. *Neuroscience Letters, 262,* 155–158.

Wiesel, T. N., & Hubel, D. H. (1963). Single-cell responses in striate cortex of kittens deprived of vision in one eye. *Journal of Neurophysiology, 26,* 1003–1017.

Wightman, F. L., & Kistler, D. J. (1989). Headphone simulation of free-field listening. I. Stimulus synthesis. *Journal of the Acoustical Society of America, 85,* 858–867.

Worchel, P. (1951). Space perception and orientation in the blind. *Psychological Monographs, 65,* 1–28.

Helen J. Neville
Daphne Bavelier

Specificity of Developmental Neuroplasticity in Humans: Evidence from Sensory Deprivation and Altered Language Experience

☐ Introduction

The term *neuroplasticity* is generally used to refer to the capacity of the nervous system to modify its organization. However, such changes may occur as a consequence of many different events, including the normal development and maturation of the organism, the acquisition of new skills ("learning") in immature and mature organisms, following damage to the nervous system and as a result of sensory deprivation. Studies to date of the molecular and cellular events underlying neural plasticity in such different conditions have revealed a limited set of mechanisms available to induce changes in the organization of the neural networks of the brain. Such reports raise the hypothesis and the hope that the diverse phenomena referred to as neuroplasticity will be elucidated in the not-too-distant future. However, while there is evidence to suggest that there may be considerable overlap in the mechanisms that mediate developmental and adult neuroplasticity following abnormal experience or damage, we think it is important at the present time to distinguish between them. Even if some of the mechanisms are similar or even identical, the fact that these mechanisms operate on nervous systems that are structurally and physiologically different is likely to result in quantitative and/or qualitative differences in neuroplasticity in immature and mature organisms. For example, in the immature human brain, the number of synapses is 50% greater than in the adult brain (Huttenlocher, 1994; Figure 18.1). This redundant connectivity exists at different times in different brain regions and almost certainly constrains the nature and extent of modification that can occur at different ages. Similarly, the metabolic profiles of different brain structures change dramatically over the first two decades of life. It is likely that these variables give rise to different profiles of plasticity at different times and for functions linked to different structures. Indeed, neurophysiological studies of animals indicate considerable variability and specificity in the types of plastic changes

Synapse Development
Human Brain

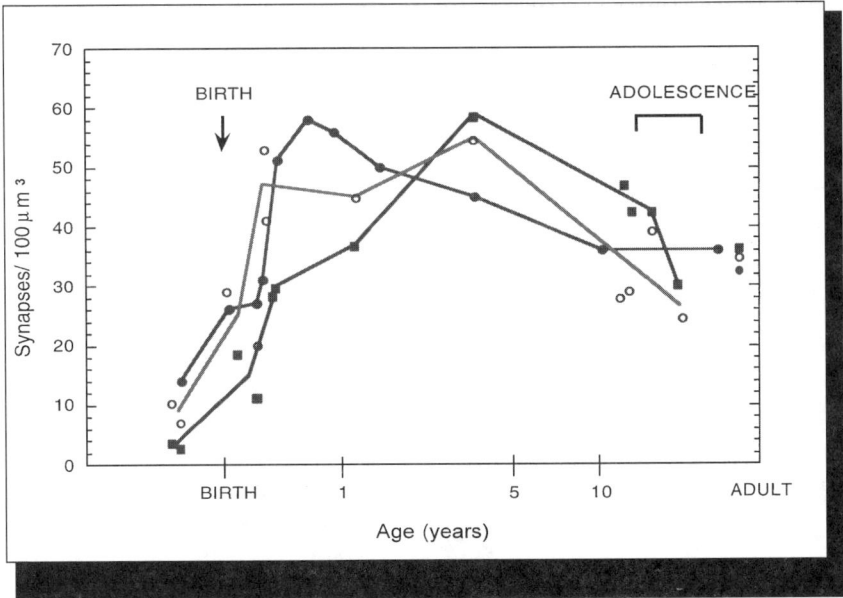

Figure 18.1. Mean synaptic density in synapses/100 um³ in auditory (filled circles), calcarine (open circles), and prefrontal (■) cortex at various ages. Adapted from "Regional Differences in Synaptogenesis in Human Cerebral Cortex," by P. R. Huttenlocher and A. S. Dabholkar, 1997, *Journal of Comparative Neurology, 387*, p. 170. Copyright 1997 by John Wiley. Also adapted from "Specificity and Plasticity in Neurocognitive Development in Humans," by H. J. Neville and D. Bavelier, 1999, p. 85. Copyright by MIT Press. Adapted with permission.

that can occur from system to system. For example, while visual experience affects the formation of ocular dominance columns only during a very limited time period in development, the remapping of the representation of the visual fields following retinal lesions extends into adulthood (Kaas et al., 1990). Similarly, while the representation of the whiskers (barrell formation) within the somatosensory cortex is modifiable only during a limited time period, remapping of the cortical representation of the digits following amputation or training can occur throughout the life of the animal (Merzenich & Jenkins, 1993).

While few in number, the available studies of human brain plasticity also suggest considerable variability and specificity in the extent of neuroplasticity within different domains of function. This is the major theme of this chapter, which focuses on developmental plasticity. Below we present first a summary of studies of the effects of auditory and visual deprivation on the organization of remaining modalities and evidence on a mechanism that may be important in these changes. Then we consider evidence on plasticity of the language systems of the brain following different language experiences, including bilingualism and acquisition of signed as compared to spoken language. The results of these studies taken as a whole raise hypotheses about the nature of the differences between neural systems that display plasticity throughout life and those that display strong constraints on the timing and extent of changes that they can undergo.

Neuroplasticity Between Modalities

While there is much anecdotal evidence claiming better audition after early blindness or better vision after early deafness, the available data are mixed. The long-held belief that multi-sensory integration is a required step to achieve full-fledged development has led research to initially focus on the disabilities caused by early vision loss or deafness. There are scores of studies, mostly from the 1970s and the early 1980s, documenting deficient spatial abilities in the blind and deficient visual perception in the deaf, for example (Thinus-Blanc & Gaunet, 1997, for a review). The recent evidence documenting the adaptability of the brain has led investigators to carefully review this issue. It appears that when the etiology and characteristics of the population tested is carefully controlled and the task appropriately chosen to not rely on encoding strategies that are not available to the deprived subjects, convincing evidence of compensatory plasticity can be established.

The mechanisms at play in compensatory plasticity is still a question of debate. While within-sensory modality plasticity appears mediated by local changes within a limited set of cortical areas, between-modality reorganization is often thought to imply more extensive modification of connectivity across areas. Most animal models of cross-modal plasticity involve forcing the input of one modality to be rerouted to the primary cortex of another modality (Frost, 1990; Sur, Pallas, & Roe, 1990; Sharma, Angelucci, & Sur, 2000; von Melchner, Pallas, & Sur, 2000). For example, when retinal inputs were rewired to innervate the auditory cortex in ferrets, cells in the primary auditory cortex A1 exhibited sensitivity to visual stimulation, but also orientation and direction selectivity as in V1 (Sharma et al., 2000; von Melchner et al., 2000). Studies of cross-modal plasticity in animal models suggest that, early on, cortical areas can change their functional specificity depending on which inputs they receive. But can such cross-modal rewiring be observed in humans? There is only scarce evidence to date that compensatory plasticity, in the absence of surgically induced rewiring, can occur in primary cortices in humans or animals; however, there is converging evidence that secondary and association cortices can compensate for the loss of one modality. This rewiring is believed to involve the stabilization of early multisensory corticocortical connections that exist in the newborn, but are eliminated in the presence of normal input. For example, in newborn kittens, projections from the auditory, somatosensory, and motor cortex to the occipital cortex (BA17,18,19) are initially observed but are eliminated around 5 weeks of life (Dehay, Kennedy, & Bullier, 1988; Innocenti & Clarke, 1984). However, in visually deprived kittens these multimodal connections are still present at 6 months of age (Berman, 1991). Thus, in the absence of competition from visual inputs, the visual cortex may become recruited for tactile or auditory processing (Hyvarinen, Carlson, & Hyvarinen, 1981). Evidence supporting this view is reviewed below.

Effects of Congenital Deafness on Vision

The data available thus far suggest a specific enhancement of behavioral performance and neural activity in response to visuospatial information presented in the peripheral visual fields. Deaf adults are better than hearing controls at detecting the onset or the direction of motion of a peripheral stimulus (Loke & Song, 1991; Neville & Lawson, 1987a, 1987b, 1987c). They are also faster at switching visual attention toward a near-periphery target in the presence of distractors located at the fixation point (Parasnis & Samar, 1985). Electrophysiological recordings while subjects monitored moving stimuli have indicated larger visually evoked responses for deaf than hearing adults over occipital sites. These group differences were specially marked for peripheral stimuli (Armstrong, 1995; Armstrong, Mitchell, Hillyard, & Neville, 2000). In a recent fMRI study, the effects of visual attention on motion processing were compared in deaf and hearing individuals (Bavelier, Tomann, Hutton et al., 2000; Bavelier, Tomann, Mitchell et al., 1998). When participants monitored the peripheral visual field, greater recruitment of the motion-selective area MT was observed in deaf than in hearing participants, whereas the two groups were comparable when attending to the central visual field. Further analysis suggested that changes in peripheral attention in the deaf are mediated through the modulation of the connections between the posterior parietal cortex and earlier sensory areas. These results suggest that the systems mediating the representation of peripheral visual field may be more modifiable than those representing central space. There is anatomical evidence that the visual periphery is represented most strongly along the dorsal visual pathway that projects from V1 to the posterior parietal cortex (Baizer, Ungerleider, & Desimone, 1991). These data have led our group to hypothesize that other dorsal pathway functions may also exhibit a greater sensitivity to altered experience. The dorsal visual pathway projects from V1 to area MT/MST and the parietal cortex and has been associated with processing of visuospatial information, such as visual motion, reaching, or visuospatial attention. To test the specificity of a dorsal pathway enhancement after early deafness, motion processing was compared to color processing. It is commonly accepted that, whereas motion processing is largely mediated by the dorsal pathway, color is strongly mediated by the ventral pathway projecting from V1 to IT. Stimuli were presented at central and peripheral locations. The color stimuli were isoluminant blue and green high spatial frequency gratings. Event-related potentials (ERPs) were evoked by a brief change in color; randomly at one location the blue bars changed to red for 100 ms. The moving stimuli consisted of low spatial frequency gratings of light and dark gray bars with a low luminance contrast. The evoking stimulus consisted of the bars at one location (random) moving transversely to the right. Subjects fixated centrally and monitored all locations for the rare occurrence of a black square at one of the locations. Whereas hearing subjects' reaction times were faster to targets occurring in the central than in the peripheral visual field, deaf subjects responded equally quickly to targets in the central and peripheral fields. In addition, deaf subjects responded more quickly than hearing subjects to peripheral moving stimuli and, beginning as early as 110 ms after stimulus onset, moving stimuli presented to the periphery elicited specific ERP components that occurred earlier from deaf than from hearing subjects. Several specific group differences occurred in the amplitude and distribution of early sensory responses recorded over anterior and temporal regions. Deaf subjects displayed significantly greater amplitudes than hearing subjects, but this effect only occurred for moving stimuli, not for color stimuli (see Figure 18.2). Further, whereas in hearing subjects, color stimuli elicited larger responses than did motion stimuli, in deaf subjects responses to motion stimuli were as large as those to color stimuli. In addition, at 150 ms ERPs to the motion stimuli displayed a source-sink generator in the temporal cortex that was clearly present in the deaf subjects but not in the hearing subjects. These data suggest that there is considerable specificity in the aspects of visual processing that are altered following auditory deprivation, specifically that several aspects of visual processing

Left Hemisphere   Right Hemisphere

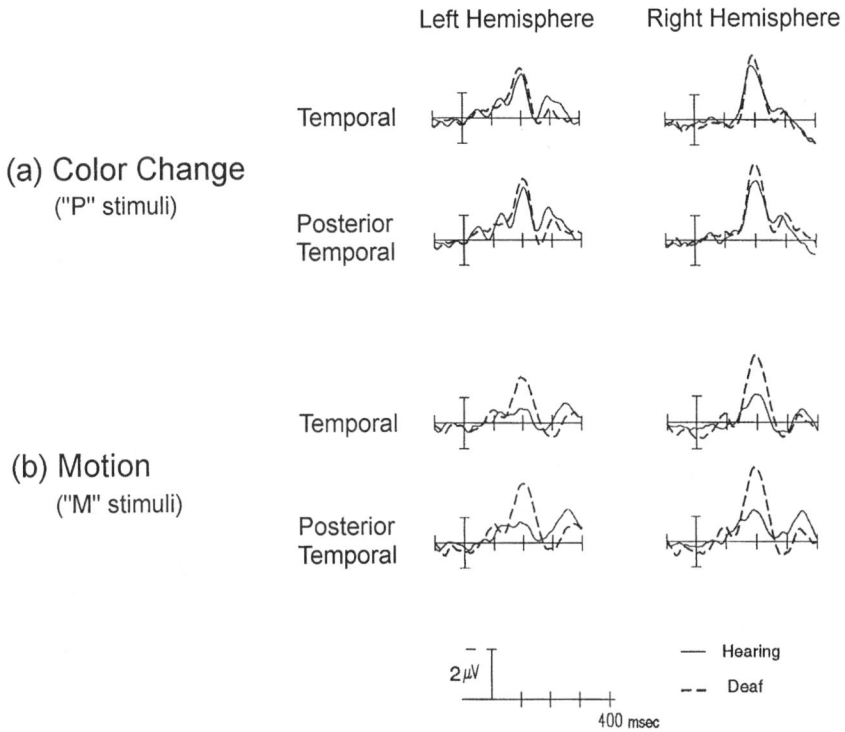

Figure 18.2. ERPs elicited by (a) color change and (b) motion in normally hearing and congenitally deaf adults. Recordings from temporal and posterior temporal regions of the left and right hemispheres. Adapted from "Specificity and Plasticity in Neurocognitive Development in Humans," by H. J. Neville and D. Bavelier, 1999, p. 85. Copyright by MIT Press. Adapted with permission.

mediated by the dorsal visual processing stream are quite modifiable in response to alterations.

Changes in these visual functions may be due to deafness or to the acquisition of a signed language. Signing has been shown to affect performance on tasks that require visuospatial transformations and are likely to recruit the dorsal pathway. Deaf native signers are both faster and more accurate than controls on tasks of mental rotation (McKee, 1987). This effect is not specific to auditory deprivation; hearing native signers also exhibit better mental rotation performance than nonsigners (Emmorey, 1998; Emmorey, Kosslyn, & Bellugi, 1993; Talbot & Haude, 1993). Emmorey and collaborators have also shown that deaf and hearing signers are faster at generating mental images than hearing nonsigners (Emmorey & Kosslyn, 1996; Emmorey, Kosslyn, & Bellugi, 1993). Deaf signers are more accurate than hearing nonsigners when identifying objects presented from a noncanonical viewpoint. This effect has been interpreted as a by-product of signing (Emmorey, 1998). This work establishes that familiarity with American Sign Language (ASL) results in behavioral enhancement in a number of visuospatial tasks that are likely to recruit structures in the dorsal pathway. Acquisition of ASL has also been linked with brain reorganization for motion processing. The few studies on that topic have reported a left-hemisphere advantage for motion detection (Bosworth & Dobkins, 1999; Neville & Lawson, 1987a, 1987b) in native signers, whereas hearing nonsigners displayed a tendency for a right-hemisphere advantage. These findings suggest the importance in future work of separating the effects of deafness from those of early acquisition of ASL by (a) comparing deaf native signers to hearing native signers, (b) comparing deaf native signers to deaf late signers, and (c) studying visual functions that are important for ASL processing but are not dorsally mediated.

Cross-Modal Changes Following Blindness

Developmental plasticity has also been documented in humans within other sensory modalities. There are several reports that early peripheral blindness leads to changes in the visually deprived cortex. Measures of glucose utilization have shown an increased metabolism in the visual cortex of early blind humans as compared to subjects who became blind after the completion of visual development. These studies reported that metabolic activity within the occipital cortex of early blind individuals is higher than that found in blindfolded sighted subjects and equivalent to that of sighted subjects with their eyes open (Uhl et al., 1994; Veraart et al., 1990; Wanet-Defalque et al., 1988). Additionally, ERP studies indicated a larger slow negative DC potential shift over the occipital lobe in early blind than sighted persons during tactile and auditory tasks (Röder, Rösler, & Hennighausen, 1997; Röder, Rösler, Hennighausen, & Näcker, 1996; Uhl, Franzen, Lindinger, Lang, & Deecke, 1991; Uhl et al., 1994). Recently, a number of studies have confirmed the functional participation of visual areas during somatosensory tasks in early blind individuals. Using positron emission tomography (PET), Sadato et al. (1996) compared tactile discrimination in early blind braille readers and control subjects. Blind subjects revealed activation of visual-cortical areas, whereas these regions were deactivated in controls. The functional relevance of visual areas in tactile discrimination was further established in a transcranial magnetic stimulation experiment (Cohen et al., 1997). Transient stimulation of the occipital cortex induced errors on a tactile task in early blind subjects but had no effect on the sighted controls. It is worth noting that not all aspects of somatosensory processing recruit visual areas in blind subjects. For example, simple tactile stimuli that did not require discrimination produced little activation in visual areas of blind subjects (Sadato et al.). This finding is in agreement with the hypothesis that different neurocognitive systems and subsystems exhibit different sensitivities to altered experience.

This point is further supported by the work of Röder et al. (1997), who have studied auditory localization abilities in blind humans. ERPs were recorded as congenitally blind adults and sighted controls attended either to central or peripheral sound sources in order to detect a rare noise burst at either the 0° or the 90° loudspeaker (on different blocks). Behavioral data revealed a higher spatial resolution in the blind, particularly when they were attending to the periphery. Gradients of ERP amplitudes suggested a sharper auditory spatial attention focus in the blind compared to the sighted. The results suggest that across auditory and visual modalities the representation of peripheral space is more altered by early sensory experience than is the representation of central space. It is interesting that in close examination of the behavioral data presented in Rice, Feinstein, & Schusterman (1965) on blind humans and Rauschecker and Kniepert (1993) on blind cats a similar effect is observed, that is, a larger advantage in sound localization for the blind at peripheral locations.

Developmental Neuroplasticity of Language Functions

It is reasonable to assume that the rules and principles that govern the development of the sensory systems also guide the development of language-relevant brain systems. Thus differences in the rate of differentiation and degree of specification may be apparent within language and help to identify different functional subsystems. In a series of experiments we have studied the development of the neural systems important in lexical, semantic, and grammatical processing. In normal, right-handed, monolingual adults nouns and verbs ("open class" words) that provide lexical/semantic information elicit a different pattern of brain activity (as measured by ERPs) than do function words, including prepositions and conjunctions ("closed class" words) that provide grammatical information in English (Neville, Mills, & Lawson, 1992; Nobre & McCarthy, 1994). In addition, sentences that are semantically nonsensical (but are grammatically intact) elicit a different pattern of ERPs than do sentences that contain a violation of syntactic structure (but that leave the meaning intact; Neville, Nicol, Barss, Forster, & Garrett, 1991; Osterhout, McLaughlin, & Bersick, 1997). These results are consistent with several other types of evidence that suggest that different neural systems mediate the processing of lexical/semantic and grammatical information in adults. Specifically, they imply a greater role for more posterior temporal-parietal systems in lexical/semantic processing and for frontal-temporal systems within the left hemisphere in grammatical processing. This overall pattern appears ubiquitous in adults, and many investigators have suggested that the central role of the left hemisphere in language processing is strongly genetically determined. Certainly the fact that most individuals, regardless of the language they learn, display left-hemisphere dominance for that language indicates that this aspect of neural development is strongly biased. Nonetheless, it is likely that language-relevant aspects of cerebral organization are dependent on and modified by language experience. Many investigators have studied this question by comparing cerebral organization in individuals who learned a second language at different times in development (Dehaene et al., 1997; Kim, Relkin, Lee, & Hirsch, 1997; Perani et al., 1996). In general, age of exposure to language appears to affect cerebral organization for that language. Moreover, there appears to be specificity in these effects: In Chinese-English bilinguals, delays of as long as 16 years in exposure to English had very little effect on the organization of the brain systems active in lexical/semantics processing. In contrast, delays of only 4 years had significant effects on those aspects of brain organization linked to grammatical processing (Weber-Fox & Neville, 1996). These results and parallel behavioral results from the same study suggest that aspects of semantic and grammatical processing differ markedly in the degree to which they depend upon language input. Specifically, grammatical processing appears more vulnerable to delays in language experience.

Studies of Deaf Adults

Further evidence on this point was provided by ERP studies of English sentence processing by congenitally deaf individuals who learned English late and as a second language (ASL was the first language of these subjects; Neville et al., 1992). Deaf subjects displayed ERP responses to nouns and to semantically anomalous sentences in written English that were indistinguishable from those of normal hearing subjects who learned English as a first language. These data are consistent with the hypothesis that some aspects of lexical/semantic processing are largely unaffected by the many different aspects of language experience that differ between normally hearing and congenitally deaf individuals. By contrast, deaf subjects displayed aberrant ERP responses to grammatical information like that presented in function words in English. Specifically they did not display the specialization of the anterior regions of the left hemisphere characteristic of native, hearing/speaking learners. These data suggest that the systems that mediate the processing of grammatical information are more modifiable and vulnerable in response to altered language experience than are those associated with lexical/semantic processing.

Studies of ASL

Recently, we have employed the ERP and fMRI techniques to further pursue this hypothesis and also to obtain evidence on the question of whether the strongly biased role of the left hemisphere in language occurs independently of the structure and modality of the language first acquired (Neville et al., 1997, 1998). ERPs recorded to response to open- and closed-class signs in ASL sentences displayed similar timing and anterior/posterior distributions to those observed in previous studies of English. However, whereas in native speakers of English responses to closed-class English words were largest over anterior regions of the left hemisphere, in native signers closed-class ASL signs elicited activity that was bilateral and that extended posteriorly to include parietal regions of both the left and right hemispheres. These results imply that the acquisition of a language that relies on spatial contrasts and the perception of motion may result in the inclusion of right-hemisphere regions into the language system. Both hearing and deaf native signers displayed this effect. However, hearing people who acquired ASL in the late teens did not show this effect, suggesting that there may be a limited time (sensitive) period during which this type of organization for grammatical processing can develop. By contrast, the response to semantic information was not affected by age of acquisition of ASL, in keeping with the results from studies of English that suggest that these different subsystems within language display different degrees of developmental plasticity.

In fMRI studies comparing sentence processing in English and ASL, we also observed evidence for biological constraints and effects of experience on the mature organization of the language systems of the brain. As seen in Figure 18.3 (top), when hearing adults read English (their first language) there is robust activation within the left (but not the right) hemisphere and in particular within the inferior frontal ("Broca's") regions. When deaf people read English (their second language, learned late and imperfectly) we did not observe activation of these regions within the left hemisphere (Figure 18.3, middle). Is the lack of left-hemisphere activation in the deaf linked to lack of auditory experience with language or to incomplete acquisition of the grammar of the language? ASL is not sound based but displays each of the characteristics of all formal languages including a complex grammar (that makes extensive use of spatial location and hand motion; Klima & Bellugi, 1979). Studies of the same deaf subjects when viewing sentences in their native ASL clearly showed activation within the same inferior frontal regions of the left hemisphere that are active when native speakers of English process English (Figure 18.3, bottom). These data suggest that there is a strong biological bias for these neural systems to mediate grammatical language regardless of the structure and modality of the language acquired. However, if the language is not acquired within

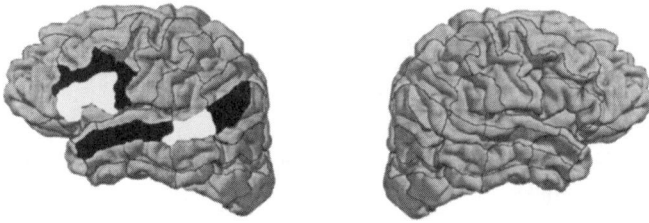

Hearing Subjects - English

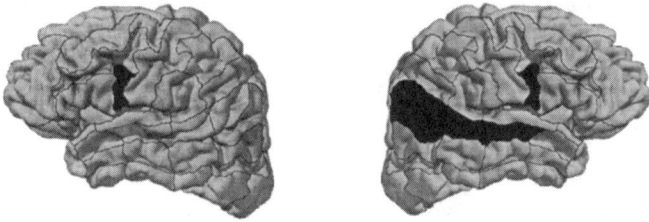

Deaf Subjects - English

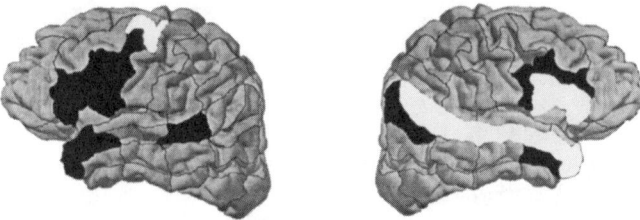

Deaf Subjects - ASL   p<.0005 .005

Figure 18.3. Cortical areas showing increases in blood oxygenation on fMRI when normal hearing adults read English sentences (top), when congenitally deaf native signers read English sentences (middle), and when congenitally deaf native signers view sentences in their native sign language (ASL). Adapted from "Specificity and Plasticity in Neurocognitive Development in Humans," by H. J. Neville and D. Bavelier, 1999, p. 85. Copyright by MIT Press. Adapted with permission.

the appropriate time window, this strong bias is not expressed. Biological constraints and language experience interact epigenetically, as has been described for many other systems described in developmental biology.

The fMRI data also indicate a robust role for the right hemisphere in processing ASL. These results suggest that the nature of the language input, in this case the co-occurrence of location and motion information with language, shape the organization of the language systems of the brain. Further research is necessary to specify the different times in human development when particular types of input are required for optimal development of the many systems and subsystems important in language processing.

Effects of Primary Language Acquisition on Cerebral Organization

The research summarized above implies that language experience determines the development and organization of language-relevant systems of the brain. A strong test of this hypothesis would be to chart the changes in brain organization as children acquire primary language and to separate these from more general maturational changes (Mills, Coffey-Corina, & Neville, 1993, 1997; Neville & Mills, 1997). We compared patterns of neural activity relevant to language processing in 13- and 20-month-old infants to determine whether or not changes in cerebral organization occur as a function of specific changes in language development when chronological age is held constant. ERPs were recorded as children listened to a series of words whose meaning was understood by the child, words whose meaning the child did not understand, and backward words. Specific and different ERP components discriminated comprehended words from unknown and from backward words. Distinct lateral and anterior/posterior specializations were apparent in ERP responses to the different types of words. At 13 months of age the effects of word comprehension were apparent over anterior and posterior regions of both the left and right hemispheres. However, at 20 months of age the effects occurred only over temporal and parietal regions of the left hemisphere. This increasing specialization of language-relevant systems is not solely dependent on chronological age, however. In comparisons of children of the same age who differ in size of vocabulary it is clear that language experience and knowledge is strongly predictive of the maturity of cerebral organization: 13-month-old infants with large vocabularies also display more focal left temporal/parietal effects of word meaning than do those with small vocabularies.

A similar effect is found in the development of the differential processing of open- and closed-class words. We compared ERPs to open- and closed-class words in infants and young children from 20 to 42 months of age. All children understood and produced both the open- and closed-class words presented. At 20 months, ERPs in response to open- and closed-class words did not differ. However, both types of words elicited ERPs that differed from those elicited by unknown and backward words. These data suggest that in the earliest stages of language development, when children are typically speaking in single-word utterances or beginning to put two words together, open- and closed-class words elicit similar patterns of brain activity. At 28–30 months of age, when children typically begin to speak in short phrases, ERPs to open- and closed-class words elicited different patterns of brain activity However, the more mature left-hemisphere asymmetry to closed-class words was not observed. By 3 years of age most children speak in sentences and use closed class words appropriately to specify grammatical relations, and, like adults, ERPs from 3-year-olds displayed a left-hemisphere asymmetry to closed-class words. The results across the three groups are consistent with the hypothesis that initially, open- and closed-class words are processed by similar brain systems, and that these systems become progressively specialized with increasing language experience. Further evidence on this hypothesis comes from an examination of ERPs from children who were the same age but who differed in language abilities. The 20-month-old children who scored below the 50th percentile for vocabulary size did not show ERP differences to open- and closed-class words. In contrast, those above the 50th percentile displayed ERP differences to open- and closed-class words that were similar to the 28- to 30-month-old patterns. These data strongly suggest that the organization of brain activity is linked to language abilities rather than to chronological age per se.

☐ Summary and Conclusions

The results from the language studies taken as a whole point to different developmental time courses and developmental vulnerabilities of aspects of grammatical and semantic/lexical processing. They thus provide support for conceptions of language that distinguish these subprocesses within language. Similarly, following auditory deprivation, processes associated with the dorsal visual pathway were more altered than were functions associated with the ventral pathway, providing support for conceptions of visual system organization that distinguish functions along these lines. A general hypothesis that may account for the different patterns of plasticity within both vision and language is that systems employing fundamentally different learning mechanisms display different patterns of developmental plasticity. It may be that systems that display experience-dependent change throughout life, including the topography of sensory maps (Gilbert, 1995; Kaas, 1995; Merzenich, Recanzone, Jenkins, Allard, & Nudo, 1988), lexical acquisition (i.e., object-word associations), and the establishment of form, face, and object representations (i.e., ventral pathway functions) rely upon very general, associative learning mechanisms that permit learning and adaptation throughout life. By contrast, systems that are important for computing dynamically shifting relations among locations, objects, and events (including the dorsal visual pathway and the systems of the brain that mediate grammar) appear dependent on and modifiable by experience primarily during more limited periods in development. This could account for both the greater developmental deficits and enhancements of dorsal pathway function following various developmental anomalies and for the greater effects of altered language experience on grammatical functions. Further research is necessary to characterize systems that become constrained in this way and those that can be modified throughout life. This type of developmental evidence can contribute to fundamental descriptions of the architecture of different cognitive systems. Additionally, in the long run, they may contribute to the design of educational and habilitative programs for both normally and abnormally developing children.

☐ Acknowledgments

This research has been supported by grants from the National Institutes of Health, DC00128, and DC00481. We are grateful to our many collaborators on the several studies summarized here, and to Linda Heidenreich for manuscript preparation.

☐ References

Armstrong, B. (1995). *Effects of auditory deprivation on color and motion processing: An ERP study.* La Jolla, CA: University of California at San Diego Press.

Armstrong, B., Mitchell, T., Hillyard, S. A., & Neville, H. J. (2000). Effects of auditory deprivation on color and motion processing: An ERP study. Manuscript in preparation.

Baizer, J. S., Ungerleider, L. G., & Desimone, R. (1991). Organization of visual inputs to the inferior temporal and posterior parietal cortex in macaques. *Journal of Neuroscience, 11*, 168–190.

Bavelier, D., Tomann, A., Hutton, C., Mitchell, T., Corina, D., Liu, G., & Neville, H. (2000). Visual attention to the periphery is enhanced in congenitally deaf individuals. *J. Neurosci., 20,* 93.

Bavelier, D., Tomann, A., Mitchell, T., Corina, D., Pouget, A., Hutton, C., Liu, G., & Neville, H. (1998). Cortical re-organization for visual functions in congenitally deaf subjects: Part I. Motion processing. *Society for Neuroscience Abstract, 24*(2), 2094.

Berman, N. E. (1991). Alterations of visual cortical connections in cats following early removal of retinal input. *Developmental Brain Research, 63*(1/2), 163–180.

Bosworth, R., & Dobkins, K. (1999). Left hemisphere dominance for motion processing in deaf signers. *Psychological Science, 10,* 256–262.

Cohen, L. G., Celnik, P., Pascual-Leone, A., Corwell, B., Faiz, L., Dambrosia, J., Honda, M., Sadato, N., Gerloff, C., Catála, M. D., & Hallett, M. (1997). Functional relevance of cross-modal plasticity in blind humans. *Nature, 389,* 180–183.

Dehaene, S., Dupoux, E., Mehler, J., Cohen, L., Perani, D., van de Moortele, P.-F., Lehérici, S. P., & Le Bihan, D. (1997). Anatomical variability in the cortical representation of first and second languages. *Neuroreport, 17,* 3809–3815.

Dehay, C., Kennedy, H., & Bullier, J. (1988). Characterization of transient cortical projections from auditory, somatosensory, and motor cortices to visual areas 17, 18, and 19 in the kitten. *The Journal of Comparative Neurology, 272,* 68–89.

Emmorey, K. (1998). The impact of sign language use on visuospatial cognition. In M. Marschark & M. D. Clark (Eds.), *Psychological perspectives on deafness* (Vol. 2, pp. 19–52). Mahwah, NJ: Erlbaum.

Emmorey, K., & Kosslyn, S. (1996). Enhanced image generation abilities in deaf signers: A right hemisphere effect. *Brain and Cognition, 32,* 28–44.

Emmorey, K. D., Kosslyn, S. M., & Bellugi, U. (1993). Visual imagery and visual-spatial language: Enhanced imagery abilities in deaf and hearing ASL signers. *Cognition, 46,* 139–181.

Frost, D. O. (1990). Sensory processing by novel, experimentally induced cross-modal circuits. In A. Diamond (Ed.), *The development and neural bases of higher cognitive function* (pp. 92–112). New York: New York Academy of Sciences Press.

Gilbert, C. D. (1995). Dynamic properties of adult visual cortex. In M. S. Gazzaniga (Ed.), *The cognitive neurosciences* (pp. 73–89). Cambridge, MA: MIT Press.

Huttenlocher, P. R. (1994). Synaptogenesis, synapse elimination, and neural plasticity in human cerebral cortex. In C. A. Nelson (Ed.), *Threats to optimal development: Integrating biological, psychological, and social risk factors* (Vol. 27, pp. 35–54). Hillsdale, NJ: Erlbaum.

Huttenlocher, P. R., & Dabholkar, A. S. (1997). Regional differences in synaptogenesis in human cerebral cortex. *Journal of Comparative Neurology, 387,* 167–178.

Hyvarinen, J., Carlson, S., & Hyvarinen, L. (1981). Early visual deprivation alters modality of neuronal responses in area 19 of monkey cortex. *Neuroscience Letters, 26*(3), 239–243.

Innocenti, G., & Clarke, S. (1984). Bilateral transitory projection to visual areas from auditory cortex in kittens. *Developmental Brain Research, 14,* 143–148.

Kaas, J., Krubitzer, L., Chino, Y., Langston, A., Polley, E., & Blair, N. (1990). Reorganization of retinotopic cortical maps in adult mammals after lesions of the retina. *Science, 248,* 229–231.

Kaas, J. H. (1995). The reorganization of sensory and motor maps in adult mammals. In M. S. Gazzaniga (Ed.), *The cognitive neurosciences* (pp. 51–71). Cambridge, MA: MIT Press.

Kim, K. H. S., Relkin, N. R., Lee, K.-M., & Hirsch, J. (1997). Distinct cortical areas associated with native and second languages. *Nature, 388,* 171–174.

Klima, E. S., & Bellugi, U. (1979). *The signs of language.* Cambridge, MA: Harvard University Press.

Loke, W., & Song, S. (1991). Central and peripheral visual processing in hearing and nonhearing individuals. *Bulletin of the Psychonomic Society, 29,* 437–440.

McKee, D. (1987). *An analysis of specialized cognitive functions in deaf and hearing signers.* Unpublished doctoral dissertation, University of Pittsburgh, Pittsburgh, PA.

Merzenich, M. M., & Jenkins, W. M. (1993). Reorganization of cortical representations of the hand following altrations of skin inputs induced by nerve injury, skin island transfers, and experience. *Journal of Hand Therapy, 6*(2), 89–104.

Merzenich, M., Recanzone, G., Jenkins, W., Allard, T., & Nudo, R. (1988). Cortical representational plasticity. In P. Rakic & W. Singer (Eds.), *Neurobiology of neocortex* (pp. 41–67). New York: John Wiley.

Mills, D. L., Coffey-Corina, S. A., & Neville, H. J. (1993). Language acquisition and cerebral specialization in 20-month-old infants. *Journal of Cognitive Neuroscience, 5*, 317–334.

Mills, D. L., Coffey-Corina, S. A., & Neville, H. J. (1997). Language comprehension and cerebral specialization from 13 to 20 months. *Developmental Neuropsychology, 13*(3), 397–445.

Neville, H. J., & Bavelier, D. (1998).*Variability of developmental plasticity within sensory and language systems: Behavioral, ERP and fMRI studies.* Paper presented at the Proceedings of the NIMH Conference on Advancing Research on Developmental Plasticity: Integrating the Behavioral Science and the Neuroscience of Mental Health, Washington, DC: U.S. Government Printing Office, pp. 174–184.

Neville, H. J., & Bavelier, D. (1999). Specificity and plasticity in neurocognitive development in humans. In M. S. Gazzaniga (Ed.), *The new cognitive neurosciences (2nd ed.*, pp. 83–98). Cambridge, MA: MIT Press.

Neville, H. J., Bavelier, D., Corina, D., Rauschecker, J., Karni, A., Lalwani, A., Braun, A., Clark, V., Jezzard, P., & Turner, R. (1998). Cerebral organization for language in deaf and hearing subjects: Biological constraints and effects of experience. *Proceedings of the National Academy of Science, USA, 95*(3), 922–929.

Neville, H. J., Coffey, S. A., Lawson, D. S., Fischer, A., Emmorey, K., & Bellugi, U. (1997). Neural systems mediating American Sign Language: Effects of sensory experience and age of acquisition. *Brain and Language, 57*, 285–308.

Neville, H. J., & Lawson, D. (1987a). Attention to central and peripheral visual space in a movement detection task: An event-related potential and behavioral study. I. Normal hearing adults. *Brain Research, 405*, 253–267.

Neville, H. J., & Lawson, D. (1987b). Attention to central and peripheral visual space in a movement detection task: An event-related and behavioral study. II. Congenitally deaf adults. *Brain Research, 405*, 268–283.

Neville, H. J., & Lawson, D. (1987c). Attention to central and peripheral visual space in a movement detection task. III. Separate effects of auditory deprivation and acquisition of a visual language. *Brain Research, 405*, 284–294.

Neville, H. J., & Mills, D. (1997). Epigenesis of language. *Mental Retardation and Developmental Disabilities Research Reviews, 3*(4), 282–292.

Neville, H. J., Mills, D., & Lawson, D. (1992). Fractionating language: Different neural subsystems with different sensitive periods. *Cerebral Cortex, 2*, 244–258.

Neville, H. J., Nicol, J., Barss, A., Forster, K., & Garrett, M. (1991). Syntactically based sentence processing classes: Evidence from event-related brain potentials. *Journal of Cognitive Neuroscience, 3*, 155–170.

Nobre, A., & McCarthy, G. (1994). Language-related ERPs: Scalp distributions and modulation by word type and semantic priming. *Journal of Cognitive Neuroscience, 6*, 233–255.

Osterhout, L., McLaughlin, J., & Bersick, M. (1997). Event-related brain potentials and human language. *Trends in Cognitive Sciences, 1*(6), 203–209.

Parasnis, I., & Samar, V. J. (1985). Parafoveal attention in congenitally deaf and hearing young adults. *Brain and Cognition, 4*(3), 313–327.

Perani, D., Dehaene, S., Grassi, F., Cohen, L., Cappa, S. F., Dupoux, E., Fazio, F., & Mehler, J. (1996). Brain processing of native and foreign languages. *Neuroreport, 7*(15–17), 2439–2444.

Rauschecker, J., & Kniepert, U. (1993). Auditory localization behaviour in visually deprived cats. *European Journal of Neuroscience, 6*, 149–160.

Rice, C., Feinstein, S., & Schusterman, R. (1965). Echo-detection ability of the blind: Size and distance factors. *Journal of Experimental Psychology, 70*, 246–251.

Röder, B., Rösler, F., & Hennighausen, E. (1997). Different cortical activation patterns in blind and sighted humans during encoding and transformation of haptic images. *Psychophysiology, 34*, 292–307.

Röder, B., Rösler, F., Hennighausen, E., & Näcker, F. (1996). Event-related potentials during auditory and somatosensory discrimination in sighted and blind human subjects. *Cognitive Brain Research, 4*, 77–93.

Röder, B., Teder-Salejarvi, W., Sterr, A., Rösler, F., Hillyard, S. A., & Neville, H. J. (1997). Auditory-spatial tuning in sighted and blind adults: Behavioral and electrophysiological evidence. *Society for Neuroscience Abstract, 23*(2), 1590.

Sadato, N., Pascual-Leone, A., Grafman, J., Ibanez, V., Deiber, M.-P., Dold, G., & Hallet, M. (1996). Activation of the primary visual cortex by Braille reading in blind subjects. *Nature, 380*, 526–528.

Sharma, J., Angelucci, A., & Sur, M. (2000). Induction of visual orientation modules in auditory cortex. *Nature, 404*, 841–847.

Sur, M., Pallas, S., & Roe, A. (1990). Cross-modal plasticity in cortical development: Differentiation and specification of sensory neocortex. *Trends in Neurosciences, 13*(6), 227–233.

Talbot, K. F., & Haude, R. H. (1993). The relationship between sign language skill and spatial visualization ability: Mental rotation of three-dimensional objects. *Perception in Motor Skills, 77*, 1387–1391.

Thinus-Blanc, C., & Gaunet, F. (1997). Representation of space in blind persons: Vision as a spatial sense? *Psychological Bulletin, 121*(1), 20–42.

Uhl, F., Franzen, P., Lindinger, G., Lang, W., & Deecke, L. (1991). On the functionality of the visually deprived occipital cortex in early blind persons. *Neuroscience Letters, 124*, 256–259.

Uhl, F., Kretschmer, T., Lindinger, G., Goldenberg, G., Lang, W., Oder, W., & Deecke, L. (1994). Tactile mental imagery in sighted persons and in patients suffering from peripheral blindness early in life. *Electroencephalography and Clinical Neurophysiology, 91*, 249–255.

Veraart, C., DeVolder, A., Wanet-Defalque, M., Bol, A., Michel, C., & Goffinet, A. (1990). Glucose utilization in human visual cortex is abnormally elevated in blindness of early onset but decreased in blindness of late onset. *Brain Research, 510*, 115–121.

von Melchner, L., Pallas, S. L., & Sur, M. (2000). Visual behavior mediated by retinal projections directed to the auditory pathway. *Nature, 404*, 871–876.

Wanet-Defalque, M., Veraart, C., DeVolder, A., Metz, R., Michel, C., Dooms, G., & Goffinet, A. (1988). High metabolic activity in the visual cortex of early blind human subjects. *Brain Research, 446*, 369–373.

Weber-Fox, C., & Neville, H. J. (1996). Maturational constraints on functional specializations for language processing: ERP and behavioral evidence in bilingual speakers. *Journal of Cognitive Neuroscience, 8*(3), 231–256.

Howard M. Lenhoff
Oligario Perales
Gregory S. Hickok

19

CHAPTER

Preservation of a Normally Transient Critical Period in a Cognitively Impaired Population: Window of Opportunity for Acquiring Absolute Pitch in Williams Syndrome

☐ Introduction

Cognitively impaired individuals may provide new avenues for the study of the dynamics of brain development and plasticity by preserving an essential, intermediate, and time-dependent "critical period" of the immature brain that no longer operates or operates differently in mature normal individuals. Until recently, most studies with various cognitively impaired populations have been concerned with defining, localizing, and quantifying diminished cognitive functions in those individuals. In contrast, we provide evidence that in the cognitively impaired individuals having Williams syndrome (WS; Williams, Barratt-Boyes, & Lowe, 1961), the brain preserves a unique transient critical period of its development, the window of opportunity which allows normal individuals to acquire with musical training up through the age of 6 the trait of absolute pitch (AP). AP is the rare ability present in 1/10,000 (Bachem, 1955; Takeuchi & Hulse, 1993) normal individuals in Western cultures to identify a wide range of specific musical tones (Baggaley, 1974; Ward, 1999).

We came to that conclusion from our research quantifying AP abilities in individuals with WS, people having an average IQ of about 55 who share a common microdeletion of about 20 genes in the q11.23 region of one of their two chromosomes number 7 (Ewart et al., 1993). Our research (a) suggests that people with WS have a higher incidence of AP than do normal individuals; (b) demonstrates that they score higher in tests for AP than do highly trained normal musicians who claim to have AP; and (c) shows that they can acquire AP at an age when normal people can no longer do so (Lenhoff, Perales, & Hickok, 2001).

In this chapter, we deal with the following topics: (a) The nature of WS; (b) musical interests and abilities of people with WS; (c) experiments on AP: participants, methods, and results; (d) interpretation of results of studies on AP; (e) brain plasticity: critical period for acquiring AP remains open in people with WS older than age 6; (f) whether people with WS are born with AP; (g) the possible role of genes; (h) brain and AP; (i) who is considered musically intelligent; and (j) mental asymmetries and uncovered intelligences of others labeled as "mentally retarded." Lastly, we provide an addendum that may prove useful to those interested in pursuing research in cognition with the cognitively impaired.

☐ The Nature of Williams Syndrome

The congenital condition called Williams syndrome (for review see Lenhoff et al., 1997) was first described in 1961. Individuals with the syndrome are estimated to make up 1/20,000 of the population; about 4,000 have been identified in the United States and 500 in Canada (this information was supplied in 1999 by the Williams Syndrome Association, USA, and the Canadian Association for Williams Syndrome). Ewart et al. (1993) found that WS was caused by a microdeletion in one of the two chromosomes number 7, regardless of whether it was of maternal or paternal origin. Most people with WS share a number of traits: an average IQ of 55 and weak academic and cognitive skills (Bellugi, Klima, & Wang, 1996), such as in simple arithmetic and in visual closure and spatial tasks (Crisco, Dobbs, & Mulhern, 1988). They are considered to have a short attention span for most cognitive tasks, but not for music related activities. Their facial features (e.g., broad forehead, upturned "pug" nose, depressed nasal bridge, wide mouth with full lips, small chin with receding jaw) are often called elf-like and compared to those of the elves or pixies of folklore (Lenhoff, 1999). Common physical and medical defects include heart problems of varying degrees of severity, early feeding and sleeping difficulties, and delays in motor development (Udwin & Yule, 1991).

They are generally viewed as friendly, outgoing, and loquacious (Von Arnim & Engel, 1964), with an intense desire to please those whom they know. Some are good storytellers (Reilly, Klima, & Bellugi, 1990) and possess relatively good language abilities compared to others with a similar average IQ (Bellugi, Klima, & Wang, 1996). They perform well on face recognition tasks and on tasks requiring recall of verbal material (Udwin & Yule, 1991). Most exhibit hyperacusis: they find relatively loud sounds uncomfortable and/or painful (Klein, Armstrong, Greer, & Brown, 1990; Van Borsel, Curfs, & Fryns, 1997).

☐ Musical Interests and Abilities of People With WS

The musical interests of children with WS were noticed as early as 1964 (Von Arnim & Engel, 1964). In subsequent years sporadic mentions were made of these special interests. But having musical interests and abilities was not considered one of their shared traits until after 1990, when a newly diagnosed 35-year-old musician with WS performed before WS researchers. Shortly thereafter, a group of parents formed a yearly week-long music camp for individuals with WS. Since then, reports by teachers and parents regarding the musicality of people with WS have become more and more common

(Lenhoff, 1998; Stambaugh, 1997). They noted that people with WS showed unusually long attention spans for listening to and participating in musical activities; surprising abilities in AP and relative pitch (RP), in rhythm, and in retention of melodies and lyrics over long periods; and a facility for harmonizing, improvising, composing, and performing.

In the past few years there have been three empirical reports on the musical abilities of individuals with WS. The first was described in the 1997 dissertation of Audrey Don of the University of Ontario (see also Don, Schellenberg, & Rourke, 1999). After investigating the language and music skills of 19 children with WS (ages 8–13), Don concluded that the children have relatively intact musical abilities "commensurate with their relatively strong receptive vocabulary." She also observed that the children with WS who participated in her study showed a relatively intense interest in music. As one child with WS told her, "Music is my favorite way of thinking" (Don, 1997).

The results of a survey returned by over 200 out of 388 parents of children with WS confirm reports that children with WS are more interested in listening to music, singing, and dancing than their siblings who are closest in age, and that these differences in interest are statistically significant, with $P < 0.001$ in all cases (Sandeen, Levine, and Lenhoff, 2000).

Another study described as preliminary by the authors (Levitin & Bellugi, 1998) deals with rhythm. It concluded that children with WS achieved accuracy scores equivalent to those of the normal comparison group and demonstrated equivalent abilities in change of meter and in maintenance of beat.

Research regarding the musical abilities of people with WS is still in its infancy. Lacking have been rigorous investigations for a number of measures of musicality, such as pitch, rhythm, timbre, harmony, composition, retention, and recall. In the study reported here we deal with aspects of AP (Lenhoff, Perales, and Hickok, 2001). Not described in this chapter are our studies in RP, recall and transposition. Those results and further details of our AP studies will be reported in a specialty journal.

Our work on pitch was made possible after we found a sufficient number of people with WS who could participate in research on AP by being able to name musical notes and associate them with tones.

☐ Absolute Pitch: Participants, Methods, and Results

Cognitive and Musical Background of the Participants

All of the participants were determined to have WS by either physicians or geneticists or by the FISH test for the elastin gene. Four of the five had been placed in segregated special education classes because they were considered cognitively impaired by their local school psychologists. All were allowed to take some classes with the non-special-education students, usually in music. WS 17 was placed in a normal classroom for his 3rd year in high school. WS 13, the youngest, has always attended regular school classes as a special needs student who was given extra help as required, such as taking modified tests and in organizational skills.

WS 13 was raised in a musical family and began his formal musical training at age 6. He is proficient in the "fixed Do" solfege method. WS 17 was raised in a musical family and began formal piano lessons at age 7. He learns by ear and can name the musical notes. WS 19 was raised in a family of five that was not musical, except for a sister who took piano and clarinet lessons and who taught WS 19 to name musical notes. WS 21's parents enjoyed music, but were not musical. At age 12 he started to play the acoustic guitar and devised his own method for tuning it. He likes singing and composing country music. He plays by ear and can name the musical notes. WS 43's parents enjoyed music, but were not musical. At age 11, she started classical voice lessons, learning by ear. At age 18 she started to play the accordion seriously. In 1996 WS 43 learned to name the natural notes, and in 1998, the accidental notes.

Because our primary interest was in comparing the quantified abilities in AP of individuals with WS versus those of normal individuals possessing AP, we decided to use the results presented in a meta-analysis of data obtained in a number of studies published from 1970 through 1971 on individuals, most of whom were well-trained musicians, claiming to possess AP.

We did not attempt to use normal individuals of comparable ages and musical training to our WS participants because we believe that "age" is a meaningless term when dealing with cognitively impaired individuals. Chronological age does not make sense for this study, and mental age regarding musical abilities is simply not defined or measurable. Similarly, it would be difficult to find comparable musical training for WS people, especially because most do not know how to name musical notes, and even a fewer number can read music. In addition, because of their congenital poor motor control, their lack of finger dexterity, and in some cases, inflexibility of the forearm caused by a fused radius and ulnus, their musical abilities in performance on a wide number of instruments is significantly limited.

Nonetheless, we did select a small group of individuals as a control group, primarily to make certain that our testing procedures were acceptable. These controls were especially useful in helping us to evaluate the tests for RP. Accordingly, we tested six university graduates. Four of them ranged from no musical training to moderate musical training. The two participants in the second group had graduate training in music and were working for Master of Fine Arts degrees.

Methods

For consistency, only the second author administered and recorded the testing sessions. All sessions were recorded using a Sony Walkman, Professional WM-D3. They lasted no more than an hour at a time so as not to tire the participants; it usually took 3 days to administer a full set of tests. Recently tuned pianos and various keyboards set for piano tones were used for all tests.

For all randomization procedures, we used Psyscope, a MacIntosh-based program developed by Carnegie Mellon University (J. D. Cohen, MacWhinney, Flatt, & Provost, 1993). For our calculations, a correct answer was given one point. Following the rationale described by Baharloo, Johnston, Service, Gitschier, and Freimer (1998), an answer that was off a semitone was given 3/4th of a point, whereas answers off by a full tone or more were given zero points.

Key Experiments and Results

All five WS participants who could name musical notes and associate them with tones performed at or near the ceiling on tests of AP. They averaged 97.5% correct on a range of tests of AP comprising over 1,000 trials. One series of tasks tested the WS participants' ability to identify natural notes, accidental notes, mixed natural and accidental notes in octave 4, and, in addition, mixed natural and accidental notes in octaves 2 through 6 (Figure 19.1, far-left bar). Their average performance on these tasks was 97% correct. In a second series of tasks testing their ability to identify the individual natural notes

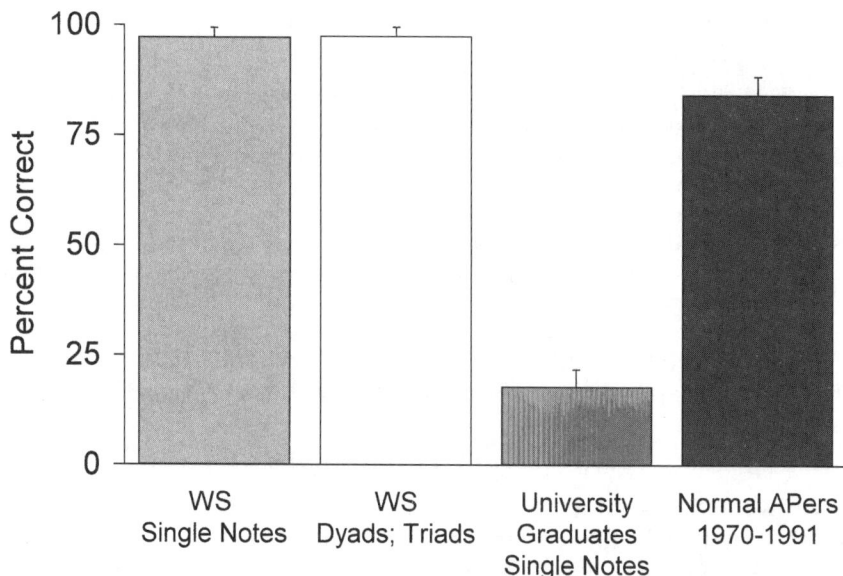

Figure 19.1. Percent correct answers in tests for AP. Far-left bar: Single-note tests of individuals with WS. Middle left bar: Identifying notes in dyads and triads by individuals with WS. Middle right bar: Single-note tests of university graduates. Far-right bar: Meta-analysis findings for normal musicians with AP (APers). The vertical lines represent standard error. For all randomization procedures, we used the program Psyscope, developed at Carnegie Mellon University (J. D. Cohen, MacWhinney, Flatt, & Provost, 1993).

presented simultaneously in sets of two (dyads) or three (triads) under a variety of conditions, the five WS participants as a group averaged 98% correct (Figure 19.1, middle left bar).

The WS participants scored much higher than the six normal university graduates we tested (including the two with graduate training in music), who averaged 18% correct (Figure 19.1, middle right bar).

☐ Interpretation of Results of Studies on AP

Exceptional Abilities in AP

Our results demonstrate that despite limitations in many areas of cognition, the five people with WS in this study scored extremely well in over 1,000 trials for AP, averaging as a group close to 98% correct. Their overall score compares favorably not only to those of our control participants, who scored 18%, but also to the performance of normal individuals who are trained musicians and who claim to possess AP; as a group, these latter individuals scored 84.3% correct on tests for AP using piano or synthesized piano tones. This latter score was determined from data summarized in a meta-analysis of studies of AP reported between 1970 and 1991 (Takeuchi & Hulse, 1993). Thus, our results clearly demonstrate that an exceptional musical talent can be developed in spite of limitations in other cognitive domains, suggesting some degree of modularity in cognitive development in WS.

Results not Altered by Familiarity With Timbre of Piano

Because all of the tests involved tones produced by a piano or an electronic keyboard set to piano tones, there existed the possibility that the WS participants' expertise in absolute pitch could have been facilitated by their familiarity with the timbre of the piano tones. This possibility was eliminated when all the participants showed great skills in another test, the production recall task. For this task the WS participants were asked to and were able to recall the melodies of a number of pieces by singing the correct names of the notes of those melodies instead of the lyrics. Because they produced the correct notes by singing them and not by identifying piano tones, those results, besides demonstrating that the WS participants possessed excellent tonal memory, including memory of the relationships between pitch and the duration of the tones, also showed clearly that they did not get cued to the correct notes in the tests for AP by their familiarity with the timbre and characteristics of the piano and keyboard tones (Lenhoff, Perales, & Hickok, 2001).

Higher Than Normal Incidence of AP Among People With WS

The results of the AP studies also provide evidence that the incidence of AP in people with WS is much higher than among the normal population. It is generally accepted that the incidence of AP among normal individuals in Western countries is 1/10,000 (Takeuchi & Hulse, 1993); in some Eastern countries, such as Japan, the incidence is thought to be somewhat higher, possibly because Japanese children start musical training earlier (Miyazaki, 1988) or because some Asian populations speak in multitonal languages, such as Vietnamese or Mandarin (Deutsch, Henthorn, & Dolson, 1999).

We emphasize that the five WS participants in this study are the only people with WS we have evaluated for AP thus far. They were selected because they were some of the very few who were able to assign verbal names to musical tones, a requisite for the identification tasks for AP. We literally had to travel to the four corners of the United States and Canada to find and test them. Most musicians with WS learn by listening and are not able to identify notes; only a few are known to be able to read musical notation.

Thus, because each of the five WS participants in our study possesses AP, the incidence of AP in the WS population appears to be greater than that found in the general population. This conclusion is based on the fact that the five were selected from the known population of 4,500 people with WS in Canada and the United States, the pool in which we found them. Thus, even if we made the highly conservative assumption that the five individuals with WS in our study were the only people with WS with AP in the United States and Canada, the incidence of AP in that population would be about 1/1,000, which is more than 10 times greater than that presumed to exist in the population of normal individuals in Western countries.

We presume that the incidence of AP in the WS population is higher, and that presumption is testable. As more and more people with WS begin to study music and learn to name the notes and eventually are tested, we venture to guess that the incidence of AP in the WS population will be closer to 1/10 or higher.

☐ Brain Plasticity: Critical Period for Acquiring AP Remains Open in WS People Older Than Age 6

If normal individuals possess AP, it is generally assumed that those individuals gained the ability by having been trained in music some time before and up to the age of 6 (Takeheuchi & Hulse, 1993). Brady (1970), Sergeant and Roche (1973), and Sloboda

(1985) have stated that AP is best learned at an early age and that it becomes more difficult to learn AP as one gets past the age of 6. Recent data indicating "that there is a correlation between early musical training and the development of AP" was recently presented by Baharloo et al. (1998). They asked 612 classically trained musicians the age at which they first started formal music lessons. Of those starting before age 4, 40% reported having AP, whereas only 3% of those who began after age 9 claimed to have AP. Furthermore, although musicians at most ages can gain abilities in RP, they cannot gain AP once they are older, no matter how much they try. Even such eminent composers as Berlioz, Schumann, Wagner, Tchaikovsky, Ravel, and Stravinsky did not possess AP (Langendorf, 1992).

Other auditory abilities appear to be age related, such as the ability to acquire rather complex accents in foreign languages. For example, German natives can come to the United States as young adults, learn to speak English, and gain an immense vocabulary, and yet the large majority of them will speak English with a German accent for the rest of their lives. If, however, a member of that German family had arrived at the age of 5–8 years, he or she could be expected to lose the German accent.

More recently Deutsch et al. (1999) have claimed that the learning of multitonal languages, such as Vietnamese and Mandarin, is best done when the individual is very young. Further, they suggested that the ability to learn multitonal languages is related to an innate ability to possess absolute musical pitch, although she provides no tests for musical pitch in her preliminary report.

Therefore, we propose that a part or parts of the brain of individuals with WS may be altered in such a way that it has preserved into adulthood a critical period, that is, the "window of opportunity" usually associated with young normal children that allows them to acquire AP. In support of this hypothesis, all five WS participants in our study possess absolute pitch, and four of the five began their relatively serious study of music from about the age of 7 or older; one started music lessons at age 6.

Additional support comes from observing our 43-year-old participant (WS 43), who at age 42 learned to name the natural notes and associate them with the correct musical tones. Only during the course of this study, at age 43, did she acquire the ability to name, identify, and produce the correct accidental notes. For a normal musician to learn to name notes at such an age and then identify and produce the correct musical tones would be highly unlikely.

We have been told by many parents and teachers that they feel other children with WS have AP. But, because those children have never learned to name those notes, they have not been tested quantitatively for AP as well as for other aspects of musicality. Most parents and music teachers of children with WS find those children to be natural musicians who can learn easily and quickly by listening. On the other hand, if one tries to teach the musician with WS the names of the musical notes, chords, and other cognitive features of music using the same methods used with normal students, it tends to confuse and frustrate them and takes away the pleasure they had for learning and performing music.

Through suitable teaching techniques that take these matters into account, it may be possible for musicians with WS to learn to name the musical notes, as did WS 43 at age 42. Then they, too, may test positively for AP.

☐ Are WS People Born With AP?

Is what we are observing an ability that people with WS have had since birth but that only became recognizable later in life, after they had learned to associate verbal labels with musical tones? That interesting possibility would be difficult to prove. From the available evidence and from examples in the literature, we conclude that in regard to AP, people with WS are like normal people with one major difference. Like normal people, people with WS are born with the critical period giving them the ability to gain AP with musical training up to and including the age of 6. With people with WS, however, the microdeletion affects their brain development in such a way that the critical period, the window of opportunity for acquiring AP, remains open much longer, probably into adulthood. Thus, people with WS, again with the requisite musical training, can gain AP, but significantly after the age of 6.

Further, it seems reasonable and eventually testable that the part(s) of the brain related to auditory functions, such as recognition of timbre, accents, multitonal languages, and rhythm, as well as the retention of auditory information, also remain open in people with WS. At present the evidence is anecdotal, as was the evidence previously with AP. But as with AP, it should be possible to test and quantify those other auditory functions in people with WS.

☐ Possible Role of Genes in AP

WS is caused by a microdeletion in the q11.23 region of one of the pair of chromosomes number 7. Approximately 20 genes are believed to be missing, and most of them are currently identified (see, e.g., Meng et al., 1998). Consequently, individuals with WS would appear to offer a genetically homogeneous population for the study of how specific genes may account for many of their physical and behavioral characteristics. The microdeletion of an elastin gene, for example, can be correlated with arterial, lung, and intestinal problems in people with WS.

Does the high incidence of AP in people with WS, a population that shares a common microdeletion of about 20 identified genes, provide any basis for thinking that 1 gene is responsible for AP, and does it give clues to the identity of that gene? If we were to make such an assumption about people with WS, it would be difficult to show that they can acquire AP because of only 1 of the 20 genes that are hemizygous as a result of the microdeletion. With normal people who have AP, it could be projected that a hemizygosity of any 1 of those same 20 genes might account for their ability to acquire AP. In such a scenario one would expect normal possessors of AP to demonstrate a specific hemizygosity for one of the genes in the q23.11 region of their chromosome number 7. That has not been demonstrated.

A more plausible alternative would be that the hemizygous condition of one or more of the missing genes affects the development of parts of the brain of people with WS, perhaps the parts dealing with specific auditory phenomena, so that they retain for a long period the ability to acquire AP. One of those genes, LIM Kinase 1 (LIMK1), is known to affect brain development in mice. It appears that the LIMK1 affects the assembly of actin fibers in neurons. Some propose that LIMK1 is responsible for some of the cognitive deficits of people with WS (Frangiskakis et al., 1996). It also might be possible that LIMK1 alters the development of nerve cells in the part of the brain in people with WS that deals with their musical abilities. One region of the brain, the left planum temporale, described in the following section, could be a candidate.

We do not postulate that the ability to acquire AP is determined either directly by specific genes or by stimuli from the environment, such as musical training. Instead, we propose that the changes in the brain of people with WS associated with the microdeletion may preserve the critical period (see, e.g., A. Cohen & Baird, 1990), giving people with WS the ability to gain absolute pitch, but that this ability will not develop unless the person with WS is exposed to music and musical training. Further, it goes without saying that people with WS have about 100,000 other genes, and these also may affect the degree of their abilities in music, just as they do with normal individuals.

☐ Brain and AP

What is known about the brain of those with WS and about the parts of the brain in normal individuals involved in auditory functions? Will such information provide clues in regard to the abilities of people with WS in AP?

The average brain size of people with WS is about 80% that of the normal-size human brain (Jernigan, Bellugi, Sowell, Doherty, & Hesselink, 1993), accounting in part for a number of their cognitive deficits. Their brains may be smaller because of developmental anomalies resulting from the hemizygous condition of some of the 20 or so genes affected by the microdeletion in chromosome 7. As mentioned above, one candidate is LIM-kinase 1, a gene known to affect brain development in other mammals. Another might be STX1A, which encodes a component of the synaptic apparatus.

Despite the relatively smaller size of the brain of people with WS, there are clues that individuals with WS may have certain preserved brain areas that might influence their musical abilities. Those clues stem from the work of Schlaug, Jancke, Huang, and Steinmetz (1995), who showed that the left planum temporale is enlarged in musicians having AP. Although that observation appears promising, there is a question of the role played by the left planum temporale in AP (Zatorre, Perry, Beckett, Westbury, & Evans, 1998).

Similar preliminary observations of asymmetries in the sizes of the left and right planum temporale in people with Williams syndrome were announced in a Letter to the Editor by Hickok, Bellugi, & Jones (1995). They observed that MRIs of the brains of a few individuals with WS showed an enlarged or preserved left planum temporale similar to those reported by Schlaug and his colleagues (1995) in trained musicians. Hickok et al. (1995) did not elaborate on their findings, however, because at the time they obtained their brain images, they had no quantitative information about the musical abilities of the people with WS analyzed in their MRI studies. With our methods of quantifying AP in people with WS now described, it seems worthwhile to expand and reevaluate MRI studies of the brains of people with WS to see if the size of the left planum temporale correlates with the ability to possess AP.

Finally, the WS population, relatively homogeneous genetically because they share a common microdeletion, may serve as a more productive model for investigating the structures and processes associated with AP than others reported to have a relatively high incidence of AP, such as some blind (Oakes, 1955) and some autistic (Treffert, 1989) individuals.

☐ Who Is Considered Musically Intelligent?

In our culture, psychologists, educators, and the public label as "mentally retarded" or "cognitively impaired" individuals whose social skills do not fit the accepted norm and who do not score well on IQ and related tests, that is, on tests designed to show skills considered normal in problem solving and spatial and visual relationships. On the other hand, that people with WS have such strengths in AP supports the view that they have a musical intelligence, as defined by Gardner (1983), in regard to pitch.

Geschwind (1984) challenges us to consider how a society in which musical skills are considered the norm would treat individuals of normal or above normal intelligence who were not musical. His example is a girls' school taught by Antonio Vivaldi in which everyone was expected to be talented and immersed in music. There, a "dysmusical" individual would be considered inept and a failure at the single activity considered most important. Perhaps, Geschwind proposed, like many of the mentally retarded in today's society (including the highly talented musicians with WS), this individual would be reminded frequently of her lack of musical abilities and probably be assigned to cleaning and cooking chores.

Geschwind (1984) also reminded us that a talented musician needs a brain capable of performing remarkable feats of neural computation. Gardner (1983) defined pitch, timbre, and rhythm as major components of musical intelligence. We demonstrate that cognitively impaired musicians with WS possess such a musical intelligence with regard to pitch, and we believe that with time, research will show that people with WS possess a high level of musical intelligence with regard to timbre and rhythm. Levitin and Bellugi (1998) have already provided some promising preliminary evidence regarding the abilities of WS people with rhythm.

☐ Do Mental Asymmetries and Uncovered Intelligences of Others Labeled as "Mentally Retarded" Offer an Approach for Investigating Phases of Brain Development?

The findings with the WS participants should raise questions about the understanding of other populations of the cognitively impaired. Once researchers learn how to ask questions that are understandable to individuals of those populations (see the addendum), as we have done with our participants with WS, they too may find previously undescribed peaks in their cognitive profiles. Accordingly, the term "mentally asymmetric" may describe more accurately and objectively the cognitive abilities of populations considered mentally retarded (Lenhoff, 1995). Scholars are only now beginning to learn of the strengths and potentials of those mentally asymmetric populations who until recently have been studied primarily for their cognitive deficits.

In addition, analogous to the rationale by which biochemical geneticists investigated an array of bacterial mutants to uncover many sequential metabolic pathways, the investigation of the behaviors of the cognitively impaired may give similarly revealing results. Specifically, by discovering and measuring quantifiable cognitive behaviors in individuals representing an array of genetic populations of the mentally asymmetric, cognitive scientists may uncover sequential patterns of development of specific regions of the human brain.

☐ Addendum: Some Difficulties in Conducting Quantitative Research With the Cognitively Impaired

We believe that at least two major obstacles impede quantitative research with the cognitively impaired: (a) There is a relative scarcity of potential research participants; (b) available methods of testing, which were developed primarily for individuals of normal or greater than normal intelligence, do not fit the cognitive profiles of the mentally handicapped.

Scarcity of "Qualified" Participants

As various cognitively impaired populations are being newly defined and their impairments pinpointed as related to specific genetic or chromosomal conditions, it is becoming apparent that most of these conditions occur in relatively small numbers of individuals. Furthermore, because many of these conditions have been identified only recently, many individuals having those congenital genetic or chromosomal conditions have yet to be identified or have been diagnosed incorrectly. Such is the case with WS, which was first reported in 1961. Only in the last 5 or 6 years, primarily because of the discovery of the microdeletion in 1993 and the interest of the media in the personality and musicality of people with WS, have physicians, professionals, and the public become aware of the syndrome. Even with current publicity, there are about 4,500 people with WS identified in Canada and the United States.

Hence, one should not expect specialized research with the cognitively impaired to involve very large populations of participants. It is noteworthy that in research on AP among "normal" populations, music cognition researchers usually seek participants from conservatories and university music classes, and usually in relatively small numbers compared to the numbers that are available.

Inadequate Testing Methods

The cognitive limits of individuals born with various kinds of brain damage may make them unsuitable participants for a number of behavioral research projects. For example, because in-depth and quantitative research on AP requires that the participants be able to name the musical notes and link those names to musical tones, it was difficult to find many WS participants to test. Of the 4,500 individuals in Canada and the United States known to have WS, those actively involved in music learn primarily by listening; most cannot name the musical notes, and only a few are known to be able to read musical notation. Among those showing musical skills, we found and tested five individuals who were able to associate verbal labels with musical notes.

To devise tests that could be comprehended by the WS participants, we found it necessary first to get a better understanding of the behavior and thought processes of people with WS in general, and particularly of those participating in this investigation. This was time consuming; it varied with each participant and with the type of pitch studies we carried out.

In addition, we also had to become aware of some of the behavioral peculiarities of people with WS and modify our testing procedures accordingly. For example, individuals with WS make a major effort to please people. They will cooperate with investigators they like and less so with those they suspect. On the other hand, their desire to please may lead them to twist their answers in a way (rightly or wrongly) that they believe will please an investigator they admire. Frequently the eyes of the WS participant will be glued to those of the investigator, partly because they want to detect if their answers please that person. A perceptive investigator will not fall into this trap and will show approval equally for both correct and incorrect answers.

We noted that our participants had difficulty in understanding the differences between such comparisons as "same" or "different," "higher" or "lower," and "more" or "less." These problems were similar to those encountered by other researchers trying to assess pitch discrimination in young normal children (Andrews & Madeira, 1977). Further, although the five WS participants were able to recognize differences in pitch, the concepts regarding musical intervals, such as a major third or perfect fifth, were foreign to most of them. Therefore, we needed to devise custom-made tests, terminology, and questions.

☐ Acknowledgments

We thank Dr. Steven Brown for his perceptive comments, Drs. Joseph Young and Christopher Shaw for their encouragement, and Sylvia G. Lenhoff and Rebecca Jane Simpson for their superb editorial help. Supported by the National Science Foundation, Division of Human Perception and Cognition (SBR-9617078), and by the Bernon Family Fund. Dedicated to the memory of K. S. Lashley, who, like the senior author (H.M.L.), began his research career investigating the fresh-water hydra.

☐ References

Andrews, M. L., & Madeira, S. S. (1977). The measurement of pitch discrimination ability in young children. *Journal of Speech and Hearing Disorders, XLII*, 279–286.

Bachem, A. (1955). Absolute pitch. *Journal of the Acoustical Society of America, 27*, 1180–1185.

Baggaley, J. (1974). Measurement of absolute pitch. *Psychology of Music, 22*, 11–17.

Baharloo, S., Johnston, P. A., Service, S. K., Gitschier, J., & Freimer, N. B. (1998). Absolute pitch: An approach for identification of genetic and nongenetic components. *American Journal of Human Genetics, 62*, 224–231.

Bellugi, U., Klima, E. S., & Wang, P. P. (1996). Cognitive and neural development clues from genetically based syndromes. In D. Magnusson (Ed.), *The Lifespan Development of Individuals: Behavioral, Neurobiological, and Psychosocial Perspectives: A Synthesis* (pp. 223–243). New York: Cambridge University Press.

Brady, P. T. (1970). The genesis of absolute pitch. *Journal of the Acoustical Society of America, 48*, 883–887.

Cohen, A., & Baird, K. (1990). Acquisition of absolute pitch: The question of critical periods. *Psychomusicology, 9*, 31–37.

Cohen, J. D., MacWhinney, B., Flatt, M., & Provost, J. (1993). A new graphic interactive environment for designing psychology experiments. *Behavioral Research Methods, Instruments, and Computers, 25*, 257–271.

Crisco, J. J., Dobbs, J. M., & Mulhern, R. K. (1988). Cognitive processing of children with Williams syndrome. *Developmental Medicine & Child Neurology, 30* (5), 650–656.

Deutsch, D., Henthorn, T., & Dolson, M. (1999, April). *Abstract 4pPP5: Absolute pitch is demonstrated in speakers of tone languages.* Presented at the 138th Meeting of the Acoustical Society of America, Columbus, OH.

Don, A. J. (1997). *Auditory pattern perception in children with Williams syndrome.* Unpublished doctoral dissertation, University of Windsor, Windsor, ON, Canada.

Don, A. J., Schellenberg, E. G., & Rourke, B. P. (1999). Music and language skills of children with Williams syndrome. *Child Neuropsychology, 5*, 154–170.

Ewart, A. K., Morris, C. A., Atkinson, D., Jin, W., Sternes, K., Spallone, P., Stock, A. D., Leppert, M., & Keating, M. T. (1993). Hemizygosity at the elastin locus in a developmental disorder, Williams syndrome. *Nature Genetics, 5*, 11–16.

Frangiskakis, J. M., Ewart, A. K., Morris , C., Mervis, C. B., Bertrand, J., Robinson, B. F., Klein, B. P., Ensing, G. J., Everett, L. A., Green, E. D., Prosche, C., Gutowski, N. J., Noble, M., Atkinson, D. L., Odelberg, S. J., & Keating, M. T. (1996). LIM-Kinase 1 hemizygosity implicated in impaired visuospatial constructive cognition. *Cell, 86*, 59–69.

Gardner, H. (1983). *Frames of mind: The theory of multiple intelligences*. New York: Basic Books.

Geschwind, N. (1984). The brain of learning-disabled individual. *Annals of Dyslexia, 34*, 319–327.

Hickok, G., Bellugi, U., & Jones, W. (1995). Asymmetrical abilities. *Science, 270*, 219–220.

Jernigan, T. L., Bellugi, U., Sowell, E., Doherty, S., & Hesselink, J. (1993). Cerebral morphologic distinctions between Williams and Down syndromes. *Archives of Neurology, 50*, 186–191.

Klein, A. J., Armstrong, B. L., Greer, M. K., Brown, F. R., III. (1990). Hyperacusis and otitis media in individuals with Williams syndrome. *Journal of Speech and Hearing Disorders, 55*(2), 339–444.

Langendorf, F. (1992). Absolute pitch: Review and speculations. *Medical Problems of Performing Arts, 7*(1), 6–13.

Lenhoff, H. M. (1995). Mentally asymmetric. *Ability Network, 3*(3), 15–16.

Lenhoff, H. M. (1998). Insights into the musical potential of cognitively impaired people diagnosed with Williams syndrome. *Music Therapy Perspectives, 16*, 32–35.

Lenhoff, H. M. (1999). Real world source for the "Little People": The relationship of fairies to individuals with Williams syndrome. In G. Westfahl & G. Slusser (Eds.), *Nursery realms: Children in the worlds of science fiction, fantasy and horror* (pp. 150–160). Athens, GA: University of Georgia Press.

Lenhoff, H. M., Perales, O., & Hickok, G. S. (2001). Quantification of absolute pitch in Williams Syndrome. *Music Perception*. In Press.

Lenhoff, H. M., Wang, P. P., Greenberg, P., & Bellugi, U. (1997). Williams syndrome and the brain. *Scientific American, 26*, 42–47.

Levitin, D. J., & Bellugi, U. (1998). Musical abilities in individuals with Williams Syndrome. *Music Perception, 15*, 357–389.

Meng, X., Lu, X., Li, Z., Green, E. D., Massa, H., Trask, B. J., Morris, C. A., & Keating, M. T. (1998). Complete physical map of the common deletion region in Williams syndrome and identification and characterization of three novel genes. *Human Genetics, 103*, 590–599.

Miyazaki, K. (1988). Musical pitch identification by absolute pitch possessors. *Perception & Psychophysics, 44*, 501–512.

Reilly, J., Klima, E. S., & Bellugi, U. (1990). Once more with feeling: Affect and language in atypical populations. *Development and Psychopathology, 2*, 367–391.

Oakes, W. F. (1955). An experimental study of pitch naming and pitch discrimination reactions. *Journal of General Psychology, 86*, 237–259.

Sandeen, B., Levine, L., & Lenhoff, H. M. (in preparation). *Parents' perceptions of the musical interests and abilities of their children with Williams Syndrome*. Manuscript in preparation.

Sergeant, D., & Roche, S. (1973). Perceptual shifts in the auditory information processing of young children. *Psychology of Music, 1*, 39–48.

Schlaug, G., Jancke, L., Huang, Y., & Steinmetz, H. (1995). In vivo evidence of structural brain asymmetry in musicians. *Science, 267*, 699–701.

Sloboda, J. A. (1985) *The musical mind*. Oxford, England: Clarendon Press.

Stambaugh, L. (1996). Special learners with special abilities. *Music Educators Journal, 83*, 19–23.

Takeuchi, A. H., & Hulse, S. H. (1993). Absolute pitch. *Psychological Bulletin, 113*, 345–361.

Treffert, D. A. (1989). *Extraordinary people: Understanding "idiot savants."* New York: Harper & Row.

Udwin, O., Davies, M., & Howlin, P. (1996). A longitudinal study of cognitive abilities and educational attainment in Williams syndrome. *Developmental Medicine and Child Neurology, 38*, 1020–1029.

Van Borsel, J., Curfs, L. M., & Fryns, J. P. (1997). Hyperacusis in Williams syndrome: A sample survey study. *Centrum voor Gehoor-en Spraakrevalidatie, 8*, 121–126.

Von Arnim, G., & Engel, P. (1964). Mental retardation related to hypercalcaemia. *Developmental Medicine and Child Neurology, 6*, 336–377.

Ward, W. D. (1999). Absolute pitch. In D. Deutsch (Ed.), *The psychology of music*. San Diego, CA: Academic Press.

Williams, J. C. P., Barratt-Boyes, B. G., & Lowe, J. B. (1961). Supravalvular aortic stenosis. *Circulation, 24*, 1311–1318.

Zatorre, R. J., Perry, D. W., Beckett, C. A., Westbury, C. F., & Evans, A. C. (1998). Functional anatomy of musical processing in listeners with absolute pitch and relative pitch. *Proceedings of the National Academy of Sciences, 95*, 3172–3177.

20

CHAPTER

Timothy Bredy
Ian Weaver
Francis C. Champagne
Michael J. Meaney

Stress, Maternal Care, and Neural Development in the Rat

☐ Introduction

Development proceeds as a constant interaction between environmental and genetic factors. These gene-environment interactions result not only in growth, but also in adaptation; long-term changes occur as a result of environmental influences. The early environment influences development in part through the "programming" of neuroendocrine systems. In the rat, naturally occurring variations in maternal care regulate the development of hypothalamic-pituitary-adrenal (HPA) responses to stress in the pups. The critical targets are the corticotropin-releasing factor (CRF) systems of the hypothalamus and amygdala. The effects of early maternal care result in enduring changes in behavior and physiology of adult offspring, and the alterations are in some cases transmitted across generations.

The quality of infant care has been demonstrated to regulate growth and adaptation during development in both rats and humans. Periods of maternal separation result in a precipitous decline in growth and heightened stress reactivity in rat pups. These effects can be prevented by gentle stroking of the pup, a procedure that mimics the maternal licking that accompanies nursing.

In human infants, the quality of early family life influences not only the immediate growth of the child, but also the development of individual differences in vulnerability to illness in later life. Poor early care, ranging from extremes such as physical or emotional abuse to more moderate neglect or detachment, greatly increases the susceptibility of the adult children to depression, anxiety, alcoholism, diabetes, and heart disease (e.g., Felitti et al., 1999; Russek & Schwartz, 1997).

A critical question to be addressed concerns the nature and underlying mechanisms of parental influence on the lifelong health of offspring. We have argued that the relationship between early life events and adult behavior and health is mediated by parental influence on the development of neural systems mediating the expression of stress-related behavioral and endocrine responses (see Francis & Meaney, 1999). Two critical assumptions underlie this hypothesis: First, that prolonged activation of neural and hormonal responses to stress can promote illness, and second, that early environmental events influence the development of these responses. In essence, we believe that vulnerability to illness in later life reflects the adaptive changes that occur in the brain in response to adversity in early life. Such changes are of considerable benefit to the organism in both the short and long term. There is, however, a cost. The cost is paid in terms of increased vulnerability to certain forms of chronic illness over the life-span.

☐ Responses to Stress

Stress is a risk factor for a variety of illnesses, ranging from autoimmune disorders to mental illness. The pathways by which stressful events can promote such divergent forms of illness involve the same hormones that ensure survival during a period of stress (McEwen & Stellar, 1997). These effects can, in part, be understood in terms of the responses elicited by stressors (see Dallman et al., 1993). The increased release of catecholamines, adrenaline, and noradrenaline, as well as the glucocorticoids, orchestrate a state of catabolism, increasing lipolysis, mobilizing glucose reserves, and insulin antagonism. The increase in circulating levels of catecholamines and glucocorticoids is also associated with increased cardiovascular tone. These actions increase the availability and distribution of energy substrates. Prolonged activation of these pathways provides a significant risk for decreased sensitivity to insulin and steroid-induced diabetes, hypertension, hyperlipidemia, hypercholesterolemia, and arterial wear and tear (see Brindley & Rolland, 1989), all of which are associated with an increased risk for heart disease (see Seeman, Singer, Rowe, Horwitz, & McEwen, 1999).

There are also cognitive responses to stressors that include systems which mediate attentional processes and learning and memory (Arnsten, 1998). During stress, individuals become hypervigilant; the level of attention directed to the surrounding environment is increased at the expense of the ability to concentrate on a focused set of tasks that are not essential for survival. As a function of these changes in attentional processes, as well as the effects of glucocorticoids on brain structures such as the hippocampus, episodic memory is less functional during periods of stress (see Lupien, Deleon et al., 1998). At the same time, glucocorticoids and noradrenaline act on areas of the brain such as the amygdala to enhance learning and memory for emotional stimuli (Ledoux, 1992). These changes in psychological arousal are also associated with altered emotional states: feelings of apprehension and fear predominate during a stressful experience, corresponding to activation of ascending noradrenergic pathways emanating from the locus coeruleus. While these responses are highly adaptive, chronic activation of these systems can promote the emergence of specific forms of cognitive impairments, states of anxiety and dysphoria, sleep disorders, etc. Herein lies the dilemma: the same stress hormones that permit survival during stress can ultimately lead to disease, as described above.

☐ Corticotropin-Releasing Hormone

Stress reactions are in large part governed by central CRF systems (Plotsky, 1991), which coordinate behavioral, emotional, autonomic, and endocrine responses to stressors. Hypothalamic CRF neurons influence the systemic release of both glucocorticoids and catecholamines. Major CRF pathways regulating the expression of stress responses include that from the parvocellular regions of the paraventricular nucleus of the hypothalamus

(PVNh) to the hypophysial-portal system of the anterior pituitary, a system that serves as a principal network for the transduction of a neural signal into a pituitary-adrenal response (Plotsky, 1991). In response to stressors, CRF, as well as cosecretagogues such as arginine vasopressin, is released from PVNh neurons into the portal blood supply of the anterior pituitary, where it provokes the synthesis and release of adrenocorticotropic hormone (ACTH; see Plotsky, 1991). Pituitary ACTH, in turn, causes the release of glucocorticoids from the adrenal gland. CRF neurons from the PVNh also project to midbrain structures, regulating sympathetic output. CRF neurons in the PVNh and the central nucleus of the amygdala (CnAmy) serve as important mediators of both behavioral and endocrine responses to stress.

These findings provide a basis for understanding how stress can influence health. One hypothesis that guides research on the development of vulnerability to pathology focuses on the role of early life events in determining individual differences in stress reactivity. This hypothesis rests firmly on the assumption that chronic activation of central and endocrine stress responses can promote illness. Thus, early life events that increase stress reactivity result in a greater vulnerability to stress-induced illness over the life-span.

☐ Environmental Regulation of HPA and Behavioral Responses to Stress

Maternal licking/grooming in the rat provides a major source of tactile stimulation for the developing pup and has been associated with the regulation of somatic growth and neural development (Schanberg & Field, 1987). In the neonate, development is fostered through specific endocrine profiles, such as exposure to normal levels of growth hormone and suppressed release of the highly catabolic adrenal glucocorticoids (e.g., Francis & Meaney, 1999; van Oers, de Kloet, & Levine, 1998). Maternal deprivation, even for periods of only a few hours, results in a dramatic reduction in growth hormone release and increased glucocorticoid levels. Glucocorticoids are known to reduce the expression of several neurotrophins, including brain-derived neurotropic factor (BDNF) (Chao, Sakai, Ma, & McEwen, 1998), and maternal separation has been associated with reduced BDNF expression. These effects of maternal deprivation are blocked by artificial "stroking" of the deprived pups with brushes, a manipulation that is thought to mimic the tactile stimulation derived from maternal licking/grooming (van Oers et al., 1998). These findings form the basis for the idea that the tactile stimulation associated with maternal licking/grooming serves to maintain a neuroendocrine state that promotes neural development.

One of the strongest models for environmental regulation of the development of responses to stress is the postnatal handling research model in rodents. Handling involves a brief (i.e., 3–15 min), daily period of separation of the pup from the mother. In the rat and mouse, postnatal handling decreases the magnitude of behavioral and endocrine responses to stress in adulthood (e.g., Bhatnagar, Shanks, & Meaney, 1995; Levine, 1957). In contrast, longer periods (i.e., 3–6 hours) of daily separation from the mother increase behavioral and endocrine responses to stress. These effects persist through the life of the animal (e.g., Meaney, Aitken, Bhatnagar, Berkel, & Sapolsky, 1988) and are associated with negative health outcomes (Bhatnagar, Shanks, & Meaney, 1995; Meaney et al., 1988).

The central CRF systems are critical targets for these effects. CRF gene expression in the PVNh and the CnAmy is decreased following handling, and increased following maternal separation. There are also potent effects on systems that are known to regulate CRF gene expression in these areas, including glucocorticoid receptor systems and GABAergic/central benzodiazepine systems. Environmental manipulations can alter the expression of behavioral and endocrine responses to stress, as illustrated by the enhancement of stress-induced activation of ascending noradrenergic systems in adult animals by maternal separation and attenuation by handling in early life (Liu, Caldji, Sharma, Plotsky, & Meaney, in press).

In addition to effects on CRF systems, maternal separation in early life alters the development of ascending serotonergic systems in both monkey (see Higley, Haser, Suomi, & Linnoila, 1991) and rat (Ladd, Owens, & Nemeroff, 1996). Kraemer, Ebert, Schmidt, and McKinney (1989) have shown that repeated periods of maternal separation in early life increase cerebrospinal fluid (CSF) measures of central noradrenaline and 5-HT responses to stress in the rhesus monkey. Given the importance of the ascending NA and 5-HT systems in depression, these findings suggest a mechanism whereby early life events might predispose an individual to depression in later life.

The decreased mother-infant contact resulting from long periods of maternal separation seems likely to be a critical variable in understanding how this procedure increases behavioral and HPA responses to stress. But does maternal care actively contribute to the development of stress-related neural systems, or is the absence of the mother so disruptive to pup physiology that it affects the development of these systems? If maternal care is the crucial factor, what are the relevant features of mother-pup interactions, and how do they influence neural development?

Although handling is merely a brief interlude in the routine of mother-pup interactions, the manipulation does alter the behavior of the mother toward the offspring (e.g., Lee & Williams, 1974). Mothers of handled (H) pups spend the same overall amount of time with their litters as mothers of nonhandled (NH) pups; however, mothers of H litters spend significantly more time licking and grooming their pups (Lee & Williams, 1974; Liu et al., 1997). The question, then, is whether this altered pattern of maternal behavior serves as a critical stimulus mediating the environmental effects on development of endocrine and behavioral responses to stress.

There are substantial, naturally occurring variations in maternal licking/grooming in rat dams. Maternal licking/grooming of pups occurs most frequently prior to or during periods where the mother nurses her young in the arched-back position, and thus the frequency of the two behaviors are closely correlated across mothers ($r = +.91$; Liu et al., 1997). Moreover, these individual differences are remarkably stable across multiple litters. In one series of studies, mothers were divided into two groups: animals high or low in licking/grooming and arched-back nursing (LG-ABN). The idea that handling-induced differences in LG-ABN are relevant for effects on HPA development is supported by the observation that offspring of high LG-ABN mothers become H animals (Liu et al., 1997). As adults, the offspring of high LG-ABN mothers showed reduced plasma ACTH and corticosterone responses to restraint stress. These animals also showed significantly increased hippocampal GC receptor mRNA expression, enhanced GC negative feedback sensitivity, and decreased hypothalamic CRF mRNA levels. In addition, we found that the adult offspring of low LG-ABN mothers showed significantly increased noradrenergic responses to stress at the level of the PVNh. These studies suggest that the critical feature for the handling effect on HPA development involves an increase in maternal licking/grooming.

The offspring of the high and low LG-ABN mothers also differed in behavioral responses to novelty (Caldji et al., 1998). As adults, the offspring of the low LG-ABN mothers showed increased startle responses, decreased open-field exploration, and longer latencies to eat food provided in a novel environment. These animals also showed increased CRF receptor levels in the locus coeruleus and decreased CBZ receptor levels in the basolateral and central nucleus of the amygdala, as well as in the locus coeruleus (Caldji et al., 1998) and increased CRF mRNA expression in the CnAmy (Francis, Diorio, & Meaney, unpublished). These differences map perfectly onto the differences in H and NH animals, and provide further support for the idea that the effects of handling are mediated by changes in maternal behavior.

The seemingly subtle variations in maternal behavior described above may have such a profound impact on development due to the fact that stimulus diversity is slight during the first weeks of life for a rat pup, and the mother serves as a primary link between the environment and the developing animal.

☐ Maternal Care and Hippocampal Development

As adults, the offspring of high and low LG mothers differ in cognitive function. In adulthood, the high LG offspring show improved spatial learning/memory in the Morris water maze, a hippocampal-dependent task. This effect emerged even when animals were afforded a 7-day preexposure period to the swim maze to habituate them to the task and decrease the impact of potential differences in emotional reaction to the test. Differences in hippocampal development and function may be related to the effect of maternal care on hippocampal plasticity and synaptogenesis: high vs. low LG offspring have been observed to differ in levels of synaptic proteins involved in synapse formation and synaptic plasticity (e.g., N-CAM, NGFI-A). Additional studies found the following differences in hippocampal measures of high relative to low LG-ABN offspring: increased levels of choline acetyltransferase (chAT) activity and acetylcholine release, suggesting greater cholinergic synapse number; higher levels of BDNF; and elevated NMDA receptor subunit mRNA expression and NMDA receptor binding. As NMDA receptor activation increases BDNF gene expression in hippocampal neurons (Constantine-Paton, Cline, & Debski, 1990) and BDNF is associated with the survival of cholinergic synapses, the observed changes are consistent with a role for maternal behavior in the development of cholinergic innervation in the hippocampus.

Thus, variations in maternal care may be considered to produce differential levels of sensory experience for the developing pup, resulting in altered levels of hippocampal synaptic development. The increased expression of NMDA receptor subunits apparent in the offspring of the high LG-ABN mothers in early postnatal life might serve as a critical mechanism in triggering this effect. Alternatively, these receptor differences might simply reflect different levels of synaptic development.

In sum, our findings suggest that in the rat, maternal care serves not only a permissive role in neural development by ensuring an appropriate endocrine/metabolic state, but also acts directly on neural systems that mediate synaptic growth and/or survival. Thus, variations in maternal care, occurring within a normal range of maternal behavior, produce substantial individual differences in neural and cognitive development.

☐ The Transmission of Individual Differences in Maternal Care to Offspring

Such effects of maternal behavior might serve as a possible mechanism by which selected traits are transmitted from one generation to the next. Interestingly, individual differences in maternal behavior show intergenerational transmission. The female offspring of high LG-ABN mothers showed significantly greater mother LG-ABN than did the female offspring of low LG-ABN mothers. The intergenerational transmission of parental behavior has also been reported in primates. In rhesus monkeys there is clear evidence for family lineages expressing infant abuse (Maestripieri, Wallen, & Carroll, 1997). There is also evidence for transmission of individual differences in parental styles falling within the normal range, including measures of physical contact and offspring rejection rate (Berman, 1990; Fairbanks, 1996). Similar findings exist in humans, where Miller, Kramer, Warner, Wickramaratne, and Weissman (1997) found that scores on parental bonding measures between a mother and her daughter were highly correlated with the same measures of bonding between the daughter and her child. These findings suggest a perhaps common process of intergenerational transmission of maternal behavior. A critical question to be answered is what mechanism underlies intergenerational transmission of individual differences in behavior?

We have provided evidence for a nongenomic transmission of individual differences in maternal behavior. In one study, we performed reciprocal cross-fostering of the offspring of low and high LG-ABN mothers. In order not to alter maternal behavior by wholesale fostering of litters (Maccari et al., 1995), no more than 2 of 12 pups were fostered into, or from, any one litter. The results of the behavioral studies are consistent with the idea that maternal care is causally related to the resultant behavior of the offspring. The biological offspring of low LG-ABN dams reared by high LG-ABN mothers were significantly less fearful under conditions of novelty than were any of the offspring reared by low LG-ABN mothers, including the biological offspring of high LG-ABN mothers. As adults, the female offspring of low LG-ABN dams reared by high LG-ABN mothers did not differ from normal, high LG-ABN offspring in the frequency of pup LG-ABN. Individual differences in fearfulness or maternal behavior mapped onto those of the rearing mother, rather than the biological mother.

A second series of studies was designed to test the effects of handling on pup development and behavior. Handling pups increases maternal LG-ABN behavior, effectively turning low LG-ABN mothers into high LG-ABN mothers. As adults, the handled offspring of such mothers act as high LG-ABN mothers, a finding that is consistent with the nongenomic transmission hypothesis. The handled offspring of low LG-ABN mothers also resemble the offspring of high LG-ABN dams on measures of hypothalamic CRF and hippocampal glucocorticoid receptor mRNA expression, as well as CBZ receptor binding (Francis, Diorio, & Meaney, 1999). These findings suggest that individual differences in gene expression can also be transmitted across generations via a nongenomic mechanism.

The Potential Effects of Maternal Behavior on the Development of Behavior and Endocrine Responses to Stress in BALBc Mice

BALBc is a mouse strain that is very fearful and shows elevated HPA responses to stress. However, BALBc mice cross-fostered to C57 mothers are significantly less fearful, with lower HPA responses to stress (Zaharia, Shanks, Meaney, & Anisman, 1996). Importantly, C57 mothers normally lick and groom their pups about twice as frequently as BALBc mothers (Anisman, Zaharia, Meaney, & Merali, 1998). Comparable findings have emerged with rat strains. Typically, Fisher 344 rats are more responsive to novelty and have increased HPA responses to acute stress, compared to Long-Evans rats. Moore and Lux (1998) reported that Long-Evans dams lick/groom their offspring significantly more often than do Fisher 344 mothers.

Genetic and environmental factors work in concert and are often correlated (Scarr & McCartney, 1983). Because parents provide both genes and environment for their biological offspring, the offspring's environment is therefore, in part, correlated with their genes. The offspring's genes are correlated with those of the parents, and the parents' genes influence the environment they provide for the offspring. The reason why many epidemiological studies based on linear regression models often find that the epigenetic factors, such as parental care, do not add predictive value above that of genetic inheritance is because of this correlation. But this is clearly different from concluding that the maternal care is not relevant, and the results of the cross-fostering studies attest to the importance of such epigenetic influences.

The value of this process is that it can provide for variation: environmental events can alter the path of the genetically established trajectory in favor of more adaptive outcomes. This, of course, is the benefit of plasticity.

In our minds, these are adaptive processes. Children inherit not only genes from their parents, but also an environment: Englishmen inherit England, as Francis Galton remarked. We believe that the transmission of individual differences in stress reactivity from mother to offspring can provide an adaptive level of "preparedness" for the offspring. Under conditions of increased environmental demand, it is commonly in the animal's interest to enhance behavioral (e.g., vigilance, fearfulness) and endocrine (HPA and metabolic/cardiovascular) responsivity to stress. These responses promote detection of potential threat, avoidance learning, and the mobilization of energy reserves that are essential under the increased demands of the stressor. Since the offspring usually inhabit a niche that is similar to their parents, it would be beneficial for parents inhabiting a very demanding environmental niche to "transmit" a high level of stress reactivity to their offspring.

☐ Maternal Responsivity in High and Low LG-ABN Mothers

What is the neural basis for individual differences in maternal behavior and its intergenerational transmission? In the rat, maternal behavior emerges as a resolution of an interesting conflict (Rosenblatt, 1994). Female rats, unless they are in late pregnancy or lactating, exhibit a fearful, neophobic reaction to pups. Habituation through continuous exposure to pups renders females more likely to exhibit maternal behavior. In the classic behavioral test for "maternal responsivity," virgin females are exposed continuously to pups of 3–6 days of age (Stern, 1997). After a number of days, most females begin to show active care of the pups, including crouching over the pups in a nursing posture and licking/grooming. In general, procedures that reduce fearfulness (e.g., amygdaloid lesions) enhance maternal responsivity, reducing the amount of time for females to exhibit maternal behavior (Fleming, Cheung, Natalie, & Ziggy, 1989). Such findings may also apply to the human condition. Fleming (1988) reported that many factors contribute to the quality of the mother's attitude toward her newborn, but none is correlated more highly than the woman's level of anxiety.

Given the differences in fearfulness in the female offspring of high and low LG-ABN rats, we expected to see differences on the maternal responsivity test in these animals. As predicted, the virgin female offspring of high LG-ABN mothers exhibited the full pattern of maternal behavior in about one-half the exposure time of the offspring of low LG-ABN (4.4 vs. 8.9 days of exposure). These findings suggest that naturally occurring variations in maternal care, including in nulliparous females, are reflected in differences in the maternal responsivity test.

The onset of maternal care in the rat is mediated by hormonal events prior to and during parturition (Bridges, 1994; Rosenblatt, 1994), including critical variations in circulating levels of progesterone and estrogen. Estrogen acts at the level of the medial preoptic area (MPOA) to enhance maternal behavior (Rosenblatt, 1994). The MPOA is also a site of action for the effects of placental lactogens, including prolactin, on maternal behavior (Bridges, 1994).

The influence of ovarian hormones on maternal behavior in the rat is mediated, in part, by effects on central oxytocinergic systems (Pederson, 1995). Estrogen induces oxytocin receptor gene expression (de Kloet et al., 1986). Intracerebroventricular administration of oxytocin rapidly stimulates maternal behavior in virgin rats (Fahrbach, Morrell, & Pfaff, 1985). The effect of oxytocin is abolished by ovariectomy and reinstated with estrogen treatment. Moreover, treatment with oxytocin-antisera or receptor antagonists blocks the effects of ovarian steroid treatments on maternal behavior (Fahrbach et al., 1985).

Oxytocin receptor levels are enriched in sites such the MPOA, the ventral tegmental area (VTA), and the CnAmy and increase following parturition in each of these regions (Pederson, 1995). Oxytocin infusion into the MPOA or the VTA increases the expression of maternal behavior (e.g., Fahrbach et al., 1985; Pederson, 1995). Oxytocinergic neurons which project to the VTA have been located in the ventral bed nucleus of the stria terminalis-lateral preoptic area as well as the PVNh (Pedersen, 1995) and lesions of these areas inhibit maternal behavior (Insel & Harbaugh, 1989; Numan, 1994). The VTA is the source for the mesocorticolimbic dopamine system, and dopamine receptor blockers suppress the expression of pup licking/grooming (Stern, 1997).

Functionally, the onset of maternal behavior emerges from the decreased fear and greater attraction of the female to her pups. The positive cues associated with pups emerge from tactile, gustatory, and auditory stimuli (e.g., Rosenblatt, 1994; Stern, 1997, for reviews). Pup stimuli can be aversive, eliciting withdrawal, or positive, eliciting approach.

For virgin females, pups elicit withdrawal and avoidance associated with odor cues transduced via both the vomeronasal and accessory olfactory bulb projections to the MPOA. The vomeronasal projections arise via the amygdala. Thus, anosmic females are more readily maternal (Fleming, 1988) and lesions of the amygdala enhance maternal responsiveness in virgin females (Numan, 1994). These findings suggest that the cues which elicit withdrawal are transmitted through the amygdala. Morgan, Watchus, and Fleming (1975) found that amygdaloid kindling, which enhances fearfulness in the rat, increases neophobia and decreases approaches to pup-related stimuli in virgin females. Additionally, oxytocin projections to the olfactory bulb may mediate a decrease in odor-induced fear responses to pups (Kendrick & Leng, 1988). Interestingly, Neumann (1999) reported that oxytocin infused directly into the CnAmy produced an anxiolytic effect in female rats. These findings suggest that oxytocin might promote the expression of maternal behavior, in part, by inhibiting fear-related neural activity.

It is interesting to consider the possibility that neural systems involved in the expression of fearfulness, notably the CRF systems, can directly influence maternal behavior. Pederson, Caldwell, McGuire, & Evans (1991) reported that central CRF infusions disrupt maternal behavior in the rat. Such CRF effects could explain, at least in part, differences in the maternal behavior of high and low LG-ABN mothers. In addition, there may be effects of maternal care on neural systems mediating attraction to pup-related stimuli. We found significantly reduced oxytocin receptor levels in the CnAmy of low LG-ABN mothers, as well as increased CRF receptor in this region. Such findings underscore the relationship between neural systems mediating fear and those involved in maternal behavior.

Individual differences in maternal care could therefore be derived from early environmental effects on the development of neural systems mediating fearfulness as well as those involved in mediating the attraction of females toward pups. The net effect is differences in maternal responsivity between high and low LG-ABN mothers. These effects, in turn, provide the basis for stable individual differences in stress reactivity and maternal behavior in the offspring. This hypothesis could partially account for the stable transmission of individual differences in maternal behavior in the rat.

☐ Environmental Regulation of Maternal Behavior

A critical issue to address here is the relationship between the environment of the mother and the nature of her behavior toward her offspring. We propose that such individual differences are functionally related to the level of environmental demand which confronts the animal. In natural conditions in the burrow, rat pups have little direct experience with the environment. Instead, conditions such as the scarcity of food, social instability, low dominance status, etc., directly affect the status of the mother, and thus maternal care. The effects of such environmental challenges on the development of the pups are then mediated by alterations in maternal care, which transduces an environmental signal to the pups. The environmentally driven alterations in maternal care influence the development of neural systems that mediate behavioral and HPA responses to stress. These effects can thus serve to increase or decrease stress reactivity in the offspring. We suggest that more fearful, anxious animals, such as the low LG-ABN mothers, are therefore more neophobic and lower in maternal responsivity to pups than are less fearful animals. These effects then serve as the basis for comparable patterns of maternal behavior in the offspring and for the transmission of these traits to the subsequent generation.

A critical assumption here is that variations in parental behavior are related to the level of environmental demand. Human research suggests that the social, emotional, and socioeconomic context are overriding determinants of the quality of the relationship between parent and child. Human parental care is disturbed under conditions of chronic stress. Conditions that most commonly characterize abusive and neglectful homes involve economic hardship, marital strife, and a lack of social and emotional support (Eisenberg, 1990). Such homes breed neglectful parents such that individual differences in parental behavior are reliably transmitted across generations. Under a high level of environmental demand, increased fearfulness and hypervigilance might be considered adaptive. However, increased stress reactivity is also associated with enhanced vulnerability to stress-induced illness. Since individual differences in parental care can influence the development of stress reactivity and thus vulnerability for chronic illness in later life, this latter trait is also transmitted across generations.

Perhaps the most compelling evidence for a connection between parental behavior and environmental demand emerges from the studies of Rosenblum and colleagues (see Rosenblum & Andrews, 1995 for a review). Bonnet macaque mother-infant dyads were maintained under one of three foraging conditions: low foraging demand (LFD), where food was readily available; high foraging demand (HFD), where ample food was available but required long periods of searching; and variable foraging demand (VFD), a mixture of the two conditions on an unpredictable basis. At the time that these conditions were imposed, there were no differences in the nature of mother-infant interactions. However, following a number of months of these conditions, there were highly significant differences in mother-infant interactions. The VFD condition was clearly the most disruptive, increasing mother-infant conflict. Infants of mothers housed under these conditions were significantly more timid and fearful, and although not separated from their mothers, showed signs of depression commonly observed in maternally separated macaque infants. As adolescents, the infants reared in the VFD conditions were more fearful and submissive and showed less social play behavior.

More recent studies have demonstrated the effects of these conditions on the development of neurobiological systems that mediate the behavioral and endocrine/metabolic response to stress. Copland, Rosenblum and colleagues (Copland et al., 1998) showed that, as adults, monkeys reared under VFD conditions showed increased CSF levels of CRF. Increased central CRF drive would suggest altered noradrenergic and serotonergic responses to stress, and this is what was observed in adolescent VFD-reared animals. Predictably, these animals show increased fearfulness. We would expect that if the environmental conditions remained stable, these differences would be transmitted to the offspring.

In summary, these studies underscore two critically important points. First, variations in maternal care falling within the normal range of the species can have a profound influence on development. One does not need to appeal to the more extreme conditions of abuse and neglect to see evidence for the importance of parental care. Second, environmental demands can alter parental care, and thus infant development. Indeed, we hypothesize that environmentally induced alterations in maternal care mediate the effect of variations in the early postnatal environment on the development of specific neural systems that mediate the development of fearfulness and response to stress. Such individual differences in turn influence the parental care behavior in the adult offspring, providing a neurobiological basis for the intergenerational transmission of specific behavioral traits.

☐ Acknowledgment

J. C. McEachern was responsible for extensive rewriting of a draft of this manuscript, aided by the helpful comments of C. A. Shaw. Document formatting was performed by R. J. Simpson.

☐ References

Anisman, H., Zaharia, M. D., Meaney, M. J., & Merali, Z. (1998). Do early-life events permanently alter behavioral and hormonal responses to stressors? *International Journal of Developmental Neuroscience, 16*, 149–164.

Arnsten, A. F. (1998). The biology of being frazzled. *Science, 280*, 1711–1712.

Berman, C. M. (1990). Intergenerational transmission of maternal rejection rates among free-ranging rhesus monkeys on Cayo Santiago. *Animal Behavior, 44*, 247–258.

Bhatnagar, S., Shanks, N., & Meaney, M. J. (1995). Hypothalamic-pituitary-adrenal function in handled and nonhandled rats in response to chronic stress. *Journal of Neuroendocrinology, 7*, 107–119.

Brindley, D. N., & Rolland, Y. (1989). Possible connections between stress, diabetes, obesity, hypertension and altered lipoprotein metabolism that may result in atheroselerosis. *Clinical Science, 77*, 453–461.

Calbresi, P., Centonze, D., Gubellini, P., Pisani, A., & Bernadi, G. (1998). Blockade of M2-like muscarinic receptors enahnces long-term potentiation at corticostriatal synapses. *European Journal of Neuroscience, 10*, 3020–3023.

Chao, H. M., Sakai, R. R., Ma, L. Y., & McEwen, B. S. (1998). Adrenal steroid regulation of neurotrophic factor expression in the rat hippocampus. *Endocrinology, 139*, 3112–3118.

Constatine-Paton, M., Cline, H. T., & Debski, E. (1990). Patterned activity, synaptic convergence, and the NMDA receptor in developing visual pathways. *Annual Review of Neuroscience, 13*, 129–154.

De Kloet, E. R., Vregdenhil, E., Oitzl, M. S., Joels, M. (1998). Brain corticosteroid receptor balance in health and disease. *Endocrinology Review, 19*, 269–301.

Eisenberg, L. (1990). The biosocial context of parenting in human families. In N. A. Krasnegor & R. S. Bridges (Eds.), *Mammalian parenting: biochemical, neurobiological, and behavioral determinants* (pp. 9–24). London: Oxford University Press.

Fahrbach, S. E., Morrell, J. L., & Pfaff, D. W. (1985). Possible role for endogenous oxytocin in estrogen-facilitated maternal behavior in rats. *Neuroendocrinology, 40*, 526–532.

Fairbanks, L. (1996). Individual differences in maternal style. *Advanced Study of Behavior, 25*, 579–611.

Felitti, V. J., Anda, R. F., Nordenberg, D., Williamson, D. F., Spitz A. M., Edwards, V., Koss, M. P., & Marks, J. S. (1998). Relationship of childhood abuse and household dysfunction to many of the leading causes of death in adults. *American Journal of Preventative Medicine, 14*, 245–258.

Fleming, A. S. (1998). Factors influencing maternal responsiveness in humans: Usefulness of an animal model. *Psychoneuroendocrinology 13*, 189–212.

Fleming, A. S., Cheung, U., Nathalie, M., & Ziggy, K. (1989). Effects of maternal hormones on 'timidity' and attraction to pup-related odors in female rats. *Physiology & Behavior, 46*, 449–453.

Fleming, A., & Corter, C. (1988). Factors influencing maternal responsiveness in humans: Usefulness of an animal model. *Psychoneuroendocrinology, 13*, 189–212.

Fleming, A. S., O'Day, D. H., & Kraemer, G. W. (1988). Neurobiology of mother-infant interactions: Experience and central nervous system plasticity across development and generations. *Neuroscience & Biobehavioral Review*, 673–685.

Francis, D. D., Diorio, J., & Meaney, M. J. (1999). Individual differences in responses to stress in the rat are transmitted across generations through variations in maternal care: Evidence for a non-genomic mechanism of inheritance. *Science, 256*, 1155–1158.

Francis, D., & Meaney, M. J. (1999). Maternal care and the development of stress responses. *Current Opinions in Neurobiology, 9*, 128–134.

Higley, J. D., Haser, M. F., Suomi, S. J., & Linnoila, M. (1991). Nonhuman primate model of alcohol abuse: Effects of early experience, personality and stress on alcohol consumption. *Proceedings of the National Academy of Sciences of the United States of America, 88*, 7261–7265.

Insel, T. R., & Harbaugh, C. R. (1989). Central administration of corticotropin releasing factor alters rat pup isolation calls. *Pharmacology Biochemistry & Behavior, 32*, 197–201.

Jablonska, B., Kossut, M., & Skangiel-Kramska, J. (1996). Transient increase of AMPA and NMDA receptor binding in the barrel cortex of mice after tactile stimulation. *Neurobiology of Learning & Memory, 66*, 36–43.

Kendrick, K. M., & Leng, G. (1988). Hemorrhage-induced release of noradrenaline, 5-hydroxytryptamine and uric acid in the supraoptic nucleus of the rat, measured by rnicrodialysis. *Brain Research, 440*, 402–411.

Kraemer, G. W., Ebert, M. H., Schmidt, D. E., & McKinney, W. T. (1989). A longitudinal study of the effect of different social rearing conditions on cerebrospinal fluinorepinephrine and biogenic amine metabolises in rhesus monkeys. *Neuropsychopharmacology, 2*, 175–189.

Laban, O., Markovic, B. M., Dimitrijevic, M., & Jankovic, B. D. (1995). Maternal deprivation and early weaning modulate experimental allergic encephalomyelitis in the rat. *Brain, Behavior & Immunology, 9*, 9–19.

Ladd, C. O., Owens, M. J., & Nemeroff, C. B. (1996). Persistent changes in corticotropin-releasing factor neuronal systems induced by maternal deprivation. *Endocrinology, 137*, 1212–1218.

Ledoux, J. E. (1992). Emotion and the amygdala. In J. P. Aggleton (Ed.), *The amygdala: Neurobiological aspects of emotion, memory, and mental dysfunction* (pp. 339–351). New York: Wiley-Liss.

Lee, M., & Williams, D. (1974). Changes in licking behavior of rat mother following handling of young. *Animal Behavior, 22*, 679–681.

Levine, S. (1957). Infantile experience and resistance to physiological stress. *Science, 126*, 405–406.

Liu, D., Diorio, J., Tannenbaum, B., Caldji, C., Francis, D., Freeman, A., Sharma, S., Pearson, D., Plotsky, P. M., & Meaney, M. (1997). Maternal care, hippocampal glucocorticoid receptors, and hypothalamic-pituitary-adrenal responses to stress. *Science, 277*, 1659–1662.

Lupien, S., Deleon, M., Desanti, S., Convit, A., Tarshish, C., Nair, N., Thakur, M., McEwen, B. S., Hauger, R. L., & Meaney, M. J. (1998). Cortisol levels during human aging predict hippocampal atrophy and memory deficits. *Nature Neuroscience, 1*, 69–73.

Maccari, S., Piazza, P. V., Kabbaj, M., Barbazanges, A., Simon, H., & LeMoal, M. (1995). Adoption reverses the long-term impairment in glucocorticoid feedback induced by prenatal stress. *Journal of Neuroscience, 15*, 110–116.

Maestripieri, D., Wallen, K., & Carroll, K. A. (1997). Genealogical and demographic influences on infant abuse and neglect in group-lining sooty mangabeys (Cerocebus atys). *Developmental Psychobiology, 31*, 175–180.

Meaney, M. J., Aitken, D. H., Bhatnagar, S., Berkel, C. V., & Sapolsky, R. M. (1988). Postnatal handling attenuates neuroendocrine, anatomical, and cognitive impairments related to the aged hippocampus. *Science, 238*, 766–768.

Miller, L., Kramer, R., Warner, V., Wickramaratne, P., & Weissman, M. (1997). Intergenerational transmission of parental bonding among women. *Journal of the American Academy of Child & Adolescent Psychiatry, 36*, 1134–1139.

Moore, C. L., & Lux, B. A. (1998). Effects of lactation on sodium intake in Fischer-344 and Long-Evans rats. *Developmental Psychobiology, 32*, 51–56.

Morgan, H. D., Watchus, J. A., & Fleming, A. S. (1975). The effects of electrical stimulation of the medial preoptic area and the medial amygdala on maternal responsiveness in female rats. *Annals of the New York Academy of Sciences, 807*, 602–605.

McEwen, B. S., & Stellar, E. (1997). Stress and the individual: Mechanisms leading to disease. *Archives of Internal Medicine, 153*, 2093–2101.

Neumann, L. (1999). *Anxiolytic effects of oxytoxin at the level of the amygdala.* Paper presented at the Annual Conference of the Maternal Brain, Bristol, UK.

Numan, M. (1994). A neural circuitry analysis of maternal behavior in the rat. *Acta Paediatrica Supplementum, 397*, 19–28.

Pederson, C. A. (1995). Oxytocin control of maternal Behavior. Regulation by sex steroids and offspring stimuli. *Annals of the New York Academy of Sciences, 807*, 126–145.

Pedersen, C. A., Caldwell, J. D., Mcguire, M., & Evans, D. L. (1991). Corticotropin-releasing hormone inhibits maternal behavior and induces pup-killing. *Life Sciences, 48*, 1537–1546.

Plotsky, P. M. (1991). Pathways to the secretion of adrenocorticotropin: A view from the portal. *Journal of Neuroendocrinology, 3*, 1–9.

Plotsky, P. M., & Meaney, M. J. (1993). Effects of early environment on hypothalamic corticotrophin-releasing factor mRNA, synthesis, and stress-induced release. *Molecular Brain Research, 18*, 195–200.

Rosenblatt, J. (1994). Psychobiology of maternal behavior: Contribution to the clinical understanding of maternal behavior among humans. *Acta Paediatrica, 397*, 3–8.

Rosenblum, L., Coplan, J., Freidman, S., Bassoff, T., Gorman, J. & Andrews, M. (in press). Adverse early experiences affect noradrenergic and serotonergic functioning in adult primates. *Biological Psychology.*

Russek, L. G., & Schwartz, G. (1997). Feelings of parental care predict health status in midlife: A 35 year follow-up of the Harvard Mastery of Stress Study. *Journal of Behavioral Medicine, 20*, 1–11.

Scarr, S., & McCartney, K. (1983). How people make their own environments. A theory of genotype-environment effects. *Child Development, 54*, 424–435.

Schanberg, S. M., & Field, T. M. (1987). Sensory deprivation stress and supplemental stimulation in the rat pup and preterm human neonate. *Child Development, 58,* 1431–1447.

Seeman, T. E., Singer, B. H., Rowe, J. W., Horwitz, R. I., & McEwen, B. S. (1997). Price of adaptation-allostatic load and its health consequences. *Archives of Internal Medicine, 157,* 2259–2268.

Stern, J. M. (1997). Offspring-induced nurturance: Animal-human parallels. *Developmental Psychobiology, 31,* 19–37.

Tang, Y. P., Shimizu, E., Dube, G. R., Rampon, C., Kerchner, G. A., Zhuo, M., Liu, G. S., & Tsien, J. Z. (1999). Genetic enhancement of learning and memory in mice. *Nature, 401,* 63–69.

Valentino, R. J., Curtis, A. L., Page, M. E., Pavcovich, L. A., & Florin-Lechner, S. M. (1998). Activation of the locus coeruleus brain noradrenergic system during stress: Circuitry, consequences, and regulation. *Advancements in Pharmacology, 42,* 781–784.

van Oers, H. J., de Kloet, E. R., & Levine, S. (1998). Maternal deprivation effect on the infant's neural stress markers is reversed by tactile stimulation and feeding but not by suppressing corticosterone. *Journal of Neuroscience, 18,* 10171–10179.

Zaharia, M. D., Shanks, N., Meaney, M. J., & Anisman, H. (1996). The effects of postnatal handling on Morris water maze acquisition in different strains of mice. *Psychopharmacology, 128,* 227–239.

Zhang, L. X., Xing, G. O., Levine, S., Post, R. M., & Smith, M. A. (1997). *Society for Neuroscience Abstracts, 23,* 1113.

H. Anisman
S. Hayley
W. Staines
Z. Merali

21

CHAPTER

Cytokines, Stress, and Neurochemical Change: Immediate and Proactive Effects

☐ Introduction

Products of activated immune cells (cytokines), which ordinarily serve as signaling molecules, may contribute to communication between the immune, endocrine, autonomic, and central nervous systems in this respect (Anisman, Zalcman, & Zacharko, 1993; Dunn, 1995; Rothwell & Hopkins, 1995). Interestingly, cytokine activation gives rise to several central and peripheral neurochemical changes reminiscent of those ordinarily elicited by stressors. Moreover, like stressors, cytokines may proactively influence the response to subsequent cytokine and stressor challenges (sensitization). Thus, it was suggested that immune activation may be interpreted by the central nervous system (CNS) as a stressor (Anisman et al., 1993; Dunn, 1995). Indeed, cytokines may be part of a regulatory loop that, by virtue of their effects on CNS functioning, might contribute to the symptoms of behavioral pathologies, including mood and anxiety-related disorders (Anisman, Ravindran, Griffiths & Merali, 1999; Maes, 1995).

It is curious that while cytokines have found a greater role in immunotherapy (Jorgensen, Apparailly, & Sany, 1999) and may play a role in neurodegenerative processes (Rothwell, 1999), scant attention has been devoted to the analyses of the behavioral and neurochemical impact of these cytokines. The present review will outline some of the similarities between the central actions of stressors and cytokines, with particular emphasis on the sensitizing effects of cytokines on neuroendocrine and central neurotransmitter functioning, and the implications of such a sensitization effect toward the provocation or exacerbation of behavioral pathologies.

☐ Cytokines as Immunotransmitters

Bioactivity and mRNA expression of several cytokines and their receptors have been documented in numerous brain regions (Ilyin & Plata-Salaman, 1996). Moreover, in addition to being constitutively expressed, central bioactivity may be provoked by various challenges, including systemic or central bacterial endotoxin administration, brain injury, cerebral ischemia, and seizure (Buttini & Boddeke, 1995; De Simoni, Del Bo, De Luigi, Simard, & Forloni, 1995; Rothwell, 1999; Yabuuchi, Minami, Katsumata, & Satoh, 1993). While the function of central cytokine activation remains to be elucidated, proinflammatory cytokines, such as interleukin-1β (IL-1β), may act in a reparative capacity in neurological diseases or brain trauma, or alternatively, IL-1β may actually promote neuronal damage following central insults (Rothwell, 1999).

Several routes of communication have been offered between the immune system and the brain. For instance, cytokines released from activated immune cells may serve to stimulate receptors present on dendrites of the vagal nerve (Ek, Kurosawa, Lundenberg, & Ericsson, 1998), which then transmits neural information, via the nodose ganglion, to brainstem regions such as the nucleus of the solitary tract (Ek et al., 1998; Dantzer et al., 1996). As well, macrophage-derived cytokines, such as IL-1β, IL-6, and tumor necrosis factor-α (TNF-α), and IL-2 secreted from T cells, may act as mediators (immunotransmitters) between the immune system and the brain. Although cytokines are large molecules, entry into the brain may occur where the blood-brain barrier is less restrictive (e.g., the organum vasculosum laminae terminalis), or by a saturable transport system (Banks, Ortz, Plotkin, & Kasten, 1991; Gutierrez, Banks, & Kastin, 1993), or in some pathological conditions (e.g., seizure)

It is, of course, well established that functional plasticity occurs within the immune system, such that once certain immune cells are exposed to antigenic challenge, they retain a memory for this antigen, exhibiting a faster and more robust immune response upon subsequent encounters with this challenge (secondary immune response). In addition to an immunological memory, a sensitization effect can also be established with respect to central neurochemical processes. This sensitization involves processes distinct from those subserving immunological memory and may occur in response to stressors and to certain cytokine challenges, hence influencing vulnerability to subsequent stressor-related behavioral and physical disturbances.

☐ Stress and Physiological Processes

Although cytokine challenges promote central neurochemical effects akin to those of traditional stressors, it is important to distinguish such systemic or metabolic stressors from conventional processive stressors, that is, those that involve higher order sensory processing (e.g., fear cues) (Herman & Cullinan, 1997). Although systemic and processive stressors promote hypothalamic-pituitary-adrenal (HPA) activation, processive stressors may involve limbic forebrain regions, which in turn may stimulate GABAergic neurons at an intervening synapse (e.g., bed nucleus of the stria terminalis) before acting upon corticotropic cells of the paraventricular nucleus (PVN) of the hypothalamus. Systemic stressors, in contrast, may promote HPA alterations via brainstem nuclei which directly innervate the PVN (Herman & Cullinan, 1997). It is thought that many of the neurochemical alterations induced by environmental insults serve in an adaptive capacity, preparing the organism to deal with the stressor, blunt its physiological and psychological impact, and stimulate processes which preclude excessive physiological activation (Munck & Guyre, 1991). The central actions of systemic stressors may likewise serve in an adaptive capacity (Maier & Watkins, 1998).

Neurochemical Response to Acute Psychogenic Stressors

Stressors provoke brain region–specific alterations of norepinephrine (NE), dopamine (DA), and serotonin (5-HT), the magnitude and duration of which are related to stressor severity as well as to experiential and organismic variables (e.g., age or strain; Anisman et al., 1993). If the stressor is uncontrollable and sufficiently severe, then utilization of NE, 5-HT, and DA in some brain regions may exceed synthesis, culminating in reduced amine levels (Anisman et al., 1993; Weiss & Simson, 1989). In addition, uncontrollable (but not controllable) stressors increased 5-HT$_{1B}$ receptor mRNA in the dorsal raphe, although comparable differentiation was not evident in the medial prefrontal cortex (PFC) or hippocampus (Neumaier, Petty, Kramer, Szot, & Hamblin, 1997). The monoamine variations are not unique to neurogenic stressors, as such effects are readily induced by purely psychogenic stressors (e.g., predator exposure; McIntyre, Kent, Hayley, Merali & Anisman, 1999).

While the stressor-elicited NE alterations are fairly widespread, the DA alterations are more restricted, being most readily detectable in the arcuate nucleus, PFC, ventral tegmentum, and the nucleus accumbens shell, whereas nigrostriatal DA activity is hardly affected (Deutch, Bourdelais, & Zahm, 1993; Kalivas & Duffy, 1995). In vivo studies (using microdialysis and chronamperometric measurements) indicated that even mild stimuli (handling, tail pinch, novelty) and psychosocial stressors increased DA release in the PFC and the nucleus accumbens (Sullivan & Gratton, 1998; Tidey & Miczek, 1996).

Neuroendocrine Responses to Acute Stressors

It is well established that stressors promote the secretion of neuroendocrine peptides within the PVN, including corticotropin releasing hormone (CRH) and arginine vasopressin (AVP), which synergistically provoke secretion of ACTH, and consequently of adrenal glucocorticoids (Lightman, 1994). While some central neurochemical alterations are sensitive to stressor controllability, not all processes are so affected. The HPA variations are exquisitely sensitive to stressors and tend not to be determined by stressor controllability per se (although differences occur in response to graded stressor severity). It would, after all, be most adaptive for neurochemical systems to react rapidly to stressors, irrespective of whether they were controllable or uncontrollable, as it may take some number of experiences for the animal to "learn" or "perceive" that a particular stressor was indeed uncontrollable. Thus, those systems that are necessary to rapidly contend with stressors (e.g., activation of the HPA axis and the sympathetic nervous system), and even fundamental immune responses that act against pathogenic stimuli, ought to react comparably to both controllable and uncontrollable stressors. It may be that only those central systems that are uniquely involved in the appraisal of processive stressors would be differentially influenced by controllable and uncontrollable insults.

In addition to the neuropeptide variations at the PVN, stressors promote CRH mRNA expression or CRH protein changes at extrahypothalamic sites, including the amygdala and bed nucleus of the stria terminalis (Merali, McIntosh, Kent, Michaud & Anisman, 1998; Sawchenko et al., 1996). It was proposed that fear-eliciting stimuli may be associated with activation of central amygdala CRH, whereas diffuse stimuli (leading to general anxiety) may be related primarily to CRH release from the bed nucleus of the stria terminalis. Stimulation of the basolateral amygdala, which innervates both regions, may be fundamental to both conditioned and unconditioned fear responses

(Davis, Walker, & Lee, 1999). It is possible, as well, that DA changes elicited by stressors may be coupled to activation of the amygdala and that the contribution of monoamines in the left and right basolateral amygdala may not play identical roles in stressor-related emotional responses (Sullivan & Gratton, 1998). Furthermore, as stressors provoke in vivo variations of NE (e.g., within the PVN, central amygdala, and bed nucleus of the stria terminalis), which elicit CRH activity, the peptide changes (and anxiety-related behaviors) may be secondary to NE variations (Pacak, Palkovits, Kopin, & Goldstein, 1995; Sawchenko et al., 1996). Furthermore, hypothalamic CRH activity may influence 5-HT functioning in PFC, thereby contributing to clinical depressive symptoms (Dinan, 1994).

☐ Neurochemical Impact of Chronic Stressors

Chronic stressors elicit a compensatory enhancement of NE and 5-HT synthesis, coupled with moderation of DA utilization (Imperato, Angelucci, Casolini, Zocchi, & Puglisi-Allegra, 1992), hence precluding the reduction of levels (Anisman et al., 1993). Additionally, chronic stressors may promote down-regulation of ß-NE receptor activity and the NE-sensitive cAMP response (Stone, 1983), as well as 5-HT$_{1B}$ receptor expression (Bolanos-Jimenez et al., 1995). When the stressor is applied on an unpredictable basis, the neurochemical adaptation was slower to develop, ß-NE subsensitivity did not occur, and 5-HT$_2$ receptor density was increased (Ferretti, Blengio, Gamalero, & Ghi, 1995). Interestingly, in contrast to neurogenic stressors, chronic psychogenic stressors may be associated with persistent alterations of c-fos expression in several brain regions (Matsuda et al., 1996), suggesting that adaptation to ethologically significant stimuli may not occur readily.

It is important to emphasize that chronic stressors are not associated with a "tolerance-like" effect, wherein the neurochemical impact of acute stressors are diminished. For instance, while CRH activity may decline with repeated stressor exposure, the accompanying increased AVP release (which acts synergistically with CRH) ensures heightened ACTH and corticosterone release (Dallman et al., 1994). With respect to monoamines, chronic stressors may promote sustained increases of synthesis, permitting levels of the substrate to be produced at sufficiently high rates. The high rate of synthesis and utilization may favor behavioral and physiological responses to deal with the stressor; however, the excessive wear and tear on neuronal functioning (termed "allostatic load") may culminate in pathological outcomes (Schulkin, Gold, & McEwen, 1998).

Sensitization Associated with Stressors Experiences

The neurochemical variations provoked by acute stressors persist for a matter of minutes or hours (Anisman et al., 1993) but are readily reestablished upon subsequent reexposure to a mild stressor (Anisman & Sklar, 1979; Doherty & Gratton, 1992; Kalivas & Duffy, 1995; Yoshioka, Matsumoto, Togashi, & Saito, 1995). This occurs even when the second session (a) involved a stressor that differed from the one to which the animal had originally been exposed (Gresch, Sved, Zigmond, & Finlay, 1994), or (b) comprised a pharmacological agent that acted as a catecholamine stimulant (Kalivas & Stewart, 1991).

Interestingly, in animals exposed to a chronic stressor, reductions of amine levels were not readily provoked upon later exposure to an acute stressor, although utilization of the amine was greatly increased. Evidently, while acute stressors induce sensitization of mechanisms associated with NE release, chronic stressors also induce sensitization of mechanisms associated with amine synthesis, thus assuring adequate NE supplies upon later stressor encounters (Anisman et al., 1993). It should be noted that following a chronic predictable stressor regimen, subsequent exposure to a novel stressor provokes a particularly marked enhancement of neurochemical activity. In effect, a predictable stressor regimen may set in motion sensitization-like effects, which may be most apparent upon exposure to a novel (heterotypic) stressor (Bhatnager, Singh, Sazawal, Saxena, & Bhan, 1998; Gresch et al., 1994).

In their analysis of the mechanisms associated with chronic stressor effects, Tilders and his associates (Tilders, Schmidt, & De Goeij, 1993; Schmidt, Binnekade, Janszen, & Tilders, 1996) indicated that paraventricular neurosecretory neurons have the capacity for phenotypic plasticity. In particular, the terminals in the external zone of the median eminence (originating from the PVN) frequently contain CRH, and in a proportion of the terminals AVP coexpression is apparent. In chronically stressed animals, or with the passage of time following acute stressors, colocalization of AVP and CRH was increased (Schmidt et al., 1996; Tilders et al., 1993). The fact that these peptides synergistically stimulate pituitary ACTH secretion might account for the increased HPA responsivity observed upon reexposure to a stressor.

Neurochemical Consequences of Cytokine Challenge

Although cytokine entry to the brain is limited, de novo synthesis may be induced centrally in microglia and in neuronal tissues (Hopkins & Rothwell, 1995), which then act on central cytokine receptors. The central circuitry activated by cytokines or by bacterial endotoxins may involve several sites of cytokine entry into the brain (Rivest, 1995), and c-fos mRNA expression may follow a biphasic temporal course across brain regions (Brady, Lynn, Herkenhan, & Gottesfeld, 1994). The initial changes may represent cytokine entry into the brain, promoting neuroendocrine changes and the neural transduction of peripheral signals, while the later variations may reflect the cellular activation associated with IL-1β along various diffusion routes or effects secondary to de novo synthesis (Brady et al., 1994; Gaballec, Griffais, Fillion, & Haour, 1996).

Both central and systemic IL-1β administration increase CRH secretion, which then serves to stimulate ACTH and corticosterone release. Predictably, the effects of the cytokines were prevented by passive immunization with antisera to CRH and by CRH receptor antagonists (Dunn, 1995). Like stressors, IL-1β increased c-fos expression of CRH-immunoreactive neurons within the PVN (Ericsson, Kovacs, & Sawchenko, 1994; Rivest & Rivier, 1994). There is reason to believe that NE may promote IL-1β–induced HPA changes, while nitric oxide restrains HPA responses to proinflammatory stimuli (Turnbull & Rivier, 1996).

Although stressors have effects similar to those of IL-1β and also influence IL-1β mRNA or protein levels within the brain and pituitary (Nguyen et al., 1998; Shintani et al., 1995; Yabuuchi et al., 1993), these treatments may involve independent inputs to CRH neurons (Whitnall, Perlstein, Mougey, & Neta, 1992). It will be recalled that while processive stressors influence HPA activity via the central amygdala, systemic stressors (e.g., IL-1) may act via an amygdala-independent mechanism (Herman & Cullinan, 1997). This is not to say that cytokines do not affect amygdaloid activity, as IL-1β increased Fos-immunoreactivity in the central amygdala and bed nucleus of the stria terminalis, as well as catecholaminergic neurons of the NTS and ventrolateral medulla (the latter projecting to the PVN; Ericsson et al., 1994; Sawchenko et al., 1996). Moreover, variations of plasma ACTH and corticosterone, as well as in vivo release of hypothalamic NE, DA, and 5-HT ordinarily elicited by a stressor, were prevented by pretreatment with an IL-1 receptor antagonist (Shintani et al., 1995).

In addition to the neuropeptide variations, systemic IL-1β or lipopolysaccharide (LPS) administration increased NE and DA activity in several hypothalamic nuclei and extrahypothalamic sites (Dunn, 1995; Lacosta, Merali, & Anisman, 1999; Mohankumar & Quadri, 1993; Shintani et al., 1995). As well, cytokine or endotoxin treatment increase tryptophan in the brainstem, hypothalamus, and PFC (Dunn, 1995) and increase the accumulation of the 5-HT metabolite, 5-HIAA (Anisman & Merali, 1999; Dunn, 1995). In vivo, IL-1β stimulated hypothalamic (Gemma, Ghezzi, & De Simoni, 1991) and hippocampal (Linthorst, Flachskamm, Muller-Preusse, Holsboer, & Reul, 1995) 5-HT release. As depicted in Figure 21.1, we likewise observed cytokine treatment to increase in vivo 5-HIAA at the nucleus accumbens, as well as at the hippocampus (Merali, Lacosta, & Anisman, 1997; Song, Merali, & Anisman, 1999).

Many of the amine and neuroendocrine changes elicited by IL-1β are typical of those seen in stressed animals (Anisman & Merali, 1999). Yet, in several respects the effects of IL-1β could be distinguished from those typically associated with stressors. For instance, while stressors enhance NE activity within the amygdala and DA within the prefrontal cortex and nucleus accumbens (Anisman et al., 1993; Deutch & Roth, 1990), such effects were not elicited by the IL-1β treatment (Lacosta, Merali, & Anisman, 1998; Merali et al., 1997; Song et al., 1999). This is not to say that immune activation will not affect accumbal DA functioning. In fact, as seen in Figure 21.2, approximately 90 min following systemic administration of an endotoxin (LPS), in vivo elevations of accumbal DA were apparent, which persisted for about 90 min. Interestingly, LPS also increased accumbal 5- HIAA; this effect not only occurred earlier, but was also more persistent. The source for the different DA and 5-HT time courses is not immediately apparent, but it seems that neuronal networks within a particular brain region may be differentially responsive to immune challenge (Borowski, Kokkinidis, Merali, & Anisman, 1998).

While the data concerning the central neurochemical actions of TNF-α are less extensive than those of IL-1β it appears that this cytokine also stimulates plasma corticosterone secretion, but the magnitude of the effect is less pronounced than that provoked by IL-1β (Brebner, Hayley, Zacharko, Merali, & Anisman, 2000; Dunn, 1995; Hayley, Brebner, Lacosta, Merali, & Anisman, 1999). Likewise, TNF-α provoked central monoamine alterations, including a reduction of NE within the locus coeruleus and dorsal hippocampus, and increased 5-HT turnover within the PVN and central amygdala. The effects of TNF-α, however, could be distinguished from those of other cytokines. For instance, unlike central IL-1β and IL-2, TNF-α did not influence hippocampal 5-HT activity (Pauli, Linthorst, & Reul 1998).

Sensitization of Cytokine Effects

A sensitization-like effect can be engendered by IL-1β, and as observed with respect to stressor and drug-induced effects, the development of the sensitization may be dependent upon the passage of time. Specifically, IL-1β engendered increased costorage of CRH and AVP within CRH terminals at the external zone of the median eminence (Schmidt, Janszen, Wouterlood, & Tilders 1995; Tilders & Schmidt, 1998). This effect became progressively more pronounced over time, peaking during the initial 2 weeks after treatment (Schmidt et al., 1995). It is particularly interesting that when these animals were later exposed to a neurogenic stressor (footshock), plasma ACTH and corticosterone release were augmented. Thus, IL-1β increased the availability of secretagogues, such that later challenges augmented glucocorticoid secretion.

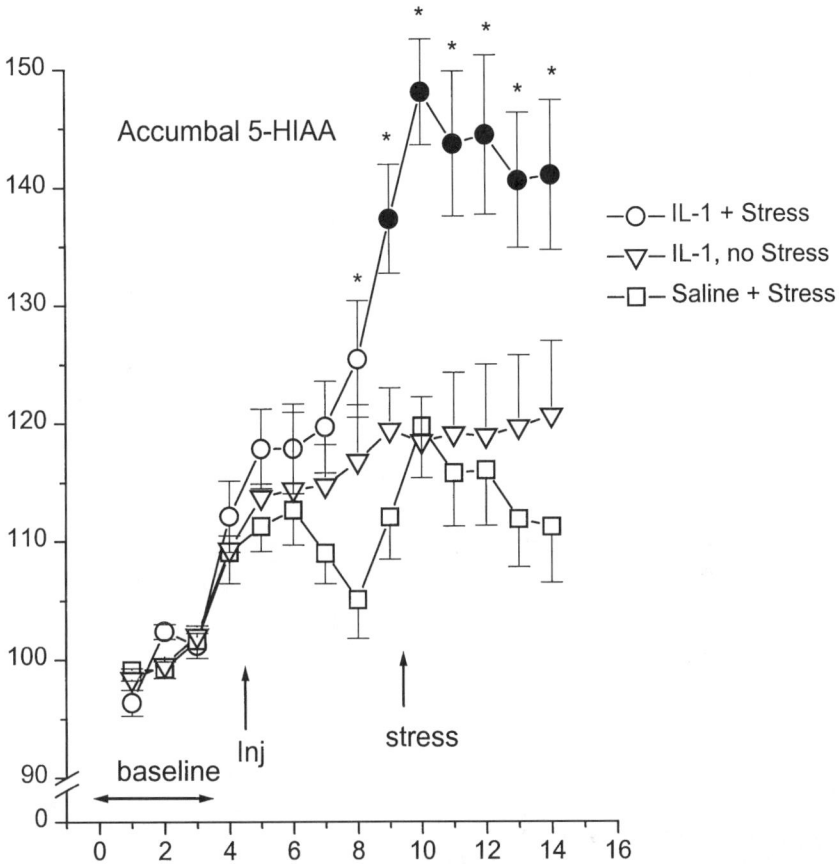

Figure 21.1. Extracellular 5HIAA at the nucleus accumbens, expressed as a percentage of baseline, over 30 min dialysate samples. Following 4 baseline samples, rats were injected with either saline (squares) or IL-1β (circles and triangles) and 5 samples were collected at 30-min intervals. Air-puff stress (5 puffs of 1 s duration) was then delivered (circles and squares) and dialysates collected over 5 additional periods. Filled-in symbols denote significant differences from the baseline, asterisks denote significant differences from saline-treated rats. Similar effects were also obtained from the hippocampus. From "Effects of Interleuken-1β and Mild Stress on Alterations of Central Monoamines: A Regional Microdialysis Study," by Z. Merali, S. Lacosta, and H. Anisman, 1997, *Brain Research, 761*, 229.

In addition to its immediate effects, TNF-α also proactively influences behavioral and neurochemical alterations in response to subsequent challenges. For example, in an in vitro rat slice preparation, TNF-α inhibited the induction of long-term hippocampal potentiation (Tancredi et al., 1992) and modulated Ca^{2+} currents in cultured sympathetic neurons (Soliven & Albert, 1992). Furthermore, this cytokine exerted protracted actions on HPA activity, central monoamine functioning, and behavior. In particular, in mice exposed to recombinant human TNF-α, at doses from 1.0 to 4.0 μg, little evidence of illness was apparent in terms of motor activity, social exploration, or the animal's general

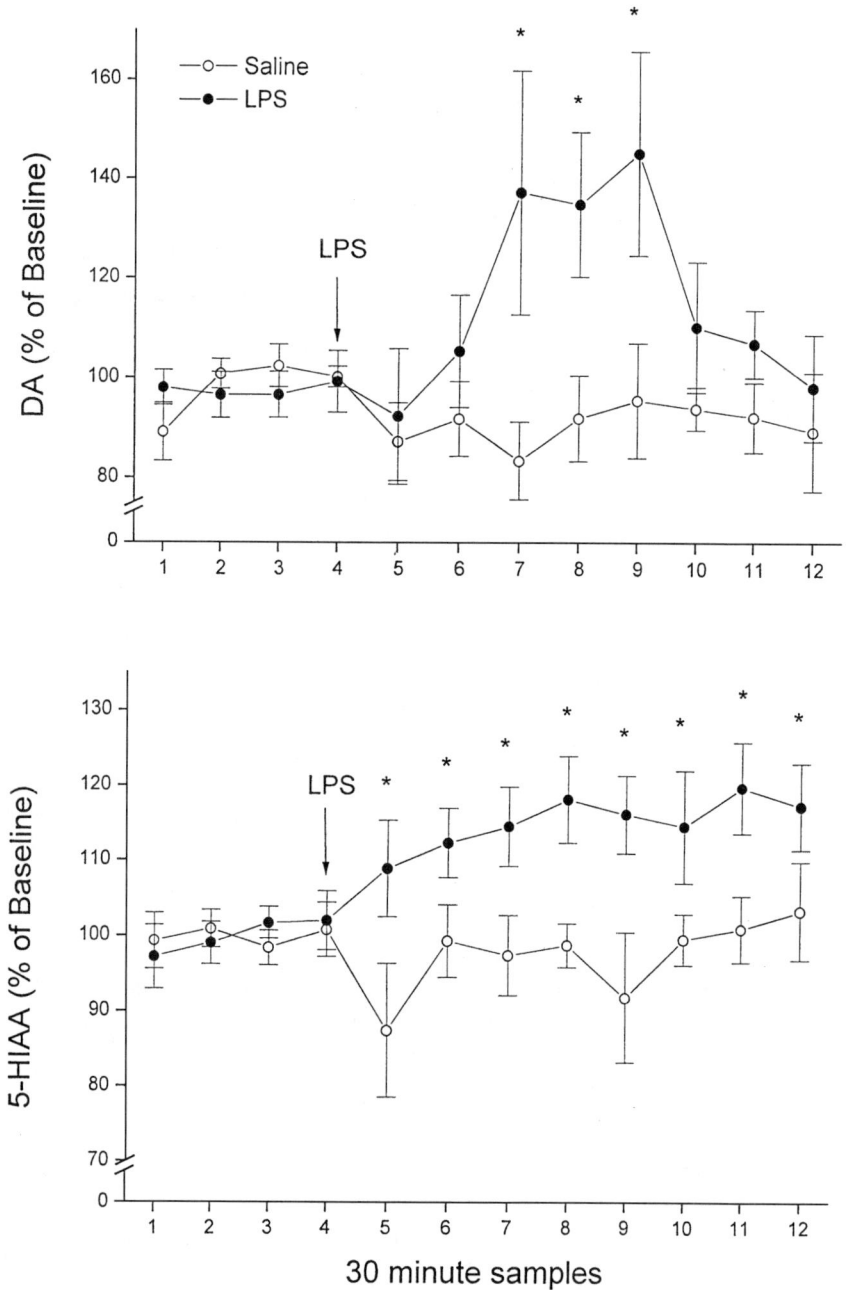

Figure 21.2. Interstitial DA (upper panel) and 5-HIAA (lower panel) at the nucleus accumbens as a percentage of baseline (four samples) and after ip administration of either saline or LPS (100 μg). Each point represents dialysates collected over a 30-min period. *$P < 0.05$ relative to saline-treated rats. From "Lipopoly Saccharide, Central in Vivo Amine Alterations, and Anhedonia," by T. Borowski, L. Kokkinidis, Z. Merali, and H. Anisman, 1998, *Neuro Report, 9*, 380.

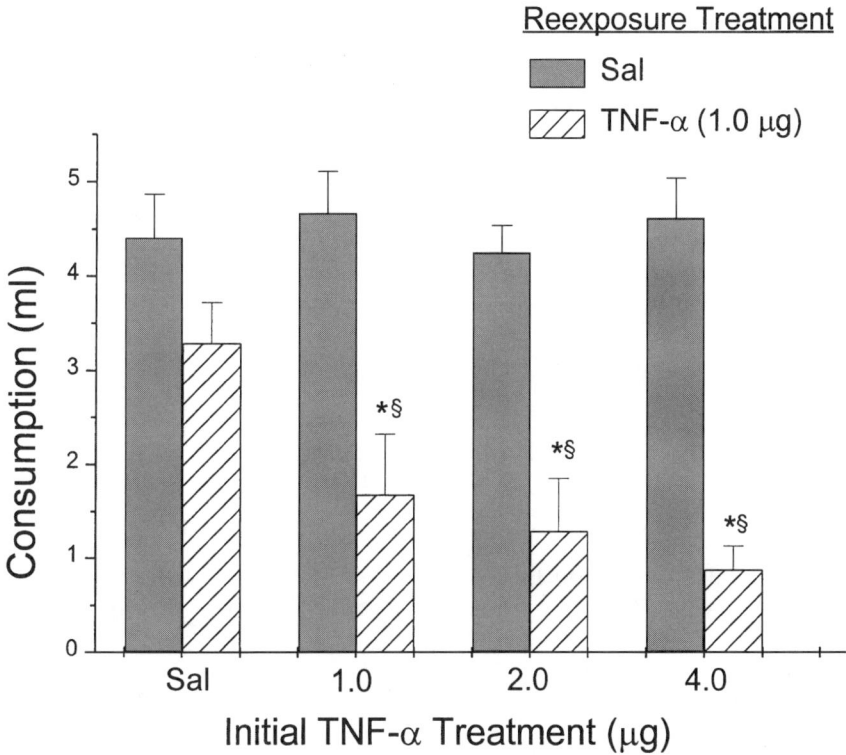

Figure 21.3. Mean (±SEM) chocolate milk consumption among mice treated with saline or TNF-α (1.0, 2.0, or 4.0 μg) and then reexposed to either saline or the 1.0 μg dose of the cytokine 2 weeks later. *$P < 0.05$ relative to saline-treated mice; §$P < 0.05$ relative to mice that received acute TNF-α injection. From "Sensitization to the Effects of Tumor Necrosis Factor-α: Neuroendocrine, Central Monoamine, and Behavioral Variations," by S. Haley, K. Brebner, S. Lacosta, Z. Merali, & H. Anisman, 1999, *Journal of Neuroscience, 19*, 5656.

appearance, although at the highest dose, mice displayed reduced consumption of a favored snack (chocolate milk), likely reflecting sickness-related anorexia. As depicted in Figure 21.3, if mice were exposed to 1.0, 2.0, or 4.0 μg of TNF-α, and then 2 weeks later treated with 1.0 μg of the cytokine, a marked decline of chocolate milk consumption was apparent. In effect, this index of illness indicated that a sensitization was induced by the initial TNF-α treatment, even if it involved a behaviorally subeffective dosage (Hayley et al., 1999).

It was subsequently demonstrated that the response to TNF-α increased with the passage of time following the initial administration. Figure 21.4 shows that social interaction rated on a 4-point scale (higher numbers reflect greater social isolation) was hardly affected by 1.0 μg of TNF-α administered 1 h earlier or 4.0 μg administered 2 weeks earlier. In animals that received 4.0 μg followed 1 or 7 days later by the 1.0 μg dosage, there was again no change in social interaction. However, when the second TNF-α treatment was administered 14 or 28 days after initial cytokine exposure, a marked decline of social exploration was apparent (Hayley et al., 1999).

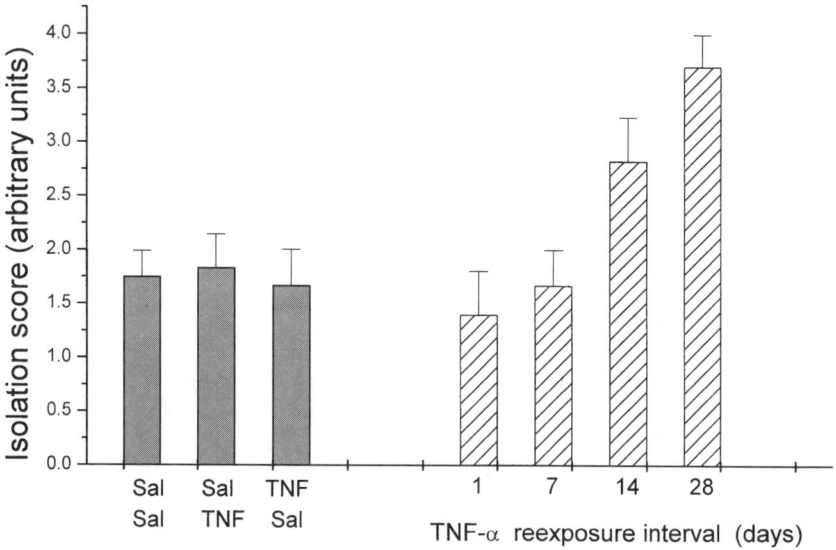

Figure 21.4. Sensitization associated with TNF-α on mouse social interaction ($x \pm$ SEM) rated on a 4-point scale (see text). The gray bars on the left depict mice injected with saline on two occasions, saline followed by TNF-α (1.0 μg), or TNF-α (4.0 μg), followed by saline (injections given ip 14 days apart). The bars on the right (hatched) show mice that were pretreated with TNF-α (4.0 μg) and then reexposed to the cytokine (1.0 μg) either 1, 7, 14, or 28 days later.

Plasma corticosterone concentrations in response to TNF-α reexposure likewise varied in a time-dependent fashion. As depicted in Figure 21.5, 1 h after administration of the 1.0 μg dose, the level of plasma corticosterone increased appreciably, while cytokine administered 14 days earlier was without effect. However, if mice were initially treated with the 4.0 μg dose, and then reexposed to 1.0 μg either 14 or 28 days later, the rise of plasma corticosterone exceeded that of acutely treated mice. In contrast, if the second treatment was given 1 day after initial TNF-α administration, a significant desensitization was apparent, wherein the plasma corticosterone levels fell below those of acutely treated mice. Evidently, the HPA axis is subject to a remarkable degree of plasticity in response to TNF-α (desensitization or sensitization), but the nature of the effect is dependent upon the timing of the cytokine treatment. Parenthetically, the sensitization was not related to the fact that a human recombinant form of the cytokine was being used in mice (particularly as human TNF-α only excites the p55 receptor, while murine TNF-α stimulates both the p55 and the p75 receptor), as the murine form of the cytokine yielded a similar enhancement of corticosterone release (Anisman, Hayley, & Merali, in press).

Given that TNF-α proactively influenced glucocorticoid secretion in response to later cytokine challenge, it was of interest to determine whether TNF-α provoked a sensitization with respect to AVP and CRH expression within the median eminence. An immunofluorscence procedure was used to double label AVP and CRH neurons within the external zone of the median eminence. Within this region, the degree of AVP and CRH immunoreactivity following TNF-α challenge varied with the passage of time. That is, the degree of fluorescence intensity and the quantity of the peptides was dependent upon the time interval that elapsed since exposure to a single 4.0 μg ip injection of TNF-α. However, while TNF-α increased both AVP and CRH immunoreactivity, the

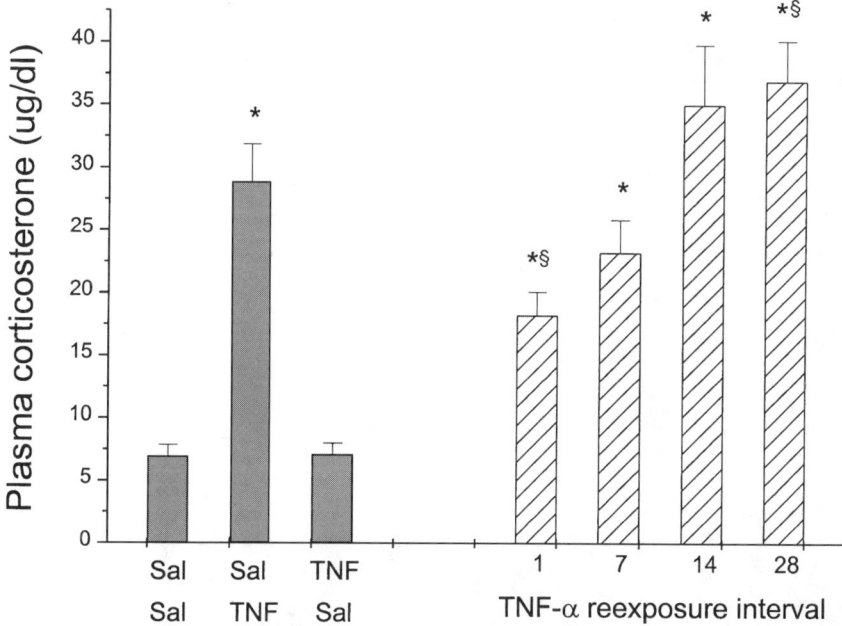

Figure 21.5. Plasma corticosterone levels ($x \pm$ SEM) among mice exposed to various TNF-α regimens. The three groups to the left (solid bars) received either saline only, saline followed 2 weeks later by the low dose of TNF-α (1.0 μg), or a high dose of TNF-α (4.0 μg) followed 2 weeks later by saline treatment. The four groups on the right (hatched bars) received two injections of TNF-α; an initial 4.0 μg dose followed by a second 1.0 μg dose either 1, 7, 14, or 28 days later. *$P < 0.05$ relative to saline treated mice; §$P < 0.05$ relative to mice that received acute TNF-α injection. From "Sensitization to the Effects of Tumor Necrosis Factor-α: Neuroendocrine, Central Monoamine, and Behavioral Variations," by S. Haley, K. Brebner, S. Lacosta, Z. Merali, & H. Anisman, 1999, *Journal of Neuroscience, 19*, 565.

time course for the up-regulation of the peptides did not correspond to the elevated plasma corticosterone levels observed upon reexposure to TNF-α. Figure 21.6 shows representative photomicrographs for both AVP and CRH immunoreactivity at various times following TNF-α challenge. AVP and CRH immunoreactivity increased within 1 h of systemic TNF-α administration, continued to increase over the ensuing 24 h, and peaked 7 days after initial cytokine administration. Although elevated immunoreactivity for the two peptides was still evident 14 days after the single TNF-α treatment, this effect was not permanent and declined towards control values by 28 days (Hayley, Staines, Merali, & Anisman, 1999). The protracted effects of TNF-α were not limited to the hypothalamus, as the cytokine also altered CRH immunoreactivity within the central amygdala. However, the cytokine-induced amygdaloid neuropeptide changes were distinguishable from those observed at the median eminence. Unlike the time-dependent CRH changes observed within the latter region, reexposure to TNF-α increased amygdaloid CRH independent of the passage of time. Specifically, reexposure to a relatively low dose of TNF-α (1.0 μg; ip) either 1, 7, or 14 days after initial treatment increased amygdaloid CRH beyond that evident in saline-treated mice or in animals acutely

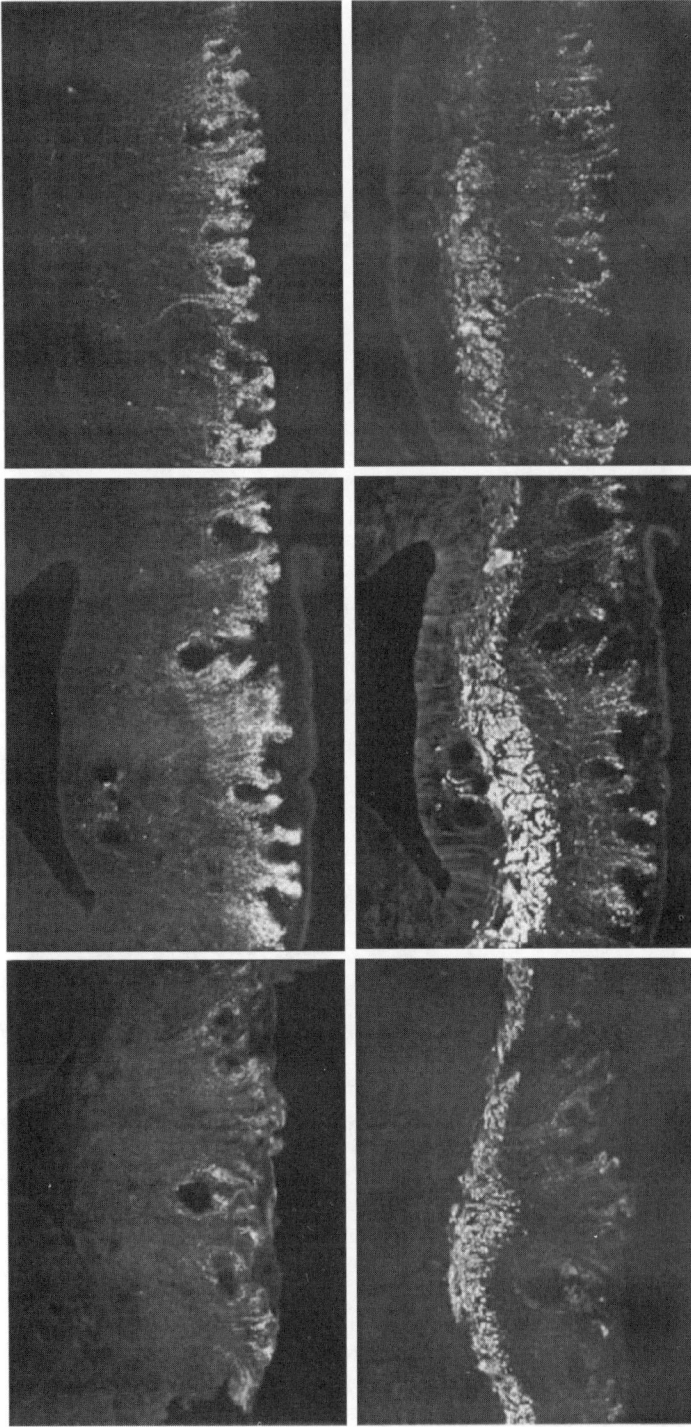

Figure 21.6. Immunoreactivity for CRH and AVP within the extremal zone of the median eminence of mice treated with saline (left), TNF-α (4.0 μg) 7 days earlier (middle), or TNF-α (4.0 μg) 14 days earlier (right). The sections were double labeled such that the CRH (labeled with FITC) and AVP (labeled using Texas Red) are depicted in the top and bottom panels, respectively. The two panels on the far left side are from saline-treated mice; the middle panels are from mice treated with TNF-α 7 days earlier; the panels on the far right are from mice treated with TNF-α 14 days earlier. Magnification × 40.

treated with the cytokine and then killed at these corresponding time periods (i.e., in the absence of the reexposure treatment). This effect was less pronounced and more variable when reexposure occurred 28 days after the initial cytokine treatment. It is important to underscore that the outcome described was evident only upon reexposure to TNF-α. In the absence of such treatment the effects of the initial TNF-α exposure were not apparent. Inasmuch as the amygdaloid CRH alterations were dependent upon reexposure to the cytokine, it is likely that the increased immunoreactivity (i.e., the sensitization) reflects de novo synthesis of the peptide, as opposed to altered storage of the peptide.

Just as TNF-α provokes the sensitization of HPA activity, this cytokine proactively influences the response to CNS neurotransmitter processes. However, the time-dependent nature of the sensitization varied across brain regions and as a function of the specific neurotransmitter under investigation. Moreover, the time-dependent nature of the sensitization could be distinguished from that seen with respect to neuroendocrine functioning. Within the PVN, the utilization of NE, as reflected by increased MHPG accumulation, was increased by the low dose of TNF-α. As in the case of the neuroendocrine changes described earlier, the extent of the increased PVN NE utilization elicited upon reexposure to the cytokine was progressively greater with the passage of time (up to 28 days). In contrast, as depicted in Figure 21.7, within the prefrontal cortex and the central amygdala a marked sensitization effect was evident in mice that were reexposed to the cytokine at the 1 day interval, but was absent at lengthier intervals. Clearly, in addition to having marked neuroendocrine and central neurotransmitter effects, TNF-α engenders a sensitization wherein the response to later neurochemical functioning is increased. Some of these effects are dependent on the passage of time, becoming progressively more pronounced over the 28 days following cytokine treatment, whereas other effects appear to be limited to a brief period. The mechanisms governing these divergent effects remain to be identified; however, these data suggest that cytokine treatment may set into motion a series of dynamic processes involving different temporal patterns and different behavioral sequelae

☐ Summary and Implications

It will be recalled that the production of some cytokines and their soluble receptors may be elevated in depressive illnesses (Anisman et al., 1999; Maes, 1995). Whether these are simply correlates of the illness or play a causal role has yet to be determined, although the finding that cytokines (used in immunotherapy) may elicit depressive-like symptoms is commensurate with a causal involvement in the disorders. Further, in rodents, chronic low-dose endotoxin treatment provokes behavioral and neuroendocrine changes reminisent of those associated with clinical depression, and such variations were antagonized by antidepressant treatment (Yirmya, 1996). It may be that a chronic low grade bacterial infection may render individuals prone to depressive states and that the mechanisms underlying such an effect may involve synergistic interactions among the multiple cytokines activated by such an immunlogical challenge.

The mechanisms by which cytokines come to provoke a depressive-like state remains to be established. However, it is clear that cytokines, like stressors, may promote HPA activation and affect central neurotransmitter systems. As well, the effects of cytokines are such that they may engender plasticity, so that later challenges, even of a different nature, may provoke neurochemical alterations and hence have an impact on affective illness. However, analyses of the effects of cytokines need to consider carefully

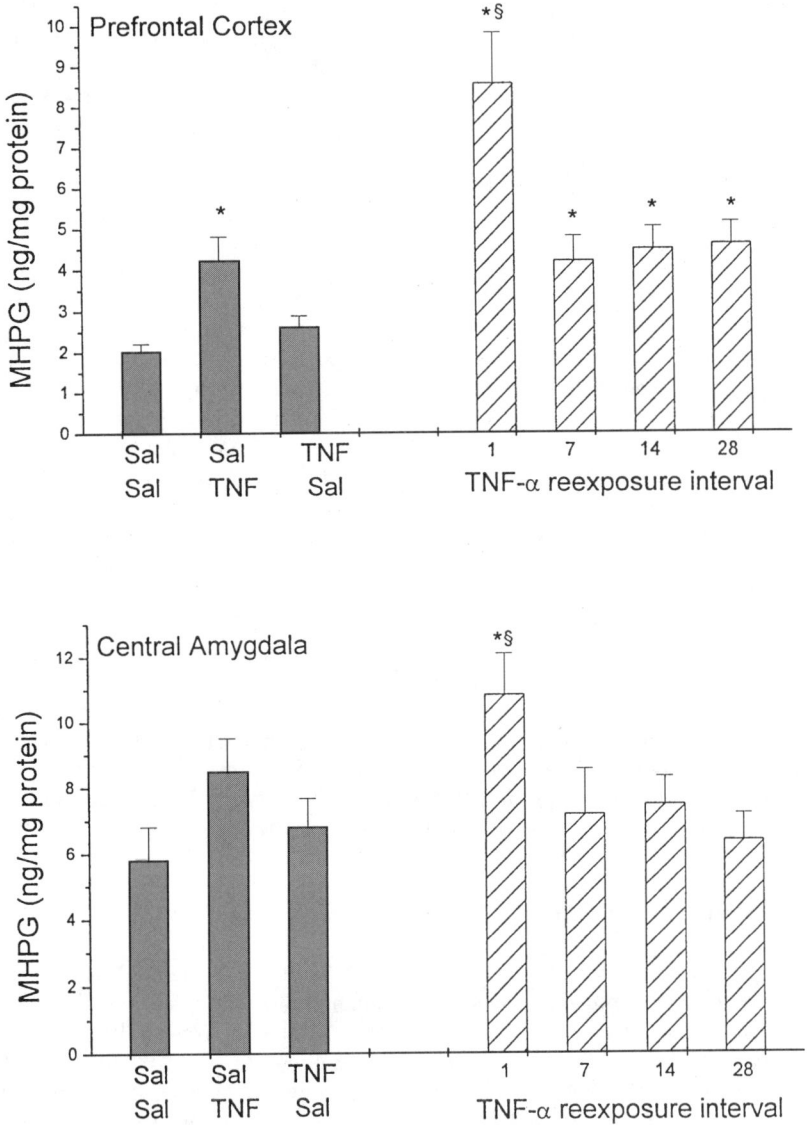

Figure 21.7. Mean (±SEM) concentrations of MHPG within the prefrontal cortex (top) and central amygdala (bottom) as a function of the TNF-α treatment. The group designations were the same as those of Figure 21.5. *$P < 0.05$ relative to saline-treated mice. From "Sensitization to the Effects of Tumor Necrosis Factor-α: Neuroendocrine, Central Monoamine, and Behavioral Variations," by S. Haley, K. Brebner, S. Lacosta, Z. Merali, & H. Anisman, 1999, *Journal of Neuroscience, 19*, 5560–5561.

the characteristics of the depressive illness. This includes not only the severity of the illness (Maes, 1995), but the specific symptom profile or course of the disorder. For instance, one could readily imagine that some cytokines may be more closely aligned with depressive illness involving certain neurovegetative features (e.g., typical vs. atypical depression; the latter being associated with increased eating, carbohydrate craving, more sleep, mood reactivity) or may be particularly notable in chronic syndromes (e.g., dysthymia), especially when onset of the illness occurred at an early age (Anisman et al., 1999).

In addition to affective illnesses, the present findings raise the possibility that cytokines ought to be considered as contributing to the neuroprotective effects that may occur under some conditions of brain trauma. In particular, it has been reported that a mild ischemic episode or electrical stimulation of the brain which promotes seizure (kindling) may protect against the marked neuronal damage that would otherwise be provoked by a later, more pronounced insult (Barone et al., 1998; Kelley & McIntyre, 1994). Interestingly, it seems that such effects may, among other things, be dependent upon the timing of the two incidents (Barone et al., 1998). To be sure, while cytokines may act in a neurodestructive manner (Rothwell, 1999), it seems that they may also act in a protective fashion (Nawasiro, Tasaki, Ruetzler, & Hallenbeck, 1997), depending on the cytokine dosage and cellular milieu (Rothwell, 1999). It is possible that the state of the CNS at the time of cytokine challenge may be important in determing whether the immune mediator acts in a protective or deleterious fashion. For instance, IL-1 has more pronounced pathophysiological effects (e.g., exacerbated corticostriatal damage) in animals subjected to excitotoxic or ischemic insults than in otherwise untreated animals (Rothwell, 1999). Likewise, the role of cytokines may change with the progression of neuropathology, such that it may be neurodestructive during the early stages (e.g., increasing blood-brain-barrier permeability or inducing the release of free radicals in neurodegenerative states) but protective at later times (e.g., through release of various trophic factors). While it is possible that several other factors could account for the divergent actions of cytokines (e.g., cofactors released from glial cells), it ought to be considered that time-dependent sensitization or desensitzation associated with challenges may contribute to the outcomes. Collectively, the available evidence suggests that cytokines may act in a modulatory role to affect CNS processes and that the nature of such actions may depend upon the demands placed upon the brain by other ongoing or prior challenges.

Acknowledgments

The work was supported by the Medical Research Council of Canada. S. H. was supported by an NSERC Fellowship. H. A. is an Ontario Mental Health Foundation Senior Research Fellow.

References

Anisman, H., & Merali, Z. (1999). Cytokines and stress in relation to anxiety and anhedonia. In: R. Dantzer, E. E. Wollmann, & R. Yirmiya (Eds.), *Cytokines, stress and depression.* (pp. 199–234) London: Plenum Press.

Anisman, H., Hayley, S., & Merali, Z. (in press). Neurochemical sequelae of cytokine activation: Parallels with stressor effects. In R. Kvetnansky (Ed.), *Seventh Symposium on Catecholamines and Other Transmitters in Stress.* Slovak Academy of Science.

Anisman, H., Ravindran, A. V., Griffiths, J., & Merali, Z. (1999). Endocrine and cytokine correlates of major depression and dysthymia with typical or atypical features. *Molecular Psychiatry, 4*, 182–188.

Anisman. H., & Sklar, L. S. (1979). Catecholamine depletion upon reexposure to stress: Mediation of the escape deficits produced by inescapable shock. *Journal of Comparative and Physiological Psychology, 93*, 610–625.

Anisman, H., Zalcman, S., & Zacharko, R. M. (1993). The impact of stressors on immune and central neurotransmitter activity: Bidirectional communication. *Reviews in the Neurosciences, 4*, 147–180.

Banks, W. A., Ortiz, L., Plotkin, S. R., & Kasten, A. J. (1991). Human interleukin (IL) 1 alpha, murine IL-1 alpha and murine IL-2 beta are transported from blood to brain in the mouse by a shared saturable mechanism. *Journal of Pharmacological and Experimental Therapeutics, 259*, 988–996.

Barone, F. C., White, R. F., Spera, T. A., Ellison, J., Currie, R. W., Wang, X., & Feuerstein, G. Z. (1998). Ischemic preconditioning and brain tolerance: Temporal histological and functional outcomes, protein synthesis requirement, and interleukin-1 receptor antagonist and early gene expression. *Stroke, 29*, 1937–1951.

Bhatnagar, S., Singh, K. D., Sazawal, S., Saxena, S. K., & Bhan, M. K. (1998). The effects of prior chronic stress on cardiovascular responses to acute restraint and formalin injection. *Brain Research, 797*, 313–320.

Bolanos-Jimenez, F., Manhaes de Casatro, R., Seguin, L., Cloez-Tayarani, I., Monneret, V., Drieu, K., & Fillion, G. (1995). Effects of stress on the functional properties of pre- and postsynaptic 5-HT1B receptors in the brain. *European Journal of Pharmacology, 294*, 531–540.

Borowski, T., Kokkinidis, L., Merali, Z., & Anisman, H. (1998). Lipopolysaccharide, central in vivo amine alterations, and anhedonia. *NeuroReport, 9*, 3797–3802.

Brady, L. S., Lynn, A. B., Herkenham, M., & Gottesfeld, Z. (1994) Systemic interleukin-1 induces early and late patterns of c-fos mRNA expression in brain. *Journal of Neuroscience, 14*, 4951–4964.

Brebner, K., Hayley, S., Zacharko, R. M., Merali, Z., & Anisman, H. (2000). Synergistic effects of interleukin-1β, interleukin-6 and tumor necrosis factor-a: Central monoamine, corticosterone and behavioral variations. *Neuropsychopharmacology* (pp. 566–580).

Buttini, M., & Boddeke, H. (1995). Peripheral lipopolysaccharide stimulation induces interleukin-1b messenger RNA in rat brain microglial cells. *Neuroscience, 65*, 523–530.

Buttini, M., Sauter, A., & Boddeke, H. W. (1994). Induction of interleukin-1 beta mRNA after focal cerebral ischemia in the rat. *Molecular Brain Research, 23*, 126–134.

Dallman, M. F., Akana, S. F., Levin, N., Walker, C. D., Bradbury, M. J., Suemaru, S., & Scribner, K. S. (1994). Corticosteroids and the control of function in the hypothalamo-pituitary-adrenal (HPA) axis. *Annals of the New York Academy of Sciences, 746*, 22–31.

Dantzer, R., Bluthe, R. M., Aubert, A., Goodall, G., Bret–Dibat, J.-L., Kent, S., Goujon, E., Laye, S., Parnet, P., & Kelley, K. W. (1996). Cytokine actions on behavior. In N. J. Rothwell (Ed.), *Cytokines and the nervous system* (pp. 117–144). London: Landes.

Davis, M., Walker, D. L., & Lee, Y. (1999). Neurophysiology and neuropharamacology of startle and its affective modification. In M. E. Dawson, A. M. Schell, & A. H. Bohmelt (Eds.), *Startle modification: Implications for neuroscience, cognitive science, and clinical science* (pp. 95–114). Cambridge, England: Cambridge University Press.

De Simoni, M. G., Del Bo, R., De Luigi, A., Simard, S., & Forloni, G. (1995). Central endotoxin induces different patterns of interleukin (IL)-1b and IL-6 messenger robonucleic acid expression and IL-6 secretion in the brain and periphery. *Endocrinology, 136*, 897–902.

Deutch, A. Y., & Roth, R. H. (1990) The determinants of stress-induced activation of the prefrontal cortical dopamine system. In H. B. M. Uylings, C. G. Van Eden, J. P. C. De Bruin, M. A. Corner, & M. G. P. Feenstra (Eds.), *Progress in brain research* (Vol. 85. pp. 367–403). New York: Elsevier.

Deutch, A. Y., Bourdelais, A. J., & Zahm, D. S. (1993). The nucleus accumbens core and shell:

Accumbal compartments and their functional attributes. In P. W. Kaliovas & C. D. Barnes (Eds.), *Limbic motor circuits and neuropsychiatry* (pp. 45–88). Boca Raton, FL: CRC Press.

Dinan, T. G. (1994). Glucocorticoids and the genesis of depressive illness: A psychobiological model. *British Journal of Psychiatry, 164*, 365–371.

Doherty, M. D., & Gratton, A. (1992). High-speed chronoamperometric measurements of mesolimbic and nigrostriatal dopamine release associated with repeated daily stress. *Brain Research, 586*, 295–302.

Dunn, A. J. (1995). Interactions between the nervous system and the immune system. In F. E. Bloom & D. J. Kupfer (Eds.), *Psychopharmacology: The fourth generation of progress* (pp. 719–731). New York: Raven Press.

Ek, M., Kurosawa, M., Lundenberg, T., & Ericsson, A. (1998). Activation of vagal afferents after intravenous injection of interleukin-1β: Role of endogenous prostaglandins. *Journal of Neuroscience, 18*, 9471–9479.

Ericsson, A., Kovacs, K. J., & Sawchenko, P. E. (1994). A functional anatomical analysis of central pathways subserving the effects of interleukin-1 on stress-related neuroendocrine neurons. *Journal of Neuroscience, 14*, 89–91.

Ferretti, C., Blengio, M., Gamalero, S. R., & Ghi, P. (1995). Biochemical and behavioral changes induced by acute stress in a chronic variate stress model of depression: The effect of amitriptyline. *European Journal of Pharmacology, 280*, 19–26.

Gaballec, M.-M., Griffais, R., Fillion, G., & Haour, F. (1996). Interleukin-1 receptors type I and type II in the mouse brain: Kinetics of mRNA expressions after peripheral administration of bacterial lipopolysaccharide. *Journal of Neuroimmunology, 66*, 65–70.

Gemma, C., Ghezzi, P., & De Simoni, M. G. (1991). Activation of the hypothalamic serotonergic system by central interleukin-1. *European Journal of Pharmacology, 209*, 139–140.

Gresch, P. J., Sved, A. F., Zigmond, M. J., & Finlay, J. M. (1994). Stress-induced sensitization of dopamine and norepinephrine efflux in medial prefrontal cortex of the rat. *Journal of Neurochemistry, 63*, 575–583.

Gutierrez, E. G., Banks, W. A., & Kastin, A. J. (1993). Murine tumor necrosis factor alpha is transported from blood to brain in the mouse. *Journal of Neuroimmunology, 47*, 169–176.

Hayley, S. Brebner, K., Lacosta, S., Merali, Z., & Anisman, H. (1999). Sensitization to the effects of tumor necrosis factor-α: Neuroendocrine, central monoamine, and behavioral variations. *Journal of Neuroscience, 19*, 5654–5665.

Hayley, S., Staines, W., Mercali, Z., & Anisman, H. (1999). Changes in immunoreactivity for AVP, CRH, NOS, and GFAP in the murine brain after tumor necrosis factor-α treatment. *Society for Neuroscience Abstracts, 25*, 1121.

Herman, J. P., & Cullinan, W. E. (1997). Neurocircuitry of stress: Central control of hypothalamo-pituitary-adrenocortical axis. *Trends in Neuroscience, 20*, 78–84.

Hopkins, S. J., & Rothwell N. J. (1995). Cytokines and the nervous system. *Trends in Neuroscience, 18*, 83–88.

Ilyin, S. E., & Plata-Salaman, C. R. (1996). In vivo regulation of the IL-1 beta system (ligand, receptors I and II, receptor accessory protein, and receptor antagonist) and TNF-alpha mRNAs in specific brain regions. *Biochemistry Biophysics Research Communication, 227*, 861–867.

Imperato, A., Angelucci, L., Casolini, P., Zocchi, A., & Puglisi-Allegra, S. (1992). Repeated stressful experiences differently affect limbic dopamine release during and following stress. *Brain Research, 577*, 194–199.

Jorgensen, C., Apparailly, F., & Sany, J. (1999) Immunological evaluation of cytokine and anti-cytokine immunotherapy in vivo: What have we learnt? *Annals of Rheumatoid Disorders, 58*, 136–141.

Kalivas, P. W., & Duffy, P. (1995). Selective activation of dopamine transmission in the shell of the nucleus accumbens by stress. *Brain Research, 675*, 325–328.

Kalivas, P. W., & Stewart, J. (1991). Dopamine transmission in the initiation and expression of drug- and stress-induced sensitization of motor activity. *Brain Research Reviews, 16*, 223–244.

Kelley, M. E., & McIntyre, D. C. (1994). Hippocampal kindling protects several structures from the neuronal damage resulting from kainic acid-induced status epilepticus. *Brain Research, 634,* 245–256.

Lacosta, S., Merali, Z., & Anisman, H. (1998). Influence of interleukin-1 on exploratory behavior, plasma ACTH and corticosterone, and central biogenic amines in mice. *Psychopharmacology, 137,* 351–361.

Lacosta, S., Merali, Z., & Anisman, H. (1999). Behavioral and neurochemical consequences of lipopolysaccharide in mice: Anxiogenic-like effects. *Brain Reseach, 818,* 291–303.

Lightman, S. L. (1994). How does the hypothalamus respond to stress? *Seminars in Neuroscience, 6,* 215–219.

Linthorst, A. C. E., Flachskamm, C., Muller-Preuss, P. Holsboer, F., & Reul, J. M. H. M. (1995). Effect of bacterial endotoxin and interleukin-1b on hippocampal serotonergic neurotransmision, behavioral activity, and free corticosterone levels: An in vivo microdialysis study. *Journal of Neuroscience, 15,* 2920–2934.

Maes, M. (1995). Evidence for an immune response in major depression: A review and hypothesis. *Progress in Neuro-psychopharmacology and Biological Psychiatry, 19,* 11–38.

Maier, S. F., & Watkins, L. R. (1998). Cytokines for psychologists: Implications of bidirectional immune-to-brain communication for understanding behavior, mood, and cognition. *Psychological Review, 105,* 83–107.

Matsuda, S., Peng, H., Yoshimura, H., Wen, T.-C., Fukuda, T., & Sakanaka, M. (1996). Persistent c-fos expression in the brains of mice with chronic social stress. *Neuroscience Research, 26,* 157–170.

McIntyre, D. C., Kent, P., Hayley, S., Merali, Z., & Anisman, H. (1999). Influence of psychogenic and neurogenic stressors on neuroendocrine and central monoamine activity in fast and slow kindling rats. *Brain Research, 840,* 65–74.

Merali, Z., McIntosh, J., Kent, P., Michaud, D., &. Anisman, H. (1998). Aversive as well as appetitive events evoke the release of corticotropin releasing hormone and bombesin-like peptides at the central nucleus of the amygdala. *Journal of Neuroscience, 18,* 4758–4766.

Merali, Z., Lacosta S., & Anisman, H. (1997). Effects of interleukin-1β and mild stress on alterations of central monoamines: A regional microdialysis study. *Brain Research, 761,* 225–235.

Mohankumar, P. S., & Quadri, S. K. (1993). Systemic administration of interleukin-1 stimulates norepinephrine release in the paraventricular nucleus. *Life Sciences, 52,* 1961–1967

Munck, A., & Guyre, P. M. (1991). Glucocorticoids and immune function. In R. Ader, D. L. Felten, & N. Cohen (Eds.), *Psychoneuroimmunology* (pp. 447–474). San Diego: Academic Press.

Nawashiro, H., Tasaki, K., Ruetzler, C. A., & Hallenbeck, J. M. (1997). TNF-alpha pretreatment induces protective effects against focal ischemia in mice. *Journal of Cereberal Flow and Metabolism, 17,* 483–490.

Neumaier, J. F., Petty, F., Kramer, G. L., Szot, P., & Hamblin, M. W. (1997). Learned helplessness increases 5-hydroxytryptamine1B receptor mRNA levels in the rat dorsal raphe nucleus. *Biological Psychiatry, 41,* 668–674.

Nguyen, K. T., Deak, T., Owens, S. M., Kohno, T., Fleshner, M., Watkins, L. R., & Maier, S. F. (1988). Exposure to acute stress induces brain interleukin-1b protein in the rat. *Journal of Neuroscience, 18,* 2239–2246.

Pacak, K., Palkovits, M., Kopin, I. J., & Goldstein, D. S. (1995). Stress-induced norepinephrine release in the hypothalamic paraventricular nucleus and pituitary-adrenal and sympathoadrenal activity: In vivo microdialysis studies. *Frontiers of Neuroedocrinology, 16,* 89–150.

Pauli S., Linthorst, A. C. E., Reul, J. M. H. M. (1998). Tumor necrosis factor-α and interlekin-2 differentially affect hippocampal serotonergic neurotransmission, behavioral activity, body temperature and hypothalamic-pituitary-adrenocortical axis activity in the rat. *European Journal of Neuroscience, 10,* 868–878.

Rivest, S. (1995). Molecular mechanisms and neural pathways mediating the influence of interleukin-1 on the activity of neuroendocrine CRF motoneurons in the rat. *International Journal of Developmental Neuroscience, 13,* 135–146.

Rivest S., & Rivier C. (1994). Stress and interleukin-1 beta-induced activation of c-Fos, Ngfi-B and CRF gene expression in the hypothalamic PVN—Comparison between Sprague-Dawley, Fisher-344 and Lewis rats. *Journal of Neuroendocrinology, 6*, 101–117.

Rothwell, N. J. (1999). Cytokines—killers in the brain. *Journal of Physiology, 514*, 3–17.

Rothwell, N. J., & Hopkins, S. J. (1995). Cytokines and the nervous system II: Actions and mechanisms of action. *Trends in Neuroscience, 18*, 130–136.

Sawchenko, P. E., Brown, E. R., Chan, R. K. W., Ericsson, A., Li, H.-Y., Roland, B. L., & Kovacs, K. J. (1996). The paraventricular nucleus of the hypothalamus and the functional neuroanatomy of visceromotor responses to stress. *Progress Brain Research, 107*, 201–222.

Schmidt, E. D., Binnekade, R., Janszen, A. W., & Tilders, F. J. H. (1996). Short stressor induced long-lasting increases of vasopressin stores in hypothalamic corticotropin-releasing hormone (CRH) neurons in adult rat. *Journal of Neuroendocrinology, 8*, 703–712.

Schmidt, E. D., Janszen, A. W. J. W., Wouterlood, F. G., & Tilders, F. J. H. (1995). Interleukin-1 induced long-lasting changes in hypothalamic corticotropin-releasing hormone (CRH) neurons and hyperresponsiveness of the hypothalamic-pituitary-adrenal axis. *Journal of Neuroscience, 15*, 7417–7426.

Schulkin, J., Gold, P. W., & McEwen, B. S. (1998). Induction of corticotropin-releasing hormone gene expression by glucocorticoids: Implication for understanding the states of fear and anxiety and allostatic load. *Psychoneuroendocrinology, 23*, 219–243.

Shintani, F., Nakaki, T., Kanba, S., Sato, K., Kato, R., & Asai, M. (1995). Role of interleukin-1 in stress responses. *Molecular Neurobiology, 10*, 47–71.

Smith, M. A., Banerjee, S., Gold, P. W., & Glowa, J. (1992). Induction of c-fos mRNA in rat brain by conditioned and unconditioned stressors. *Brain Research, 578*, 135–141.

Soliven, B., & Albert, J. (1992). Tumor necrosis factor modulates Ca^{2+} currents in cultured sympathetic neurons. *Journal of Neuroscience, 12*, 2665–2671.

Song, C., Merali, Z., & Anisman, H. (1999). Variations of nucleus accumbens dopamine and serotonin following systemic interleukin-1, interleukin-2 or interleukin-6 treatment. *Neuroscience, 88*, 823–836.

Stone, E. A. (1983). Adaptation to stress and brain nonadrenergic receptors. *Neuroscience and Biobehavioral Reviews, 1*, 503–509.

Sullivan, R. M., & Gratton, A. (1998). Relationships between stress-induced increases in medial prefrontal cortical dopamine band plasma corticosterone levels in rats. Role of cerebral laterality. *Neuroscience, 83*, 81–91.

Tancredi, V., D'Arcangelo, G., Grassi, F., Tarroni, P., Palmieri, G., Santoni, A., & Eusebi, F. (1992). Tumor necrosis factor alters synaptic transmission in rat hippocampal slices. *Neuroscience Letters, 146*, 176–178.

Tidey, J. W., & Miczek, K. A. (1996). Social defeat stress selectively alters mesocorticolimbic dopamine release: An in vivo microdialysis study. *Brain Research, 721*, 140–149.

Tilders, F. J. H., & Schmidt, E. D., (1998). Interleukin-1-induced plasticity of hypothalamic CRH neurons and long-term stress hyperresponsiveness. *Annals of the New York Academy of Science, 840*, 65–73.

Tilders, F. J. H., Schmidt, E. D., & De Goeij, D. C. E. (1993). Phenotypic plasticity of CRF neurons during stress. *Annals of the New York Academy of Science, 697*, 39–52.

Turnbull, A. V., & Rivier, C. (1996). Cytokine effects on neuroendocrine axes: Influence of nitric oxide and carbon monoxide. In N. J. Rothwell (Ed.), *Cytokines in the nervous system* (pp. 93–116). London: Landes.

Weiss, J. M., & Simson, P. E. (1989). Electrophysiology of the locus coeruleus: Implications for stress-induced depression. In G. F. Koob, C. L. Ehlers, & D. J. Kupfer (Eds.), *Animal models of depression* (pp. 111–134). Boston: Birkhauser.

Whitnall, M. H., Perlstein, R. S., Mougey, E. H., & Neta, R. (1992). Effects of interleukin-1 on the stress responsive and nonresponsive subtypes of corticotropin-releasing hormone neurosecretory axons. *Endocrinology, 131*, 37–44.

Yabuuchi, K., Minami, M., Katsumata, S., & Satoh, M. (1993). In situ hybridization study of interleukin-1β mRNA induced by kainic acid in the rat brain. *Molecular Brain Research, 20,* 153–161.

Yirmiya, R. (1996). Endotoxin produces a depressive-like episode in rats. *Brain Research, 711,* 163–174.

Yoshioka, M., Matsumoto, M., Togashi, H., & Saito, H. (1995). Effects of conditioned fear stress on 5-HT release in the rat prefrontal cortex. *Pharmacology, Biochemistry & Behavior, 51,* 515–519.

"PATHOLOGICAL" NEUROPLASTICITY AND THE RESPONSE TO INJURY

The Mutability of Sensory Representations After Injury in Adult Mammals

☐ Introduction

Until recently, the general opinion was common that the mature brain is rather stable or fixed in functional organization. This general opinion seemed to be based on two major lines of evidence. As an example of one type of evidence, Sperry (1943) showed that altering inputs into the mature brain of mature rats failed to produce adaptive adjustments in behavior. Specifically, Sperry crossed sensory nerves from one hindlimb to the other and allowed regeneration of the cut nerve into the skin of the wrong limb. When the newly innervated skin was pinched, the rats retracted the original limb rather than the newly innervated limb, and this behavior persisted. We repeated these experiments with exactly the same behavioral results (Wunderlick, Wall, & Kaas, 1981). Rats consistently retracted the original rather than the pinched leg. Recordings in the somatosensory cortex showed no adaptive reorganization that would alter this behavior. In regard to this manipulation, no adaptive change in behavior occurred, and no relevant reorganization of the somatosensory system was observed. Sperry, on the basis of the behavioral observations alone, concluded that the mature nervous system was not very plastic.

A similar conclusion emerged from the studies of Hubel and Wiesel (1970) on the developmental effects of visual deprivation in kittens. Unilateral eyelid closure altered the growth of neurons in the deprived layers of the lateral geniculate nucleus of the thalamus and reduced the number of binocularly activated neurons in the primary visual cortex. The magnitudes of these effects depended on the age of the kitten. The effects of deprivation were most profound in young kittens, soon after natural eye opening, and no changes were apparent in adult cats. Experiments of this type repeatedly produced similar results, and they led to the general conclusion that a period of developmental susceptibility to the effects of injury and deprivation is followed by a lack of such plasticity in the mature brain.

Both types of experiments point out that the developing brain may be more plastic, or differently plastic, than the mature brain, and that significant brain changes may not occur after some manipulations. We should also consider the possibility that brain reorganizations may occur that do not lead to adaptive changes in the brain. While Sperry (1943) concluded from the fixed and maladaptive behavior of rats that the brain was not very plastic, changes in the brain might have occurred that did not relate to the observed behavior.

☐ An Early Study of the Effects of Sensory Deafferentation on the Somatosensory Cortex

In the early 1980s, we wondered what the effects on the somatosensory cortex might be of a major loss of sensory input. Previous studies on subcortical sensory representations in the spinal cord and brainstem after sensory nerve sections were highly suggestive of considerable plasticity (e.g., Wall & Egger, 1971), but measuring changes in small subcortical representations was difficult, and the described changes were questioned (see Snow & Wilson, 1991; Jain, Florence, & Kaas, 1995). New World owl monkeys and squirrel monkeys have large systematic representations of the glabrous hand as an important sensory surface, and these representations were on the surface of the brain in these primates with a short and shallow or a missing central sulcus. Cutting the median nerve subserving the thumb half of the glabrous skin of the hand effectively removed the activating inputs to about half of the large hand representations in area 3b (primary somatosensory cortex or S1; see Kaas, 1983). Detailed maps of this deprived cortex made with microelectrodes months after the injury revealed no regions of unresponsive cortex. Instead, neurons throughout the deprived zone of the cortex responded to new inputs, largely those from the dorsal hairy surface of the hand (Merzenich et al., 1983). Thus, we had changed the cortical representation of the rather limited and unimportant sensory inputs from the dorsal hand from a tiny fraction of the total hand representation to over half. We still don't know if this has any perceptual consequences, but one might expect mislocalizations so that touch on the back of the hand is felt on the front (see below). The major importance of this discovery is that the magnitude of the change showed beyond doubt that significant reorganization could occur in the mature brain. By implication, all brain systems might be similarly plastic in adults, and there might be many ways of altering mature systems. These suppositions have now been extensively supported by experimental evidence. We also know more about mediating mechanisms and the functional consequences of brain reorganization.

☐ Sensory Deafferentations Alter Somatosensory, Visual, and Auditory Cortical Maps

While nerve section clearly demonstrated the capacity for reorganization of the somatosensory cortex in mature primates, other types of deafferentations also result in reorganizations. Monkeys sometimes injure and lose a finger, and the cortex normally responsive to inputs from that finger becomes responsive to inputs from adjoining fingers and the palm (Jain, Catania, & Kaas, 1998; Merzenich et al., 1984). Larger reorganizational changes were observed in monkeys that had lost all or most of sensory inputs from an arm, either after section of the dorsal sensory roots of sensory nerves entering the spinal cord (Pons et al., 1991) or after therapeutic amputations of severely injured arms (Florence & Kaas, 1995; Wu & Kaas, 1999). The deprived section of the somatosensory cortex (area 3b) became responsive to inputs from the face, stump of the amputated limb, or both. Extensive reactivations also occur after ascending branches of sensory afferents have been cut as they travel to the brainstem in the dorsal columns of the spinal cord. Such sections leave terminations on spinal cord neurons and other ascending systems in the lateral and ventral spinal cord intact, but they do deactivate much of the primary somatosensory cortex, including the hand and forearm representations. The inputs from the face enter the brainstem above the spinal cord section without damage. After such deafferentations, the hand and forearm sections of the somatosensory cortex become responsive to inputs from the face (Jain, Catania, & Kaas, 1997).

Similar cortical reorganizations have been observed in the visual system after deafferentations produced by retinal lesions. Lasers are commonly used to place small restricted lesions in the human retina to protect remaining parts of the retina, with little thought to how or if this affects the rest of the brain. However, we know from many experiments in cats (Chino, Kaas, Smith, Langston, & Cheng, 1992; Kaas et al., 1990; Schmid, Rosa, Calford, & Ambler, 1996) and monkeys (Gilbert & Wiesel, 1992; Heinen & Skavenski, 1991), that the deprived neurons in the primary visual cortex acquire new receptive fields based on preserved inputs from portions of the retina surrounding the lesion. Thus, there is no unresponsive zone in the visual cortex, and the retinotopic map distorts to omit the cortical scotoma produced by the lesion.

The auditory cortex also reorganizes after a hearing loss. The potential for such reorganization has not been extensively studied but reorganization has been demonstrated. Robertson and Irvine (1989) first demonstrated the capacity for the primary auditory cortex to tonotopically reorganize by lesioning the middle portion of the cochlea in guinea pigs. After weeks or more of recovery, neurons in the deprived middle frequency zone of the cortex responded instead to tones that were lower or higher in frequency than normal. Similar results have been obtained after partial lesions of the cochlea in cats (Rajan, Irvine, Wise, & Heil, 1993) and monkeys (Schwaber, Garraghty, & Kaas, 1993). Neurons deprived of their normal source of activation after a partial loss of sensory afferents come to respond to remaining auditory afferents.

☐ Subcortical Reorganization

Deafferentations have also been shown to produce reorganizations in subcortical nuclei. The most convincing evidence came from studies of the large hand subnucleus of the ventroposterior thalamic nucleus of monkeys. Removal of afferents from half of all of the glabrous hand by cutting the median nerve or the median and ulnar nerves is followed over time by the reactivation of the complete subnucleus by the relatively few afferents from the dorsal hand that course in the intact radial nerve (Garraghty & Kaas, 1991). In monkeys with longstanding therapeutic arm amputations, the hand subnucleus is reactivated by arm stump and face inputs (Florence, Hackett, & Strata, 2000). Microelectrode recordings and stimulations in the thalamus of humans with amputations also suggest that the hand subnucleus of the ventroposterior nucleus is reactivated by the stump (Davis et al., 1998; Lenz, Gracely, Baker, Richardson, & Dougherty, 1998). In monkeys long deprived of sensory inputs from the arm after sectioning of the dorsal roots of nerves to the arm, the hand subnucleus is reactivated by inputs from the face (Jones & Pons, 1998). A more limited reorganization of the cuneate nucleus of the brainstem appears to occur after median nerve section, so that a substantial number but not all of the deprived neurons acquire receptive fields in the dorsal hand (Xu & Wall, 1997).

Visual and auditory brainstem structures may reorganize after partial deafferentations as well. What is known is that the reorganization of the dorsal lateral geniculate nucleus is much less extensive after retinal lesions than the cortical reorganization over the same time period (Darian-Smith & Gilbert, 1995; Eysel, 1982). Partial lesions of the cochlea in adult cats produced no obvious reorganization in the dorsal cochlear nucleus of the brainstem over a time course that would produce extensive reorganization in auditory cortex (Rajan & Irvine, 1998).

Reorganization After Cortical Lesions

Reorganization can occur in cortical representations after partial lesions of those representations or after lesions of cortical areas feeding into cortical representations. Jenkins and Merzenich (1987) selectively removed the part of area 3b of monkeys representing digit 3 and later found neurons responsive to digit 3 in cortex around the lesion. Since areas 1 and 3a receive inputs from area 3b, larger lesions of 3b altered the organizations of areas 1 and 3a (Xerri, Merzenich, Peterson, & Jenkins, 1998). Large lesions of the hand representations in areas 3a, 3b, 1, and 2 caused one of their targets, the second somatosensory area or S2, to reorganize so that the deprived hand portion of S2 came to represent the foot (Pons, Garraghty, & Mishkin, 1988). Thus, cortical areas can reorganize to recover missing portions of their representations, when the missing part is small. Furthermore, cortical areas can reorganize to use remaining inputs when some direct inputs are removed.

Reorganization Due to Experience

While the focus of this chapter is on the impressive plasticity that occurs after injury, more restricted changes in sensory representations occur as a consequence of notable changes in sensory experience, for example, as more sensory activity seems to enlarge the representation of a stimulated skin surface. This is perhaps most clearly demonstrated by the simple procedure of electrically stimulating a digit of the forepaw in rats for several hours. This stimulation increased the size of the representation of that digit in the primary somatosensory cortex (Li, Waters, McCandlish, & Johnson, 1996). In a similar manner, electrically stimulating a site in area 3b of monkeys with a microelectrode enlarged the cortical territory representing that site (Recanzone, Merzenich, & Dinse, 1992). Jenkins, Merzenich, Ochs, Allard, and Guic-Robles (1990) reported that monkeys trained to maintain contact with the fingertips on a rotating disk had enlarged representations of the digit tips in area 3b. Other training experiences have altered receptive field sizes and neuron response properties (see Buonomano & Merzenich, 1998, for review).

Typically, experience-related changes in cortical representations are seen as mediating wanted changes in behavior. However, some types of experience can lead to reorganizations that may relate to impairments in behavior. Monkeys overtrained on a hand-grasp task to the extent that they developed a dystonia-like motor disorder had a degraded map of the hand in area 3b (Bly, Merzenich, & Jenkins, 1996).

Motor Cortex Reorganization

Procedures that have been used to cause motor cortex maps to reorganize have been quite different in concept from those used to alter sensory maps. Instead of altering sensory input and activity, motor representations have been altered by the loss of the motor targets. The first demonstrations were in rats, where electrical stimulation of a large portion of the primary motor cortex moves the behaviorally important sensory whiskers of the face. Sectioning the facial motor nerve to the muscles of the facial vibrissae creates a large portion of motor cortex where electrical stimulation can no longer move whiskers. Instead, normal levels of electrical stimulation with microelectrodes in this cortex come to move the eyelid and forelimb (Donoghue, Suner, & Sanes, 1990; Sanes, Suner, Lando, & Donoghue, 1988). More recently, it has been possible to study motor cortex in monkeys with long-standing therapeutic amputations of a forelimb (Qi, Stepneiwska, & Kaas, 2000; Schieber & Deuel, 1997; Wu & Kaas, 1999). Normally, most stimulation sites in the forelimb section of primary motor cortex in monkeys are devoted to digit movements. In the monkeys with forelimb loss, most sites are devoted to moving the stump and shoulder of the amputated limb. While some of these sites require higher than normal levels of electrical stimulation to evoke these movements, more sites than normal evoke upper arm (stump) movement at normal or lower thresholds. Stump movements can also be evoked from more sites in premotor cortex (Wu & Kaas, 1999). Thus, the globally topological motor maps of both primary motor and premotor cortex are capable of reorganizing after the loss of muscle targets.

☐ Mechanisms of Reorganization

The main mechanisms of reorganization are the potentiation of existing connections and the growth of new connections. The strengths of local connections in sensory and motor systems appear to be in a constant state of flux, and they are adjusted by changes in neural activity patterns. Extreme depressions of activity, as with major deafferentations, and the loss of normal targets for neuron projections appear to provoke growth of new connections, even over considerable distances. Extensive new growth is provoked by unusual circumstances, but local new growth involving the arbors of axons and dendrites may be quite common. Some of the changes in neurons that are related to plasticity are noted below.

Neurons in the central nervous system are under the influence of many factors that alter ongoing spike activity. Response properties are maintained through a dynamic balance of these influences, and the balance is easily altered (see Nicolelis, 1997; Xing & Gerstein, 1996, for review). Neuron response properties are influenced by stimuli outside receptive field, preceding stimuli, and motivational factors. In many deafferentation experiments, slight changes in receptive field locations for partially deprived neurons are recorded immediately, largely as a result of shifting the dynamic balance. The most probable course of such immediate changes is the loss of afferent drive of the neurons that then stimulate the inhibitory neurons that are parts of local circuits. The loss of inhibition that spreads laterally ("lateral inhibition") in structures allows remaining subthreshold excitatory contact to become suprathreshold. This type of change has been called unmasking (Wall, 1977) or disinhibition (e.g., Calford & Tweedale, 1988), and it is usually rather limited in extent.

Damage to sensory structures and afferents can also sensitize afferents and thereby alter inputs. In addition, external events and internal states can activate neural modulating systems such as the acetylcholine-releasing neurons in the brainstem that project widely to the cortex. Electrical stimulation of the basal forebrain to trigger acetylcholine release in the cortex promotes experience-related plasticity in the cortex (see Kilgard & Merzenich, 1998), and depletion of acetylcholine reduces plasticity. The neuromodulators presumably work to promote plasticity by increasing activity and temporarily creating a window of opportunity when other sources of activation can be strengthened. Thus, Dykes (1997) has described the role of neuromodulators as creating a "permissive state" for neural plasticity. Acetylcholine and noradrenaline have long been considered important modulators of developmental plasticity in the visual cortex (e.g., Bear & Singer, 1986).

The major mechanism for creating experience-related plasticity is referred to as Hebbian plasticity (see Rauschecker, 1991) after Donald Hebb, the psychologist who proposed that changes in synaptic strength are responsible for learning. Hebbian plasticity may be based in part on long-term potentiation (LTP, see Teyler, Chapter 9, and Cain, Chapter 10 of this volume). After intense stimulation of inputs on a neuron, a long period of increased sensitivity is created so that a previously ineffective input becomes effective. For example, if input A activates a neuron, while input B does not, the coactivation of A and B for a time may potentiate the effectiveness of B so that B becomes effective, thereby changing the response properties of the activated neuron. Coactive neuromodulatory inputs may help. Discorrelated activity may weaken or depress the effectiveness of inputs, creating long-term depression (LTD). LTP depends on the glutamatergic activation of NMDA receptors on neurons and possibly nitric oxide (NO) as a retrograde messenger (Brenman & Bredt, 1977). Changes in sensory representations as a result of experience, training, and even injury have been attributed to Hebbian cellular mechanisms (Buonomano & Merzenich, 1998).

Activity-dependent changes in gene expression in neurons is another factor that could alter neuron response properties. In particular, the expression of the inhibitory neural transmitter, GABA, and the receptors for GABA seem to be activity dependent (see Jones, 1993). Reduced levels of GABA and GABA receptors would reduce inhibition and allow otherwise subthreshold inputs to be expressed.

Although difficult to detect without detailed quantitative study, neurons probably commonly modify numbers and locations of synaptic contacts through local growth of dendritic and axonal arbors. Early studies showed that rats given new learning experiences, enhanced social environments, or greater sensory stimulation developed more complex dendrites and more dendritic spines on cortical neurons (e.g., Withers & Greenough, 1989). Axon arbor growth or rearrangement as a result of experience has been described in the developing brain, and it likely occurs in the adult brain, but this has not been clearly documented. However, axon growth typically occurs after injury, and such growth may be extensive enough to be easily detected (see below).

The major reactivations of the sensory cortex that occur after an extensive loss of sensory inputs often appear to depend, at least in part, on new axon growth. Sometimes the central processes of injured neurons sprout beyond their normal territory as part of the recovery and regeneration process (see Florence, Garraghty, Carlson, & Kaas, 1993), but uninjured neurons sprout into deactivated territories as well. Normally, afferents from the hand terminate in an orderly somatotopic pattern in the cuneate nucleus of the lower brainstem (e.g., Florence, Wall, & Kaas, 1989). In this nucleus, each glabrous digit and pad of palm is represented in a distinct cluster of neurons surrounded by fibers. The sparse inputs from the back of the digits and hand terminate on neurons in the same clusters as their more numerous counterparts on the glabrous surface. After median or ulnar nerve section, a rather modest growth of the afferents from the back of the hand and digits probably occurs to activate some of the neurons in the cuneate nucleus that have been deprived of their normal sources of activation; this limited reactivation of neurons in the cuneate nucleus is likely to be the critical factor in the much more extensive reactivation of the cortex (see Florence et al., 1989; Garraghty & Kaas, 1991). The effects of the reactivation of only a few neurons by new growth in the brainstem could be amplified by changes in the thalamus and cortex so that an extensive reorganization in the cortex occurs.

While such limited new growth after median nerve section has only been postulated, more extensive new growth is easier to document and it has been demonstrated. In monkeys with arm amputation, afferents from the arm stump that normally terminate only in a restricted part of the cuneate nucleus grow into the part of the nucleus normally innervated by the missing digits (Florence & Kaas, 1995). The new growth is sparse, and for it to fully reactivate deprived cortex, some amplification at higher levels would be required. We already know of a further cortical mechanism. The horizontal connections within the deprived somatosensory cortex also grow to potentially activate more neurons (Florence, Taub, & Kaas, 1998). Thus, activity in a few cortical neurons could be spread laterally to others. In the visual cortex deprived of normal activation by a focal retinal lesion, horizontal connections are also enhanced (Darian-Smith & Gilbert, 1994). New growth at the level of the brainstem can be even more extensive. Inputs from the face normally terminating in the trigeminal complex of the brainstem sprout and grow, again sparsely, into the cuneate nucleus when most of the afferents to the cuneate nucleus are lost after spinal cord injury or arm amputation (Jain, Florence, & Kaas, 2000). This new growth appears to develop slowly, so that the reactivation of the hand sector of the somatosensory cortex by face afferents takes 6–8 months to emerge (Jain et al., 1997). These recent results suggest that the growth of new connections may often occur and contribute to the reactivation of deprived parts of the brain. As another possibility, other recent studies indicate that at least a few new neurons can be generated in the mature brain (e.g., Gould, Beylin, Tanapat, Reeves, & Shors, 1999). These new neurons could help repair damaged brain circuits, and they may be generated in response to brain injury.

Finally, some of the mechanisms involved in reorganization of the motor system, after the section of motor nerves or the loss of limbs and muscles, probably differ from those involved in sensory loss and change. However, lateral connections might be altered in the motor cortex as in the sensory cortex. In addition, corticospinal neurons might grow and change their termination sites to include motor neurons innervating intact muscles. Furthermore, motor neurons with severed axons due to the loss of the limb might survive and regenerate connections to upper arm shoulder muscles moving the stump. Thus, the great increase, after amputation, in the proportion of cortical sites where upper arm movements are evoked (see Wu & Kaas, 1999) could depend on new functional roles for neurons formerly terminating on muscles moving the digits.

☐ The Functional Consequences of Neural Plasticity

Neural activity arising from a response to events in the environment provides a powerful source of information and feedback. To the extent that neural activity patterns maintain and alter neural circuits, the maintained and altered neural properties are likely to have beneficial consequences. Yet, while each neuron probably participates in a number of local circuits, it remains logical to assume that reassignments both improve and impair. Any reassignment of neurons from one circuit to another would seemingly improve some abilities while impairing others, but reassignments based on practice and experience would place neurons in needed, valuable circuits. A common finding in studies of cortical plasticity is that, as training improves performance, more neurons are assigned to the task. Thus, a major role for cortical plasticity in the mature brain is to allow for the acquisition of new motor and perceptual skills. Without maintained practice, neurons are altered by other activities, and skills and abilities deteriorate. The skilled basketball player needs to continue to practice. Some improvements in perceptual and motor skills, when learned on a particular finger for a particular location in the visual field, do not transfer well when other parts of the sensory surface—other fingers, for example—are used. Other improvements do transfer (see Ahissar & Hockstein, 1997). A reasonable interpretation is that if the improvements depend on local reorganizations in the highly topographic primary sensory or motor maps, transfer will be limited. In contrast, if the improvements are mediated in higher order, less topographic representations, transfer of new abilities from finger to finger or from upper to lower visual field may occur.

Brain changes related to practice and experience may not always produce desirable results. Extensive practice, especially under conditions of high stress or injury when modulating systems are active and are capable of promoting cortical plasticity, may modify brain circuits to such an extent that an acceptable range of performance is lost. Such an excessive modification of cortical circuits may be responsible for some types of practice-induced local dystonias (see Bly et al., 1996). For example, after extensive practice, musicians sometimes develop stereotyped hand movements that interfere with proper performance. If these problems stem from excessive rewiring, improvements might follow changes in the practice program that restore beneficial circuits.

Brain plasticity might also lead to misperceptions and other impairments rather than compensations or improvements. Small retinal lesions are not always noticed by the observer, presumably because reactivated neurons in the visual cortex "fill in" missing information with information from the surroundings, and the observer is unaware of what inputs are absent. Nearly all amputees have the sensation that the missing limb is still present, the so-called phantom limb (Melzack, 1990), and this presumably is a consequence of neural activity, induced or spontaneous, in the deprived cortex. Such misperceptions become serious when the missing limb has pain, since this pain is not generated by peripheral stimuli and can't be treated in the usual ways.

Sometimes sensations in a phantom limb can be evoked by touching other parts of the body. Specifically, touch on the face or arm stump might be felt on the missing arm (see Ramachandran & Hirstein, 1998), as well as normally on the face and stump. These misperceptions most probably result from the skin afferents activating both normal and abnormal locations in cortical representations. Face and stump inputs activate both face or stump regions of cortex and hand cortex. Indeed, electrical stimulation of neurons responsive to the stump of an amputated arm in the hand subnucleus of the somatosensory thalamus evokes sensations on the hand, not the stump (Davis et al., 1998). While the person with the reorganized brain may regard these misperceptions as no more than distracting, the plasticity is not beneficial. As another example, tinnitus, the perception of sound in the absence of an auditory stimulus, has been associated with peripheral hearing losses (see Lockwood et al., 1998). Quite possibly, these phantom sounds are a consequence of plasticity in the auditory system as deprived neurons acquire other sources of activation. However, the mechanisms that cause referred sensations on a missing limb, such as those caused by touch on trigger zones on the face or stump, are not fully understood. Some perceptual changes occur too soon after injury (see Doetsch, 1997) to be explained by the growth of new connections.

These two sides of neural plasticity, the beneficial and the detrimental, indicate that we should seek a fuller understanding of the mechanisms and consequences of plasticity in order to develop ways of influencing outcomes. In the clinical setting, we would like to promote beneficial changes and prevent harmful ones.

Acknowledgments

This paper was prepared while the author was a Fellow at the Center for Advanced Study in the Behavioral Sciences at Stanford University. Financial support at the Center was provided by the John D. and Catherine T. MacArthur Foundation. Research by the author was funded by NIH grant NS16446.

References

Ahissar, M., & Hochstein, S. (1997). Task difficulty and the specificity of perceptual learning. *Nature, 387*, 401–406.

Bear, M. F., & Singer, W. (1986). Modulation of visual cortical plasticity by acetylcholine and non-adrenaline. *Nature, 320*, 172–176.

Brenman, J. E., & Bredt, D. S. (1997). Synaptic signaling by nitric oxide. *Current Opinion in Neurobiology, 7*, 374–378.

Buonomano, D. V., & Merzenich, M. M. (1998). Cortical plasticity: From synapses to maps. *Annual Review of Neuroscience, 21*, 149–186.

Byl, N. N., Merzenich, M. M., & Jenkins, W. M. (1996). A primate genesis model of focal dystonia and repetitive strain injury: I. Learning-induced dedifferentiation of the representation of the hand in the primary somatosensory cortex in adult monkeys. *Neurology, 47*, 508–520.

Calford, M. B., & Tweedale, R. (1988). Immediate and chronic changes in responses of somatosensory cortex in adult flying-fox after digit amputation. *Nature, 332*, 446–448.

Chino, Y. M., Kaas, J. H., Smith, E. L., III, Langston, A. L., & Cheng, H. (1992). Rapid organization of cortical maps in adult cats following restricted deafferentation in retina. *Vision Research, 32*, 789–796.

Darian-Smith, C., & Gilbert, C. D. (1994). Axonal sprouting accompanies functional reorganization in adult cat striate cortex. *Nature, 368*, 737–740.

Darian-Smith, C., & Gilbert, C. D. (1995). Topographic reorganization in the striate cortex of the adult cat and monkey is cortically mediated. *Journal of Neuroscience, 15*, 1631–1647.

Davis, K. D., Kiss, Z. H., Luo, L., Tasker, R. R., Lozano, A. M., & Dostrovsky, J. O. (1998). Phantom sensations generated by thalamic microstimulation. *Nature, 391*, 385–387.

Doetsch, G. S. (1997). Progressive changes in cutaneous trigger zones for sensation referred to a phantom hand: A case report and review with implications for cortical reorganization. *Somatosensory and Motor Research, 14*, 6–16.

Donoghue, J. P., Suner, S., & Sanes, J. N. (1990). Dynamic organization of primary motor cortex output to target muscles in adult rats. II. Rapid reorganization following motor nerve lesions. *Experimental Brain Research, 79*, 492–503.

Dykes, R. W. (1997). Mechanisms controlling neuronal plasticity in somatosensory cortex. *Canadian Journal of Physiology and Pharmacology, 75*, 535–545.

Eysel, U. T. (1982). Functional reconnections without new axonal growth in a partially denervated visual relay nucleus. *Nature, 299*, 442–444.

Florence, S. L., & Kaas, J. H. (1995). Large-scale reorganization at multiple levels of the somatosensory pathway follows therapeutic amputation of the hand in monkeys. *Journal of Neuroscience, 15*, 8083–8095.

Florence, S. L., Garraghty, P. E., Carlson, M., & Kaas, J. H. (1993). Sprouting of peripheral nerve axons in the spinal cord of monkeys. *Brain Research, 601*, 343–348.

Florence, S. L., Hackett, T., & Strata, F. (2000). Thalamic and cortical contributions to neural plasticity after limb amputation. *Journal of Neurophysiology, 83*, 3154–3159.

Florence, S. L., Taub, H. B., & Kaas, J. H. (1998). Large-scale sprouting of cortical connections after peripheral injury in adult macaque monkeys. *Science, 282*, 1117–1121.

Florence, S. L., Wall, J. T., & Kaas, J. H. (1989). Somatotopic organization of inputs from the hand to the spinal gray and cuneate nucleus of monkeys with observations on the cuneate nucleus of humans. *Journal of Comparative Neurology, 286*, 48–70.

Garraghty, P. E., & Kaas, J. H. (1991). Functional reorganization in adult monkey thalamus after peripheral nerve injury. *NeuroReport, 2*, 747–750.

Gilbert, C. D., & Wiesel, T. N. (1992). Receptive field dynamics in adult primary visual cortex. *Nature, 356*, 150–152.

Gould, E., Beylin, A., Tanapat, P., Reeves, A., & Shors, T. J. (1999). Learning enhances adult neurogenesis in the hippocampal formation. *Nature Neuroscience, 2*, 260–265.

Heinen, S. J., & Skavenski, A. A. (1991). Recovery of visual responses in foveal V1 neurons following bilateral foveal lesions in adult monkey. *Experimental Brain Research, 83*, 670–674.

Hubel, D. H., & Wiesel, T. N. (1970). The period of susceptibility to the physiological effects of unilateral eye closure in kittens. *Journal of Physiology, 206*, 419–436.

Jain, N., Catania, K. C., & Kaas, J. H. (1997). Deactivation and reactivation of somatosensory cortex after dorsal spinal cord injury. *Nature, 386*, 495–498.

Jain, N., Catania, K. C., & Kaas, J. H. (1998). A histologically visible representation of the fingers and palm in primate area 3b and its immutability following long-term deafferentations. *Cerebral Cortex, 8*, 227–236.

Jain, N., Florence, S. L., & Kaas, J. H. (1995). Limits on plasticity in somatosensory cortex of adult rats: Hindlimb cortex is not reactivated after dorsal column section. *Journal of Neurophysiology, 73*, 1537–1546.

Jain, N., Florence, S. L., & Kaas, J. H. (2000). Growth of new brainstem connections in adult monkeys massive sensory loss. *Proceedings of the National Academy of Sciences, 97*, 5546–5550.

Jenkins, W. M., & Merzenich, M. M. (1987). Reorganization of neocortical representations after brain injury: A neurophysiological model of the bases of recovery from stroke. *Progress in Brain Research, 71*, 249–266.

Jenkins, W. M., Merzenich, M. M., Ochs, M. T., Allard, T., & Guic-Robles, E. (1990). Functional reorganization of primary somatosensory cortex in adult owl monkeys after behaviorally controlled tactile stimulation. *Journal of Neurophysiology, 63*, 82–104.

Jones, E. G. (1993). GABAergic neurons and their role in cortical plasticity in primates. *Cerebral Cortex, 3*, 361–372.

Jones, E. G., & Pons, T. P. (1998). Thalamic and brainstem contributions to large-scale plasticity of primate somatosensory cortex. *Science, 282*, 1121–1125.

Kaas, J. H. (1983). What, if anything, is SI? Organization of first somatosensory area of cortex. *Physiological Reviews, 63*, 206–231.

Kaas, J. H., Krubitzer, L. A., Chino, Y. M., Langston, A. L., Polley, E. H., & Blair, N. (1990). Reorganization of retinotopic cortical maps in adult mammals after lesions of the retina. *Science, 248*, 229–231.

Kilgard, M. P., & Merzenich, M. M. (1998). Cortical map reorganization enabled by nucleus basalis activity. *Science, 279*, 1714–1718.

Lenz, F. A., Gracely, R. H., Baker, F. H., Richardson, R. T., & Dougherty, P. M. (1998). Reorganization of sensory modalities evoked by microstimulation in region of the thalamic principal sensory nucleus in patients with pain due to nervous system injury. *Journal of Comparative Neurology, 399*, 125–138.

Li, C. X., Waters, R. S., McCandlish, C. A., & Johnson, E. F. (1996). Electrical stimulation of a forepaw digit increases the physiological representation of that digit in layer IV of SI cortex in rat. *NeuroReport, 7*, 2395–2400.

Lockwood, A. H., Salvi, R. J., Coad, M. L., Towsley, M. L., Wack, D. S., & Murphy, B. W. (1998). The functional neuroanatomy of tinnitus: Evidence for limbic system links and neural plasticity. *Neurology, 50*, 114–120.

Melzack, R. (1990). Phantom limbs and the concept of a neuromatrix. *Trends in Neuroscience, 13,* 88–92.

Merzenich, M. M., Kaas, J. H., Wall, J. T., Nelson, R. J., Sur, M., & Felleman, D. (1983). Topographic reorganization of somatosensory cortical areas 3b and 1 in adult monkeys following restricted deafferentation. *Neuroscience, 8,* 33–55.

Merzenich, M. M., Nelson, R. J., Stryker, M. P., Cynader, M. S., Schoppmann, A., & Zook, J. M. (1984). Somatosensory cortical map changes following digit amputation in adult monkeys. *Journal of Comparative Neurology, 224,* 591–605.

Nicolelis, M. A. (1997). Dynamic and distributed somatosensory representations as the substrate for cortical and subcortical plasticity. *Seminars in the Neurosciences, 9,* 24–33.

Pons, T. P., Garraghty, P. E., & Mishkin, M. (1988). Lesion-induced plasticity in the second somatosensory cortex of adult macaques. *Proceedings of the National Academy of Sciences of the United States of America, 85,* 5279–5281.

Pons, T. P., Garraghty, P. E., Ommaya, A. K., Kaas, J. H., Taub, E., & Mishkin, M. (1991). Massive cortical reorganization after sensory deafferentation in adult macaques. *Science, 252,* 1857–1860.

Qi, H.-X., Stepneiwska, I., & Kaas, J. H. (2000). Reorganization of primary motor cortex in adult macaque monkeys with long-standing amputations. *Journal of Neurophysiology.* In press.

Rajan, R., & Irvine, D. R. (1998). Absence of plasticity of the frequency map in dorsal cochlear nucleus of adult cats after unilateral partial cochlear lesions. *Journal of Comparative Neurology, 399,* 35–46.

Rajan, R., Irvine, D. R., Wise, L. Z., & Heil, P. (1993). Effect of unilateral partial cochlear lesions in adult cats on the representation of lesioned and unlesioned cochleas in primary auditory cortex. *Journal of Comparative Neurology, 338,* 17–49.

Ramachandran, V. S., & Hirstein, W. (1998). The perception of phantom limbs. The D. O. Hebb lecture. *Brain, 121,* 1603–1630.

Rauschecker, J. P. (1991). Mechanisms of visual plasticity: Hebb synapses, NMDA receptors, and beyond. *Physiological Reviews, 71,* 587–615.

Recanzone, G. H., Merzenich, M. M., & Dinse, H. R. (1992). Expansion of the cortical representation of a specific skin field in primary somatosensory cortex by intracortical microstimulation. *Cerebral Cortex, 2,* 181–196.

Robertson, D., & Irvine, D. R. (1989). Plasticity of frequency organization in auditory cortex of guinea pigs with partial unilateral deafness. *Journal of Comparative Neurology, 282,* 456–471.

Sanes, J. N., Suner, S., Lando, J. F., & Donoghue, J. P. (1988). Rapid reorganization of adult rat motor cortex somatic representation patterns after motor nerve injury. *Proceedings of the National Academy of Sciences of the United States of America, 85,* 2003–2007.

Schieber, M. H., & Deuel, R. K. (1997). Primary motor cortex reorganization in a long-term monkey amputee. *Somatosensory and Motor Research, 14,* 157–167.

Schmid, L. M., Rosa, M. G., Calford, M. B., & Ambler, J. S. (1996). Visuotopic reorganization in the primary visual cortex of adult cats following monocular and binocular retinal lesions. *Cerebral Cortex, 6,* 388–405.

Schwaber, M. K., Garraghty, P. E., & Kaas, J. H. (1993). Neuroplasticity of the adult primate auditory cortex following cochlear hearing loss. *American Journal of Otology, 14,* 252–258.

Snow, P. J., & Wilson, P. (1991). Plasticity in the somatosensory system of developing and mature mammals: The effects of injury to the central and peripheral nervous system. *Progress in sensory physiology* (Vol. 2). New York: Plenum.

Sperry, R. W. (1943). Functional results of crossing sensory nerves in rats. *Journal of Comparative Neurology, 78,* 59–90.

Wall, P. D. (1977). The presence of ineffective synapses and the circumstances which unmask them. *Philosophical Transactions of the Royal Society of London Series B Biological Sciences, 278,* 361–372.

Wall, P. D., & Egger, M. D. (1971). Formation of new connexions in adult rat brains after partial deafferentation. *Nature, 232,* 542–545.

Withers, G. S., & Greenough, W. T. (1989). Reach training selectively alters dendritic branching in subpopulations of layer II-III pyramids in rat motor-somatosensory forelimb cortex. *Neuropsychologia, 27*, 61–69.

Wu, C. W. H., & Kaas, J. H. (1999). The organization of motor cortex of squirrel monkeys with longstanding therapeutic amputations. *Journal of Neuroscience, 19*, 7679–7697.

Wunderlich, D., Wall, J., & Kaas, J. (1981). Unpublished observations.

Xerri, C., Stern, J. M., & Merzenich, M. M. (1994). Alterations of the cortical representation of the rat ventrum induced by nursing behavior. *Journal of Neuroscience, 14*, 1710–1721.

Xerri, C., Merzenich, M. M., Peterson, B. E., & Jenkins, W. (1998). Plasticity of primary somatosensory cortex paralleling sensorimotor skill recovery from stroke in adult monkeys. *Journal of Neurophysiology, 79*, 2119–2148.

Xing, J., & Gerstein, G. L. (1996). Networks with lateral connectivity. III. Plasticity and reorganization of somatosensory cortex. *The American Physiological Society, 75*, 217–231.

Xu, J., & Wall, J. T. (1997). Rapid changes in brainstem maps of adult primates after peripheral injury. *Brain Research, 774*, 211–215.

23
CHAPTER

Gernot S. Doetsch

Phantoms and Other Perceptual Phenomena Related to Plasticity in Somatosensory Cortex

☐ Introduction

The experiential phenomenon of "phantom limbs" following amputation has been recognized for centuries but was first described in detail by S. W. Mitchell (1872) in his classic studies of peripheral nerve injuries. During the last 15 years, phantoms have attracted renewed interest, due primarily to the dramatic results of research on cerebral plasticity induced by peripheral denervation. This line of investigation was sparked by the pioneering work of P. D. Wall and associates (see Merrill & Wall, 1978), who found that somatosensory neurons deprived of their dominant afferent drive begin to respond to new peripheral inputs. The findings of studies such as these have provided insight into the neural mechanisms responsible for some of the sensory-perceptual phenomena associated with phantoms.

☐ Cortical Mapping Studies

Electrophysiological mapping in adult animals revealed that selective loss of afferent input to primary somatosensory (SI) cortex caused the partially-deafferented cortical neurons to respond to stimulation of new receptive fields (RFs) on skin regions adjacent to the denervated skin territory. This switching or rerouting of input to SI results in local reorganization of somatotopic cortical maps, whereby the representations of skin sites adjoining the denervation are enlarged (for reviews, see Buonomano & Merzenich, 1998; Garraghty, Kaas, & Florence, 1993; Kaas, 1991, 1995; Merzenich & deCharms, 1996; Merzenich, Recanzone, Jenkins, Allard, & Nudo, 1988). For instance, after amputation of a digit, neurons in the SI area formerly representing that digit developed responses to stimulation of other digits adjoining the amputation site, thereby altering the cortical representation of the hand (Calford & Tweedale, 1988; Doetsch, Harrison, MacDonald, & Litaker, 1996; Kelahan & Doetsch, 1984; Merzenich et al., 1984; Rasmusson, 1982).

Similarly, transection of the median nerve in monkeys caused neurons in the median nerve zone of SI to be activated by stimulation of skin regions innervated by the radial and ulnar nerves, resulting in a new cortical representation of inputs from the hand (Garraghty & Kaas, 1991; Kolarik, Rasey, & Wall, 1994; Merzenich et al., 1983; Silva, Rasey, Wu, & Wall, 1996). Reorganization in SI has also been demonstrated in rats following partial denervation of the hindpaw (Dykes & Lamour, 1988; Wall & Cusick, 1984) and selective removal of mystacial vibrissae (Kossut, Hand, Greenberg, & Hand 1988; Levin & Dunn-Meynell, 1991). An unusually extensive case of SI reorganization was found in monkeys 12 years after denervation of one arm; the large SI zone normally representing the arm had developed responsiveness to stimulation of the face (Pons et al., 1991).

Recent mapping studies of somatosensory cortex in humans with partial denervations or amputations have shown similar plasticity effects. Evoked potential recordings and magnetic source imaging in amputees revealed that the cortical area usually representing the now-absent limb showed enhanced responses to stimulation of skin regions proximal to the amputation stump (Elbert et al., 1994; Flor et al., 1995; Ramachandran, 1993; Sica, Panizza, Reich, & Correale, 1988; Yang et al., 1994). Similar changes in the cortical representation of the body surface were recently observed using positron emission tomography in two patients with total denervation of an arm (Kew et al., 1997). In patients with spinal cord transection (Lenz et al., 1994) or limb amputation (Davis et al., 1998), microelectrode mapping of the somatosensory thalamus showed that many neurons located in the representational zones of the now-denervated body regions were activated by stimulation of cutaneous sites adjoining the denervated skin territory.

These studies confirm the idea that selective peripheral denervation in adult mammals can greatly alter the response properties of neurons in the somatosensory cortex (and subcortical areas, as well). In species from rats to humans, neurons in a cortical area deprived of its dominant afferent drive become responsive to entirely new inputs from the skin and show enhanced responses to previously effective but weak inputs. The appearance of new RFs on formerly ineffective skin fields results in local modification of somatosensory maps.

☐ Perceptual Phenomena

The physiological cortical changes produced by selective denervation of a body part are accompanied by profound changes in the sensory-perceptual characteristics of that body region and neighboring skin. Two primary effects can be identified. First, the denervated skin territory or lost appendage is almost invariably experienced as a phantom that appears immediately after the subject can attend to the injury (Doetsch, 1997; Katz, 1992; Melzack, 1990, 1992; Ramachandran, 1994; Ramachandran & Hirstein, 1998; Sunderland, 1968). Second, stimulation of skin sites near, and sometimes distant from, the deprived zone typically evokes two distinct sensations, one referred to the stimulated site and the other to a location on the phantom (Cronholm, 1951; Doetsch, 1997, 1998; Ramachandran, 1994; Ramachandran & Hirstein, 1998). The characteristics of phantoms and the phenomena associated with sensation that is referred to intact skin or to a phantom are discussed below. Neural mechanisms responsible for the various perceptual phenomena are explored, although a detailed discussion of synaptic and neurochemical mechanisms of plasticity is beyond the scope of this chapter.

Phantoms

Phantom limbs are experienced by the vast majority of patients with amputation of an arm, leg, or other appendage, and are also common after injury to a nerve plexus and transection of the spinal cord (Katz, 1992; Melzack, 1990, 1992; Mitchell, 1872; Ramachandran, 1994; Ramachandran & Hirstein, 1998; Sunderland, 1968). The incidence of phantoms in child amputees less than 7 years of age is considerably lower than that in adult amputees (Simmel, 1958). Early reports suggested that individuals with congenitally missing limbs do not experience phantoms at all, but recent studies have shown that some of these individuals do indeed have phantoms (Lacroix, Melzack, Smith, & Mitchell, 1992; Saadah & Melzack, 1994; Weinstein, Sersen, & Vetter, 1964).

An acquired phantom is typically perceived as quite vivid and real, closely resembling the intact limb. Over time, the phantom may become less distinct, begin to fade, and shorten or "telescope" into the amputation stump. However, a phantom can also remain intact for many years or, if it fades, can suddenly reappear in response to strong peripheral stimulation, mental concentration or attention to the phantom, intense emotional experiences, and other central or peripheral factors. Finally, the phantom may be painless and described as having a tingling quality, with associated normal sensations of touch-pressure, temperature, and movement, etc. Or the phantom can be painful, giving rise to intense shooting or burning pains and often assuming a cramped, unnatural position associated with severe pain.

The frequent occurrence of a persistent phantom (or a phantom that can be recalled) indicates that the neural mechanisms for representation of the now-denervated or lost body part remain intact, despite any rerouting of input or reorganization that takes place in SI and other cortical areas (Doetsch, 1997, 1998). This means that the brain circuits and neuronal activity patterns which subserve the percept of the denervated body region remain functional over time. Melzack (1990, 1992) has referred to the network responsible for the body schema as a "neuromatrix," which is (to a large extent) genetically determined or "prewired" and includes the somatosensory thalamus and cortex, the parietal lobe, and the limbic system. The body image or schema is thought to be represented by a unique pattern of neuronal activity distributed across the neuromatrix, referred to as the "neurosignature" of the matrix, which can be modified by experience. This notion is consistent with modern neuronal population coding models (Doetsch, 1998, 2000; Erickson, 1982). The body image and changes in that image are mediated (encoded) by specific population activity patterns within a highly distributed neural system (the matrix); these activity patterns do not require input from external stimuli, but are maintained by endogenous brain activity. (In contrast, stimulation of localized regions of the body evokes sensations that are mediated by specific population response patterns limited to certain parts of the neural network, depending on the properties of the stimulus and the site of stimulation.) Finally, it should be noted that the body schema (including phantoms) is strongly influenced by input from visual and vestibular systems, feedback or corollary discharge from motor systems, and activation of systems dealing with memory, emotion, and attention (Melzack, 1990, 1992; Ramachandran, 1994; Ramachandran & Hirstein, 1998). Figure 23.1 shows the basic neural network thought to subserve the body schema and illustrates the changes that may occur in one of the network components following amputation.

There is relatively little evidence regarding the specific role of different brain areas in maintaining a phantom. Phantom percepts, including a painful phantom, may be suppressed by lesions of the contralateral posterior parietal cortex but not by removal of the SI cortex alone; the latter causes deficits in somatosensory localization, discrimination,

A. Neural Circuits Mediating Body Schema

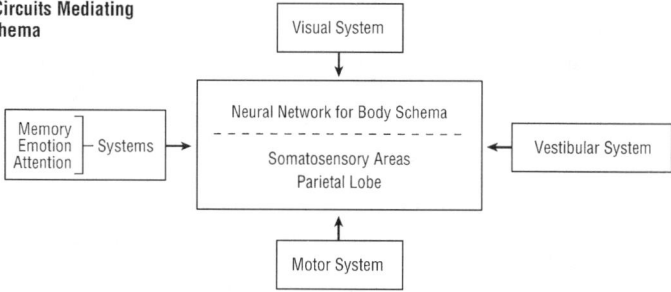

B. Intact Arm

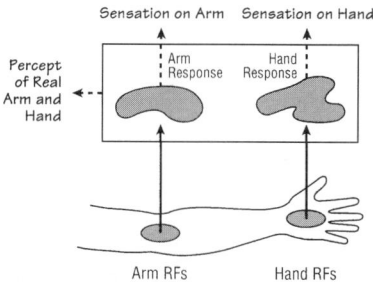

C. After Amputation of Hand

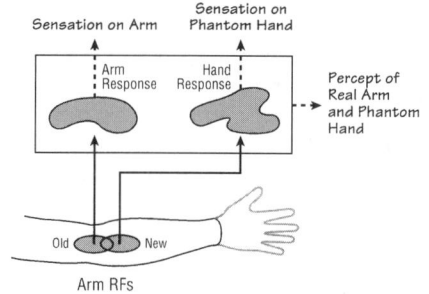

Figure 23.1. Diagram illustrating the basic neural circuits contributing to the body schema, and showing the effects of amputation. (A) The somatosensory system and parietal lobe are central components of the neural network, receiving input or feedback from other systems (visual, vestibular, motor, etc.). (B) and (C) Boxes represent the somatosensory network component responsible for perception of a limb, independent of afferent input. Shaded areas in the boxes represent neuronal population responses evoked by stimulation of neuronal RFs on the arm and hand (shaded areas). (B) In the normal state, stimulation of RFs on the arm and hand evokes different response patterns, giving rise to sensations projected to the arm and hand, respectively. (C) After amputation of the hand, the network for perception of the limb remains intact despite cortical reorganization; hence, the percept of the real arm is retained, and a phantom hand is perceived that closely resembles the real hand. Stimulation of the "old" RFs on the arm elicits "old" neuronal response patterns that still produce sensations projected to the arm. Stimulation of "new" RFs on the arm evokes afferent input that has been switched (rerouted) to the neural hand area, producing response patterns similar to those formerly elicited by stimulation of the hand. The "old" hand response patterns still generate sensations referred to the (phantom) hand.

and object recognition (Appenzeller & Bicknell, 1969; Head & Holmes, 1911; White & Sweet, 1969). This indicates that the neural circuits responsible for awareness of the body image may involve SI, but are certainly not limited to it. In contrast, the circuits mediating somatosensory discriminative abilities depend greatly on the integrity of the SI cortex.

The subjective phantom may actually be more vivid in the patient's awareness than the intact contralateral limb, suggesting higher levels of neuronal activity in phantom-related circuits, presumably due to central hyperexcitability or supersensitivity (Coderre, Katz, Vaccarino, & Melzack, 1993; Woolf & Doubell, 1994). In patients with spinal cord transection, the spontaneous activity of neurons in the deafferented portion of the somatosensory thalamus seems to be characterized by increased high-frequency bursting (Lenz et al., 1994). Greater neuronal firing rates could increase the magnitude of the population activity that signals the phantom, resulting in a more intense phantom percept. The cortical (and subcortical) circuits mediating the body percept can be modified by afferent input but are not dependent on that input, since blockade of afferent signals from the stump usually does not erase the phantom permanently (Sunderland, 1968). Any significant alterations in the phantom percept with time must be due to modifications of the neural circuits and their activity patterns. For instance, fading of a phantom may be due to silencing or loss of scattered cells throughout the endogenously active neuronal population. Telescoping of the phantom into the stump could result from quiescence of a set of neurons specifically related to proximal regions of a phantom limb. These changes are often temporary, since a full-blown phantom can reappear under certain stimulus conditions or behavioral (mental) states.

Sensation Referred to Intact Skin Near a Phantom

Stimulation of skin regions adjoining a denervated cutaneous zone often elicits sensation that is projected correctly to the stimulated site and has modality characteristics that are typically associated with the particular features of the stimulus (Sunderland, 1968). Interestingly, the sensation projected to the intact skin is often weaker than the sensation referred to a phantom, suggesting increased levels of neuronal excitability in neural circuits subserving phantom sensations. The place and modality characteristics of the sensory percept projected to the intact skin are presumably mediated by relatively normal patterns of activation in neuronal ensembles representing that skin region (Doetsch, 1997, 1998).

In cases of sensory denervation by complete nerve transection, the cutaneous area of anesthesia is usually separated from skin with normal tactile sensibility by a marginal zone of diminished sensation (Sunderland, 1968). This fringe area is a region where terminal branches of different nerves overlap, with the remaining sensibility due to the surviving nerve branch. Thus, the reduced tactile sensitivity is probably due to a decrease in innervation density that results in the activation of fewer neurons and less intense population responses. The degree to which normal sensation returns in the affected skin regions is dependent on the extent of nerve regeneration and the accuracy of reinnervation of the denervated skin.

In contrast, the skin near an amputation line is often hypersensitive, with stimulation giving rise to intense, sometimes unpleasant sensations (Sunderland, 1968). Furthermore, there is evidence that the cutaneous surface of the amputation stump may have greater sensitivity to stimulation (lower tactile thresholds), better point localization, and enhanced two-point discrimination compared with corresponding skin regions on the intact limb (Haber, 1955; Teuber, Krieger, & Bender, 1949). This enhanced stump sensibility may be especially characteristic of patients with telescoped phantoms: point localization (but not absolute thresholds or two-point discrimination) was found to be significantly greater when phantoms were perceived as receded into the stump, compared with those felt as extending out of the stump into space (Haber, 1955).

The general hypersensitivity of an amputation stump appears to be due largely to axonal sprouting from the severed nerves and the formation of neuromas that are highly sensitive to physical and chemical changes (e.g., levels of norepinephrine and acetylcholine) as well as local pathology (Katz, 1992; Sunderland, 1968). Furthermore, the formation of numerous sprouts from each axon increases peripheral innervation density (number of axon terminals per unit area of skin), resulting in greater convergence and summation of input from the skin to primary afferent neurons. This may increase firing rates at all levels of the somatosensory system, enhancing neuronal population responses and thereby leading to lower tactile thresholds and increased sensitivity.

Better point localization, as well as lower thresholds, on the stump could be due to increases in the sensitivity and density of the RFs of neurons located in cortical zones near the border between partially deafferented and normal cortex. Denervation (amputation) truncates the RFs of neurons straddling the boundary between intact skin and "denervated" skin. The small surviving portions of those fields usually expand from the denervation line into normal skin, and the neurons increase their responsiveness to stimulation of that skin (Doetsch et al., 1996). This process may result in more RF overlap (density) on the stump skin and greater rates of firing, producing more differentiated population response patterns that lead to improved point localization and increased sensitivity.

Enhanced two-point discrimination on the stump probably involves decreases in the size of the RFs of cortical neurons normally representing that skin, as well as increased response rates. Some regenerating axons in the stump may reinnervate the skin with sprouts that form smaller-than-usual terminal branches (RFs). In fact, neurons in partially deafferented SI cortex are known to have RFs on or near the stump that are often smaller than normal (Kelahan & Doetsch, 1984; Merzenich et al., 1984). Furthermore, use-dependent RF changes on the stump may be a factor, since decreases in the RF size of SI neurons have been found after extensive cutaneous stimulation of normal skin (Jenkins, Merzenich, Ochs, Allard, & Guic-Robles, 1990; Xerri, Coq, Merzenich, & Jenkins, 1996). Excitation of neurons with smaller RFs or greater firing rates would increase the differentiation of neuronal response patterns generated by simultaneous stimulation of different skin locations, resulting in improved two-point discrimination.

Sensation Referred to a Phantom

Stimulation of certain skin regions (trigger zones) on or near an amputation stump usually elicits sensation that is projected to a phantom in addition to the skin site stimulated. This phenomenon raises one of the central issues regarding the perceptual significance of SI cortical reorganization following denervation. Specifically, does the reorganized cortical area begin to signal (represent) the skin regions containing the new RFs of partially deafferented neurons, and does stimulation of the new RFs elicit sensation projected to those new skin fields or to the original, now-missing fields?

Evidence regarding the referral of sensation was recently reviewed by the author (Doetsch, 1997, 1998) and is briefly summarized here. The data include:

- the ubiquitous appearance of phantoms after amputation and other types of denervation (Katz, 1992; Melzack, 1990, 1992; Mitchell, 1872; Ramachandran, 1994; Ramachandran & Hirstein, 1998; Sunderland, 1968);
- the referral of sensation to a phantom by stimulation of cutaneous trigger zones (Aglioti, Bonazzi, & Cortese, 1994; Cronholm, 1951; Doetsch, 1997; Halligan, Marshall, Wade, Davey & Morrison, 1993; Ramachandran, 1994; Ramachandran & Hirstein, 1998);
- the "incorrect" projection of skin sensation after peripheral nerve lesions and faulty regeneration (Hallin, Wiesenfeld, Lindblom, 1981; Hawkins, 1948; Head, 1920);

- the referral of sensation to the original donor site following neurovascular island transplants (Dyck, Lambert, Wood & Linscheid, 1988; Murray, Ord, & Gavelin, 1967; Omer, 1980);
- and the projection of sensation to a phantom by stimulation of transected nerve fibers in an amputation stump (Anani & Korner, 1979; Carlen, Wall, Nadvorna, & Steinback, 1978; Schady, Braune, Watson, Torebjork, & Schmidt, 1994).

Additional evidence comes from patients with spinal cord injury or amputation in whom sensation can be referred to anesthetic regions of the body or a phantom, following transcranial magnetic stimulation of the cortex (Cohen, Bandinelli, Findlay, & Hallett, 1991; Cohen, Topka, Cole, & Hallett, 1991) or microstimulation of the thalamus (Lenz et al., 1994; Davis et al., 1998). Finally, there is the interesting case of a patient who had his arm amputated 24 years earlier, developed a phantom limb, and then lost it 14 years later—electrical stimulation of the patient's hand and arm somatosensory cortex, 10 years after the phantom had disappeared, elicited sensations projected once again to his reemergent phantom limb (Ojemann & Silbergeld, 1995).

The findings obtained from these diverse sources are remarkably consistent. (a) They support the idea that central neural mechanisms representing a body region remain intact after denervation and are manifest subjectively as a phantom. (b) Sensation projected correctly to a stimulated site is presumably mediated by activation of the original neuronal ensembles representing that site. (c) The sensation referred to locations on the phantom is most likely due to rerouting of afferent input and excitation of neuronal ensembles in the reorganized cortex. Although driven by new inputs, response patterns in these ensembles produce sensations—referred not to a new skin region—but still projected to the original (now-phantom) body part. (d) This leads to the conclusion that the perceptual significance of the neuronal population responses remains essentially unchanged (activity patterns in a set of neurons are not functionally respecified), although the responses can now be elicited by stimulation of new skin sites (Doetsch, 1997, 1998). These ideas are illustrated in Figures 23.1b and 23.1c.

Several important features are associated with sensation referred to a phantom. (a) The cutaneous trigger zones from which sensation is projected to the phantom are usually located on skin near the site of denervation (amputation), but can sometimes be remote. In his comprehensive study, Cronholm (1951) found great variation in the locations of the trigger zones of different amputees. Some zones were confined to a small area immediately surrounding the amputation line, and others covered large portions of the ipsilateral body and face, sometimes including contralateral skin regions. These results have been confirmed by more recent studies which have tended to stress unusual findings, such as circumscribed trigger zones on the face in arm amputees (Halligan et al., 1993; Ramachandran, 1994; Ramachandran & Hirstein, 1998). Trigger zones and their associated phantom can appear immediately after amputation and can change considerably over time (Doetsch, 1997). (b) The referred sensation can be vague and poorly localized, especially on a fading phantom (Cronholm, 1951), but can also be distinctly localized to the phantom. (c) A close topographic relationship often exists between the site of stimulation in a trigger zone and the location of the sensation projected to the phantom. This topographic correspondence can be maintained despite time-dependent changes in the size and location of the trigger zones (Doetsch, 1997), or the somatotopy can break down and become "disorganized" over time (Halligan, Marshall, & Wade, 1994). (d) The sensation projected to the phantom may be "non-adequate in quality, intensified, diffuse and unpleasant" (Cronholm, 1951), or may closely resemble the quality and intensity of the sensation elicited at the site of stimulation. Ramachandran and

Hirstein (1993, 1994, 1998) reported that sensations referred to a phantom were modality specific: touching a trigger zone with cotton was experienced as tingling on the phantom, skin vibration and the application of warm and cold water elicited corresponding phantom sensations, and the flow of water across the skin was felt as "trickling" down the phantom. (e) The phantom sensation is often stronger than the sensation projected correctly to the skin, and thresholds for the phantom sensation can be lower than those for the skin (Carlen et al., 1978).

Several mechanisms can account for these findings. The cutaneous trigger zones mapped in human amputees and the new RFs of neurons mapped in reorganized SI cortex are most likely expressions of the same basic phenomenon (Doetsch, 1997, 1998). Both show time- and use-dependent changes in skin location, size, and modality sensitivity. The trigger zones may be formed by aggregates of new RFs expressed by the partially deafferented SI neurons. They may also represent circumscribed skin regions innervated by afferent fibers that formerly had no excitatory access to those SI neurons, but gain that access by various mechanisms including disinhibition, facilitation, synaptogenesis, etc. The appearance of trigger zones (RFs) adjoining the denervation site can be mediated partly by activation of the extensive axon terminals of some thalamocortical fibers (Garraghty & Sur, 1990), but the more distant trigger zones may be due to facilitation of long-range cortical interconnections (Doetsch, 1988). The net effect is that stimulation of cutaneous regions close to, or distant from, the site of denervation evokes sensation projected to the original skin location by generating population response patterns representing that location.

The close somatotopic relationship sometimes found between the site of skin stimulation and the location of sensory referral to a phantom indicates a greater degree of topographic order in subthreshold or weak thalamocortical and intracortical connections than might be expected. The same is true for the connections that preserve the modality, intensity, and temporal features of stimulus-induced phantom sensations. Such specificity implies that the neuronal circuitry and response patterns signaling those stimulus characteristics survive cortical reorganization after denervation and suggests that they can be maintained by use-dependent, Hebbian mechanisms.

At least for a time, the phantom may be very distinct and more vivid than a real limb, and stimulus thresholds for sensation referred to the phantom may be lower than those for sensation projected to the stimulated skin. Even spatial resolution may be better on a phantom hand than on adjacent skin (Doetsch, 1996). This is actually not surprising if the denervated skin (e.g., the hand) has a larger cortical magnification factor (number of neurons per unit area of skin) than that of the intact skin (e.g., the arm). Greater sensitivity and discriminability on the phantom suggest that the response patterns representing the now-denervated skin regions are more highly differentiated than the response patterns for intact skin. However, the salient phantom and its heightened sensitivity often do not last, both tending to fade with time. Vague, diffuse phantom sensations presumably reflect degraded neuronal response patterns and are often associated with a fading phantom and its own deteriorating functional activity.

Finally, there are some surprising twists in the story. A recent study showed that the amount of phantom pain experienced by human amputees is highly correlated with the spatial extent of cortical reorganization (Flor et al., 1995). A similar relationship between pain and plasticity may exist in patients with chronic back pain (Flor, Braun, Elbert, & Birbaumer, 1997). Many pathological pain states seem to involve sensitization of central neurons via glutamate- and neuropeptide-mediated increases in excitatory synaptic transmission, as in the dorsal horn of the spinal cord (Coderre et al., 1993; Woolf & Doubell, 1994). These findings indicate that peripheral reference may be retained (as in a phantom), but that sensory quality can change considerably from a nonpainful to a painful state. This modality change is not completely understood, but is probably due to changes in neuronal population activity and recruitment of cortical (and subcortical) neurons with pain-related activity. In any case, it is clear that cortical plasticity can be maladaptive and contribute to neurological dysfunction, especially when denervation is traumatic and evokes strong injury discharges in peripheral nerve fibers.

☐ Summary

Phantoms may be viewed as parts of the body schema or body image that survive peripheral denervation. The body schema is thought to be represented by a unique pattern of activity across a widely distributed neural network, and a limb (or its phantom) is presumably mediated by a specific component of that overall activity pattern. This idea is entirely consistent with neuronal population coding models (Doetsch, 1998, 2000; Erickson, 1982).

Furthermore, the place and modality characteristics of stimulus-induced sensations referred to a phantom are presumably subserved by patterns of responses in neuronal populations originally representing the (now-denervated) skin region. As is the case for somatosensory perception in normal individuals, the location and quality of phantom sensations are mediated by different population response profiles, whereas the perceived intensity of phantom sensations is subserved by the magnitude (neural mass) of those response profiles. Similarly, the time-varying aspects of the sensory experience are given by the temporal features of the response patterns. Thus, the integrity of the phantom and its associated stimulus-related sensations indicate that the neural mechanisms for somatosensory perception of the now-missing limb remain intact, despite so-called cortical reorganization.

☐ Acknowledgments

I thank S. David Stoney, Jr. for helpful comments regarding this manuscript, and for many stimulating discussions of neural plasticity, sensory coding, and other topics. I also thank Laura McKie for help in preparing the illustration.

☐ References

Aglioti, S., Bonazzi, A., & Cortese, F. (1994). Phantom lower limb as a perceptual marker of neural plasticity in the mature human brain. *Proceedings of the Royal Society of London. Series B: Biological Sciences, 255*, 273–278.

Anani, A., & Korner, L. (1979). Discrimination of phantom hand sensations elicited by afferent electrical nerve stimulation in below-elbow amputees. *Medical Progress Through Technology, 6*, 131–135.

Appenzeller, O., & Bicknell, J. M. (1969). Effects of nervous system lesions on phantom experience in amputees. *Neurology, 19*, 141–146.

Buonomano, D. V., & Merzenich, M. M. (1998). Cortical plasticity: From synapses to maps. *Annual Review of Neuroscience, 21*, 149–186.

Calford, M. B., & Tweedale, R. (1988). Immediate and chronic changes in responses of somatosensory cortex in adult flying-fox after digit amputation. *Nature, 332*, 446–449.

Carlen, P. L., Wall, P. D., Nadvorna, H., & Steinbach, T. (1978). Phantom limbs and related phenomena in recent traumatic amputations. *Neurology, 28,* 211–217.

Coderre, T. J., Katz, J., Vaccarino, A. L., & Melzack, R. (1993). Contribution of central neuroplasticity to pathological pain: Review of clinical and experimental evidence. *Pain, 52,* 259–285.

Cohen, L. G., Bandinelli, S., Findlay, T., & Hallett, M. (1991). Motor reorganization after upper limb amputation in man. *Brain, 114,* 615–627.

Cohen, L. G., Topka, H., Cole, R. A., & Hallett, M. (1991). Leg paresthesias induced by magnetic brain stimulation in patients with thoracic spinal cord injury. *Neurology, 41,* 1283–1288.

Cronholm, B. (1951). Phantom limbs in amputees. *Acta Psychiatra et Neurologica Scandinavica. Supplementum, 72,* 1–310.

Davis, K. D., Kiss, Z. H. T., Luo, L., Tasker, R. R., Lozano, A. M., & Dostrovsky, J. O. (1998). Phantom sensations generated by thalamic microstimulation. *Nature, 391,* 385–387.

Doetsch, G. S. (1996). Spatial discrimination on a phantom hand. Unpublished observations.

Doetsch, G. S. (1997). Progressive changes in cutaneous trigger zones for sensation referred to a phantom hand: A case report and review with implications for cortical reorganization. *Somatosensory and Motor Research, 14,* 6–16.

Doetsch, G. S. (1998). Perceptual significance of somatosensory cortical reorganization following peripheral denervation. *NeuroReport, 9,* R29–R35.

Doetsch, G. S. (2000). Patterns in the brain: Neuronal population coding in the somatosensory system. *Physiology and Behavior, 69,* 187–201.

Doetsch, G. S., Harrison, T. A., MacDonald, A. C., & Litaker, M. S. (1996). Short-term plasticity in primary somatosensory cortex of the rat: Rapid changes in magnitudes and latencies of neuronal responses following digit denervation. *Experimental Brain Research, 112,* 505–512.

Doetsch, G. S., Standage, G. P., Johnston, K. W., & Lin, C.-S. (1988). Intracortical connections of two functional subdivisions of the somatosensory forepaw cerebral cortex of the raccoon. *Journal of Neuroscience, 8,* 1887–1900.

Dyck, P. J., Lambert, E. H., Wood, M. B., & Linscheid, R. L. (1988). Assessment of nerve regeneration and adaptation after median nerve reconnection and digital neurovascular flap transfer. *Neurology, 38,* 1586–1591.

Dykes, R. W., & Lamour, Y. (1988). An electrophysiological laminar analysis of single somatosensory neurons in partially deafferented rat hindlimb granular cortex subsequent to transection of the sciatic nerve. *Brain Research, 449,* 1–17.

Elbert, T., Flor, H., Birbaumer, N., Knecht, S., Hampson, S., Larbig, W., & Taub, E. (1994). Extensive reorganization of the somatosensory cortex in adult humans after nervous system injury. *NeuroReport, 5,* 2593–2597.

Erickson, R. P. (1982). The "across-fiber pattern" theory: An organizing principle for molar neural function. In W. D. Neff (Ed.), *Contributions to sensory physiology, Vol. 6* (pp. 79–110). New York: Academic Press.

Flor, H., Braun, C., Elbert, T., & Birbaumer, N. (1997). Extensive reorganization of primary somatosensory cortex in chronic back pain patients. *Neuroscience Letters, 224,* 5–8.

Flor, H., Elbert, T., Knecht, S., Wienbruch, C., Pantev, C., Birbaumer, N., Larbig, W., & Taub, E. (1995). Phantom-limb pain as a perceptual correlate of cortical reorganization following arm amputation. *Nature, 375,* 482–484.

Garraghty, P. E., & Kaas, J. H. (1991). Large-scale functional reorganization in adult monkey cortex after peripheral nerve injury. *Proceedings of the National Academy of Sciences of the United States of America, 88,* 6976–6980.

Garraghty, P. E., Kaas, J. H., & Florence, S. L. (1993). Plasticity of sensory and motor maps in adult and developing mammals. In V. A. Casagrande & P. G. Shinkman (Eds.), *Advances in neural and behavioral development, Vol. 4* (pp. 1–36). Norwood, NJ: Ablex.

Garraghty, P. E., & Sur, M. (1990). Morphology of single intracellularly stained axons terminating in area 3b of macaque monkeys. *Journal of Comparative Neurology, 294,* 583–593.

Haber, W. B. (1955). Effects of loss of limb on sensory functions. *Journal of Psychology, 40,* 115–123.

Halligan, P. W., Marshall, J. C., & Wade, D. T. (1994). Sensory disorganization and perceptual plasticity after limb amputation: A follow-up study. *NeuroReport, 5,* 1341–1345.

Halligan, P. W., Marshall, J. C., Wade, D. T., Davey, J., & Morrison, D. (1993). Thumb in cheek? Sensory reorganization and perceptual plasticity after limb amputation. *NeuroReport, 4*, 233–236.

Hallin, R. G., Wiesenfeld, Z., & Lindblom, U. (1981). Neurophysiological studies on patients with sutured median nerves: Faulty sensory localization after nerve regeneration and its physiological correlates. *Experimental Neurology, 73*, 90–106.

Hawkins, G. L. (1948). Faulty sensory localization in nerve regeneration. *Journal of Neurosurgery, 5*, 11–18.

Head, H. (1920). *Studies in neurology, Vol. 1*. London: Oxford University Press.

Head, H., & Holmes, G. (1911). Sensory disturbances from cerebral lesions. *Brain, 34*, 102–254.

Jenkins, W. M., Merzenich, M. M., Ochs, M. T., Allard, T., & Guic-Robles, E. (1990). Functional reorganization of primary somatosensory cortex in adult owl monkeys after behaviorally controlled tactile stimulation. *Journal of Neurophysiology, 63*, 82–104.

Kaas, J. H. (1991). Plasticity of sensory and motor maps in adult mammals. *Annual Review of Neuroscience, 14*, 137–167.

Kaas, J. H. (1995). The reorganization of sensory and motor maps in adult mammals. In M. S. Gazzaniga (Ed.), *The cognitive neurosciences* (pp. 51–71). Cambridge, MA: MIT Press.

Katz, J. (1992). Psychophysiological contributions to phantom limbs. *Canadian Journal of Psychiatry, 37*, 282–298.

Kelahan, A. M., & Doetsch, G. S. (1984). Time-dependent changes in the functional organization of somatosensory cerebral cortex following digit amputation in adult raccoons. *Somatosensory Research, 2*, 49–81.

Kew, J. J. M., Halligan, P. W., Marshall, J. C., Passingham, R. E., Rothwell, J. C., Ridding, M. C., Marsden, C. D., & Brooks, D. J. (1997). Abnormal access of axial vibrotactile input to deafferented somatosensory cortex in human upper limb amputees. *Journal of Neurophysiology, 77*, 2753–2764.

Kolarik, R. C., Rasey, S. K., & Wall, J. T. (1994). The consistency, extent, and locations of early-onset changes in cortical nerve dominance aggregates following injury of nerves to primate hands. *Journal of Neuroscience, 14*, 4269–4288.

Kossut, M., Hand, P. J., Greenberg, J., & Hand, C. (1988). Single vibrissal cortical column in SI cortex of rat and its alterations in neonatal and adult vibrissae deafferented animals - a quantitative 2 DG study. *Journal of Neurophysiology, 60*, 829–852.

Lacroix, R., Melzack, R., Smith, D., & Mitchell, N. (1992). Multiple phantom limbs in a child. *Cortex, 28*, 503–507.

Lenz, F. A., Kwan, H. C., Martin, R., Tasker, R., Richardson, R. T., & Dostrovsky, J. O. (1994). Characteristics of somatotopic organization and spontaneous neuronal activity in the region of the thalamic principal sensory nucleus in patients with spinal cord transection. *Journal of Neurophysiology, 72*, 1570–1587.

Levin, B. E., & Dunn-Meynell, A. (1991). Adult rat barrel cortex plasticity occurs at 1 week but not at 1 day after vibrissectomy as demonstrated by the 2-deoxyglucose method. *Experimental Neurology, 113*, 237–248.

Melzack, R. (1990). Phantom limbs and the concept of a neuromatrix. *Trends in Neuroscience, 13*, 88–92.

Melzack, R. (1992). Phantom limbs. *Scientific American, 266*, 120–126.

Merrill, E. G., & Wall, P. D. (1978). Plasticity of connection in the adult nervous system. In C. W. Cotman (Ed.), *Neuronal plasticity* (pp. 97–111). New York: Raven Press.

Merzenich, M. M., & deCharms, R. C. (1996). Neural representations, experience, and change. In R. Llinas & P. S. Churchland (Eds.), *The mind-brain continuum* (pp. 61–81). Cambridge, MA: MIT Press.

Merzenich, M. M., Kaas, J. H., Wall, J. T., Sur, M., Nelson, R. J., & Felleman, D. J. (1983). Progression of change following median nerve section in the cortical representation of the hand in areas 3b and 1 in adult owl and squirrel monkeys. *Neuroscience, 10*, 639–665.

Merzenich, M. M., Nelson, R. J., Stryker, M. P., Cynader, M. S., Schoppmann, A., & Zook, J. M. (1984). Somatosensory cortical map changes following digit amputation in adult monkeys. *Journal of Comparative Neurology, 224*, 591–605.

Merzenich, M. M., Recanzone, G., Jenkins, W. M., Allard, T. T., & Nudo, R. J. (1988). Cortical representational plasticity. In P. Rakic & W. Singer (Eds.), *Neurobiology of neocortex* (pp. 41–67). New York: Wiley.

Mitchell, S. W. (1872). *Injuries of nerves and their consequences*. Philadelphia: J. B. Lippincott.

Murray, J. F., Ord, J. V. R., & Gavelin, G. E. (1967). The neurovascular island pedicle flap. *Journal of Bone and Joint Surgery, 49,* 1285–1297.

Ojemann, J. G., & Silbergeld, D. L. (1995). Cortical stimulation mapping of phantom limb rolandic cortex. *Journal of Neurosurgery, 82,* 641–644.

Omer, G. E., Jr. (1980). Neurovascular cutaneous island pedicle flaps. In G. E. Omer, Jr. & M. Spinner (Eds.), *Management of peripheral nerve problems* (pp. 779–790). Philadelphia: Saunders.

Pons, T. P., Garraghty, P. E., Ommaya, A. K., Kaas, J. H., Taub, E., & Mishkin, M. (1991). Massive cortical reorganization after sensory deafferentation in adult macaques. *Science, 252,* 1857–1860.

Ramachandran, V. S. (1993). Behavioral and magnetoencephalographic correlates of plasticity in the adult human brain. *Proceedings of the National Academy of Sciences of the United States of America, 90,* 10413–10420.

Ramachandran, V. S. (1994). Phantom limbs, neglect syndromes, repressed memories, and Freudian psychology. *International Review of Neurobiology, 37,* 291–333.

Ramachandran, V. S., & Hirstein, W. (1998). The perception of phantom limbs. *Brain, 121,* 1603–1630.

Rasmusson, D. D. (1982). Reorganization of raccoon somatosensory cortex following removal of the fifth digit. *Journal of Comparative Neurology, 205,* 313–326.

Saadah, E. S. M., & Melzack, R. (1994). Phantom limb experiences in congenital limb-deficient adults. *Cortex, 30,* 479–485.

Schady, W., Braune, S., Watson, S., Torebjork, H. E., & Schmidt, R. (1994). Responsiveness of the somatosensory system after nerve injury and amputation in the human hand. *Annals of Neurology, 36,* 68–75.

Sica, R. E. P., Panizza, M., Reich, E., & Correale, J. (1988). Modifications of the N1-P1 component of the somatosensory evoked potential in humans after partial limb amputation as a manifestation of central nervous system remodeling. *Electromyography and Clinical Neurophysiology, 28,* 227–231.

Silva, A. C., Rasey, S. K., Wu, X.-F., & Wall, J. T. (1996). Initial cortical reactions to injury of the median and radial nerves to the hands of adult primates. *Journal of Comparative Neurology, 366,* 700–716.

Simmel, M. L. (1958). The conditions of occurrence of phantom limbs. *Proceedings of the American Philosophical Society, 102,* 492–500.

Sunderland, S. (1968). *Nerves and nerve injuries*. Edinburgh, Scotland: Churchill Livingstone.

Teuber, H. L., Krieger, H. P., & Bender, M. B. (1949). Reorganization of sensory function in amputation stumps: Two-point discrimination. *Federation Proceedings, 8,* 156.

Wall, J. T., & Cusick, C. G. (1984). Cutaneous responsiveness in primary somatosensory (S-I) hindpaw cortex before and after partial hindpaw deafferentation in adult rats. *Journal of Neuroscience, 4,* 1499–1515.

Weinstein, S., Sersen, E. A., & Vetter, R. J. (1964). Phantoms and somatic sensation in cases of congenital aplasia. *Cortex, 1,* 276–290.

White, J. C., & Sweet, W. H. (1969). *Pain and the neurosurgeon*. Springfield, IL: Charles C. Thomas.

Woolf, C. J., & Doubell, T. P. (1994). The pathophysiology of chronic pain–increased sensitivity to low threshold A-fibre inputs. *Current Opinion in Neurobiology, 4,* 525–534.

Xerri, C., Coq, J. O., Merzenich, M. M., & Jenkins, W. M. (1996). Experience-induced plasticity of cutaneous maps in the primary somatosensory cortex of adult monkeys and rats. *Journal of Physiology (Paris), 90,* 277–287.

Yang, T. T., Gallen, C. C., Ramachandran, V. S., Cobb, S., Schwartz, B. J., & Bloom, F. E. (1994). Non-invasive detection of cerebral plasticity in adult human somatosensory cortex. *NeuroReport, 5,* 701–704.

G. Campbell Teskey

Using Kindling to Model the Neuroplastic Changes Associated With Learning and Memory, Neuropsychiatric Disorders, and Epilepsy

Epilepsy is the price that we pay for learning and memory.
—*Whytsie Wadman*

Kindling provides a model for conceptualizing physiological and behavioral abnormalities that progress in severity in response to the same inducing stimulation over time.
—*Robert M. Post*

The kindling preparation may be used to model either generalized convulsive seizures or a variety of focal seizures.
—*McIntyre Burnham*

☐ Using Stimulation to Cause Changes in Brain Function

As a general statement, derived from Heisenberg's uncertainty principle, the act of observation can change the phenomena being observed. This principle applies to attempts to study brain function by using electrical stimulation. That is, electrical stimulation used to reveal the workings of the brain can persistently or permanently alter the workings of the brain (Corcoran, 1988). The use of electrical stimulation to investigate brain function and plasticity can be traced (no pun intended) back to Sechenov's book, *Reflexes of the Brain*, published in 1866. Sechenov described physiological evidence for the "capacity of retention" after briefly stimulating a nerve in a frog's leg and observing a persistent contraction. Romanes in 1882 published an account of his research with several invertebrate preparations and argued that the enhanced responses produced by low-intensity electrical stimulation served as the basis for many physiological and psychological phenomena. Around the time of Hebb's book (circa 1950) it was well documented that moderately long-lasting changes in synaptic transmission could be induced in invertebrate preparations, mammalian neuromuscular junctions, and the spinal cord, but long-lasting changes had not yet been discovered in the mammalian forebrain. In the late 1960s and early 1970s two models, kindling and long-term potentiation (LTP), were discovered which demonstrated long-lasting changes in synaptic efficacy in the mammalian forebrain. Today, there is still a need for stimulation models, which produce changes in brain function, that will allow us to test the assertions of our theories and to guide us in reformulating better theories and descriptions of brain function.

While investigating the effect of electrical stimulation of the amygdala on avoidance conditioning Goddard (1967) observed what at first appeared to be an irritant and an experimental confound: that repeated electrical stimulation, while initially ineffective, eventually resulted in the development and growth of seizure activity. The seizures became more prolonged and severe even though the intensity of the stimulating current had remained unchanged. Furthermore, stimulated animals that displayed seizure activity and were then left unstimulated for prolonged periods of time, when restimulated again displayed well-developed seizure activity. Thus, the phenomenon appeared permanent. Although earlier researchers had made similar observations, it was Goddard who recognized the potential significance of the phenomenon: that this apparently permanent change in brain functioning in response to an invariant stimulus may be similar to those believed to underlie the neuroplastic processes related to learning (Goddard & Douglas, 1975; Goddard, McIntyre, & Leech, 1969). Goddard named the phenomenon "kindling" in analogy to starting a fire with an initially ineffective stimulus.

☐ What Is Kindling?

Kindling refers to the eventual development of persistent seizure activity following repeated exposure to an initially subconvulsant epileptogenic agent. This epileptogenic agent can be either a train of electrical stimulation or a chemical, as long as it elicits an EEG event termed epileptiform discharge or afterdischarge (AD). In electrical kindling the stimulation is applied, via permanently implanted wire electrodes, in brief trains of electrical pulses to a brain site, usually once daily. When the intensity of stimulation is strong enough, ADs are evoked. It is the elicitation of the AD that is the prerequisite for kindling to occur (Goddard et al., 1969; Racine 1972a, 1972b). As the kindling stimulation is repeated over successive trials, several primary changes occur. The first is the growth of several measures of the AD itself, including duration, amplitude, frequency, and spike complexity. Second, the threshold for the AD is reduced, that is, less intense stimulation can elicit an AD. Third, the AD propagates from the focal region around the stimulating electrode and can be recorded in regions of the brain distant from the stimulated site. The fourth change is the appearance of seizure behaviors that are associated with the AD propagation to motoric regions of the brain. It is the AD that drives the seizure behaviors. Racine (1972b) classified the seizure behaviors elicited by kindling the amygdala of rats into five stages, with the earliest stage involving rostral (facial) musculature and the successive stages recapitulating the earlier stages and involving progressively more caudal (hind quarters) skeletal musculature. The stage 5 seizure is characterized by a fully generalized convulsion with bilateral forelimb and hindlimb clonus. Thus, kindling represents both a phenomenon and a technique. As a phenomenon it describes various features of progressive states in the brain, while as a technique, kindling is used as a procedure to carry out various manipulations of the brain.

Useful Features of Kindling

Electrical kindling may be one of the best-suited techniques for investigating progressive changes in brain function for several reasons. First, kindling itself is a robust phenomenon that is highly predictable and reliable. The kindled seizures themselves are well defined and easily scored. The physiological and behavioral changes that occur are slow and graded enough to allow measurement and manipulation at many points during the kindling development. Because kindling results in large, easily measurable changes in anatomy, neurochemistry, metabolism, electrophysiology, and behavior, the signal-to-noise ratio problem that occurs with learning experiments doesn't occur. Furthermore, as a technique, kindling allows the experimenter control over when and how the stimulation is delivered. Because all brain structures, except the cerebellum, support kindling, the experimenter can study the development of the phenomenon in different neuroanatomical regions. Kindling also allows for investigations that examine the relationship between brain and behavior. Unlike other models of plasticity (i.e., LTP), including those in reduced preparations (i.e., whole brain, slices) the kindling model allows for an interface between brain and behavior. The experimenter can induce the behavioral seizures and then measure the resultant changes in brain function and interictal behaviors. Furthermore, kindling is a pan-species phenomenon that has been found in all vertebrates studied, including amphibians (frogs), reptiles (lizards), and a variety of mammals (mice, rats, rabbits, guinea pigs, gerbils, cats, dogs, baboons, and monkeys). It would be surprising to find a phenomenon that spans vertebrates, including amphibians, reptiles, and mammals that didn't include humans, and indeed, Sramka, Sedlak, & Nadvornik (1977) reported that a human has been kindled. This underscores the applicability of the animal model for humans. Furthermore, different animal species have different kindling characteristics, which make comparisons useful in determining mechanisms (Teskey, Valentine, Sainsbury, & Trepel, 1995). There are also rat strains that manifest differences in kindling rate and susceptibility to anticonvulsant drugs (Dufresne, Kelly, & McIntyre, 1989; Loscher, Cramer, & Ebert, 1998). Finally the development of knockout and transgenic mice allows causal questions related to kindling to be addressed and answered. Thus, kindling has several useful features that make it attractive as a model for neuroplasticity. The following sections will deal with kindling as a model for learning and memory, neuropsychiatric disorders, and partial epilepsy.

Kindling as a Model of Learning and Memory

Graham Goddard et al. (1969) completed an extensive set of experiments that reinforced his belief in the overlap between memory and kindling. Subsequently, he and others have documented a number of similarities between learning and kindling. For example, kindling can be defined as "a process that results in a relatively permanent change in behavior resulting from stimulation," while learning can be defined as "a process that results in a relatively permanent change in behavior resulting from experience." Both phenomena share the feature of a long-term change in behavior resulting from an externally imposed event that is not the result of damage or due to some contamination of the inducing agent (Goddard & Douglas, 1975). Spaced electrical stimulation is also more effective than massed stimulation in producing kindling, as is spaced practice more effective than massed practice in promoting learning (Leech & McIntyre, 1976). Positive and negative transfer effects are also shared by learning and kindling. Prior kindling of one structure results in faster kindling of a second structure (positive transfer) and is analogous to facilitated learning with prior learning. Kindling of one structure can interfere with concurrent kindling of a second structure (kindling antagonism effect) and is analogous to the interference effects observed when learning two different things at the same time. Furthermore, retroactive and proactive interference effects and spontaneous recovery (event jumps back) are also properties shared between kindling and learning (D. C. McIntyre, personal communication, 1999). Thus, kindling does share with learning a variety of similarities that may be considered analogous.

Kindling and learning may have other similarities that may be more homologous. For example, kindling proceeds more rapidly in structures thought to be involved in memorial processes (i.e., forebrain). Older animals kindle more slowly (deToledo-Morrell, Morrell, & Fleming, 1984) and learn more slowly (Barnes, 1988). Pharmacological agents that retard kindling rate also retard learning rate. A number of biochemical changes associated with kindling also appear to be associated with learning (e.g., NMDA). Moreover, when something is well learned there appears to be a shorter latency to respond, while in the well-kindled animal there is a shorter latency to express behavior (e.g., forelimb clonus).

Tests of the hypothesis that kindling shares common mechanisms with learning include examinations of whether a kindled brain inhibits or blocks normal learning and memory. This approach has suggested that lasting deficits in short- and long-term spatial memory and place learning may be observed in kindled animals (deToledo-Morrell et al., 1984). However, other studies have failed to replicate this finding. The failure to replicate may be reflected, at least in part, in the different temporal intervals between the kindling stimulations and the behavioral test (Mohapel & McIntyre, 1998). Behavioral and learning impairments are likely to be most evident when testing occurs shortly after a seizure, but these deficits appear to be somewhat transient in nature.

Some researchers have used a novel approach to explore the relationship between kindling mechanisms and learning and memory mechanisms by correlating predisposed learning rates with subsequent differences in kindling parameters. Based on the notion that kindling and learning and memory mechanisms are, at least to some degree, shared, one could predict that animals that kindle rapidly should learn rapidly, while animals that kindle slowly should learn more slowly. Leech and McIntyre (1976) reported that two inbred mice strains that differed in their ability to learn an inhibitory avoidance task also differed, in the appropriate direction, in their rate of amygdala kindling. Unfortunately, two subsequent studies have reported the opposite correlation, with fast learners kindling slower and slow learners kindling faster. Zaide (1974) observed that Tryon Maze-Dull rats had longer ADs than Tryon Maze-Bright rats. The "fast" and "slow" kindling rat strains, which are differentiated by a dramatic discrepancy in their kindling rates (Dufresne, Kelly, & McIntyre, 1989), have also been tested on a number of learning and memory tasks (Mohapel & McIntyre, 1998). The result was that the slow-strain rats learned the tasks faster than the fast-strain animals. Thus, the relationship between kindling rate and learning rate is not a simple or straightforward one.

The belief that learning and memory are mediated by an alteration in synaptic efficacy is a long-standing postulate in psychology and neuroscience. Thus, the finding that kindling alters synaptic connectivity (deJonge & Racine, 1987; Maru & Goddard,

1987) was one of the most exciting findings for proponents of kindling as a memory model. Interestingly, kindling-induced potentiation (KIP) appears to decay at a much slower rate than LTP, and depending on the anatomical pathway, KIP may even be permanent (Racine & Cain, 1991; Teskey & Valentine, 1998). These persistent alterations in neuronal interactions are presumed to be based on mechanisms available to the normal brain, although it is possible that kindling results in the distortion of normal plastic mechanisms and in a "pathological" condition.

In summary, while there are a number of similarities between learning and memory on one hand and kindling on the other, shared neurobiological mechanisms are still to be determined. At the very least, the kindling preparation can be used to guide researchers in their pursuit of neuroplasticity mechanisms such as synaptic efficacy, synaptogenesis, neuronal growth, and neurogenesis mechanisms, which may be related to those that underlie learning and memory.

☐ Kindling as a Model of Some Neuropsychiatric Disorders

A number of researchers have suggested that the kindling paradigm shows a set of attributes that are similar to some neuropsychiatric illnesses and that kindling may be pertinent to the understanding of the long-term and developing patterns of non-seizure-related disorders (for a review, see Bolwig & Trimble, 1989). In kindling, repeated intermittent stimulation over time results in a progressive increase in behavioral and physiological responsivity and a decrease in the threshold for an event (i.e., seizure) and can eventually result in spontaneous events (i.e., spontaneous seizures). The seizure can be used as a convenient endpoint marker for behavioral and physiological responsivity to the same, or even to a smaller, stimulus over time. Post and Weiss (1998) argued that the kindling model can be used to understand the progression of a variety of neuropsychiatric illnesses. These illnesses include those that are initially expressed with minor physiological and behavioral perturbations, to later more serious full-blown pathology, and then finally to those that eventually appear in the absence of any obvious external inducing stimulus. An important caveat is that the kindling model appears to lack direct mechanistic homology, and therefore its utility is based on suggesting principles and general pathophysiological characteristics of progressive limbic-related abnormalities (Weiss & Post, 1995).

The recurrent nature of many neuropsychiatric disorders has been documented for nearly as long as the illnesses have been studied (Kraepelin, 1921). While there is substantial variation between and within patients, the course of untreated illnesses is generally characterized by a decreasing well-interval between episodes and a transition from episodes that are precipitated by external events (losses and stressors) to those that occur more spontaneously. The observation of the potential for minor episodes to give way to more major ones is often made in bipolar (manic-depression) and unipolar (depression) disorders. The patterns and forms of these illnesses can change from episodes that were isolated and intermittent to more continuous rhythmic varieties and then to rapid cycling with chaotic manifestations. The aspects of the kindling model that resemble the course of recurrent affective illness are its progressive feature, with threshold lowering and the move from induced to spontaneous occurrence.

In panic disorders it is apparent that some patients move from highly intermittent panic attacks that are precipitated by a cue or context, to those that begin to occur more frequently and spontaneously. In addition, some patients become increasingly more paralyzed by agoraphobia, which may increase to the point of complete incapacitation. In the case of cocaine-related panic attacks, some patients who have a history of persistently and repeatedly self-administering cocaine without anxiety or panic, can suddenly express a full blown cocaine-related panic attack. Furthermore, spontaneous panic attacks may begin to emerge in the absence of cocaine administration (Post, Weiss, Pert, & Uhde, 1987). Once again, kindling's progressive feature with threshold lowering and the move from induced to spontaneous events appears to model panic disorders.

In obsessive compulsive disorder (OCD), initial minor obsessions and ritualistic compulsions often increase in severity and lead to incapacitation. This progressive feature of OCD is modeled by kindling. Perhaps OCD shares some homologous mechanisms with seizure-related disorders, because in a model of OCD, canine paw licking, many of the dogs also had seizures (Luescher, McKeown, & Halip, 1991). Individuals with posttraumatic stress disorder (PTSD) who have experienced prior traumatic life events also appear more likely to suffer from PTSD upon repeated exposure to trauma (Post, Weiss, & Smith, 1995). Repeated inducing events may also yield more severe and long-lasting consequences than isolated events. There may be progression in the emergence of flashbacks, which are initially triggered by cues linked to the original event and then occur more spontaneously. The decreases in AD threshold observed in kindling may model greater episode recurrence in this disorder. These neuropsychiatric phenomena are perhaps only analogous and not homologous to kindling because these disorders are not usually associated with seizures. However, because of many phenomenological similarities, kindling may be pertinent to the understanding of the long-term and developing patterns of these disorders.

☐ Kindling as a Model of Epilepsy

Epilepsy is a chronic brain disorder characterized by recurrent seizures due to excessive discharge of neurons, with a spectrum of severity ranging from mild and benign to severe and intractable. It is estimated to affect about 1% of the population. Epileptiform activity includes the mechanisms involved in its triggering and generalization, while epileptogenesis is the process that underlies the transformation of normal brain tissue to a chronic epileptic state. Epilepsy is a condition that can be brought about by a wide range of external perturbations such as infectious disease, and head injury, or by internal factors such as anomalous alleles or tumors. These perturbations and factors can disrupt normal developmental or plasticity mechanisms, ultimately giving rise to the metabolic, neurochemical, and structural abnormalities that generate the hypersynchronous and hyperexcitable discharges that drive seizures.

Research has uncovered much information on the cellular and synaptic mechanisms of seizures and epileptogenesis, but many unanswered questions remain. Because of the ethical impediment to using humans and the inherent limitations of using excised "epileptic" human tissue, we still require the use of animal models. Animal models have been, and will continue to be, invaluable for (a) modeling the clinical condition, (b) determining the basic mechanisms underlying the genesis and progression of seizures, as well as for, (c) screening potential anticonvunlsant drugs. While an ideal model would possess properties identical to *all* aspects of a particular human condition, this is probably not attainable. The characteristics of a valuable model should possess a substantial degree of similarity to at least some aspect of the disorder of interest. Thus, a good animal model should be able to provide new insight into the disorder it models and respond in a reproducible and predictable manner. An ideal model would possess the following characteristics: (a) evoked or spontaneous seizures; (b) long-lasting seizure susceptibility; (c) similar ictal and interictal behaviors; (d) similar electrophysiologic, metabolic, anatomic, and neurochemical characteristics; and (e) similar anticonvulsant pharmacology and pharmacokinetics. Many other pragmatic characteristics are also important, with better models being available and inexpensive to obtain, the animals easily maintained, genetically uniform and controlled, amenable to behavioral testing, and providing unlimited access to antemortem and postmortem sampling. The kindling preparation, depending on the species, possesses many of these characteristics and is an excellent model for certain clinical seizure disorders and their underlying mechanisms and as a screening tool.

☐ Clinical Condition

Kindling provides a model for many aspects of seizures and epilepsy. In this context it is important to ask what human state or pathology is modeled by the kindling preparation. This is a complex question because kindling may be used in multiple ways. Since kindling is both a phenomenon and a technique, both the phenomenal properties and technical aspects will be summarized with respect to the clinical condition. Kindling can be used to model (a) the *development* of seizures, (b) the *occurrence* of partial (focal) and/or secondary generalized seizures, (c) either the *progression* in severity of seizures or the *stability* of seizures over time, (d) *spontaneous* seizures, and (e) interictal *behaviors*.

In the case of posttraumatic epilepsy, brain tissue that was presumably once normal becomes disrupted in a manner that eventually gives rise to spontaneous seizures. Apparently, it is not the case that the acute reactive ictal events that occur during the immediate posttraumatic period necessarily cause the appearance of a chronic epileptic condition. Furthermore, the risk factors for reactive seizures are different from those for chronic epilepsy (Jennett, 1975). Thus, some other mechanism, working over months or years and causing some structural reorganization of the injured tissue, eventually results in spontaneous seizures. Penfield and Jasper (1954) referred to this process as a "ripening of the scar." In the naïve animal, stimulation which doesn't initially give rise to an AD, if it is repeated over several sessions, can eventually come to give rise to an AD (Racine, 1972a). In this way repeated subthreshold stimulation could model the "irritation" and lower seizure threshold in the clinical syndrome.

Kindling is most obviously a seizure model because seizures can be evoked following brief trains of suprathreshold electrical stimulation. In people with epilepsy, where activity is generated from a particular brain focus, the seizure or convulsion is remarkably similar to that shown by the kindled animal stimulated in a similar locus. Manifestations of both tonic and clonic behaviors are readily induced in the kindled animal. Initial kindled seizures from the amygdala or the cortical loci model either simple or complex partial attacks, while later seizures that secondarily generalize into a convulsion model tonic-clonic attacks.

The progression of seizure severity in epileptic populations is somewhat controversial because the widespread use of anticonvulsant drugs prevents an uncontaminated examination of the phenomenon. However, before the introduction of anticonvulsant pharmacological treatments, it was observed that as seizures recurred, there was an increasing tendency for minor attacks to lead to major ones and for the interval between attacks to decrease (Morrell, 1973). The famous quote, "Seizures beget more seizures," captures this general tendency. It is probably the case that certain subpopulations of epileptics tend to show seizure progression while other subpopulations tend to show stability in their seizure severity (Engel, 1998). The aspects of kindling that model seizure progression are: (a) the unambiguous progression of electrographic and seizure severity with repeated kindling stimulations, (b) the occurrence of focal seizures in one hemisphere leading to the development of independent foci in the homotopic site in the contralateral hemisphere, (c) the lowering of the afterdischarge threshold with repeated *supra*threshold (afterdischarge-inducing) stimulation, (d) the increased trans-synaptic excitability, and (e) the increase in neuronal burst-firing. Furthermore, concurrent multiple-site kindling leads to a more rapid progression and greater seizure severity (Teskey, Thiessen & Gilbert, 1999), which probably models the more rapid and severe seizures in individuals with multiple lesions. If kindling in animals models progressive changes in seizure severity, then one can ask whether humans kindle. Sramka et al. (1977) described a case of a 47-year-old woman who had depth electrodes located in 3 structures of the left thalamus and was stimulated daily to relieve pain. During the third week of stimulation she perceived spontaneous mild movements in the right half of her face and parts of her right hand. Although the electrodes were removed she continued to have seizures and paroxysmal brain activity. The seizures became secondarily generalized, and the patient became epileptic. These are good reasons to believe that the progressive advances in clinical seizure severity are well modeled when animals are kindled.

However, as mentioned above, it is likely that some epileptics do not show progression and instead have stable seizures over long periods of time (Engel, 1998). My laboratory has observed that single-site-kindled guinea pigs initially show a progression of kindling but then fail to proceed beyond unilateral forelimb clonus, even after as many as 250 stimulations. Wada (1998) has obtained similar findings for the rhesus monkey.

Typically, kindled seizures are elicited, while human epileptic seizures occur spontaneously. However, some species of animals (baboons, dogs, cats, and rats) can be kindled to the point where they exhibit spontaneous seizures, thus undermining the position that kindling lacks relevance because the seizures *are* induced and not spontaneous. Furthermore, the spontaneous seizures that patients express, while not induced by trains of electrical stimulation, *are* induced by some stimulus, even though that trigger may not be obvious.

On somewhat of a tangential point, some authors have made the claim that there is a relationship between phylogenetic status and the development of spontaneous seizures, with lower animals being less prone and higher animals being more resistant (Schmutz, 1987). This is an error for a very good theoretical reason: there is *no* phylogenetic scale with humans at the top and other animals beneath. All life forms today stem from a single progenitor that lived approximately 4 billions years ago. That is to say that all life is the same evolutionary age. Furthermore, no species can be considered more or less evolved than any other species because evolution is nondirectional, only shaping adaptations to fit local conditions. If we were to replace the failed concept of higher and lower species with brain size and postulate that smaller brains kindle faster and larger brains kindle more slowly, we would still be in error. Some larger brained species like baboons kindle more rapidly than some smaller brained species like guinea pigs, who kindle more slowly (Wada, 1998).

Cognitive and behavioral abnormalities have been reported to occur in human epileptics (Adamec, 1990). These include deficits in verbal and visual memory that may not be directly linked to the occurrence of seizures. Changes in fear and anxiety are some of the most common emotional disturbances associated with temporal lobe epilepsy (Gloor, 1992). It is often difficult to determine whether behavioral impairments are a result of seizures or other factors, such as medication. Furthermore, given the difficulties with the stigma associated with epilepsy, it is important to make absolutely sure that any causal relationship between seizures and persistent aberrant behavior is real and unimagined. However, identifying psychosocial problems and their underlying neurobiological substrates may allow us to prevent or reverse their expression. The fact that certain epileptic-related interictal behaviors can disappear after successful surgical treatment implies a relationship between the two. Kindling the amygdala has been used to study the relationship between emotionality and limbic epileptogensis (Adamec, 1990). Repeatedly inducing seizures in the amygdala can produce various changes in emotional responses, particularly those involving fear and anxiety (Adamec & Morgan, 1994; Kalynchuk, Pinel, Treit, & Kippin, 1997). It is, however, important to note that other researchers have found no, or even diminished, changes in fear and anxiety responses with amygdala kindling. These apparently contradictory results require resolution. It is likely that methodological differences involving different tasks, stages of kindling, number of stimulations, and treatments to one or both hemispheres account for the contradictory results.

☐ Underlying Mechanism

Kindling can be used to explore physiological and anatomical alterations that cannot be explored in humans. However, the recording of EEG with surface electrodes or with depth electrodes during surgery, the use of MRI and PET scans to measure metabolism and gross anatomical changes, and the use of excised epileptic tissue to examine microanatomy, electrophysiology, neuropharmacology, and biochemistry allows us to compare the data from human epileptics with the body of knowledge generated from the kindling model. Unfortunately, the lack of human "control" tissue makes comparisons difficult and the interpretation of the data from excised epileptic tissue should be done with caution (Glass & Dragunow, 1995).

In people with epilepsy, epileptiform activity is identified by large amplitude "spikes" in an EEG record that is often followed by a depression of the EEG signal. In kindled animals, AD evoked by electrical stimulation is similar in morphology, amplitude, and frequency. After prolonged discharges in the kindled animal, postictal depression of the EEG is also clearly identified. In both the epileptic human and the kindled animal, large transient waveforms in the EEG record are observed (Racine, Mosher, & Kairiss, 1988). At the individual cell level, the progression to a burst-type firing pattern is also an electrophysiological commonality between kindled neurons and human epileptic neurons (Teskey & Racine, 1993). Anatomical examination of brains from kindled animals and excised epileptic tissue from humans has revealed cell loss; loss of dendritic length, branching and spine density (Teskey, Hutchinson, & Kolb, 1999), and increased sprouting in the dentate gyrus, as revealed by Timm stain (Sutula, Cascino, Cavazos, Parada, & Ramirez, 1989). With respect to ictal events, epileptic patients have hypermetabolic signatures that are consistent from seizure to seizure but are highly variable between patients. Kindled guinea pigs also show a great deal of interanimal variability in their ictal metabolic signatures (Valentine et al., 1996). Medial temporal lobe epilepsy has a hypometabolic focus in the interictal state, while kindled brains appear to have no altered metabolic signature during the interictal state. However, more work on the kindling model needs to be done, perhaps with a species manifesting kindling-induced spontaneous seizures. There are also impressive numbers of parallels (and differences) between biochemical changes in kindled tissue and excised human tissue (Corcoran & Moshe, 1998; Glass & Dragunow, 1995).

Anticonvulsant Screening

Determining the usefulness of seizure models for the screening of anticonvulsant medications is important. Models with high predictive validity for partial epilepsy should show a close correspondence between the effectiveness of the anticonvulsants in the human condition and the model. Likewise, the demonstration of the effectiveness of an anticonvulsant in generalized epilepsy, and ineffectiveness in focal or partial epilepsy, should also correspond with ineffectiveness in the model. It is important to note that the kindled limbic focus appears to provide the only validated animal model of partial seizures (Albright & Burnham, 1980). Using the amygdala-kindled rat as a model, the traditional anticonvulsant medications, phenytoin, carbamazepine, valproate, phenobarbital, and clonazapam, are all effective at either reducing seizure severity and AD duration and/or raising AD thresholds (for review, see Loscher, 1998). The newer anticonvulsant medications, such as topiramate, felbamate, lamotrigine, and vigabatrin, also appear to be effective in kindled animals, although more work is needed to fully determine their efficacy for both patients and kindled animals. With respect to the anticonvulsant ethosuximide, used in the treatment of absence epilepsy, it is not effective in the kindling model at nontoxic doses (Albright & Burnham, 1980). When the response of the kindling model is properly scored, there is a general parallel with the clinical drug response indicating the usefulness of kindling as a screening tool for partial epilepsy.

Summary

Kindling has been studied for over three decades and has generated a substantial literature. It shows a number of similarities to learning and neuropsychiatric disorders and may share some common mechanisms. With respect to partial epilepsy, kindling has value as a model for certain aspects of the clinical condition and the understanding of brain mechanisms and as a tool for screening the anticonvulsant properties of pharmacological drugs. In the future, the kindling model should continue to provide a useful model for the identification and verification of neuroplastic mechanisms, as well as assisting in the conceptualization of learning and memory theories and various progressive disorders.

Acknowledgments

The author thanks Dr. Rod Cooper, Marie Monfils, Isaac Bogoch, and Pamela Valentine for commenting on an earlier version of this chapter.

References

Adamec, R. (1990). Kindling, anxiety and limbic epilepsy: Human and animal perspectives. In J. A. Wada (Ed.), *Kindling 4* (pp. 329–341). New York: Raven Press.

Adamec, R. E., & Morgan, H. D. (1994). The effect of kindling of different nuclei in the left and right amygdala on anxiety in the rat. *Physiology and Behaviour, 55*, 1–12.

Albright, P. S., & Burnham, W. M. (1980). Development of a new pharmacological seizure model: Effects of anticonvulsants on cortical- and amygdala-kindled seizures in the rat. *Epilepsia, 21*, 681–689.

Barnes, C. A. (1988). Aging and the physiology of spatial memory. *Neurobiology of Aging, 9*, 563–568.

Bolwig, T. G., & Trimble, M. R. (1989). *The clinical relevance of kindling*. New York: Wiley.

Corcoran, M. E. (1988). Characteristics and mechanisms of kindling. In C. Barnes and P. Kavivas (Eds.), *Sensitization of the nervous system* (pp. 82–116). Caldwell, NJ: Telford Press.

Corcoran, M. E., & Moshe, S. L. (1998). *Kindling 5*. New York: Plenum Press.

deJonge, M., & Racine, R. J. (1987). The development and decay of kindling-induced increases in paired-pulse depression in the dentate gyrus. *Brain Research, 412*, 318–328.

deToledo-Morrell, L., Morrell, F., & Fleming, S. (1984). Age-dependent deficits in spatial memory are related to impaired hippocampal kindling. *Behavioural Neuroscience, 98*, 902–907.

Dufresne, C., Kelly, M. E., & McIntyre, D. C. (1989). New fast and slow kindling rat strains. *Epilepsia, 30 (Suppl.)*, 652.

Engel, J., Jr. (1998). The syndrome of mesial temporal lobe epilepsy: A role for kindling. In M. E. Corcoran & S. L. Moshe (Eds.), *Kindling 5* (pp. 469–484). New York: Plenum Press.

Glass, M., & Dragunow, M. (1995). Neurochemical and morphological changes associated with human epilepsy. *Brain Research Reviews, 21*, 29–41.

Gloor, P. (1992). The role of the amygdala in temporal lobe epilepsy. In J. P. Aggleton (Ed.), *The amygdala: Neurobiological aspects of emotion, memory, and mental dysfunction* (pp. 505–538). New York: Wiley-Liss.

Goddard, G. V. (1967). Development of epileptic seizures through brain stimulation at low intensity. *Nature, 214*, 1020–1021.

Goddard, G. V., & Douglas, R. M. (1975). Does the engram of kindling model the engram of normal long-term memory? *Canadian Journal of Neurological Science, 2*, 385–394.

Goddard, G. V., McIntyre, D. C., & Leech, C. K. (1969). A permanent change in brain function resulting from daily electrical stimulation. *Experimental Neurology, 25*, 90–112.

Jennett, B. (1975). *Epilepsy after non-missle head injuries* (2nd ed). Chicago: William Heinemann.

Kalynchuk, L. E., Pinel, J. P. J., Treit, D., & Kippin, T. E. (1997). Changes in emotional behaviour produced by long-term amygdala kindling in rats. *Biological Psychiatry, 41*, 438–451.

Kraepelin, E. (1921). *Manic-depressive insanity and paranoia* (R. M. Barclay, Trans.; G. M. Robertson, ed.). Edinburgh, Scotland: E. S. Livingstone.

Leech, C. K., & McIntyre, D. C. (1976). Kindling rates in inbred mice: An analog to learning? *Behavioral Biology, 16*, 439–452.

Loscher, W. (1998). New visions in the pharmacology of anticonvulsion. *European Journal of Pharmacology, 342*, 1–13.

Loscher, W., Cramer, S., & Ebert, U. (1998). Differences in kindling development in seven outbred and inbred rat strains. *Experimental Neurology, 154*, 551–559.

Luescher, U. A., McKeown, D. B., & Halip, J. (1991). Stereotypic or obsessive-compulsive disorders in dogs and cats. *Advances in Companion Animal Behavior, 21*, 401–413.

Maru, E., & Goddard, G. V. (1987). Alteration in dentate neuronal activities associated with perforant-path kindling. I. Long-term potentiation of excitatory transmission. *Experimental Neurology, 96*, 19–32.

Mohapel, P., & McIntyre, D. C. (1998). Amygdala kindling-resistant (SLOW) or -prone (FAST) rat strains show differential fear responses. *Behavioral Neuroscience, 112*, 1402–1413.

Morrell, F. (1973). Goddard's kindling phenomenon: A new model of the mirror focus. In H. C. Sabelli (Ed.), *Chemical modulation of brain function*. New York: Raven Press.

Penfield, W., & Jasper, H. (1954). *Epilepsy and the functional anatomy of the human brain*. Boston: Little Brown.

Post, R. M., & Weiss, S. R. B. (1998). Sensitization and kindling phenomena in mood, anxiety, and obsessive-compulsive disorders: The role of serotonergic mechanisms in illness progression. *Biological Psychiatry, 44*, 193–206.

Post, R. M., Weiss, S. R. B., Pert, A., & Uhde, T. W. (1987). Chronic cocaine administration: Sensitization and kindling effects. In A. Raskin & S. Fisher (Eds.), *Cocaine: Clinical and biobehavioural aspects* (pp. 109–173). New York: Oxford University Press.

Post, R. M., Weiss, S. R. B., & Smith, M. (1995). Sensitization and kindling: Implications for the evolving neural substrate of PTSD. In M. J. Friedman, D. S. Charney, & A. Y. Deutch (Eds.),

Neurobiology and clincal consequences of stress: From normal adaptations to PTSD (pp. 203–224). Philadelphia: Lippincott-Raven.

Racine, R. J. (1972a). Modification of seizure activity by electrical stimulation. I. After-discharge threshold. *Electroencephalography and Clinical Neurophysiology, 32,* 269–279.

Racine, R. J. (1972b). Modification of seizure activity by electrical stimulation. II. Motor seizure. *Electroencephalography and Clinical Neurophysiology, 32,* 281–284.

Racine, R. J., & Cain, D. P. (1991). Kindling-induced potentiation. In F. Morrell (Ed.), *Kindling and synaptic plasticity: The legacy of Graham Goddard.* (pp. 38–53). Boston: Birkhauser.

Racine, R. J., Mosher, M., & Kairiss, E. W. (1988). The role of the pyriform cortex in the generation of interictal spikes in the kindling preparation. *Brain Research, 454,* 251–263.

Romances, G. J. (1970). *Animal intelligence* (originally published 1882). Westmead, UK: Gress International.

Schmutz, M. (1987). Relevance of kindling and related processes to human epileptogenesis. *Progress in Neuro-Psychopharmacology and Biological Psychiatry, 11,* 505–525.

Sechenov, I. M. (1970). *Reflexes of the brain* (originally published 1866). Cambridge, MA: M. I. T. Press.

Sramka, M., Sedlak, P., & Nadvornik, P. (1977). Observation of kindling phenomenon in treatment of pain by stimulation in thalamus. In W. H. Sweet, S. Obrador, & J. G. Martin-Rodriguez (Eds.), *Neurosurgical treatment in psychiatry, pain and epilepsy* (pp. 651–654). Baltimore: University Park Press.

Sutula, T., Cascino, G., Cavazos, J., Parada, I., & Ramirez, L. (1989). Mossy fiber synaptic reorganization in the epileptic human temporal lobe. *Annual Neurology, 26,* 321–330.

Teskey, G. C., Hutchinson, J. E., & Kolb, B. (in press). Sex differences in cortical plasticity and behaviour following anterior cortical kindling in rats. *Cerebral Cortex.*

Teskey, G. C., & Racine, R. J. (1993) Increased spontaneous unit discharge rates following electrical kindling in the rat. *Brain Research, 624,* 11–18.

Teskey, G. C., Thiessen, L. J., & Gilbert, T. H. (1999) Alternate-site kindling in the guinea-pig results in accelerated seizure progression and generalization. *Epilepsy Research, 34,* 151–159.

Teskey, G. C., & Valentine, P. A. (1998). Post-activation potentiation in the neocortex of awake freely moving rats. *Neuroscience and Biobehavioural Reviews, 22,* 195–207.

Teskey, G. C., Valentine, P. A., Sainsbury, R. S., & Trepel, C. (1995). Evolution of afterdischarge characteristics during electrical kindling of the guinea pig. *Brain Research, 672,* 137–147.

Valentine, P. A., Thiessen, E. J., Gilbert, T. H., Peyton, C., Cooper, R. M., & Teskey, G. C. (1996). Local cerebral glucose utilization during electrical and pentylenetetrazol-induced seizures in the naive and kindled guinea-pig. *Society for Neuroscience Abstract, 22,* 2085.

Wada, J. A. (1998). Genetic predisposition and kindling susceptibility in primates. In M. E. Corcoran & S. L. Moshe (Eds.), *Kindling 5* (pp. 1–11). New York: Plenum Press.

Weiss, S. R. B., & Post, R. M. (1995). Caveats in the use of the kindling model of affective disorders. *Journal of Toxicological and Industrial Health, 10,* 421–447.

Zaide, J. (1974). Differences between Tryon Bright and Dull rats in seizure activity evoked by amygdala stimulation. *Physiology and Behavior, 12,* 527–534.

Marina E. Wolf

The Neuroplasticity of Addiction

☐ Introduction

This chapter will evaluate the idea that drug addiction is a form of neuroplasticity that employs cellular mechanisms common to more thoroughly characterized forms of plasticity such as long-term potentiation (LTP). It will focus on cocaine and the amphetamines, and present evidence that addiction to these substances is an inappropriate form of glutamate-dependent "learning."

Neuroplasticity may be defined as the ability of the nervous system to modify its response to a stimulus in response to prior experience. Addiction meets this criterion, since its development implies a change in the reaction of an individual to the abused drug. However, exactly what "changes" is a matter of debate. Do the pleasurable effects of the drug increase, or are addicts motivated by the desire to alleviate a withdrawal syndrome? It is useful to begin by defining addiction as the gradual evolution, which occurs only in some individuals, from casual or controlled use into a compulsive pattern of drug-seeking and drug-taking behavior. Even after abstinence is achieved, patients remain vulnerable to episodes of craving and relapse triggered by stimuli previously associated with the availability of drugs or the act of drug taking (e.g., Ehrman, Robbins, Childress, & O'Brien, 1992).

Robinson and Berridge (1993, in press) have argued for an incentive-sensitization view of addiction. The idea is that addictive drugs produce long-lasting adaptations in brain systems involved in incentive-motivational effects, leading to "sensitization" of these systems to drugs and to environmental stimuli that are associated with drug-taking behavior. "The brain systems that are sensitized do not mediate the pleasurable or euphoric effects of drugs (drug 'liking'), but instead they mediate a subcomponent of reward we have termed incentive salience (drug 'wanting')" (Robinson & Berridge, 2000). A key element of this theory is that "liking" and "wanting" have dissociable neural substrates, and it is the latter that sensitizes with repeated drug use. Sensitization models of addiction will be discussed further in the next section.

The mesotelencephalic dopamine (DA) projections and their targets are strongly implicated in incentive-motivational effects (Robinson & Berridge, 1993; Wise & Bozarth, 1987). Particular emphasis has been placed on the mesoaccumbens DA projection, which originates in the ventral tegmental area (VTA; A10) of the midbrain and projects to the nucleus accumbens (NAc; also termed ventral striatum). This system exhibits profound adaptations following chronic stimulant administration (White & Kalivas, 1998). The nigrostriatal DA pathway, originating in substantia nigra (A9) and projecting to dorsal striatum, also plays an important role in sensitization and displays many of the same cellular correlates of sensitization (Wolf, 1998).

Historically, drug abuse research has focused on the idea that adaptations in DA transmission must play a primary role in addiction. As discussed below, it is now appreciated that many (and perhaps all) of these adaptations are enabled by glutamate-dependent forms of plasticity. This is not surprising given the universal importance of glutamate in plasticity and the anatomical relationship between glutamate and DA systems. Thus, glutamate-containing neurons provide the major source of excitatory drive to DA cell bodies in the midbrain and converge with DA terminals on common postsynaptic targets in forebrain regions (e.g., Sesack & Pickel, 1992).

Behavioral Sensitization: A Model for Intensification of Drug Craving in Addiction

Imaging studies in cocaine users have demonstrated that brain areas rich in glutamate, such as cortical and limbic regions, display profound metabolic responses during cocaine-induced euphoria and craving as well as during cue-elicited craving (e.g., Breiter et al., 1997; Childress et al., 1999; Grant et al., 1996). These findings implicate glutamate in responses to drugs and drug-related cues, but not necessarily in addiction-related neuroadaptations. The most direct evidence for the latter role comes from studies of behavioral sensitization.

In general terms, behavioral sensitization refers to the progressive enhancement of species-specific behavioral responses that occurs during repeated drug administration and persists even after long periods of withdrawal. Sensitization occurs in humans (Strakowski & Sax, 1998), but most studies have focused on sensitization of locomotor activity in rodents. These studies provide one important foundation for the incentive-motivational theory of addiction discussed in the previous section, since the same DA systems are implicated in sensitization of locomotor activity and sensitization of incentive-motivational effects (Wise & Bozarth, 1987; Robinson & Berridge, 1993). Another strong argument for the relevance of locomotor sensitization to addiction comes from studies of drug self-administration, in which rats press a lever or perform a nose-poke to obtain intravenous drug. Prior exposure to cocaine or amphetamine, resulting in locomotor sensitization, promotes drug self-administration (see Lorrain, Arnold, & Vezina, 2000 and references therein), and the expression of sensitization is associated with reinstatement of self-administration following long-term extinction (De Vries, Schoffelmeer, Binnekade, Mulder, & Vanderschuren, 1998). Finally, environmental stimuli and conditioning strongly modulate sensitization in rats, as well as drug craving in humans (Robinson, Browman, Crombag, & Badiani, 1998). At the very least, behavioral sensitization provides an animal model for the induction of persistent changes in the neural circuitry of motivation and reward as a result of chronic exposure to drugs of abuse.

Glutamate and Behavioral Sensitization

It was first demonstrated in 1989 that the development of behavioral sensitization in rats and mice was prevented if each injection of amphetamine or cocaine in a chronic regimen was preceded by systemic injection of the noncompetitive N-methyl-D-aspartate receptor (NMDA) antagonist MK-801 (Karler, Calder, Chaudhry, & Turkanis, 1989). Many groups have reported similar effects with different classes of NMDA receptor antagonists, and with AMPA and metabotropic glutamate receptor antagonists (Wolf, 1998). Importantly, coadministration of glutamate antagonists with psychostimulants also prevents the ability of prior drug exposure to promote drug self-administration (Schenk et al., 1993; reviewed in Wolf, 1998). Another key observation is that glutamate antagonist treatments that prevent behavioral sensitization also prevent the development of biochemical and electrophysiological adaptations that normally accompany sensitization (Wolf, 1998; Li et al., 1999). This indicates that glutamate receptor stimulation is a necessary step in the cascade leading to sensitization, and argues strongly against the alternative theory that MK-801 prevents sensitization through mechanisms related to state-dependent learning (e.g., Carlezon, Mendrek, & Wise, 1995).

Glutamate receptor antagonists are probably acting in the A9/A10 region (containing DA cell bodies) to prevent the initiation of sensitization. Earlier studies showed that microinjection of amphetamine into this region, but not others, was sufficient to produce sensitization (Kalivas & Stewart, 1991). More recent studies have shown that direct injection of glutamate receptor antagonists into the VTA prevents the development of sensitization in response to intra-VTA amphetamine or systemic cocaine (Cador, Bjijou, Cailhol, & Stinus, 1999; Kalivas & Alesdatter, 1993; Kim & Vezina, 1998). It is likely that glutamate receptor antagonists prevent sensitization by attenuating excitatory drive to midbrain DA neurons. This is consistent with the ability of all three classes of glutamate receptor antagonists (NMDA, AMPA, and metabotropic) to prevent sensitization, since all three contribute to glutamate-mediated excitation of DA neurons (White, 1996). If this hypothesis is correct, lesions of glutamate-containing projections to the VTA should have a similar effect. In fact, excitotoxic lesions of the prefrontal cortex, a major source of glutamate-containing projections to VTA DA neurons, prevent the development of amphetamine and cocaine sensitization (Cador et al., 1999; Li et al., 1999; Tzschentke & Schmidt, 1998; Wolf, Dahlin, Hu, Xue, & White, 1995). As discussed below, considerable interest is focused on the possibility of drug-induced plasticity at excitatory synapses between prefrontal cortical projections and VTA DA neurons.

The *expression* of sensitization refers to the ability of an animal, after chronic drug treatment, to exhibit a sensitized behavioral response when challenged with drug. Once sensitization has been established by repeated systemic or intra-VTA drug administration, a sensitized locomotor response will be expressed in response to systemic drug challenge or in response to drug injection directly into the striatal or accumbal DA terminal fields (Kalivas & Stewart, 1991). Thus, sensitization is initiated in the VTA but expressed in the striatal complex. The ventral striatum, or NAc, is more important in locomotor responses, while the striatum contributes more to stereotypy. Glutamate's role in the expression of sensitization is controversial and has been reviewed elsewhere (Wolf, 1998). We will consider instead its role in the *maintenance* of sensitization, that is, the underlying and persistent changes in brain function that maintain the animal in an altered state such that subsequent exposure to drugs (or stress, or conditioned cues) results in a sensitized behavioral response. The NAc is believed to be an important site of neuroadaptations contributing to the maintenance of sensitization (White & Kalivas, 1998).

☐ Sensitization and LTP: An Overview

While analogies between LTP and sensitization have been suggested ever since the glutamate dependence of sensitization was demonstrated (Karler et al., 1989; Wolf &

Khansa, 1991), it is clear that sensitization is not LTP. There are two major distinctions. First, LTP is manifest as increased sensitivity to glutamate agonists, whereas the hallmark of sensitization is increased responsiveness to drugs that potentiate DA transmission. Having said this, it is important to emphasize that sensitization is not a simple leftward shift in the dose-response curve to psychostimulants, but a qualitative change in the behavioral response (Segal & Kuczenski, 1987). Second, LTP occurs at the level of a single glutamatergic synapse. Sensitization is a complex phenomenon that is elicited by systemic drug administration and requires a cascade of sequential steps involving multiple brain regions, neurotransmitters, and alterations in gene expression.

Our hypothesis is that LTP-like steps participate in the sensitization cascade. First, this hypothesis will be discussed as it relates to events in the VTA that are believed to contribute to the induction of sensitization during repeated drug exposure and at early withdrawal times. Second, we will consider the possible contribution of LTP-like steps to more persistent forms of plasticity underlying the maintenance of sensitization in the NAc.

Synaptic Plasticity in the VTA

The prefrontal cortex sends monosynaptic excitatory inputs to both DA and non-DA cells of the VTA (Sesack & Pickel, 1992). These are very important in regulating DA cell firing rate and pattern (Overton & Clark, 1997). Considerable evidence suggests that the induction of sensitization involves a transient potentiation of excitatory transmission between the prefrontal cortex and VTA DA neurons. Thus, sensitization can be elicited by diverse treatments that have in common the ability to produce brief but intense activation of VTA DA cells. These include repeated electrical stimulation of the prefrontal cortex (Schenk & Snow, 1994) or the VTA (Ben-Shahar & Ettenberg, 1994), and pharmacological disinhibition of VTA DA cells (Steketee & Kalivas, 1991). A similar activation of DA cells may underlie the ability of overexpression of GluR1 in VTA to increase sensitivity to the locomotor stimulatory and rewarding effects of morphine (Carlezon et al., 1997). Excitotoxic lesions of the prefrontal cortex performed prior to repeated amphetamine or cocaine administration prevent the development of behavioral sensitization, presumably by depriving VTA DA neurons of excitatory drive (see above). All of these findings are consistent with other evidence, both biochemical and electrophysiological, indicating that the firing rate of VTA DA neurons is transiently increased at short withdrawal times (White, 1996; Zhang, Hu, White, & Wolf, 1997).

What mechanisms are responsible for enhanced excitatory transmission between the prefrontal cortex and VTA during early withdrawal? Some contributing effects may occur at the level of the prefrontal cortex. For example, we have found that repeated amphetamine administration produces a transient increase in GluR1 expression in the prefrontal cortex (Lu, Chen, Xue, & Wolf, 1997; Lu & Wolf, 1999), accompanied by increased electrophysiological responsiveness of prefrontal cortex neurons to the excitatory effects of glutamate (Peterson, Wolf, & White, 2000). However, most attention has been focused on mechanisms at the level of the VTA. We have found that VTA DA neurons recorded 3 but not 14 days after discontinuing repeated cocaine or amphetamine administration show increased responsiveness to the excitatory effects of glutamate or AMPA, when these agonists are applied directly to the DA cell body regions by microiontophoresis (White, Hu, Zhang, & Wolf, 1995; Zhang, Hu, White, & Wolf, 1997). Thus, there is a transient enhancement of AMPA receptor transmission in the VTA at early withdrawal times. This could account for biochemical and electrophysiological findings indicative of increased DA cell activity at short withdrawal times (above). This increase in DA cell activity is important because it may "transfer" sensitization to forebrain regions important in its expression.

One mechanism that could account for potentiation of AMPA transmission at early withdrawal times is increased glutamate receptor expression by VTA DA neurons. The initial impetus for this hypothesis was a Western blotting study showing increased expression of the AMPA receptor subunit GluR1 (and in some cases the NMDA receptor subunit NMDAR1) in the VTA of rats killed 16–18 hrs after discontinuation of chronic cocaine, morphine, or stressors (Fitzgerald, Ortiz, Hamedani, & Nestler, 1996). However, using the same chronic drug regimens used to demonstrate electrophysiological supersensitivity to AMPA after 3 days of withdrawal from amphetamine (White et al., 1995; Zhang et al., 1997; see also above), we have failed to find increased expression of GluR1 or NMDAR1 in the VTA or substantia nigra using quantitative immunoautoradiographic techniques (Lu, Monteggia, & Wolf, 1999, submitted). These results question the idea that a simple increase in glutamate receptor expression accounts for increased activity of VTA DA neurons at short withdrawal times. Another possibility is that it reflects a more subtle change in glutamate transmission, perhaps related to LTP. As a first step towards evaluating this hypothesis, several laboratories have begun to characterize synaptic plasticity in the VTA.

Bonci & Malenka (1999) showed that DA (but not GABA neurons) of the VTA exhibit LTP and that its induction requires NMDA but not metabotropic glutamate receptor activation. Substantia nigra DA neurons also exhibit NMDA receptor-dependent LTP (Overton, Richards, Berry, & Clark, 1999). Most recently, it was found that VTA DA neurons express long-term depression (LTD) in addition to LTP and that bath application of amphetamine 10–15 min prior to an LTD-inducing protocol blocks LTD induction (Jones, Kornblum, & Kauer, 2000). These authors proposed that "LTD normally acts to protect VTA dopamine neurons from excessive glutamatergic excitation, but that in the presence of amphetamine this brake is removed, permitting unrestricted excitation of dopamine neurons." We have shown that amphetamine produces a long-lasting increase in extracellular glutamate levels in the VTA (Xue, Ng, Li, & Wolf, 1996) through a mechanism involving glutamate transporters (Wolf, Xue, Li & Wavak, submitted). Increased glutamate levels, combined with the absence of braking effects normally provided by LTD, may promote "pathological" strengthening of excitatory synapses on DA neurons via LTP.

It should be noted that other electrophysiological studies, not focusing directly on activity-dependent plasticity, also provide strong support for the idea that interactions between GABA, glutamate, and DA receptors in VTA are profoundly altered during drug withdrawal (Bonci & Williams, 1996; Manzoni & Williams, 1999).

Synaptic Plasticity in the Nucleus Accumbens

Electrophysiological and neurochemical adaptations produced in the VTA by chronic stimulant administration occur at short withdrawal times and are transient, consistent with the idea that sensitization is initiated in the VTA. In contrast, those produced in the NAc are more persistent and may require a withdrawal period of 7–10 days to become evident, in keeping with its role in the maintenance and expression of sensitization. This section will focus on stimulant-induced adaptations in glutamate transmission within the NAc.

Several studies have now assessed glutamate receptor expression in the NAc after chronic stimulant administration. As might be expected, no changes are detected at short withdrawal times (16 h, 3 days; Churchill, Swanson, Urbina, & Kalivas, 1999; Fitzgerald et al., 1996; Lu et al., 1997; Lu et al., 1999; Lu & Wolf, 1999). However, after 2 weeks of withdrawal, we have observed substantial (~20%) reductions in mRNA and protein levels for GluR1 and GluR2 (Lu et al., 1997; Lu & Wolf, 1999). Levels of NR1, an obligatory subunit of the NMDA receptor, were also reduced in NAc as well as in portions of substantia nigra and in the prefrontal cortex (Lu et al., 1999). In electrophysiological studies which examined the responsiveness of NAc neurons to iontophoretic glutamate after the same amphetamine regimen or after repeated cocaine administration, we found that neurons recorded from sensitized rats after 3 days of withdrawal were subsensitive to the excitatory effects of glutamate (White et al., 1995). Subsequent studies found that this subsensitivity persisted for at least 14 days and reflected decreased responsiveness to AMPA and NMDA, but not the metabotropic agonist 1S,3R-t-ACPD (White, Hu, Zhang, & Li, in press). The mechanism underlying subsensitivity after 3 days of withdrawal is unclear. However, decreased responsiveness to NMDA and AMPA after 14 days may reflect the decreases in NMDA and AMPA receptor subunit expression described above. In contrast, after a different cocaine regimen and 3 weeks of withdrawal, Kalivas and coworkers found increased GluR1 protein levels (Churchill et al., 1999), a trend towards increased GluR1 mRNA, and decreased GluR3 and mGluR5 mRNA levels in the NAc (Ghasemzadeh, Nelson, Lu, & Kalivas, 1999).

What is the functional significance of these changes? GABAergic medium spiny neurons comprise 90% to 95% of cells in the striatal complex and are its output neurons. Their activity is determined by convergent DA and glutamate input. It is generally believed that DA modulates glutamate- mediated synaptic responses, enabling DA to influence the signal-to-noise ratio (Cepeda & Levine, 1998). However, the nature of the modulatory effect is controversial and seems to depend on the recording preparation, the subtypes of DA and glutamate receptors involved, and the concentration of DA. Moroever, medium spiny neurons are a heterogeneous population characterized by different projection targets and neuropeptide expression. Thus, determining the functional consequences of altered glutamate receptor expression will require identification of the cell types in the NAc exhibiting such alterations and a better understanding of how the activity of afferent inputs to NAc neurons is altered by chronic drug administration.

Activity-dependent forms of synaptic plasticity may also contribute to drug-induced adaptations in the NAc and the dorsal striatum. In drug-naïve rats, in vitro recording studies first showed that repetitive activation of corticostriatal glutamatergic fibers produces LTD of excitatory synaptic transmission in the striatum (e.g., Calabresi, Maj, Pisani, Mercuri, & Bernardi, 1992). Striatal LTD requires membrane depolarization and action potential discharge of the postsynaptic cell during the conditioning tetanus, coactivation of D1 and D2 DA receptors, and activation of metabotropic glutamate receptors (Calabresi, Maj, Pisani, & Mercuri, & Bernardi, 1992). Striatal LTP was subsequently reported under in vitro conditions that enhance NMDA receptor activation and in vivo after tetanic stimulation of cortical fibers (e.g., Charpier & Deniau, 1997). Interestingly, pulsatile application of DA during a conditioning protocol that normally results in LTD shifted the effect towards potentiation of EPSP amplitude (Wickens, Begg, & Arbuthnott, 1996). This is similar to the effect of amphetamine in VTA (Jones et al., 2000; see above). Excitatory synapses in the NAc also exhibit activity-dependent plasticity. Recordings from an in vitro slice preparation of the NAc showed that tetanic stimulation of prefrontal cortical afferents produced both LTP and LTD, although LTP was observed more frequently (Pennartz, Ameerun, Groeneweger, & Lopes da Silva, 1993). Using in vivo recording techniques, LTP of accumbens field potentials has been observed after tetanization of the fimbria-fornix (Boeijinga, Mulder, Pennartz, Manshanden, & Lopes da Silva, 1993). A single NAc neuron can exhibit LTD of NMDA receptor–mediated responses and LTP of AMPA receptor–mediated responses (Kombian & Malenka, 1994).

Activation of normally quiescent striatal neurons requires synchronous activation of multiple excitatory inputs. For example, stimulation of hippocampal inputs enables NAc neurons to enter a depolarized, active state, and this is required for generation of spike firing by activation of prefrontal cortical inputs (O'Donnell & Grace, 1995). Insofar as LTP or LTD would affect the likelihood of synchronized activation, they would be expected to have profound effects on striatal output. It is therefore exciting that several recent studies have found alterations in corticostriatal plasticity after chronic drug treatment.

Pulvirenti, Criado, Balducci, Koob, and Henriksen (1998) compared evoked field responses in the NAc after stimulation of fimbria afferents in rats exposed to either one or five days of cocaine self-administration. The latter group showed an NMDA receptor– and AMPA receptor–dependent increase in paired pulse facilitation of the long-latency P25 component of the evoked potential in the NAc shell, an effect also produced by tetanic stimulation of NAc afferents. This was not observed after a single day of cocaine self-administration or in yoked-control animals (which receive the same amount of cocaine as their self-administering counterparts, but not on a "voluntary" basis). These results suggest that the acquisition of cocaine-seeking behavior is associated with enhancement of hippocampal-accumbens transmission. This may increase outflow through corticothalamic circuits, which could have widespread behavioral consequences and play a particularly important role in context-sensitive gating of behavioral output (see O'Donnell & Grace, 1995).

Another very interesting set of studies examined plasticity in the rat neostriatum following chronic exposure to ethanol (Yamamoto et al., 1999) or methamphetamine (Nishioku, Shimazoe, Yamamoto, Nakanishi, & Watanabe, 1999). Tetanic stimulation induced LTD in naïve rats or saline-treated rats, whereas a slowly developing form of LTP was observed in slices prepared 15–20 h after ethanol withdrawal or 6 days after discontinuation of methamphetamine injections. In both cases, the development of LTP required NMDA receptor activation. D2 receptor activation depressed the magnitude of LTP in ethanol-withdrawn rats. Drawing upon these and other findings, the authors speculated that the "switch" to LTP might reflect increased NMDA receptor tone coupled with the loss of normal D2 receptor–mediated negative control over LTP induction (Yamamoto et al., 1999).

LTP-like steps contribute to sensitization and other forms of drug-induced plasticity An important goal, for both LTP and sensitization research, is to identify changes in synaptic structure and biochemistry that are responsible for the plasticity that is detected with electrophysiological techniques. In this section we will discuss general similarities between activity-dependent plasticity in the hippocampus and drug-induced plasticity. Then, we will consider specific changes in glutamate receptor function that may contribute in both cases.

One important general similarity is the critical role of protein kinase and phosphatase cascades in both phenomena. This is well established for LTP and LTD (Roberson, English, & Sweatt, 1996), and it is increasingly clear that similar cascades are involved in long-term responses to drugs of abuse. In particular, there is compelling evidence for potentiated D1 receptor signaling in the NAc (Henry & White, 1995; White et al., in press) and up-regulation of the associated cAMP-PKA pathway (Self & Nestler, 1995). Interestingly, D1 receptor stimulation and protein kinase A (PKA) activation are necessary for late phases of LTP at CA1 Schaffer collateral synapses (e.g., Frey, Huang, &

Kandel, 1993; Huang & Kandel, 1995; Matthies et al., 1997), and chronic administration of cocaine or morphine alters synaptic plasticity in the hippocampus (e.g., Mansouri, Motamedi, & Fathollahi, 1999; Sarnyai et al., 1998).

A second general similarity between LTP/LTD and drug-induced plasticity is that both are associated with synaptic remodeling. Repeated treatment with either amphetamine or cocaine increased dendritic branching, spine density, and the number of branched spines in Golgi-stained medium spiny neurons in the NAc, effects which persisted at least a month (Robinson & Kolb, 1997, 1999a). Similar effects were observed in the prefrontal cortex (Robinson & Kolb, 1997; 1999a). Interestingly, chronic morphine produced effects opposite to those observed after cocaine or amphetamine, that is, decreases in spine density and dendritic branching (Robinson & Kolb, 1999b).

A final general similarity is that changes in gene expression contribute to both activity-dependent plasticity and the enduring changes produced by drugs of abuse. This may be linked to the involvement of the D1-PKA pathway in both processes (see above). Through this pathway, drugs of abuse induce phosphorylation and activation of the cAMP response element-binding protein (CREB), as well as expression of IEG transcription factors (Hyman, 1996). Glutamate transmission is required for both responses (e.g., Konradi, Leveque, & Hyman, 1996; Wang & McGinty, 1996). CREB, of course, is strongly implicated in LTP and many types of memory (Silva, Kogan, Frankland, & Kida, 1998).

In recent years, considerable progress has been made towards understanding the role of glutamate receptor phosphorylation and trafficking in LTP and LTD. According to the "silent synapse" hypothesis of LTP, tetanic stimulation converts synapses that are silent at normal resting membrane potentials (because they contain NMDA receptors but lack AMPA receptors) to synapses which contain functional AMPA receptors (Malenka & Nicoll, 1997). One way to explain this rapid conversion is that stores of receptor are located in the dendritic spines awaiting signals for membrane insertion and functional expression. Supporting this possibility, tetanic synaptic stimulation in hippocampal cultures induced a rapid redistribution of GluR1 from the dendritic shaft (the site of most labeling under basal conditions) into dendritic spines and also induced clustering within the dendritic shaft or at the base of spines (Shi et al., 1999). Conversely, induction of LTD caused a decrease in synaptic GluR1 clusters (Carroll, Lissin, Zastrow, Nicoll, & Malenka, 1999). Other studies suggest an important role for AMPA receptor subunit phosphorylation in LTP and LTD. GluR1 is phosphorylated on the carboxyl terminus by Ca^{2+}/calmodulin–dependent protein kinase type II (CaM-KII), protein kinase C (PKC), and PKA, resulting in potentiation of agonist-activated currents (e.g., Roche, O'Brien, Mammen, Bernhardt, & Huganir, 1996). Phosphorylation of GluR1 by CaMKII is strongly implicated in LTP (e.g., Barria, Muller, Derkach, Griffith, & Soderling, 1997), whereas dephosphorylation of GluR1 at the PKA site accompanies LTD (Lee, Kameyama, Huganir, & Bear, 1998). Perhaps phosphorylation of GluR1 mediates a rapid enhancement of synaptic strength in LTP that is subsequently augmented by activity-dependent redistribution of AMPA receptor subunits. It is also possible, by analogy to G-protein-coupled receptors, that phosphorylation of glutamate receptors influences regulation of their trafficking.

Similar mechanisms probably contribute to drug-induced changes in glutamate transmission. For example, the potentiation of AMPA transmission in VTA at short withdrawal times could reflect the addition of AMPA receptors to previously "silent" synapses. Strong GluR1 labeling associated with the internal surface of the plasma membrane was found in DA neurons of the squirrel monkey VTA (Paquet, Tremblay,

Soghomonian, & Smith, 1997), providing a potential receptor pool for recruitment to synaptic compartments. Potentiation of AMPA transmission could also involve GluR1 phosphorylation, a notion that is consistent with the requirement for protein kinase activity in the VTA in the induction process (e.g., Tolliver, Ho, Fox, & Berger, 1999). Likewise, changes in glutamate receptor expression and transmission in the NAc that result from chronic drug administration may reflect alterations in glutamate receptor phosphorylation or trafficking.

If we propose that such mechanisms contribute to amphetamine- and cocaine-induced plasticity, we must address the question of how these stimulants, which initially target the DA transporter, are ultimately able to influence glutamate neurotransmission. One mechanism may be through D1 receptor–mediated phosphorylation of glutamate receptor subunits through PKA-dependent mechanisms. This has been demonstrated for NR1 in NAc slices (Snyder, Fienberg, Huganir, & Greengard, 1998) and for GluR1 in embryonic striatal neurons (Price, Kim, & Raymond, 1999) and postnatal NAc neurons (Chao, Lu, Lee, Huganir, & Wolf, 1999). In hippocampus, GluR1 phosphorylation increases AMPA receptor–mediated currents (above). Thus, our results (Chao et al., 1999) suggest that AMPA receptor transmission in the NAc will be potentiated by concurrent D1 receptor stimulation. After repeated administration of cocaine or amphetamine, D1 transmission in the NAc is augmented (Henry & White, 1995; White & Kalivas, 1998), perhaps resulting in an increase in the ambient level of GluR1 phosphorylation. This, in the long run, may trigger mechanisms leading to more persistent changes in glutamate receptor trafficking and expression. Of course, changes in the level of DA receptor stimulation could also produce changes in glutamate receptor function indirectly, by influencing neuronal activity in glutamate-containing pathways.

☐ Conclusions

Activity-dependent forms of synaptic plasticity (LTP and LTD) involve a complex cascade of biochemical changes leading to posttranslational modification and altered trafficking of glutamate receptors, as well as other changes in synaptic structure. Recent work suggests that the brain may employ similar mechanisms to produce the maladaptive forms of synaptic plasticity that contribute to drug addiction. After discontinuation of drug administration, key brain regions display alterations in glutamate release, electrophysiological responses to glutamate, glutamate receptor expression, and synaptic structure. An important challenge is to characterize the pharmacological and cellular basis of drug-induced plasticity. This will help to identify targets for pharmacological intervention. In this respect, it is encouraging to note that pharmacological treatments involving manipulation of glutamate and DA transmission are capable of reversing established behavioral sensitization in rats (DeMontis, Gambarana, Ghiglieri, & Tagliamonte, 1995; Li, White, & Wolf, 2000).

☐ References

Andersen, P., & Soleng, A. F. (1998). Long-term potentiation and spatial training are both associated with the generation of new synapses. *Brain Research Review*, 26, 353–359.

Barria, A., Muller, D., Derkach, V., Griffith, L. C., & Soderling, T. R. (1997). Regulatory phosphorylation of AMPA-type glutamate receptors by CaM-KII during long-term potentiation. *Science*, 276, 2042–2045.

Ben-Shahar, O., & Ettenberg, A. (1994). Repeated stimulation of the ventral tegmental area sensitizes the hyperlocomotor response to amphetamine. *Pharmacology Biochemistry and Behavior, 48,* 1005–1009.

Boeijinga, P. H., Mulder, A. B., Pennartz, C. M. A., Manshanden, I., & Lopes da Silva, F. H. (1993). Reponses of the nucleus accumbens following fornix/fimbria stimulation in the rat. Identification and long-term potentiation of mono- and polysynaptic pathways. *Neuroscience, 53,* 1049–1058.

Bonci, A., & Malenka, R. C. (1999). Properties and plasticity of excitatory synapses on dopaminergic and GABAergic cells in the ventral tegmental area. *Journal of Neuroscience, 19,* 3723–3730.

Bonci, A., & Williams, J. T. (1996). A common mechanism mediates long-term changes in synaptic transmission after chronic cocaine or morphine. *Neuron, 16,* 631–639.

Breiter, H. C., Gollub, R. L., Weisskoff, R. M., Kennedy, D. N., Makris, N., Berke, J. D., Goodman, J. M., Kantor, H. L., Gastfriend, D. R., Riorden, J. P., Mathew, R. T., Rosen, B. R., & Hyman, S. E. (1997). Acute effects of cocaine on human brain activity and emotion. *Neuron, 19,* 591–611.

Cador, M., Bjijou, Y., Cailhol, S., & Stinus, L. (1999). Amphetamine-induced behavioral sensitization: Implication of a glutamatergic medial prefrontal cortex-VTA innervation. *Neuroscience, 94,* 705–721.

Calabresi, P., Maj, R., Pisani, A., Mercuri, N. B., & Bernardi, G. (1992). Long-term synaptic depression in the striatum: Physiological and pharmacological characterization. *Journal of Neuroscience, 12,* 4224–4233.

Carlezon, W. A., Jr., Mendrek, A., & Wise, A. (1995). MK-801 disrupts the expression but not the development of bromocriptine sensitization: A state-dependency interpretation. *Synapse, 20,* 1–9.

Carlezon, W. A., Boundy, V. A., Haile, C. N., Lane, S. B., Kalb, R. G., Neve, R. L., & Nestler, E. J. (1997). Sensitization to morphine induced by viral-mediated gene transfer. *Science, 277,* 812–814.

Carroll, R. C., Lissin, D. V., Zastrow, M. V., Nicoll, R. A., & Malenka, R. C. (1999). Rapid redistribution of glutamate receptors contributes to long-term depression in hippocampal cultures. *Nature Neuroscience, 2,* 454–460.

Cepeda, C., & Levine, M. S. (1998). Dopamine and N-methyl-D-aspartate receptor interactions in the neostriatum. *Developmental Neuroscience, 20,* 1–18.

Chao, S. Z., Lu, W. X., Lee, H.-K., Huganir, R. L., & Wolf, M. E. (1999). D1 dopamine receptor stimulation increases GluR1 phosphorylation in postnatal nucleus accumbens cultures. *Society for Neuroscience Abstracts, 25,* 2211.

Charpier, S., & Deniau, J. M. (1997). *In vivo* activity-dependent plasticity at cortico-striatal connections: Evidence for physiological long-term potentiation. *Proceedings of the National Academy of Sciences of the United States of America, 94,* 7036–7040.

Childress, A. R., Mozley, P. D., McElgin, W., Fitzgerald, J., Reivich, M., & O'Brien, C. P. (1999). Limbic activation during cue-induced cocaine craving. *American Journal of Psychiatry, 156,* 11–18.

Churchill, L., Swanson, C. J., Urbina, M., & Kalivas, P. W. (1999). Repeated cocaine alters glutamate receptor subunit levels in the nucleus accumbens and ventral tegmental area of rats that develop behavioral sensitization. *Journal of Neurochemistry, 72,* 2397–2403.

DeMontis, M. B., Gambarana, C., Ghiglieri, O., & Tagliamonte, A. (1995). Reversal of stable behavioral modifications through NMDA receptor inhibition in rats. *Behavioral Pharmacology, 6,* 562–567.

De Vries, T. J., Schoffelmeer, A. N. M., Binnekade, R., Mulder, A. H., & Vanderschuren, L. J. M. J. (1998). Drug-induced reinstatement of heroin- and cocaine-seeking behaviour following long-term extinction is associated with expression of behavioral sensitization. *European Journal of Neuroscience, 10,* 3565–33571.

Ehrman, R. N., Robbins, S. J., Childress, A. R., & O'Brien, C. P. (1992). Conditioned responses to cocaine-related stimuli in cocaine abuse patients. *Psychopharmacology, 107,* 523–529.

Fitzgerald, L. W., Ortiz, J., Hamedani, A. G., & Nestler, E. J. (1996). Drugs of abuse and stress increase the expression of GluR1 and NMDAR1 glutamate receptor subunits in the rat ventral tegmental area: Common adaptations among cross-sensitizing agents. *Journal of Neuroscience,* *16,* 274–282.

Frey, U., Huang, Y.-Y., & Kandel, E. R. (1993). Effects of cAMP stimulate a late stage of LTP in hippocampal CA1 neurons. *Science, 260,* 1661–1664.

Ghasemzadeh, M. B., Nelson, L. C., Lu, X.-Y., & Kalivas, P. W. (1999). Neuroadaptations in ionotropic and metabotropic glutamate receptor mRNA produced by cocaine treatment. *Journal of Neurochemistry, 72,* 157–165.

Grant, S., London, E. D., Newlin, D. B., Villemagne, V. L., Liu, X., Contoreggi, C., Phillips, R. L., Kimes, A. S., & Margolin, A. (1996). Activation of memory circuits during cue-elicited cocaine craving. *Proceedings of the National Academy of Sciences of the United States of America, 93,* 12040–12045.

Henry, D. J., & White, F. J. (1995). The persistence of behavioral sensitization to cocaine parallels enhanced inhibition of nucleus accumbens neurons. *Journal of Neuroscience, 15,* 6287–6299.

Huang, Y. Y., & Kandel, E. R. (1995). D1/D5 receptor agonists induce a protein synthesis-dependent late potentiation in the CA1 region of the hippocampus. *Proceedings of the National Academy of Sciences of the United States of America, 92,* 2446–2450.

Hyman, S. E. (1996). Addiction to cocaine and amphetamine. *Neuron, 16,* 901–904.

Jones, S., Kornblum, J. L., & Kauer, J. A. (2000). Amphetamine blocks long-term synaptic depression in the ventral tegmental area. *Journal of Neuroscience, 20,* 5575–5580.

Kalivas, P. W., & Alesdatter, J. E. (1993). Involvement of N-methyl-D-aspartate receptor stimulation in the ventral tegmental area and amygdala in behavioral sensitization to cocaine. *Journal Pharmacology and Experimental Therapeutics, 267,* 486–495.

Kalivas, P. W., & Stewart, J. (1991). Dopamine transmission in the initiation and expression of drug- and stress-induced sensitization of motor activity. *Brain Research Review, 16,* 223–244.

Karler, R., Calder, L. D., Chaudhry, I. A., & Turkanis S. A. (1989). Blockade of 'reverse tolerance' to cocaine and amphetamine by MK-801. *Life Sciences, 45,* 599–606.

Kim, J.-H., & Vezina, P. (1998). Metabotropic glutamate receptors are necessary for sensitization by amphetamine. *NeuroReport, 9,* 403–306.

Kombian, S. B., & Malenka, R. C. (1994). Simultaneous LTP of non-NMDA- and LTD of NMDA-receptor-mediated responses in the nucleus accumbens. *Nature, 368,* 242–246.

Konradi, C., Leveque, J.-C., & Hyman, S. E. (1996). Amphetamine and dopamine-induced immediate early gene expression in striatal neurons depends on postsynaptic NMDA receptors and calcium. *Journal of Neuroscience, 16,* 4231–42329.

Lee, H.-K., Kameyama, K., Huganir, R. L., & Bear, M. F. (1998). NMDA induces long-term synaptic depression and dephosphorylation of the GluR1 subunit of AMPA receptors in hippocampus. *Neuron, 21,* 1151–1162.

Li, Y., Hu, X.-T., Berney, T. G., Stine, C., Vartanian, A. J., Wolf, M. E., & White, F. J. (1999). Both glutamate receptor antagonists and prefrontal cortex lesions prevent the induction of cocaine sensitization and associated neuroadaptations. *Synapse, 34,* 169–180.

Li, Y., White, F. J., & Wolf, M. E. (2000). Pharmacological reversal of behavioral and cellular indices of cocaine sensitization. *Psychopharmacology,* in press.

Li, Y., & Wolf, M. E. (1999). Can the "state-dependency" hypothesis explain prevention of amphetamine sensitization in rats by NMDA receptor antagonists? *Psychopharmacology, 141,* 351–361.

Lorrain, D. S., Arnold, G. M., & Vezina, P. (2000). Previous exposure to amphetamine increases incentive to obtain the drug: Long-lasting effects revealed by the progressive ratio schedule. *Behavioural Brain Research, 107,* 9–19.

Lu, W., Chen, H., Xue, C.-J., & Wolf, M. E. (1997). Repeated amphetamine administration alters the expression of mRNA for AMPA receptor subunits in rat nucleus accumbens and prefrontal cortex. *Synapse, 26,* 269–280.

Lu, W., Monteggia, L. M., & Wolf, M. E. (1999). NMDAR1 expression in the rat mesocorticolimbic dopamine system is decreased after withdrawal from repeated amphetamine administration. *European Journal of Neuroscience, 11,* 3167–3177.

Lu, W., Monteggia, L. M., & Wolf, M. E. (in press). Repeated amphetamine administration does not alter AMPA receptor subunit expression in the rat midbrain.

Lu, W., & Wolf, M. E. (1999). Repeated amphetamine administration alters immunoreactivity for AMPA receptor subunits in rat nucleus accumbens and medial prefrontal cortex. *Synapse, 32,* 119–131.

Malenka, R. C. & Nicoll, R. A. (1997). Silent synapses speak up. *Neuron, 19,* 473–476.

Mansouri, F. A., Motamedi, F., & Fathollahi, Y. (1999). Chronic in vivo morphine administration facilitates primed-bursts-induced long-term potentiation of Schaffer collateral-CA1 synapses in hippocampal slices in vitro. *Brain Research, 815,* 419–423.

Manzoni, O. J., & Williams, J. T. (1999). Presynaptic regulation of glutamate release in the ventral tegmental area during morphine withdrawal. *Journal of Neuroscience, 19,* 6629–6636.

Matthies, H., Becker, A., Schroeder, H., Kraus, J., Hollt, V., & Krug, M. (1997). Dopamine D_1-deficient mutant mice do not express the late phase of hippocampal long-term potentiation. *NeuroReport, 8,* 3533–3535.

Nishioku, T., Shimazoe, T., Yamamoto, Y., Nakanishi, H., & Watanabe, S. (1999) Expression of long-term potentiation of the striatum in methamphetamine-sensitized rats. *Neuroscience Letters, 268,* 81–84.

O'Donnell, P., & Grace, A. A. (1995). Synaptic interactions among excitatory afferents to nucleus accumbens neurons: Hippocampal gating of prefrontal cortical input. *Journal of Neuroscience, 15,* 3622–3639.

Overton, P. G., & Clark, D. (1997). Burst firing in midbrain dopaminergic neurons. *Brain Research Review, 25,* 312–334.

Overton, P. G., Richards, C. D., Berry, M. S., & Clark D. (1999). Long-term potentiation at excitatory amino acid synapses on midbrain dopamine neurons. *NeuroReport, 10,* 221–226.

Paquet, M., Tremblay, M., Soghomonian, J.-J., & Smith, Y. (1997). AMPA and NMDA glutamate receptor subunits in midbrain dopaminergic neurons in the squirrel monkey: An immunohistochemical and in situ hybridization study. *Journal of Neuroscience, 17,* 1377–1396.

Pennartz, C. M. A., Ameerun, R. F., Groenewegen, H. J., & Lopes da Silva, F. H. (1993). Synaptic plasticity in an in vitro slice preparation of the rat nucleus accumbens. *European Journal of Neuroscience, 5,* 107–117.

Peterson, J. D., Wolf, M. E., & White, F. J. (2000). Altered responsiveness of medial prefrontal cortex neurons to glutamate and dopamine after withdrawal from repeated amphetamine treatment. *Synapse, 36,* 342–344.

Price, C. J., Kim, P., & Raymond, L. A. (1999). D1 dopamine receptor-induced cyclic AMP-dependent protein kinase phosphorylation and potentiation of striatal glutamate receptors. *Journal of Neurochemistry, 73,* 2441–2446.

Pulvirenti, L., Criado, J., Balducci, C., Koob, G. F., & Henriksen, S. J. (1998). Enhanced synaptic efficacy in the nucleus accumbens during the acquisition of cocaine-seeking behavior. *Society for Neuroscience Abstracts, 24,* 779.

Roberson, E. D., English, J. D., & Sweatt, J. D. (1996). A biochemist's view of long-term potentiation. *Learning & Memory, 3,* 1–24.

Robinson, T. E., & Berridge, K. C. (1993). The neural basis of drug craving: An incentive-sensitization theory of addiction. *Brain Research Review, 18,* 247–291.

Robinson, T. E., & Berridge, K. C. (2000). The psychology and neurobiology of addiction: An incentive-sensitization view. *Addiction, 95*(Suppl. 2), in press.

Robinson, T. E., Browman, K. E., Crombag, H. S., & Badiani, A. (1998). Modulation of the induction or expression of psychostimulant sensitization by the circumstances surrounding drug administration. *Neuroscience and Biobehavioral Reviews, 22,* 347–354.

Robinson, T. E., & Kolb, B. (1997). Persistent structural modifications in nucleus accumbens and prefrontal cortex neurons produced by previous experience with amphetamine. *Journal of Neuroscience, 17,* 8491–8497.

Robinson, T. E., & Kolb, B. (1999a). Alterations in the morphology of dendrites and dendritic spines in the nucleus accumbens and prefrontal cortex following repeated treatment with amphetamine or cocaine. *European Journal of Neuroscience, 11,* 1598–1604.

Robinson, T. E., & Kolb, B. (1999b). Morphine alters the structure of neurons in the nucleus accumbens and neocortex of rats. *Synapse, 33,* 160–162.

Roche, K. W., O'Brien, R. J., Mammen, A. L., Bernhardt, J., & Huganir, R. L. (1996). Characterization of multiple phosphorylation sites on the AMPA receptor GluR1 subunit. *Neuron, 16,* 1179–1188.

Sarnyai, Z., Conrad, C. D., Lev, S., Paylides, C., Beck, K. D., Luine, V., Kreek, M. J., & McEwen, B. S. (1998). Impaired spatial memory and long-term potentiation (LTP) and neuronal atrophy in the dentate gyrus after chronic cocaine administration in rats. *Society for Neuroscience Abstracts, 24,* 779.

Schenk, S., Valadez, A., McNamara, C., House, D. T., Higley, D., Bankson, M. G., Gibbs, S., & Horger, B. A. (1993). Development and expression of sensitization to cocaine's reinforcing properties: Role of NMDA receptors. *Psychopharmacology, 11,* 332–338.

Schenk, S., & Snow, S. (1994). Sensitization to cocaine's motor activating properties produced by electrical kindling of the medial prefrontal cortex but not of the hippocampus. *Brain Research, 659,* 17–22.

Segal, D. S., & Kuczenski, R. (1987). Behavioral and neurochemical characteristics of stimulant-induced augmentation. *Psychopharmacology Bulletin, 23,* 417–424.

Self, D. W., & Nestler, E. J. (1995). Molecular mechanisms of drug reinforcement and addiction. *Annual Review of Neuroscience, 18,* 463–495.

Sesack, S. R., & Pickel, V. M. (1992). Prefrontal cortical efferents in the rat synapse on unlabeled neuronal targets of catecholamine terminals in the nucleus accumbens septi and on dopamine neurons in the ventral tegmental area. *Journal of Comparative Neurology, 320,* 145–160.

Silva, A. J., Kogan, J. H., Frankland, P. W., & Kida, S. (1998). CREB and memory. *Annual Review of Neuroscience, 21,* 127–148.

Shi, S.-H., Hayashi, Y., Petralia, R. S., Zaman, S. H., Wenthold, R. J., Svoboda, K., & Malinow, R. (1999). Rapid spine delivery and redistribution of AMPA receptors after synaptic NMDA receptor activation. *Science, 284,* 1811–1816.

Snyder, G. L., Fienberg, A. A., Huganir, R. L., & Greengard, P. (1998). A dopamine/D1 receptor/protein kinase A/dopamine- and cAMP-regulated phosphoprotein (M_r 32 kDa)/protein phosphatase-1 pathway regulates dephosphorylation of the NMDA receptor. *Journal of Neuroscience, 18,* 10297–10303.

Steketee, J. D., & Kalivas, P. W. (1991). Sensitization to psychostimulants and stress after injection of pertussis toxin into the A10 dopamine region. *Journal of Pharmacology and Experimental Therapeutics, 259,* 916–924.

Strakowski, S. M., & Sax, K. W. (1998). Progressive behavioral response to repeated d-amphetamine challenge: Further evidence for sensitization in humans. *Biological Psychiatry, 44,* 1171–1177.

Tolliver, B. K., Ho, L. B., Fox, L. M., & Berger, S. P. (1999). Necessary role for ventral tegmental area adenylate cyclase and protein kinase A in induction of behavioral sensitization to intraventral tegmental area amphetamine. *Journal of Pharmacology and Experimental Therapeutics, 289,* 38–47.

Tzschentke, T. M., & Schmidt, W. J. (1998). The development of cocaine-induced behavioral sensitization is affected by discrete quinolinic acid lesions of the prelimbic medial prefrontal cortex. *Brain Research, 795,* 71–76.

Wang, J. Q., & McGinty, J. F. (1996). Glutamatergic and cholinergic regulation of immediate early gene and neuropeptide gene expression in the striatum. In K. Merchant (Ed.), *Pharmacological regulation of gene expression in the CNS* (pp. 81–113). Boca Raton, FL: CRC Press.

White, F. J. (1996). Synaptic regulation of mesocorticolimbic dopamine neurons. *Annual Review of Neuroscience, 19,* 405–436.

White, F. J., Hu, X.-T., Zhang, X.-F., & Li, Y. (in press). Neuroadaptations in cocaine addiction and withdrawal: A neurophysiological perspective. *Psychopharmacology.*

White, F. J., Hu, X.-T., Zhang, X.-F., & Wolf, M. E. (1995). Repeated administration of cocaine or amphetamine alters neuronal responses to glutamate in the mesoaccumbens dopamine system. *Journal of Pharmacology and Experimental Therapeutics, 273,* 445–454.

White, F. J., & Kalivas, P. W. (1998). Neuroadaptations involved in amphetamine and cocaine addiction. *Drug and Alcohol Dependence, 51,* 141–153.

Wickens, J. R., Begg, A. J., & Arbuthnott, G. W. (1996). Dopamine reverses the depression of rat corticostriatal synapses which normally follows high-frequency stimulation of cortex in vitro. *Neuroscience, 70,* 1–5.

Wise, R. A., & Bozarth, M. A. (1987). A psychomotor stimulant theory of addiction. *Psychological Review, 94,* 469–492.

Wolf, M. E. (1998). The role of excitatory amino acids in behavioral sensitization to psychomotor stimulants. *Progress in Neurobiology, 54,* 679–720.

Wolf, M. E., & Khansa, M. R. (1991). Repeated administration of MK-801 produces sensitization to its own locomotor stimulant effects but blocks sensitization to amphetamine. *Brain Research, 562,* 164–168.

Wolf, M. E., Dahlin, S. L., Hu, X.-T., Xue C.-J., & White, K. (1995). Effects of lesions of prefrontal cortex, amygdala, or fornix on behavioral sensitization to amphetamine: Comparison with N-methyl-D-aspartate antagonists. *Neuroscience, 69,* 417–439.

Wolf, M. E., Xue, C.-J., Li, Y., & Wavak, D. (2000). Amphetamine increases glutamate efflux in the rat ventral tegmental area by a mechanism involving glutamate transporters and reactive oxygen species. *Journal of Neurochemistry,* in press.

Xue, C.-J., Ng, J. P., Li, Y., & Wolf, M. E. (1996) Acute and repeated systemic amphetamine administration: Effects on extracellular glutamate, aspartate, and serine levels in rat ventral tegmental area and nucleus accumbens. *Journal of Neurochemistry, 67,* 352–363.

Yamamoto, Y., Nakanishi, H., Takai, N., Shimazoe, T., Watanabe, S., & Kita, H. (1999). Expression of N-methyl-D-aspartate receptor-dependent long-term potentiation in the neostriatal neurons in an in vitro slice after ethanol withdrawal of the rat. *Neuroscience, 91,* 59–68.

Zhang, X.-F., Hu, X.-T., White, F. J., & Wolf, M. E. (1997). Increased responsiveness of ventral tegmental area dopamine neurons to glutamate after repeated administration of cocaine or amphetamine is transient and selectively involves AMPA receptors. *Journal of Pharmacology and Experimental Therapeutics, 281,* 699–706.

Gytis Baranauskas

Pain-Induced Plasticity in Spinal Cord

☐ Two Types of Pain: Nociceptive and Chronic

Pain is a subjective phenomenon, which is usually described as unpleasant experience associated with exposure to potentially damaging stimuli. Such pain signaling is termed acute pain and is of clear functional significance: it allows an organism to avoid dangerous situations (Millan, 1999). Nevertheless, in some cases pain sensation can occur without any clear external stimuli and can persist for months. Such pain is called *chronic pain* and it is not clear if it has any functional meaning (Woolf & Doubell, 1994). It is likely that chronic pain simply reflects a malfunction in pain signaling. There is the intermediate case when pain lasts for hours or days. This type of pain, called *prolonged pain*, occurs during injury or inflammation and prevents unnecessary disturbance of the tissue while undergoing healing. Normally, acute pain does not induce long-lasting (>5 min) changes in the sensory perception. Repeated application of painful stimuli and injury can produce long-lasting changes in pain perception (Sandkuhler & Liu, 1998). The main focus of this review will be synaptic and cellular plasticity in the spinal cord evoked by acute or prolonged pain or an analogous stimulus.

I do not intend to present a comprehensive review of pain-induced plasticity. The main aim is to assess critically the data on neuroplasticity obtained in the spinal cord, thus providing enough information for the readers to compare these changes with analogous events in other parts of the brain.

☐ Pain-Induced Plasticity

Definitions and Function

Prolonged pain and injury can induce several types of changes in the perception of mechanical, chemical and temperature stimuli. The most common is hyperalgesia, which is defined as an increase in pain elicited by a noxious stimulus. Primary hyperalgesia occurs in the region of tissue damage, and secondary hyperalgesia, in the surrounding region. Allodynia, defined as pain evoked by a normally innocuous stimulus, is often also reported to be present after injury and inflammation. The increased sensitivity to external stimuli serves to protect the injured area from unnecessary disturbances and thus facilitates the healing process.

These changes in perception may be due to changes in several places along the pain pathways; thus a brief description of the pathways will follow.

Pain Pathways and Pain-Induced Changes in Periphery

Surgical evidence indicates that pain sensation is formed in the thalamus and possibly also in the neocortex: pain from lower parts of the body can be relieved by cutting the axons ascending from the spinal cord to the thalamus (Willis & Westlund, 1997).

Noxious inputs, which are perceived as a pain, arrive to the spinal cord from receptors in skin, muscles, and viscera (see Figure 26.1). These receptors are formed by specialized structures or axon terminals capable of detecting various types of stimuli: mechanical (pressure, vibration), temperature (heat, cold), and chemical (Willis & Coggeshall, 1991). Many of these receptors are specialized to react to strong, potentially dangerous stimuli only, and they are called nociceptors. Nociceptor fiber types C and Aδ are differentiated on the basis of size, conduction speed, myelination, and neurotransmitter localization: Aδ fibers are medium sized, of intermediate conduction velocity, and myelinated, and possess glutamate alone. C-type fibers are thin, slowly conducting, unmyelinated, and a large fraction contain, in addition to glutamate, a whole spectrum of peptidergic neurotransmitters: substance P, neurokinin A (NKA), and calcitonin-gene-related peptide (CGRP; Willis & Coggeshall, 1991). A third type of fiber, termed Aβ, normally transmits non-nociceptive information from the periphery to the spinal cord, and is thick, fast conducting, myelinated, and possess glutamate alone. During inflammation or nerve injury, all three types of fibers can undergo dramatic changes resulting in change of threshold, appearance of spontaneous firing (Millan, 1999), and even change in phenotype: Aβ fibers become positive to substance P (Neumann, Doubell, Leslie, & Woolf, 1996). These phenomena alone may account for much of pain-induced plasticity. In addition, spontaneous or increased peripheral receptor activity can indirectly change signal transmission in the spinal cord (see below).

The axons of neurons forming all three types of fibers are originate in dorsal root ganglia (DRG), which form a series of small structures along both sides of the spinal cord (see Figure 26.1). These neurons are bipolar, and their second axon branch terminates in the spinal cord on spinal interneurons, motoneurons, or ascending pathway neurons. Most of the ascending pathway nociceptive cells send their axons to the thalamus and are termed spinothalamic tract (STT) neurons. There are also several types of descending pathways, which arrive from brainstem nuclei (Figure 26.1). They can strongly modulate pain transmission in the spinal cord and therefore can participate in pain-induced plasticity in the spinal cord (M. O. Urban & Gebhart, 1999).

Pain-Induced Central Plasticity

The presented brief review of pain pathways demonstrates that plastic changes in pain transmission can occur both in the periphery (receptors, dorsal ganglia neurons) and in the central nervous system (CNS) (spinal cord, brainstem, thalamus). Moreover, each section of the pathway is influenced by the activity in other sections (see below). Pain-induced plasticity in the CNS was first introduced as a central component of

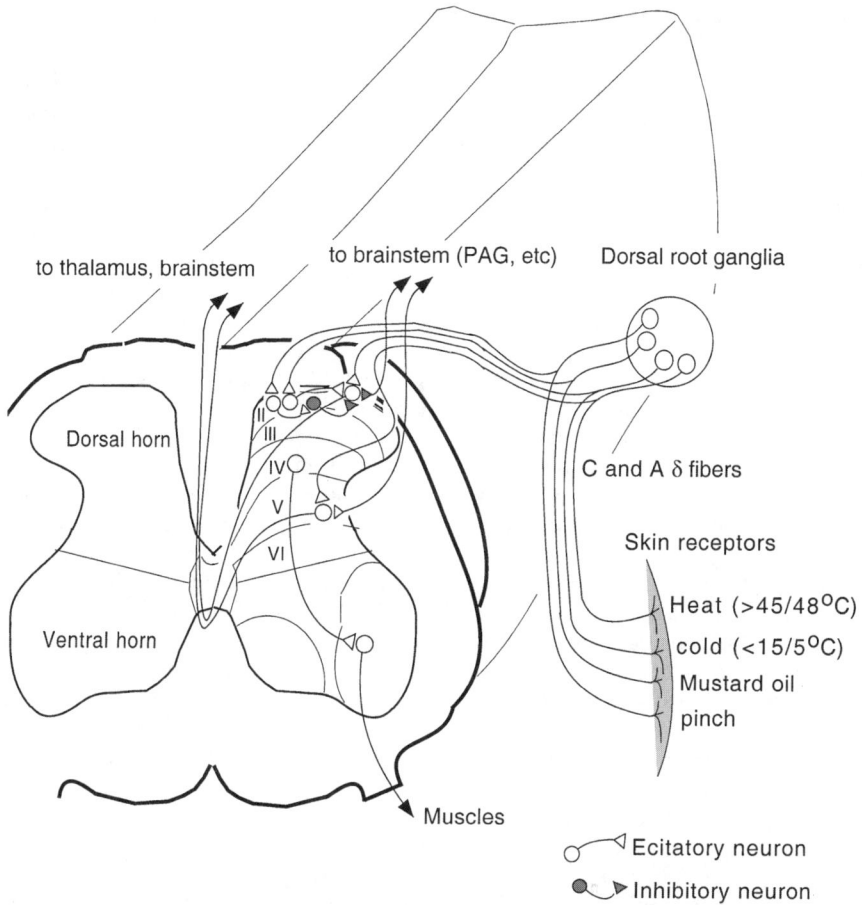

Figure 26.1. Simplified diagram of nociceptive pathways in the spinal cord. Visceral nociceptive receptors are omitted for simplicity. The left part of the diagram shows a transverse section of the lumbar part of the spinal cord. The right side of the section is subdivided into laminae: laminae I–VI make up the dorsal horn. Laminae I-II are often referred to as the superficial dorsal horn and laminae V–VI are called the deep dorsal horn. Most C fibers terminate in laminae I–II and VI and in the ventral horn. DRG neurons are mainly bipolar: the first axon endings terminate in the skin, forming contacts on receptor structures or serving as receptors; the second axon endings terminate in the spinal cord, forming synapses on spinal neurons. Two major types of neurons receive these synapses: interneurons (in laminae I–II on the left side) and ascending pathway neurons (in laminae I and V on the right side; see text for details).

injury-induced hypersensitivity (Woolf, 1983). It was defined as increased excitability of the spinal cord, which may account, in part, for pain-induced hyperalgesia or/and allodynia. Pain-induced synaptic plasticity is found in brainstem and forebrain also, but this review will be limited to discussion of changes in the spinal cord.

☐ Neuroplasticity in the Spinal Cord

Several forms of synaptic plasticity can be induced in the spinal cord by nociceptive stimuli. Action potential windup is defined as an increase in the number of spikes generated by a neuron after each successive stimulus during a pulse train (Mendell & Wall, 1966). It lasts only for the duration of a single response (<1 min), but associated phenomena can be observed for >1 hour. Since both hyperalgesia and allodynia can last for many hours, windup itself is normally not included in the definition of central sensitization (Woolf, 1996). Nevertheless, it can be viewed as a form of short-term plasticity able in some cases to trigger long-term changes. Another form of short-term plasticity is an increase of the responses of STT neurons to chemical and mechanical stimuli induced by intradermal injection of capsaicin (Simone et al., 1991) which lasts ~1 hour.

Repetitive noxious heating or pinching of the skin, nerve injury, or high-frequency stimulation of C fibers can facilitate neuronal responses for >6 hours (Liu & Sandkuhler, 1995). This form of synaptic plasticity resembles hippocampal long-term potentiation (LTP) in many respects (for definitions of LTP and long-term depression, LTD, see Teyler, Chapter 9 of this volume). Low-frequency stimulation of Aδ fibers leads to a depression of synaptic responses which can last >3 hours and resembles hippocampal LTD (Sandkuhler, Chen, Cheng, & Randic, 1997). Peripheral nerve injury can result in Aβ-type fiber innervation of spinal areas normally free of fiber terminals of this type (Woolf, Shortland, & Coggeshall, 1992). This is called axon sprouting and can be regarded as neuroplasticity even though there is no direct evidence of impact of these changes on synaptic transmission. Neuropathic pain, which is produced by nerve injury, differs in mechanisms from prolonged pain (Basbaum, 1999). Hence, this type of neuroplasticity will be discussed only briefly. Inflammation and nerve injury can also change receptor expression and it may lead to changed sensitivity of pain-induced behavior (Goff, Burkey, Goff, & Jasmin, 1998).

All these forms of pain-induced plasticity are not strictly separate. For instance, LTP in non-nociceptive pathways can potentially influence pain-induced plasticity in the spinal cord (Woolf & Wall, 1982). In addition, in most experiments it is impossible to stimulate C fibers only as Aδ fibers have a lower threshold of activation than C fibers. Hence, Aδ fiber–induced changes will add to C fiber–evoked changes.

The functional significance of pain-induced plasticity in the CNS is still debated (Cleland & Gebhart, 1997) and peripheral drive can strongly control it (Cervero, 1995), but there is no doubt that pain does induce changes in the spinal cord. I will discuss forms of plasticity according to the time scale of their persistence. This division is somewhat arbitrary but it helps to illustrate the differences between various types of changes.

☐ Action Potential Windup: A Form of Short-Term Plasticity

Definition of Phenomenon

Historically, the first form of synaptic plasticity found in the spinal cord was action potential windup (Mendell & Wall, 1966; I do not consider paired pulse facilitation here). Windup is an increase in the number of action potentials generated by a neuron after each constant strength stimulus in a train (Figure 26.2). This increase in number of spikes represents the cellular equivalent of pain facilitation found in human subjects

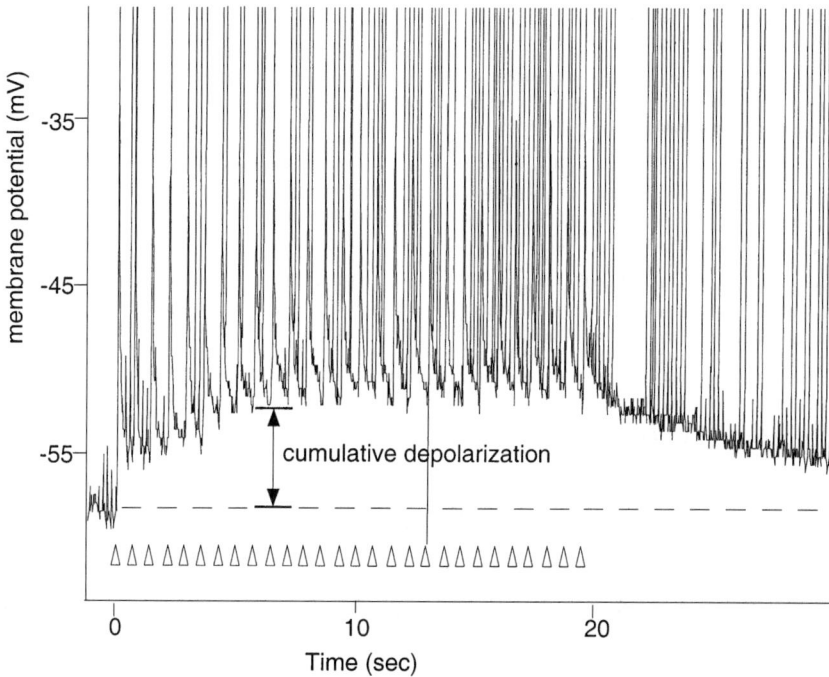

Figure 26.2. Example of a windup response recorded intracellularly from a lumbar motoneuron of the rat spinal cord in vitro. A train of electrical pulses (1 msec; 10 V intensity; 1 Hz, open triangles) were applied to the segmental dorsal root at intensity sufficient to activate C fibers. The cell was slightly depolarized by a constant current injection. The cell gradually depolarized from the baseline membrane potential (dashed line) to the final level indicated by the upper arrow. Cumulative depolarization is defined as the difference between the baseline potential before the train and the potential achieved before each successive stimulus. Large upward deflections which reach the top of the figure represent action potentials. Note a dramatic increase in the number of action potentials after each stimulus (windup) by the end of the train.

with an analogous stimulus pattern (Arendt-Nielsen et al., 1995). Windup is only observed in the frequency range 0.5–2 Hz with a stimulus sufficient to activate C fibers (see Urban, Thompson, & Dray, 1994). Under pathological conditions or during inflammation, windup can also be observed in myelinated fibers (Thompson, Dray, & Urban, 1994). Windup phenomena and the underlying mechanisms have been discussed in several reviews (Baranauskas & Nistri, 1998; Urban, Thompson, & Dray, 1994b), so I will describe only briefly the main features which distinguish it from other forms of plasticity.

Means of Induction and Basic Properties

Windup can only be elicited in a subset of cells; in the remaining cells the number of action potentials after each stimulus in the train does not change or even decreases

(Thompson, King, & Woolf, 1990). The only good predictor of action potential windup is the rate of the rise of cumulative depolarization which accompanies low-frequency C fiber–induced neuronal responses (Sivilotti, Thompson, & Woolf, 1993; Figure 26.2). Even though windup seems to result from summation of long excitatory postsynaptic potentials (EPSPs), in control conditions there is no correlation between the size and duration of C fiber–evoked EPSPs and rate of rise of cumulative depolarization. Nevertheless, in the presence of NMDA receptor antagonists the amplitude of slow component of C fiber–evoked EPSPs correlates with the rate of rise of cumulative depolarization and the presence of windup in rat motoneurones (Baranauskas & Nistri, 1996). No such data are currently available for dorsal horn neurons. Membrane depolarization enhances windup and hyperpolarization depresses windup in neonatal rat motoneurones (Baranauskas & Nistri, 1996) and in some, but not all dorsal horn cells (Sivilotti et al., 1993).

Receptors Involved

In most of the cases windup can be blocked by NMDA receptor antagonists (Arendt-Nielsen et al., 1995; Thompson et al., 1990). Nevertheless, NMDA receptor antagonist–resistant forms are found in adult rat dorsal horn (Xu, Dalsgaard, & Wiesenfeld-Hallin, 1992) and neonatal rat motoneurones (Baranauskas & Nistri, 1996). Tachykinin NK1 receptor antagonists reduced or abolished windup in most of the cases tested, while NK2 receptor antagonists were ineffective (Russo, Nagy & Hounsgaard, 1997; Xu et al., 1992). Metabotropic glutamate receptor antagonists reduced cumulative depolarization and windup (Russo et al., 1997). Opioids can control slow EPSP and might modify cumulative depolarization and windup (Chapman & Dickenson, 1992).

Putative Mechanisms

Several mechanisms have been proposed for action potential windup. The prevailing hypothesis is that NMDA receptor–mediated responses are facilitated by tachykinin receptor activation through the protein kinase C (PKC) pathway (Urban, Thompson, & Dray, 1994). However, there is no direct evidence that PKC inhibitors can block windup. Moreover, in some cases NMDA receptor antagonists are ineffective. There are three additional proposed mechanisms underlying windup: (a) slow synaptic potential summation, possibly mediated by tachykinin receptor activation (Baranauskas & Nistri, 1996); (b) increase of L-type calcium channel currents by metabotropic glutamate and tachykinin receptor effects; and (c) a decrease in tonic and/or phasic GABAergic and glycinergic inhibition.

☐ Central Sensitization: Pain-Induced Long-Term Plasticity

Three Types of Plasticity Found in the Spinal Cord

The central component of pain-induced sensitization was first defined as increase of spinal cord excitability after injury (Woolf, 1983). Central sensitization is comprised of several phenomena, which can be divided into three groups:

1. LTP/LTD–like synaptic facilitation/depression, including the relief of tonic inhibition;

2. global changes in synaptic contacts expressed as axon sprouting and/or changes of ganglion cell phenotypes;
3. changes in receptor density and/or expression patterns in the spinal cord.

1. LTP (and LTD) in the hippocampus can be defined as a long-lasting (>1 hour) increase (or decrease) in EPSP amplitude, which is believed to reflect the increase in synaptic connection strength (Linden, 1999). If the increased EPSP amplitude reaches spike threshold, it will result in an increase in the number of spikes evoked by synaptic stimulation. Central sensitization in the spinal cord was first described as a simple increase in the number of spikes induced by constant strength stimulus after injury (Woolf, 1983). This increase lasted for at least several hours. Later studies demonstrated that such increases can last for >8 hours (Sandkuhler & Liu, 1998). Similarly, an increase in field potential amplitude, which probably reflects the increase in EPSP amplitude (Baba, Doubell, & Woolf, 1999), was also observed for the same time period (Liu & Sandkuhler, 1995). More complex changes are also found in the spinal cord: reduced inhibition of descending pathways, reduced sensitivity to external inhibitory neurotransmitters GABA and glycine, and reduced activity of inhibitory interneurons. The first two are found in spinothalamic tract neurons (Lin, Peng, & Willis, 1994). There are indirect data that also suggest the presence of tonic inhibition from local interneurons: topical application of $GABA_A$ and glycine receptor antagonists evoke allodynia- and hyperalgesia-like states (Yaksh, 1989). Nevertheless, such a mechanism implies that synaptic connections from inhibitory interneurons are reduced in strength for long periods of time, the definition of LTD. There is the additional possibility that inhibitory interneurones die during nerve injury. It is currently unclear how much this latter mechanism contributes to changes in transmission of nociceptive information in the spinal cord.
2. Axon sprouting has been found after injury, as evidenced by the detection of axon terminals in areas of the dorsal horn previously free of these terminal types (Woolf et al., 1992).
3. Changes in receptor density have been observed as global (in the whole dorsal horn or in one particular lamina) changes in expression of receptor mRNA or changes in staining by specific antibodies (Ji et al., 1995). More local changes are likely to occur, but to date no experimental data exist at a cellular level.

The three types of plasticity in the spinal cord can be distinguished by the time course of their onset. LTP/LTD can be detected within minutes (Lozier & Kendig, 1995), while changes in receptor density are detectable within 24 hours (Pellegrini-Giampietro, Fan, Ault, Miller, & Zukin, 1994) and axon sprouting can be clearly visible after one week (Woolf et al., 1992). Hence, all three types of plasticity are relatively independent even though one cannot ignore cross-talk between them.

Means of Induction

All three forms of plasticity can be induced by pain. Central sensitization can be induced by the strong chemical irritant mustard oil, painful repetitive heat application, intradermal capsaicin injection, and nerve injury (Lin, Peng, & Willis, 1996a; Sandkuhler & Liu, 1998; Woolf & Wall, 1986). For experimental purposes, more controlled electrical stimulation is used. Both low- and high-frequency electrical stimulation parameters are able to induce long-term changes in spinal cord transmission.

Low-frequency (0.5–2 Hz) C fiber–activating stimulation can cause an increase in spinal cord excitability of variable duration (Woolf & Wall, 1986). The persistence depends on stimulus duration, the nerve stimulated and on the presence/absence of prolonged painful experience of an experimental animal (Thompson et al., 1994). Under normal conditions, only C fiber activation induces a long lasting increase in excitability of the spinal cord (Woolf & Doubell, 1994). $A\beta$ and $A\delta$ fiber stimulation at such frequencies leads to depression of synaptic transmission (Lev-Tov & Pinco, 1992; Sandkuhler et al., 1997).

High-frequency (100 Hz for 1–5 sec) stimulation leads to synaptic transmission facilitation for >2 hours (Randic, Jiang, & Cerne, 1993). This form of synaptic plasticity in many respects resembles LTP in hippocampus. High-frequency (100 Hz) stimulation can induce LTP of all three types of EPSP: $A\beta$, $A\delta$, and C fiber evoked (Liu & Sandkuhler, 1995; Randic et al., 1993; Sandkuhler et al., 1997). $A\beta$ fiber stimulation at 100 Hz can lead to both potentiation and depression in slice preparation (Randic et al., 1993). In intact spinal cord, muscle blockade can result in elimination of $A\beta$ fiber LTP, suggesting the presence of peripheral control of $A\beta$ fiber plasticity (Svendsen, Tjolsen, & Hole, 1998).

Short-term potentiation (STP)-like phenomena can also be induced by the combined application of substance P and NMDA receptor agonists on STT neurons in monkeys (Dougherty & Willis, 1991). LTP can be induced in dorsal horn neurons by the separate application of substance P or NKA or NMDA receptor agonists on dorsal horn of spinalized rats and not in the rats with intact spinal cord (Liu & Sandkuhler, 1998). LTP can also be induced by the application of serotonin in slices (Hori, Endo, & Takahashi, 1996).

Receptors Involved

Similar to windup, LTP in the spinal cord is sensitive to ionotropic glutamatergic and tachykinin receptor antagonists.

The NMDA receptor antagonist CPP completely eliminated LTP of C fiber–evoked field potential responses in superficial dorsal horn (Liu & Sandkuhler, 1995). These field potentials have been demonstrated to be evoked by C fiber stimulation only (Schouenborg, 1984) and were insensitive to CPP before LTP induction (Liu & Sandkuhler, 1995). Hence, CPP blocked LTP induction or a CPP-sensitive fraction was added by high-frequency stimuli. In contrast, in deeper dorsal horn neurons, another NMDA receptor antagonist, D-AP5, reduced the number of late spikes evoked by C fiber stimulation both before and after LTP induction (Svendsen et al., 1998). As a consequence, D-AP5 only slightly reduced LTP-associated increase in number of action potentials in these neurons (Svendsen et al., 1998). Similarly, AP-5 did not block slow ventral root potential LTP (Lozier & Kendig, 1995). However, the latter study was done in neonatal rats (P3-7) and there is a switch in sensitivity of slow ventral root potentials to NMDA receptor antagonists at P10-11. These potentials are more sensitive to tachykinin receptor antagonists at P3-8 and are more sensitive to NMDA receptor antagonists at P12-21 (Gibbs & Kendig, 1992). Hence, it is likely that the sensitivity of LTP induction to NMDA receptor antagonists also develops at P10-11. The C fiber response, defined as the number of spikes between 30/70 and 300 msec after a stimulus (used by Svendsen et al., 1998) has its own caveats. Even though late spikes can only be obtained by C fiber strength stimulation, it is unlikely that they are completely independent of $A\beta$ and $A\delta$ fiber–evoked potentials and circuitry (Woolf & Wall, 1982). It would be more appropriate to have pure C fiber responses by blocking myelinated fiber transmission by low concentrations of TTX (Jeftinija, 1994) or by anodal depolarization (Schouenborg, 1984). Nevertheless, these data suggest that both NMDA receptor–dependent and –independent components of C fiber high-frequency stimulation–evoked LTP can be found in the spinal cord.

Non-NMDA receptor antagonists can block slow EPSPs in dorsal horn cells (Miller & Woolf, 1996) and motoneurons (Baranauskas & Nistri, 1998). Therefore, a complete block of non- NMDA receptors would eliminate C fiber–evoked response, and hence no direct evidence of a non-NMDA receptor role in the induction of LTP in the spinal cord is available. Partial block of C fiber–evoked responses in deep dorsal horn neurons had little effect on LTP induction (Svendsen et al., 1998).

Tachykinin receptor NK1 and NK2 antagonists completely blocked the induction of LTP of C fiber–evoked field potentials in superficial dorsal horn (Liu & Sandkuhler, 1997), while the NK1 receptor antagonist RP67580 was ineffective in neonatal rats (Lozier & Kendig, 1995). The latter result can be explained by the age of the animals used in the study (<P8, see above).

Pharmacologically induced STP in STT cells in monkeys seems to be no different from painful stimuli–evoked facilitation: it is evoked by co-application of tachykinins and NMDA receptor agonists (Dougherty & Willis, 1991); conversely, the blockade of the same receptors prevents STT neuron facilitation (Dougherty, Palecek, Paleckova, & Willis, 1994).

Behavioral studies show that many other receptor systems can modify pain-induced responses, including serotonin, adrenergic, and opioid (Millan, 1999). These studies are likely to reflect the influence of descending pathways, which are known to modulate pain sensation and have terminals which release all above-mentioned neurotransmitters (Willis & Coggeshall, 1991). It should be noted that pain-induced changes of transmitter release from descending fibers will result in modified synaptic transmission in the spinal cord (Urban & Gebhart, 1999). However, cellular changes related to the release of the transmitters will occur in projecting neurons in supraspinal structures (brainstem or thalamus, which are beyond the scope of this review). Part of the events underlying such plasticity may occur in spinal presynaptic terminals and most of the studies on second messenger systems involved in spinal plasticity do not distinguish between processes in spinal neurons and synaptic terminals from extraspinal neurons. Therefore, in the next section both possibilities will be discussed.

Second Messenger Systems and Putative Mechanisms

The best-studied case of synaptic transmission facilitation induced by painful stimuli (intradermal capsaicin injection) is an increase in responsivness of STT neurons in the monkey (Simone et al., 1991). This type of synaptic facilitation resembles hippocampal STP since it lasts <1.5 hours. The main mechanism of this facilitation is believed to be the reduction of tonic inhibition received mainly from the brainstem periaqueductal gray (PAG; Lin, Peng, & Willis, 1996c). Several second messenger systems acting at different sites seem to be involved in this facilitation: PKC and nitric oxide synthase (NOS; Lin, Peng, & Willis, 1996b). PKC activation reduced responses of STT neurons to GABA and glycine, the main neurotransmitters thought to mediate tonic inhibition from PAG (Lin et al., 1996a). PKC and NOS inhibitors act differentially on superficial and deep STT neurons, and their site of action is likely to be presynaptic (Lin, Peng, Wu, & Willis, 1997). Neurotransmitters GABA and glycine are believed to be released from PAG terminals (Lin et al., 1994). Nevertheless, there is no demonstration that the application of antagonists for GABA or glycine receptors can block this kind of facilitation.

There is no direct evidence of involvement of second messenger systems in electrically induced LTP. Aδ fiber–induced LTD is insensitive to phosphatase inhibitors (Sandkuhler et al., 1997).

Studies of gene mutations show that PKCγ knockout mice have unchanged acute and reduced nerve injury–related neuropathic pain (Malmberg, Chen, Tonegawa, & Basbaum, 1997), while PKA knockout mice possess reduced second phase of nociceptive response (between 10 and 60 min) and inflammation and unchanged neuropathic pain (Malmberg et al., 1997). This parallels LTP modifications in hippocampus: in PKC knockout mice STP is preserved, while LTP is suppressed (Abeliovich et al., 1993). In contrast, in PKA knockout mice a late-phase LTP was reduced and only STD could be induced (Qi et al., 1996). It is difficult to deduce how these results relate to pain signaling the spinal cord and it is likely that both PKC and PKA act as modulators of sensitization, as has been proposed for hippocampal LTP (Winder, Mansuy, Osman, Moallem, & Kandel, 1998).

☐ Axon Sprouting and/or Changes in Ganglion Cell Phenotype

Axon sprouting is described as the detection of axon terminals in areas previously free of those types of axon endings (Woolf et al., 1992). It occurs after nerve injury or section (Doubell, Mannion, & Woolf, 1997) and can be detected within 1–2 weeks.

Phenotypic switch of dorsal ganglia cells and axons is defined as appearance of myelinated fibers positive to substance P, which is normally present only in unmyelinated fibers (Neumann et al., 1996). There is a corresponding change in the distribution of substance P positive neurons in dorsal ganglia. This switch can be induced by inflammation; changes in expression of other fiber markers are also reported (Kerr et al., 1999).

Nerve injury seems to induce a similar switch, and axon sprouting might be explained by it (Tong et al., 1999). Axon sprouting is revealed by the appearance after injury of cholera toxin B-subunit (CTB) binding in laminae II (Figure 26.1), which is free of this type of binding in control conditions. Normally, CTB binds only in myelinated fibers, so a change in toxin binding pattern can explain the appearance of CTB-marked axons in laminae II.

Axon sprouting and phenotypic switching occur during conditions of neuropathic pain following nerve group dysfunction or damage. This type of pain seems to be related more closely to chronic pain (Basbaum, 1999). Hence, it is possible that such plasticity does not occur even during repeated acute noxious stimuli such as that used to induce spinal LTP. Nevertheless, it is an intriguing possibility that the new contacts made by non-nociceptive fibers on nociceptive neurons might explain allodynia when a normally nonpainful stimulus induces pain sensation. Moreover, a phenotypic switch can occur during inflammation and is detectable within 48 hours (Kerr et al., 1999; Neumann et al., 1996), hence it is likely to contribute to prolonged pain-induced plasticity in the spinal cord.

☐ Changes in Receptor and Transmitter Expression

Inflammation and peripheral nerve injury can also change the gene expression of many receptors, including tachykinin, glutamate, opioid, galanin, and neuropeptide Y receptors (Abbadie, Brown, Mantyh & Basbaum, 1996; Ji et al., 1995; Pellegrini-Giampietro et al., 1994). Experimental data suggest that these changes can contribute to altered modulation of pain pathways after inflammation or injury (Goff et al., 1998; Wiesenfeld-Hallin et al., 1992). Slow onset of receptor expression (~24 hours) suggests that such a phenomenon is unlikely to contribute significantly to most of the forms of LTP. Moreover, these changes are considered to be induced by neuropathic pain or inflammation and there are no reports of acute pain–induced changes. Nevertheless, studies on knockout mice suggest that there is a link between the acute pain and inflammation–induced plasticity (Malmberg, Brandon et al., 1997a; Malmberg, Chen et al., 1997) and it is likely that receptor density changes contribute to the late phase of long term plasticity in the spinal cord.

☐ Conclusions

In summary, there are many common features between pain-induced synaptic plasticity and LTP/LTD in the hippocampus. First, several types of kinases, PKA and PKC, control or modulate synaptic plasticity in both the hippocampus and the spinal cord. Moreover, similar to LTP in the hippocampus, PKC controls long-term changes induced by neuropathic pain. Second, NMDA receptors control some, but not all, forms of synaptic plasticity. There are more parallels, but their significance is as yet unclear. For example, Ca^{2+} signaling in spinal cord neurons is clearly crucial for some types of sensitization, but direct evidence for functional linkage with other signaling pathway elements is lacking. There are also clear differences between hippocampal synaptic plasticity and pain-induced plasticity in the spinal cord. In the hippocampus, low-frequency stimulation leads to LTD, while spinal C fiber stimulation can lead to windup or STP, lasting for >3 hours in some cases. This may reflect the specific nature of C fiber–mediated EPSPs; their duration can exceed 1 sec and many slow transmitters can be released simultaneously, overcoming the LTD observed at these frequencies in Aδ fibers. A second major difference is a crucial dependence of pain-induced synaptic plasticity on peptidergic neurotransmission. It is interesting that the tachykinin NK1 receptor is implicated in status epilepticus in the hippocampus (Basbaum, 1999), suggesting that this is not a fundamental difference. Third, the densities of many receptors (e.g., tachykinin, CGRP) are changed dramatically after a painful experience, which, to my knowledge, has not been reported for other parts of the brain during sensory stimulation, although nonmeasurable local changes are likely.

In conclusion, both fields of investigation, LTP/LTD in the hippocampus and pain-induced sensitization in the spinal cord, are benefiting from parallel discoveries. Currently there is much more influence from hippocampal studies to spinal cord research, but influences in the opposite direction are likely.

☐ References

Abbadie, C., Brown, J. L., Mantyh, P. W., & Basbaum, A. I. (1996). Spinal cord substance P receptor immunoreactivity increases in both inflammatory and nerve injury models of persistent pain. *Neuroscience, 70*, 201–209.

Abeliovich, A., Chen, C., Goda, Y., Silva, A. J., Stevens, C. F., & Tonegawa, S. (1993). Modified hippocampal long-term potentiation in PKC gamma-mutant mice. *Cell, 75*, 1253–1262.

Arendt-Nielsen, L., Petersen-Felix, S., Fischer, M., Bak, P., Bjerring, P., & Zbinden, A. M. (1995). The effect of N-methyl-D-aspartate antagonist (ketamine) on single and repeated nociceptive stimuli: A placebo-controlled experimental human study. *Anesthesia and Analgesia, 81*, 63–8.

Baba, H., Doubell, T. P., & Woolf, C. J. (1999). Peripheral inflammation facilitates Abeta fiber-mediated synaptic input to the substantia gelatinosa of the adult rat spinal cord. *Journal of Neuroscience, 19*, 859–67.

Baranauskas, G., & Nistri, A. (1996). NMDA receptor-independent mechanisms responsible for the rate of rise of cumulative depolarization evoked by trains of dorsal root stimuli on rat spinal motoneurones. *Brain Research, 738*, 329–32.

Baranauskas, G., & Nistri, A. (1998). Sensitization of pain pathways in the spinal cord: Cellular mechanisms. *Progress in Neurobiology, 54*, 349–65.

Basbaum, A. I. (1999). Distinct neurochemical features of acute and persistent pain [In Process Citation]. *Proceedings of the National Academy of Sciences of the United States of America, 96*, 7739–7743.

Cervero, F. (1995). Visceral pain: Mechanisms of peripheral and central sensitization. *Annals of Medicine, 27*, 235–239.

Chapman, V., & Dickenson, A. H. (1992). The combination of NMDA antagonism and morphine produces profound antinociception in the rat dorsal horn. *Brain Research, 573*, 321–323.

Cleland, C. L., & Gebhart, G. F. (1997). Does central nervous system plasticity contribute to hyperalgesia? *Behavioral and Brain Sciences, 20*.

Doubell, T. P., Mannion, R. J., & Woolf, C. J. (1997). Intact sciatic myelinated primary afferent terminals collaterally sprout in the adult rat dorsal horn following section of a neighbouring peripheral nerve. *Journal of Comparative Neurology, 380*, 95–104.

Dougherty, P. M., Palecek, J., Paleckova, V., & Willis, W. D. (1994). Neurokinin 1 and 2 antagonists attenuate the responses and NK1 antagonists prevent the sensitization of primate spinothalamic tract neurons after intradermal capsaicin. *Journal of Neurophysiology, 72*, 1464–1475.

Dougherty, P. M., & Willis, W. D. (1991). Enhancement of spinothalamic neuron responses to chemical and mechanical stimuli following combined micro-iontophoretic application of N-methyl-D-aspartic acid and substance P. *Pain, 47*, 85–93.

Gibbs, L. M., & Kendig, J. J. (1992). Substance P and NMDA receptor-mediated slow potentials in neonatal rat spinal cord: Age-related changes. *Brain Research, 595*, 236–41.

Goff, J. R., Burkey, A. R., Goff, D. J., & Jasmin, L. (1998). Reorganization of the spinal dorsal horn in models of chronic pain: Correlation with behaviour. *Neuroscience, 82*, 559–574.

Hori, Y., Endo, K., & Takahashi, T. (1996). Long-lasting synaptic facilitation induced by serotonin in superficial dorsal horn neurones of the rat spinal cord. *Journal of Physiology (London), 492*, 867–876.

Jeftinija, S. (1994). The role of tetrodotoxin-resistant sodium channels of small primary afferent fibers. *Brain Research, 639*, 125–34.

Ji, R. R., Zhang, Q., Law, P. Y., Low, H. H., Elde, R., & Hokfelt, T. (1995). Expression of mu-, delta-, and kappa-opioid receptor-like immunoreactivities in rat dorsal root ganglia after carrageenan-induced inflammation. *Journal of Neuroscience, 15*, 8156–8166.

Kerr, B. J., Bradbury, E. J., Bennett, D. L., Trivedi, P. M., Dassan, P., French, J., Shelton, D. B., McMahon, S. B., & Thompson, S. W. (1999). Brain-derived neurotrophic factor modulates nociceptive sensory inputs and NMDA-evoked responses in the rat spinal cord. *Journal of Neuroscience, 19*, 5138–5148.

Lev-Tov, A., & Pinco, M. (1992). In vitro studies of prolonged synaptic depression in the neonatal rat spinal cord. *Journal of Physiology (London), 447*, 149–69.

Lin, Q., Peng, Y., & Willis, W. D. (1994). Glycine and GABAA antagonists reduce the inhibition of primate spinothalamic tract neurons produced by stimulation in periaqueductal gray. *Brain Research, 654*, 286–302.

Lin, Q., Peng, Y. B., & Willis, W. D. (1996a). Inhibition of primate spinothalamic tract neurons by spinal glycine and GABA is reduced during central sensitization. *Journal of Neurophysiology, 76*, 1005–1014.

Lin, Q., Peng, Y. B., & Willis, W. D. (1996b). Possible role of protein kinase C in the sensitization of primate spinothalamic tract neurons. *Journal of Neuroscience, 16*, 3026–34.

Lin, Q., Peng, Y. B., & Willis, W. D. (1996c). Role of GABA receptor subtypes in inhibition of primate spinothalamic tract neurons: Difference between spinal and periaqueductal gray inhibition. *Journal of Neurophysiology, 75*, 109–23.

Lin, Q., Peng, Y. B., Wu, J., & Willis, W. D. (1997). Involvement of cGMP in nociceptive processing by and sensitization of spinothalamic neurons in primates. *Journal of Neuroscience, 17*, 3293–3302.

Linden, D. J. (1999). The return of the spike: Postsynaptic action potentials and the induction of LTP and LTD. *Neuron, 22*, 661–666.

Liu, X., & Sandkuhler, J. (1997). Characterization of long-term potentiation of C-fiber-evoked potentials in spinal dorsal horn of adult rat: Essential role of NK1 and NK2 receptors. *Journal of Neurophysiology, 78*, 1973–1982.

Liu, X. G., & Sandkuhler, J. (1995). Long-term potentiation of C-fiber-evoked potentials in the rat spinal dorsal horn is prevented by spinal N-methyl-D-aspartic acid receptor blockage. *Neuroscience Letters, 191*, 43–46.

Liu, X. G., & Sandkuhler, J. (1998). Activation of spinal N-methyl-D-aspartate or neurokinin receptors induces long-term potentiation of spinal C-fibre-evoked potentials. *Neuroscience, 86*, 1209–1216.

Lozier, A. P., & Kendig, J. J. (1995). Long-term potentiation in an isolated peripheral nerve-spinal cord preparation. *Journal of Neurophysiology, 74*, 1001–1009.

Malmberg, A. B., Brandon, E. P., Idzerda, R. L., Liu, H., McKnight, G. S., & Basbaum, A. I. (1997). Diminished inflammation and nociceptive pain with preservation of neuropathic pain in mice with a targeted mutation of the type I regulatory subunit of cAMP-dependent protein kinase. *Journal of Neuroscience, 17*, 7462–7470.

Malmberg, A. B., Chen, C., Tonegawa, S., & Basbaum, A. I. (1997). Preserved acute pain and reduced neuropathic pain in mice lacking PKCgamma [see comments]. *Science, 278*, 279–283.

Mendell, L. M., & Wall, P. D. (1966). Response of single dorsal horn cells to peripheral cutaneous unmyelynated fibers. *Nature, 206*, 97–99.

Millan, M. J. (1999). The induction of pain: An integrative review. *Progress in Neurobiology, 57*, 1–164.

Miller, B. A., & Woolf, C. J. (1996). Glutamate-mediated slow synaptic currents in neonatal rat deep dorsal horn neurons in vitro. *Journal of Neurophysiology, 76*, 1465–1476.

Neumann, S., Doubell, T. P., Leslie, T., & Woolf, C. J. (1996). Inflammatory pain hypersensitivity mediated by phenotypic switch in myelinated primary sensory neurons. *Nature, 384*, 360–4.

Pellegrini-Giampietro, D. E., Fan, S., Ault, B., Miller, B. E., & Zukin, R. S. (1994). Glutamate receptor gene expression in spinal cord of arthritic rats. *Journal of Neuroscience, 14*, 1576–1583.

Qi, M., Zhuo, M., Skalhegg, B. S., Brandon, E. P., Kandel, E. R., McKnight, G. S., & Idzerda, R. L. (1996). Impaired hippocampal plasticity in mice lacking the Cbeta1 catalytic subunit of cAMP-dependent protein kinase. *Proceedings of the National Academy of Science of the United States of America, 93*, 1571–1576.

Randic, M., Jiang, M. C., & Cerne, R. (1993). Long-term potentiation and long-term depression of primary afferent neurotransmission in the rat spinal cord. *Journal of Neuroscience, 13*, 5228–5241.

Russo, R. E., Nagy, F., & Hounsgaard, J. (1997). Modulation of plateau properties in dorsal horn neurones in a slice preparation of the turtle spinal cord. *Journal of Physiology (London), 499*, 459–474.

Sandkuhler, J., Chen, J. G., Cheng, G., & Randic, M. (1997). Low-frequency stimulation of afferent Adelta-fibers induces long-term depression at primary afferent synapses with substantia gelatinosa neurons in the rat. *Journal of Neuroscience, 17*, 6483–6491.

Sandkuhler, J., & Liu, X. (1998). Induction of long-term potentiation at spinal synapses by noxious stimulation or nerve injury. *European Journal of Neuroscience, 10*, 2476–2480.

Schouenborg, J. (1984). Functional and topographical properties of field potentials evoked in rat dorsal horn by cutaneous C-fibre stimulation. *Journal of Physiology (London), 356*, 169–192.

Simone, D. A., Sorkin, L. S., Oh, U., Chung, J. M., Owens, C., LaMotte, R. H., & Willis, W. D. (1991). Neurogenic hyperalgesia: Central neural correlates in responses of spinothalamic tract neurons. *Journal of Neurophysiology, 66*, 228–246.

Sivilotti, L. G., Thompson, S. W., & Woolf, C. J. (1993). Rate of rise of the cumulative depolarization evoked by repetitive stimulation of small-caliber afferents is a predictor of action potential windup in rat spinal neurons in vitro. *Journal of Neurophysiology, 69*, 1621–1631.

Sugimoto, T., Bennett, G. J., & Kajander, K. C. (1990). Transsynaptic degeneration in the superficial dorsal horn after sciatic nerve injury: Effects of a chronic constriction injury, transection, and strychnine. *Pain, 42*, 205–213.

Svendsen, F., Tjolsen, A., & Hole, K. (1998). AMPA and NMDA receptor-dependent spinal LTP after nociceptive tetanic stimulation. *NeuroReport, 9,* 1185–1190.

Thompson, S. W., Dray, A., & Urban, L. (1994). Injury-induced plasticity of spinal reflex activity: NK1 neurokinin receptor activation and enhanced A- and C-fiber mediated responses in the rat spinal cord in vitro. *Journal of Neuroscience, 14,* 3672–3687.

Thompson, S. W. N., King, A. E., & Woolf, C. J. (1990). Activity-dependent changes in rat ventral horn neurons in vitro—summation of prolonged afferent evoked postsynaptic depolarizations produce a D-2-amino-5-phosphonovaleric acid sensitive windup. *European Journal of Neuroscience, 2,* 638–649.

Tong, Y. G., Wang, H. F., Ju, G., Grant, G., Hokfelt, T. & Zhang, X. (1999). Increased uptake and transport of cholera toxin B-subunit in dorsal root ganglion neurons after peripheral axotomy: possible implications for sensory sprouting. *Journal of Comparative Neurology, 404,* 143–58.

Urban, L., Thompson, S. W. & Dray, A. (1994). Modulation of spinal excitability: Co-operation between neurokinin and excitatory amino acid neurotransmitters. *Trends in Neuroscience, 17,* 432–438.

Urban, M. O., & Gebhart, G. F. (1999). Supraspinal contributions to hyperalgesia [In Process Citation]. *Proceedings of the National Academy of Sciences of the United States of America, 96,* 7687–7692.

Wiesenfeld-Hallin, Z., Xu, X. J., Langel, U., Bedecs, K., Hokfelt, T., & Bartfai, T. (1992). Galanin-mediated control of pain: Enhanced role after nerve injury. *Proceedings of the National Academy of Sciences of the United States of America, 89,* 3334–3337.

Willis, W. D., & Coggeshall, R. E. (1991). *Sensory mechanisms of the spinal cord.* New York: Plenum Press.

Willis, W. D., & Westlund, K. N. (1997). Neuroanatomy of the pain system and of the pathways that modulate pain. *Journal of Clinical Neurophysiology, 14,* 2–31.

Winder, D. G., Mansuy, I. M., Osman, M., Moallem, T. M., & Kandel, E. R. (1998). Genetic and pharmacological evidence for a novel, intermediate phase of long-term potentiation suppressed by calcineurin. *Cell, 92,* 25–37.

Woolf, C. J. (1983). Evidence for a central component of post-injury pain hypersensitivity. *Nature, 306,* 686–688.

Woolf, C. J. (1996). Windup and central sensitization are not equivalent [editorial]. *Pain, 66,* 105–108.

Woolf, C. J., & Doubell, T. P. (1994). The pathophysiology of chronic pain–increased sensitivity to low threshold A beta-fibre inputs. *Current Opinion in Neurobiology, 4,* 525–534.

Woolf, C. J., Shortland, P., & Coggeshall, R. E. (1992). Peripheral nerve injury triggers central sprouting of myelinated afferents. *Nature, 355,* 75–78.

Woolf, C. J., & Wall, P. D. (1982). Chronic peripheral nerve section diminishes the primary afferent A- fibre mediated inhibition of rat dorsal horn neurones. *Brain Research, 242,* 77–85.

Woolf, C. J., & Wall, P. D. (1986). Relative effectiveness of C primary afferent fibers of different origins in evoking a prolonged facilitation of the flexor reflex in the rat. *Journal of Neuroscience, 6,* 1433–1442.

Xu, X. J., Dalsgaard, C. J., & Wiesenfeld-Hallin, Z. (1992). Spinal substance P and N-methyl-D-aspartate receptors are coactivated in the induction of central sensitization of the nociceptive flexor reflex. *Neuroscience, 51,* 641–648.

Yaksh, T. L. (1989). Behavioral and autonomic correlates of the tactile evoked allodynia produced by spinal glycine inhibition: Effects of modulatory receptor systems and excitatory amino acid antagonists. *Pain, 37,* 111–123.

27

David Neill

Maladaptive and Dysfunctional Synaptoplasticity in Relation to Alzheimer's Disease and Schizophrenia

☐ Introduction

Areas of the brain associated with higher order cognitive functions have reached their highest level of evolutionary advancement in humans. This has enabled complex problem solving and foresight, processes which have ultimately led to the development of the complexities of human society. Participation in such a complex environment requires continual cognitive analysis and ability to learn from experience, processes which at the neuronal level involve synaptoplasticity. It would not be surprising if such synatoplasticity has advanced in the human brain and that maladaption or dysfunction could lead to mental disorders which could be human specific. This chapter proposes etiological models for Alzheimer's disease (AD) and schizophrenia which are related to this hypothesized evolutionary advanced synaptoplastic potential of the mature human brain. Relative background information regarding evolution, ontogeny, higher order cognitive functions, and brain involution will be described initially, prior to elucidation of these theories.

☐ Evolution of the Human Brain

Relevant to the proposed "maladaptive synaptoplasticity hypotheses" (MSH) for AD and "dysfunctional synaptoplasticity hypotheses" for schizophrenia is the evolutionary principal of *neoteny*. Neoteny relates to retarded development resulting in the retention of juvenile characteristics in the adult form (Gould, 1977). Although neoteny as a general principal may not explain all aspects of evolution, retarded brain development and the retention of juvenile qualities in the adult brain may have played a fundamental role in the evolution of humans. Retarded brain development in humans can be observed in several forms and is especially relevant to the most evolutionary advanced brain areas. Attainment of final cranial capacity at birth is 65% achieved in Macaca mulatta compared to 40.5% in chimpanzees and only 23% in humans. Cognitive development in humans is prolonged, taking up to 16 years to complete (Piaget, 1963). The retention of juvenile qualities in the adult brain is, however, less obvious. It is the main proposal of the present chapter that such juvenile qualities in the form of increased synapto-plastic potential are maintained in evolutionary advanced regions of the adult human brain.

Over the last 5 million years since human (Hominid)- and chimpanzee (Pan)-like ancestors diverged from a common ancestor, there has been a relative 3-fold increase in brain size in humans. The earliest fossil remains of Australopithecus (ancient hominid) had a brain volume only slightly larger than the modern chimpanzee. The beginnings of brain enlargement occurred 2.3 million years ago with the emergence of the genus Homo. Brain size has remained stable in Homo sapiens (modern hominids) over the last 50,000–100,000 years. The neocortex and especially association cortex expanded more rapidly during hominid evolution than during evolution of nonhuman primates (Passingham, 1973). Broadmann (1912) calculated that prefrontal association areas constitute 29% of the neocortex in humans, 17% in chimpanzees, and 11% in macaques, and Passingham (1973) calculated that the human prefrontal cortex was 2-fold larger than expected by extrapolation from primates. As emphasized by Rapoport (1990) areas of the brain which retain prominent connections with the association cortex evolve with it as functional units. Increased size in humans compared to nonhuman primates is most evident in subcortical regions with direct association to cortical connections such as layer II entorhinal cortex, subiculum, CA1 of hippocampus, and basolateral amylgdala.

Although research so far has not focused on the present proposal of increased synaptoplastic potential in evolutionary advanced brain regions, the evidence available is supportive. Qualitative and quantitative changes in association cortical areas continue well into the human life-span, as reflected in a prolonged myelination cycle (Yakovlev & Lecours, 1967). The mature human association cortex continues to express GAP43 (Neve, Finch, Bird, & Benowitz, 1988), a presynaptic membrane phosphoprotein associated with functional modulation and regeneration of synaptic relationships. This distribution of GAP43 in the adult human brain is similar to that in the developing rat brain rather than the mature rat brain (Masliah et al., 1991). Functionally linked brain areas that have co-evolved, such as the hippocampus, entorhinal cortex, and nucleus basalis, also appear to retain "plastic" qualities in the mature nervous system (Neill, 1995). Also supportive is the evolutionary determined increased brain glial-neuronal ratio in higher species, reaching its maximum in humans (Reichenbach, 1989). These cells have important roles in synaptoplastic mechanisms (Bacci, Verderio, Pravettoni, & Matteoli, 1999) and have been implicated in adaptation to complex environments (Sirevaag & Greenough, 1991).

☐ Development of Cortex and Functionally Associated Brain Areas

Neurons destined for primate cerebral cortex originate prenatally in the ventricular and subventricular germinal zones of the fetal telencephalic wall. Mitosis of germinal cells leads to the development of proliferative units. Cells from each proliferative unit migrate along radial glia bundles to form ontogenetic columns. Rakic (1988) argued evolutionary change has affected the number of proliferative units, leading to larger surface area of the cortex with little change in thickness. The neocortex in primitive placental animals is 1,000 times smaller in surface area but only 2 times smaller in thickness. The increased number of proliferative units could easily be produced by delayed development, which allows further divisions of progenitor cells and is therefore compatible with neoteny. According to the "parcellation" theory (Ebbesson, 1984) an increased number of association cortical neurons would be followed by increased specialization by selective loss of connections. This is evident in the increased asymmetry of the human brain (Geschwing, 1979).

Early postnatal development of the association cortex (frontal cortex) has been divided into two phases (Huttenlocher, 1979). The first phase for up to 1 or 2 years is associated with rapid decline in neuronal density and increased synaptic density, dendritic growth, and expansion of cortical volume. The second phase, from 2–16 years, is associated with a slow decline in synaptic density. This prolonged second developmental phase allows time for interaction with the complex human environment and is presumably influenced by this interaction. The general sequence is, however, developmentally programmed, as is evident in the stages of cognitive development (Piaget, 1963).

☐ Higher Order Cognitive Functions

The main manifestation of the evolutionary advancement of the human cortex is the operation of higher order cognitive functions. These cognitive functions separate humans from all other animals, including primates. Fundamental to higher order cognitive functioning is "working memory" (Goldman-Rakic, 1990). Working memory relates to the ability to bring to mind representations, for example, of the outside world and past experience, in the absence of direct stimulation and through this to direct behavior by thoughts and ideas. It is likely to have been instrumental, together with the ability to store vast memories of past experiences and the ongoing ability to learn throughout life, in the establishment of the extremely complex environment of human society (De Bruin, 1990; Goldman-Rakic, 1990). This ability to adapt to the complexities of human society, referred to as social or Machiavellian intelligence, is one of the most complex functions of the human brain (Brothers, 1990; Byrne & Whiten, 1988). As structural and functional modification of existing synapses together with new synapse formation are involved in the operation of such functions (Greenough & Chang, 1985), the association cortex and functionally linked brain areas must retain a vast synaptoplastic potential throughout life. Structural synaptic modification includes changes in synaptic size, curvature, plate perforations, and dendritic spines (Greenough & Chang, 1985; Neill, 1995). New synapse formation involves growth-associated responses in the pre- and postsynaptic sites and can be estimated by extent of dendritic tree and number of synapses per neuron.

An important question is, How does synaptoplasticity in the mature brain relate to synaptoplasticity in the developing brain? Greenough and Chang (1985) have defined two types of synaptoplasticity: "experience-expected synaptoplasticity" and "experience-dependent synaptoplasticity." The former is associated with, for example, the visual cortex and cerebellum, as environmental experience related to vision, balance, and coordination would be expected to be obtained by the end of the developmental period; the latter is associated with processes, such as social learning in humans, which require ongoing experience throughout life. In general terms, developmental (experience expected) synaptoplasticity may relate mainly or entirely to an initial overproduction of synapses followed by selective preservation of a subpopulation of these synapses. Experience-dependent synaptoplasticity involves enhancing the potential of mature synapse functional units, by either increasing the efficacy of existing synapses (synaptic remodeling) or forming new synapses. The delayed development of the association cortex and functionally linked brain areas indicates that experience-dependant synaptoplasticity in these evolutionary advanced brain regions may not be fully functional until late adolescence. From late adolescence to early adult life areas of the brain most actively engaged in experience-dependant synaptoplasticity are likely to show changes in synaptic efficacy and growth-associated responses such as increased dendritic arborization, synapse number, and a consequential increased neuronal perikaryol size (Greenough & Chang, 1985; Rutledge, Wright, & Duncan, 1974; Uylings, Kuypers, Diamond, & Veltman, 1978). In gross anatomical terms this could result in increased gray matter volume of the relevant brain area.

☐ Brain Involution

Involution of the human brain would appear to start as early as 50 years of age and it would seem that phylogenetically recent brain areas such as the prefrontal cortex are the first to be involved (Neill, 1995). The involution involves a dendritic regression, a shrinkage, and possibly the death of a subpopulation of large pyramidal neurons. Compared to humans, there have been fewer studies of involution in nonhuman primates, however, overall, the findings would appear to be superficially similar (Brizzee, Ordy, & Bartus, 1980; Cupp & Uemura, 1980). The gradual involution will lead to a progressive loss of synapses and hence a compensatory synaptoplastic response. Glial cells involved in both synaptic remodeling and new synapse formation (Bacci, Verderio, Pravettoni, & Matteoli, 1999) accumulate in the aged brain (Neill, 1995). Changes in efficacy of existing synapses in the aged human brain have been documented in terms of increased size and increased numbers of plate perforations. New synapse formation is methodologically difficult to study in the aging human brain, but its prerequisite sprouting of dendrites has been documented in the hippocampus (see Neill, 1995).

☐ Maladaptive Synaptoplasticity and AD

AD is the most common form of dementia in the elderly. Its prevalence increases exponentially with age, rising to as much as 50% affected in the over-90 age group. It is characterized by a specific brain pathology consisting of neurofibrillary tangles (NFT) and senile plaques (SP). NFT consist of aggregated hyperphosphorylated forms of the microtubule-associated protein tau, occurring in a vulnerable subpopulation of pyramidal neurons (Braak & Braak, 1991; Neill, 1995). SP consist of extracellular deposits of β-amyloid surrounded by abnormal neurites. The β-amyloid is formed from aggregates of a 40–42 amino acid peptide which is derived from a membrane-bound glycoprotein termed amyloid precursor protein (APP). NFT would appear to be specific for the human brain, whereas SP occur in the brains of aged animals (Neill, 1995).

The only definite genetic association for the common late-onset (>65 years) form of AD is with the ε4 allele of the apolipoproten E (APOE) gene (Saunders et al., 1993). APOE4, as apposed to E2 or E3, operates as a susceptibility factor leading to an earlier age of onset (Roses, 1994). Mutations in three separate genes, however, are known to cause autosomal dominant early onset (<65 years) forms of AD (Levy-Lahad & Bird,

1996). These genes are the APP gene on chromosome 21 and the presenilin 1 and 2 genes on chromosomes 14 and 1.

Despite these genetic discoveries the pathological process which leads to the development of AD remains a topic of conjecture. There are several important facts that any complete theory for the etiology of AD has to address.

1. Exponential increase in prevalence with age.
2. Why is only a particular subpopulation of neurons vulnerable to NFT formation?
3. Specificity for NFT formation for the aged human brain.
4. Progression of NFT formation in a characteristic sequence.
5. Pathological role of all genetic susceptibility and causative factors.
6. Association with previous head trauma.
7. Association with Down's syndrome.
8. Increased prevalence in families in which Down syndrome babies have been born to young mothers.
9. Protective effect of education.

One theory that can adequately explain all these facts is the maladaptive synaptoplasticity hypothesis (MSH; Neill, 1995; see also Figure 27.1). This theory relates to a maladaptive compensatory synaptoplastic response in a vulnerable subpopulation of postsynaptic neurons in the aged brain. Although the synaptoplasticity in these neuronal systems is initially adaptive in compensating for lost synaptic input, with increasing synaptic loss, it eventually bypasses a threshold and becomes maladaptive. It is entirely compatible with an exponential increase in AD with age as the brain involution, responsible for the compensatory synaptoplastic response, increases with age. The maladaptive synaptoplastic response leads directly to NFT formation in the vulnerable postsynaptic neurons. NFT formation eventually leads to death of neurons and progression of the pathological process along anatomically linked vulnerable neuronal systems (Neill, 1995). The vulnerable neurons are large pyramidal projection neurons in layers III and V of the association cortex, together with neurons in functionally linked brain areas. This constitutes the most phylogenetically advanced brain functional system containing neurons involved in higher order cognitive functioning and with advanced synaptoplastic capability (Arendt, Bruckner, Gertz, & Marcova, 1998; Neill, 1995). Brain involution, and presumably a degree of compensatory synaptoplasticity, also occurs in aged animals. However, according to the MSH, any compensatory synaptoplastic response will be less vigorous than in humans and therefore will not become maladaptive.

Pre-α neurons in layer II of the entorhinal cortex, the recipient neurons of major converging polysynaptic pathways from all association cortical areas (Neill, 1995), will be the first vulnerable postsynaptic neurons to be affected by synaptic loss during brain involution. It is precisely these neurons that are the first to develop NFT in AD (Braak & Braak, 1991; Gomez-Isla et al., 1996). NFT formation leads to death of pre-α neurons with resulting deafferentation of vulnerable postsynaptic neurons in CA1 and subiculum of the hippocampus. NFT formation and death then results in these neurons. NFT formation then progresses to vulnerable postsynaptic neurons which receive projection form CA1 and the subiculum and to other areas affected by the increasing involution of the association cortex. This leads to NFT formation in the basolateral nucleus of the amygdala and in subcortical nuclei such as the nucleus basalis, dorsal raphe nucleus, and the locus coeruleus. In the final stage, feedback projection to association cortical regions leads to NFT in pyramidal neurons of layers III and V (see Neill, 1995).

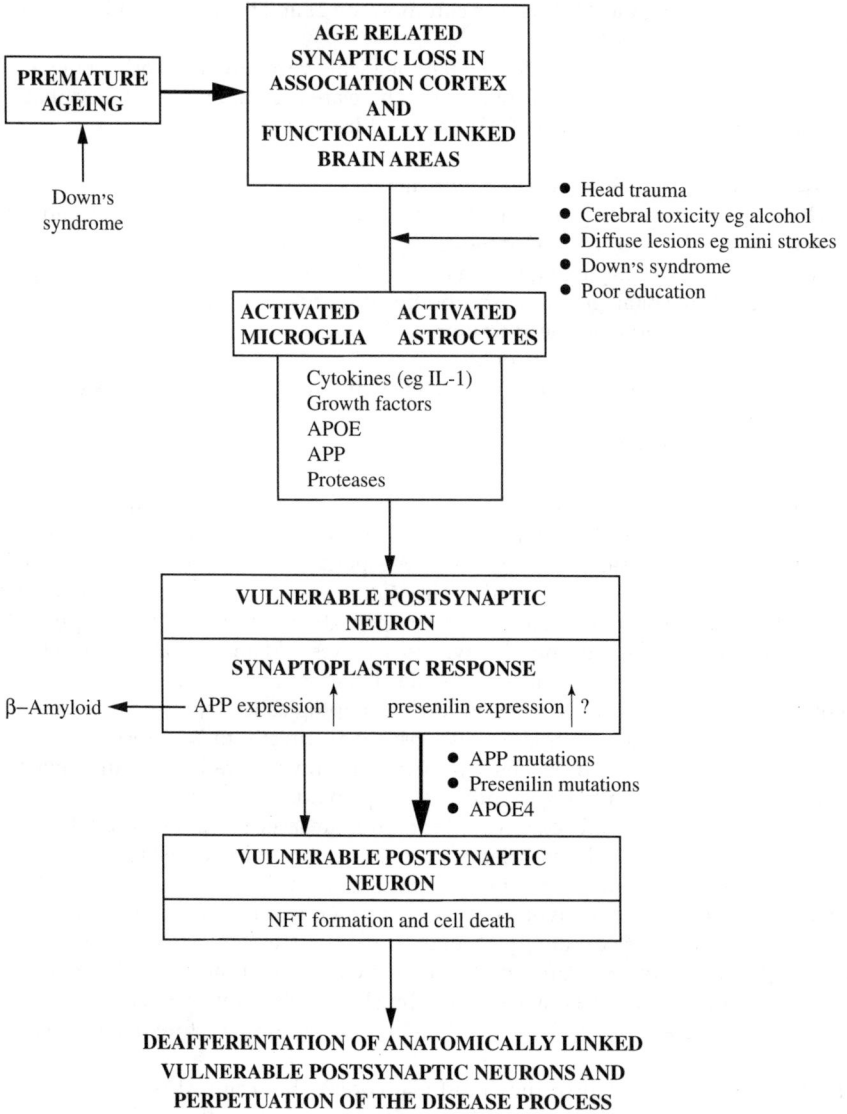

Figure 27.1. Alzheimer's disease: maladaptive synaptoplasticity hypothesis.

Fundamental support for a maladaptive synaptoplastic response in AD is the fact that all genetic susceptibility and causative factors appear to have roles in neuritic growth, a prerequisite for new synapse formation, with the AD-associated forms being detrimental to this process. APOE is abundant in the brain being synthesized and secreted by astrocytes (Boyles, Pites, Wilson, Manley, & Taylor, 1985). Within the brain, APOE has a major role in neuritic growth and synaptogenesis via facilitating the transport of phospholipids and cholesterol into neurons (Poirier, Minnich, & Davignon, 1995). The AD-associated E4 isoform has been demonstrated to be less effective at promoting neurite extension than the E3 isoform (Neill, 1995). APOE-deficient mice, with advancing age, have been shown to lose nerve terminals and dendrites in the neocortex and hippocampus (Masliah et al., 1995). Arendt et al (1997) have also demonstrated that AD patients with an APOE ε4 allele, compared to AD patients with ε3 alleles, have impaired dendritic remodeling. APP is developmentally regulated, with maximum expression coinciding with synaptogenesis (Neill, 1995). In the mature brain APP continues to be expressed at high levels in areas that retain high levels of synaptoplasticity (Loffler & Huber, 1992). It is located at synaptic sites and shows a similar distribution to GAP43 (Neill, 1995). Its expression increases during neural lesions in the CNS (Leanza, 1998) and it is involved in neuritogenesis in cultured neuronal cell lines (Qiu, Ferreira, Miller, Koo, & Selkoe, 1995). Synaptoplastic roles for APP in the cortex and hippocampus have also been demonstrated using APP transgenic and knockout mice (Mucke et al., 1994; Seabrook et al., 1999). In AD, APP has been colocalized with GAP43 in aberrant sprouting neurites (Neill, 1995). Defective neurite extension has been associated with APP, containing AD-causing mutations (Li et al., 1997). The presenilin proteins have only recently been identified in humans. They are integral membrane proteins possessing 6–8 transmembrane domains (Doan et al., 1996). In non-neuronal cells they are found mainly in the endoplasmic reticulum, whereas, as in neurons they are also found in vesicular structures and membranes within the somatodendritic compartment (Beher et al., 1999; Capell et al., 1997). They have been implicated in developmental signaling by the cell surface protein Notch (Levitan & Greenwald, 1995). PS-1 and Notch knockout mice manifest severe developmental abnormalities, which result from defects in somite segmentation and cell differentiation (Shen et al., 1997; Wong et al., 1997). In the case of neurons their role in differentiation involves growth of neurites (Dowjat, Wisniewski, Efthimiopoulos, & Wisniewski, 1999; Furukawa, Guo, Schellenberg, & Mattson, 1998), a major requirement for compensatory synaptogenesis. They are expressed at higher levels in brain areas, such as the hippocampus and entorhinal cortex, which retain synaptoplastic potential (Lee et al., 1996). The AD-causing PS-1 mutations have been demonstrated to inhibit neuritic outgrowth (Dowjat et al., 1999; Furukawa et al., 1998).

Epidemiological and pathological studies have shown an association between AD and previous head trauma. In head trauma the orbitofrontal cortex, temporal poles, and long-projection corticocortical fibers are most susceptible to damage. As these are the same neuronal systems subject to involution in senescence, the effects on synaptic loss will be additive. This will lead to earlier development of a critical loss in synaptic density and premature malfunction of compensatory synaptoplastic mechanisms in vulnerable postsynaptic neurons (Neill, 1995; Figure 27.1).

Practically every person with Down's syndrome (DS) will develop AD pathological lesions in their brain by the fifth decade of life. In DS there is premature age-related brain atrophy and regression of the dendritic tree of cortical pyramidal neurons which starts in early childhood and continues into adulthood. This will result in a premature cortical involution, and according to the MSH will be compatible with the early development of Alzheimer's pathology in these individuals (Neill, 1995; Figure 27.1).

In addition to an association between AD and DS, there is an additional association between AD and young mothers (<35 years) that give birth to DS babies (Schupf, Kapell, Lee, Ottman, & Mayeux, 1994). The chance of conceiving a DS baby increases exponentially with maternal age. The association of young mothers that give birth to DS babies and AD may therefore relate to premature aging in the mother. This premature aging will presumably involve earlier cortical involution and hence development of AD (Figure 27.1).

Epidemiological studies have consistently shown an association between education and a lower prevalence of AD. Increased use of higher order cognitive processing could result in more extensive dendritic trees and increased number of synapses in association cortical neurons (Rutledge et al., 1974). This could delay the development of AD due to an increased synaptic reserve capacity of these neurons. Development of a critical loss in synaptic number will be delayed and may not develop within the life-span of the individual (Neill, 1995; Figure 27.1).

☐ Dysfuntional Synaptoplasticity and Schizophrenia

Schizophrenia is a common mental illness that affects some 0.85% of the population worldwide. Onset is rare before puberty, thereafter rising to a peak in the third decade of life. The onset, as well as relapses of the illness, are often provoked by stress especially in relation to social situations (Norman & Malla, 1993). It has been suggested that schizophrenia develops when the threshold for stress tolerance in a vulnerable individual has been exceeded (Zubin & Spring, 1977). Diagnosis is based on symptomatology that can be divided into two groups termed positive and negative symptoms. The positive symptoms include delusions, hallucinations, positive formal thought disorder, and bizarre behavior (Andreasen & Olsen, 1982). They have been interpreted as a failure to integrate intrinsically generated representations and concurrent perception. The negative symptoms consist of alogia, affective flattening, avolition-apathy, anhedonia-associality, and attentional impairment (Andreasen, 1982). They may develop chronically or after acute episodes of positive symptoms, accumulating until a plateau is reached, and are irreversible. The chronic handicap resulting from the irreversibility of negative symptoms is often referred to as a defect state. In general terms, approximately one third of schizophrenics develop acute episode(s) of positive symptoms from which they recover, one third continue to have repeated episodes of positive symptoms, and one third develop a deteriorating course marked by negative symptoms. Positive symptoms are more responsive to treatment with antipsychotic drugs than negative symptoms, and treatment of acute episodes of positive symptoms may prevent development of negative symptoms (Wyatt, 1991). The therapeutic action of traditional antipsychotic drugs is correlated with blockade of dopamine (D2) receptors, suggesting a role for dopaminergic systems in the disease process (Snyder, Banerjee, Yamamura, & Greenberg, 1974). Atypical antipsychotic drugs, however, have lower D2 affinities and more pronounced blockade of 5-HT2A receptors (Meltzer, 1996), suggesting that other neurotransmitter systems in addition to dopamine could be involved.

Unlike in AD, there are no diagnostic pathological lesions in the brains of schizophrenics. However, there is evidence for minor structural abnormalities in the association cortex and medial temporal lobes (Harrison, 1999). Brain imaging studies have demonstrated a 40% increase in size of the lateral and third ventricles (Lawrie & Abukmeil, 1998). This is reflected in a loss of brain tissue in association cortex and medial temporal lobe structures. Physiological brain imaging techniques (Andreasen et al., 1992) and psychological testing (Goldberg & Weinberger, 1988) have suggested prominent involvement of the prefrontal cortex. Also, negative symptoms such as poor motivation, lack of drive, and emotional blunting are similar to the clinical manifestations of frontal lobe damage (Blumer & Benson, 1975). Postmortem studies in general have confirmed the imaging findings by showing enlarged lateral ventricles and reduced size of temporal lobe structures (Harrison). The brain tissue lost would appear to be predominately gray matter as opposed to white matter (Lawrie & Abukmeil, 1998). The gray matter loss appears to be due to a reduction in neuronal size rather than number. A reduced neuronal size has been reported for pyramidal neurons in the hippocampus, subiculum, and lamina III neurons in the dorsolateral prefrontal cortex (Harrison). As perikaryal size is related to the extent of dendritic arborization, reduced arborization and hence number of synapses may be present on these pyramidal neurons. Studies of dendritic extent and concentration of synaptic marker proteins have generally supported this proposition, although there have been some negative findings (Harrison). In general these finding would support an underdevelopment or regression of pyramidal neurons in the areas of the brain such as the prefrontal cortex and functionally associated areas such as the hippocampus and entorhinal cortex. The fact that these pyramidal neurons are glutamatergic together with induction of schizophrenic-like positive symptoms by phencyclidine (indirect antagonist of NMDA glutamate receptor) suggests involvement of glutamatergic pathways in the disease process (Tamminga, 1998). The brain changes described above are present in first episode cases and would appear to be nonprogressive or at least show minimal change after the onset of illness (Harrison). They are therefore part of the disease process and not some secondary effect, for example, due to administration of antipsychotic drugs.

Schizophrenia runs in families and has a much higher concordance in monozygotic (MZ; 50%) as opposed to dizygotic (DZ; 15%) twins, indicating a genetic component to the etiology (Gottesman, 1991). Offspring of both affected and nonaffected MZ twin pairs have a similar morbid risk for schizophrenia (Gottesman & Bertelsen, 1989), suggesting differences in expressivity of a vulnerable genotype. Such differences in expressivity could relate to environmental (Waddington, 1993), epigenetic, or chance events (Kurnit, Layton, & Matthysse, 1987; Woolf, 1997). In MZ twins the affected twin has larger ventricles (Suddath, Christison, Torrey, Casanova, & Weinberger, 1990) and smaller cortical and hippocampal size (Noga, Bartley, Jones, Torrey, & Weinberger, 1996), suggesting that expression of the schizophrenic genotype has led directly to these changes. Although there is likely to be a genetic influence in most cases of schizophrenia, it is possible that brain damage may be primarily responsible for some cases (Waddington, 1993; see also Figure 27.2).

Theories for the etiology of schizophrenia have to be compatible with several important facts:

1. Age of onset in early adulthood.
2. Involvement of evolutionary recent brain areas and, in particular, prefrontal cortex and functionally linked brain regions.
3. Involvement of stress in precipitation and relapse.
4. Reduced neuronal size, dendritic arborization, and synapses rather than loss of neurons.
5. Defects in item 4 above are present at onset and are not or minimally progressive.
6. Strong genetic component.
7. Environmental influences.
8. Chronicity of defect state.

To be compatible with these facts, currently proposed theories are generally based on an evolutionary framework, with some specifying specific brain developmental abnormalities in the prefrontal cortex and functionally related brain areas. Specific development insults could occur anytime from the initial stages of development right up to the completion of synaptic pruning at around the age of 16. Proposed theories include abnormal neuronal migration (Bloom, 1993), abnormal synaptic pruning (Feinberg, 1983), abnormal connectivity (Randall, 1983), and abnormal cerebral asymmetry (Crow et al., 1998). The main problem with developmental theories in general is how to explain the gap

```
                    ┌─────────────────────────────────────┐
                    │  PREFRONTAL CORTEX AND FUNCTIONALLY  │
                    │        CONNECTED BRAIN AREAS         │
         VIRUS      ├─────────────────────────────────────┤
                    │       ABNORMAL DEVELOPMENT           │◄── BRAIN DAMAGE
                    └─────────────────────────────────────┘

   ┌──────────────┐ ┌─────────────────────────────────────┐
   │   GENETIC    │ │      ABNORMAL CONNECTIVITY           │
   │VULNERABILITY │ │  NEUROTRANSMITTER IMBALANCE          │◄── BRAIN DAMAGE
   └──────────────┘ └─────────────────────────────────────┘

   CHANCE
                    ┌─────────────────────────────────────┐
                    │  PREFRONTAL CORTEX AND FUNCTIONALLY  │
                    │        CONNECTED BRAIN AREAS         │
                    ├─────────────────────────────────────┤
                    │   DYSFUNCTIONAL EXPERIENCE           │
                    │  DEPENDANT SYNAPTOPLASTICITY         │
                    └─────────────────────────────────────┘

                    ┌─────────────────────────────────────┐
                    │  PREFRONTAL CORTEX AND FUNCTIONALLY  │
                    │        CONNECTED BRAIN AREAS         │
                    ├─────────────────────────────────────┤
                    │       IMPAIRED MATURATION            │
                    └─────────────────────────────────────┘

   SOCIAL STESS ──────────►
                         ┌──────────────────┐
                         │  SCHIZOPHRENIA   │
                         └──────────────────┘
```

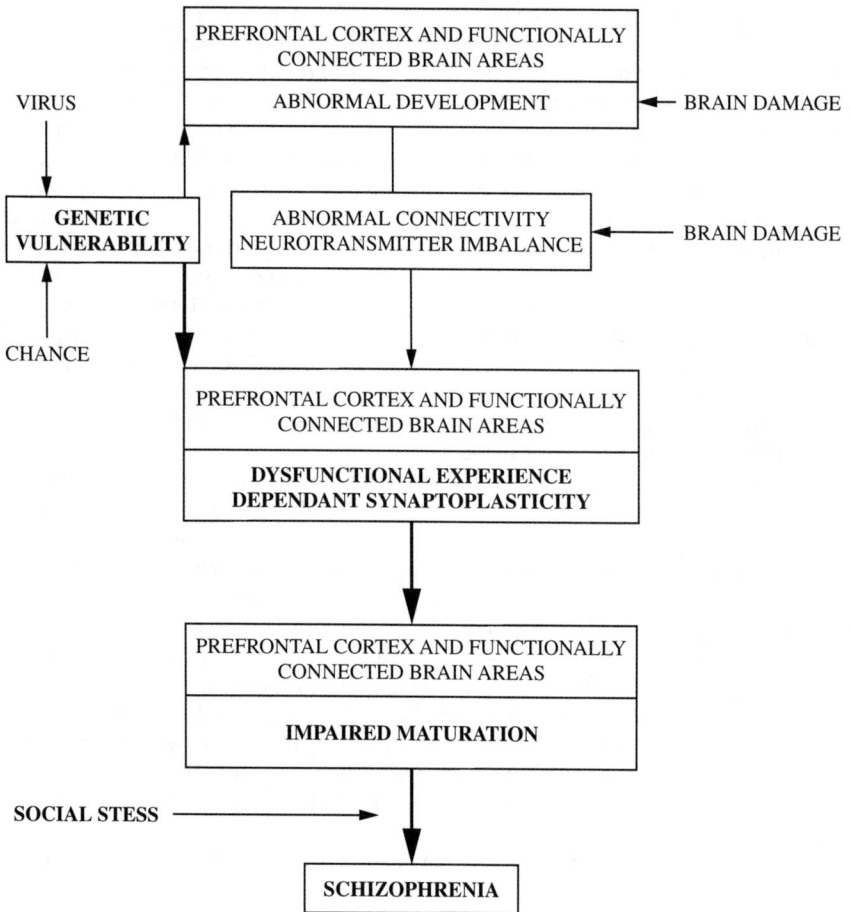

Figure 27.2. Schizophrenia: dysfunctional synaptoplasticity hypothesis.

between the developmental abnormality and the onset of schizophrenia in early adulthood. Also, in the majority of schizophrenics there is no evidence for premorbid defects, which might be expected to be present if there was a brain developmental abnormality. To circumvent these difficulties it has been suggested that schizophrenia only becomes manifest after full maturation of the brain. This was originally emphasized by Weinberger (1987), who suggested that minor developmental brain abnormalities early in life become manifest as schizophrenia after normal maturation of the dopaminergic innervation of the prefrontal cortex. Weinberger's theory is compatible with the involvement of stress in schizphrenia, as the dopaminergic systems innervating the prefrontal cortex are especially sensitive to stress (Roth, Tam, Ida, Yang, & Deutch, 1988). Weinberger proposed that schizophrenia relates to a defective input of dopamine to the prefrontal cortex, leading to a compromised ability to regulate stress. Lieberman, Sheitman, and Kinon (1997), using a similar framework to that of Weinberger's theory, has implicated sensitization in the disease process. Sensitization is a specific synaptoplastic response which relates to an augmented behavioral or motor response resulting from prior exposure to noxious stimuli. Its proposed involvement in schizophrenia is derived from its production in rodents by pharmacological agents such as dopamine, and noncompetitive NMDA antagonists, which in humans can produce delusions and hallucinations similar to those in schizophrenia. In Lieberman's theory a developmental abnormality of the cortex leads to deficient inhibitory control of the cortex on subcortical structures. This leads to sensitization by defects in the regulatory capacity of the cortex on perturbations of neuronal activity produced by stress or psychostimulant drug abuse. The defect state, according to this theory, could result from excitatory neurotoxicity which develops after prolonged sensitization. One problem with this theory is why sensitization does not lead to symptoms prior to the onset of schizophrenia in the third decade. The authors attempted to explain this by suggesting that sensitization only occurs after completion of synaptic pruning, as the increased numbers of synapses present prior to this were more able to compensate.

The implication of the evolutionary advanced prefrontal cortex and associated functional brain units in schizophrenia, together with environmental influences relating to adaptation to the complexities of human society, suggests the possibility that experience-dependent synaptoplastic mechanisms are involved in its etiology. As suggested in the MSH for AD, these synaptoplastic mechanisms may have advanced in humans, allowing for dysfunction to produce mental disorders that are human specific. The prolonged and complex development of the prefrontal cortex and associated brain functional units in humans could be considered to end, after the completion of synaptic pruning, around 16 years of age. This functional system, however, does not become static at this time, as it matures in relation to environmental exposure. This maturation involves experience-dependent synaptoplasticity, which leads to potentiation of function. This is mediated through strengthening existing synapses together with dendritic growth and new synapse formation. The dysfunction synaptoplasticity theory for schizophrenia proposes that the common underlying mechanism responsible for the development of schizophrenia is dysfunction of this maturation process (Figure 27.2). This could result in retarded growth and possibly a degree of regression. In the normally functioning system dendritic growth and new synapse formation will be paralleled by an increase in neuronal size and hence volume of the relevant brain area. Dysfunction resulting in retardation of this process would hence result in smaller dendritic arborization decrease in neuronal size and smaller volume of the relevant brain area. This is entirely compatible with pathological studies in schizophrenia, which confirm such abnormalities in the prefrontal cortex and hippocampus (Harrison, 1999). Although experience-dependent synaptoplasticity may be at its peak around late adolescence, when synaptic pruning is completed, its effects on growth retardation or regression will take time to develop. This would make this hypothesis entirely compatible with the age of onset for schizophrenia in early adulthood. The environmental exposure relevant to the maturation of the prefrontal cortex and associated functional unit will include adaptation to the complexities of human society. Adolescence to early adulthood involves leaving the protective environment of the family and having to adjust as an independent individual in society and to responsibilities such as having a job or going to university, etc. The onset of schizophrenia could occur when the inadequately matured prefrontal cortex functional unit becomes "overloaded" in a situation of acute environmental stress. The precise mechanism by which this leads to development of schizophrenic positive symptoms and to the defect state is entirely speculative at the present time. It is likely, however, that prefrontal dopaminergic and glutamatergic pathways are involved, with the effects of stress being mediated through the mesocortical dopaminergic system. One possible mechanism that has already been described is the sensitization process proposed by Leiberman et al. (1977). Genetic influences could operate by affecting experience-dependent synaptoplasticity directly or indirectly by producing minor brain developmental defects. The developmental defects could produce abnormal connectivity, which in turn could lead to neurotransmitter imbalance and dysfunction of experience-dependent synaptoplasticity. Environmental influences are entirely compatible with this theory and they could operate by several different routes which are not mutually exclusive. Experience-dependent synaptoplasticity operates through environmental exposure and, therefore, could be affected directly by inadequate or adverse environmental experience. It is unlikely that these environmental effects would be enough to produce schizophrenia themselves; however, they may contribute in a genetically vulnerable individual. Environmental influences could also operate through effects on brain development. As for genetic effects this could lead to abnormal connectivity, neurotransmitter imbalance, and hence dysfunctional synaptoplasticity. The environmental effects on brain development could be mediated through affecting the expressivity of a vulnerable genotype (e.g., an intrauterine viral infection) or via direct brain damage (e.g., obstetric complications).

In summary, the etiology of schizophrenia is likely to be multifactorial and complex. It is unlikely that any previously suggested theory is complete in itself, however certain aspects of these theories may well be involved. The present theory differs from previous theories; while accepting brain developmental contributions in some cases, it suggests that the pivotal defect is in experience-dependent synaptoplasticity leading to defective maturation of the prefrontal cortex and associated functional units. The main strength of this theory is that it is entirely compatible with age of onset of schizophrenia in the third decade of life, the brain pathology, and the involvement of social stress.

☐ References

Andreasen, N. C. (1982). Negative symptoms in schizophrenia. *Archives of General Psychiatry, 39,* 784–788.

Andreasen, N. C., & Olsen, S. (1982). Negative v positive schizophrenia: Definition and validation. *Archives of General Psychiatry, 39,* 789–794.

Andreasen, N. C., Rezai, K., Alliger, R., Swayze, V. W., Flaum, M., Kirchner, P., Cohen, G., & O'Leary, D. S. (1992). Hypofrontality in neuroleptic-naive patients and in patients with chronic schizophrenia. *Archives of General Psychiatry, 49,* 943–958.

Arendt, T., Bruckner, M. K., Gertz, H. J., & Marcova, L. (1998). Cortical distribution of neurofibrillary tangles in Alzheimer's disease matches the pattern of neurons that retain their capacity of plastic remodelling in the adult brain. *Neuroscience, 83,* 991–1002.

Arendt, T., Schindler, C., Bruckner, M. K., Eschrich, K., Bigl, V., Zedlick, D., & Marcova, L. (1997). Plastic neuronal remodeling is impaired in patients with Alzheimer's disease carrying apolipoprotein e4 allele. *Journal of Neuroscience, 17,* 516–529.

Bacci, A., Verderio, C., Pravettoni, E., & Matteoli, M. (1999). The role of glial cells in synaptic function. *Philosophical Transactions of the Royal Society of London. Series B: Biological Sciences, 354,* 403–409.

Beher, D., Elle, C., Underwood, J., Davis, J. B., Ward, R., Karran, E., Masters, C. L., Beyreuther, K., & Malthaup, G. (1999). Proteolytic fragments of Alzheimer's disease-associated presenilin 1 are present in synaptic organelles and growth cone membranes of rat brain. *Journal of Neurochemistry, 72,* 1564–1573.

Bloom, F. E. (1993). Advancing a neurodevelopmental origin for schizophrenia. *Archives of General Psychiatry, 50,* 224–227.

Blumer, D., & Benson, D. F. (1975). *Psychiatric aspects of neurologic disease: Personality changes with frontal and temporal lobe lesions.* New York: Grune and Stratton.

Boyles, J. K., Pitas, R. E., Wilson, E., Mahley, R. W., & Taylor, J. M. (1985). Apolipoprotein E associated with astrocytic glia of the central nervous system and with nonmyelinating glia of the peripheral nervous system. *Journal of Clinical Investigation, 76*, 1501–1513.

Braak, H., & Braak, E. (1991). Neuropathological staging of Alzheimer-related changes. *Acta Neuropathologica, 82*, 239–259.

Brizzee, K. R., Ordy, J. M., & Bartus, R. T. (1980). Localization of cellular changes within multimodal sensory regions in aged monkey brain: Possible implications of age related cognitive loss. *Neurobiology of Aging, 1*, 45–52.

Broadmann, K. (1912). Neue ergebnisse uber die vergleichende histolische lokalisation der grosshirnrinde. *Verhandl Anat Anz, 26*, 157–216.

Brothers, L. (1990). The social brain: A project for integrating primate behavior and neurophysiology in a new domain. *Concepts in Neuroscience, 15*, 27–51.

Byrne, R., & Whitten, A. (1988). *Machiavellian intelligence: Social expertise and the evolution of intellect in monkeys, apes and humans.* Oxford, England: Clarendon Press.

Capell, A., Saffrich, R., Olivo, J. C., Meyn, L., Walter, J., Grunber, J., Mathews, P., Nixon, R., Dotti, C., & Haass, C. (1997). Cellular expression and proteolytic processing of presenilin proteins is developmentally regulated during neuronal differentiation. *Journal of Neurochemistry, 69*, 2432–2440.

Crow, T. J., Ball, J., Bloom, S. R., Brown, R., Burton, C. J., Colter, N., Firth, C. D., Johnstone, E. C., Owens, D. G. C., & Roberts, G. W. (1998). Schizophrenia as an anomaly of development of cerebral asymmetry. *Archive of General Psychiatry, 46*, 1145–1150.

Cupp, C. J., & Uemura, E. (1980). Age-related changes in prefrontal cortex of Macaca mulatta: Quantitative analysis of dendritic branching patterns. *Experimental Neurology, 69*, 143–163.

De Bruin, J. P. C. (1990). Social behaviour and the prefrontal cortex. *Progress in Brain Research, 85*, 485–497.

Doan, A., Thinakaran, G., Borchelt, D. R., Slunt, H. H., Ratovitsky, T., Podlisny, M., Selkoe, D. J., Seeger, M., Gandy, S. E., Price, D. L., & Sisodia, S. S. (1996). Protein topology of presenilin 1. *Neuron, 17*, 1023–1030.

Dowjat, W. K., Wisniewski, T., Efthimiopoulos, S., & Wisniewski, H. M. (1999). Inhibition of neurite outgrowth by familial Alzheimer's disease-linked presenilin-1 mutations. *Neuroscience Letters, 267*, 141–144.

Ebbesson, S. O. E. (1984). Evolution and ontogeny of neural circuits. *Behavioral and Brain Sciences, 7*, 321–366.

Feinberg, I. (1983). Schizophrenia: Caused by a fault in programmed synaptic elimination during adolescence? *Journal of Psychiatric Research, 17*, 319–334.

Furukawa, K. S., Guo, Q., Schellenberg, G. D., & Mattson, M. P. (1998). Presenilin-1 mutation alters NGF-induced neurite outgrowth, calcium homeostasis, and transcription factor (AP-1) activation in PC12 cells. *Journal of Neuroscience Research, 52*, 618–624.

Geschwing, N. (1979). Specializations of the human brain. *Scientific American, 241*, 180–201.

Goldberg, T. E., & Weinberger, D. R. (1988). Probing prefrontal function in schizophrenia with neuropsychological paradigms. *Schizophrenia Bulletin, 14*, 179–183.

Goldman-Rakic, P. S. (1990). Cellular and circuit basis of working memory in prefrontal cortex of nonhuman primates. *Progress in Brain Research, 85*, 325–336.

Gomez-Isla, T., Price, J. L., McKeel, D. W., Morris, J. C., Growdon, J. H., & Hyman, B. T. (1996). Profound loss of laye II entorhinal cortex neurons occurs in very mild Alzheimer's disease. *Journal of Neuroscience, 16*, 4491–4500.

Gottesman, I. I. (1991). *Schizophrenia genesis—The origins of madness.* New York: Freeman.

Gottesman, I. I., & Bertelsen, A. (1989). Confirming unexpressed genotypes for schizophrenia. Results in the offspring of Fisher's Danish identical and fraternal discordant twins. *Archives of General Psychiatry, 46*, 867–872.

Gould, S. J. (1977). *Ontogeny and phylogeny.* Cambridge, MA: Harvard: Belknap Press.

Greenough, W. T., & Chang, F.-L. F. (1985). *Synaptic plasticity: Synaptic structural correlates of information storage in mammalian nervous systems.* New York: Guilford.

Harrison, P. J. (1999). The neuropathology of schizophrenia. A critical review of the data and their interpretation. *Brain, 122,* 593–624.

Huttenlocher, P. R. (1979). Synaptic density in human frontal cortex: Developmental changes and effects of aging. *Brain Research, 163,* 195–205.

Kurnit, D. M., Layton, W. M., & Matthysse, S. (1987). Genetics, chance, and morphogensis. *American Journal of Human Genetics, 41,* 979–995.

Lawrie, S. M., & Abukmeil, S. S. (1998). Brain abnormality in schizophrenia. A systematic and quantitative review of volumetric magnetic resonance imaging studies. *British Journal of Psychiatry, 172,* 110–120.

Leanza, G. (1998). Chronic elevation of amyloid precursor protein expression in the neocortex and hippocampus of rats with selective cholinergic lesions. *Neuroscience Letters, 257,* 53–56.

Lee, M. K., Slunt, H. H., Martin, L. J., Thinakaran, G., Kim, G., Gandy, S. E., Seeger, M., Koo, E., Price, D. L., & Sisodia, S. S. (1996). Expression of presenilin 1 and 2 (PS1 and PS2) in human and murine tissue. *Journal of Neuroscience, 16,* 7513–7525.

Levitan, D., & Greenwald, I. (1995). Facilitation of lin-12-mediated signalling by SEL-12, a Caenorhabditis elegans S182 Alzheimer's disease gene. *Nature, 377,* 351–354.

Levy-Lahad, E., & Bird, T. D. (1996). Genetic factors in Alzheimer's disease: A review of recent advances. *Annals of Neurology, 40,* 829–840.

Li, H. L., Roch, J. M., Sundsmo, M., Otero, D., Sisodia, S., Thomas, R., & Saitoh, T. (1997). Defective neurite extension is caused by a mutation in amyloid b/A4 (Ab) protein precursor found in familial Alzheimer's disease. *Journal of Neurobiology, 32,* 469–480.

Lieberman, J. A., Sheitman, B. B., & Kinon, B. J. (1997). Neurochemical sensitization in the pathophysiology of schizophrenia: Deficits and dysfunction in neuronal regulation and plasticity [Review]. *Neuropsychopharmacology, 17,* 205–229.

Loffler, J., & Huber, G. (1992). b-Amyloid precursor protein isoforms in various rat brain regions and during brain development. *Journal of Neurochemistry, 59,* 1316–1324.

Masliah, E., Mallory, M., Hansen, L., Alford, M., Albright, T., DeTeresa, R., Terry, R., Baudier, J., & Saitoh, T. (1991). Patterns of aberrant sprouting in Alzheimer's disease. *Neuron, 6,* 729–739.

Masliah, E., Mallory, M., Ge, N., Alford, M., Veinbergs, I., & Roses, A. D. (1995). Neurodegeneration in the central nervous system of apoE deficient mice. *Experimental Neurology, 136,* 107–122.

Meltzer, H. (1996). Pre-clinical pharmacology of atypical antipsychotic drugs: A selective review. *British Journal of Psychiatry, 168 (suppl),* 23–31.

Mucke, L., Masliah, E., Johnson, W. B., Ruppe, M. D., Alford, M., Rockenstein, E. M., Forss-Petter, S., Pietropaolo, M., Mallory, M., & Abraham, C. R. (1994). Synaptotrophic effects of human amyloid b protein precursors in the cortex of transgenic mice. *Brain Research, 666,* 151–167.

Neill, D. (1995). Alzheimer's disease: 'Maladaptive Synaptoplasticity Hypothesis'. *Neurodegeneration, 4,* 217–232.

Neve, L. N., Finch, E. A., Bird, E. D., & Benowitz, L. (1988). Growth-associated protein GAP-43 is expressed selectively in associative regions of the adult human brain. *Proceedings of the National Academy of Sciences of the United States of America, 85,* 3638–3642.

Noga, J. T., Bartley, A. J., Jones, D. W., Torrey, E. F., & Weinberger, D. R. (1996). Cortical gyral anatomy and gross brain dimensions in monozygotic twins discordant for schizophrenia. *Schizophrenia Research, 22,* 27–40.

Norman, R. M., & Malla, A. K. (1993). Stressful life events and schizophrenia. I: A review of the research. *British Journal of Psychiatry, 162,* 161–166.

Passingham, R. E. (1973). Anatomical differences between the neocortex of man and other primates. *Brain, Behavior and Evolution, 7,* 337–359.

Piaget, J. (1963). *The origins of intelligence in children.* New York: Norton.

Poirier, J., Minnich, A., & Davignon, J. (1995). Apolipoprotein E, synaptic plasticity and Alzheimer's disease. *Annals of Medicine, 27,* 663–670.

Qiu, Q. W., Ferreira, A., Miller, C., Koo, E. H., & Selkoe, D. J. (1995). Cell-surface b-amyloid precursor protein stimulates neurite outgrowth of hippocampal neurons in an isoform-dependent manner. *Journal of Neuroscience, 15,* 2157–2167.

Rakic, P. (1988). Specification of cerebral cortical areas. *Science, 227,* 154–156.

Randall, P. L. (1983). Schizophrenia, abnormal connection, and brain evolution. *Medical Hypothesis, 10,* 247–280.

Rapoport, S. I. (1990). Integrated phylogeny of the primate brain, with special reference to humans and their diseases. *Brain Research Review, 15,* 267–294.

Reichenbach, A. (1989). Glia-Neuron Index: Review and hypothesis to account for different values in various mammals. *Glia, 2,* 71–77.

Roses, A. D. (1994). Apolipoprotein E affects the rate of Alzheimer's disease expression: Beta-amyloid burden is a secondary consequence dependant of ApoE genotype and duration of disease. *Journal of Neuropathology and Experimental Neurology, 53,* 429–437.

Roth, R. H., Tam, S. Y., Ida, Y., Yang, J. X., & Deutch, A. Y. (1988). Stress and the mesocorticolimbic dopamine system. *Annals of the New York Academy of Sciences, 537,* 138–147.

Rutledge, L. T., Wright, C., & Duncan, J. (1974). Morphological changes in pyramidal cells of mammalian neocortex associated with increased use. *Experimental Neurology, 44,* 209–228.

Saunders, A. M., Strittmatter, W. J., Schmechel, D., St. George-Hyslop, P. H., Pericak-Vance, M. A., Joo, S. H., Rosi, B. L., Gusella, J. F., Crapper-MacLachlan, D. R., Alberts, M. J., Huletts, C., Crain, B., Goldgaber, D., & Roses, A. D. (1993). Association of apolipoprotein E allele e4 with late-onset familial and sproadic Alzheimer's disease. *Neurology, 43,* 1467–1473.

Schupf, N., Kapell, D., Lee, J. H., Ottman, R., & Mayeux, R. (1994). Increased risk of Alzheimer's disease in mothers of adults with Down's syndrome. *Lancet, 344,* 353–356.

Seabrook, G. R., Smith, D. W., Bowery, B. J., Easter, A., Reynolds, T., Fitzjohn, S. M., Morton, R. A., Zheng, H., Dawson, G. R., Sirinathsinghji, D. J. S., Davies, C. H., Collingridge, G. L., & Hill, R. G. (1999). Mechanisms contributing to the deficits in hippocampal synaptic plasticity in mice lacking amyloid precursor protein. *Neuropharmacology, 38,* 349–359.

Shen, J., Bronson, R. T., Chen, D. F., Xia, W., Selkoe, D. J., & Tonegawa, S. (1997). Skeletal and CNS defects in Presenilin-1-deficient mice. *Cell, 89,* 629–639.

Sirevaag, A. M., & Greenough, W. T. (1991). Plasticity of GFAP-immunoreactive astrocyte size and number in visual cortex of rats reared in complex environments. *Brain Research, 540,* 273–278.

Snyder, S. H., Banerjee, S. P., Yamamura, H. I., & Greenberg, D. (1974). Drugs, neurotransmitters, and schizophrenia. *Science, 184,* 1243–1253.

Suddath, R. L., Christison, G. W., Torrey, E. F., Casanova, M. F., & Weinberger, D. R. (1990). Anatomical abnormalities in the brains of monozygotic twins discordant for schizophrenia. *New England Journal of Medicine, 322,* 789–794.

Tamminga, C. A. (1998). Schizophrenia and glutamatergic transmission. *Critical Reviews in Neurobiology, 12,* 21–36.

Uylings, H. B., Kuypers, K., Diamond, M. C., & Veltman, W. A. (1978). Effects of differential environments on plasticity of dendrites of cortical pyramidal neurons in adult rats. *Experimental Neurology, 62,* 658–677.

Waddington, J. (1993). Schizophrenia: Developmental neuroscience and pathobiology. *Lancet, 341,* 531–535.

Weinberger, D. R. (1987). Implications of normal brain development for the pathogenesis of schizophrenia. *Archives of General Psychiatry, 44,* 660–669.

Wong, P. C., Zheng, H., Chen, H., Becher, M. W., Sirinathsinghji, D. J. S., Trembauer, M. E., Chen, H. Y., Price, D. L., Van der Ploeg, L. H. T., & Sisodia, S. S. (1997). Presenilin 1 is required for Notch 1 and Dll1 expression in the paraxial mesoderm. *Nature, 387,* 288–292.

Woolf, C. M. (1997). Does the genotype for schizophrenia often remain unexpressed because of canalization and stochastic events during development? *Psychological Medicine, 27,* 659–668.

Wyatt, R. L. (1991). Neuroleptics and the natural course of schizophrenia. *Schizophrenia Bulletin, 17,* 325–351.

Yakovlev, P. T., & Lecours, A-R. (1967). *Regional development of the brain in early life: The myelogenetic cycles of regional maturation of the brain.* Philadelphia: Davis.

Zubin, J., & Spring, B. (1977). Vulnerability—a new view of schizophrenia. *Journal of Abnormal Psychology, 86,* 103–126.

Mark P. Mattson
Wenzhen Duan
Sic L. Chan
Zhihong Guo

Apoptotic and Antiapoptotic Signaling at the Synapse: From Adaptive Plasticity to Neurodegenerative Disorders

☐ Neuronal Life and Death Signals: All Roads Pass Through the Synapse

The synapse is a highly complex, finely tuned, and integrated signal transduction machine. The most heavily studied categories of signaling pathways engaged at the synapse are those that involve neurotransmitters and neurotrophic factors. Activation of such neurotransmitter and neurotrophic factor signaling pathways has been shown to play an important role in synaptogenesis (Martinez et al., 1998; Mattson, 1988), fast synaptic transmission (Edwards, 1995; Levine, Dreyfus, Black, & Plummer, 1995), long-term changes in synaptic function (Albensi & Mattson, 1999; Figurov, Pozzo-Miller, Olafsson, Wang, & Lu, 1996), synaptic degeneration/pruning (Mattson, 1988; Mattson, Keller, & Begley, 1998), and cell death (Mattson, 1988; Mattson & Furukawa, 1996; Oppenheim, 1991). It is well established that activity in neuronal circuits plays a major role in synaptic organization and programmed neuronal death during development of the nervous system and that synaptic signals involving neurotransmitters and neurotrophic factors are key mediators of activity-dependent neuronal plasticity (Purves, Snider, & Voyvodic, 1988). Programmed cell death in neurons, a form of apoptosis that occurs during development, appears to be controlled by synaptic signaling. Neurons that receive at least a threshold level of activation of neurotrophic factor receptors in presynaptic terminals survive, whereas neurons not receiving sufficient target-derived trophic factor undergo apoptosis. On the other hand, overactivation of glutamate receptors located in postsynaptic regions of dendrites may trigger neuronal death, particularly when levels of neurotrophic factors are low (see Mattson, 1996).

There are many lessons to be learned from studies of mechanisms of neuronal plasticity and death on both ends of life. The mature nervous system is relatively stable with regard to the number of neurons it contains and their synaptic connectivity. Subtle changes in synaptic structure do occur in the healthy adult nervous system and such changes appear to subserve adaptive processes such as learning and memory (Jones, Klintsova, Kilman, Sirevaag, & Greenough, 1997). Unfortunately, the structure and adaptive plasticity of neuronal circuits is often disrupted by disease and the aging process. Indeed, neurodegenerative disorders are defined by the loss of synapses and death of neurons in specific regions of the nervous system. For example, Alzheimer's disease (AD) involves degeneration of neurons in the hippocampus and connected cortical regions (Braak & Braak, 1991); Parkinson's disease (PD) results from degeneration of dopaminergic neurons in the substantia nigra (Marsden, 1994); and amyotrophic lateral sclerosis (ALS) involves degeneration of spinal cord motor neurons (Tandan & Bradley, 1985). Aberrancies in the same synaptic signal transduction pathways that sculpt neuronal architecture and connectivity during development and adult plasticity appear to be central to synaptic degeneration and neuronal death in neurodegenerative disorders (see Mattson, 1989, for review).

Until recently the concept of a development–adult plasticity–cell death signaling continuum was based largely on experimental cell culture and animal models that suggested important roles for neurotrophic factors (particularly nerve growth factor and basic fibroblast growth factor) and neurotransmitters (particularly glutamate) in regulating neuronal plasticity and survival (see Mattson, 1988; Mattson & Lindvall, 1997, for review). During the past few years, however, more direct evidence has been obtained that better defines the specific molecular and biochemical bases of synaptic degeneration and neuronal death in various neurodegenerative disorders. The present chapter describes some of these new findings with a focus on "apoptotic" and "anti-apoptotic" signaling pathways and their roles in modulating synaptic plasticity and cell death. The general theme of this chapter is that neuronal plasticity and survival are regulated by the interactions of "apoptotic" and "antiapoptotic" signaling pathways in a manner that normally allows for adaptive changes in neuronal connectivity (Figure 28.1). In this view, physiological and pathological neuronal degeneration occurs when the degenerative cascades become predominant and/or anti-apoptotic signaling is insufficient.

☐ Programmed Cell Death: Classic and Revised Views of Apoptosis

The bulk of evidence that apoptosis is an "active" process comes from studies of a few model systems in which it was reported that RNA synthesis inhibitors (e.g., actinomycin D) and protein synthesis inhibitors (e.g., cycloheximide) prevent neuronal death. For example, Johnson and colleagues found that such macromolecular synthesis inhibitors can delay the death of cultured rat sympathetic neurons following withdrawal of nerve growth factor (Martin et al., 1988). However, more recent findings have clearly shown that gene transcription is not required for cell death in many paradigms of neuronal apoptosis and that protein synthesis is only required in some cases (Mattson & Furukawa, 1996). Rapid progress in elucidating the molecular and biochemical underpinnings of apoptotic cell death has been of great value in advancing our understanding of developmental and pathological neuronal death and, as will be discussed below, is providing novel insight into mechanisms that regulate the synaptic plasticity–cell death continuum.

ANTI-APOPTOTIC   SIGNALS
Neurotrophic   Factors
Cytokines
Antioxidant   Enzymes
Calcium-Regulating   Proteins
Protective   Bcl-2   Members
Telomerase

DEVELOPMENT

ADULT   PLASTICITY

APOPTOTIC   SIGNALS
Reduced   Trophic   Support
Glutamate
Reactive   Oxygen   Species
Caspases
Death-inducing   Bcl-2   members
Decreased   Telomerase

NEURODEGENERATIVE
DISORDERS

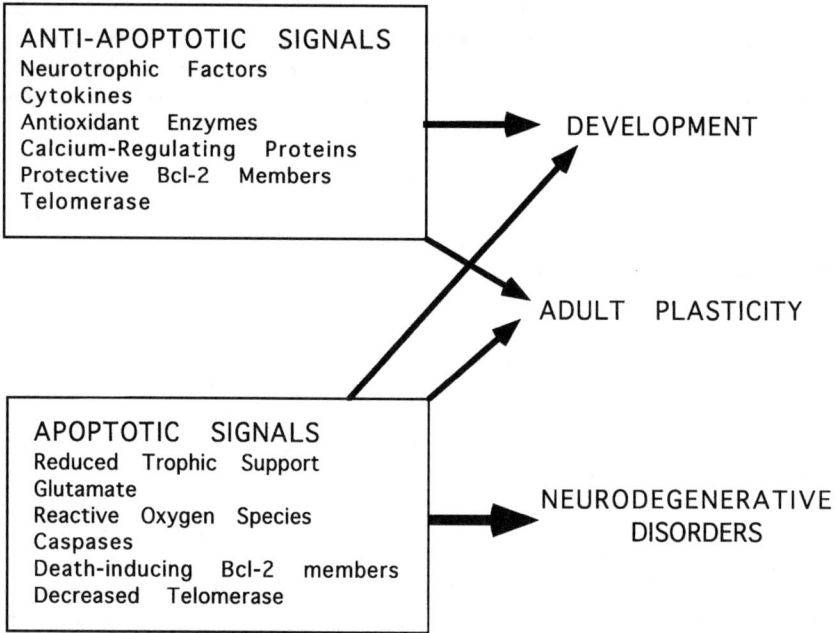

Figure 28.1. Regulation of development, plasticity, and degeneration of neuronal circuits by interactions of apoptotic and antiapoptotic signals.

Morphological and Biochemical Features of Apoptosis

A combination of morphological and biochemical criteria are used to define the form of cell death called apoptosis (Pettmann & Henderson, 1998; Wyllie, Kerr, & Currie, 1990). The morphological characteristics of apoptosis include plasma membrane blebbing, nuclear DNA condensation and fragmentation, and maintenance of organellar integrity. Biochemical alterations in cells undergoing apoptosis include loss of plasma membrane phospholipid asymmetry, mitochondrial membrane depolarization and oxyradical production, activation of one or more cysteine proteases of the caspase family, cellular calcium overload (in many cases), and release of factors from mitochondria that can induce nuclear chromatin condensation and DNA fragmentation (see Bredesen, 1995; Kroemer, Zamzami, & Susin, 1997, for review). Apoptosis is distinct from necrosis in that necrosis involves cell swelling, loss of organellar integrity, lack of caspase activation and nuclear DNA condensation and fragmentation (in most cases), and cell lysis. Another important distinction between apoptosis and necrosis is that apoptotic cells are removed (by macrophages and microglia) without adversely affecting neighbor cells, whereas necrotic cells release toxic substances and elicit an immune response that results in destruction of neighboring cells. Neuronal deaths that occur during development of the nervous system (Oppenheim, 1991) and in several different neurodegenerative disorders including stroke (Linnik, Zobrist, & Hatfield, 1993; MacManus, Buchan, Hill, Rasquinha, & Preston, 1993; Nitatori et al., 1995), AD (Guo, Fu et al., 1998; Kruman, Bruce-Keller, Bredesen, Waeg, & Mattson, 1997), and Huntington's disease (Portera-Cailliau, Hedreen, Price, & Koliatsos, 1995) fullfill the criteria of apoptosis. Cell culture and in vivo studies of experimental models of developmental neuronal death and of

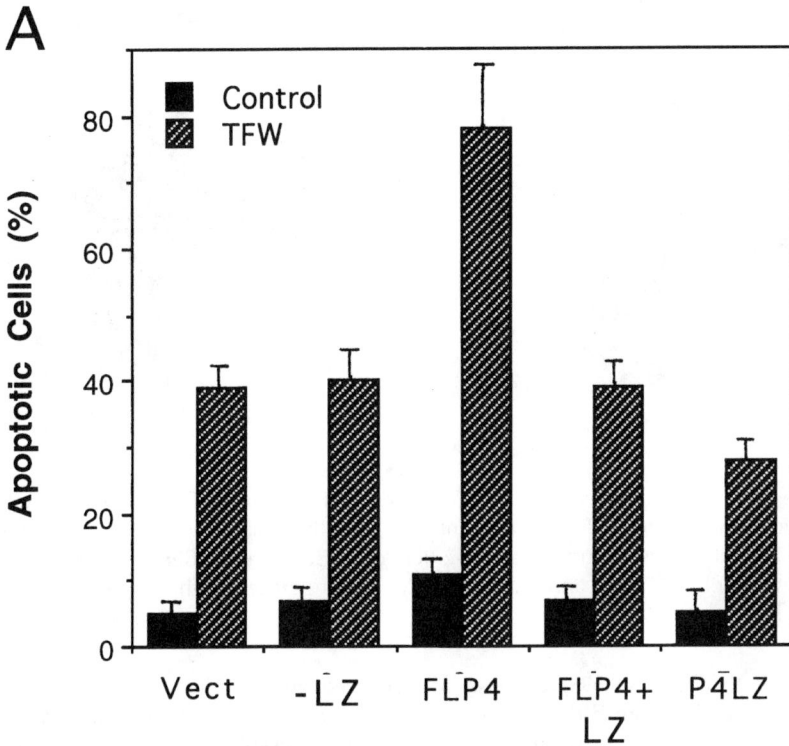

Figure 28.2. The leucine zipper domain is required for the function of Par-4 in neuronal apoptosis. Cultures of the indicated PC12 cell clones (Vect, vector-transfected cells; -LZ, cells overexpressing Par-4 lacking the leucine zipper domain; FLP4, cells overexpressing full-length Par-4; FLP4+LZ, cells overexpressing both full-length Par-4 and the Par-4 leucine zipper domain; P4LZ, cells overexpressing the Par-4 leucine zipper domain) were maintained in the presence of serum (Control) or were subjected to serum withdrawal (TFW) for 48 h. The percentage of cells with apoptotic nuclei in each culture was quantified. Values are the mean and SE of determinations made in 4-6 cultures.

neurodegenerative disorders have identified several prominent triggers of neuronal apoptosis. They include: trophic factor withdrawal (Deshmukh & Johnson, 1997; Mattson & Furukawa, 1996), oxidative insults (Keller, Kindy et al., 1998; Mattson, Goodman, Luo, Fu, & Furukawa, 1997), metabolic compromise (Keller, Guo, Holtsberg, Bruce-Keller, & Mattson, 1998; Pang & Geddes, 1997), overactivation of glutamate receptors (Ankarcrona et al., 1995; Tenneti, D'Emilia, Troy, & Lipton, 1998), and exposure to bacterial toxins such as staurosporine (Koh et al., 1995; Kruman, Guo, & Mattson, 1998).

Several proteins have been shown to play central roles in either effecting or preventing neuronal apoptosis. They include caspases such as caspases 1, 2, 3, and 8 (Dodel et al., 1999; Mattson, Keller et al., 1998), Bcl-2 and related proteins such as Bax and Bad (Datta, Dudek et al., 1997; Johnson et al., 1998; Xiang et al., 1998), prostate apoptosis response-4 (Par-4; Guo, Fu et al., 1998), p53 (Johnson et al., 1998; Xiang et al., 1998), and cytochrome C (Neame, Rubin, & Philpott, 1998) and Apaf-1 (Cecconi, Alvarez-Bolado,

Bcl-2

PKCzeta

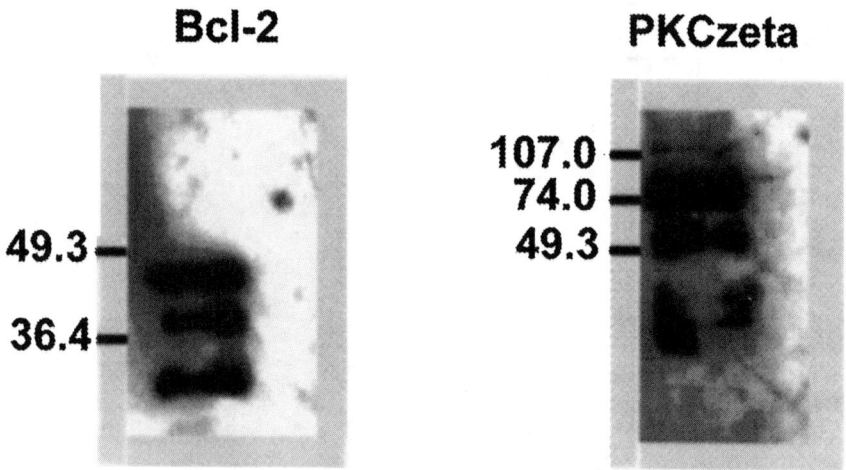

49.3—

36.4—

107.0 —
74.0 —
49.3 —

Figure 28.3. Par-4 interacts with Bcl-2 and PKCzeta. Proteins in PC12 cell homogenates were immunoprecipitated with Par-4 antibody, and then subjected to Western blot analysis using antibodies against either Bcl-2 (left) or PKCzeta (right). Bands corresponding to full-length Bcl-2 (26 kDa) and PKCzeta (76 kDa) were present in the respective immunoprecipitates.

Meyer, Roth, & Gruss, 1998). Caspases are activated, and caspase inhibitors clearly prevent cell death, in many different paradigms of neuronal apoptosis (see Chan & Mattson, 1999, for review). A rapidly growing number of caspase substrates are being identified and include procaspases (Nunez, Benedict, Hu, & Inohara, 1998), cytoskeletal proteins such as actin and spectrin (Cryns, Bergeron, Zhu, Li, & Yuan, 1996; Mashima et al., 1997), Bcl-2 family members (E. H. Cheng et al., 1997), protein kinases (Datta, Kojima, Yoshida, & Kufe, 1997; McGinnis, Whitton, Gnegy, & Wang, 1998), glutamate receptor subunits (Chan, Griffin, & Mattson, 1999), and disease-related proteins such as the Alzheimer amyloid precursor protein (Barnes et al., 1998) and presenilins (Kim, Pettingell, Jung, Kovacs, & Tanzi, 1997). Cleavage of some caspase substrates (e.g., actin and nuclear lamins) cause morphological changes associated with apoptosis (e.g., nuclear disintigration and membrane blebbing), while cleavage of other substrates (e.g., glutamate receptor subunits and Bcl-2) may modulate biochemical processes that regulate the apoptotic cascade (e.g., calcium influx and mitochondrial function).

Triggers of Neuronal Apoptosis

Oxidative stress and perturbed neuronal calcium homeostasis have long been implicated in neuronal degeneration that occurs in many different settings. For example, sustained elevations of intracellular calcium levels and increased oxyradical production occur in neurons in cell culture and in vivo models of excitotoxic and ischemic brain injury (Mattson, Lovell, Furukawa, & Markesbery, 1995). Such aberrant calcium homeostasis and free radical metabolism is central to the cell death process because agents that stabilize calcium homeostasis and antioxidants can prevent neuronal death in these models. Studies of postmortem brain tissue from AD patients have provided evidence for increased oxidative stress and intracellular calcium levels in degenerating neurons (Lovell, Ehmann, Mattson, & Markesbery, 1997; Nixon et al., 1994). Experimental models of AD support roles for oxidative stress and dysregulation of calcium homeostasis in the neurodegenerative process (Goodman and Mattson, 1994; Mark, Hensley, Butterfield, & Mattson, 1995). Studies of developmental neuronal apoptosis support the involvement of oxidative stress (Greenlund, Deckwerth, & Johnson, 1995) and perturbed calcium homeostasis (Mattson et al., 1989). Indeed, two major mechanisms whereby neurotrophic factors prevent neuronal apoptosis are by stabilizing calcium homeostasis (B. Cheng & Mattson, 1991) and suppressing oxyradical production (Mattson et al., 1995).

Alterations in many different signaling pathways can result in disruption of neuronal calcium homeostasis and increased oxyradical production. Receiving much attention in this regard is the excitatory neurotransmitter glutamate, which activates receptors linked to calcium influx. Overactivation of glutamate receptors, particularly under conditions of impaired energy availability and oxidative stress, can result in neuronal calcium overload and either apoptosis or necrosis (Ankarcrona et al., 1995). Activation of glutamate receptors may contribute to neuronal apoptosis during development of the nervous system (Mattson et al., 1989) and to disorders ranging from stroke (Linnik et al., 1993) to AD (Mattson, Barger et al., 1993) to ALS (Rothstein, 1995). The discovery that neurotrophic factors (e.g., bFGF, NGF, BDNF, and IGFs) can protect neurons against excitotoxic and oxidative insults (see Mattson & Furukawa, 1996; Mattson & Lindvall, 1997, for review) led to the elucidation of the underlying mechanisms. It was found that neurotrophic factors can modulate the expression of several different calcium-regulating proteins (e.g., calcium-binding proteins and glutamate receptor subunits; B. Cheng, Christakos, & Mattson, 1994; Mattson, Kumar, Cheng, Wang, & Michaelis, 1993) and antioxidant enzymes (Mattson et al., 1995, 1997). The latter findings suggest that disengagement of neurotrophic factor signaling pathways may promote neuronal death by impairing the ability of the neurons to regulate calcium homeostasis and free radical metabolism. Another emerging signaling pathway that regulates neuronal survival involves membrane proteins called integrins that mediate cell-substrate and cell-cell interactions. Engagement of integrins activates a signaling pathway involving an enzyme called focal adhesion kinase. We have found that such integrin-mediated signaling can reduce neuronal vulnerability to excitotoxicity and apoptosis by a mechanism involving stabilization of calcium homeostasis (Gary & Mattson, 1998). As is the case with glutamate and neurotrophic factor signaling pathways, the components of the integrin signaling pathway are highly concentrated in synaptic terminals.

How do calcium and oxyradicals induce neuronal apoptosis? Calcium activates proteases, including caspases and calpains, which then cleave various substrates resulting in cell degeneration (Chan & Mattson, 1999). Importantly, calcium and oxyradicals interact in a cross-amplifying manner such that increased oxidative stress disrupts calcium homeostasis, and increased intracellular calcium levels induce oxyradical production (Mark, Pang, Geddes, Uchida, & Mattson, 1997; Mattson et al., 1995). Calcium and oxyradicals adversely affect mitochondria, resulting in mitochondrial membrane depolarization and generation of apoptotic factors (Keller, Kindy et al., 1998; Kruman, Pang, Geddes, & Mattson, 1999).

☐ Programmed Cell Life: The Emerging View of Antiapoptotic Signaling

From an evolutionary perspective it makes sense that the nervous system would have developed a variety of mechanisms that guard against unwanted neuronal degeneration. One view of neuronal apoptosis is that it occurs only when such antiapoptotic signaling pathways are insufficiently activated or overwhelmed by adverse environmental conditions. Recent advances in our understanding of the specific mechanisms whereby antiapoptotic signals act are enhancing our understanding of both apoptosis and synaptic plasticity.

Transcription-Dependent Life Programs

Among antiapoptotic signaling pathways, those activated by neurotrophic factors and cytokines have been the most heavily studied. Neurotrophins (NGF, BDNF, NT-3, NT4/5), basic fibroblast growth factor (bFGF), and insulin-like growth factor-1 (IGF-1) activate receptors with intrinsic tyrosine kinase activity. Each of these neurotrophic factors can protect cultured neurons against various apoptotic insults (e.g., oxidative, metabolic, and excitotoxic insults) by mechanisms involving stabilization of cellular calcium homeostasis and suppression of oxyradical production (B. Cheng & Mattson, 1991; Mattson et al., 1989; Mattson et al., 1995). By preventing the calcium overload and oxyradical production the neurotrophic factors suppress the apoptotic process at an early step, prior to mitochondrial dysfunction and caspase activation. A major mechanism whereby neurotrophic factors prevent apoptosis is by modulating expression of genes that encode proteins involved in calcium regulation and free radical metabolism (Keller, Guo et al., 1998; Mattson et al., 1995). For example, bFGF suppresses the expression of an N-methl-D-aspartate (NMDA) receptor protein (Mattson, Kumar et al., 1993) and increases expression of a non-NMDA receptor protein (B. Cheng et al., 1995), in cultured hippocampal neurons. Basic FGF also induces the expression of the antioxidant enzyme Cu/Zn-SOD (Mattson et al., 1995).

Cyokines also modulate neuronal apoptosis by transcription-mediated mechanisms. For example, the cytokine tumor necrosis factor-α (TNF) can prevent neuronal excitotoxicity and apoptosis (Mattson, Culmsee, Yu, & Camandola, 1999). Pretreatment of cultured rat hippocampal neurons with TNF results in increased resistance to excitotoxicity (B. Cheng et al., 1994) and apoptosis induced by exposure to amyloid β-peptide or iron (Barger et al., 1995; Mattson et al., 1997). Studies of TNF receptor knockout mice have shown that injury-induced TNF plays a role in protecting neurons against excitotoxicity and apoptosis in vivo (Bruce et al., 1996). The mechanism whereby TNF prevents neuronal apoptosis involves activation of the transcription factor NF-κB (Barger et al., 1995; Mattson et al., 1997). TNF induces NF-κB activation in cultured neurons, and several manipulations that more directly activate NF-κB (e.g., suppression of I-κB expression or treatment of cells with C2-ceramide) mimic the excitoprotective and antiapoptotic actions of TNF (Barger et al., 1995; Goodman & Mattson, 1996). Activation of NF-κB is required for the neuroprotective actions of TNF because treatment of cells with κB decoy DNA abolishes the protective effect of TNF (Mattson et al., 1997). Neurons exhibit a constitutive level of NF-κB activity, and suppression of this basal activity enhances neuronal apoptosis (Figure 28.4). The gene targets regulated by NF-κB that may mediate its antiapoptotic actions include those encoding antioxidant enzyme manganese superoxide dismutase (Mattson et al., 1997), the calcium-binding protein calbindin D28k (B. Cheng et al., 1994), members of the inhibitor of apoptosis (IAP) family of proteins (Deveraux & Reed, 2000), and glutamate receptor subunits (Furukawa & Mattson, 1998). NF-κB appears to play a broad role in preventing neuronal apoptosis because it is activated in response to oxidative stress which occurs in both developmental and pathological neuronal apoptosis (Barger & Mattson, 1996; Guo, Robinson, & Mattson, 1998).

It is now well established that when cells are under stress they activate mechanisms designed to help them resist further stress. A classic example is the heat shock response in which cells up-regulate levels of "heat-shock proteins" such as HSP-70

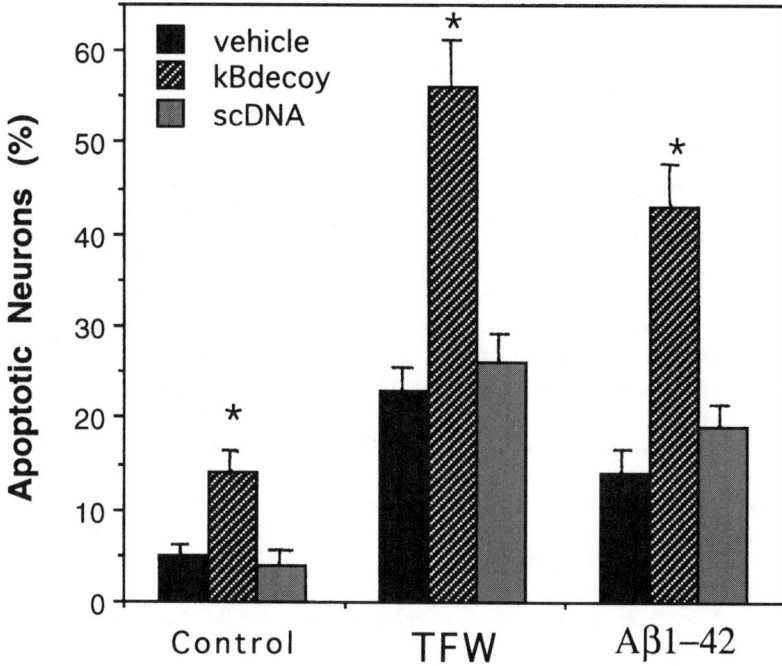

Figure 28.4. Suppression of NF-κB DNA-binding activity enhances neuronal apoptosis. Cultures of embryonic rat hippocampal neurons were pretreated for 2 h with vehicle (water), 20 μM αB decoy DNA or 20 μM scrambled DNA (scDNA). Cultures were then subjected to trophic factor withdrawal (TFW), or were exposed to 10 μM Aβ1-42 or saline (Control) for 24 h. The percentage of neurons with apoptotic nuclei in each culture was determined. Values are the mean and SE of determinations made in 4 cultures. *$p < 0.01$ compared to value for cultures treated with vehicle or scDNA.

(Latchman, 1995). Neurons respond to stressors such as increased levels of oxyradicals and metabolic compromise by increasing expression of heat-shock proteins and other cytoprotective proteins. Examples include induction of HSP-70 and GRP-78 (glucose-regulated protein 78) by excitotoxic, metabolic, and oxidative insults (Lowenstein, Chan, & Miles, 1991; Yu, Luo, Fu, & Mattson, 1999). The latter studies showed that the induction of such stress proteins protects neurons against more severe, potentially lethal insults. Increased levels of intracellular calcium levels, such as occur following overactivation of glutamate receptors, can also trigger additional protective mechanisms. For example, calcium induces activation of transcription factors such as CREB, AP-1, and NF-κB (Finkbeiner & Greenberg, 1998). These transcription factors play important roles in synaptic plasticity and in neuronal responses to injury (Deisseroth, Bito, & Tsien, 1996; Mattson, Culmsee et al., 1999).

Additional Life Programs

Several different signaling mechanisms that rapidly effect neuroprotective changes in synaptic terminals have recently been identified. It has long been recognized that activation of inhibitory neurotransmitter receptors, such as those responsive to gamma-aminobutyric acid (GABA), can protect neurons against excitotoixicty (Mattson & Kater, 1989). Similarly, activation of receptors linked to cyclic AMP production can protect neurons against death, apparently by modulating the activity of ion channels that regulate calcium influx (Mattson & Kater, 1988).

Another example includes elevation of intracellular cyclic guanosine monophosphate (GMP) levels in response to receptor activation or activation of soluble guanylate cyclase by nitric oxide. The secreted form of APP (sAPPα) induces cyclic GMP production in dissociated cell cultures and in hippocampal slices (Barger et al., 1995; Ishida, Furukawa, Keller, & Mattson, 1997). Cyclic GMP in turn activates a kinase, resulting ultimately in activation of potassium channels and membrane hyperpolarization (Furukawa, Barger, Blalock, & Mattson, 1996). The latter signaling pathway can protect synapses and neurons against excitotoxic injury (Mattson, Barger et al., 1993; Mattson, Guo, Geiger, 1999). Another rapid neuroprotective signaling pathway involves actin filaments. Calcium activates gelsolin, a protein that cleaves actin filaments. Actin depolymerization, in turn, modulates the activity of voltage-dependent calcium channels and NMDA receptors such that the channels run down more rapidly, resulting in less calcium influx (Furukawa, Fu, Witke, Kwiatkowski, & Mattson, 1997; Furukawa, Smith-Swintosky, & Mattson, 1995). A third example is the Bcl-2-mediated preservation of mitochondrial function. It was previously demonstrated that Bcl-2 associates with mitochondria and that this association is important for the antiapoptotic function of Bcl-2 (Kroemer et al., 1997). We have found that such translocation of Bcl-2 to mitochondria can occur in synaptosomes, suggesting a role for Bcl-2 in local protection of synaptic terminals.

DNA damage is an important trigger for apoptosis in many paradigms. DNA damage results in a cascade of events, including mitochondrial dysfunction and casapse activation, that culminate in cell death. The tumor suppressor gene product p53 is believed to play an important role in effecting cell death following DNA damage (Xiang et al., 1998). Telomerase is an enzyme complex consisting of a reverse transcriptase catalytic subunit, an RNA component, and several telomerase-associated proteins (Weng, Hathcock, & Hodes, 1998). The established function of telomerase is to add a six-base DNA sequence (TTAGGG) to the ends of chromosomes, which prevents their shortening and protects them against end-to-end fusion. Telomerase activity is absent or reduced in most fully differentiated cells and in association with cellular senescence, and is increased during cell transformation and immortalization. Recent findings suggest that telomerase can prevent apoptosis by a mechanism involving suppression of a death signal from the nucleus (Fu, Begley, Killen, & Mattson, 1999). Thus, telomerase inhibitors enhance apoptosis, whereas manipulations that increase telomerase activity can prevent apoptosis. The antiapoptotic action of telomerase appears to be exerted at an early step in the cell death pathway prior to mitochondrial alterations and caspase activation (Fu et al., 1999). Interestingly, telomerase activity is present in neurons during embryonic and early postnatal development, although its roles in developmental cell death are unknown.

☐ Synaptic Apoptotic and Antiapoptotic Cascades

The data described above were obtained largely in studies that examined classic cell body changes such as nuclear DNA fragmentation and mitochondrial alterations, or they involved biochemical analyses on entire cells. In our view, this focus on the cell body has (to a considerable extent) impeded progress in understanding the contributions of altered synaptic signaling to neuronal apoptosis. The relative dearth of cell death studies that examine events that occur in synapse is quite surprising in light of the compelling evidence that both developmental and pathological neuronal deaths appear to be triggered by altered signaling in synaptic compartments. Because of the evidence that signaling pathways known to be concentrated in synapses play major roles in determining whether or not a neuron lives or dies in various physiological and pathological settings, we initiated a series of experiments aimed at elucidating whether "apoptotic" cascades occur locally in synaptic terminals and whether such cascades play roles in synaptic plasticity and degeneration.

Dogma in the natural neuronal death field is that a critical determinant of neuronal life or death is whether or not a neuron receives a sufficient level of survival signals from the target cells they innervate. In the case of sympathetic neurons, for example, target-derived nerve growth factor (NGF) activates receptors in axonal terminals that communicate a "life" signal to the cell body; accordingly, neurons in which the NGF signaling cascade is not sufficiently activated undergo apoptosis. There are several general ways in which lack of trophic signaling in a presynaptic terminal might lead to neuronal cell death (Figure 28.5). One possibility is that the lack of neurotrophic factor engagement of receptors results in a signal that is transmitted to the cell body that therein initiates the apoptotic cascade. A second possibility is that the apoptotic machinery is activated locally in the axon terminal and that the apoptotic changes then spread to the cell body. Although very little information is available on this topic, data emerging from our studies suggest that the apoptotic events are activated first within the axon following trophic factor withdrawal. When placed in culture, primary embryonic rat hippocampal neurons establish a distinct polarity, with one process differentiating into an axon and the other processes differentiating into dendrites. These neurons undergo apoptosis when deprived of trophic factors, and such apoptosis can be suppressed by caspase inhibitors (Chan, Tammariello, Estus, & Mattson, 1999). Using a novel in situ method for localization and quantification of activated caspase-3 (Mattson, Keller et al., 1998), we have found that caspase activation occurs in the axon of hippocampal neurons following trophic factor withdrawal (Mattson & Duan, 1999). Analysis of data from a time course study indicates that caspase activation occurs first in the axon and then "propagates" to the cell body.

Additional data suggest that apoptotic cascades can be activated in postsynaptic terminals. Par-4 (a protein that appears to play an early and pivotal role in neuronal apoptosis; Guo, Fu et al., 1998) is induced at the translational level in synaptosomes exposed to apoptotic insults (Duan, Rangnekar, & Mattson, 1999). The apoptotic insults also induce mitochondrial membrane depolarization and release of factors into the cytosol that are capable of inducing nuclear DNA condensation and fragmentation. When synaptosomes are treated with the caspase inhibitor zVAD-fmk, mitochondrial function is maintained following exposure to apoptotic insults (Mattson, Keller et al., 1998). Double-label confocal imaging of activated caspases and the synaptic vesicle-associated protein synaptophysin in cultured hippocampal neurons confirm that caspase activation can occur in presynaptic terminals following exposure of intact cells to apoptotic insults (Mattson & Duan, 1999). Similar double-labeling studies have provided evidence that Par-4 protein levels increase in presynaptic terminals of hippocampal neurons exposed to apoptotic insults (Duan, Rangnekar et al., 1999). We recently found that three different neurotrophic factors, sAPPα, activity-dependent neurotrophic factor (ADNF), and bFGF can suppress neurodegenerative cascades induced by oxidative and apoptotic insults in synaptosomes (Guo & Mattson, 1999; Mattson, Guo et al., 1999). In the case of sAPPα, the signal transduction pathway involves activation of cyclic GMP-dependent

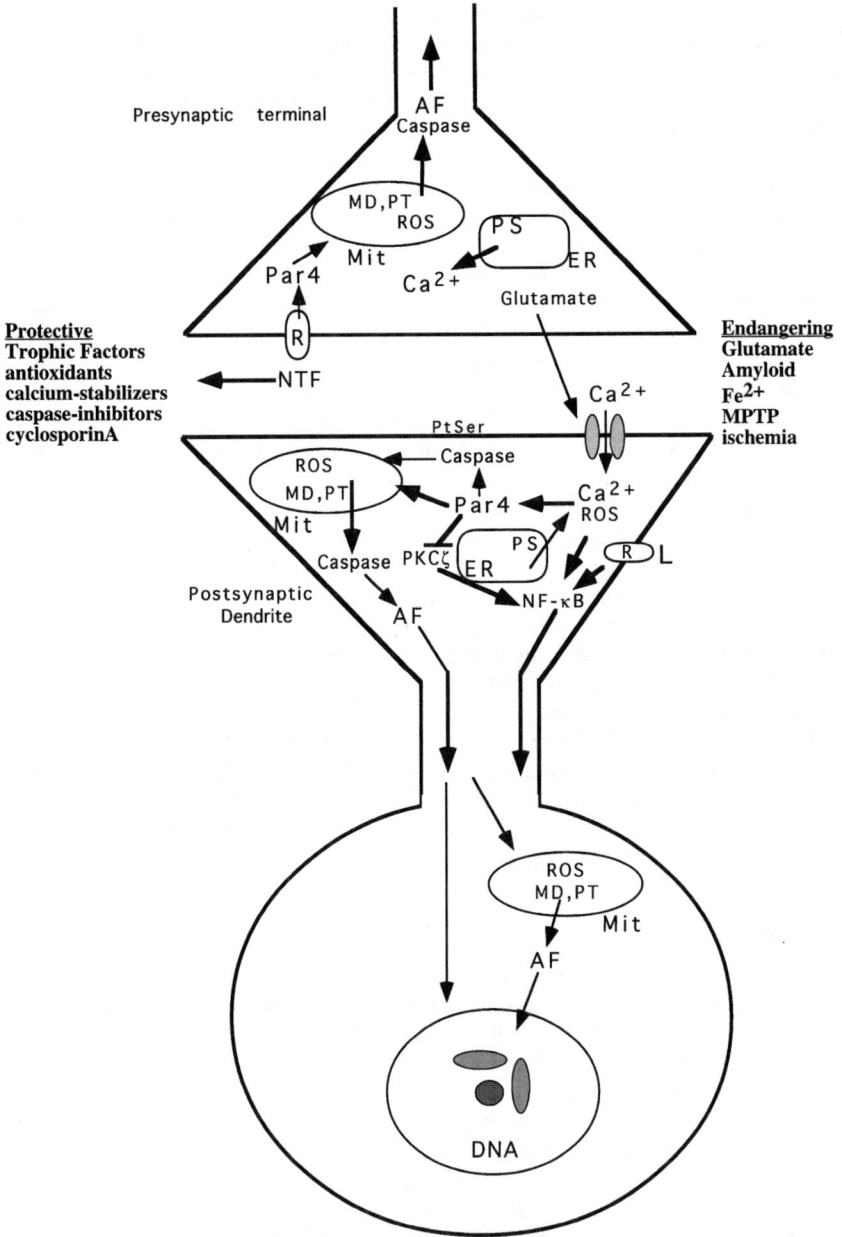

Figure 28.5. Model for regulation of synaptic remodelling and neuronal survival by synaptic signaling. See text for discussion. AF, apoptotic factor; ER, endoplasmic reticulum; L, ligand; MD, membrane depolarization; PS, presenilin; PT, permeability transition; PtSer, phosphatidylserine; R, receptor. Modified from "Evidence for Synaptic Apoptosis," by M. P. Mattson, J. N. Keller, and J. G. Begley, 1998, *Experimental Neurology, 153*, 45.

protein kinase (Mattson, Guo et al., 1999). The latter study showed that sAPPα can enhance glucose and glutamate transport in synaptosomes, indicating that this activity-dependent signal can modulate energy availability and glutamate metabolism locally in synaptic terminals.

Neuronal apoptosis can also be induced by anterograde death signals initiated in postsynaptic regions of dendrites. The best example of such a mechanism of synaptic degeneration comes from the literature on excitotoxicity, a process in which overactivation of postsynaptic glutamate receptors induces cell death (see Mattson, 1996, for review). Excessive calcium influx, increased oxidative stress, and mitochondrial dysfunction have each been implicated in the apoptosis that occurs in response to glutamate receptor overaction (Guo, Fu et al., 1999; Mattson, Kumar et al., 1993). Evidence that apoptotic cascades can be activated in dendrites comes from studies of cultured embryonic rat hippocampal neurons and cortical synaptosomes (Duan, Rangnekar et al., 1999; Mattson, Keller et al., 1998; Mattson, Partin, & Begley, 1998). The latter studies demonstrate that caspase activation occurs in dendrites following exposure of neurons to apoptotic stimuli such as staurosporine and amyloid β-peptide. Exposure of hippocampal neurons to glutamate resulted in increased caspase activation in dendrites, followed by a "spreading" of the caspase activation towards the cell body. Following exposure to glutamate, mitochondrial membrane depolarization also occurred first in dendrites and later in the cell body. Par-4 levels increase in dendrites of cultured hippocampal neurons and in cortical synaptosomes following exposure to apoptotic and oxidative insults (Duan, Rangnekar et al., 1999). The increases in Par-4 levels occur very rapidly (within 1–2 h of exposure to glutamate or amyloid β-peptide) and appear to be required for mitochondrial dysfunction in dendrites because mitochondrial function is preserved in neurons and synaptosomes treated with Par-4 antisense oligonucleotides. Further data demonstrated that Par-4 is induced at the translational level in synaptic terminals (Duan, Rangnekar et al., 1999), a finding that provides the first evidence that production of a "killer protein" can be regulated locally in synaptic terminals.

Increases in levels of intracellular calcium, and intramitochondrial calcium, are believed to play important roles in neuronal apoptosis in several different paradigms, including following overactivation of glutamate receptors and exposure to some oxidative insults (Kruman et al., 1999). Such increases in calcium levels occur most prominently in postsynaptic terminals, because that is where glutamate receptors and voltage-dependent calcium channels are concentrated. Calcium-regulating proteins are often concentrated in synaptic terminals and dendrites of neurons.

☐ Roles for Synaptic Apoptotic and Antiapoptotic Cascades in Neuronal Plasticity and Neurodegenerative Disorders

Calcium and reactive oxygen species play important roles in both synaptic plasticity and neuronal apoptosis. Postsynaptic influx of calcium, resulting from glutamate receptor activation, is required for induction of both long-term potentiation (LTP) and long-term depression (LTD; Soderling, Tan, McGlade-McCulloh, Yamamoto, & Fukunaga, 1994). Nitric oxide, an oxyradical, may play an important role in maintenance of LTP, apparently by acting as a retrograde signal that diffuses from postsynaptic cells to presynaptic terminals (Zorumski & Izumi, 1993). Both calcium and nitric oxide can also activate apoptotic cascades involving Par-4 induction, caspase activation, and mitochondrial dysfunction (Chan, Tammariello et al., 1999; Keller, Kindy et al., 1998). These observations suggest a role for apoptotic signaling in synaptic plasticity. We have recently obtained data suggesting that caspases may play roles in synaptic plasticity (Chan, Griffin et al., 1999). Two caspase substrates, actin and spectrin (Kayalar, Ord, Testa, Zhong, & Bredesen, 1996; Wang et al., 1998), may modulate synaptic plasticity (Furukawa et al., 1997; Wheal et al., 1998). A mechanism whereby cytoskeletal changes may modulate synaptic plasticity was suggested by recent studies showing that changes in actin polymerization can affect NMDA-induced currents and voltage-dependent calcium currents, and calcium responses to glutamate in cultured hippocampal neurons (Furukawa et al., 1995; Furukawa et al., 1997). Interestingly, the calcium-activated actin-severing protein gelsolin appears to serve as an important transducer of elevations of intracellular calcium levels into changes in NMDA and calcium currents (Furukawa et al., 1997).

Subunits of the AMPA type of glutamate receptor are proteolytically degraded in cultured hippocampal neurons following exposure to apoptotic insults such as trophic factor withdrawal, staurosporine, and amyloid β-peptide (Chan, Griffin et al., 1999). The caspase inhibitor zVAD-fmk prevents degradation of the AMPA receptor subunits, indicating that caspases mediate the proteolysis of the receptor subunits. Calcium imaging studies showed that a functional consequence of caspase-mediated cleavage of AMPA receptor subunits, is a decreased calcium response to glutamate (Figure 28.6). The data suggest that caspase-mediated cleavage of AMPA receptor subunits may prevent excitotoxic necrosis and thereby steer the cells to apoptosis. It remains to be established whether caspase-mediated cleavage of AMPA receptor subnits occurs during, and/or is involved in, synaptic plasticity. However, caspases can be activated in response to physiological stimuli, including membrane depolarization and glutamate receptor activation (Mattson, Partin, & Begley 1998).

Emerging findings suggest that the endoplasmic reticulum (ER) plays important roles in both synaptic plasticity and apoptosis. Studies of the mechanisms underlying LTD of synaptic transmission at climbing fiber–Purkinje cell synpases have shown that calcium release from IP3- sensitive ER stores is necessary for induction of LTD (Finch & Augustine, 1998; Takechi, Eilers, & Konnerth, 1998). The ER is present in dendritic spines, where it is positioned to modulate intracellular calcium levels locally. Studies of the pathogenic mechanism of mutations in presenilin-1 that cause early-onset autosomal dominant AD have revealed a surprising role for altered ER calcium regulation in this disorder (see Mattson & Guo, 1999, for review). Expression of presenilin-1 mutations in cultured neural cell lines and knockin mice results in increased vulnerability of the cells to apoptosis and excitotoxicity (Guo et al., 1996, 1997; Guo, Fu et al., 1999; Guo, Sebastian et al., 1999). Neurons expressing presenilin-1 mutations exhibit enhanced calcium release from ER stores following stimulation with muscarinic agonists and glutamate (Guo et al., 1996, 1997). The enhanced calcium release mediates the endangering action of the presenilin-1 mutations because treatment of cells with agents that suppress calcium release from ER (e.g., dantrolene and xestospongin) abolish the death-enhancing effect of the mutations (Guo et al., 1996, 1997; Mattson et al., 2000). Recent studies of synaptosomes from wild-type and presenilin-1 mutant transgenic mice indicate that the alteration in ER calcium homeostasis, and its degenerative consequences, can occur locally in synaptic terminals (Begley, Duan, Duff, & Mattson, 1999).

Glial cells play important roles in modulating synaptic function. For example, astrocytes express high levels of glutamate transporters and thereby provide a major mechanism for rapidly decreasing the concentration of extracellular glutamate following its

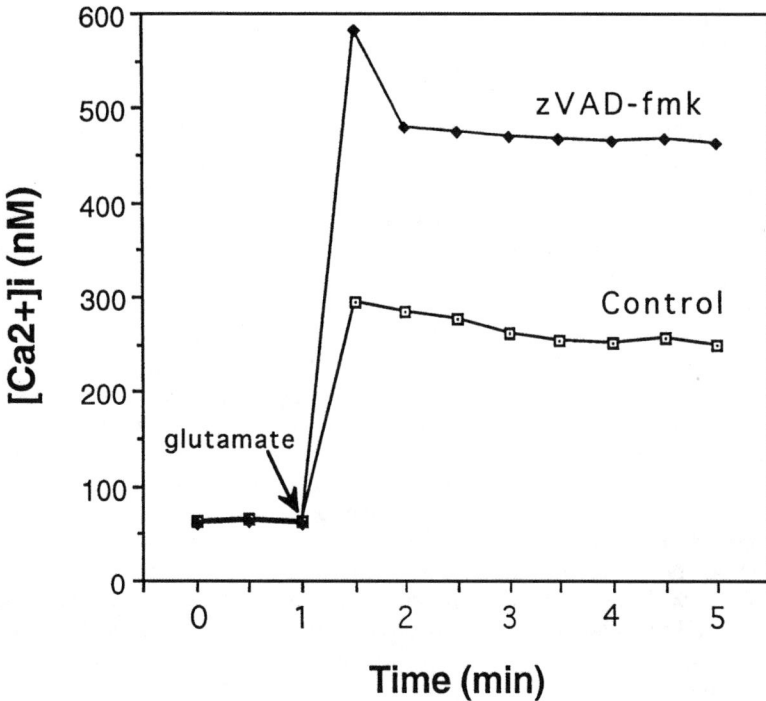

Figure 28.6. Hippocampal cultures were pretreated for 2 h with the caspase inhibitor zVAD-fmk (100 μM) or vehicle (Control). Levels of intracellular calcium were then measured by imaging of the dye fura-2 at 30 sec intervals prior to and following exposure to 100 μM glutamate. Values are the mean of measurements made in 23–29 neurons. The calcium response to glutamate was much greater in the neurons treated with zVAD-fmk, suggesting that caspase activity reduces glutamate responses.

synaptic release (Blanc, Keller, Fernandez, & Mattson, 1998; Keller et al., 1997). Synaptic glutamate transport, which is mediated mainly by astrocytes, can be enhanced by sAPPα and may thereby protect synaptic terminals against excitotoxic injury (Mattson et al., 1999). Microglia serve as immune cells in the nervous system, and indeed, they are activated in response to injury (Moore & Thanos, 1996). Microglia recognize cells undergoing apoptosis as the result of exposure of phosphatidylserine on the surface of the apoptotic cell. We have shown that phosphatidylserine exposure can be induced to occur in synaptic terminals following exposure to glutamate and amyloid β-peptide (Mattson, Keller et al., 1998; Mattson, Partin et al., 1998), suggesting that exposure of phosphatidylserine on the membrane surface of synaptic terminals may elicit a local microglial response that participates in remodeling of synaptic connections.

Synaptic degeneration precedes neuronal cell death in many different neurodegenerative disorders including AD, stroke, epileptic seizures, traumatic brain injury, PD, and Huntington's disease. The evidence that alterations in synaptic homeostasis play roles in the pathogenesis of neurodegenerative disorders is quite extensive, and it is beyond the scope of this chapter to consider such evidence (see Mattson, 1997, for review). The following paragraphs describe recent data from this laboratory that have identified synaptic signaling mechanisms that either promote or prevent synaptic degeneration in experimental models of neurodegenerative disorders.

The first example comes from studies of the cell biology of the APP and the involvement of aberrant APP metabolism in the pathogenesis of AD (see Mattson, 1997, for review). APP is a large (695–770) amino acid integral membrane protein with one membrane-spanning domain; APP contains amyloid β-peptide, a 40–42 amino acid peptide which appears to be partially embedded in the membrane at the cell surface. APP is axonally transported, localizes to presynaptic terminals, and can be proteolytically processed in at least two different ways. One processing pathway involves activity-dependent cleavage of APP in the middle of the $A\beta$ sequence, which releases a large extracellular portion of APP called sAPPα into the synaptic cleft. A second processing pathway involves cleavage of APP at the N-terminus of the amyloid β-peptide sequence, which leaves a C-terminal fragment containing intact amyloid β-peptide associated with the plasma membrane; this C-terminal fragment can be endocytosed and further processed such that intact $A\beta$ is produced. In AD, APP processing is altered such that levels of amyloid β-peptide are increased, while levels of sAPPα are decreased.

Amyloid β-peptide may directly impair synaptic function and may induce degeneration of synapses. Exposure of cortical synaptosomes to amyloid β-peptide results in membrane lipid peroxidation and impairment of membrane ion-motive ATPases and glucose and glutamate transporters (Keller et al., 1997; Mark, Pang et al., 1997; Mark, Keller et al., 1997). Amyloid β-peptide also induces Par-4 production, caspase activation, and mitochondrial dysfunction in cortical synaptosomes and in dendrites of cultured hippocampal neurons (Duan, Rangnekar et al., 1999; Mattson, Keller et al., 1998). Because amyloid β-peptide appears to be deposited in synaptic regions in AD (Mattson, 1997), these findings suggest that synaptic degenerative changes are likely to be early and pivotal events in the neurodegenerative process in AD. Other neurodegenerative disorders may involve a similar degenerative cascade initiated by different, disorder-specific, factors.

Data suggest that sAPPα plays an important role in regulating developmental and synaptic plasticity. sAPPα promotes neurite outgrowth and cell survival in cultured embryonic hippocampal neurons (Mattson, 1994; Mattson, Barger et al., 1993); sAPPα is released from hippocampal slices in response to stimulation that induces LTP (Nitsch, Farber, Growdon, & Wurtman, 1993). Whole-cell perforated patch clamp analysis of ion currents in cultured primary hippocampal neurons have shown that sAPPα activates high-conductance potassium channels resulting in membrane hyperpolarization (Furukawa, Barger et al., 1996; Furukawa, Sopher et al., 1996); sAPPα modulates synaptic plasticity in hippocampal slices by shifting the frequency-dependence for induction of LTD and increasing the amplitude of LTP (Ishida et al., 1997). sAPPα can protect neurons against excitotoxicity and apoptosis by a signaling mechanism involving cyclic GMP production. The sAPPα signaling pathway results in activation of NF-κB, which may induce production of neuroprotective proteins (Barger & Mattson, 1996).

We recently found that sAPPα can enhance glucose and glutamate transport in synaptosomes (Mattson, Guo, & Geiger, 1999). Pretreatment of synaptosomes with sAPPα increased their resistance to amyloid β- peptide and Fe^{2+}-induced impairment of glucose and glutamate transport. Cyclic GMP mediates sAPPα-induced enhancement of glucose and glutamate transport (Mattson, Guo et al., 1999). These findings demonstrate that a trophic factor released in an activity-dependent manner can act locally on synaptic terminals to enhance the function of two membrane transporters that play important roles in protecting neurons against excitotoxicity and apoptosis. In subsequent studies we have found that at least two other neurotrophic factors, ADNF and bFGF can also activate signaling pathways within synaptic terminals that directly protect those compartments (Guo & Mattson, 1999).

A well-established animal model of PD involves administration of the toxin I-methyl-4-phenyl-1,2,3,6-tetrahydropyridine (MPTP), which induces mitochondrial oxidative stress in synaptic terminals resulting in excitotoxic degeneration of dopaminergic neurons in the substantia nigra (Jenner & Olanow, 1998). Following administration of MPTP to monkeys and mice, there is a rapid (hours) increase in levels of Par-4 protein in substantia nigra dopaminergic neurons followed by subsequent loss of tyrosine hydroxylase and cell death (Duan, Gash, Rangnekar, & Mattson, 1999). The latter studies further showed that the complex I inhibitor rotenone and iron (two insults relevant to the pathogenesis of PD) induce Par-4 production in cultured human dopaminergic cells. Dopaminergic cells pretreated with Par-4 antisense DNA were resistant to cell death induced by rotenone and iron, indicating a key role for Par-4 in the cell death process.

"Stress" proteins and Bcl-2 are present in synaptic compartments and may act locally therein to protect synapses against various insults. Cell culture studies have provided direct evidence that increased levels of stress proteins such as HSP-70 and GRP-78 can protect neurons against excitotoxic, apoptotic, and oxidative insults (Lowenstein et al., 1991; Yu et al., 1999). Administration of 2-deoxyglucose (2DG, a non-metabolizable analog of glucose that induces a mild metabolic stress) to rats and mice in vivo increases levels of HSP-70 and GRP-78 in hippocampus, cortex, and striatum (Duan & Mattson, 1999; Yu & Mattson, 1999). We have found that levels of HSP-70 and GRP-78 are also increased in synaptosomes prepared from cortex of 2DG-treated rats compared to control rats.

Another example of the mounting evidence supporting a primary role for aberrant synaptic signaling in neurodegenerative disorders comes from studies of the pathogenic action of mutations in the presenilin-1 gene, which cause early-onset autosomal dominant AD. Presenilin-1 mutations increase neuronal vulnerability to apoptosis (Guo et al., 1997; Guo, Sebastian et al., 1999) and excitotoxicity (Guo, Fu et al., 1999). When mutant presenilin-1 is expressed in cultured PC12 cells or primary hippocampal neurons, ER calcium homeostasis is perturbed such that more calcium is released when the cells are stimulated with muscarinic cholinergic agonists or glutamate (Guo et al., 1996; Guo, Fu et al., 1998, 1999). The endangering actions of presenilin-1 mutations result from perturbed calcium regulation in that agents that block calcium release from ER or buffer cytoplasmic calcium counteract the cell death–promoting action of the presenilin-1 mutations (Guo et al., 1996; Guo, Fu et al., 1998). Synaptic calcium handling is perturbed in neurons from presenilin-1 mutant transgenic mice in a manner that promotes mitochondrial dysfunction (Begley et al., 1999).

☐ Future Directions

The findings described above suggest that apoptotic cascades function in a continuum in which low levels of activation play roles in adaptive responses to physiological activity and subtoxic levels of stress, whereas higher levels of activation mediate synaptic degeneration and cell death. Much further work will be required to better understand the molecular and cellular mechanisms that regulate pro- and antiapoptotic responses in synapses. A key goal will be to dissect the pathways of communication from the synapse to the nucleus and back. Synaptic signaling clearly has profound effects on gene expression, and the specific molecular cascades subserving this important aspect of synaptic function merits intense investigation.

☐ **References**

Albensi, B. C., & Mattson, M. P. (2000). Evidence for the involvement of TNF and NF-κB in hippocampal synaptic plasticity. *Synapse, 35*, 151–159.

Ankarcrona, M., Dypbukt, J. M., Bonfoco, E., Zhivotovsky, B., Orrenius, S., Lipton, S. A., & Nicotera, P. (1995). Glutamate-induced neuronal death: a succession of necrosis or apoptosis depending on mitochondrial function. *Neuron, 15*, 961–973.

Barger, S. W., Horster, D., Furukawa, K., Goodman, Y., Krieglestein, J., & Mattson, M. P. (1995). Tumor necrosis factors α and β protect neurons against amyloid β-peptide toxicity: Evidence for involvement of a κB-binding factor and attenuation of peroxide and Ca^{2+} accumulation. *Proceedings of the National Academy of Sciences of the United States of America, 92*, 9328–9332.

Barger, S. W., & Mattson, M. P. (1996). Induction of neuroprotective κB-dependent transcription by secreted forms of the Alzheimer's β-amyloid precursor. *Molecular Brain Research, 40*, 116–126.

Barnes, N. Y., Li, L., Yoshikawa, K., Schwartz, L. M., Oppenheim, R. W., & Milligan, C. E. (1998). Increased production of amyloid precursor protein provides a substrate for caspase-3 in dying motoneurons. *Journal of Neuroscience, 18*, 5869–5880.

Begley, J. G., Duan, W., Duff, K., & Mattson, M. P. (1999). Altered calcium homeostasis and mitochondrial dysfunction in cortical synaptic compartments of presenilin-1 mutant mice. *Journal of Neurochemistry, 72*, 1030–1039.

Blanc, E. M., Keller, J. N., Fernandez, S., & Mattson, M. P. (1998). 4-hydroxynonenal, a lipid peroxidation product, inhibits glutamate transport in astrocytes. *Glia, 22*, 149–160.

Braak, H., & Braak, E. (1991). Neuropathological stageing of Alzheimer-related changes. *Acta Neuropathologica, 82*, 239–259.

Bredesen, D. E. (1995). Neural apoptosis. *Annals of Neurology, 38*, 839–851.

Bruce, A. J., Boling, W., Kindy, M. S., Peschon, J., Kraemer, P. J., Carpenter, M. K., Holtsberg, F. W., & Mattson, M. P. (1996). Altered neuronal and microglial responses to brain injury in mice lacking TNF receptors. *Nature Medicine, 2*, 788–794.

Cecconi, F., Alvarez-Bolado, G., Meyer, B. I., Roth, K. A., & Gruss P. (1998). Apaf1 (CED-4 homolog) regulates programmed cell death in mammalian development. *Cell 94*, 727–737.

Chan, S. L., Griffin, W. S. T., & Mattson, M. P. (1999). Evidence for caspase-mediated cleavage of AMPA receptor subunits in neuronal apoptosis and in Alzheimer's disease. *Journal of Neuroscience Research, 57*, 315-323.

Chan, S. L., & Mattson, M. P. (1999). Caspase and calpain substrates: roles in synaptic plasticity and cell death. *Journal of Neuroscience Research, 58*, 167–190.

Chan, S. L., Tammariello, S. P., Estus, S., & Mattson, M. P. (1999). Involvement of Par-4 in trophic factor withdrawal-induced apoptosis of hippocampal neurons: Actions prior to mitochondrial dysfunction and caspase activation. *Journal of Neurochemistry, 73*, 502–512.

Cheng, B., Christakos, S., & Mattson, M. P. (1994). Tumor necrosis factors protect neurons against excitotoxic/metabolic insults and promote maintenance of calcium homeostasis. *Neuron, 12*, 139–153.

Cheng, B., Furukawa, K., O'Keefe, J. A., Goodman, Y., Kihiko, M., Fabian, T., & Mattson, M. P. (1995). Basic fibroblast growth factor selectively increases AMPA-receptor subunit GluR1 protein level and differentially modulates Ca^{2+} responses to AMPA and NMDA in hippocampal neurons. *Journal of Neurochemistry, 65*, 2525–2536.

Cheng, B., & Mattson, M. P. (1991). NGF and bFGF protect rat and human central neurons against hypoglycemic damage by stabilizing calcium homeostasis. *Neuron, 7*, 1031–1041.

Cheng, E. H., Kirsch, D. G., Clem, R. J., Ravi, R., Kastan, M. B., Bedi, A., Ueno, K., & Hardwick, J. M. (1997). Conversion of Bcl-2 to a Bax-like death effector by caspases. *Science, 278*, 1966–1968.

Cryns, V. L., Bergeron, L., Zhu, H., Li, H., & Yuan, J. (1996). Specific cleavage of alpha-fodrin during Fas- and tumor necrosis factor-induced apoptosis is mediated by an interleukin-1beta-converting enzyme/Ced-3 protease distinct from the poly (ADP-ribose) polymerase protease. *Journal of Biological Chemistry, 271*, 31277–31282.

Datta, S. R., Dudek, H., Tao, X., Masters, S., Fu, H., Gotoh, Y., & Greenberg, M. E. (1997). Akt phosphorylation of BAD couples survival signals to the cell-intrinsic death machinery. *Cell 91*, 231–241.

Datta, R., Kojima, H., Yoshida, K., & Kufe, D. (1997). Caspase-3-mediated cleavage of protein kinase C theta in induction of apoptosis. *Journal of Biological Chemistry, 272*, 20317–20320.

Deisseroth, K., Bito, H., & Tsien, R. W. (1996). Signaling from synapse to nucleus, postsynaptic CREB phosphorylation during multiple forms of hippocampal synaptic plasticity. *Neuron, 16*, 89–101.

Deshmukh, M., & Johnson, E. M. (1997). Programmed cell death in neurons: Focus on the pathway of nerve growth factor deprivation-induced death of sympathetic neurons. *Molecular Pharmacology, 51*, 897–906.

Deveraux, Q. L., & Reed, J. C. (2000). Inhibitor of apoptosis proteins (IAPs). In M. P. Mattson, V. Rangnekar, & S. Estus (Eds.), *Programmed cell death, advances in cell and aging gerontology* (Vol. 1), Greenwich, CT: JAI Press.

Dodel, R. C., Du, Y., Bales, K. R., Ling, Z., Carvey, P. M., & Paul, S. M. (1999). Caspase-3-like proteases and 6-hydroxydopamine induced neuronal cell death. *Molecular Brain Research, 64*, 141–148.

Duan, W., Gash, D. M., Rangnekar, V., & Mattson, M. P. (1999). Participation of Par-4 in degeneration of dopaminergic neurons in primate and rodent models of Parkinson's disease. *Annals of Neurology, 46*, 587–597.

Duan, W., & Mattson, M. P. (1999). Dietary restriction and 2-deoxyglucose administration improve behavioral outcome and reduce degeneration of dopaminergic neurons in models of Parkinson's disease. *Journal of Neuroscience Research, 57*, 195–206.

Duan, W., Rangnekar, V., & Mattson, M. P. (1999). Par-4 production in synaptic compartments following apoptotic and excitotoxic insults: Evidence for a pivotal role in mitochondrial dysfunction and neuronal degeneration. *Journal of Neurochemistry, 72*, 2312–2322.

Edwards, F. A. (1995). Anatomy and electrophysiology of fast central synapses lead to a structural model for long-term potentiation. *Physiological Reviews, 75*, 759–787.

Figurov, A., Pozzo-Miller, L. D., Olafsson, P., Wang, T., & Lu, B. (1996). Regulation of synaptic responses to high-frequency stimulation and LTP by neurotrophins in the hippocampus. *Nature, 381*, 706–709.

Finch, E. A., & Augustine, G. J. (1998). Local calcium signaling by inositol-1,4,5-triphosphate in Purkinje cell dendrites. *Nature, 396*, 753–756.

Finkbeiner, S., & Greenberg, M. E. (1998). Ca^{2+} channel-regulated neuronal gene expression. *Journal of Neurobiology, 37*, 171–189.

Fu, W., Begley, J. G., Killen, M. W., & Mattson, M. P. (1999). Anti-apoptotic role of telomerase in pheochromocytoma cells. *Journal of Biological Chemistry, 274*, 7264–7271.

Furukawa, K., Barger, S. W., Blalock, E., & Mattson, M. P. (1996). Activation of K^+ channels and suppression of neuronal activity by secreted β-amyloid precursor protein. *Nature, 379*, 74–78.

Furukawa, K., Fu, W., Witke, W., Kwiatkowski, D. J., & Mattson, M. P. (1997). The actin-severing protein gelsolin modulates calcium channel and NMDA receptor activities and vulnerability to excitotoxicity in hippocampal neurons. *Journal of Neuroscience, 17*, 8178–8186.

Furukawa, K., & Mattson, M. P. (1998). The transcription factor NF-κB mediates increases in calcium currents and decreases in NMDA and AMPA/kainate-induced currents in response to TNFα in hippocampal neurons. *Journal of Neurochemistry, 70*, 1876–1886.

Furukawa, K., Smith-Swintosky, V. L., & Mattson, M. P. (1995). Evidence that actin depolymerization protects hippocampal neurons against excitotoxicity by stabilizing $[Ca^{2+}]_i$. *Experimental Neurology, 133*, 153–163.

Furukawa, K., Sopher, B. L., Rydel, R. E., Begley, J. G., Martin, G. M., & Mattson, M. P. (1996). Increased activity-regulating and neuroprotective efficacy of β-secretase-derived secreted APP is conferred by a C-terminal heparin-binding domain. *Journal of Neurochemistry, 67*, 1882–1896.

Gary, D. S., & Mattson, M. P. (1998). A role for the extracellular matrix in attenuating neuronal death. *Molecular Biology of the Cell, 9*, 425a.

Goodman, Y., & Mattson, M. P. (1994). Secreted forms of β-amyloid precursor protein protect hippocampal neurons against amyloid β-peptide-induced oxidative injury. *Experimental Neurology, 128*, 1–12.

Goodman, Y., & Mattson, M. P. (1996). Ceramide protects hippocampal neurons against excitotoxic and oxidative insults, and amyloid β-peptide toxicity. *Journal of Neurochemistry, 66,* 869–872.

Greenlund, L. J., Deckwerth, T. L., & Johnson, E. M. (1995). Superoxide dismutase delays neuronal apoptosis: A role for reactive oxygen species in programmed neuronal death. *Neuron, 14,* 303–315.

Guo, Q., Fu, W., Sopher, B. L., Miller, M. W., Ware, C. B., Martin, G. M., & Mattson, M. P. (1999). Increased vulnerability of hippocampal neurons to excitotoxic necrosis in presenilin-1 mutant knockin mice. *Nature Medicine, 5,* 101–107.

Guo, Q., Fu, W., Xie, J., Luo, H., Sells, S. F., Geddes, J. W., Bondada, V., Rangnekar, V., & Mattson, M. P. (1998). Par-4 is a novel mediator of neuronal degeneration associated with the pathogenesis of Alzheimer's disease. *Nature Medicine, 4,* 957–962.

Guo, Q., Furukawa, K., Sopher, B. L., Pham, D. G., Robinson, N., Martin, G. M., & Mattson, M. P. (1996). Alzheimer's PS-1 mutation perturbs calcium homeostasis and sensitizes PC12 cells to death induced by amyloid β-peptide. *NeuroReport, 8,* 379–383.

Guo, Z. H., & Mattson, M. P. (1999). Neurotrophic factors protect cortical synaptic terminals against amyloid- and oxidative stress-induced impairment of glucose transport, glutamate transport and mitochondrial function. *Cerebral Cortex, 10,* 50–57.

Guo, Q., Robinson, N., & Mattson, M. P. (1998). Secreted APPα counteracts the pro-apoptotic action of mutant presenilin-1 by activation of NF-κB and stabilization of calcium homeostasis. *Journal of Biological Chemistry, 273,* 12341–12351.

Guo, Q., Sebastian, L., Sopher, B. L., Miller, M. W., Ware, C. B., Martin, G. M., & Mattson, M. P. (1999). Increased vulnerability of hippocampal neurons from presenilin-1 mutant knock-in mice to amyloid β-peptide toxicity: Central roles of superoxide production and caspase activation. *Journal of Neurochemistry, 72,* 1019–1029.

Guo, Q., Sopher, B. L., Pham, D. G., Furukawa, K., Robinson, N., Martin, G. M., & Mattson, M. P. (1997). Alzheimer's presenilin mutation sensitizes neural cells to apoptosis induced by trophic factor withdrawal and amyloid β-peptide: Involvement of calcium and oxyradicals. *Journal of Neuroscience, 17,* 4212–4222.

Ishida, A., Furukawa, K., Keller, J. N., & Mattson, M. P. (1997). Secreted form of β-amyloid precursor protein shifts the frequency dependence for induction of LTD, and enhances LTP in hippocampal slices. *NeuroReport, 8,* 2133–2137.

Jenner, P., & Olanow, C. W. (1998). Understanding cell death in Parkinson's disease. *Annals of Neurology, 44,* S72–S84.

Johnson, M. D., Xiang, H., London, S., Kinoshita, Y., Knudson, M., Mayberg, M., Korsmeyer, S. J., & Morrison, R. S. (1998). Evidence for involvement of Bax and p53, but not caspases, in radiation-induced cell death of cultured postnatal hippocampal neurons. *Journal of Neuroscience Research, 54,* 721–733.

Jones, T. A., Klintsova, A. Y., Kilman, V. L., Sirevaag, A. M., & Greenough, W. T. (1997). Induction of multiple synapses by experience in the visual cortex of adult rats. *Neurobiology of Learning and Memory, 68,* 13–20.

Kayalar, C., Ord, T., Testa, M. P., Zhong, L. T., & Bredesen, D. E. (1996). Cleavage of actin by interleukin 1 β-converting enzyme to reverse DNase I inhibition. *Proceedings of the National Academy of Sciences of the United States of America, 93,* 2234–2238.

Keller, J. N., Guo, Q., Holtsberg, F. W., Bruce-Keller, A. J., & Mattson, M. P. (1998). Increased sensitivity to mitochondrial toxin-induced apoptosis in neural cells expressing mutant presenilin-1 is linked to perturbed calcium homeostasis and enhanced oxyradical production. *Journal of Neuroscience, 18,* 4439–4450.

Keller, J. N., Kindy, M. S., Holtsberg, F. W., St. Clair, D. K., Yen, H. C., Germeyer, A., Steiner, S. M., Bruce-Keller, A. J., Hutchins, J. B., & Mattson, M. P. (1998). Mitochondrial MnSOD prevents neural apoptosis and reduces ischemic brain injury: Suppression of peroxynitrite production, lipid peroxidation and mitochondrial dysfunction. *Journal of Neuroscience, 18,* 687–697.

Keller, J. N., Pang, Z., Geddes, J. W., Begley, J. G., Germeyer, A., Waeg, G., & Mattson, M. P. (1997). Impairment of glucose and glutamate transport and induction of mitochondrial oxidative stress and dysfunction in synaptosomes by amyloid β-peptide: Role of the lipid peroxidation product 4- hydroxynonenal. *Journal of Neurochemistry, 69,* 273–284.

Kim, T. W., Pettingell, W. H., Jung, Y. K., Kovacs, D. M., & Tanzi, R. E. (1997). Alternative cleavage of Alzheimer-associated presenilins during apoptosis by a caspase-3 family protease. *Science, 277,* 373–376.

Koh, J. Y., Wie, M. B., Gwag, B. J., Sensi, S. L., Canzoniero, L. M., Demaro, J., Csernansky, C., & Choi, D. W. (1995). Staurosporine-induced neuronal apoptosis. *Experimental Neurology, 135,* 153–159.

Kroemer, G., Zamzami, N., & Susin, S. A. (1997). Mitochondrial control of apoptosis. *Immunology Today, 18,* 44–51.

Kruman, I., Bruce-Keller, A. J., Bredesen, D. E., Waeg, G., & Mattson, M. P. (1997). Evidence that 4-hydroxynonenal mediates oxidative stress-induced neuronal apoptosis. *Journal of Neuroscience, 17,* 5089–5100.

Kruman, I., Guo, Q., & Mattson, M. P. (1998). Calcium and reactive oxygen species mediate staurosporine-induced mitochondrial dysfunction and apoptosis in PC12 cells. *Journal of Neuroscience Research, 51,* 293–308.

Kruman, I., Pang, Z., Geddes, J. W., & Mattson, M. P. (1999). Pivotal role of mitochondrial calcium uptake in neural cell apoptosis and necrosis. *Journal of Neurochemistry, 72,* 529–540.

Latchman, D. S. (1995). Cell stress genes and neuronal protection. *Neuropathology and Applied Neurobiology, 21,* 475–477.

Levine, E. S., Dreyfus, C. F., Black, I. B., & Plummer, M. R. (1995). Brain-derived neurotrophic factor rapidly enhances synaptic transmission in hippocampal neurons via postsynaptic tyrosine kinase receptors. *Proceedings of the National Academy of Sciences of the United States of America, 92,* 8074–8077.

Linnik, M. D., Zobrist, R. H., & Hatfield, M. D. (1993). Evidence supporting a role for programmed cell death in focal cerebral ischemia in rats. *Stroke, 24,* 2002–2008.

Loo, D. T., Copani, A., Pike, C. J., Whittemore, E. R., Walencewicz, A. J., & Cotman, C. W. (1993). Apoptosis is induced by β-amyloid in cultured central nervous system neurons. *Proceedings of the National Academy of Sciences of the United States of America, 90,* 7951–7955.

Lovell, M. A., Ehmann, W. D., Mattson, M. P., & Markesbery, W. R. (1997). Elevated 4- hydroxynonenal in ventricular fluid in Alzheimer's disease. *Neurobiology of Aging, 18,* 457–461.

Lowenstein, D. H., Chan, P., & Miles, M. (1991). The stress protein response in cultured neurons: Characterization and evidence for a protective role in excitotoxicity. *Neuron, 7,* 1053–1060.

MacManus, J. P., Buchan, A. M., Hill, I. E., Rasquinha, I., & Preston, E. (1993). Global ischemia can cause DNA fragmentation indicative of apoptosis in rat brain. *Neuroscience Letters, 164,* 89–92.

Mark, R. J., Hensley, K., Butterfield, D. A., & Mattson, M. P. (1995). Amyloid β-peptide impairs ion-motive ATPase activities: Evidence for a role in loss of neuronal Ca^{2+} homeostasis and cell death. *Journal of Neuroscience, 15,* 6239–6249.

Mark, R. J., Keller, J. N., Kruman, I., & Mattson, M. P. (1997). Basic FGF attenuates amyloid β-peptide-induced oxidative stress, mitochondrial dysfunction, and impairment of Na^+/K^+-ATPase activity in hippocampal neurons. *Brain Research, 756,* 205–214.

Mark, R. J., Pang, Z., Geddes, J. W., Uchida, K., & Mattson, M. P. (1997). Amyloid β-peptide impairs glucose uptake in hippocampal and cortical neurons: Involvement of membrane lipid peroxidation. *Journal of Neuroscience, 17,* 1046–1054.

Marsden, C. D. (1994). Parkinson's disease. *Journal of Neurology, Neurosurgery and Psychiatry, 57,* 672–681.

Martin, D. P., Schmidt, R. E., DiStefano, P. S., Lowry, O. H., Carter, J. G., & Johnson, E. M. Jr. (1988). Inhibitors of protein synthesis and RNA synthesis prevent neuronal death caused by nerve growth factor deprivation. *Journal of Cell Biology, 106,* 829–844.

Martinez, A., Alcantara, S., Borrell, V., Del Rio, J. A., Blasi, J., Otal, R., Campos, N., Boronat, A., Barbacid, M., Silos-Santiago, I., & Soriano, E. (1998). TrkB and TrkC signaling are required for maturation and synaptogenesis of hippocampal connections. *Journal of Neuroscience, 18,* 7336–7350.

Mashima, T., Naito, M., Noguchi, K., Miller, D. K., Nicholson, D. W., & Tsuruo, T. (1997). Actin cleavage by CPP-32/apopain during the development of apoptosis. *Oncogene, 14,* 1007–1012.

Mattson, M. P. (1988). Neurotransmitters in the regulation of neuronal cytoarchitecture. *Brain Research, 472,* 179–212.

Mattson, M. P. (1989). Cellular signaling mechanisms common to the development and degeneration of neuroarchitecture. A review. *Mechanisms of Ageing Development, 50,* 103–157.

Mattson, M. P. (1994). Secreted forms of β-amyloid precursor protein modulate dendrite outgrowth and calcium responses to glutamate in cultured embryonic hippocampal neurons. *Journal of Neurobiology, 25,* 439–450.

Mattson, M. P. (1996). Calcium and free radicals: Mediators of neurotrophic factor- and excitatory transmitter-regulated developmental plasticity and cell death. *Perspectives on Developmental Neurobiology, 3,* 79–91.

Mattson, M. P. (1997). Cellular actions of β-amyloid precursor protein, and its soluble and fibrillogenic peptide derivatives. *Physiological Reviews, 77,* 1081–1132.

Mattson, M. P., Barger, S. W., Cheng, B., Lieberburg, I., Smith-Swintosky, V. L., & Rydel, R. E. (1993). β-amyloid precursor protein metabolites and loss of neuronal calcium homeostasis in Alzheimer's disease. *Trends in Neuroscience, 16,* 409–415.

Mattson, M. P., Culmsee, C., Yu, Z., & Camandola, S. (1999). Roles of NF-κB in neuronal survival and plasticity. *Journal of Neurochemistry, 74,* 443–456.

Mattson, M. P., & Duan, W. (1999). "Apoptotic" biochemical cascades in synaptic compartments: Roles in adaptive plasticity and neurodegenerative disorders. *Journal of Neuroscience Research, 58,* 152–166.

Mattson, M. P., & Furukawa, K. (1996). Programmed cell life: Anti-apoptotic signaling and therapeutic strategies for neurodegenerative disorders. *Restorative Neurology and Neuroscience, 9,* 191–205.

Mattson, M. P., Goodman, Y., Luo, H., Fu, W., & Furukawa, K. (1997). Activation of NF-κB protects hippocampal neurons against oxidative stress-induced apoptosis: Evidence for induction of Mn-SOD and suppression of peroxynitrite production and protein tyrosine nitration. *Journal of Neuroscience Research, 49,* 681–697.

Mattson, M. P., & Guo, Q. (1999). The presenilins. *The Neuroscientist, 5,* 112–124.

Mattson, M. P., Guo, Z. H., & Geiger, J. D. (1999). Secreted form of amyloid precursor protein enhances basal glucose and glutamate transport, and protects against oxidative impairment of glucose and glutamate transport in synaptosomes by a cyclic GMP-mediated mechanism. *Journal of Neurochemistry, 73,* 532–537.

Mattson, M. P., & Kater, S. B. (1988). Intracellular messengers in the generation and degeneration of hippocampal neuroarchitecture. *Journal of Neuroscience Research, 21,* 447–464.

Mattson, M. P., & Kater, S. B. (1989). Excitatory and inhibitory neurotransmitters in the generation and degeneration of hippocampal neuroarchitecture. *Brain Research, 478,* 337–348.

Mattson, M. P., Keller, J. N., & Begley, J. G. (1998). Evidence for synaptic apoptosis. *Experimental Neurology, 153,* 35–48.

Mattson, M. P., Kumar, K., Cheng, B., Wang, H., & Michaelis, E. K. (1993). Basic FGF regulates the expression of a functional 71 kDa NMDA receptor protein that mediates calcium influx and neurotoxicity in cultured hippocampal neurons. *Journal of Neuroscience, 13,* 4575–4588.

Mattson, M. P., & Lindvall, O. (1997). Neurotrophic factor and cytokine signaling in the aging brain. In M. P. Mattson & J. W. Geddes (Eds.), *The aging brain, advances in cell and aging gerontology, 2* (pp. 299–345). Greenwich, CT: JAI Press.

Mattson, M. P., LaFerla, F. M., Chan, S. L., Leissring, M. A., Shepel, P. N., & Geiger, J. D. (2000). Calcium signaling in the ER: Its role in neuronal plasticity and neurodegenerative disorders. *Trends Neurosci. 23,* 222–229.

Mattson, M. P., Lovell, M. A., Furukawa, K., & Markesbery, W. R. (1995). Neurotrophic factors attenuate glutamate-induced accumulation of peroxides, elevation of $[Ca^{2+}]_i$ and neurotoxicity, and increase antioxidant enzyme activities in hippocampal neurons. *Journal of Neurochemistry, 65,* 1740–1751.

Mattson, M. P., Partin, J., & Begley, J. G. (1998). Amyloid β-peptide induces apoptosis-related events in synapses and dendrites. *Brain Research, 807,* 167–176.

McGinnis, K. M., Whitton, M. M., Gnegy, M. E., & Wang, K. K. (1998). Calcium/calmodulin- dependent protein kinase IV is cleaved by caspase-3 and calpain in SH-SY5Y human neuroblastoma cells undergoing apoptosis. *Journal of Biological Chemsitry, 273,* 19993–20000.

Moore, S., & Thanos, S. (1996). The concept of microglia in relation to central nervous system disease and regeneration. *Progress in Neurobiology, 48,* 441–460.

Neame, S. J., Rubin, L. L., & Philpott, K. L. (1998). Blocking cytochrome c activity within intact neurons inhibits apoptosis. *Journal of Cell Biology, 142,* 1583–1593.

Nitatori, T., Sato, N., Waguri, S., Karasawa, Y., Araki, H., Shibanai, K., Kominami, E., & Uchiyama, Y. (1995). Delayed neuronal death in the CA1 pyramidal cell layer of the gerbil hippocampus following transient ischemia is apoptosis. *Journal of Neuroscience, 15,* 1001–1011.

Nitsch, R., Farber, A. S., Growdon, H. J., & Wurtman, J. R. (1993). Release of amyloid β-protein precursor derivatives by electrical depolarization of rat hippocampal slices. *Proceedings of the National Academy of Sciences of the United States of America, 90,* 5191–5193.

Nixon, R. A., Saito, K. I., Grynspan, F., Griffin, W. R., Katayama, S., Honda, T., Mohan, P. S., Shea, T. B., & Beerman, M. (1994). Calcium-activated neutral proteinase (calpain) system in aging and Alzheimer's disease. *Annals of the New York Academy of the Sciences, 747,* 77–91.

Nunez, G., Benedict, M. A., Hu, Y., & Inohara, N. (1998). Caspases: The proteases of the apoptotic pathway. *Oncogene, 17,* 3237–3245.

Oppenheim, R. W. (1991). Cell death during development of the nervous system. *Annual Review of Neuroscience, 14,* 453–501.

Pang, Z., & Geddes, J. W. (1997). Mechanisms of cell death induced by the mitochondrial toxin 3-nitropropionic acid: Acute excitotoxic necrosis and delayed apoptosis. *Journal of Neuroscience, 17,* 3064–3073.

Pettmann, B., & Henderson, C. E. (1998). Neuronal cell death. *Neuron, 20,* 633–647.

Portera-Cailliau, C., Hedreen, J. C., Price, D. L., & Koliatsos, V. E. (1995). Evidence for apoptotic cell death in Huntington disease and excitotoxic animal models. *Journal of Neuroscience, 15,* 3775–3787.

Purves, D., Snider, W. D., & Voyvodic, J. T. (1988). Trophic regulation of nerve cell morphology and innervation in the autonomic nervous system. *Nature, 336,* 123–128.

Rothstein, J. D. (1995). Excitotoxicity and neurodegeneration in amyotrophic lateral sclerosis. *Clinical Neuroscience, 3,* 348–359.

Soderling, T. R., Tan, S. E., McGlade-McCulloh, E., Yamamoto, H., & Fukunaga, K. (1994). Excitatory interactions between glutamate receptors and protein kinases. *Journal of Neurobiology, 25,* 304–311.

Takechi, H., Eilers, J., & Konnerth, A. (1998). A new class of synaptic response involving calcium release in dendritic spines. *Nature, 396,* 757–760.

Tandan, R., & Bradley, W. G. (1985). Amyotrophic lateral sclerosis. Part 1. Clinical features, pathology and ethical issues in management. *Annals of Neurology, 18,* 271–280

Tenneti, L., D'Emilia, D. M., Troy, C. M., & Lipton, S. A. (1998). Role of caspases in N-methyl-D- aspartate-induced apoptosis in cerebrocortical neurons. *Journal of Neurochemistry, 71,* 946–959.

Wang, K. K., Posmantur, R., Nath, R., McGinnis, K., Whitton, M., Talanian, R.V., Glantz, S. B., & Morrow, J. S. (1998). Simultaneous degradation of alphaII- and betaII-spectrin by caspase 3 (CPP32) in apoptotic cells. *Journal of Biological Chemistry, 273,* 22490–22497.

Weng, N. P., Hathcock, K. S., & Hodes, R. J. (1998). Regulation of telomere length and telomerase in T and B cells: A mechanism for maintaining replicative potential. *Immunity, 9,* 151–157.

Wheal, H. V., Chen, Y., Mitchell, J., Schachner, M., Maerz, W., Wieland, H., Van Rossum, D., & Kirsch, J. (1998). Molecular mechanisms that underlie structural and functional changes in the postsynaptic membrane during synaptic plasticity. *Progress in Neurobiology, 55,* 611–640.

Wyllie, A. H., Kerr, J. F. R., & Currie, A. R. (1990). Cell death: The significance of apoptosis. *International Review of Cytology, 68,* 251–306.

Xiang, H., Kinoshita, Y., Knudson, C. M., Korsmeyer, S. J., Schwartzkroin, P. A., & Morrison, R. S. (1998). Bax involvement in p53-mediated neuronal cell death. *Journal of Neuroscience, 18,* 1363–1373.

Yu, Z. F., Luo, H., Fu, W., & Mattson, M. P. (1999). The endoplasmic reticulum stress-responsive protein GRP78 protects neurons against excitotoxicity and apoptosis: Suppression of oxidative stress and stabilization of calcium homeostasis. *Experimental Neurology, 155,* 302–314.

Yu, Z. F., & Mattson, M. P. (1999). Dietary restriction and 2-deoxyglucose administration reduce focal ischemic brain damage and improve behavioral outcome: Evidence for a preconditioning mechanism. *J. Neurosci. Res., 57,* 830–839.

Zorumski, C. F., & Izumi, Y. (1993). Nitric oxide and hippocampal synaptic plasticity. *Biochemical Pharmacology, 46,* 777–785.

IS THERE
A THEORY OF
NEUROPLASTICITY?

29

CHAPTER

Christopher A. Shaw
Jill C. McEachern

Traversing Levels of Organization: A Theory of Neuronal Plasticity and Stability

We can characterize the picture we begin to get of the development of behaviour as a series, or rather a web, of events, starting with innate programming instructions contained in the zygote, which straightaway begin to interact with the environment; this interaction may be discontinuous, in that periods of predominantly internal development alternate with periods of interaction, or sensitive periods. The interaction is enhanced by active exploration; it is steered by selective Sollwerte *[ideal or template to which response is compared] of great variety; and stage by stage this process ramifies; level upon level of ever-increasing complexity is being incorporated into the programming.*

N. Tinbergen, 1968

☐ Introduction

A primary goal of this book is to determine whether or not there is any rational basis for grouping all forms of neural modification under the umbrella of *neuroplasticity*. If there is, the commonalities among neuroplasticity subfields should be greater than a simple sharing of certain of the large, but finite, number of structures and signaling pathways used in everyday nervous system function. Unless either the similarities go much deeper or plasticity is found to be a specialized characteristic of only a subset of neurons and behaviors, the term neuroplasticity cannot be accorded a meaning more specific than that of a general term such as "brain function." If the different subfields are each found to have unique principles of operation, any theory of neuroplasticity as a whole will have to be sufficiently general to encompass a broad range of largely unrelated phenomena. More specific theories will only be possible within subfields, for example, memory, cortical map reorganization, or neurological disease—and even these divisions will almost certainly be too broad. Thus, without the identification of common principles, no general theory is likely to emerge.

The question of just what the different forms of neuroplasticity have in common is one we have tried to address by gaining an overall perspective of the field. And although the survey of nervous system function and dysfunction gleaned from the chapters collected in this book is by no means comprehensive, it nevertheless includes samples of research from different species, developmental stages, and levels of neural organization from genetic through behavioral. Within these chapters are revealed a number of key themes (themes that no doubt would differ with a different sample of research by other editors), but in addition are found what appear to be general principles that are, we hope, of wide relevance across many of the subfields of neuroplasticity. These themes and principles will be presented below in the first half of the chapter, along with conclusions and implications for the direction of future research. The second half will be devoted to an outline of a general theory of plasticity and stability in the nervous system. This combination represents our best first attempt to flesh out such a theory.

☐ Synthesis of Chapter Key Themes and General Principles

A major caveat of this section concerns the selectivity of what we considered key themes and principles. First, space and priority dictate that they be derived almost exclusively from the chapters of this book, so many important ideas from the wider literature will unavoidably be omitted. Second, these reflect our personal choices, which may differ from those of the authors. The concepts are no more than a starting point that will, without doubt, be built up and torn down in further attempts at a similar synthesis.

Where Plasticity Is Found

While stability is an important characteristic of neural function, the research presented in this book does not indicate that there is a distinct subset of neuronal structures or behaviors that is *incapable* of plasticity. Plasticity of neural structure and function is evident in species from very simple organisms (e.g., habituation reflex in *C. elegans*, Rose & Rankin, Chapter 14 of this volume) up the scale to humans (e.g., response to injury, Doetsch, Chapter 23; language, Neville & Bavelier, Chapter 18; musical pitch, Lenhoff, Perales, & Hickok, Chapter 19; visual adaptation, Sugita, Chapter 5). The cortex, although initially quite resistant to long-term potentiation (LTP) induction, may now have succumbed to an in vivo stimulation protocol (Trepel & Racine, 1998). Similarly, motor reflex arcs were previously considered essentially "hard-wired" and invariant, but are now seen to be quite plastic (see Latash, 1988). These examples are mentioned in order to highlight the problem of distinguishing a true lack of plasticity from an ineffectual stimulation or training paradigm, or means of measuring such changes (McEachern & Shaw, 1996).

What Types of Stimuli Induce Plasticity?

Nervous system function can be persistently altered by a vast number of molecules, manipulations, perturbations, and stressors. A short list of those discussed in this book includes experience, neural activity, hormones, stress (however defined, but see below), neurotransmitters, modulators, neurotrophic factors, injury, immune response, and various categories of drugs (Wheal et al., 1998; see also Mattson, Duan, Chan, & Guo, Chapter 28 of this volume). Some of the characteristics that influence whether a given stimulus reaches the threshold for inducing change may include the intensity, duration, and temporal pattern; however, this is an area that remains poorly understood.

Progressive Response Potentiation

"Kindling" is a term that was coined to describe the progressive increase in neural response and seizure expression in a model of (among other things) epilepsy (see Teskey, Chapter 24). However, a kindling-like increase in response also appears to be characteristic of other forms of neuroplasticity, including drug addiction (Wolf, Chapter 25), central nervous system (CNS) response to immune activation (Anisman, Hayley, Staines, & Merali, Chapter 21), and psychiatric disease (Teskey, Chapter 24). Characteristic elements of increased response can include decreased latency, decreased threshold, greater amplitude, greater duration, decreased refractoriness, and greater spontaneity (vs. requirement for an eliciting stimulus). A major challenge for neuroplasticity research is to determine why some stimuli undergo response potentiation while others are "damped out."

Cross-Sensitization

Another general principle among some forms of neuroplasticity is that the kindling-like increase in response to a stimulus of one modality transfers to another modality (a "heterotopic" stimulus) or transfers among neural structures. As an example of transfer between brain sites, seizure kindling in the amygdala greatly decreases the threshold for subsequent kindling of the hippocampus (e.g., Teskey, Chapter 24). Cross-sensitization also occurs between cytokine exposure and a stressor (e.g., footshock). Cytokine treatment induces lasting changes in characteristics of CNS neurotransmitter and receptor function, and neural phenotype. The sensitized central response induced by cytokine treatment "transfers" to footshock exposure, that is, the heterotopic stimulus elicits a similar increased central response as that induced by the original, or homotopic, stimulus (Anisman et al., Chapter 21). Similarly, certain sensitization effects of addictive drugs can be reactivated by stress or reexposure to drug-related environmental cues (Wolf, Chapter 25). Cross-sensitization may occur as a result of "ramping up" the function in convergent signaling pathways, whether acting via shared circuitry, molecular mechanisms, or both.

Interestingly, the CNS seems to unleash a somewhat stereotypical activation of immune and stress response systems as a result of quite different stimuli (see Anisman et al., Chapter 21; Bredy, Weaver, Champagne, & Meaney, Chapter 20). It may be that through evolution and experience the nervous system has come to use a "best guess" response strategy that is adaptive in the most important situations, for example, those affecting survival (e.g., fear conditioning). The consequence of this strategy, however, is that the typical response will be maladaptive in some cases. For example, activation of stereotypical neural "stress" and immune responses following exposure to a stressor may be beneficial if that stressor is an injury or infectious agent, but not if it's a traffic jam. We believe that such maladaptive or inappropriate use of plasticity mechanisms is an important general principle of neuroplasticity. We will return to this subject in other sections; it is also a major focus in our recent reviews (McEachern & Shaw, 1996, 1999, 2000).

Age-Dependence

A general principal that seems to apply across many facets of neuroplasticity phenomena is that there are both quantitative and qualitative differences in the properties of the plasticity at different developmental stages. Quantitatively, there seems to be a greater amount of plasticity in young animals, both for experience- or activity-dependent learning processes and for recovery from injury (Debello & Knudsen, Chapter 3; Mower, Chapter 13; Kolb, Gibb, & Gonzalez, Chapter 16; however, see Sugita, Chapter 5).

Qualitative differences are observed in critical period plasticity, such that following the end of a "critical period," certain neural modifications are no longer inducible (Debello & Knudsen, Chapter 3; Mower, Chapter 13; but see also Lenhoff et al., Chapter 19). In the same category of differences, the large-scale remodeling of neuronal and synaptic connectivity that occurs in early development is not characteristic of adult stages (see Neville & Bavelier, Chapter 18) except perhaps as a compensatory response to disease or injury (Kolb et al., Chapter 16; Rauschecker, Chapter 17; Kaas, Chapter 22; see also McEachern & Shaw, 2000). The aging brain also exhibits a host of changes different in amount and/or type from young and adult stages. Among these are the involution and regression of neurons and loss of synapses. Neurite outgrowth can compensate for these losses, but the process may also become maladaptive (Neill, Chapter 27). There are, of course, innumerable other age-related differences that will not be addressed here.

Characteristics of Activity-Dependent and Experience-Dependent Change

Presented below are a number of general characteristics that are shared among many neuroplasticity subfields and also various mechanisms observed in individual research models that we considered important despite the fact that their general relevance is currently unknown.

Stimulus/Training Pattern.   Spaced activation is superior to massed activation for causing lasting increases in neural and behavioral function. This is discussed with regard to the temporal pattern of stimulation used to induce kindling (Teskey, Chapter 24) and the paradigm used for training the tap withdrawal reflex in *C. elegans* (Rose & Rankin, Chapter 14). The greater effectiveness of intermittent stimuli for inducing plasticity may be a general principle of both short and long time scale processes. The tetanic stimulation used to induce some forms of LTP is an example of a short time scale intermittent stimulus. Learning and/or memory of various kinds, kindling, and some drug sensitization processes are induced by intermittent stimuli that operate on a longer time scale.

Context.   The concurrent encoding of environmental cues and context is well known in mammalian models of learning and memory, but also affects retention time of the tap withdrawal response in *C. elegans* (Rose & Rankin, Chapter 14) and addictive drug recidivism (Wolf, Chapter 25). Molecular context is also very important, such that the outcome of a given perturbation is dependent on the physiological milieu of the brain: for example, Anisman et al. (Chapter 21) found that the state of the CNS at the time of cytokine challenge determined whether the cytokine acted in a neuroprotective or deleterious fashion; moreover, the effect varied as the pathology progressed. The importance of fine details of molecular context is also evident in the research of Wolf into dopaminergic regulation of glutamate receptor activity in addiction (Chapter 25). Wolf and colleagues found that receptor regulation varied in a complex way, depending on the preparation, the concentration of dopamine, and the subtypes of receptors involved.

Persistence.   The longevity of neuroplastic alterations spans a range from very short to essentially permanent. The search for the mechanisms and substrates of lasting change is a prime focus of neuroplasticity research and is addressed in several of the chapters in this book. Notable among the ways of maintaining changes were the following phenomena and mechanisms: a lasting form of LTP that cannot be depotentiated (Teyler, Chapter 9); activation of the cAMP/CREB pathway, manipulation of which interferes with various stages of memory, including the late stages (Saitoe & Tully, Chapter 15); and the existence of a "refresh" mechanism during sleep that returns synaptic activity to a "dedicated value" (Kavanau, Chapter 6). Striking evidence of the persistence of cortical representations is presented in chapters on the subjects of phantom limbs (Doetsch, Chapter 23) and auditory space map plasticity (Debello & Knudsen, Chapter 3). In both cases, the representations persisted following cortical map reorganization, despite the fact that the representations had decreased adaptiveness for function. Long-term potentiation is considered by many of these authors to be an important player in the formation and/or maintenance of changes in neural function, a theme we will elaborate upon below.

Memory Code.   One author (N. M. Weinberger, Chapter 4) has suggested that the pertinent neural change for learning in auditory cortex is an increase in the *number* of cells tuned to an important stimulus. At the single cell level, this would translate to increased response by one neuron. The increased "tuning" of response to significant stimuli may be a mechanism widely used in the nervous system, but it raises certain questions, for example, What prevents neurons from "switching" their tuning to the next relevant stimulus? The fact that representations are not constantly erased may suggest that new infrastructure is built to encode new information (see Rao, Raju, & Meti, 1999, and citations in this article), or that there is a strict specificity and separation of neural pathways that prevents overlap and obliteration of previous encodings.

Also at the cortical level, Debello and Knudsen (Chapter 3) report on changes in cortical map representations induced by altered visual and auditory input from the periphery (e.g., by using a prism to alter visual input). They believe cortical map changes occur through an increase in new functional connections and a decrease in nonadaptive connections. They speculate that new functional connections are created by axon outgrowth and synaptogenesis and/or potentiation of existing weak or silent synapses. Nonadaptive connections are silenced by an intriguing cause-effect relationship in which an initial decrease in synaptic strength leads to further masking of the connections by activating strong inhibition. On the subject of newly formed functional connections, it will be important to determine the circumstances of, and the extent to which, the nervous system creates completely novel pathways versus embellishing genetically and experientially dictated infrastructure. Evidence from a variety of preparations suggests that novel synaptic structures must be created in many circumstances (Rao et al., 1999; Toni, Buchs, Nikonenko, Bron, & Muller, 1999).

Other chapters in this book detail the types of changes in molecular cascades that might underlie the changes in functional connections and tuning of neural activity discussed above. Activity-dependent activation of immediate early genes (IEGs) is one possible mechanism proposed for tying alterations in neural activity to gene expression. Mower (Chapter 13) describes a complex and specific signaling system achievable through the particular combination and time course of IEG induction and the interaction between IEGs to form different, functionally unique heterodimers. The complexity and specificity of signaling possible with such molecular combinations and interactions may not be unique to IEGs, but rather may reflect a more general rule of molecular signal transduction in the CNS.

Assigning Significance to Stimuli

Weinberger (Chapter 4, pp. 33) states that "virtually all learning situations involve 'tagging' or 'assigning' significance or importance to experience, from simplest habituation to sophisticated cognition in humans." This is a crucial concept and a general principle of neuroplasticity. An important question that remains to be answered for many levels of neural organization is, How do organisms and neural structures signal that a particular stimulus is important or, alternatively, irrelevant? This question may be closely related to another regarding homeostasis versus change: What determines whether a particular stimulus, whether behavioral, molecular, or other, induces processes that result in altered neural function versus homeostatic processes that return activity and function to baseline?

Cell Birth and Cell Death

The recent rediscovery of new cell proliferation in the adult brain is certain to revolutionize many areas of neuroplasticity, both experience-dependent and injury-related. Omerod and Galea (Chapter 8) provide an introduction to these data, which form a counterpart to the mechanisms underlying apoptotic and antiapoptotic signaling in development and neurological disease (Mattson et al., Chapter 28).

Signaling Mechanisms in Homeostasis and Plasticity

Contributors to this book have elucidated a number of important biochemical signaling mechanisms. Desai, Nelson, and Turrigiano (Chapter 11) draw attention to two serious drawbacks to LTP- and LTD-like alterations of neural activity levels without homeostatic mechanisms to balance them: First, neural firing rates could saturate, or fall silent, without a method to return activity to a baseline functional range. Second, Hebbian and LTP-like potentiations have a positive feedback nature such that higher activation levels will, in turn, lead to increasingly large potentiations. Both of these factors would be uncontrollable without homeostatic regulation. We would add that not only would this situation be detrimental to normal neural function, but activation levels beyond a tolerable range would initiate calcium-mediated molecular cascades, culminating in excitotoxic cell death (this subject is treated in detail in McEachern & Shaw, 1999, 2000; see also Mattson et al., Chapter 28 of this volume). Desai et al. describe two forms of homeostatic regulation that may act to balance Hebbian plasticity and prevent neural dysfunction: (a) scaling up or down of synaptic strengths in a manner that preserves previously encoded relative differences in strength, and (b) control of intrinsic neural excitability via ion conductance regulation.

Liu and Wang (Chapter 12) also describe tightly coupled molecular mechanisms of plasticity and stability. Synaptic stability occurs through tight control of excitatory AMPA receptor endocytosis and insertion processes at the plasma membrane. This is a *constitutive* process that maintains a constant number of receptors even in the face of neural perturbations. Plasticity, in contrast, is achieved through an *activity-dependent* mechanism. Release of insulin overrides the constitutive homeostatic processes and results in an enduring change in receptor number at the plasma membrane. Other ionotropic receptors may operate using similar mechanisms (Pasqualotto & Shaw, 1996, 2000).

We consider the concept of constitutive stability versus regulated plasticity to be a general principle of neural function. According to this idea, only special forms of stimuli have the ability to bypass the strong homeostatic mechanisms that are the mainstay of brain function. We return to this idea later in the chapter.

Plasticity-Pathology Connection and Reuse of Developmental Mechanisms

Studies of maladaptive plasticity reveal that some stimuli can co-opt normal plasticity mechanisms, bypassing homeostatic controls and inducing inappropriate or pathological alterations in brain function. Included here are kindling (Teskey, Chapter 24) and drug addiction (Wolf, Chapter 25), both of which involve glutamate-dependent mechanisms also linked to beneficial processes like learning and memory, cortical reorganization (Doetsch, Chapter 23, phantom limbs; Sugita, visual field adaptation), and neurite outgrowth during aging and neural injury repair (Neill, Chapter 27; Kaas, Chapter 22), these latter having beneficial *and* detrimental consequences for function. Neill views the process of neurite outgrowth during aging as a "reuse" of developmental mechanisms of sprouting. The reuse of developmental plasticity mechanisms and the relationship between beneficial and pathological plasticity processes are likely to be general principles of brain function common to many areas of neuroplasticity.

LTP- and LTP-Like Phenomena

Best-known as a putative model of memory and/or learning processes, LTP is the subject of two chapters in this book (Cain, Chapter 10; Teyler, Chapter 9) that analyze it in these and similar roles. In addition, however, LTP-like processes have repeatedly arisen as a key theme in chapters on the subject of maladaptive neuroplasticity. Whatever the function (if any) of LTP in the intact animal, it is abundantly clear that it warrants close examination here as a "key theme." The recurrence of LTP in a number of chapters may suggest that it is a general mechanism used in many forms of neuroplasticity. Alternatively, it may simply reflect a heavy focus on this currently dominant paradigm. This is a question we will attempt to address in this section.

Cain, in Chapter 10, looks at the evidence for and against the existence of a connection between LTP and learning and/or memory. In the end, he states that, "No definitive conclusion whether LTP subserves any form of learning and memory is available as yet." (Cain, pp. 126). Teyler's position is that "LTP is a generic mechanism for increasing synaptic gain throughout the brain whenever increases in synaptic strength are needed." (Teyler, Chapter 9, pp. 105).

Our own view is that those who unequivocally equate learning or memory with LTP often do so on the basis of a selective interpretation of "a neurophysiological postulate" put forward by D. O. Hebb (1949) to explain long-lasting changes in synaptic strength. Hebb made the assumption that, "When an axon of cell A is near enough to excite a cell B and repeatedly or persistently takes part in firing it, some growth process or metabolic change takes place in one or both cells such that A's efficiency, as one of the cells firing B, is increased" (pp. 62). Thus, since LTP seems to reflect such a relationship between pre- and postsynaptic elements, it is often taken that LTP *itself* is a clear example of the sort of modification that Hebb thought might underlie learning and memory. It seems, however, that this conclusion is somewhat at odds with a statement Hebb wrote immediately preceding his famous postulate, namely, that,

> To account for the permanence [of memory], some structural change seems necessary, but a structural growth presumably would require an appreciable time. If some way can be found of supposing that a reverberatory trace might cooperate with the structural change, and *carry the memory until the growth change is made* [italics, D. O. Hebb], *we should be able to recognize the theoretical value of the trace which is an activity only, without having to ascribe all memory to it. The conception of a transient, unstable reverberatory trace is therefore useful, if it is possible to suppose also that some more permanent structural change reinforces it* [italics ours].
> (Hebb, 1949, p. 62)

Hebb goes on to state that a choice does not have to be made between reverberatory activity and structural change as the basis of memory. The foregoing makes clear that making the so-called Hebbian rules synonymous with the dogma of LTP typifies a classic error of confusing a process (learning/memory) with a potential (LTP).

It may be the case that this is an argument of semantics, and those who call LTP the substrate of memory equate the term LTP with the totality of processes from the time neurons are activated, on through all of the ensuing biochemical cascades up to and including structural changes. However, no discussion of the substrate of "memory" or "learning" can be undertaken separate from the changes that occur at levels of neural organization higher than the molecular and cellular levels to alter large-scale structure and system activity. The interactions, processes, and changes at higher levels are not reducible to LTP any more than a house is reducible to a brick. Therefore, if LTP occurs naturally in the behaving animal, it can at best be said to underlie *circuit* formation, not learning or memory.

In addition to the proposed connection of LTP to learning and/or memory, authors of chapters on the subjects of pain-induced plasticity (Baranauskas, Chapter 26) and addiction (Wolf, Chapter 25) have noted common features among these forms of neuroplasticity and LTP- and LTD-like processes. The commonalities include long-lasting changes in neural activity attributable to activation of the NMDA receptor/PKC cascade (in pain and addiction), as well as characteristics such as an LTP-like progression of the alterations, involvement of the hippocampus, and changes in synaptic and dendritic structure (in addiction). Allusion is also made to a role for LTD in addiction. In this context, amphetamine is said to "remove the brake" that normally protects neurons from pathological strengthening of excitatory synapses through LTP (Kornblum, Jones, Bonci, Malenka, & Kauer, 1999). The ability of certain stimuli to interfere with inhibitory or depotentiating mechanisms is consistent with our idea that normal mechanisms of plasticity can produce pathology when certain stimuli are able to overcome homeostatic processes (McEachern & Shaw, 1996, 1999, 2000).

Research devoted to uncovering the molecular underpinnings of LTP and other forms of neuroplasticity have repeatedly turned up the NMDA receptor and protein kinase and phosphatase cascades as pivotal players. For example, NMDA receptor action is found to be involved across the board in varieties of learning, memory, developmental processes, LTP, kindling, potentiation of pain pathways, cell birth in the adult brain, cell death (apoptosis), addictive drug-induced behavioral sensitization, cortical map reorganization, and critical period plasticity. But does this widespread involvement of certain molecules point to a general principle or commonality among the diverse types of plasticity, or merely to a surface similarity based upon the use of an almost global signaling mechanism in the CNS? Commonalities based on shared molecules such as the NMDA receptor and mechanisms such as LTP have been discussed above. The story is not straightforward, however: the literature details a vast number of molecules and mechanisms that induce or block plasticity, and many of the results are mutually contradictory (e.g., see Table 1 in McEachern & Shaw, 1996; or Wheal et al., 1998). Therefore, when attempting to find similarities between subtypes of neuroplasticity, a match of one kind or another will almost always be possible. While discovering similarities at the level of individual molecules may reflect nothing more than usage of a mechanism that is widespread and not unique to plasticity processes, comparisons that elucidate general principles, for example, "rules" of regulation that determine homeostasis versus change, are more significant.

In addition to the sheer number and complexity of molecular players, matters are often further complicated by those who make the assumption that receptor function or neural activity is equivalent to LTP, even without any measure of the longevity of the phenomenon in question. This easy substitution is prevalent in the neuroplasticity literature (e.g., Teyler, Chapter 9, p. 110) and most likely contributes to the momentum of the dominant view, that is, that LTP is a pivotal mechanism in many forms of neuroplasticity.

While there are many similarities in molecular cascades across neuroplasticity models, some quite startling differences can also be found in this book. For example, research in *C. elegans* (Rose & Rankin, Chapter 14) reveals that the glutamate receptor involved in tap withdrawal response plasticity activates a *chloride* channel, illustrating that not all glutamate-gated receptors are created equal with respect to their effect on excitation versus inhibition. In addition, Rose and Rankin found that two different subcircuits involved in habituation used different mechanisms. Therefore, even in subcircuits of a single behavior in a very simple organism, plasticity mechanisms are heterogeneous. Furthermore, octopamine, a molecule that is important in plasticity in the honey bee (Mercer, Chapter 7), is not even known in vertebrates. Similar to the case in *C. elegans*, the details of the molecular cascades underlying mammalian LTP differ in hippocampal fields CA3 and CA1, and even vary from CA1 apical to basal dendrites, although the phenomenology is said to be the same (Teyler, Chapter 9). The above makes obvious the fact that great variability exists in the molecular substrates of plasticity, not only across different species and behaviors (which is perhaps unsurprising), but also regardless of how narrow a focus is placed on species, structure, and behavior.

But is this variability a serious blow to the possibility of there being a cohesive theory of neuroplasticity? Perhaps not in itself, if, as mentioned above by Teyler, the phenomenology is the same. While it is true that the molecules differ, molecules are not identical to mechanisms. This is the rationale for our emphasis on general principles. A given phenomenon may be produced by different molecules governed according to certain general rules in the same way that a given play may be produced by different sets of actors following the same script. It is still possible that various forms of neuroplasticity will be found to be governed by general principles that are common at a neural level higher than the molecular level.

Conclusions and Implications for Neuroplasticity Research

At the current time, the biggest problem for attempting to find a theory of neuroplasticity is that there are still so many gaps in our knowledge, in particular *across* levels of neural organization. For instance, most research is highly reductionist and/or focused at only one level, and often there is no attempt to relate molecular plasticity up through the levels to a relevant behavior, or behavioral plasticity back down through levels to the substrate circuit/cellular alterations. We make no claim that this is an easy task, and unfortunately it would appear that such level-crossing needs to be done within individual models and laboratories. Otherwise, the number of confounding variables becomes even larger, and the difficulty in finding connections escalates. Without such cross-level connections, however, we are unable to assess whether there is a true correspondence between, for example, LTP and cortical map reorganization. Attempting to "jump" levels, for example, by looking for a relationship between LTP and learning in a behavior where the underlying circuit is poorly understood, is likely to continue to prove unrewarding. An example of the latter is spatial learning, where strict separation between hippocampal-dependent and -independent tasks is a subject of dispute and no unambiguous conclusion about the importance of LTP in this form of learning is possible (Cain, Chapter 10 of this volume; McEachern & Shaw, 1996, 1999, 2000). A technique that might prove more fruitful is to proceed sequentially through levels, for example, from behavior to whole brain waves, to cortical receptive field alterations, on down through circuit formation via LTP-like processes. Some researchers have made successful efforts in this direction (e.g., Freeman, 1981). In this book, Rose and Rankin, Chapter 14, and Saitoe and Tully, Chapter 15, have crossed all levels from behavioral to genetic, and most of the remaining authors have traversed at least one level.

Having discussed the similarities, differences, and common principles, we now attempt to apply these in a general theory of neuroplasticity.

☐ Plasticity and Stability Across Levels of Neural Organization

In the following, we will present our view that a general theory of neuroplasticity is plausible, a view that we attempt to validate by reference to the material presented by the various contributors to this book and, in a limited way due to length constraints, to the primary literature.

Our theory of neural modifiability and stability across levels of nervous system organization represents a partial synthesis of a variety of concepts and of the incredibly diverse data that make up the subject matter of neuroplasticity. While we feel that our particular formulation is novel in many respects, we stress that we do not claim that it is totally unique; neither do we feel that it is exclusive of, or antithetical to, older concepts, for example, Hebbian synapses and ensembles (Hebb, 1949). Space limitations in this chapter preclude a detailed comparison and discussion of previous theories of plasticity and learning and memory (e.g., Amit, 1995, with commentaries; Hebb, 1949; Latash, 1988) to ours, an omission that will be addressed in a later forum.

In many respects what follows is still rudimentary, and until many aspects of our model are tested experimentally, much of it will remain purely speculative. We emphasize, however, that the goal of this book is to provide a direction and framework for a general theory of neuroplasticity; at this stage, the journey is as important as the destination.

Questions the Theory Must Address

Any theory that attempts to deal with a subject as complex as neuroplasticity must be able to contend with a variety of questions, of which the following are key:

1. How does the nervous system achieve flexibility, yet stability? Neurons must be able to adapt (e.g., learn) yet cannot be totally labile, for if they were, memory and stable learned responses would not be possible.

2. Do neurons and neural circuits saturate their ability to be modified over time? How does repetition change learning? What constitutes forgetting, and how is retrieval of memory possible?
3. What age-dependent changes are there in neuroplastic processes from young to old CNS?
4. What are the natural events that can induce neuroplasticity, and how do these differ from those employed in vitro?
5. How do various types of neuropathology arise and progress, and how are these changes similar to or different from the normal processes of neuroplasticity across developmental stages from early life to old age?

Proposed Levels of Neural Organization

We begin by describing various basic levels of organization similar to those we have proposed earlier (Shaw, Lanius, & van den Doel, 1994; McEachern & Shaw, 2000), albeit with some changes from our original formulation. Overall, we conceptualize the interactive levels as a form of neural "web," with interactions occurring laterally within layers of the web and hierarchically across levels.

Gene- and Transcription-Level Events.   The most basic level is that of gene expression acting via DNA, mRNA, and protein expression to affect the nervous system and each of its elements. The first consequence of alterations in genetic activity/function will be observed at the single cell level, where they will be manifest as changes in a variety of molecular reactions. An example of this would be the age-dependent expression of a particular ionotropic receptor population in a particular type of neuron.

Molecular-Level Events.   Any biochemical reactions occurring within the cell are part of this level. These may include receptor or second messenger signaling (including expression of proteins such as receptors, structural proteins, anchoring proteins, etc.). This level also includes the interactions between receptors and various protein kinases and phosphatases (including also the actions of other regulatory processes for receptors), activation of IEGs, etc. The most immediate consequence for neural signaling and neural modification at a molecular level will occur at the synapse. Molecules produced at this level can then affect the amount of activation by feedback at the genetic level. Continuing the example of the first level, increased activity through ionotropic receptors leads to a genomic down-regulation of protein expression for that receptor.

Synaptic-Level Events.   The expression of various molecules affects synaptic function in the following manner: receptor distribution and characteristics are controlled by protein expression at structures such as the postsynaptic density and receptor anchoring proteins. In terms of neural signaling, subunit protein expression will control the types and ratios of the various receptor populations at the synapse, including those for neurotransmitters and neuromodulators. The enzymes controlling the synthesis, release, and degradation of the respective neurotransmitters will also be affected by protein expression, as will those involved in the modulation of receptor activity (e.g., protein kinases and phosphatases). The activity of each of the above will affect synaptic function by altering synaptic thresholds. Synaptic activity and the currents that are generated in turn feed back to trigger second messenger cascades, which in some cases will lead to the activation of IEGs and to the regulation of receptor, second messenger, kinase/phosphatase, and other elements via feedback. The regulation of stimulated receptors by down-regulation is an example of such feedback in which the numbers and properties of the receptors (and their regulatory enzymes) are highly and mutually controlled. This control by ongoing activity occurs both developmentally and in the adult CNS, although differences in the nature of the feedback may occur (see Shaw et al., 1994). The feedback between pre- and postsynaptic elements is key for both stability and modifiability at this level, and the so-called Hebbian rules for synaptic modification via association of activity in pre- and postsynaptic elements may be present. In regard to such rules, we note that synchrony in activity across the synapse (e.g., repetitive activation of a synapse by the presynaptic activity at a particular terminal) may facilitate level crossing. Any net alteration in total synaptic activity and modulation in concert with other cellular changes leads to the next level.

Cellular (Neuronal)-Level Events.   These include the cumulative effects of synapses on a neuron via ionic current flow, kinase/phosphatase activity (homologous and heterologous receptor regulation), subcellular actions that affect overall changes in total cellular response (e.g., whether or not the neuron produces an action potential). Cellular activity, in turn, reciprocally regulates activity at the level of the constituent synapses, activates other molecules, and affects cellular metabolism. Cell to cell communication, for example, the crossing to the next level, may occur as the result of synchrony in pre- and postsynaptic elements via Hebbian associativity.

Circuit-Level Interactions.   Such interactions occur among cells in a neural circuit and involve the electrical, chemical, and other transduction pathways (e.g., communication by trophic factors). Interactions within a neural circuit also include cell to cell feedforward and feedback excitation and inhibition, lateral inhibition, etc. Alterations in the activity of any neuron in the circuit impacts circuit activity as a whole and, as a result, the activity of other component neurons (see Fregnac, 1996). It is important to note that the concept of a circuit does not imply a "fixed" circuit of unvarying neuronal combinations as in a barrel field or cortical "blob," but can include circuits composed of changing ensembles of neurons allied for a particular time to provide the basis for specific tasks (Freeman, 1994, 1995; Nicolelis, Fanselow, & Ghazanfar, 1997; see also Chrobak & Buzsaki, 1998; Hebb, 1949). Neuron-glial interactions are also included at this level. Circuit-level activity builds the next level as the net activity across a number of interacting circuits.

System-Level Events.   These include coordination of excitation or inhibition among circuits of the same modality to produce a cohesive overall response which acts to synchronize or desynchronize the activity in the component circuits, for example, visual images produced by successive and integrative actions across the visual system. (We note that subunits of the visual and other systems can be considered systems in their own right, for example, retina, lateral geniculate nucleus, visual cortex, etc.) It is also worth noting at this stage that a possible emergent property of systems may be that system complexity increases across phylogeny. For example, visual cortex as a system becomes a dominant CNS component beginning in mammals; further, in the higher mammals, particularly humans, polysensory association cortex with its unique properties and possibly unique plasticity becomes the largest overall component of the cerebral cortex. The addition of these additional features may lead to nonlinear increases in function. As was the case for previous levels, system-level activity can influence circuit activity at lower levels; at the next higher level, system-level activity leads to coordination among systems.

Whole CNS Actions.   At this level we are referring to the coordination/integration of activity in various systems, for example, sensory and motor acting to generate a behavioral response. Alterations in CNS function affect the activity of various individual systems relative to one another. Thoughts and conscious action arise at this level, leading to the final level.

Behavior.   Behavior is the response of the animal to externally or internally generated stimuli. Such responses can be instinctual, reflexive, or learned. Persistent behavioral responses alter CNS activity (e.g., conditioned response), feeding downward across levels of organization.

☐ General Overview of the Theory

The central idea of the theory is that neural activity and its modification or stability does not occur at one level of organization, but rather through the interactions and relationships at numerous levels. Each level is nested in those above and below it, with novel properties emerging at each successive level in a "hierarchy." For example, while LTP is usually induced and measured as an action potential or field potential representing activity at the cellular or circuit level, respectively, these levels are only some of those that clearly exist in a continuum from genetic instruction to behavior. Between these extremes are synaptic, cellular, neural circuit, neural system, and coordination between systems, to mention but a few of the major delineations as discussed in detail above. Activity at each level is dependent on the ones above and below. Taking again the example of the *synaptic* level, synaptic strengths and activities are controlled in part by the expression of various proteins, for example, structural elements, receptors, kinases and phosphatases. Much of the expression of these molecules is under *genetic* control, which determines which molecules are expressed, how they are transported, and where they are used, etc. In turn, synaptic activity can affect *genomic* expression of such molecules via negative and positive feedback processes. Although much is still unknown about the mutual interactions between genetic expression and the activity of the synapse, it is quite clear that such interactions exist and regulate overall synaptic activity (e.g., receptor regulation; see Shaw et al., 1994). Above the synaptic level is the level of the individual neural *cell*, whose net activity is determined by the individual activity of hundreds or thousands of individual synapses and which impacts back upon the activity at any given synapse, thus establishing yet another feedback mechanism between levels (see Desai et al., Chapter 11). The response at a given synapse can be strengthened by particular types of cellular activity or weakened by others (the types as yet uncertain; but see Stent, 1973). If the activities at synapse and cell are mutually reinforcing, cellular activity becomes altered and the process repeats at the next level. The series of mutually reinforcing alterations across levels of nervous system organization can be described as a "trajectory," which can be either narrow or wide. This point will be elaborated further below. The detailed mechanisms leading to reinforcement at various levels remain to be fully understood, but may include LTP-like processes (e.g., Hebbian rules; Teyler, Chapter 9), increased neural "tuning" to a relevant stimulus (Weinberger, Chapter 4), or alterations in cortical map representations following either learning or injury (Debello & Knudsen, Chapter 3; Kaas, Chapter 22; Rauschecker, Chapter 17; Neville & Bavelier, Chapter 18).

Viewed in this way, external stimuli and behavior, if they are sufficiently "strong" (i.e., frequent enough, or of particular intensity or "relevance" to the animal) make their way down across levels to ultimately impact on genomic function and expression (e.g., in a fear conditioning response evoking CREB-dependent gene transcription; see Saitoe & Tully, Chapter 15). Similarly, information derived from genetic instructions is expressed progressively across levels, culminating in systems-level activity and, finally, behavior (e.g., protein kinase deletion affecting particular behavioral responses; see Silva, Paylor, Whehner, & Tonegawa, 1995; Silva, Stevens, Whehner, & Tonegawa, 1992). Each level contains powerful negative feedback mechanisms that normally serve to control alterations in overall activity, thus maintaining stability. For example, at the synapse, receptors are regulated, in part, by the opposing action of protein kinases and phosphatases: overstimulation is normally followed by receptor down-regulation (Pasqualotto & Shaw, 1996). Negative feedback *between* levels serves the same function: overstimulation at a synapse causes down-regulation of genomic receptor expression (Kim, Olsen, & Tobin, 1996) and initiates homeostatic controls at the cellular level (Desai et al., Chapter 11). The net consequence of such feedback is twofold: First, only the most relevant stimuli trigger cascading modifications that have a trajectory across levels. Second, by traversing levels, the stimulus leads to mutually reinforcing activity across levels. Another consequence of the above is that stimuli that exceed the built-in constraints can induce pathology. In our view, LTP as typically induced out of context in in vitro preparations provides such an example: by exceeding constraints of context, longevity, and/or strength, it may induce pathological processes (see McEachern & Shaw, 1996, 1999, 2000). In contrast, a natural stimulus in vivo may potentiate synaptic response only transiently and, before decaying, may activate a biochemical cascade that serves to reset the other levels of organization. The final stabilization of this change in neural activity may occur as a change in synaptic or cellular morphology (for recent evidence, see Rao et al., 1999; Toni et al., 1999; Mercer, Chapter 7 of this volume) that serves as a more permanent substrate for altered behavior (Hebb, 1949). The altered behavior, if adaptive, reinforces the lower levels. The latter may serve to explain why the durability of a behavioral modification (e.g., spatial learning) may not have an obvious electrophysiological modification linked to a particular anatomical locus (e.g., LTP in dentate gyrus). For example, once distributed to a larger system (cortex), alterations in neural activity in hippocampal circuits can return to near prestimulation levels and thus avoid a potential excitotoxic outcome. It is interesting to speculate that normal in vivo activity may occasionally exceed the tolerance of the system and induce cell death. Since the dentate gyrus shows neuronal birth in adulthood (Gould, Tanapat, McEwen, Flugge, & Fuchs, 1998; Omerod & Galea, Chapter 8 of this volume), it is a possibility that new neurons are added to this "hair-trigger" circuit to replace those killed in normal activity.

Based on the above general scheme, we discuss below some proposed rules for the interactions between levels of neural organization.

Proposed Rules for Interactions Within and Between Levels of Organization

The following postulates form the core assumptions of the theory.

1. Interactions in the nervous system include those *within* as well as *between* levels, that is, lateral and "hierarchical." Hierarchical is used here in the sense that each level arises from simpler building blocks, with more complex and/or novel properties *emergent* at each as one progresses from genomic to behavioral levels.

2. Interactions between levels are bidirectional. For example, at the gene/transcription level, there is a genomically determined creation of a number of specific molecules during development; these molecules affect the type and function of the various neural cells and their elements (i.e., synapses). In turn, the activity of the neurons feeds back to partially regulate gene function and activity, whether during development, under the partial influence of environmental factors (e.g., experience-dependent modification), or in context to nondevelopmentally mediated activity in the adult nervous system. In the same manner, synaptic/cellular function is also controlled by higher level action: the activity patterns of the network(s) in which a given neuron acts will control, to an extent, the neuron's output properties. In turn, activity at the cellular level will regulate the types of molecules (e.g., receptors, enzymes, etc.) that are active at the various synapses. Such interactions occur between all levels with those above and below them.

3. Given the above mutuality of feedback between levels, alterations at the genetic level can ultimately propagate up to the behavioral level (Lenhoff et al., Chapter 19). In the same way, responses to the sensory environment and experience can percolate back down through the various levels to impact ultimately on the genetic level, leading, potentially, to changes in gene expression (see Saitoe & Tully, Chapter 15; Mercer, Chapter 7; Kaas, Chapter 22). As discussed in the preceding sections, each level is acted upon *directly* by those above and below, and indirectly by all the others. This is true even at the two ends of the continuum, at both the gene and the behavioral level: the gene level is affected by the molecular/synapse level above it in the web, and by free radicals, toxins, radiation, and other energies at the 'extra'-gene level. By the same token, the behavioral level is directly affected by the whole CNS level below and the effects of the environment above. Since the whole system is nested, in some sense behavioral and environmental events must make their ways down through the levels to the genome (for an example of such a modification in the context of a nonneuronal context, see Rutherford & Lindquist, 1998) to affect genetic expression in at least some fraction of genes, perhaps as a function of age (Saitoe & Tully, Chapter 15; e.g., CREB expression following fear conditioning).

4. In a general sense, any alteration in neural activity generated at any level is a 'perturbation' in that activity. Such perturbations can be acute or chronic; they can reflect either internally or externally generated stimuli; they can be the response to beneficial stimuli (e.g., those leading to learning) or can be more traditionally noxious or pathological "stressors"; and they can further be naturally or artificially (e.g., experimentally) induced (see Bredy et al. Chapter 20; Anisman et al., Chapter 21). An example of a natural perturbation would be any learning or internally generated, activity-dependent neural potentiation that operates under strict regulations to produce a long-term modification of neural activity by restructuring relationships among levels of organization. In contrast, an artificial perturbation such as an electrically induced tetanus can induce a response potentiation (e.g., LTP or kindling) that might not normally have been maintained but occurs because the circuit is further "tricked" by overriding the normal inhibitory feedback mechanisms that are present in vivo (see McEachern & Shaw, 1999, for details).

5. To a great extent, the relative "strength" of any perturbation will depend on relevance to the animal. As an example at the behavioral level, diffuse stimuli (e.g., activation of sensory modalities in a multiple or unrelated fashion) will lead to interference or inhibition acting to diminish the strength of the perturbation. Taking an anecdotal example, this might occur when unrelated auditory stimuli interfere with the acquisition of short-term memory for a phone number. Similar examples exist

for all sensory modalities. In contrast, focused, relevant stimuli (e.g., coordination of the visual identification of a specific object with directed hand movement to pick up that object; for specific examples, see Sugita, Chapter 5) will favor level crossing as it will be reinforcing rather than inhibitory.

6. The specificity of neural modification is achieved by a narrow "trajectory" or path of activity across levels: the more focused the trajectory, the greater the specificity and ability to bypass homeostatic mechanisms and to traverse levels; in contrast, wider trajectories will generate powerful negative feedback within and across levels, acting to retain overall homeostasis. As above, lateral spread will be more severely limited by lateral inhibition within a given level. Specificity as detailed here has two components, those of age and level. Concerning age, early developmental genetic instructions may be more widespread across the CNS than those arising from particular neural subsets in the adult CNS. In the first case, the trajectory will be wide, affecting a large numbers of neurons (e.g., genetic instructions for synaptogenesis). The relative lack of inhibitory mechanisms allows such wide trajectories to effectively alter circuitry in the young brain. In contrast, genetic alterations in the adult CNS will have a narrow trajectory, regulated by powerful inhibitory mechanisms, impacting on a specific and limited number of neurons (e.g., activation of IEGs or CREB in a distinct subset of neurons following particular perturbations). Behavior- and systems-generated stimuli will be more "global" in both cases; depending on relevance, such stimuli may cause greater or fewer specific alterations as they make their way across levels to impact on the genome.

7. The spread of activity within and across levels will depend on the balances of positive and negative feedback among elements: less appropriate or "weaker" alterations in activity will be damped out by homeostatic mechanisms; more appropriate/relevant or "stronger" alterations will propagate by overcoming feedback inhibition and the lateral inhibition within any one level. This lateral inhibition will limit lateral spread more within a level than across levels. These feedback mechanisms determine that within each level there exists the basis for neuronal stability (e.g., homeostasis: see Desai et al., Chapter 11; Liu & Wang, Chapter 12), transient modifications of neuronal function (some forms of short- or long-term potentiation–like events), as well as long-lasting, perhaps permanent, modifications, (e.g., some forms of learning; see Cain, Chapter 10; Teyler, Chapter 9; Teskey, Chapter 24).

8. The longevity of any potential modification will depend on stimulus strength as defined above, and by the reinforcing contribution by other levels. The contribution of other levels may include the durability, number of repetitions, or strength of the inducing neural activity. As discussed previously, each level is acted upon by stimuli traversing from levels above and below. This is also true at both ends of the continuum, the genetic and the behavioral level. The levels of the system are nested: behavioral/environmental events percolate down through the levels to the genome, and stimuli likewise move up from the genomic level. The persistence of the signal in an either direction alters previously stable relationships, resulting in an altered response. When it occurs top-down in response to environmental stimuli, the result may be a learned response. Top-down stimuli may be further reinforced by complementary bottom-up genetic events favoring change during development and maintained by changed genetic instructions, for example, for alterations in structural elements. Similarly, genetic alterations should ultimately impact on behavior: the studies of Silva et al. (1992a, 1992b) demonstrated that dramatic alterations occurred in some types of behavior following the deletion of genes encoding specific protein kinases.

9. The following are examples of the types of perturbations that will fail or succeed in crossing levels of neural organization, and hence be the basis of either neural stability or plasticity. As an example of a perturbation that will not cross levels, potentiation of activity in one neuron (or circuit) as a result of "natural" stimuli may only occur transiently until returned to baseline response by inhibitory feedback mechanisms. Repetitive or stronger stimuli in the same pathway may succeed in forcing level crossing. In contrast, artificial stimulation of the same neuron or circuit in vitro may experimentally lack the normal context and interactions that might prevent overstimulation. A stimulus of excessive or inappropriate strength or frequency may be unable to traverse levels in a manner that rebalances activity at the circuit and other levels. Such circumstances may favor a pathological outcome (McEachern & Shaw, 1999, 2000). The key may be the distribution of the perturbation across levels in a relevant manner. For example, a neural response to strong genetic stimuli (CREB activation) or environmental stimuli (fear conditioning), or even internally generated activity, may traverse levels and force each into a new steady state. Given the mutuality between levels, such state changes may become reinforcing within and across levels, that is, provide the basis for a permanent or semipermanent modification in behavior and function. The above, clearly, is speculative and the experimental or natural conditions favoring variations in longevity to various stimuli remain to be fully elucidated.

10. The dynamic changes associated with neural development early in life will be weighed in favor of genetic instruction as the main driving force. Neuropathological events in development (e.g., Down's syndrome) or maturity (familial neurological disorders) may arise from abnormal genetic instructions that lead to inappropriate alterations across levels. These points will be elaborated below.

The Theory as Applied to Developmental Neuroplasticity

Other speculative aspects of the theory include the following in relation to the changing nature of plasticity during development and in neuropathological conditions in which different levels of neural organization make differing contributions.

1. Early in life, genetic information contributes more significantly than environmental input in order to sculpt the developing neural levels (see Bredy et al., Chapter 20). The genetic contribution may include instructions for the various molecules present at the synapse, for neuronal sprouting, and for synaptogenesis and synaptic pruning, etc.

2. During the critical periods for various neurons when neuroplastic modifications are greatest, environmental influences *combine* with genetic instructions, that is, there is simultaneous bottom-up and *synergistic* top-down influence, to provide major modifications in long-term neural activity. Included in this stage is the peak of synaptogenesis and receptor proliferation, both regulated, in part, by external stimuli. Leading up to and including this stage, inhibitory feedback mechanisms may still be relatively weak and hence provide less homeostatic feedback (McEachern & Shaw, 2000). The greater number and contribution of levels driving and maintaining the changes in neurons in the developing CNS may partially explain why young neurons almost always exhibit greater plasticity compared to those in the adult.

3. Beyond the critical periods (occurring after puberty for many well-studied neural circuits), environmental influences become the greatest factor for changing neural activity. At this stage, homeostatic regulation of receptors and synapses becomes

paramount, and lateral inhibition becomes a dominant feature of neural circuits and the interactions between systems. Given such mechanisms of global homeostasis, the alterations that do occur in the adult CNS only do so in response to the strongest stressors and may reflect "fine tuning" of neuronal function. Note that small changes in neural properties, however, can nevertheless amount to significant alterations in behavior when *amplified* across neuronal levels of organization. This latter amplification, or nonlinearity, may be an emergent property of level crossing at various stages of neural development. In the adult CNS, neurons may be less readily modifiable except under precise, and in some cases pathological, conditions. For example, in the adult nervous system, large-scale changes in neuron number or connectivity, or in receptor characteristics may reflect a pathological process arising in response to injury, or gene dysfunction (see Neill, Chapter 27), or neural overstimulation. An example of the latter form of pathological plasticity is kindling, which may arise due to bypassed receptor regulation mechanisms (McEachern & Shaw, 1999, 2000). (In contrast, pain-induced forms of neuroplasticity may reflect appropriate, or at least ambiguous, regulatory mechanisms similar to those more conventionally thought of as beneficial [i.e., learning; see Baranauskas, Chapter 26], while addiction may represent a combination of appropriate and inappropriate responses [see Wolf, Chapter 25].)

4. Neuronal *plasticity* thus reflects the restructuring of activity across levels of neural organization due to the dynamic interplay between levels; neuronal *stability* reflects the homeostatic controls at and between each level. Large-scale changes in connectivity may be more likely to occur in the young nervous system, which lacks certain feedback controls (e.g., inhibitory processes; see Cherubini, Rovira, Gaiarsa, Corradetti, & Ben-Ari, 1990), or in response to CNS injury (see Kolb et al., Chapter 16; Doetsch, Chapter 23). Stability against large-scale alterations may be more a feature of adult nervous systems, where only fine tuning is required and which occurs only under precisely defined and controlled conditions.

The Theory as Applied to Neuropathology

Neuropathological events follow from inappropriate stimuli acting within and across levels of organization. Examples are the following.

1. Artificially induced electrical stimuli that evade normal inhibitory feedback mechanisms can lead to neuron death. Examples of such types of stimuli are LTP and kindling (see McEachern & Shaw, 1996, 1999, 2000).
2. Inappropriate activation of genetic programs can induce more global activation of particular molecules (particularly when induced out of context to normal developmental sequelae) whose action may be powerful enough to activate activity across neural levels, leading to programmed (apoptosis) cell death (see Mattson et al., Chapter 28). Examples of this are the genetically based early onset forms of various neurological disorders or those potentially caused by potent neurotoxins or by multiple stressors acting synergistically in adult CNS.
3. Maladaptive forms of neuroplasticity, for example, modifications in pain pathways (Baranauskas, Chapter 26) and chemical addiction (Wolf, Chapter 25) arise from stressor stimuli powerful enough to exert influences across all levels of neural organization, perhaps by bypassing normal inhibitory feedback controls.
4. Reorganization of sensory maps occurs as a result of top-down changes at the sensory periphery or within the cortex that traverse levels to impact at the genetic level. In turn, genetic bottom-up instructions working back through the levels lead to

the reorganization of cortical (and other) areas to allow for expansion/recovery of function.

We note that the level of recovery that can be attained is also age-dependent, differing from the adult CNS in the amount of reorganization possible (see Kolb et al., Chapter 16; Rauschecker, Chapter 17; Kaas, Chapter 22; Neville & Bavelier, Chapter 18). Such age-dependent factors include the extent of the "exuberant" connections still present (connections that would normally be subject to pruning during normal development), expression of various neural growth factors to spur axonal sprouting, etc.

☐ Conclusions and Future Directions

In this chapter, we have presented an attempt at synthesis of what we believe to be the key elements of similarity in properties and mechanisms in neuroplasticity between different levels of the nervous system and across different species and preparations. Our analysis is that the similarities exist in many domains and provide the basis for core principles of neuroplasticity. Many of the dissimilarities can be attributable to variations in technique and level of analysis. Other differences arise due to the strong possibility that while general principles may be followed in all cases, individual elements (e.g., particular molecules) may vary in either ontogeny or phylogeny. Superimposed on the synthesis of key principles is our attempt to provide the framework for a general theory of neuroplasticity. We believe that in most instances the theory and the data synthesis are in accord.

The theory describes the basis for neuronal plasticity and stability based on interactions among levels of neural organization. It embodies within this core concept the key principles derived from consideration of the chapters in this book. The theory as presented here is sufficiently comprehensive to encompass aspects of both developmental and pathological plasticity, the former often confused with plasticity in the adult, and the latter a frequently discordant note in the attempt to create a general theory. The fit to many other aspects of neuroplasticity, for example, those not considered in this chapter and those yet to be determined experimentally, as well as specific and explicit predictions of this theory, will serve as tests of its ultimate validity. Our formulation of the theory is as yet incomplete and undoubtedly overly simplistic in some regards. Notably, it lacks detailed explanation of issues such as the saturability of plasticity; the manner in which repetition affects neural modification, where the "sink" for modification lies at various levels of organization; what constitutes "forgetting," and how retrieval of percepts and memories is possible, to name just a few. Many of these issues will be pursued in an upcoming review. An additional goal is to provide a mathematical treatment of the intra- and interlevel relationships, a facet that would enhance the predictive ability of the theory. Despite these shortcomings, for those who accept its fundamental premises, we hope the theory will serve as a basis for future discussion and experimentation. For those who do not, we welcome alternative theories that will serve to advance our understanding of this all-important subject.

☐ Acknowledgments

This work was supported by a MITACS Centre of Excellence scholarship to J. C. McEachern. The assistance of Rebecca Simpson is gratefully acknowledged—her dedication and efforts have greatly enhanced this project.

☐ References

Amit, D. J. (1995). The Hebbian paradigm reintegrated: Local reverberations as internal representations. *Behavioral and Brain Sciences, 18*, 617–657.

Cherubini, E., Rovira, C., Gaiarsa, J. L., Corradetti, R., & Ben-Ari, Y. (1990). GABA mediated excitation in immature rat CA3 hippocampal neurons. *International Journal of Developmental Neuroscience, 8*, 481–490.

Chrobak, J. J., & Buzsáki, G. (1998). Gamma oscillations in the entorhinal cortex of the freely behaving rat. *Journal of Neuroscience, 18* (1), 388–398.

Freeman, W. J. (1981). A physiological hypothesis of perception. *Perspectives in Biology and Medicine, 24*, 561–592.

Freeman, W. J. (1994). Neural networks and chaos. *Journal of Theoretical Biology, 171*, 13–18.

Freeman, W. J. (1995). The Hebbian paradigm reintegrated: Local reverberations as internal representations. *Behavioral and Brain Sciences, 18* (4), 631.

Fregnac, Y. (1996). Dynamics of functional connectivity in visual cortical networks: An overview. *Journal of Physiology (Paris), 90*, 113–139.

Gould, E., Tanapat, P., McEwen, B. S., Flugge, G., & Fuchs, E. (1998). Proliferation of granule cell precursors in the dentate gyrus of adult monkeys is diminished by stress. *Proceedings of the National Academy of Sciences of the United States of America, 95*, 3168–3171.

Hebb, D. O. (1949). *The organization of behavior: A neuropsychological theory.* New York: Wiley.

Kim, H. Y., Olsen, R. W., & Tobin, A. J. (1996). GABA and GABA$_A$ receptors: Development and regulation. In C. A. Shaw (Ed.), *Receptor dynamics in neural development*, pp. 59–72. Boca Raton, FL: CRC Press.

Kornblum, J. L., Jones, S., Bonci, A., Malenka, R. C., & Kauer, J. A. (1999). Amphetamine blocks long-term depression (LTD) in the ventral tegmental area (VTA). *Society for Neuroscience Abstracts, 25*, 1738.

Latash, L. P. (1988). Automation of movement: Challenges to the notions of the orienting reaction and memory. In M. L. Latash (Ed.), *Progress in motor control, Vol. 1. Bernstein's traditions in movement studies* (pp. 51–88). Champaign, IL: Human Kinetics.

McEachern, J. C., & Shaw, C. A. (1996). An alternative to the LTP orthodoxy: A plasticity-pathology continuum model. *Brain Research Reviews, 22*, 51–92.

McEachern, J. C., & Shaw, C. A. (1999). The plasticity-pathology continuum: Defining a role for the LTP phenomenon. *Journal of Neuroscience Research, 58* (1), 42–61.

McEachern, J. C., & Shaw, C. A. (2000). Revisiting the LTP orthodoxy: Plasticity versus pathology. In C. Holscher (Ed.). *Neuronal mechanisms of memory formation.* Cambridge, UK: Cambridge University Press.

Neville, H. J., Bavelier, D., Corina, D., Rauschecker, J., Karni A., Lalwani, A., Brauni, A., Clark, V., Jezzard, P., & Turner, R. (1998). Cerebral organization for language in deaf and hearing subjects: Biological constraints and effects of experience. *Proceedings of the National Academy of Sciences of the United States of America, 95*, 922–929.

Nicolelis, M. A. L., Fanselow, E. E., & Ghazanfar, A. A. (1997). Hebb's dream: The resurgence of cell assemblies. *Neuron, 19*, 219–221.

Pasqualotto, B. A., & Shaw, C. A. (1996). Regulation of ionotropic receptors by protein phosphorylation. *Biochemical Pharmacology, 51* (11), 1417–25.

Pasqualotto, B. A., & Shaw, C. A. (2000). Tuning up the signal. *Cellular and Mollecular Life Sciences.* In press.

Polley, D. B., Chen-Bee, C. H., & Frostig, R. D. (1999). Two directions of plasticity in the sensory-deprived adult cortex. *Neuron, 24*, 1–20.

Rao, B. S. S., Raju, T. R., & Meti, B. L. (1999). Self-stimulation rewarding experience induced alterations in dendritic spine density in CA3 hippocampal and layer V motor cortical pyramidal neurons. *Neuroscience, 89* (4), 1067–1077.

Rutherford, S. L., & Lindquist, S. (1998). HSP90 as a capacitor for morphological evolution. *Nature, 396* (6709), 336–342.

Shaw, C. A., Lanius, R. A. & van den Doel, K. (1994). The origin of synaptic neuroplasticity: crucial molecules or a dynamical cascade? *Brain Research Reviews, 19*, 241–263.

Silva, A. J., Paylor, R., Whehner, J. M., & Tonegawa, S. (1992). Impaired spatial learning in α-calcium calmodulin kinase II mutant mice. *Science, 257*, 206–211.

Silva, A. J., Stevens, C. F., Tonegawa, S., & Wang Y. (1992). Deficient hippocampal long-term potentiation in α-calcium-calmodulin kinase II mutant mice. *Science, 257*, 201–206.

Stent, G. S. (1973). A physiological mechanism for Hebb's postulate of learning. *Proceedings of the National Academy of Sciences of the United States of America, 70* (4), 997–1001.

Tinbergen, N. (1968). On war and peace in animals and man. *Science, 160*, 1411–1418.

Toni, N., Buchs, P.-A., Nikonenko, I., Bron, C. R., & Muller, D. (1999). LTP promotes formation of multiple spine synapses between a single axon terminal and a dendrite. *Nature, 402*, 421–425.

Trepel C., & Racine R. J. (1998). Long-term potentiation in the neocortex of the adult, freely moving rat. *Cerebral Cortex, 8* (8), 719–729.

Wheal, H. V., Chen, Y., Mitchell, J., Schachner, M., Maerz, W., Wieland, H., Van Rossum, D., & Kirsch, J. (1998). Molecular mechanisms that underlie structural and functional changes at the postsynaptic membrane during synaptic plasticity. *Progress in Neurobiology, 55*, 611–640.

INDEX